CIMA

D1495015

MANAGEMENT

PAPER F2

FINANCIAL MANAGEMENT

Our text is designed to help you study **effectively** and **efficiently**.

In this edition we:

- **Highlight** the **most important elements** in the syllabus and the **key skills** you will need

- **Signpost** how each chapter links to the syllabus and the learning outcomes

- Use **overview and summary diagrams** to develop understanding of interrelations between topics

- **Provide** lots of **exam alerts** explaining how what you're learning may be tested

- **Include examples** and **questions** to help you apply what you've learnt

- **Emphasise key points** in **section summaries**

- **Test your knowledge** of what you've studied in **quick quizzes**

- **Examine your understanding** in our **practice question bank**

SUITABLE FOR EXAMS IN 2015

BPP
LEARNING MEDIA

First edition 2014

ISBN 9781 4727 1444 2
eISBN 9781 4727 2048 1

British Library Cataloguing-in-Publication Data
A catalogue record for this book is available from the British
Library

Published by

BPP Learning Media Ltd
BPP House, Aldine Place,
London W12 8AA

www.bpp.com/learningmedia

Printed in the United Kingdom by

RICOH UK Limited
Unit 2
Wells Place
Mertsham
RH1 3LG

Your learning materials, published by BPP Learning Media
Ltd, are printed on paper sourced from sustainable,
managed forests.

We are grateful to the Chartered Institute of Management Accountants
for permission to reproduce past examination questions. The suggested
solutions in the exam answer bank have been prepared by BPP Learning
Media Ltd.

Contents

How our Study Text can help you pass

Streamlined studying	• We show you the best ways to study efficiently
	• Our Text has been designed to ensure you can easily and quickly navigate through it
	• The different features in our Text emphasise important knowledge and techniques
Exam expertise	• **Studying F2** on page xii introduces the key themes of the syllabus and summarises how to pass
	• We highlight throughout our Text how topics may be tested and what you'll have to do in the exam
	• We help you see the complete picture of the syllabus, so that you can answer questions that range across the whole syllabus
	• Our Text covers the syllabus content – no more, no less
Regular review	• We frequently summarise the key knowledge you need
	• We test what you've learnt by providing questions and quizzes throughout our Text

Our other products

BPP Learning Media also offers these products for the F2 exam:

i-Pass	Providing computer-based testing in a variety of formats, ideal for self-assessment
Objective Test Kit	Providing helpful guidance on how to pass the objective test and more question practice
Passcards	Summarising what you should know in visual, easy to remember, form
Integrated Case Study Kit	Providing help with exam skills and question practice for the integrated case study exam

You can purchase these products by visiting www.bpp.com/cimamaterials

CIMA Distance Learning

BPP's distance learning packages provide flexibility and convenience, allowing you to study effectively, at a pace that suits you, where and when you choose.

Online classroom live	Through live interactive online sessions it provides you with the traditional structure and support of classroom learning, but with the convenience of attending classes wherever you are
Online classroom	Through pre-recorded online lectures it provides you with the classroom experience via the web with the tutor guidance & support you'd expect from a face to face classroom

You can find out more about these packages by visiting www.bpp.com/cimadistancelearning

Features in our Study Text

Chapter Overview Diagrams illustrate the connections between the topic areas you are about to cover

 Section Introductions explain how the section fits into the chapter

 Key Terms are the core vocabulary you need to learn

KEY TERM

 Key Points are points that you have to know, ideas or calculations that will be the foundations of your answers

KEY POINT

 Exam Alerts show you how subjects are likely to be tested

 Exam Skills are the key skills you will need to demonstrate in the exam, linked to question requirements

 Formulae To Learn are formulae you must remember in the exam

LEARN

 Exam Formulae are formulae you will be given in the exam

EXAM

 Examples show how theory is put into practice

 Questions give you the practice you need to test your understanding of what you've learnt

 Case Studies link what you've learnt with the real-world business environment

CASE STUDY

 Links show how the syllabus overlaps with other parts of the qualification, including Knowledge Brought Forward that you need to remember from previous exams

 Website References link to material that will enhance your understanding of what you're studying

 Further Reading will give you a wider perspective on the subjects you're covering

Section Summary Diagrams allow you to review each section

Streamlined studying

What you should do	In order to
Read the Chapter and Section Introductions and look at the Chapter Overview Diagram	See why topics need to be studied and map your way through the chapter
Go quickly through the explanations	Gain the depth of knowledge and understanding that you'll need
Highlight the Key Points, Key Terms and Formulae To Learn	Make sure you know the basics that you can't do without in the exam
Focus on the Exam Skills and Exam Alerts	Know how you'll be tested and what you'll have to do
Work through the Examples and Case Studies	See how what you've learnt applies in practice
Prepare Answers to the Questions	See if you can apply what you've learnt in practice
Review the Chapter Summary Diagrams	Remind you of, and reinforce, what you've learnt
Answer the Quick Quiz	Find out if there are any gaps in your knowledge
Answer the Question(s) in the Practice Question Bank	Practise what you've learnt in depth

Should I take notes?

Brief notes may help you remember what you're learning. You should use the notes format that's most helpful to you (lists, diagrams, mindmaps).

Further help

BPP Learning Media's *Learning to Learn Accountancy* provides lots more helpful guidance on studying. It is designed to be used both at the outset of your CIMA studies and throughout the process of learning accountancy. It can help you **focus your studies on the subject and exam**, enabling you to **acquire knowledge, practise and revise efficiently and effectively**.

Syllabus and learning outcomes

Paper F2 Financial Management

The syllabus comprises:

Topic and Study Weighting

A	Sources of long-term finance	15%
B	Financial reporting	60%
C	Analysis of financial performance and position	25%

Learning Outcomes				
Lead		**Component**		**Syllabus content**
A	**Sources of long-term finance**			
1	Discuss types and sources of long-term finance for an incorporated entity.	(a)	Discuss the characteristics of different types of long-term debt and equity finance	(i) Characteristics of ordinary and preference shares and different types of long-term debt.
		(b)	Discuss the markets for and methods of raising long-term finance.	(ii) Operation of the stock and bond markets.
				(iii) Share and bond issues.
				(iv) Role of advisors.
2	Calculate a weighted average cost of capital (WACC) for an incorporated entity.	(a)	Calculate the cost of equity for an incorporated entity using the dividend valuation model	(i) Cost of equity using the dividend valuation model, with and without growth in dividends.
		(b)	Calculate the post-tax cost of debt for an incorporated entity	(ii) Post-tax cost of bank borrowings.
				(iii) Yield to maturity of bonds and post-tax cost of bonds.
				(iv) Post-tax cost of convertible bonds up to and including conversion.
		(c)	Calculate the weighted average cost of capital (WACC) for an incorporated entity.	(v) WACC and its use.

Learning Outcomes				
Lead		**Component**		**Syllabus content**
B	**Financial reporting**			
1	Produce consolidated primary financial statements, incorporating accounting transactions and adjustments, in accordance with relevant international accounting standards, in an ethical manner.	(a)	Produce primary financial statements for a group of entities in accordance with relevant international accounting standards	(i)	Production of: • Consolidated statement of comprehensive income • Consolidated statement of financial position • Consolidated statement of changes in equity • Consolidated statement of cash flows including the adoption of both full consolidation and the principles of equity accounting, in accordance with the provisions of IAS 1, IAS 27, IAS 28, IFRS 3, IFRS 10 and IFRS 11.
		(b)	Discuss the need for and nature of disclosure of interests in other entities	(ii)	The need for and nature of disclosure of interests in other entities, in accordance with IFRS 12.
		(c)	Discuss the provisions of relevant international accounting standards in respect of the recognition and measurement of revenue, leases, financial instruments, provisions, share-based payments and deferred taxation	(iii)	The need for and nature of disclosures of contingent assets and liabilities, in accordance with IAS 37.
				(iv)	Recognition and measurement of: • revenue, in accordance with IAS 18 and the provisions of the framework • operating and finance leases, in accordance with IAS 17
		(d)	Produce the accounting entries, in accordance with relevant international accounting standards		• financial instruments, in accordance with IAS 32 and IAS 39 (excluding hedge accounting) • provisions, in accordance with IAS 37 • share-based payments, in accordance with IFRS 2 • provision for deferred taxation, in accordance with IAS 12.

BPP LEARNING MEDIA

Learning Outcomes				
Lead		**Component**		**Syllabus content**
	(e)	Discuss the ethical selection and adoption of relevant accounting policies and accounting estimates.	(v)	Ethics in financial reporting.
2 Demonstrate the impact on the preparation of the consolidated financial statements of certain complex group scenarios.	(a)	Demonstrate the impact on the group financial statements of: (i) Acquiring additional shareholdings in the period (ii) Disposing of all or part of a shareholding in the period	(i)	Additional acquisition in the period resulting in a simple investment becoming a controlling interest, in accordance with the provisions of IFRS 3.
			(ii)	Calculation of the gain/loss on the disposal of a controlling interest in a subsidiary in the year, in accordance with the provisions of IFRS 3.
			(iii)	Adjustment to parent's equity resulting from acquiring or disposing of shares in a subsidiary, in accordance with the provisions of IFRS 3.
	(b)	Demonstrate the impact on the group financial statements of consolidating a foreign subsidiary	(iv)	Provisions of IAS 21 in respect of consolidating a foreign subsidiary and the calculation of the foreign exchange gains and losses in the period.
	(c)	Demonstrate the impact on the group financial statements of acquiring indirect control of a subsidiary.	(v)	Impact of indirect effective holdings on the preparation of group financial statements.
3 Discuss the need for and nature of disclosure of transactions between related parties.	(a)	Discuss the need for and nature of disclosure of transactions between related parties.	(i)	The need for and nature of disclosure of related party transactions, in accordance with IAS 2.
4 Produce the disclosures for earnings per share.	(a)	Produce the disclosures for earnings per share.	(i)	Calculate basic and diluted earnings per share, in accordance with IAS 33.

Learning Outcomes				
Lead		**Component**		**Syllabus content**
C	**Analysis of financial performance and position**			
1	Evaluate the financial performance, financial position and financial adaptability of an incorporated entity.	(a)	Calculate ratios relevant for the assessment of an entity's profitability, financial performance, financial position and financial adaptability	(i)	Ratios for profitability, performance, efficiency, activity, liquidity and gearing.
		(b)	Evaluate the financial performance, financial position and financial adaptability of an entity based on the information contained in the financial statements provided	(ii)	Interpretation of the primary financial statements and any additional information provided.
		(c)	Advise on action that could be taken to improve an entity's financial performance and financial position.	(iii)	Action that could be realistically taken by the entity's management to improve financial performance and strengthen financial position, taking into account ethical considerations and internal and external constraints.
2	Discuss the limitations of ratio analysis.	(a)	Discuss the limitations of ratio analysis based on financial statements that can be caused by internal and external factors.	(i)	Inter-segment comparison
				(ii)	International comparisons.

D	Developments in external reporting				
1	Discuss contemporary developments in financial and non-financial reporting	(a)	Discuss pressures for extending the scope and quality of external reports to include prospective and non-financial matters, and narrative reporting generally	(i)	Increasing stakeholder demands for information that goes beyond historical financial information and frameworks for such reporting, including as an example of national requirements and guidelines, the UK's Business Review and the Accounting Standard Board's best practice standard, RS1, and the Global Reporting Initiative
		(b)	Explain how information concerning the interaction of a business with society and the natural environment can be communicated in the published accounts	(ii)	Environmental and social accounting issues, differentiating between externalities and costs internalised through, for example, capitalisation of environmental expenditure, recognition of future environmental costs by means of provisions, taxation and the costs of emissions permit trading schemes
		(c)	Discuss social and environmental issues which are likely to be most important to stakeholders in an organisation	(iii)	Non-financial measures of social and environmental impact
		(d)	Explain the process of measuring, recording and disclosing the effect of exchanges between a business and society – human resource accounting	(iv)	Human resource accounting
				(v)	Major differences between IFRS and US GAAP, and progress towards convergence
		(e)	Discuss major differences between IFRS and US GAAP, and the measures designed to contribute towards their convergence		

Studying F2

1 What's F2 about

The Paper F2 syllabus is in three parts:

- Sources of long-term finance
- Financial reporting
- Analysis of financial performance and position

1.1 Sources of long-term finance

This part of the syllabus covers the structure of the financial markets, the different sources of long-term finance available, and how to evaluate the suitability of each source of finance. You will also need to be able to calculate the cost of finance, through cost of equity, cost of debt and weighted average cost of capital calculations.

Weighted at 15% of the syllabus, it's important that you are familiar with the more discursive, concept-based side of the topic, as well as the numerical workings.

1.2 Financial reporting

This is by the biggest component of the syllabus, at a weighting of 60%. Essentially, this component can be divided into two parts: group reporting, and issues in recognition and measurement.

As you work through the progressively advanced topics on **group reporting**, it is vital that you get a good grasp of the basics and the principles. There are a lot of easy marks available for basic consolidation techniques. You should not, however, concentrate on the 'hows' of the calculation to the exclusion of the 'whys', which will always be tested through objective test questions.

The **recognition and measurement** part of the financial reporting component involves explaining the problems of profit measurement. Thus you will need to understand the principles contained in the Conceptual Framework. Very importantly, you will need to apply these principles to relevant accounting standards, all of which are covered in this Study Text.

1.3 Analysis of financial performance and position

With a weighting of 25%, this is an important area, unsurprisingly, given that the title of the paper is Financial Management, rather than Financial Accounting.

Again, discussion is every bit as important as calculation in this section. It is important that you are able not just to calculate the ratios, but also to explain the implication of each ratio. The OTQs will test your understanding in a precise way.

2 What's required

2.1 Knowledge

The exam requires you to demonstrate knowledge as much as application. Bear in mind this comment from the examiner, from her report on an exam under the old syllabus:

> *At the top end, some candidates scored very highly indeed, producing a full complement of excellent answers. However, a substantial minority of candidates appeared to have virtually no useable knowledge of the syllabus.*

2.2 Explanation

As well as stating your knowledge, you will also sometimes be asked to demonstrate the more advanced skill of explaining the requirements of accounting standards. Explaining means providing simple definitions and covering the reasons why regulations have been made and what the problems are that the standards are designed to counter. In an OTQ exam, you will still need to demonstrate your ability to 'explain' – questions may require you to select the correct definitions and make inferences in a short scenario, based on your understanding of the topics.

2.3 Calculations

Calculations are of course an important part of this exam. Make sure you learn the formulas by heart, through repeated practice. It's important (especially when it comes to ratios) that you learn the formulas as provided in this Study Text. The precision of objective testing means that if you use a wrong figure in one part of your workings, and thus choose the wrong answer, you will not gain the allocated marks.

3 How to pass

3.1 Cover the whole syllabus?

Yes! You need to be comfortable with **all areas of the syllabus**, as questions in the objective test exam will cover all syllabus areas.

3.2 Lots of question practise

You can **develop application skills** by attempting questions in the Practise Question Bank. While these might not be in the format that you will experience in your exam, doing the full question will enable you to answer the exam questions. For example, you will only be able to answer a question on an element of a consolidated statement of financial position if you know how to prepare the complete consolidated statement of financial position. Similarly, in the integrated case study exam, you will have to answer questions that combine F2 syllabus areas with E2 and P2. However, by answering questions on F2 you will develop the technical knowledge and skills in order to answer those questions.

However, you should practice exam standards questions, which you will find in the BPP Objective Test Kit and Integrated Case Study Kit.

3.3 Answering questions in the Integrated Case Study

Well-judged, **clear recommendations** grounded in the scenario will always score well as markers for this paper have a wide remit to reward good answers. You need to be **selective**.

Scenario details should only be used if they support the points you're making, but they should be used when relevant.

Answers should be well-structured, clear and concise. They should demonstrate a clear and logical thought process. If the question asks for a discussion, a list of single-line bullet points will not be an adequate answer.

3.4 The pre-seen

The pre-seen provides an idea of what may be in the integrated case study exam, and enables you to put questions into context. You will be expected to use the information in the pre-seen when answering questions, as well as using the additional unseen information that you will be given in the exam.

3.5 Develop business awareness

Candidates with good business awareness can score well in a number of areas.

- Reading articles in CIMA's *Financial Management* magazine and the business press will help you understand the practical rationale for accounting standards and make it easier for you to apply accounting requirements correctly

- Looking through the accounts of major companies will familiarise you with the contents of accounts and help you comment on key figures and changes from year-to-year

4 Brought forward knowledge

The examiner may test knowledge or techniques you've learnt at lower levels. As F2 is part of the Financial pillar, the content of paper F1 will be significant.

5 What the examiner means

The table below has been prepared by CIMA to help you interpret the syllabus and learning outcomes and the meaning of questions.

You will see that there are 5 levels of Learning objective, ranging from Knowledge to Evaluation, reflecting the level of skill you will be expected to demonstrate. CIMA Certificate subjects only use levels 1 to 3, but in CIMA's Professional qualification the entire hierarchy will be used.

At the start of each chapter in your study text is a topic list relating the coverage in the chapter to the level of skill you may be called on to demonstrate in the exam.

Learning objectives	Verbs used	Definition
1 Knowledge		
What are you expected to know	• List	• Make a list of
	• State	• Express, fully or clearly, the details of/facts of
	• Define	• Give the exact meaning of
2 Comprehension		
What you are expected to understand	• Describe	• Communicate the key features of
	• Distinguish	• Highlight the differences between
	• Explain	• Make clear or intelligible/state the meaning or purpose of
	• Identify	
	• Illustrate	• Recognise, establish or select after consideration
		• Use an example to describe or explain something
3 Application		
How you are expected to apply your knowledge	• Apply	• Put to practical use
	• Calculate/ compute	• Ascertain or reckon mathematically
		• Prove with certainty or to exhibit by practical means
	• Demonstrate	
	• Prepare	• Make or get ready for use
	• Reconcile	• Make or prove consistent/compatible
	• Solve	• Find an answer to
	• Tabulate	• Arrange in a table
4 Analysis		
How you are expected to analyse the detail of what you have learned	• Analyse	• Examine in detail the structure of
	• Categorise	• Place into a defined class or division
	• Compare and contrast	• Show the similarities and/or differences between
		• Build up or compile
	• Construct	• Examine in detail by argument
	• Discuss	• Translate into intelligible or familiar terms
	• Interpret	• Place in order of priority or sequence for action
	• Prioritise	• Create or bring into existence
	• Produce	
5 Evaluation		
How you are expected to use your learning to evaluate, make decisions or recommendations	• Advise	• Counsel, inform or notify
	• Evaluate	• Appraise or assess the value of
	• Recommend	• Propose a course of action

Competency Framework

CIMA has developed a competency framework detailing the skills, abilities and competencies that finance professionals need. The CIMA syllabus has been developed to match the competency mix as it develops over the three levels of the professional qualification. The importance of the various competencies at the strategic level is shown below.

CIMA COMPETENCY FRAMEWORK

39%
CORE ACCOUNTING AND FINANCE SKILLS
Do accounting and finance work

BUSINESS ACUMEN
In the context of the business
24%

16% **LEADERSHIP SKILLS**
And lead within the organisation

PEOPLE SKILLS
To influence people
21%

ETHICS, INTEGRITY AND PROFESSIONALISM

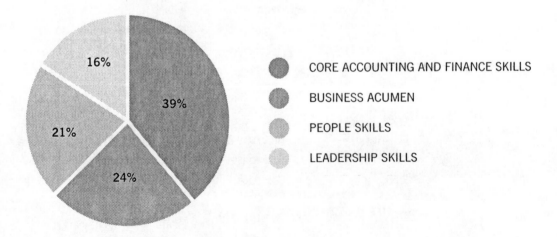

MANAGEMENT LEVEL

16%
39%
21%
24%

● CORE ACCOUNTING AND FINANCE SKILLS

● BUSINESS ACUMEN

● PEOPLE SKILLS

● LEADERSHIP SKILLS

Assessment

The CIMA assessment is a two-tier structure with objective tests for each subject and an integrated case study at each level.

Objective test

The objective tests are computer based and can be taken on demand. The student exam preparation on the CIMA website has additional information and tools to help you become familiar with the test style. Make sure you check back regularly as more information may be added.

The web link is: http://www.cimaglobal.com/Students/2015-syllabus/assessment/

The objective tests will test all levels in the CIMA hierarchy of verbs.

Integrated case study

Candidates must pass or receive exemptions from the three objective tests at each level, before attempting the integrated case study exam for that level.

The integrated case studies will be available four times a year.

The integrated case study exams will combine the knowledge and learning from all the pillars. They will be set in the context of a fictional organisation based on a real business or industry.

The management level will require long and short essays supported by calculations and analysis. The role of the candidate will be that of a manager reporting to the CFO and senior business managers.

LONG-TERM FINANCE

Part A

2

SOURCES OF LONG-TERM FINANCE

Obtaining finance to support the business's operations is crucial to any company's survival. We shall start our CIMA F2 studies by looking at the structure of the financial markets. We will introduce the different sources of long-term finance, how they can be obtained, and the advantages and disadvantages of each. This is a new topic, added to the syllabus in 2014, so likely to come up in the exams.

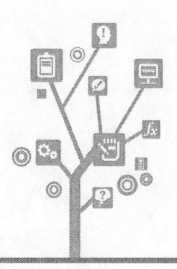

1

Topic list	learning outcomes	syllabus references
1 The operation of stock and bond markets	A1	A1(b)
2 Sources of equity finance	A1	A1(a)
3 Sources of long-term debt finance	A1	A1(a)

Chapter Overview

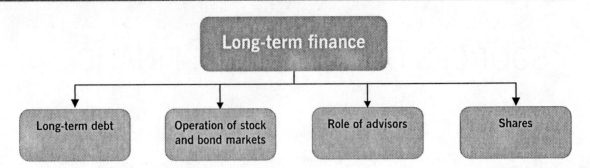

1   The operation of stock and bond markets

In this chapter we will explore and evaluate the different options for long-term finance – debt and equity – and discuss the process for obtaining each form of finance.

Before a company determines what form of long-term finance is most appropriate, it is important to understand how financial markets operate.

1.1 Financial markets

Introduction

Financial markets are the markets where individuals and organisations with surplus funds provide funds to other individuals and organisations that require financing.

This function is shown diagrammatically below.

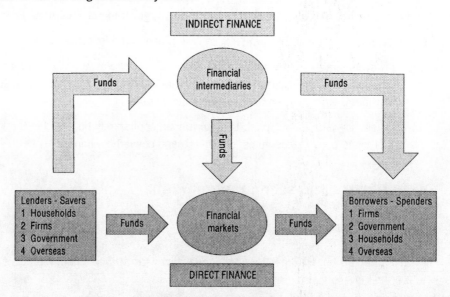

Those who have saved and are lending funds, the **lender–savers**, are on the left, and those who must borrow funds to finance their spending, the **borrower–spenders**, are on the right. The principal lender–savers are **households** and **firms**, as well as **overseas institutions** and their **governments**, who sometimes also find themselves with excess funds and so lend them out. The most important borrower–spenders are corporations and governments, although individuals also borrow to finance the acquisition of durable goods or houses. The arrows show that funds flow from lender–savers to borrower–spenders via two routes.

The first route is the direct finance route at the bottom of the diagram, when borrowers borrow funds directly from lenders in financial markets by selling them **securities** (also called **financial instruments**), which are **claims** on the **borrowers' future income** or **assets**.

The second, indirect, route, involves the borrowers obtaining funds through **financial intermediaries** such as banks and stock exchanges. We will look a the role of financial intermediaries in more detail as we progress through this chapter.

The channelling of funds from **savers** to **spenders** is a crucial function for the economy because the people who save are frequently not the same people who have profitable investment opportunities available to them ie the entrepreneurs. Without financial markets it is hard to transfer funds from a person with surplus funds and no investment opportunities, to one who has investment opportunities but no funds. They would be unable to transact and both would be worse off as a result. Financial markets are thus essential to promoting **economic efficiency**.

1.2 Capital markets

Introduction

A **stock market** (in the UK: the main market plus the Alternative Investment Market (AIM)) acts as a **primary market** for raising finance, and as a **secondary market** for the trading of existing securities.

Securities are tradable financial instruments. They can take the form of equity (such as shares), debt (such as bonds) or derivatives.

Capital markets are markets for trading in **medium and long-term finance**, in the form of financial instruments such as equities and corporate bonds.

In the UK the principal capital markets are:

(a)   The Stock Exchange **main market** (for companies with a full Stock Exchange listing)
(b)   The more loosely regulated second tier **Alternative Investment Market (AIM)**

The Stock Exchange is also the market for dealing in **government securities**.

Firms obtain long-term or medium-term capital in one of the following ways.

(a)   They may raise **share capital**. Most new issues of share capital are in the form of ordinary share capital. Firms that issue ordinary share capital are inviting investors to take an **equity stake** in the business, or to increase their existing equity stake.

(b)   They may raise **loan capital**. Long-term loan capital may be raised in the form of loan notes, corporate bonds, debentures, unsecured and convertible bonds.

1.3 Primary and secondary markets

Introduction

Primary markets enable organisations to raise new finance. **Secondary** markets enable existing investors to sell their investments.

The financial markets serve two main purposes.

(a)   As **primary markets** they enable organisations to **raise new finance** by issuing new shares or new bonds. In the UK a company must have public company status (be a publicly listed company, or plc) to be allowed to raise finance from the public on a capital market.

(b)   As **secondary markets** they enable existing investors to **sell their investments**, should they wish to do so. The marketability of securities is a very important feature of the capital markets, because investors are more willing to buy stocks and shares if they know that they can sell them easily.

Here are two examples of how primary and secondary markets work.

Primary markets: When one company wants to **take over** another, it is common to do so by issuing shares to finance the takeover. Takeovers by means of a share exchange are only feasible if the shares that are offered can be readily traded on a stock market, and so have an identifiable market value.

Secondary markets: When a company comes to the stock market for the first time and **floats** its shares on the market, the owners of the company can **realise** some of the **value of their shares** in cash because they will offer a proportion of their personally-held shares for sale to new investors.

1.4 Exchange and over the counter (OTC) markets

Introduction

Secondary markets can be organised as **exchanges** or **over the counter (OTC) markets**.

Secondary markets for financial securities can be organised as **exchanges**, where buyers and sellers of securities buy and sell securities in one location, the exchange. Examples of exchanges include the London Stock Exchange and the New York Stock Exchange for the trading of shares, the Chicago Board of Trade for the trading of commodities and the London International Financial Futures and Options Exchange (LIFFE) for the trading of derivatives.

Alternatively, secondary markets can operate as **over the counter** markets where buyers and sellers transact with each other not through an exchange but by **individual negotiation**.

The prices at which securities are bought over the counter may be the same as the corresponding transactions in an exchange, because the buyers and sellers agree the most competitive price based on constant contact through computers with other market participants.

Securities that are issued in an over the counter market can be negotiable or non-negotiable.

* **Negotiable** securities can be resold.
* **Non-negotiable** securities cannot be resold.

1.5 Capital market participants

The various participants in the capital markets are summarised in the diagram below.

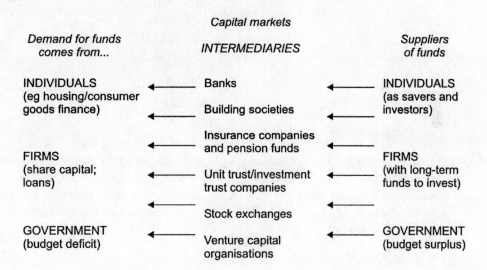

1.6 The role of advisors

Raising finance on the capital market requires input from a wide range of experts. The diagram below, adapted from the London Stock Exchange website, summarises the advisors involved in a listing and their respective responsibilities.

The legal requirements concerning advisors vary from one jurisdiction to another. In this section, we will take the example of the London Stock Exchange to give you an overview of the role of advisors in the capital market.

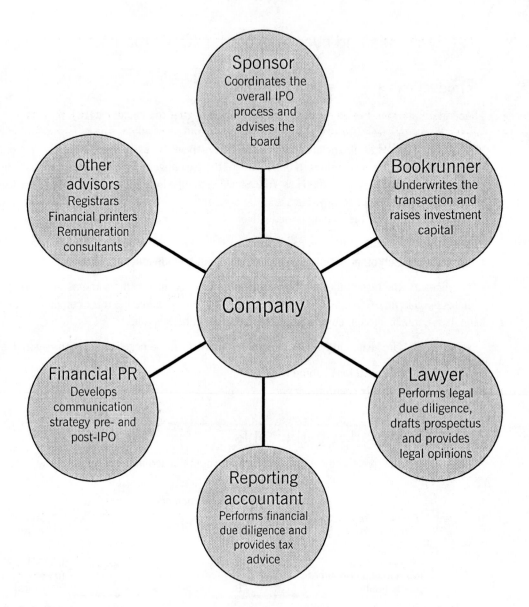

1.6.1 Sponsor

A **sponsor**, typically an investment bank or large accountancy firm, acts as the lead advisor in an **Initial Public Offer (IPO)** on the Main Market. We cover IPOs in Section 2.4 below. Firms offering services as sponsors must be approved by the **UK Listing Authority (UKLA)** which forms part of the UK's **Financial Conduct Authority (FCA)**. A list of approved sponsors can be found on the FCA's website: http://www.fca.org.uk/.

The sponsor's functions include:

(a)   Project managing the IPO process

(b)   Co-ordinating the due diligence and the drafting of the prospectus (the **prospectus** is the document in which the company offers its shares for sale)

(c)   Ensuring compliance with the applicable rules

(d)   Developing the investment case, valuation and offer structure

(e)   Managing the communication between the London Stock Exchange and the UKLA

(f)   Advising the company's board both before the IPO and after

While the sponsor advises the company, its primary responsibilities are owed to the UKLA. For example, the sponsor is required to submit an eligibility letter to the UKLA setting out how the company satisfies the admission criteria for its category of listing.

For listings on AIM the role of the sponsor is fulfilled by the **nominated advisor (Nomad)**, also approved by the FCA.

1.6.2 Bookrunner

As will be explained in section 2 below, share issues in the primary market may be **underwritten** by a financial institution, such as an investment bank. The issue of debt may be underwritten in the same way. The underwriter is referred to as the **bookrunner**.

The bookrunner undertakes to raise finance from investors on behalf of the company. In the process, it helps to determine the appropriate pricing for the share or debt. If the bookrunner is unable to find enough investors, it will hold some of the shares itself.

In a public offering, shares are often underwritten by a **syndicate** of several bookrunners.

1.6.3 Reporting accountant

The directors bear legal responsibility for the integrity of the listing documents (including the prospectus). The sponsor, as the company's lead advisor, risks considerable damage to its reputation should the prospectus be deficient.

For this reason, the sponsor would usually require the company to engage a **reporting accountant** to review and report on the company's readiness for the transaction.

The reporting accountant would typically report on the following:

(a) **Financial reporting procedures** – whether the company would be able to meet its reporting obligations as a public company

(b) **Financial historical records** – the equivalent of an audit opinion on the company's entire financial track record

(c) **Working capital** – whether the basis for the directors' working capital statement in the prospectus is sound

(d) **Other information** – any other additional information provided in the prospectus, such as profit forecasts and pro-forma financial information (for example, to illustrate the effects of an IPO)

In addition, the reporting accountant also issues a **long form report**, a private due diligence report covering the significant aspects of the company's business.

1.6.4 Lawyer

The London Stock Exchange is governed by EU law, UK Acts of Parliament, the FCA's Listing Rules and the Exchange's own rules. Lawyers therefore play an important part in ensuring that the company meets the eligibility criteria for the listing, and continues to comply with the ongoing obligations of a public company.

2 Sources of equity finance

Introduction

Equity finance is raised through the sale of **ordinary shares** to investors. We will focus on the new issue of shares for now.

2.1 Ordinary shares

Ordinary shares are issued to the owners of a company. In many countries, including the UK, ordinary shares have a **nominal** or **face** value, typically $1 or £1.

You should understand that the **market value** of a quoted company's shares bears **no relationship** to their nominal value, except that when ordinary shares are issued for cash, the issue price must be equal to or (more usually) more than the nominal value of the shares. Outside the UK it is not uncommon for a company's shares to have no nominal value.

Ordinary shareholders have **rights** as a result of their ownership of the shares.

(a)   Shareholders can attend company general meetings.

(b)   They can vote on important company matters such as the appointment and re-election of directors; approving a takeover bid for another company, where the financing arrangements will involve a large new issue of shares; the appointment of auditors; or (possibly, as in the UK) approving the company's remuneration policy for senior executives.

(c)   They are entitled to receive a share of any agreed dividend.

(d)   They will receive the annual report and accounts.

(e)   They will receive a share of any assets remaining after liquidation.

(f)   They can participate in any new issue of shares.

Ordinary shareholders are the ultimate bearers of **risk** as they are at the bottom of the **creditor hierarchy** in a liquidation. This means there is a significant risk they will receive nothing after the settlement of all the company's liabilities.

This risk means that shareholders expect the **highest return** of all long-term providers of finance in the form of dividend yields, dividend growth and share price growth. The cost of equity finance is therefore always **higher** than the cost of debt.

2.2 Advantages of a stock market listing

2.3 Disadvantages of a stock market listing

The owners of a company seeking a stock market listing must take the following disadvantages into account:

(a)   There will be significantly greater **public regulation**, **accountability** and **scrutiny**. The legal requirements the company faces will be greater, and the company will also be subject to the rules of the stock exchange on which its shares are listed.

(b)   A **wider circle of investors** with more exacting requirements will hold shares.

(c)   There will be additional costs involved in making share issues, including **brokerage commissions** and **underwriting fees**.

2.4 Methods of obtaining a listing

An unquoted company can obtain a listing on the stock market by means of a:

- **Initial public offer (IPO)**
- **Placing**
- **Introduction**

2.4.1 Initial public offering (IPO)

KEY TERM

An INITIAL PUBLIC OFFERING (IPO) is an invitation to apply for shares in a company based on information contained in a prospectus.

An **IPO** is a means of selling the shares of a company to the public at large for the first time.

When companies **go public** for the first time, a **large** issue will probably take the form of an IPO. This is known as a **flotation**. Subsequent issues are likely to be **placings** (described later) or **rights issues** which we will cover in F3.

An IPO entails the **acquisition by an issuing house** of a large block of shares of a company, with a view to offering them for sale to the public and investing institutions.

An issuing house is usually an investment bank (or sometimes a firm of stockbrokers). It may acquire the shares either as a direct allotment from the company or by purchase from existing members. In either case, the issuing house publishes an invitation to the public to apply for shares, either at a fixed price or on a tender basis. The issuing house **accepts responsibility** to the public, and gives to the issue the support of its own standing.

In an IPO the company's shareholders may take the opportunity to sell some of their shares. They receive the money from these share sales. In addition, the company will issue new shares in the IPO to raise equity finance for investment.

2.4.2 A placing

A **placing** is an arrangement whereby the shares are not all offered to the public. Instead, the sponsoring market maker arranges for most of the issue to be bought by a **small number of investors**, usually institutional investors such as pension funds and insurance companies.

2.4.3 The choice between an IPO and a placing

Is a company likely to prefer an IPO of its shares, or a placing?

(a)   **Placings** are much **cheaper**. Approaching institutional investors privately is a much cheaper way of obtaining finance, and thus placings are often used for smaller issues.

(b)   Placings are likely to be **quicker**.

(c)   Placings are likely to involve **less disclosure** of **information**.

(d)   However, most of the shares will be placed with a **relatively small number of (institutional) shareholders**, which means that most of the shares are **unlikely to be available for trading** after the flotation and **institutional shareholders** will have **control of the company**.

(e)   When a company first comes to the market, there may be a restriction on the proportion of shares that can be placed, or a minimum proportion that must be offered to the general public.

2.4.4 A stock exchange introduction

By this method of obtaining a quotation, no shares are made available to the market, neither existing nor newly created shares; nevertheless, the stock market grants a quotation. This will only happen where shares in a large private company are already widely held, so that a market can be seen to exist. A company might want an **introduction** to obtain **greater marketability** for the shares, or to acquire a share valuation for inheritance tax purposes or to gain easier access in the future to additional capital.

2.5 The cost of share issues on the stock market

Companies may incur the following costs when issuing shares:

- Underwriting costs (see Section 2.5.1)
- Stock market listing fee (the initial charge) for the new securities
- Fees of the issuing house, lawyers, reporting accountants and public relations consultant
- Charges for printing and distributing the prospectus
- Advertising in national newspapers

2.5.1 Underwriting

A company about to issue new securities in order to raise finance might decide to have the issue underwritten. **Underwriters** are financial institutions which agree (in exchange for a fixed fee, perhaps 2.25% of the finance to be raised) to buy, at the issue price, any securities which are **not subscribed** for by the investing public.

Underwriters **remove** the **risk** of a share issue being undersubscribed, but at a cost to the company issuing the shares. It is not compulsory to have an issue underwritten. Ordinary offers for sale are likely to be underwritten, and rights issues may be as well.

Underwriters are an important component of the syndicate of advisers involved in helping a company to raise finance on the capital market.

2.6 Pricing shares for a stock market launch

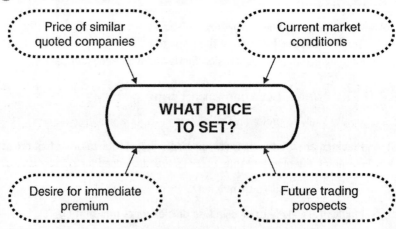

Companies will be keen to avoid **overpricing an issue**, which could result in the **issue** being **undersubscribed**, leaving underwriters with the unwelcome task of having to buy up the unsold shares. On the other hand, if the **issue price** is **too low** then the issue will be **oversubscribed** and the company would have been able to raise the required capital by issuing fewer shares.

The share price of an issue is usually advertised as being based on a certain **Price/Earnings (P/E) ratio**, the ratio of the company's current share price to their most recent **earnings per share** figure in its audited accounts. The issuer's P/E ratio can then be compared by investors with the P/E ratios of similar quoted companies. We will cover the P/E ratio in Chapter 19.

3 Sources of long-term debt finance

Introduction

A range of long-term sources of finance is available to businesses including **debt finance**, **leasing**, **venture capital** and **equity finance**.

The choice of debt finance that a company can issue depends upon:

- The size of the business (a public issue of bonds is only available to a large company)

- The duration of the loan

- Whether a fixed or floating interest rate is preferred (fixed rates are more expensive, but floating rates are riskier)

- The security that can be offered

During your F1 studies you learned about the different sources of short-term finance. In order for businesses to be sustainable, however, its managers must carefully consider its long-term finance options. We will now evaluate the different sources of long-term finance, starting with debt finance, and then moving on to equity finance.

Long-term finance is used for major investments and is usually more expensive and less flexible than short-term finance.

3.1 Reasons for seeking debt finance

Sometimes businesses may need long-term funds, but may not wish to issue equity capital. Perhaps the current shareholders will be unwilling or unable to **contribute additional capital**; possibly the company does not wish to involve outside shareholders who may have more onerous requirements than current members.

Other reasons for choosing debt finance may include a **lower cost** and **easier availability**, particularly if the company has little or no existing debt finance. Debt finance provides **tax relief** on interest payments.

3.2 Sources of debt finance

If a company does wish to raise debt finance, it will need to consider what **type** of finance will be available. If it is seeking medium-term bank finance, it ought to be in the form of a **loan**, although an overdraft is a virtually permanent feature of many companies' statements of financial position. Bank finance, in the form of bank loans, is a most important source of debt for small companies.

If a company is seeking to issue bonds, it must decide whether the bonds will be **repaid (redeemed)**, whether there will be **conversion rights** into shares, and whether **warrants** (a security entitling the holder to buy shares in the company at a fixed price in the future) will be attached.

3.3 Factors influencing the choice of debt finance

Generally, the following considerations influence what type of debt finance is sought.

(a)   **Availability**

Only listed companies will be able to make a **public issue of bonds** on a stock exchange. With a public issue the bonds are listed on a stock market, although most bond trading is off-exchange. Most investors will not invest in bonds issued by small companies. Smaller companies are only able to obtain significant amounts of debt finance from a bank.

(b)   **Credit rating**

Large companies may prefer to issue bonds if they have a strong credit rating. Credit ratings are given to bond issues by credit rating agencies, such as Standard & Poor's and Moody's. The credit rating given to a bond issue affects the interest yield that investors will require. If a company's bonds would only be given a sub-investment grade rating (**junk bond** rating), the company may prefer to seek debt finance from a bank loan.

(c)   **Amount**

Bond issues are usually for large amounts. If a company wants to borrow only a small amount of money, a bank loan would be appropriate.

(d)   **Term**

If loan finance is sought to buy a particular asset to generate revenues for the business, the length of the loan should **match** the length of time that the asset will be generating revenues.

(e)   **Fixed or floating rate**

Expectations of interest rate movements will determine whether a company chooses to borrow at a fixed or floating rate. Fixed-rate finance may be more expensive, but the business runs the risk of adverse upward rate movements if it chooses floating rate finance. Banks may refuse to lend at a fixed rate for more than a given period of time.

(f)   **Security and covenants**

The choice of finance may be determined by the assets that the business is willing or able to offer as **security**, also on the restrictions in **covenants** that the lenders wish to impose.

3.4 Term loans

A **term loan** is a loan for a fixed amount for a specified period, usually from a bank. The loan may have a specific purpose, such as the purchase of an asset. It is drawn in full at the beginning of the loan period and repaid at a specified time or in defined instalments. Term loans are offered with a variety of **repayment schedules**. Often, the interest and capital repayments are predetermined.

The bank establishes a separate loan account for the loan, charging interest to the account and setting off loan payments against the balance on the account.

Shorter-term loans can be considered a form of short-term finance, as an alternative to a bank overdraft. The main advantage of lending on a loan account for the bank is that it makes **monitoring** and **control** of the advance much easier, because the loan cash flows are recorded in a separate account. The bank can see immediately when the customer is falling behind with his repayments, or struggling to make the payments. With overdraft lending, a customer's difficulties might be obscured for some time by the variety of transactions on his current account. The lower risk that loans represent is reflected in a lower rate of interest than for overdrafts.

(a)   The customer knows what he will be **expected** to **pay back** at regular intervals and the bank can also predict its future income with more certainty (depending on whether the interest rate is fixed or floating).

(b)   Once the loan is agreed, the **term** of the loan must be **adhered** to provided that the customer does not fall behind with his repayments. It is not repayable on demand by the bank.

(c)   Because the bank will be committing its funds to a customer for a number of years, it may wish to insist on **building certain written safeguards** into the loan agreement to prevent the customer from becoming over-extended with his borrowing during the course of the loan. A loan **covenant** is a condition that the borrower must comply with. If the borrower does not act in accordance with the covenants, the loan can be considered in **default** and the bank can demand repayment.

3.5 Tax relief on loan interest

As far as companies are concerned, debt capital is a potentially attractive source of finance because interest charges **reduce the profits** chargeable to corporation tax.

(a) A new issue of bonds is likely to be preferable to a new issue of preference shares. (Preference shares are shares carrying a fixed rate of dividends, but in the UK. dividends paid are not allowable against tax)

(b) Companies might wish to **avoid dilution of shareholdings** and **increase gearing** (the ratio of fixed-interest capital to equity capital) in order to improve their earnings per share by benefiting from tax relief on interest payments.

3.6 Bonds

Introduction

The term **bond** describes various forms of long-term debt a company may issue, such as **loan notes** or **debentures**, which may be:

- **Redeemable**
- **Irredeemable**

Bonds or loans come in various forms, including:

- **Floating rate debentures**
- **Zero coupon bonds**
- **Convertible bonds**

3.6.1 Conventional bonds

Conventional bonds are fixed-rate redeemable bonds.

KEY TERM

BONDS are long-term debt capital raised by a company for which interest is paid, usually half yearly and at a fixed rate. Holders of bonds are therefore long-term creditors of the company.

Bonds have a nominal value, which is the debt owed by the company, and interest is paid at a stated **coupon** on this amount. For example, if a company issues 10% bonds, the coupon will be 10% of the nominal value of the bonds, so that $100 of bonds will receive $10 interest each year. The rate quoted is the gross rate, before tax.

Unlike shares, debt is often issued **at par** ie with $100 payable per $100 nominal value, or close to par value. Bond prices are quoted per $100 nominal value of bonds, so a price of 98.65 means a market price of $98.65 per $100 nominal value.

Where the coupon rate is fixed at the time of issue, it will be set according to **prevailing market conditions** given the **credit rating** of the company issuing the debt. Subsequent changes in market (and company) conditions will cause the **market value** of the bond to fluctuate, although the coupon will stay at the fixed percentage of the nominal value.

Bonds issued by large companies are marketable, but bond markets are small. When a company issues new equity shares, the new shares rank equally with all existing equity shares, and can be bought and sold in the same market. In contrast, each bond issue is different with its own interest rate and redemption date; the market for different bond issues by the same company cannot be combined. This is why equities may be extensively traded on a stock market, but bonds are not.

KEY TERM

DEBENTURES are a form of bond or loan note, the written acknowledgement of a debt incurred by a company, normally containing provisions about the payment of interest and the eventual repayment of capital.

3.7 Deep discount bonds

KEY TERM

DEEP DISCOUNT BONDS are bonds or loan notes issued at a price which is at a large discount to the nominal value of the bonds/notes, and which will be redeemable at par (or above par) when they eventually mature.

For example, a company might issue $1,000,000 of bonds in 20X1, at a price of $50 per $100 of bond, and redeemable at par in the year 20X9. The coupon rate of interest will be very low compared with yields on conventional bonds with the same maturity.

Investors might be attracted by the **large capital gain** offered by the bonds, which is the difference between the **issue price** and the **redemption value**. However, deep discount bonds will carry a much **lower rate of interest** than other types of bond. The only tax advantage is that the gain is taxed (as **income**) in one lump on maturity or sale, not as amounts of interest each year. The borrower can, however, **deduct notional interest** each year in computing profits.

The main benefit of deep discount bonds for a company is that the interest yield on the bonds is lower than on conventional, fixed-rate redeemable bonds. However, it will have to pay a much larger amount at maturity than it borrowed when the bonds were issued. Deep discount bonds defer much of the cost of the debt.

3.8 Zero coupon bonds

KEY TERM

ZERO COUPON BONDS are bonds that are issued at a discount to their redemption value, but no interest is paid on them.

Zero coupon bonds are an extreme form of deep discount bond. For example, a company may issue zero coupon discount bonds at $75, pay no interest at all, but at maturity (say, five years later) redeem the bonds at $100. The investor gains from the difference between the issue price and the redemption value ($25 per $75 invested). There is an implied interest rate in the amount of discount at which the bonds are issued (or subsequently resold on the market).

(a)   The advantage for borrowers is that zero coupon bonds can be used to **raise cash immediately**, and there is **no cash repayment** until redemption date. The cost of redemption is known at the time of issue. The borrower can plan to have funds available to redeem the bonds at maturity.

(b)   The **advantage for lenders** is **restricted,** unless the rate of discount on the bonds offers a high yield. The only way of obtaining cash from the bonds before maturity is to sell them. Their **market value** will depend on the **remaining term** to maturity and **current market interest rates**.

The tax advantages of zero coupon bonds are the same as those for deep discount bonds (see Section 3.7 above).

Deep discount bonds and zero coupon bonds are not common. Companies must want to pay little or no interest and incur the main cost at redemption. Investors must have reasons for wanting to invest in these bonds, rather than in conventional bonds.

3.9 Convertible bonds

Introduction

Convertible bonds are bonds that give the holder the right to convert to other securities, normally ordinary shares, at a predetermined price/rate and time.

Convertible bonds are fixed-rate bonds. The coupon rate of interest is lower than on similar conventional bonds. They give the bondholders the right (but not an obligation) to convert their bonds at a specified future date into new equity shares of the company, at a conversion rate that is also specified when the bonds are issued.

There may be more than one date on which the bonds can be converted into equity. If so, the conversion rate normally differs for each conversion date.

For example, the conversion terms for a convertible bond may be that on 1 April 20X0, $100 of bonds can be converted into 40 ordinary shares, whereas on 1 April 20X1, the conversion rate is 45 ordinary shares per $100 of bonds. Once converted, convertible bonds cannot be converted back into the original fixed-rate bond.

If bondholders choose not to convert their bonds into shares, the bonds will be redeemed at maturity, usually at par.

3.9.1 The conversion value and the conversion premium

The current market value of ordinary shares into which a bond may be converted is known as the **conversion value**. The conversion value will be below the value of the bond at the date of issue, but will be expected to increase as the date for conversion approaches on the assumption that a company's shares ought to increase in market value over time.

Conversion value = Conversion ratio × market price per share

Conversion premium = Current market value − current conversion value

Example: Convertible bonds 1

The 5% convertible bonds of Starchwhite are quoted at $142 per $100 nominal. The earliest date for conversion is in four years' time, at the rate of 30 ordinary shares per $100 nominal bond. The share price is currently $4.15. Annual interest on the bonds has just been paid.

Required

(a) Calculate the current conversion value.

(b) Calculate the conversion premium and comment on its meaning.

Solution

(a) Conversion ratio is $100 bond = 30 ordinary shares
     Conversion value = 30 × $4.15 = $124.50

(b) Conversion premium = $(142 − 124.50) = $17.50 or $\dfrac{17.50}{124.50} \times 100\% = 14\%$

The share price would have to rise by 14% before the conversion rights became attractive.

3.9.2 The issue price and the market price of convertible bonds

A company will aim to issue bonds with the **greatest possible conversion premium** as this will mean that, for the amount of capital raised, it will, on conversion, have to issue the lowest number of new ordinary shares. The premium that will be accepted by potential investors will depend on the company's growth potential and therefore on the prospects for a sizeable increase in the share price.

Convertible bonds issued at par normally have a **lower coupon rate of interest** than conventional fixed return bonds. This lower interest rate is the price the investor has to pay for the conversion rights. It is, of course, also one of the reasons why the issue of convertible bonds is attractive to a company.

A large company may issue convertible bonds rather than conventional bonds in order to benefit from lower interest costs, even if this means having to issue new shares in the future when profits and cash flows are stronger.

When convertible bonds are traded on a stock market, their **minimum market price** or **floor value** will be the price of conventional bonds with the same coupon rate of interest. If the market value falls to this minimum, it follows that the market attaches no value to the conversion rights.

The actual market price of convertible bonds will depend on:

- The **price of straight debt**

- The **current conversion value**

- The **length of time** before conversion may take place

- The **market's expectation** as to future equity returns and the risk associated with these returns

Most companies issuing convertible bonds expect them to be **converted**. They view the bonds as delayed equity. They are often used because either the company's ordinary share price is considered particularly depressed at the time of issue, or the issue of equity shares would result in an immediate and significant drop in earnings per share. There is no certainty, however, that the security holders will exercise their option to convert; therefore the bonds may run their full term and need to be redeemed.

Example: Convertible bonds 2

CD has issued 50,000 units of convertible bonds, each with a nominal value of $100 and a coupon rate of interest of 10% payable yearly. Each $100 of convertible bonds may be converted into 40 ordinary shares of CD in three years' time. Any bonds not converted will be redeemed at 110 (that is, at $110 per $100 nominal value of bond).

Required

Estimate the likely current market price for $100 of the bonds if investors in the bonds now require a pre-tax return of only 8%, and the expected value of CD ordinary shares on the conversion day is:

(a) $2.50 per share
(b) $3.00 per share

Solution

(a) **Shares are valued at $2.50 each**

If shares are only expected to be worth $2.50 each on conversion day, the value of 40 shares will be $100, and investors in the debt will presumably therefore redeem their debt at 110 instead of converting them into shares.

The market value of $100 of the convertible debt will be the discounted present value of the expected future income stream.

Year		Cash flow $	Discount factor 8%	Present value $
1	Interest	10	0.926	9.26
2	Interest	10	0.857	8.57
3	Interest	10	0.794	7.94
3	Redemption value	110	0.794	87.34
				113.11

The estimated market value is $113.11 per $100 of debt. This is also the floor value.

(b) **Shares are valued at $3.00 each**

If shares are expected to be worth $3.00 each, the debtholders will convert their debt into shares (value per $100 of bonds = 40 shares × $3.00 = $120) rather than redeem their debt at 110.

Year		Cash flow/value	Discount factor	Present value
		$	8%	$
1	Interest	10	0.926	9.26
2	Interest	10	0.857	8.57
3	Interest	10	0.794	7.94
3	Value of 40 shares	120	0.794	95.28
				121.05

The estimated market value is $121.05 per $100 of debt.

3.9.3 Security

Bonds may be secured. Bank loans are often secured. **Security** may take the form of either a **fixed charge** or a **floating charge**.

Fixed charge	Floating charge
Security relates to specific asset/group of assets (for example, land and buildings).	Security in event of default is whatever assets of the class secured (inventory/trade receivables) the company then owns.
Company can't dispose of these assets without providing substitute/consent of lender.	Company can dispose of assets until default takes place.
	In event of default, lenders appoint receiver rather than lay claim to the asset.

Investors are likely to expect a higher yield with **unsecured bonds** to compensate them for the extra risk. Similarly, a bank may charge higher interest for an unsecured loan compared with a similar secured loan.

3.10 The redemption of bonds

KEY TERM

REDEMPTION is the repayment of preference shares and bonds at maturity.

Bonds are usually redeemable. They are issued for a term of 10 years or more, and perhaps 25 to 30 years. At the end of this period, they will **mature** and become redeemable (at par or possibly at a value above par).

Most redeemable bonds have an earliest and a latest redemption date. For example, 12% Debenture Stock 20X7/X9 is redeemable at any time between the earliest specified date (in 20X7) and the latest date (in 20X9). The **issuing company** can choose the date.

Some bonds do not have a redemption date, and are **irredeemable** or undated. Undated bonds might be redeemed by a company that wishes to pay off the debt, but there is no obligation on the company to do so.

3.10.1 How will a company finance the redemption of long-term debt?

There is no guarantee that a company will be able to raise a new loan to pay off a maturing debt. One item investors should look for in a company's statement of financial position is the **redemption date** of current loans, to establish how much new finance is likely to be needed by the company and when.

Occasionally, perhaps because the secured assets have fallen in value and would not realise much in a forced sale, or perhaps out of a belief that the company can improve its position soon, unpaid debenture holders may be persuaded to surrender their debentures. In exchange they may get an **equity interest** in

the company or **convertible debentures**, paying a lower rate of interest, but carrying the option to convert the debentures into shares at a specified time in the future.

Case Study

CASE STUDY

Wage costs at Europe's top-tier football clubs have been growing at an incredible rate, and are eating up nearly two-thirds of their revenues, according to a report published by UEFA, the football governing body.

Examining the 2008 accounts of the 700-plus clubs it licenses, UEFA found that like for like staff costs grew by what UEFA said was an 'incredible 18 per cent in the year', outstripping a 10.6 per cent rise in revenues.

With wages accounting for 61 per cent of the €11.5bn ($15.5bn) of revenues, overall costs have risen 11.1 per cent to €12.1bn, exceeding revenues.

Michel Platini, UEFA's chairman, said while many clubs operated on a sustainable basis, 'there are many ... finding it increasingly hard to coexist and compete with clubs that incur costs and transfer fees beyond their means and report losses year after year'.

The debt carried by top English clubs such as Liverpool and Manchester United worries UEFA. The governing body estimated net debt across the clubs at €6.3bn, with England's share at nearly €4bn.

UEFA found that nearly half the 733 clubs in Europe's top divisions could not break even. There was also a wide discrepancy across clubs, with the biggest 10 per cent claiming two-thirds of all revenues and paying 70 per cent of all wages.

Financial Times, 25 February 2010

3.11 Issuing debt instruments

3.11.1 Bank loans

Bank loans are obtained through a direct contractual agreement with a bank. Traditionally, the conventional bank loan is simpler to access, and often cheaper, than other forms of debt funding. The downside of such loans lies in the restrictive terms and conditions (**bank covenants**) which, if breached, cause the loan to be withdrawn.

Since the financial crisis in 2008, banks worldwide have been required to hold more capital (through the Basel II and Basel III accords) and as a result, they have adopted a more conservative approach to lending. From the companies' perspective, this uncertainty about the banks' willingness and ability to lend has caused companies to consider other, more flexible, forms of finance, with less onerous terms and conditions.

3.11.2 Corporate bonds

Corporate bonds are most commonly issued on the **primary market**. Typically, the issue of corporate bonds is **underwritten**. As we have seen in relation to share issues, the underwriters – normally financial institutions such as banks – buy the issue of bonds and sell them on to investors.

Bonds are often **traded over the counter**, that is to say sold and bought directly through financial institutions without the supervision of recognised exchanges.

However, corporate bonds can also be **traded publicly** in bond markets. Many of the recognised exchanges, such as the London Stock Exchange and the New York Stock Exchange, have an associated bond market. The issue of bonds on an exchange resembles the process for share issues: a prospectus must be prepared, which must be approved by the listing authority in order for the bonds to be admitted to trading. Bonds traded on exchanges can then be resold on **secondary markets**.

The OTC markets for bonds are less transparent, and therefore riskier, for investors, as they lack the oversight of the recognised exchanges. Investors in OTC markets therefore demand a higher yield, making bonds traded in such markets more expensive for the issuing companies.

Chapter Summary

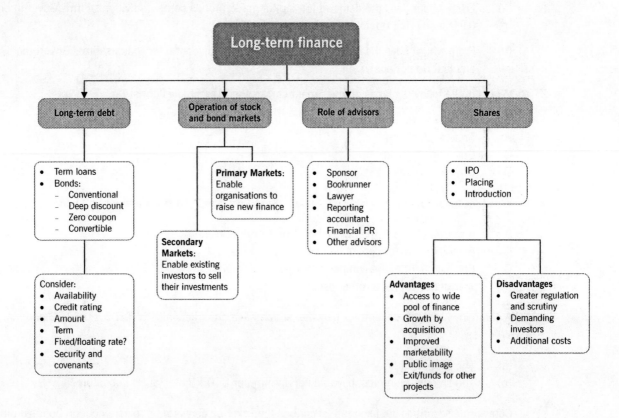

Quick Quiz

1   (a)   From whom does the **demand** for capital market funds come: Individuals/Firms/Government? (Delete any that do not apply).

      (b)   From whom does the **supply** of capital market funds come: Individuals/Firms/Government? (Delete any that do not apply).

2   Which of the following types of investment carries the highest level of risk?

     A   Corporate bonds
     B   Preference shares
     C   Government bonds
     D   Ordinary shares

3   Which of the following is least likely to be a reason for seeking a stock market flotation?

     A   Improving the existing owners' control over the business
     B   Access to a wider pool of finance
     C   Enhancement of the company's image
     D   Transfer of capital to other uses

4   A company has 12% debentures in issue, which have a market value of $135 per $100 nominal value. What is:

      (a)   The coupon rate?
      (b)   The amount of interest payable per annum per $100 (nominal) of debenture?

5   Convertible securities are fixed-rate securities that may be converted into zero coupon bonds/ordinary shares/warrants. (Delete as appropriate.)

6   What is the value of $100 12% debt redeemable in three years' time at a premium of 20c per $ if the loanholder's required return is 10%?

Answers to Quick Quiz

1   (a) and (b): You should have deleted none.

2   D   Ordinary shares

3   A   Flotation is likely to involve a significant loss of control to a wider circle of investors.

4   (a)   12%
     (b) $12

5   Ordinary shares

6

Years		$	Discount factor 10%	Present value $
1–3	Interest	12	2.487	29.84
3	Redemption premium	120	0.751	90.12
Value of debt				119.96

Now try these questions from the Practice Question Bank

Number	Level	Marks	Time
Q1	Introductory	N/A	15 mins
Q2	Introductory	N/A	18 mins

COST OF CAPITAL

Having learned about the different sources of debt and equity finance available to companies, we will now look at how the cost of such finance is calculated. In considering financing options, it is important to estimate the value of each type of debt or equity finance in today's terms. Each company's financing structure changes the level of risk undertaken by the company's shareholders, and therefore the shareholders' required level of return also changes. The calculation of the weighted average cost of capital takes this into account. Like the previous chapter, this is a new topic, so make sure you are well-prepared to answer questions on the topic in the exams.

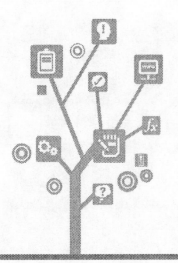

Topic list	learning outcomes	syllabus references
1 Discounted cash flows	A2	A2(a)
2 The cost of capital	A2	A2(c)
3 The cost of equity – the dividend growth model	A2	A2(a)
4 The cost of debt	A2	A2(b)
5 The weighted average cost of capital (WACC)	A2	A2(b)

Chapter Overview

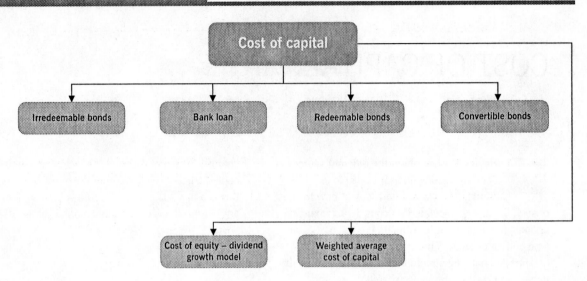

1 Discounted cash flows

Introduction

Discounted cash flows (DCF) is a technique which calculates how much cumulative future cash flows are worth in today's terms.

1.1 The time value of money

In this chapter, we will look at how to calculate the cost of debt and the cost of equity. This will enable you to determine the cost of capital in a company, given the level of debt and equity finance it takes on.

Before we launch into the key topics in this chapter, however, you will need to first understand the concept of discounted cash flows. The discounted cash flow technique will underlie the exam formulae for both dividend valuation and the cost of various types of debt.

Exam alert

It is essential for you to understand the concept of **discounting**, in order to calculate the cost of capital in the exam.

Discounted cash flow (DCF) is a valuation technique which takes into account both the timings of cash flows and also total profitability over the life of an investment.

The **timing** of cash flows is taken into account by **discounting them**. $1 earned today will be worth more than $1 earned after two years. This is partly due to the effect of inflation, and partly due to the greater certainty in having $1 in hand today compared to the promise of $1 in the future. In addition, cash we have in hand today can be spent or invested elsewhere for example, put into a savings account to earn annual interest.

1.2 Compounding

Suppose that a company has $10,000 to invest, and can earn a return of 10% (compound interest) on its investments. This means that if the $10,000 could be invested at 10%, the value of the investment with interest would build up as follows.

(a) After 1 year $10,000 × (1.10) = $11,000
(b) After 2 years $10,000 × (1.10)^2 = $12,100
(c) After 3 years $10,000 × (1.10)^3 = $13,310 and so on.

This is **compounding**. Compounding tells us how much an investment will be worth at the end, and can be used to compare two projects with the same duration. The formula for the future value of an investment plus accumulated interest after n time periods is:

$$FV = PV (1 + r)^n$$

where FV is the future value of the investment with interest

PV is the initial or **present value** of the investment

r is the compound rate of return per time period, expressed as a proportion (so 10% = 0.10, 5% = 0.05 and so on)

n is the number of time periods

1.3 Discounting

KEY TERM

PRESENT VALUE is the cash equivalent, now, of a sum of money receivable or payable at a stated future date, discounted at a specified rate of return.

Discounting starts with the future value, and converts a future value to a present value. Discounting tells us how much an investment will be worth in today's terms. This method can be used to compare two investments with different durations.

For example, if a company expects to earn a (compound) rate of return of 10% on its investments, how much would it need to invest now to have the following investments?

(a) $11,000 after 1 year
(b) $12,100 after 2 years
(c) $13,310 after 3 years

The answer is $10,000 in each case, and we can calculate it by discounting. The discounting formula to calculate the present value of a future sum of money at the end of n time periods is as follows.

LEARN

Present value of $1 = (1+r)^{-n}$ or $\dfrac{1}{(1+r)^n}$

(a)   After 1 year $11,000 \times \dfrac{1}{1.10} = £10,000$

(b)   After 2 years $12,100 \times \dfrac{1}{1.10^2} = £10,000$

(c)   After 3 years $13,310 \times \dfrac{1}{1.10^3} = £10,000$

Discounting can be applied to both money receivable and also to money payable at a future date. By discounting all payments and receipts from a capital investment to a present value, they can be compared on a common basis at a value which takes account of when the various cash flows will take place.

Example: Present value

Spender Co expects the cash inflow from an investment to be $40,000 after 2 years and another $30,000 after 3 years. Its target rate of return is 12%. Calculate the present value of these future returns, and explain what this present value signifies.

Solution

(a)

Year	Cash flow $	Discount factor 12%	Present value $
2	40,000	$\dfrac{1}{(1.12)^2} = 0.797$	31,880
3	30,000	$\dfrac{1}{(1.12)^3} = 0.712$	21,360
		NPV =	53,240

(b)   The present value of the future returns, discounted at 12%, is $53,240. This means that if Spender Ltd can invest now to earn a return of 12% on its investments, it would have to invest $53,240 now to earn the equivalent of $40,000 after 2 years plus $30,000 after 3 years.

1.4 The discount factor

In the compounding and discounting examples above, we used the company's required rate of return as the discount factor. How do companies decide the rate of return that they require?

Imagine Company A has a bank account earning 5% interest. When considering whether or not to invest in a project, the company's directors may use the bank interest rate as a benchmark. If the investment's rate of return is 3%, would Company A invest? Probably not, because a higher level of return can be earned by simply depositing the same amount of money in the bank account. However, if the investment's rate of return is 8%, then the company will probably choose to invest.

On the other hand, consider Company B which has no cash in hand. It will be required to borrow from a bank, should it decide to invest in a project. Company B's directors may use the loan interest rate as a benchmark when evaluating investments, to ensure that they only accept projects which sufficiently reward the company for the additional costs the company has to bear in making the investment. If the company borrows at 6%, it will most likely reject a project which yields a rate of return of 3%. However, it may consider a project that is expected to yield a rate of return of 8%.

These examples are two simplistic ways of thinking about the **cost of capital**, often used to derive a **discount rate** for DCF analysis and investment appraisal.

The cost of capital has two aspects to it.

(a)   It is the **cost of funds** that a company raises and uses.

(b)   It is the return that investors expect to be paid for putting funds into the company. It is therefore the **minimum return** that a company should make from its own investments, to earn the cash flows out of which investors can be paid their return.

Later in this chapter, we will look at how to calculate the cost of capital.

1.5 Net present value (NPV)

Introduction

Net present value or **NPV** is the value obtained by discounting all cash outflows and inflows of a capital investment project by a chosen target rate of return or **cost of capital**.

An **annuity** is a constant cash flow for a number of years.

A **perpetuity** is a constant annual cash flow (an annuity) that will last for ever.

The NPV method compares the **present value (PV)** of all the **cash inflows** from an investment with the PV of all the **cash outflows** from an investment. The NPV is thus calculated as the PV of **cash inflows** minus the PV of **cash outflows**.

Example: Net present value

A company is considering a capital investment, where the estimated cash flows are as follows.

Year		Cash flow
		$
0	(ie now)	(100,000)
1		60,000
2		80,000
3		40,000
4		30,000

The company's cost of capital is 15%. You are required to calculate the NPV of the project and to assess whether it should be undertaken.

Solution

Year	Cash flow $	Discount factor 15%	PV $
0	(100,000)	1.000	(100,000)
1	60,000	$\frac{1}{(1.15)} = 0.870$	52,200
2	80,000	$\frac{1}{(1.15)^2} = 0.756$	60,480
3	40,000	$\frac{1}{(1.15)^3} = 0.658$	26,320
4	30,000	$\frac{1}{(1.15)^4} = 0.572$	17,260
		NPV =	56,260

Note. The discount factor for any cash flow now (year 0) is always = 1, regardless of what the cost of capital is.

In this example, the PV of cash inflows exceeds the PV of cash outflows by $56,160, which means that the project will earn a net discounted cash inflow in excess of 15%. It should therefore be undertaken.

1.5.1 Using discount tables

The discount factor that we use in discounting is $\dfrac{1}{(1+r)^n} = (1+r)^{-n}$

Instead of having to calculate this factor every time, we can use tables. Discount tables for the present value of $1, for different values of r and n, are shown in the Appendix to this Study Text. Use these tables to work out your own solution to the following question.

Question 2.1   Net present value

Learning outcome A1

A company is planning an investment for which the following cash flows have been estimated.

Year	Net cash flow $
0	(10,000)
1	5,000
2	5,000
3	4,000

Using tables, what is the net present value of the investment if cost of capital is 14%?

1.6 Annuity tables

Where there is a **constant cash flow** from year to year, we can calculate the present value by adding together the discount factors for the individual years.

These total factors could be described as **same cash flow per annum** factors, **cumulative present value** factors or **annuity factors**.

The present value of an annuity can be calculated by multiplying the annual cash flow in the annuity by the sum of all the discount factors for the years in the annuity.

Annuity factors for annuities beginning in Year 1 (and for different costs of capital) are shown in the table for cumulative PV of $1 factors, which is shown in the Appendix to this Study Text. (2.402 for example, is in the column for 12% per annum and the row for year 3.)

Example: Annuity

If you have not used them before, check that you can understand annuity tables by trying the following exercise.

(a)   What is the present value of $1,000 in contributions earned each year from years 1 to 10, when the required return on investment is 11%?

(b)   What is the present value of $2,000 costs incurred each year from years 3 to 6 when the cost of capital is 5%?

Solution

(a)   The PV of $1,000 earned each year from year 1 to 10 when the required earning rate of money is 11% is calculated as follows.

$1,000 × 5.889 = $5,889

(b)   The PV of $2,000 in costs each year from years 3 to 6 when the cost of capital is 5% per annum is calculated as follows.

PV of $1 per annum for years 1 to 6 at 5% =	5.076
Less PV of $1 per annum for years 1 to 2 at 5% =	1.859
PV of $1 per annum for years 3 to 6 =	3.217

PV = $2,000 × 3.217 = $6,434

1.7 Annual cash flows in perpetuity

Exam alert

Make sure that you learn the formula for a perpetuity. It forms the basis of the dividend valuation model, and the calculation of the cost of irredeemable debt – both of which can be tested in the exam!

Perpetuities are constant cash flows which are assumed to occur forever. The formula for a perpetuity therefore captures the cumulative present value of cash flows being paid/received every year in perpetuity (that is, forever).

LEARN

$$PV = \frac{c}{r}, \text{ or } r = \frac{c}{PV}$$

Where PV is the **cumulative present value**, c is the constant cash flow each period and r is the cost of capital.

When the cost of capital is r, the cumulative present value of $1 per annum in perpetuity is **$1/r**.

For example, the PV of $1 per annum in perpetuity at a discount rate of 10% would be $1/0.10 = $10.

Similarly, the PV of $1 per annum in perpetuity at a discount rate of 15% would be $1/0.15 = $6.67 and at a discount rate of 20% it would be $1/0.20 = $5.

An annuity in perpetuity is unlikely to exist. However, the annuity factor in perpetuity is a good approximation for the value of an annuity **for a very long time**. This is because discount factors for years in the distant future are very small and insignificant.

Example: Perpetuities

An organisation with a cost of capital of 14% is considering investing in a project costing $500,000. The project would yield nothing in Year 1, but from Year 2 would yield cash inflows of $100,000 per annum in perpetuity.

Required

Assess whether the project should be undertaken.

Solution

Year	Cash flow $	Discount factor 14%	Present value $
0	(500,000)	1.000	(500,000)
1	0	0.877	0
2 to ∞	100,000	1/0.14 × 0.877 = 6.264	626,400
		NPV =	126,400

A perpetuity of $100,000 per annum is calculated by multiplying $100,000 by 1/0.14. This gives a cumulative present value of cash inflows at Year 2 of $714,300.

However, because the cash inflows start only at Year 2, we need to discount the cash inflows back to today's value. This is done by using the present value factor of 0.877 (or $\dfrac{1}{(1+0.14)}$).

The NPV is positive and so the project should be undertaken.

2 The cost of capital

Introduction

The **cost of capital** is the rate of return that the enterprise must pay to satisfy the providers of funds, and it reflects the risk of providing funds.

2.1 Aspects of cost of capital

As we saw in Section 1, the cost of capital has two aspects to it:

(a)   The **cost of funds** that a company raises and uses
(b)   The **return** that investors expect to be paid for putting funds into the company

It is therefore the **minimum return** that a company should make on its own investments, to earn the cash flows out of which investors can be paid their return.

The cost of capital can therefore be measured by studying the returns required by investors. It can then be used to derive a discount rate for DCF analysis and investment appraisal.

Each form of capital has its own cost. For example, equity has a cost and each bank loan or bond issue has a different cost. A company must make sufficient returns from its investments to satisfy the requirements for return of all the different finance providers.

2.2 An opportunity cost of finance

The cost of capital is an **opportunity cost of finance**, because it is the minimum return that investors require. If they do not get this return, they will transfer some or all of their investment somewhere else. Here are two examples.

(a) If a bank offers to lend money to a company, the interest rate it charges is the **yield** that the bank wants to receive from investing in the company, because it can get just as good a return from lending the money to someone else. In other words, the interest rate is the opportunity cost of lending for the bank.

(b) When shareholders invest in a company, the returns that they can expect must be sufficient to persuade them not to sell some or all of their shares and invest the money somewhere else. The yield on the shares is therefore the **opportunity cost** to the **shareholders of not investing somewhere else**.

2.3 The cost of capital and risk

The cost of capital has three elements.

> **Risk-free rate of return +**
> **Premium for business risk +**
> **Premium for financial risk**
> **COST OF CAPITAL**

(a) **Risk-free rate of return**

This is the return which would be required from an investment if it were completely free from risk. Typically, a risk-free yield would be the **yield on government securities**.

(b) **Premium for business risk**

This is an increase in the required rate of return due to the existence of **uncertainty** about the future and about a **firm's business prospects**. The actual returns from an investment may not be as high as they are expected to be. Business risk will be higher for some firms than for others, and some types of project undertaken by a firm may be more risky than other types of project that it undertakes.

(c) **Premium for financial risk**

This relates to the danger of high debt levels (high gearing). The higher the gearing of a company's capital structure, the greater will be the financial risk to ordinary shareholders, and this should be reflected in a higher risk premium and therefore a higher cost of capital.

Because different companies are in different types of business (varying business risk) and have different capital structures (varying financial risk), the cost of capital applied to one company may differ radically from the cost of capital of another.

2.4 The relative costs of finance

The cost of debt (the rate a firm pays on its current loans, bonds and other debts) is likely to be **lower** than the cost of equity (the return paid to its shareholders). This is because debt is **less risky** from the debtholders' viewpoint. In the event of liquidation, the **creditor hierarchy** dictates the priority of claims and debt finance is paid off before equity. This makes debt a safer investment than equity, and hence debt investors demand a lower rate of return than equity investors.

Debt interest is also corporation **tax deductible** (unlike equity dividends) making it even cheaper to a tax-paying company. Arrangement costs are usually lower on debt finance than equity finance and once again, unlike equity arrangement costs, they are also tax deductible.

2.4.1 The creditor (payables) hierarchy

Increasing risk

1	Creditors with a fixed charge
2	Creditors with a floating charge
3	Unsecured creditors
4	Preference shareholders
5	Ordinary shareholders

This means that the **cheapest type of finance is debt** (especially if secured) and the **most expensive type of finance is equity** (ordinary shares).

3   The cost of equity – the dividend growth model

Introduction

The **dividend growth model** can be used to estimate a cost of equity, on the assumption that the market value of a share is directly related to the expected future dividends from the shares.

3.1 The cost of ordinary share capital

New funds from equity shareholders are obtained either from **new issues of shares** or from **retained earnings**. Both of these sources of funds have a cost.

(a)   Shareholders will **not** be prepared to **provide funds** for a **new issue** of **shares** unless the return on their investment is sufficiently attractive.

(b)   Retained earnings also have a cost. This is an **opportunity cost**, the dividend forgone by shareholders.

3.2 The dividend valuation model

If we begin by ignoring share issue costs then the cost of equity, both for new issues and retained earnings, could be estimated by means of a **dividend valuation model**, on the assumption that the market value of shares is directly related to expected future dividends on the shares.

Remember the formula for a perpetuity:

$$PV = \frac{c}{r} \text{ or } r = \frac{c}{PV}$$

Where c is the constant cash flow each period, and r is the cost of capital.

If the future dividend per share is expected to be **constant** in amount, the present value of future dividends is a perpetuity. It is no surprise then that the **ex dividend** share price is calculated by the formula:

$$P_0 = \frac{d}{(1+k_e)} + \frac{d}{(1+k_e)^2} + \frac{d}{(1+k_e)^3} + ... = \frac{d}{k_e} \text{ so } k_e = \frac{d}{P_0}$$

Where k_e is the cost of equity capital

   d   is the annual dividend per share, starting at year 1 and then continuing annually in perpetuity

   P_0 is the ex dividend share price (the price of a share where the share's new owner is **not** entitled to the dividend that is soon to be paid)

Example: Dividend valuation model with no growth

Cygnus has a dividend cover ratio of 4.0 times and expects zero growth in dividends. The company has one million $1 ordinary shares in issue and the market capitalisation (value) of the company is $50 million. After-tax profits for next year are expected to be $20 million.

What is the cost of equity capital?

Solution

Total dividends = 20m shares/4 = $5m

k_e = 5/50 = 10%

3.3 The dividend growth model

Shareholders will normally expect dividends to increase year by year and not to remain constant in perpetuity. The **fundamental theory of share values** states that the market price of a share is the present value of the discounted future cash flows of revenues from the share, so the market value given an expected constant annual growth in dividends would be:

$$P_0 = \frac{d_0(1+g)}{(1+k_e)} + \frac{d_0(1+g)^2}{(1+k_e)^2} + ...$$

where P_0 is the current market price (ex div)

d_0 is the current net dividend

k_e is the cost of equity capital

g is the expected annual growth in dividend payments

and both k_e and g are expressed as proportions

It is often convenient to assume a constant expected dividend growth rate in perpetuity. The formula above then simplifies to:

$$P_0 = \frac{d_0(1+g)}{(k_e - g)} = \frac{d_1}{(k_e - g)}$$

Rearranging this, we get a formula for the ordinary shareholders' cost of capital.

LEARN

Cost of ordinary (equity) share capital, having a current ex div price, P_0, having just paid a dividend, d_0, with the dividend growing in perpetuity by a constant g% per annum:

$$k_e = \frac{d_0(1+g)}{P_0} + g \text{ or } k_e = \frac{d_1}{P_0} + g$$

Look at the second formula above, and you will notice how it is consistent with the formula for constant dividends in Section 3.2. This will help you to remember the formula in the exam.

Example: Cost of equity

A share has a current market value of 96c, and the last dividend was 12c. If the expected annual growth rate of dividends is 4%, calculate the cost of equity capital.

Solution

$$\text{Cost of capital} = \frac{12(1 + 0.04)}{96} + 0.04$$

$$= 0.13 + 0.04$$

$$= 0.17$$

$$= 17\%$$

3.3.1 Estimating the growth rate

There are two methods for estimating the growth rate that you need to be familiar with.

Firstly, the future growth rate can be predicted from an **analysis of the growth in dividends** over the past few years.

Year	Dividends $	Earnings $
20X1	150,000	400,000
20X2	192,000	510,000
20X3	206,000	550,000
20X4	245,000	650,000
20X5	262,350	700,000

Dividends have risen from $150,000 in 20X1 to $262,350 in 20X5. The increase represents four years' growth. (Check that you can see that there are four years' growth, and not five years' growth, in the table.) The average growth rate, g, may be calculated as follows.

$$\text{Dividend in 20X1} \times (1 + g)^4 = \text{Dividend in 20X5}$$

$$(1+g)^4 = \frac{\text{Dividend in 20X5}}{\text{Dividend in 20X1}}$$

$$= \frac{\$262,350}{\$150,000}$$

$$= 1.749$$

$$1 + g = \sqrt[4]{1.749} = 1.15$$

$$g = 0.15 \text{ ie } 15\%$$

The growth rate over the last four years is assumed to be expected by shareholders into the indefinite future. If the company is financed entirely by equity and there are 1m shares in issue, each with a market value of $3.35 ex div, the cost of equity, K_e, is:

$$\frac{d_0(1+g)}{P_0} + g = \frac{0.26235(1.15)}{3.35} + 0.15 + 0.15 = 0.24 \text{ ie } 24\%$$

3.3.2 Gordon's growth approximation

Alternatively, the growth rate can be estimated using **Gordon's growth approximation**. The **rate of growth in dividends** is sometimes expressed, theoretically, as:

Gordon's growth approximation: g = br

Where g is the annual growth rate in dividends
       b is the proportion of profits that are retained
       r is the rate of return on new investments

So, if a company retains 65% of its earnings for capital investment projects it has identified and these projects are expected to have an average return of 8% then:

g = br = 65% × 8 = 5.2%

4 The cost of debt

Introduction

The cost of debt is the return an enterprise must pay to its lenders.

- For irredeemable debt, this is the (post-tax) interest as a percentage of the ex interest market value of the bonds (or preferred shares).

- For redeemable debt, the cost is given by the internal rate of return of the cash flows involved (interest and capital gain or loss on redemption).

The cost of debt is measured initially as a pre-tax cost of debt. It can then be adjusted to an after-tax cost of debt.

4.1 The cost of debt capital

Lenders are only willing to lend if their initial outlay of money is fully compensated by future cash inflows. Therefore, the cost of capital is the rate at which lenders recover their initial outlay of money, and the price of debt equals the present value of cash inflows. For the borrowing company this represents:

(a)   The cost of **continuing to use the finance** rather than redeem the securities at their current market price.

(b)   The cost of raising **additional fixed-interest capital** if we assume that the cost of the additional capital would be equal to the cost of that already issued. If a company has not already issued any fixed-interest capital, it may estimate the cost of doing so by making a similar calculation for another company which is judged to be similar as regards risk.

4.2 Irredeemable debt capital

Again, remember the formula for a perpetuity is $PV = \dfrac{c}{r}$

Irredeemable debt capital is a perpetuity. Rearrange the perpetuity formula and the cost of irredeemable debt capital, paying interest **i** in perpetuity, and having a current ex interest price, P_0, is as follows:

$$P_0 = \frac{i}{K_d} \text{ and } k_d = \frac{i}{P_0}$$

Example: Cost of debt capital 1

Lepus has issued bonds of $100 nominal value with annual interest of 9% per year, based on the nominal value. The current market price of the bonds is $90. What is the cost of the bonds?

Solution

$k_d = 9/90 = 10\%$

Example: Cost of debt capital 2

Henryted has 12% irredeemable bonds in issue with a nominal value of $100. The market price is $95 ex interest. Calculate the cost of capital if interest is paid half-yearly.

Solution

If interest is 12% annually, therefore 6% is payable half-yearly.

$$\text{Cost of loan capital} = \left(1 + \frac{6}{95}\right)^2 - 1 = 13.0\%$$

4.3 Redeemable debt capital

If the debt is **redeemable** then in the year of redemption the interest payment will be received by the holder as well as the amount payable on redemption, so, ignoring tax for now:

$$P_0 = \frac{i}{(1+k_{d\,net})} + \frac{i}{(1+k_{d\,net})^2} + ... + \frac{i+p_n}{(1+k_{d\,net})^n}$$

where p_n = the amount payable on redemption in year n

The above equation cannot be simplified, so $k_{d\,net}$ will have to be calculated by trial and error, as an **internal rate of return (IRR)**.

The best trial and error figure to start with in calculating the cost of redeemable debt is to take the cost of debt capital as if it were irredeemable and then add the annualised capital profit that will be made from the present time to the time of redemption.

Example: Cost of debt capital 3

Owen Allot has in issue 10% bonds of a nominal value of $100. The market price is $90 ex interest. Calculate the cost of this capital if the bonds are:

(a)   Irredeemable
(b)   Redeemable at par after ten years

Ignore taxation.

Solution

(a)   The cost of irredeemable debt capital is $\frac{i}{P_0} = \frac{\$10}{\$90} \times 100\% = 11.1\%$

(b)   The cost of redeemable debt capital. The capital profit that will be made from now to the date of redemption is $10 ($100 – $90). This profit will be made over a period of ten years which gives

an annualised profit of $1 which is about 1% of current market value. The best trial and error figure to try first is therefore 12%.

Year		Cash flow $	Discount factor 12%	PV $	Discount factor 11%	PV $
0	Market value	(90)	1.000	(90.00)	1.000	(90.00)
1–10	Interest	10	5.650	56.50	5.889	58.89
10	Capital repayment	100	0.322	32.20	0.352	35.20
				(1.30)		+4.09

The approximate cost of redeemable debt capital is therefore:

$$(11 + \frac{4.09}{(4.09 - -1.30)} \times 1) = 11.76\%$$

4.4 Redeemable debt capital and tax

The interest on debt capital is likely to be an allowable deduction for the purposes of taxation and so the cost of debt capital and the cost of share capital are not properly comparable costs. This tax relief on interest ought to be recognised in computations. The after-tax cost of irredeemable debt capital is:

$$k_{d\,net} = \frac{i(1-T)}{P_0}$$

where $k_{d\,net}$ is the cost of debt capital

i   is the annual interest payment

P_0 is the current market price of the debt capital ex interest (that is, after payment of the current interest)

T   is the rate of corporation tax

Note. This is only a variant of the cost of irredeemable debt capital formula in Section 4.2.

Cost of irredeemable debt capital, paying annual net interest i(1 – T), and having a current ex interest price, P₀:

$$k_{d\,net} = \frac{i(1-T)}{P_0}$$

Therefore, if a company pays $10,000 a year interest on irredeemable bonds with a nominal value of $100,000 and a market price of $80,000, and the rate of tax is 30%, the cost of the debt would be:

$$\frac{10,000}{80,000}(1-0.30) = 0.0875 = 8.75\%$$

The higher the rate of tax the greater the tax benefits in having debt finance will be compared with equity finance. In the example above, if the rate of tax had been 50%, the cost of debt would have been, after tax:

$$\frac{10,000}{80,000}(1-0.50) = 0.0625 = 6.25\%$$

Exam alert

Students often don't remember that debt attracts tax relief in most countries and jurisdictions.

In the case of **redeemable debt**, the capital repayment is not allowable for tax. There are two approaches to calculating the after-tax cost of redeemable debt.

- One approach is to calculate the after-tax cost to the company of the specific debt issue, recognising the fact that interest charges are allowable costs for tax purposes but the redemption of capital is not.

- A second approach is to calculate the pre-tax cost of the debt, and adjust it to an after-tax cost by applying the factor × (1 – t) to the pre-tax cost. This approach ignores the tax implications of redemption. **However, it is the method most commonly used when calculating the weighted average cost of capital for a company.**

Example: Cost of debt capital 4

(a) A company has outstanding $660,000 of 8% bonds on which the interest is payable annually on 31 December. The debt is due for redemption at par on 1 January 20X6. The market price of the bonds at 28 December 20X2 was $95. Ignoring any question of personal taxation, what do you estimate to be the current cost of debt?

(b) If the pre-tax cost of debt rises to 12% early in 20X3, what effect will this have on the market price?

(c) If the effective rate of tax on company profits is 30%, what would be the after-tax cost of debt of the bonds in (a) above? Assume that payments of tax occur in the same year as the item that gives rise to the increase or reduction in tax.

Solution

(a) The current cost of debt is found by calculating the pre-tax internal rate of return of the cash flows shown in the table below. A discount rate of 10% is chosen for a trial and error start to the calculation. This is the pre-tax cost of debt.

Item and date		Year	Cash flow	Discount factor	Present value
			$	10%	$
Market value	28.12.X2	0	(95)	1.000	(95.0)
Interest	31.12.X3	1	8	0.909	7.3
Interest	31.12.X4	2	8	0.826	6.6
Interest	31.12.X5	3	8	0.751	6.0
Redemption	1.01.X6	3	100	0.751	75.1
NPV					0.0

By coincidence, the cost of debt is 10% since the NPV of the cash flows above is zero.

(b) If the cost of debt rises to 12% in 20X3 the market price will fall to reflect the new rate of return required by each bondholder. The new market price will be the discounted value of all future cash flows up to the redemption date in 20X6, using a discount rate of 12%.

Item and date		Year	Cash flow	Discount factor	Present value
			$	12%	$
Interest	31.12.X3	1	8	0.893	7.1
Interest	31.12.X4	2	8	0.797	6.4
Interest	31.12.X5	3	8	0.712	5.7
Redemption	01.01.X6	3	100	0.712	71.2
NPV					90.4

The estimated market price would be $90.40.

(c) There are two approaches to calculating an after-tax cost of debt. One is to calculate a cost that recognises the difference between tax relief on interest payments, but no tax relief on capital redemption. Using this approach, the after-tax cost may be calculated as follows.

Item and date		Year	Cash flow ex int $	PV 5% $	PV 10% $
Market value		0	(95.0)	(95.0)	(95.0)
Interest (8 × (1 – 0.3))	31.12.X3	1	5.6	5.3	5.1
Interest	31.12.X4	2	5.6	5.1	4.6
Interest	31.12.X5	3	5.6	4.8	4.2
Redemption	01.01.X6	3	100.0	86.4	75.1
NPV				6.6	(6.0)

The estimated after-tax cost of debt is: $5\% + (\dfrac{6.6}{(6.6+6)} \times 5\%) = 7.6\%$

The **second approach to calculating the after-tax cost of this redeemable debt** is the approach used in the calculation of a company's weighted average cost of capital. This simply takes the pre-tax cost of the debt and reduces it by a factor $(1 - t)$.

Here, the pre-tax cost is 10%. The after-tax cost is therefore $10\% \times (1 - 0.30) = 7.0\%$

Exam alert

Make sure that you know the difference in methods for calculating the cost of irredeemable and redeemable debt, as this is often a weakness in exams.

4.5 The cost of floating rate debt

If a firm has variable or **floating rate debt**, then the cost of an equivalent fixed-interest debt should be substituted. **Equivalent** usually means fixed-interest debt with a similar term to maturity in a firm of similar standing, although if the cost of capital is to be used for project appraisal purposes, there is an argument for using debt of the same period to completion as the project under consideration.

4.6 The cost of bank loans

The cost of bank loans is the current interest being charged on such funds. Alternatively, the cost of debt of ordinary or straight bonds could be used.

For example, a $30,000 loan is taken out by a business at a rate of 12% over 5 years. What will be the annual payment, assuming that payments are made every 12 months and the loan provides for gradual repayment over the term of the loan?

The annuity factor for 12% over 5 years is 3.605. Therefore $30,000 = 3.605 × annual payment.

$$\text{Annual payment} = \frac{30,000}{3.605}$$

$$= \$8,321.78$$

The after-tax cost is calculated by applying a factor $(1 - t)$ to the pre-tax cost of the debt.

4.6.1 The split between interest and capital repayment

A loan of $100,000 is to be repaid to the bank, over five years, in equal annual year-end instalments made up of capital repayments and interest at 9% pa.

The annual payment $= \dfrac{\$100,000}{3.890} = \$25,707$

Each payment can then be split between the repayment of capital and interest.

Year	Balance b/f $	Interest @ 9% $	Annual payment $	Balance c/f $
1	100,000	9,000	(25,707)	83,293
2	83,293	7,496	(25,707)	65,082
3	65,082	5,857	(25,707)	45,232
4	45,232	4,071	(25,707)	23,596
5	23,596	2,111*	(25,707)	

* Rounding difference

4.7 The cost of convertible debt

The cost of capital of convertible debt is harder to determine. The calculation will depend on whether or not conversion is likely to happen. Debt holders will only convert if the value of the shares is greater than the redemption value of the debt.

(a)   If conversion is **not** expected, the conversion value is ignored and the bond is treated as **redeemable debt**, using the IRR method described in Section 4.3.

(b)   If conversion **is** expected, the IRR method for calculating the cost of redeemable debt is used, but the number of years to redemption is replaced by the **number of years to conversion** and the redemption value is replaced by the **conversion value** ie the market value of the shares into which the debt is to be converted.

Conversion value $= P_0 (1 + g)^n R$

Where P_0 is the current ex dividend ordinary share price

g   is the expected annual growth of the ordinary share price

n   is the number of years to conversion

R   is the number of shares received on conversion

Example: The cost of convertible debt

A company has issued 8% convertible bonds which are due to be redeemed in five years' time. They are currently quoted at $82 per $100 nominal. The bonds can be converted into 25 shares in five years' time. The share price is currently $3.50 and is expected to grow at a rate of 3% pa. Assume a 30% rate of tax.

Calculate the after tax cost of the convertible debt, recognising tat payments on conversion are not allowable against tax.

Solution

Conversion value $= P_0(1+g)^n R$

$= 3.50 \times (1+0.03)^5 \times 25$

$= \$101.44$

As the redemption value is $100, investors would **choose to convert** the bonds so the **conversion value** is used in the IRR calculation.

Year		Cash flow $	Discount factor 8%	PV $	Discount factor 12%	PV $
0	Market value	(82.00)	1.000	(82.00)	1.000	(82.00)
1 – 5	Interest (8 ×(1 – 0.3))	5.60	3.993	22.36	3.605	20.19
5	Conversion value	101.44	0.681	69.08	0.567	57.52
				9.44		(4.29)

Cost of debt $= 8\% + \dfrac{9.44}{9.44 + 4.29}(12\% - 8\%) = 10.75\%$

4.8 The cost of preference shares

For preference shares, the future cash flows are the dividend payments in perpetuity. The relationship between the market price of the preference shares and the annual dividend is expressed by the formula:

$$P_0 = \frac{d}{(1+k_{pref})} + \frac{d}{(1+k_{pref})^2} + \frac{d}{(1+k_{pref})^3} + \text{(in perpetuity)}$$

where
- P_0 is the current market price of preference share capital after payment of the current dividend
- d is the dividend received
- k_{pref} is the cost of preference share capital

$$P_0 = \frac{d}{(1+k_{pref})} + \frac{d}{(1+k_{pref})^2} + \frac{d}{(1+k_{pref})^3} + \dots..$$

This simplifies to $P_0 = \dfrac{d}{k_{pref}}$

Rearranging gives $k_{pref} = d/P_0$.

The cost of preference shares can be calculated as:

$$k_{pref} = \frac{d}{P_0}$$

Again, this is the in perpetuity formula.

5 The weighted average cost of capital (WACC)

Introduction

The **weighted average cost of capital (WACC)** is the average cost of capital for all the company's long-term sources of finance, weighted to allow for the **relative** proportions of each type of capital in the overall capital structure.

The WACC is calculated by weighting the costs of the individual sources of finance according to their relative importance as sources of finance.

The WACC represents the return that the company should make on its investments to be able to provide the returns required by its finance providers.

5.1 Computing a discount rate

We have looked at the costs of individual sources of capital for a company. But how does this help us to work out the cost of capital as a whole, or the discount rate to apply in discounted cash flow investment appraisals?

In many cases, it will be difficult to associate a particular project with a particular form of finance. A company's funds may be viewed as a **pool of resources**. Money is withdrawn from this pool of funds to invest in new projects and added to the pool as new finance is raised or profits are retained. Under these circumstances, it is appropriate to use an average cost of capital as the discount rate.

The correct cost of capital to use in investment appraisal is the **marginal cost of the funds** raised (or earnings retained) to finance the investment. WACC might be considered the most **reliable guide** to the **marginal cost of capital**, but only on the assumption that the company continues to invest in the future, in projects of a standard level of business risk, by raising funds in the same proportions as its existing capital structure.

KEY TERM

WEIGHTED AVERAGE COST OF CAPITAL is the average cost of the company's finance (equity, bonds, bank loans) weighted according to the proportion each element bears to the total pool of capital

5.2 General formula for the WACC

A general formula for WACC k_0 is as follows.

LEARN

$$WACC = \left[\frac{V_e}{V_e + V_d}\right] k_e + \left[\frac{V_d}{V_e + V_d}\right] k_d (1 - T)$$

where k_e is the cost of equity

k_d is the cost of debt

V_e is the market value of equity in the firm

V_d is the market value of debt in the firm

T   is the rate of company tax

Example: Weighted average cost of capital

An entity has the following information in its statement of financial position.

	$'000
Ordinary shares of 50 cents	2,500
12% unsecured bonds	1,000

The ordinary shares are currently quoted at 130 cents each and the bonds are trading at $72 per $100 nominal. The ordinary dividend of 15 cents has just been paid with an expected growth rate of 10%. Corporation tax is currently 30%.

Calculate the weighted average cost of capital for this entity.

Solution

Market values:

		$'000
Equity (V_e):	$\frac{2,500}{0.5} \times 1.30$	6,500
Bonds (V_d):	$1,000 \times 0.72$	720
		7,220

Cost of equity:

$$k_e = \frac{d_0(1+g)}{P_0} + g = \frac{0.15(1+0.1)}{1.3} + 0.1 = 0.2269 = 22.69\%$$

Cost of debt:

$$k_d = \frac{i}{P_0} = \frac{0.12}{0.72} = 0.1667 = 16.67\%$$

Weighted average cost of capital:

$$WACC = \left[\frac{V_e}{V_e + V_d}\right] k_e + \left[\frac{V_d}{V_e + V_d}\right] k_d (1 - T)$$

$$V_E + V_D = 7,220$$

$$WACC = \left[\left(\frac{6,500}{7,220}\right) \times 22.69\%\right] + \left[\left(\frac{720}{7,220}\right) \times 16.67\% \times 0.7\right] = 20.43\% + 1.16\% = 21.59\%$$

5.3 Weighting methods

Two methods of weighting could be used.

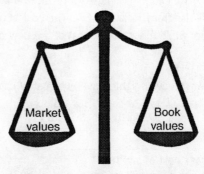

Market values should always be used if data is available. Although book values are often easier to obtain, they are based on historical costs and their use will seriously **understate** the impact of the cost of equity finance on the average cost of capital. If the WACC is underestimated, unprofitable projects may be accepted.

5.4 The marginal cost of capital approach

The **marginal cost of capital** approach involves calculating a marginal cut-off rate for acceptable investment projects by:

(a)   **Establishing rates of return** for each component of capital structure, except retained earnings, based on its value if it were to be raised under current market conditions

(b)   **Relating dividends or interest** to these values to obtain a marginal cost for each component

(c)   **Applying the marginal cost** to each component depending on its proportionate weight within the capital structure and adding the resultant costs to give a weighted average

It can be argued that the current weighted average cost of capital should be used to evaluate projects. Where a company's capital structure changes only very **slowly** over time, the marginal cost of new capital should be roughly **equal** to the weighted average cost of current capital.

Where gearing levels fluctuate significantly, or the finance for new projects carries a significantly different level of risk to that of the existing company, there is good reason to seek an alternative marginal cost of capital.

Example: Marginal cost of capital

Georgebear has the following capital structure:

Source	After-tax cost %	Market value $m	After-tax cost x Market value
Equity shares	12.0	10	1.2
Preference shares	10.0	2	0.2
Bonds	7.5	8	0.6
		20	2.0

$$\text{WACC} = \frac{2 \times 100\%}{20}$$

$$= 10\%$$

Note. This is a simplified calculation of WACC. The full calculation will give the same answer of 10%.

Georgebear's directors have decided to embark on major capital expenditure, which will be financed by a major issue of funds. The estimated project cost is $3,000,000, 1/3 of which will be financed by equity, 2/3 of which will be financed by bonds. As a result of undertaking the project, the cost of equity (existing and new shares) will rise from 12% to 14%. The cost of preference shares and the cost of existing bonds will remain the same, while the after-tax cost of the new bonds will be 9%.

Required

Calculate the company's new weighted average cost of capital, and its marginal cost of capital.

Solution

New weighted average cost of capital

Source	After-tax cost %	Market value $m	After-tax cost x Market value
Equity shares	14.0	11	1.54
Preference shares	10.0	2	0.20
Existing bonds	7.5	8	0.60
New bonds	9.0	2	0.18
		23	2.52

$$\text{WACC} = \frac{2.52 \times 100\%}{23}$$

$$= 11.0\%$$

$$\text{Marginal cost of capital} = \frac{(2.52 - 2.0) \times 100\%}{23 - 20}$$

$$= 17.3\%$$

Chapter Summary

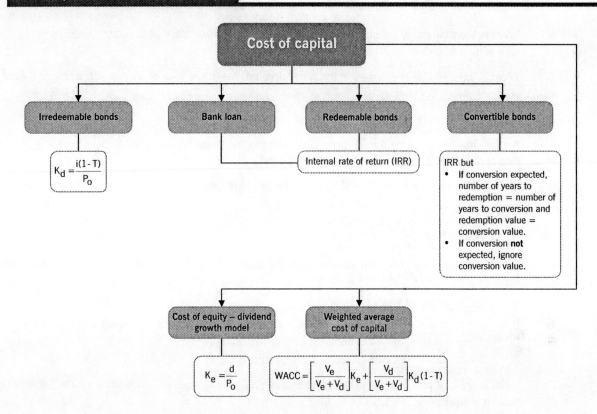

Cost of capital

Irredeemable bonds

$$K_d = \frac{i(1-T)}{P_o}$$

Bank loan

Redeemable bonds

Internal rate of return (IRR)

Convertible bonds

IRR but
- If conversion expected, number of years to redemption = number of years to conversion and redemption value = conversion value.
- If conversion **not** expected, ignore conversion value.

Cost of equity – dividend growth model

$$K_e = \frac{d}{P_o}$$

Weighted average cost of capital

$$WACC = \left[\frac{V_e}{V_e + V_d}\right]K_e + \left[\frac{V_d}{V_e + V_d}\right]K_d(1-T)$$

Quick Quiz

1   What is the formula for calculating the future value of an investment plus accumulated compound interest after n time periods?

2   What is the formula for calculating the present value of a future sum of money at the end of n time periods?

3   What is the formula for the present value of a perpetuity?

4   A share has a current market value of 120c and the last dividend was 10c. If the expected annual growth rate of dividends is 5%, calculate the cost of equity capital.

5   Identify the variables k_e, k_d, V_e and V_d in the following weighted average cost of capital formula.

$$WACC = \left[\frac{V_e}{V_e + V_d} \right] k_e + \left[\frac{V_d}{V_e + V_d} \right] k_d (1 - T)$$

6   When calculating the weighted average cost of capital, which of the following is the preferred method of weighting?

A   Book values of debt and equity
B   Average levels of the market values of debt and equity (ignoring reserves) over five years
C   Current market values of debt and equity
D   Book value of debt and current market value of equity

7   What is the cost of $1 irredeemable debt capital paying an annual rate of interest of 7% and having a current market price of $1.50?

Answers to Quick Quiz

1    $FV = PV (1 + r)^n$

2    $PV = FV \dfrac{1}{(1+r)^n}$

3   PV = Annual cash flow/discount rate

4    $\dfrac{10(1+0.05)}{120} + 0.05 = 13.75\%$

5   k_e is the cost of equity

      k_d is the cost of debt

      V_e is the market value of equity in the firm

      V_d is the market value of debt in the firm

6   C   Current market values of debt and equity

7   Cost of debt $= \dfrac{0.07}{1.50} = 4.67\%$

Answers to Questions

2.1 Net present value

Year	Cash flow	DF @ 14%	PV
	$		$
0	(10,000)	1	(10,000)
1	5,000	0.877	4,385
2	5,000	0.769	3,845
3	4,000	0.675	2,700
NPV =			930

Now try these questions from the Practice Question Bank

Number	Level	Marks	Time
Q3	Introductory	N/A	16 mins

ACCOUNTING STANDARDS

Part B

FINANCIAL INSTRUMENTS

 Financial instruments sounds like a daunting subject, and indeed this is a complex and controversial area. The numbers involved in financial instruments are often huge, but don't let this put you off. In this chapter we aim to simplify the topic as much as possible and to focus on the important issues. Before delving into the main topic, however, we will first introduce the **IASB's** *Conceptual Framework*. The *Conceptual Framework* provides the principles which underly financial reporting, and it is important that you are familiar with them.

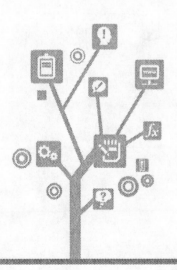

Topic list	learning outcomes	syllabus references
1 The *Conceptual Framework*	B1	B1(c)
2 Financial instruments	B1	B1(c)
3 Presentation of financial instruments	B1	B1(d)
4 Recognition of financial instruments	B1	B1(d)
5 Measurement of financial instruments	B1	B1(d)

Chapter Overview

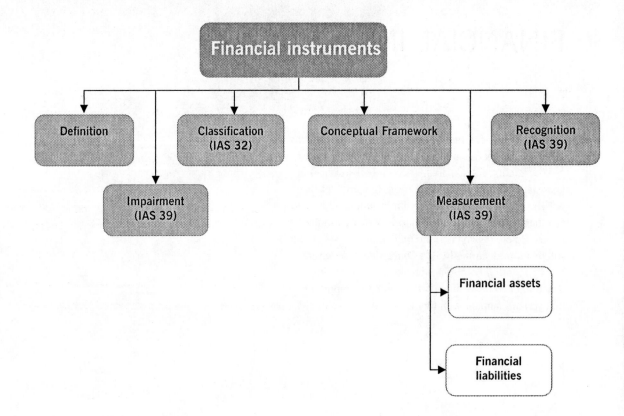

1 The Conceptual Framework

Introduction

Substance over form is an important concept that underlies many international accounting standards. It is the principle that accounting for items according to their substance and **economic reality** and not merely legal form is a key determinant of faithfully represented information.

(a)   For the majority of transactions there is **no difference** between the two and therefore no issue.

(b)   For other transactions **substance and form diverge** and the choice of treatment can give different results due to non-recognition of an asset or liability, even though benefits or obligations result.

1.1 Relationship to International Financial Reporting Standards (IFRSs)

Where the *Conceptual Framework* interacts with financial standards, whichever rules are the more specific should be applied, given that IFRSs should be consistent with the *Conceptual Framework*.

Leasing provides a good example: straightforward leases which fall squarely within the scope of IAS 17 *Leases* should be accounted for without any need to refer to the *Conceptual Framework*, but where their terms are more complex, or the lease is only one element in a larger series of transactions, then the *Conceptual Framework* comes into play. In addition, the general principle of substance over form should apply in the application of other existing rules.

1.2 Qualitative characteristics

The *Conceptual Framework* argues that, in order for financial information to be useful, it must possess both of the following **fundamental qualitative characteristics**:

(a)   **Relevance**: capable of making a difference in the decisions taken by users. Information is relevant if it has:

     (i)   **Predictive value** – it can be used by users to predict future outcomes

     (ii)   **Confirmatory value** – it either confirms or changes previous evaluations

(b)   **Faithful representation**: as far as possible, information should be:

     (i)   **Complete** – provides all the information necessary for the user to understand the account balance or transaction being depicted, including all necessary descriptions and explanations

     (ii)   **Neutral** – presents financial information in a way that is free from bias

     (iii)   **Free from error** – the account balance or transaction has been accurately described, and the process used to produce the reported information has been selected and applied correctly. Faithful representation does not mean being perfectly accurate in all respects

In addition to the fundamental characteristics, there are four **enhancing qualitative characteristics**:

(a)   **Comparability** – Information about a reporting entity is more useful if it can be compared with similar information about other entities and with similar information about the same entity for another period or another date.

(b)   **Verifiability** – Information is verifiable if different knowledgeable and independent observers could reach a consensus that a particular depiction is a faithful representation.

(c)   **Timeliness** – Information is timely if it is made available to decision-makers in time to be capable of influencing their decisions.

(d)   **Understandability** – Information is understandable if it is classified, characterised and presented clearly and concisely.

The first step in determining whether a transaction should be recorded or disclosed in the financial statements is deciding whether the transaction concerned meets the definition of an **element** of the financial statements according to the *Conceptual Framework*, or changes an existing element.

If the definition of an element is met, the transaction will be recognised if it meets the **recognition criteria**, as described in Section 1.4 below.

1.3 Elements of the financial statements

The elements of the financial statements are defined as follows in the *Conceptual Framework*.

KEY TERMS

An ASSET is a resource **controlled** by an entity as a result of **past events** and from which **future economic benefits** are expected to flow to the entity.

A LIABILITY is a **present obligation** of the entity arising from **past events**, the settlement of which is expected to result in an **outflow** from the entity of resources embodying economic benefits.

Identification of **who has the risks** relating to an asset will generally indicate **who has the benefits** and hence **who has the asset**. If an entity is, in certain circumstances, unable to avoid an **outflow of benefits**, this will provide evidence that it has a liability.

The definitions given in the *Conceptual Framework* of income and expenses are not as important as those of assets and liabilities. This is because income and expenses are **described in terms of changes in assets and liabilities**, so that they are secondary definitions.

KEY TERMS

INCOME is increases in economic benefits during the accounting period in the form of inflows or enhancements of assets or decreases of liabilities that result in increases in equity, other than those relating to contributions from equity participants.

EXPENSES are decreases in economic benefits during the accounting period in the form of outflows or depletions of assets or incurrences of liabilities that result in decreases in equity, other than those relating to distributions to equity participants.

The key point to note here is the way the *Conceptual Framework* defines assets and liabilities. The definitions ensure that assets and liabilities which meet the criteria, and which are expected to result in inflows/outflows of economic benefits, are recognised as such in the financial statements – regardless of their legal form.

1.4 Recognition criteria

KEY TERM

RECOGNITION is the process of incorporating in the statement of financial position or statement of profit or loss and other comprehensive income an item that meets the definition of an element, and satisfies the criteria for recognition set out below. It involves the depiction of the item in words and by a monetary amount, and the inclusion of that amount in the statement of financial position or statement of profit or loss and other comprehensive income totals.

The next key question is deciding **when** an asset or a liability has to be recognised in the statement of financial position. Where a transaction results in an item that meets the definition of an asset or liability, that item should be recognised in the statement of financial position if:

(a)   It is **probable** that any **future economic benefit** associated with the item will flow **to** or **from the entity** and

(b)   The item has a cost or value that can be **measured reliably**

This effectively prevents entities abusing the definitions of the elements by recognising items that are vague in terms of likelihood of occurrence and measurability. If this were not in force, entities could

manipulate the financial statements in various ways eg recognising assets when the likely future economic benefits cannot yet be determined.

Probability is assessed based on the situation at the end of the reporting period. For example, it is usually expected that some customers of an entity will not pay what they owe. The expected level of non-payment is based on past experience and the receivables asset is reduced by a percentage (the general bad debt provision).

Measurement must be reliable, but this does not preclude the use of **reasonable estimates**, which is an essential part of the financial statement preparation.

Even if something does not qualify for recognition now, it may meet the criteria **at a later date**.

1.5 Substance over form

KEY TERM

SUBSTANCE OVER FORM is the principle that transactions and other events are accounted for and presented in accordance with their substance and economic reality, and not merely their legal form.

Full disclosure is not enough: all transactions must be **accounted for** correctly, with full disclosure of related details as necessary to give the user of accounts a full understanding of the transactions.

Substance over form was enshrined in the International Accounting Standards Board's (IASB's) Framework for the *preparation and presentation of the financial statements (1989)*, which is in the process of being revised as the **Conceptual Framework for Financial Reporting (Conceptual Framework)**. Pending a full revision of the Conceptual Framework, the principle of substance over form has been provisionally carried over from the 1989 Framework.

Exam skills

The F2 exam will be based on the *Conceptual Framework*. Because substance over form still forms part of the Conceptual Framework to date, and because it is so critical to current financial reporting you should ensure that you understand this concept.

1.6 Other standards

The *Conceptual Framework* provides the general guidance for reporting the substance of transactions. The IASB has developed guidance for specific transactions. These will be covered in various parts of this text. You should consider the question of substance over form as you study them.

- IAS 17 *Leases* (see Chapter 4)

- IAS 18 *Revenue* (see Chapter 8)

- IAS 39 *Financial instruments: recognition and measurement* (in respect of the recognition and derecognition of financial assets and liabilities, such as loans. (See later in this chapter.)

Other areas where the *Framework* is important include:

- IFRS 10 *Consolidated financial statements* (see Chapter 9)
- IAS 24 *Related Party disclosures* (see Chapter 16)
- Human resource accounting

Section summary

Substance over form means that a transaction is accounted for according to its economic reality rather than its legal form.

Important points to remember from the *Conceptual Framework* are:

- The **qualitative characteristics** of useful financial information
- Definitions of **assets** and **liabilities**
- Definition of **recognition**
- **Criteria** for recognition

2 Financial instruments

Introduction

If you read the financial press, you will probably be aware of **rapid international expansion** in the use of financial instruments. These vary from straightforward, traditional instruments eg bonds, through to various forms of so-called **derivative instruments**.

Exam alert

IAS 39 is being replaced by IFRS 9 *Financial Instruments,* currently a work in progress. However, IFRS 9, which will not come into force until 2015, is not yet examinable in this paper.

2.1 Background

The dynamic nature of international financial markets has resulted in the widespread use of a variety of financial instruments. Prior to the issue of IAS 32 *Financial instruments: presentation*, many financial instruments were **off-balance-sheet**, being neither recognised nor disclosed in the financial statements while still exposing the shareholders to significant risks.

Why was a project to create a set of accounting standards for financial instruments considered necessary?

(a) The **significant growth of financial instruments** over recent years has outstripped the development of guidance for their accounting.

(b) The topic is of **international concern**.

(c) There have been recent **high-profile disasters** involving derivatives (eg Barings) which, while not caused by accounting failures, have raised questions about accounting and disclosure practices.

These are three standards on financial instruments:

(a) IAS 32 *Financial instruments: presentation*, which deals with:

(i) The classification of financial instruments between liabilities and equity
(ii) Presentation of certain compound instruments

(b) IFRS 7 *Financial instruments: disclosures*, which revised, simplified and incorporated disclosure requirements previously in IAS 32.

(c) IAS 39 *Financial instruments: recognition and measurement*, which deals with:

(i) Recognition and derecognition
(ii) The measurement of financial instruments
(iii) Hedge accounting

2.2 Classifications (IAS 32)

Financial instruments fall into three categories, summarised in the diagram below.

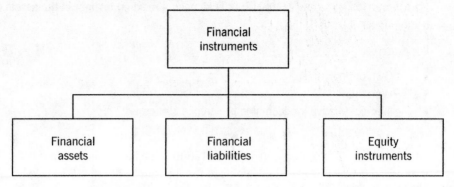

Financial liabilities are treated as **debt** in financial analysis and equity instruments as **equity**. Their classification is therefore fundamental to the accuracy of the gearing calculation.

2.3 Definitions

The most important definitions are common to all three standards.

KEY TERMS

FINANCIAL INSTRUMENT. Any contract that gives rise to both a financial asset of one entity and a financial liability or equity instrument of another entity.

FINANCIAL ASSET. Any asset that is:

(a)   Cash

(b)   An equity instrument of another entity

(c)   A contractual right:

     (i)   To receive cash or another financial asset from another entity or

     (ii)   To exchange financial assets or financial liabilities with another entity under conditions that are potentially favourable to the entity

(d)   A contract that will or may be settled in the entity's own equity instruments

For example:

- Trade receivables
- Bondsbonds held in another entity
- Sharesshares held in another entity
- Forward contracts standing at a gain

KEY TERM

FINANCIAL LIABILITY. Any liability that is:

(a)   A contractual obligation:

     (i)   To deliver cash or another financial asset to another entity or

     (ii)   To exchange financial assets or financial liabilities with another entity under conditions that are potentially unfavourable to the entity

(b)   A contract that will or may be settled in the entity's own equity instruments

For example:

- Trade payables
- Debenture loans (payable)
- Mandatorily redeemable preference shares

- Cumulative irredeemable preference shares
- Forward contracts standing at a loss

EQUITY INSTRUMENT. Any contract that evidences a residual interest in the assets of an entity after deducting all of its liabilities.

For example:

- Own ordinary shares
- Warrants
- Non-cumulative irredeemable preference shares

KEY TERMS

FAIR VALUE is the price that would be received to sell an asset or paid to transfer a liability in an orderly transaction between market participants at the measurement date.*(IFRS 13)*

DERIVATIVE. A financial instrument or other contract with all three of the following characteristics:

(a)   Its value changes in response to the change in an underlying variable (for example, share price or interest rate)

(b)   It requires little or no initial net investment and

(c)   It is settled at a future date

Exam alert

These definitions are very important – particularly for financial assets, financial liabilities and equity instruments – so learn them.

We should clarify some points arising from these definitions. Firstly, one or two terms above should be themselves defined.

(a)   A **contract** need not be in writing, but it must comprise an agreement that has **clear economic consequences** and which the parties to it cannot avoid, usually because the agreement is enforceable in law.

(b)   An **entity** could be an individual, partnership, incorporated body or government agency.

The definitions of **financial assets and financial liabilities** may seem rather circular, referring as they do to the terms financial asset and financial instrument. The point is that there may be a chain of contractual rights and obligations, but it will lead ultimately to the receipt or payment of cash or the acquisition or issue of an equity instrument.

For the purposes of this paper, the main financial instruments you will see most often include:

- Cash
- Trade receivables and trade payables
- Loans (bonds, debentures, loan notes)
- Shares
- Derivatives

IAS 32 makes it clear that the following items are not financial instruments.

- **Physical assets** eg inventories, property, plant and equipment, leased assets and intangible assets (patents, trademarks etc)

- **Prepaid expenses**, deferred revenue and most warranty obligations

- Liabilities or assets that are **not contractual** in nature

- Contractual rights/obligations that **do not involve transfer of a financial asset** eg commodity futures contracts, operating leases

Question 3.1

Learning outcome B1

Can you give the reasons why the first two items listed above do not qualify as financial instruments?

Contingent rights and obligations meet the definition of financial assets and financial liabilities respectively, even though many do not qualify for recognition in financial statements. The reason for this is the contractual rights or obligations exist because of a past transaction or event (eg assumption of a guarantee).

2.4 Derivatives

A **derivative** is a financial instrument that **derives** its value from the price or rate of an underlying item. As seen above, it has three characteristics, as follows.

(a)   Its value changes in response to an underlying variable eg share price or interest rate.
(b)   It requires little or no initial net investment.
(c)   It is settled at a future date.

Common **examples** of derivatives include:

(a)   **Forward contracts**: agreements to buy or sell an asset at a fixed price at a fixed future date

(b)   **Futures contracts**: similar to forward contracts except that contracts are standardised and traded on an exchange

(c)   **Options**: rights (but not obligations) for the option holder to exercise at a pre-determined price; the option writer loses out if the option is exercised

(d)   **Swaps**: agreements to swap one set of cash flows for another (normally interest rate or currency swaps)

The nature of derivatives often gives rise to **particular problems**. The **value** of a derivative (and the amount at which it is eventually settled) depends on **movements** in an underlying item (such as an exchange rate). This means that settlement of a derivative can lead to a very different result from the one originally envisaged. A company which has derivatives is exposed to **uncertainty and risk** (potential for gain or loss) and this can have a very material effect on its financial performance, financial position and cash flows.

Yet, because a derivative contract normally has **little or no initial cost**, under traditional accounting it **may not be recognised** in the financial statements at all. Alternatively, it may be recognised at an amount which bears no relation to its current value. This is clearly **misleading** and leaves users of the financial statements unaware of the **level of risk** that the company faces. IAS 32 and IAS 39 were developed in order to correct this situation.

Remember, under IAS 32 and IAS 39, derivatives may be recognised either as financial assets or as financial liabilities, depending on whether they are favourable or unfavourable at the end of the reporting period.

If a derivative is favourable at the year end (ie standing at a gain), it is a financial asset. The double entry to record this derivative would be:

DEBIT   Financial asset
CREDIT   Profit or loss

If a derivative is unfavourable at the year end (ie standing at a loss), it is a financial liability. The double entry to record this derivative would be:

DEBIT   Profit or loss
CREDIT   Financial liability

2.5 Overview

- Three accounting standards are relevant:

  - IAS 32 *Financial instruments: presentation*
  - IFRS 7 *Financial instruments: disclosures*
  - IAS 39 *Financial instruments: recognition and measurement*

- The definitions of **financial asset**, **financial liability** and **equity instrument** are fundamental to the standards.

Section summary

Financial instruments can be very complex, particularly **derivative instruments**.

The important definitions to learn are:

- **Financial asset**
- **Financial liability**
- **Equity instrument**

3 Presentation of financial instruments

Introduction

The presentation of financial instruments is covered by IAS 32.

3.1 Objective

The objective of IAS 32 is to establish principles for presenting financial instruments as liabilities or equity and for offsetting financial assets and financial liabilities.

3.2 Scope

IAS 32 should be applied in the presentation of **all types of financial instruments**, whether recognised or unrecognised.

Certain items are **excluded**:

- Interests in subsidiaries (IFRS 10 see Chapter 9)

- Interests in associates and joint ventures (IAS 28 see Chapter 10)

- Interests in joint arrangements (IFRS 11 see Chapter 10)

- Pensions and other post-retirement benefits (IAS 19 *Employee benefits*)

- Insurance contracts

- Contracts for contingent consideration in a business combination

- Contracts that require a payment based on climatic, geological or other physical variables

- Financial instruments, contracts and obligations under share-based payment transactions (IFRS 2 see Chapter 7)

3.3 Liabilities and equity   5/11

The main thrust of IAS 32 here is that financial instruments should be presented according to their **substance, not merely their legal form**. In particular, entities which issue financial instruments should classify them (or their component parts) as **either financial liabilities, or equity**.

The classification of a financial instrument as a liability or as equity depends on the following.

- The substance of the contractual arrangement on initial recognition
- The definitions of a financial liability and an equity instrument

How should a financial liability be distinguished from an equity instrument? The critical feature of a **liability** is an **obligation** to transfer economic benefit. Therefore a financial instrument is a financial liability if there is a **contractual obligation** on the issuer, either to deliver cash or another financial asset to the holder or to exchange another financial instrument with the holder under potentially unfavourable conditions to the issuer.

The financial liability exists **regardless of how the contractual obligation will be settled**. The issuer's ability to satisfy an obligation may be restricted eg by lack of access to foreign currency, but this is irrelevant as it does not remove the issuer's obligation or the holder's right under the instrument.

Where the above critical feature is not met, then the financial instrument is an **equity instrument**. IAS 32 explains that although the holder of an equity instrument may be entitled to a pro rata share of any distributions out of equity, the issuer does not have a contractual obligation to make such a distribution.

Although substance and legal form are often **consistent with each other**, this is not always the case. In particular a financial instrument may have the legal form of equity, but in substance it is in fact a liability. Other instruments may combine features of both equity instruments and financial liabilities.

For example, many entities issue **preference shares** which must be **redeemed** by the issuer for a fixed (or determinable) amount at a fixed (or determinable) future date. In such cases, the issuer has an **obligation**. Therefore the instrument is a **financial liability** and should be classified as such.

Another example is **cumulative irredeemable preference shares**. While the issuer does not redeem the preference shares, there is an obligation on the issuer to pay fixed dividends. If the entity has insufficient retained earnings in a given year, the dividends still must be paid in future years. Again, because the issuer has an obligation, the instrument should be classified as a financial liability.

The classification of the financial instrument is made when it is **first recognised** and this classification will continue until the financial instrument is removed from the entity's statement of financial position.

3.4 Contingent settlement provisions

An entity may issue a financial instrument where the way in which it is settled depends on:

(a)   The occurrence or non-occurrence of uncertain future events or
(b)   The outcome of uncertain circumstances

that are beyond the control of both the holder and the issuer of the instrument. For example, an entity might have to deliver cash instead of issuing equity shares. In this situation, it is not immediately clear whether the entity has an equity instrument or a financial liability.

Such financial instruments should be classified as **financial liabilities** unless the possibility of settlement is remote.

3.5 Settlement options

When a **derivative financial instrument** gives one party a **choice** over how it is settled (eg the issuer can choose whether to settle in cash or by issuing shares), the instrument is a **financial asset** or a **financial liability** unless **all the choices** would result in it being an equity instrument.

3.6 Compound financial instruments   5/11

Some financial instruments contain both a liability and an equity element. In such cases, IAS 32 requires the component parts of the instrument to be **classified separately**, according to the substance of the contractual arrangement and the definitions of a financial liability and an equity instrument.

One of the most common types of compound instrument is **convertible debt**. This creates a primary financial liability of the issuer and grants an option to the holder of the instrument to convert it into an equity instrument (usually ordinary shares) of the issuer. This is the economic equivalent of the issue of conventional debt plus a warrant to acquire shares in the future.

Although in theory there are several possible ways of calculating the split, the following method is recommended:

(a)   Calculate the value for the **financial liability** component as follows:

	$
Present value of principal *	X
Present value of interest *	X
	X

* Discounted using the market interest rate of non-convertible debt

(b)   Calculate the **equity component**:

Equity component = Proceeds – financial liability component

The reasoning behind this approach is that an entity's equity is its residual interest in its assets amount after deducting all its liabilities.

The **sum of the carrying amounts** assigned to liability and equity will always be equal to the carrying amount that would be ascribed to the instrument **as a whole**.

Example: Valuation of compound instruments

Rathbone Co issues 2,000 convertible bonds at the start of 20X2. The bonds have a three-year term, and are issued at par with a face value of $1,000 per bond, giving total proceeds of $2,000,000. Interest is payable annually in arrears at a nominal annual interest rate of 6%. Each bond is convertible at any time up to maturity into 250 common shares.

When the bonds are issued, the prevailing market interest rate for similar debt without conversion options is 9%. At the issue date, the market price of one common share is $3. The dividends expected over the three-year term of the bonds amount to 14c per share at the end of each year. The risk-free annual interest rate for a three-year term is 5%.

Required

Prepare the accounting entry to record the issue of the convertible bonds.

Solution

DEBIT	Cash	$2,000,000	
CREDIT	Financial liability		$1,847,720
CREDIT	Equity		$152,280

Being recognition of convertible bonds

The liability component is valued first, and the difference between the proceeds of the bond issue and the fair value of the liability is assigned to the equity component. The present value of the liability component is calculated using a discount rate of 9%, the market interest rate for similar bonds having no conversion rights, as shown.

	$
Present value of the principal: $2,000,000 payable at the end of three years ($2m × 0.772)*	1,544,000
Present value of the interest: $120,000 payable annually in arrears for three years ($120,000 × 2.531)*	303,725
Total liability component	1,847,720
Equity component (balancing figure)	152,280
Proceeds of the bond issue	2,000,000

* These figures can be obtained from discount and annuity tables.

The split between the liability and equity components remains the same throughout the term of the instrument, even if there are changes in the **likelihood of the option being exercised**. This is because it is not always possible to predict how a holder will behave. The issuer continues to have an obligation to make future payments until conversion, maturity of the instrument or some other relevant transaction takes place.

3.7 Treasury shares

If an entity **reacquires its own equity instruments**, those instruments (**treasury shares**) shall be **deducted from equity**. No gain or loss shall be recognised in profit or loss on the purchase, sale, issue or cancellation of an entity's own equity instruments. Consideration paid or received shall be recognised directly in equity.

3.8 Interest, dividends, losses and gains

As well as looking at statement of financial position presentation, IAS 32 considers how financial instruments affect the profit or loss (and movements in equity). The treatment varies according to whether interest, dividends, losses or gains relate to a financial liability or an equity instrument.

(a)   Interest, dividends, losses and gains relating to a financial instrument (or component part) classified as a **financial liability** should be recognised as **income or expense** in profit or loss.

(b)   Distributions to holders of a financial instrument classified as an **equity instrument** should be **debited directly to equity** by the issuer.

(c)   **Transaction costs** of an equity transaction shall be accounted for as a **deduction from equity** (unless they are directly attributable to the acquisition of a business, in which case they are accounted for under IFRS 3 *Business Combinations*).

You should look at the requirements of IAS 1 *Presentation of financial statements* for further details of disclosure, and IAS 12 *Income Taxes* for disclosure of tax effects.

3.9 Key points

- Financial instruments issued to raise capital must be classified as **liabilities** or **equity**.

- The **substance** of the financial instrument is more important than its **legal form**.

- The **critical feature of a financial liability** is the contractual obligation to deliver cash or another financial instrument.

- **Compound instruments** are split into equity and liability parts and presented accordingly.

- **Interest, dividends, losses and gains** are treated according to whether they relate to an equity instrument or a financial liability.

Section summary

Financial instruments must be classified as **liabilities** or **equity** according to their **substance**.

The critical feature of a financial liability is the **contractual obligation to deliver cash** or another financial asset.

Compound instruments are split into **equity** and **liability** components and presented accordingly in the statement of financial position.

4 Recognition of financial instruments 9/12, 11/12

Introduction

IAS 39 *Financial Instruments: recognition and measurement* establishes principles for recognising and measuring financial assets and financial liabilities.

4.1 Scope

IAS 39 applies to **all entities** and to **all types of financial instruments except** those specifically excluded, as listed below.

(a) Investments in **subsidiaries, associates and joint arrangements** that are accounted for under IFRS 10 *Consolidated financial statements*, IAS 27 *Separate financial statements* or IAS 28 *Investments in associates and joint ventures*.

(b) Employers' rights and obligations **under employee benefit plans** covered in IAS 19

(c) **Forward contracts** for a sale that will result in a **business combination** at a later date

(d) Rights and obligations under **insurance contracts** (although IAS 39 applies where the insurance contract principally involves the transfer of financial risks and derivatives embedded in insurance contracts)

(e) Equity instruments **issued by the entity** eg ordinary shares issued, or options and warrants

(f) Financial instruments, contracts and obligations under **share-based payment transactions**, covered in IFRS 2 *Share-based payment*

(g) Rights to **reimbursement payments** to which IAS 37 *Provisions, contingent liabilities and Contingent Assets* applies

4.2 Initial recognition

Financial instruments should be recognised in the statement of financial position when the entity becomes a party to the **contractual provisions of the instrument**.

KEY POINT

An important consequence of this is that all derivatives should be included in the statement of financial position.

In practical terms, this means that financial instruments are recognised as follows:

Type of financial instrument	Recognition
Trade receivable/payable	On delivery of goods or performance of service
Loans (bonds, debentures, loan notes)	On issue

Type of financial instrument	Recognition
Shares	On issue
Derivatives	On the commitment date

Notice that this is **different** from the recognition criteria in the *Conceptual Framework*, which states that items are normally recognised when there is a probable inflow or outflow of resources and the item has a cost or value that can be measured reliably.

4.3 Example: initial recognition

An entity has entered into two separate contracts.

(a)   A firm commitment (an order) to buy a specific quantity of iron

(b)   A forward contract to buy a specific quantity of iron at a specified price on a specified date, provided delivery of the iron is not taken

Contract (a) is a **normal trading contract**. The entity does not recognise a liability for the iron until the goods have actually been delivered. (Note that this contract is not a financial instrument because it involves a physical asset, rather than a financial asset.)

Contract (b) is a **financial instrument**. Under IAS 39, the entity recognises a financial liability (an obligation to deliver cash) on the **commitment date**, rather than waiting for the closing date on which the exchange takes place.

Note that planned future transactions, no matter how likely, are not assets and liabilities of an entity – the entity has not yet become a party to the contract.

Question 3.2	Recognition

Learning outcome B1

DEF has a 31 December 20X2 year end. On 1 January 20X2 DEF issues 100,000 $1 ordinary shares for $1.50 each. Shareholders are required to pay for their shares in two equal instalments on 31 March 20X2 and 30 June 20X2.

Required

At what date(s) should DEF record the accounting entry to recognise the share capital and share premium in relation to these shares?

A   1 January 20X2 only
B   31 March 20X2 only
C   31 March 20X2 and 30 June 20X2
D   31 December 20X2 only

4.4 Derecognition

Derecognition is the removal of a previously recognised financial instrument from an entity's statement of financial position.

An entity should derecognise a **financial asset** when:

(a)   The **contractual rights** to the cash flows from the financial asset **expire** or

(b)   The entity **transfers substantially all the risks and rewards of ownership** of the financial asset to another party

Question 3.3   Risks and rewards

Learning outcome B1

Can you think of an example of a situation of the sale of a financial asset in which:

(a)   An entity has transferred substantially all the risks and rewards of ownership?
(b)   An entity has retained substantially all the risks and rewards of ownership?

Exam alert

The principle here is that of **substance over form**.

When a financial asset is derecognised, there are three steps to follow.

    Revalue at fair value

    Recognise proceeds

    Derecognise financial asset

Example: Derecognition

In July 20X8 AB sold 12,000 shares for $16,800 (their market value at that date). It had purchased the shares through a broker in 20X7 for $1.25 per share. The quoted price at the 20X7 year end was $1.32 – $1.34 per share. The broker charges transaction costs of 1% purchase/sale price.

What were the journal entries to record the derecognition?

Solution

The shares were originally recorded at their cost of $15,150 in 20X7 and revalued to market value at the 20X7 year end with a gain of $690 reported in other comprehensive income:

	$
20X7 Purchase ((12,000 × $1.25) + (1% × $15,000))	15,150
Fair value gain at 31.12.20X7 β	690 → OCI 20X5 20X7
Fair value at 31.12.20X7 (12,000 × $1.32 bid price)	15,840

At the date of the derecognition in July 20X8, the shares must first be remeasured to their fair value (ie the sales price as they were sold at market price) and the gain is reported in other comprehensive income (items that will not be reclassified to profit or loss):

| DEBIT | Financial asset (16,800 – 15,840) | $960 | |
| CREDIT | Other comprehensive income | | $960 |

On derecognition the transaction costs are charged to profit or loss:

DEBIT	Cash (16,800 – (1% × 16,800))	$16,632	
DEBIT	Profit or loss (1% × 16,800)	$168	
CREDIT	Financial asset		$16,800

A **financial liability** should be removed from the statement of financial position when, and only when, it is **extinguished** – that is, when the obligation specified in the contract is either **discharged** or **cancelled** or **expires**.

Exam alert

No gain or loss will arise on the derecognition of an investment unless it is sold at a price different from fair value.

Section summary

IAS 39 *Financial Instruments: recognition and measurement* is a controversial standard.

IAS 39 states that all financial assets and liabilities should be recognised in the statement of financial position, including derivatives.

5 Measurement of financial instruments   11/10, 3/11, 9/12

Introduction

Financial assets are initially measured at the **fair value** of the consideration given or received (ie **cost**) **plus** (in most cases) **transaction costs** that are **directly attributable** to the acquisition or issue of the financial instrument.

5.1 Financial assets

The diagram below summarises how different types of financial assets are measured. We will look at the initial and subsequent measurement of each type of financial asset one by one.

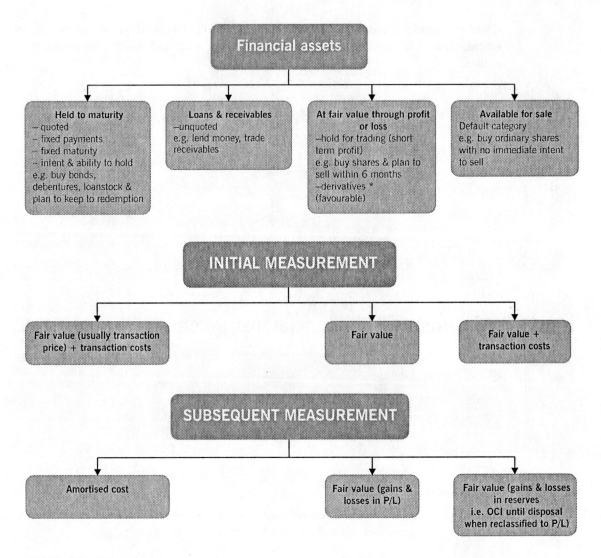

5.1.1 Classification

There is a certain amount of flexibility in that **any** financial instrument can be designated as fair value through profit or loss. However, this is a **once and for all choice** and has to be made on initial recognition. Once a financial instrument has been classified in this way, it **cannot be reclassified**, even if it would otherwise be possible to measure it at cost or amortised cost.

In contrast, it is quite difficult for an entity **not** to remeasure financial instruments to fair value.

5.1.2 Initial measurement

Financial assets are measured at fair value plus transaction costs, except when they are designated as **at fair value through profit or loss**.

Where a financial instrument is designated as **at fair value through profit or loss** (this term is explained below), then **transaction costs** are **not** added to fair value at initial recognition.

The **fair value** of the consideration is normally the **transaction price** or market price. If market prices are not reliable, the fair value may be **estimated** using a valuation technique (for example, by discounting cash flows).

5.1.3 Subsequent measurement

As you can see in the diagram above, IAS 39 classifies financial assets into four categories. These are defined here. Note particularly the criteria for a financial asset or liability to be classified **at fair value through profit or loss**.

KEY TERMS

A FINANCIAL ASSET OR LIABILITY AT FAIR VALUE THROUGH PROFIT OR LOSS meets either of the following conditions:

(a)   It is classified as **held for trading**. A financial instrument is classified as held for trading if it is:

   (i)   Acquired or incurred principally for the purpose of selling or repurchasing it in the short term

   (ii)   Part of a portfolio of identified financial instruments that are managed together and for which there is evidence of a recent actual pattern of short-term profit-taking or

   (iii) A derivative (unless it is a designated and effective hedging instrument)

(b)   Upon initial recognition it is **designated** by the entity on initial recognition as one to be measured at fair value, with fair value changes being recognised in profit or loss. An entity may only use this designation in severely restricted circumstances:

   (i)   It **eliminates** or **significantly reduces an accounting mismatch** that would otherwise arise

   (ii)   A **group** of financial assets/liabilities is managed and its performance is evaluated **on a fair value basis**

LOANS AND RECEIVABLES are non-derivative financial assets with **fixed or determinable payments** that **are not quoted in an active market**, other than:

(a)   Those that the entity intends to sell immediately or in the near term, which should be classified as held for trading

(b)   Those that the entity upon initial recognition designates as at fair value through profit or loss or

(c)   Those that the entity upon initial recognition designates as available for sale.

Those for which the holder may not recover substantially all of the initial investment, other than because of credit deterioration, shall be classified as **available for sale.**

HELD TO MATURITY INVESTMENTS are non-derivative financial assets with fixed or determinable payments and fixed maturity that an entity has the **positive intent and ability to hold to maturity**, and that:

(a)   Are not designated as at fair value through profit or loss

(b)   Do not meet the definition of loans and receivables

AVAILABLE FOR SALE FINANCIAL ASSETS are those financial assets that are classified on initial recognition as available for sale, or those which are not classified as:

(a)   Loans and receivables originated by the entity

(b)   Held to maturity investments or

(c)   Financial assets at fair value through profit or loss   *(IAS 39)*

After initial recognition, all financial assets should be **remeasured to fair value**, without any deduction for transaction costs that may be incurred on sale or other disposal, except for:

(a)   Loans and receivables – measured at amortised cost

(b)   Held to maturity investments – measured at amortised cost

(c)   Investments in equity instruments that do not have a quoted market price in an active market and whose **fair value cannot be reliably measured** (and derivatives indexed to such equity instruments) – measured at **cost**

Loans and receivables and **held to maturity investments** should be measured at **amortised cost** using the **effective interest method.**

Exam alert

Notice that derivatives **must** be remeasured to fair value. This is because it would be misleading to measure them at cost.

5.1.4 Amortised cost

KEY TERMS

AMORTISED COST of a financial asset or financial liability is the amount at which the item is recorded at initial recognition, less principal repayments, plus or minus the cumulative amortisation of any difference between that initial amount and the maturity amount, and minus any write-down (directly or through the use of an allowance account) for impairment or non-collectability.

The EFFECTIVE INTEREST METHOD is a method of calculating the amortised cost of a financial instrument and of allocating the interest income or interest expense over the relevant period.

The EFFECTIVE INTEREST RATE is the rate that exactly discounts estimated future cash payments or receipts through the expected life of the financial instrument to the net carrying amount of the financial asset or liability.   (IAS 39)

Example: Amortised cost

On 1 January 20X1 Abacus Co purchases a debt instrument for its fair value of $1,000. The debt instrument is due to mature on 31 December 20X5. The instrument has a principal amount of $1,250 and the instrument carries fixed interest at 4.72% that is paid annually. (The effective interest rate is 10%.)

How should Abacus Co account for the debt instrument over its five-year term?

Solution

Abacus Co will receive interest of $59 (1,250 × 4.72%) each year and $1,250 when the instrument matures.

Abacus must allocate the discount of $250 and the interest receivable over the five-year term at a constant rate on the carrying amount of the debt. To do this, it must apply the effective interest rate of 10%.

The following table shows the allocation over the years:

Year	Amortised cost at beginning of year	Profit or loss: Interest income for year (@10%)	Interest received during year (cash inflow)	Amortised cost at end of year
	$	$	$	$
20X1	1,000	100	(59)	1,041
20X2	1,041	104	(59)	1,086
20X3	1,086	109	(59)	1,136
20X4	1,136	113	(59)	1,190
20X5	1,190	119	(1,250+59)	–

Each year the carrying amount of the financial asset is increased by the interest income for the year and reduced by the interest actually received during the year.

Investments whose **fair value cannot be reliably measured** should be measured at **cost**.

The proforma and double entries for recording amortised cost are as follows:

Financial asset

	$	Post to:		
Balance b/d	X		DEBIT	(↑) Financial asset
			CREDIT	(↓) Cash
			(if initial recognition at start of year)	
Finance income (effective interest × b/f)	X	P/L	DEBIT	(↑) Financial asset
			CREDIT	(↑) Finance income
Interest received (coupon × par value)	(X)		DEBIT	(↑) Cash
			CREDIT	(↓) Financial asset
Balance c/d	X	SOFP		

Financial liability

	$	Post to:		
Balance b/d	X		DEBIT	(↑) Cash
			CREDIT	(↑) Financial liability
			(if initial recognition at start of year)	
Finance cost (effective interest × b/f)	X	P/L	DEBIT	(↑) Finance cost
			CREDIT	(↑) Financial liability
Interest paid (coupon × par value)	(X)		DEBIT	(↓) Financial liability
			CREDIT	(↓) Cash
Balance c/d	X	SOFP		

5.1.5 Held to maturity assets

For a financial instrument to be **held to maturity**, it must meet several extremely narrow criteria. The entity must have a **positive intent** and a **demonstrated ability** to hold the investment to maturity. These conditions are not met if:

(a)   The entity intends to hold the financial asset for an undefined period

(b)   The entity stands ready to sell the financial asset in response to changes in interest rates or risks, liquidity needs and similar factors (unless these situations could not possibly have been reasonably anticipated)

(c)   The issuer has the right to settle the financial asset at an amount significantly below its amortised cost (because this right will almost certainly be exercised)

(d)   It does not have the financial resources available to continue to finance the investment until maturity

(e)   It is subject to an existing legal or other constraint that could frustrate its intention to hold the financial asset to maturity

In addition, an **equity** instrument is **unlikely** to meet the criteria for classification as held to maturity.

There is a **penalty** for selling or reclassifying a held to maturity investment other than in certain very tightly defined circumstances. If this has occurred during the **current** financial year or during the **two preceding** financial years, **no** financial asset can be classified as held to maturity.

If an entity can no longer hold an investment to maturity, it is no longer appropriate to use amortised cost and the asset must be remeasured to fair value. **All** remaining held to maturity investments must also be remeasured to fair value and classified as available for sale (see above).

5.1.6 Gains and losses

Instruments at **fair value through profit or loss**: gains and losses are recognised **in profit or loss**.

For **available for sale** financial assets: gains and losses are recognised in **reserves (ie other comprehensive income)**. When the asset is disposed of and derecognised, the cumulative gain or loss previously recognised in other comprehensive income should be **reclassified to profit or loss**.

Financial instruments carried at **amortised cost**: gains and losses are recognised **in profit or loss** as a result of the amortisation process and when the asset is derecognised.

Financial assets and financial liabilities that are **hedged items**: special rules apply.

Question 3.4	Finance cost 1

Learning outcome B1

On 1 January 20X3 Deferred Co issued $600,000 loan notes. Issue costs were $200. The loan notes do not carry interest, but are redeemable at a premium of $152,389 on 31 December 20X4. The effective finance cost of the loan notes is 12%.

What is the finance cost in respect of the loan notes for the year ended 31 December 20X4?

A $72,000
B $76,194
C $80,613
D $80,640

Question 3.5	Extended example

Learning outcome B1

Palermo, a public limited company, has requested your advice for the following financial instrument transactions:

(a)   Palermo purchased a deep discount bond during the previous accounting period on 1 January 20X0 for $157,563 plus $200 transaction costs. Interest of 4% is payable annually on 31 December. The bond will be redeemed on 31 December 20X4 for $200,000 (its par value). The bond will be held until redemption. The effective interest rate of the bond is 9.5%.

(b)   Palermo issued 60,000 redeemable $1 preference shares on 1 January 20X1 paying an annual (cumulative) dividend of 7% per annum, redeemable in ten years' time.

(c)   Palermo purchased 12,000 shares in ABC Co through a broker on 1 July 20X0 for $1.25 a share. The market price at 31 December 20X0 was $1.32 a share. On 30 September 20X1, Palermo sold the shares in ABC for $16,800. The broker charges transaction costs of 1% purchase/sale price.

(d)   On 1 November 20X1 Palermo took out a speculative forward contract to buy coffee beans for delivery on 30 April 20X2 at an agreed price of $6,000 intending to settle net in cash. Due to a surge in expected supply, a forward contract for delivery on 30 April 20X2 would have cost $5,000 at 31 December 20X1.

Required

Explain how the above transactions should be accounted for in the year ended 31 December 20X1, showing relevant calculations where appropriate.

5.2 Impairment and non-collectability of financial assets

At each year end, an entity should assess whether there is any objective evidence that a financial asset or group of assets is impaired.

Where there is objective evidence of impairment, the entity should **determine the amount** of any impairment loss. Examples of indications of impairment include:

- Financial difficulty of issuer
- Breach of contract in repayments
- Granting a concession to a borrower not normally given
- High probability of bankruptcy of borrower

5.2.1 Financial assets carried at amortised cost

For **loans and receivables** and **held to maturity investments**, the impairment loss is the **difference** between the asset's **carrying amount** and its **recoverable amount**.

The asset's recoverable amount is the present value of estimated future cash flows, discounted at the financial instrument's **original** effective interest rate.

The amount of the loss should be **recognised in profit or loss**. The carrying amount of the asset is either reduced directly or through the use of an allowance account.

If the impairment loss decreases at a later date (and the decrease relates to an event occurring **after** the impairment was recognised) the reversal is recognised in profit or loss. The carrying amount of the asset must not exceed the original amortised cost.

5.2.2 Financial assets carried at cost

Unquoted equity instruments are carried at cost if their fair value cannot be reliably measured. The impairment loss is the difference between the asset's **carrying amount** and the **present value of estimated future cash flows**, discounted at the current market rate of return for a similar financial instrument.

Such impairment losses cannot be reversed.

5.2.3 Available for sale financial assets

Available for sale financial assets are carried at fair value and gains and losses are recognised directly in equity.

Where an available for sale financial asset suffers an impairment loss, the loss is charged first against any cumulative **gains** on fair value adjustments previously recognised in equity (and is shown as an expense in other comprehensive income), and then to profit or loss.

If there are cumulative **losses** held in equity, they are reclassified (**recycled**) from equity to profit or loss in addition to the impairment loss.

The impairment loss is the difference between its **acquisition cost** (net of any principal repayment and amortisation) and **current fair value** (for equity instruments) or recoverable amount (for debt instruments), less any impairment loss on that asset previously recognised in profit or loss.

Impairment losses relating to equity instruments cannot be reversed. Impairment losses relating to debt instruments may be reversed if, in a later period, the fair value of the instrument increases and the increase can be objectively related to an event occurring after the loss was recognised.

Example: Impairment

Broadfield Co purchased 5% debentures in X Co on 1 January 20X3 (their issue date) for $100,000. The term of the debentures was five years and the maturity value is $130,525. The effective rate of interest on the debentures is 10% and the company has classified them as a held to maturity financial asset.

At the end of 20X4 X Co went into liquidation. All interest had been paid until that date. On 31 December 20X4 the liquidator of X Co announced that no further interest would be paid and only 80% of the maturity value would be repaid, on the original repayment date.

The market interest rate on similar bonds is 8% on that date.

Required

(a)   What value should the debentures have been stated at just before the impairment became apparent?

(b)   At what value should the debentures be stated at 31 December 20X4, after the impairment?

(c)   How will the impairment be reported in the financial statements for the year ended 31 December 20X4?

Solution

(a)   The debentures are classified as a held to maturity financial asset and so they would have been stated at amortised cost:

	$
Initial cost	100,000
Interest at 10%	10,000
Cash at 5%	(5,000)
At 31 December 20X3	105,000
Interest at 10%	10,500
Cash at 5%	(5,000)
At 31 December 20X4	110,500

(b)   After the impairment, the debentures are stated at their recoverable amount (using the **original** effective interest rate of 10%):

80% × $130,525 × 0.751 = $78,419

(c)   The impairment of $32,081 ($110,500 – $78,419) should be recorded:

DEBIT	Profit or loss	$32,081	
CREDIT	Financial asset		$32,081

Being impairment of held to maturity financial asset

5.3 Financial liabilities

5.3.1 Initial measurement

Financial liabilities are measured at fair value less transaction costs, except when they are designated as **at fair value through profit or loss**.

As for financial assets, where a financial liability is designated as **at fair value through profit or loss**, **transaction costs** are **not** added to fair value at initial recognition.

5.3.2 Subsequent measurement

After initial recognition, all financial liabilities should be measured at **amortised cost**, with the exception of financial liabilities **at fair value through profit or loss** (including most derivatives). The calculation of amortised cost was introduced when we looked at the subsequent measurement of financial assets above.

Financial liabilities **at fair value through profit or loss** should be measured at **fair value**. Where the fair value **is not capable of reliable measurement**, they should be measured at **cost**.

5.4 Calculating fair value

IFRS 13 *Fair value measurement* provides extensive guidance on how the fair value of assets and liabilities should be established.

KEY TERM

FAIR VALUE. The price that would be received to sell an asset or paid to transfer a liability in an orderly transaction between market participants at the measurement date.   *(IFRS 13)*

The following should be considered in determining fair value:

(a)   The asset or liability being measured

(b)   The principal market (ie where the most activity takes place) or where there is no principal market, the most advantageous market (ie that in which the best price could be achieved) in which an orderly transaction would take place for the asset or liability

(c)   The highest and best use of the asset or liability and whether it is used on a standalone basis or in conjunction with other assets or liabilities

(d)   Assumptions that market participants would use when pricing the asset or liability

Having considered these factors, IFRS 13 provides a hierarchy of inputs for arriving at fair value. It requires that Level 1 inputs are used where possible.

Level 1   Quoted prices in active markets for identical assets that the entity can access at the measurement date

Level 2   Inputs other than quoted prices that are directly or indirectly observable for the asset

Level 3   Unobservable inputs for the asset

5.5 Recap

- On initial recognition, financial instruments are measured at fair value plus transaction costs, except when they are designated as at fair value through profit or loss.

- Subsequent measurement depends on how a financial asset is **classified**.

- Financial assets at **fair value through profit or loss** are measured at **fair value**; gains and losses are recognised in **profit or loss**.

- **Available for sale** assets are measured at **fair value**; gains and losses are taken to **equity**, through other comprehensive income.

- **Loans and receivables** and **held to maturity** investments are measured at **amortised cost**; gains and losses are recognised in **profit or loss**.

- Financial **liabilities** are normally measured at **amortised cost**, unless they have been classified as at fair value through profit or loss.

Section summary

Financial assets should initially be measured at cost = fair value.

Subsequently they should be remeasured to fair value except for

(a)   Loans and receivables not held for trading
(b)   Other held to maturity investments
(c)   Financial assets whose value cannot be reliably measured

Chapter Summary

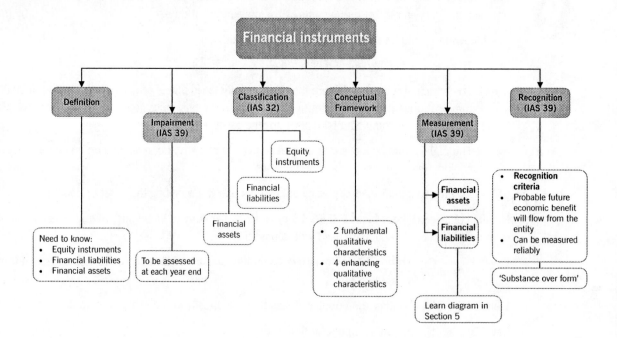

Quick Quiz

1   State two issues are dealt with by IAS 32.

2   Give examples of items which are not financial instruments according to IAS 32.

3   What is the critical feature used to identify a financial liability?

4   How should compound instruments be presented in the statement of financial position?

5   When should a financial asset be derecognised?

6   How are financial instruments initially measured?

Answers to Quick Quiz

1   Classification, and presentation, of financial instruments

2   Physical assets, prepaid expenses, non-contractual assets or liabilities, contractual rights not involving transfer of financial assets

3   The contractual obligation to deliver cash or another financial asset to the holder

4   By calculating the present value of the liability component and then deducting this from the instrument as a whole to leave a residual value for the equity component

5   Financial assets should be derecognised when the rights to the cash flows from the asset expire or where substantially all the risks and rewards of ownership are transferred to another party.

6   At fair value plus transaction costs, except when they are designated as at fair value through profit or loss (in which case, at fair value).

Answers to Questions

3.1   Why not?

Refer to the definitions of financial assets and liabilities given above.

(a)   **Physical assets**: Control of these creates an opportunity to generate an inflow of cash or other assets, but it does not give rise to a present right to receive cash or other financial assets.

(b)   **Prepaid expenses etc**: The future economic benefit is the receipt of goods/services rather than the right to receive cash or other financial assets.

3.2   Recognition

A   1 January 20X2

The share capital and share premium should be recorded when DEF becomes a party to the contractual provisions of the instrument. This is the date that DEF issues the shares rather than when they are paid for. On 1 January 20X2 a receivable would be recognised as the other side of the double entry.

3.3   Risks and rewards

IAS 39 includes the following examples:

(a)   (i)   An unconditional sale of a financial asset

    (ii)   A sale of a financial asset together with an option to repurchase the financial asset at its fair value at the time of repurchase

(b)   (i)   A sale and repurchase transaction where the repurchase price is a fixed price or the sale price plus a lender's return

    (ii)   A sale of a financial asset together with a total return swap that transfers the market risk exposure back to the entity

3.4 Finance cost 1

C   The premium on redemption of the loan notes represents a finance cost. The effective rate of interest must be applied so that the debt is measured at amortised cost (IAS 39).

At the time of issue, the loan notes are recognised at their net proceeds of $599,800 (600,000 – 200).

The finance cost for the year ended 31 December 20X4 is calculated as follows:

	B/f	Interest @ 12%	C/f
	$	$	$
20X3	599,800	71,976	671,776
20X4	671,776	80,613	752,389

3.5 Extended example

Item (a)

The bond is a financial asset held to maturity. It is therefore held at amortised cost calculated as follows.

Total finance income:		$
	$	
Coupon receipts (5 × 4% × 200,000)		40,000
Deep discount income (200,000 – (157,563 + 200))	42,237	
Total income		82,237

Spread using effective interest rate of the bond, 9.5%, as follows.

	$
Cash at 1 January 20X0 (157,563 + 200)	157,763
Interest 20X0 (9.5% × 157,763)	14,988
Coupon received (4% × 200,000)	(8,000)
At 31 December 20X0	164,751
Interest 20X1 (9.5% × 164,751)	15,651
Coupon received (4% × 200,000)	(8,000)
At 31 December 20X1	172,402

Item (b)

Despite being called shares, the redeemable preference shares are, in substance, debt and are therefore accounted for as a financial liability.

They are held at amortised cost as a company's own shares cannot be classified as held for trading. They will be shown under non-current liabilities. The annual dividend payments of 7% × 60,000 × $1 = $4,200 will be classified as interest payable.

Item (c)

Unless held for short-term profit making, shares held as an investment fall into the category available for sale financial assets. They are originally recorded at their cost (plus transaction costs) on 1 July 20X0 and revalued to fair value at the year end (31 December 20X0) with a gain of $690 reported in other comprehensive income (**items that may be reclassified subsequently to profit or loss**):

	$
Fair value at 31.12.X0 (12,000 shares × $1.32)	15,840
Cost (01.01.X0) [(12,000 shares × $1.25 = $15,000) + (1% × $15,000)]	(15,150)
Fair value gain (to other comprehensive income)	690

When the shares are sold, this fair value gain is reclassified from other comprehensive income to profit or loss and a profit on derecognition is recognised:

	$
Proceeds ($16,800 – (1% × $16,800))	16,632
Less carrying value of financial asset	(15,840)
	792
Fair value gain reclassified from OCI	690
Total gain to be recognised in profit or loss	1,482

Item (d)

A forward contract to be settled net in cash and not held for hedging purposes is accounted for at fair value through profit or loss.

The value of the contract at inception is zero.

The value of the contract at the year end is:

	$
Market price of forward contract at year end for delivery on 30 April 20X2	5,000
Palermo's forward price	(6,000)
Loss (as Palermo have to pay $1,000 more under their forward than they would at year-end prices)	(1,000)

A financial liability of $1,000 is therefore recognised with a corresponding charge of $1,000 to profit or loss.

Now try these questions from the Practice Question Bank

Number	Level	Marks	Time
Q4	Introductory	N/A	11 mins
Q5	Introductory	10	18 mins
Q6	Introductory	10	18 mins

IAS 17 LEASES

This is an **important practical** subject. Leasing transactions are extremely common, especially in recent years where there has been considerable growth in leasing agreements for example, **hire purchase agreements** in the UK. IAS 17 *Leases* standardises the accounting treatment and disclosure of assets held under lease.

In this chapter we look at the characteristics of operating and finance leases according to IAS 17, and how to account for both of these in the lessees' financial statements.

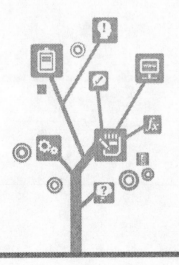

Topic list	learning outcomes	syllabus references
1 Characteristics of leases	B1	B1(c)
2 Accounting for leases	B1	B1(d)

Chapter Overview

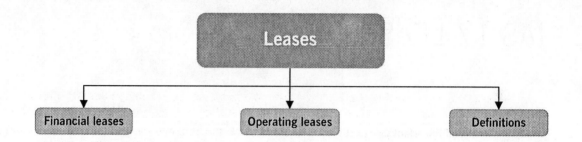

1 Characteristics of leases

Introduction

This section examines the characteristics of operating and finance leases according to IAS 17 *Leases* and explains how to distinguish between them.

1.1 The need for IAS 17 *Leases*

Before the introduction of IAS 17 *Leases*, there was widespread abuse in the use of lease accounting by companies. The lessee companies owned an asset and owed a debt for its purchase, but showed neither the asset nor the liability on the statement of financial position because the lease agreement for the asset was made to look like a rental agreement. The substance of the transaction was in fact for the purchase of an asset on credit.

This form of **off-balance sheet financing** was used by companies to make their financial statements look better by reducing the level of borrowing shown on the statement of financial position.

IAS 17 was issued to combat the abuse of lease accounting in this way by basing the accounting treatment of a leasing arrangement on the **substance of the transaction** rather than **its strict legal form**.

1.2 What is a lease?

Where goods are acquired other than on immediate cash terms, arrangements have to be made in respect of the future payments on those goods. In the simplest case of **credit sales**, the purchaser is allowed a period of time (say one month) to settle the outstanding amount and the normal accounting procedure in respect of receivables/payables will be adopted.

In a leasing transaction there is a **contract** between the lessor and the lessee for the hire of an asset. The lessor retains legal ownership but conveys to the lessee the right to use the asset for an agreed period of time in return for specified rentals.

In this chapter the **user** of an asset will often be referred to simply as the **lessee**, and the **supplier** as the **lessor**.

IAS 17 defines a lease and recognises two types.

KEY TERMS

LEASE. An agreement whereby the lessor conveys to the lessee in return for a payment or a series of payments the **right to use an asset** for an agreed period of time.

FINANCE LEASE. A lease that transfers substantially all the **risks and rewards** incidental to ownership of an asset. Title may or may not eventually be transferred.

OPERATING LEASE. A lease other than a finance lease.   (*IAS 17*)

1.3 Operating leases

Operating leases do not really pose an accounting problem. The lessee pays amounts periodically to the lessor, and these are charged to the **statement of profit or loss**. The lessor treats the leased asset as a non-current asset and depreciates it in the normal way. Rentals received from the lessee are credited to the statement of profit or loss in the lessor's books.

1.4 Finance leases

For assets held under **finance leases**, the accounting treatment described above for operating leases would not disclose the reality of the situation. If a **lessor** leases out an asset on a finance lease, the asset will probably never be seen on the lessor's premises or used in his business again. It would be inappropriate for a lessor to record such an asset as a non-current asset. In reality, what the lessor owns is a **stream of cash flows receivable** from the lessee. **The asset is an amount receivable rather than a tangible non-current asset.**

Similarly, **lessees** may use a finance lease to fund the acquisition of a major asset, which they will then use in their business perhaps for many years. **The substance of the transaction is that the lessee has acquired a non-current asset**, and this is reflected in the accounting treatment prescribed by IAS 17, even though in law the lessee never becomes the owner of the asset.

1.4.1 Characteristics of a finance lease

Remember the definition of a finance lease, which we saw in the section above:

KEY TERM

A FINANCE LEASE is a lease that transfers substantially all the **risks and rewards of ownership** of an asset to the lessee.

Deciding whether a lease is an operating lease or a finance lease requires judgement and can often be complex. The lease arrangement as a whole needs to be looked at to determine who has the significant risks and rewards associated with owning the asset.

IAS 17 gives five examples of situations that would normally lead to a lease being classified as a finance lease.

(a)   The **present value of the minimum lease payments** amounts to at least substantially all of the leased asset's **fair value** at inception. (The present value should be calculated by using the **interest rate implicit in the lease**. See the Key Terms definitions below.)

(b)   The **lease term** is for the major part of the **economic life** of the asset even if title is not transferred to the lessee.

(c)   The lease **transfers ownership** of the asset to the lessee by the end of the lease term.

(d)   The lessee has the **option to purchase** the asset at a price **sufficiently below fair value** that it is reasonably certain at the inception of the lease that the lessee will exercise the option.

(e)   The leased assets are so **specialised** that only the lessee can use them without major modifications.

The section above refers to a number of key terms:

KEY TERMS

MINIMUM LEASE PAYMENTS. The payments over the lease term that the lessee is required to make.

INTEREST RATE IMPLICIT IN THE LEASE. The discount rate that, at the inception of the lease, causes the aggregate present value of the:

(a)   Minimum lease payments
(b)   Unguaranteed residual value

To be equal to the sum of:

(a)   The fair value of the leased asset
(b)   Any initial direct costs of the lessor

LEASE TERM. The **non-cancellable** period for which the lessee has contracted to lease the asset together with any further terms for which the lessee has the option to continue to lease the asset, with or without further payment, when at the inception of the lease it is reasonably certain that the lessee will exercise the option.

ECONOMIC LIFE is either the:

(a)   Period over which an asset is expected to be economically usable by one or more users or

(b)   The number of production or similar units expected to be obtained from the asset by one or more users

USEFUL LIFE is the estimated remaining period from the beginning of the lease term over which the economic benefits embodied in the asset are expected to be consumed by the entity.

IAS 17 also gives additional indicators of situations that could lead to a lease being classified as a finance lease.

•   The lessee can cancel the lease, but must then bear any losses suffered by the lessor associated with the cancellation

•   The lessee has the ability to continue the lease for a secondary period at a rent that is substantially lower than market rent

•   Gains or losses due to fluctuation in the fair value of the residual value of the asset accrue to the lessee

Exam skills

In your exam you may be required to comment or decide on whether a lease is an operating lease or a finance lease. You should use the characteristics given in IAS 17 to assess the lease and work out what the accounting treatment should be.

Question 4.1	Finance lease or operating lease?

Learning outcome B1

On 1 January 20X8, PH leased a machine under a five-year lease. The present value of the minimum lease payments and the fair value of the asset were both $24 million. The useful life of the asset was six years, and there is no residual value. At the end of the lease term, legal title of the asset is transferred to PH.

Required

Explain whether this is an operating or a finance lease.

1.4.2 Leases of land and buildings

Under IAS 17, the land and buildings elements of a lease of land and buildings are **considered separately** for the purposes of lease classification.

A lease of land is normally treated as an operating lease, unless title is expected to pass at the end of the lease term.

A lease of buildings will be treated as a finance lease if it satisfies the requirements for a finance lease given above. The minimum lease payments are allocated between the land and buildings elements in proportion to the relative fair values of the leasehold interests in the land and the buildings. If the value of the land is immaterial, classification will be according to the buildings.

If payments cannot be reliably allocated, the entire lease is classified as a finance lease, unless both elements are operating leases, in which case the entire lease is classified as an operating lease.

Section summary

Under IAS 17, a lease of an asset can either be a **finance lease** or an **operating lease**.

A finance lease is a lease that transfers substantially all the **risks and rewards** of ownership to the lessee.

An operating lease is a lease other than a finance lease.

IAS 17 gives examples of situations that indicate that an agreement is a finance lease.

Leases of land are usually classified as operating leases.

2 Accounting for leases

Introduction

This section explains the accounting treatment of a lease in the books of the lessee.

2.1 Accounting for operating leases

The accounting treatment for an operating lease in the books of the lessee is straightforward. With an operating lease, the **lessor** has the **risks and rewards**. Therefore, the **lessee** should **not record the asset** in their statement of financial position.

KEY POINT

Operating lease payments are treated as an **expense** of the entity and should be **charged to profit or loss** on a systematic (normally **straight-line**) basis over the lease term.

2.1.1 Operating lease accounting entry

The operating lease is recorded in the financial statements as follows:

DEBIT   Operating lease charges (statement of profit or loss)
CREDIT   Cash

Assuming rentals are paid on a straight-line basis.

Example: Operating lease 1

Ginny Co enters into a non-cancellable three-year operating lease costing $6,000 per annum for three years. The machine has an estimated useful life of ten years.

Required

What is the accounting entry in respect of this operating lease?

Solution

The annual cost will be spread straight-line over the three years.

DEBIT	Operating lease charges	$6,000	
CREDIT	Cash		$6,000

Being operating lease rental expense for the year

2.1.2 Incentives and deposits

Where the lessee is offered an incentive such as a **rent-free period** or **cashback incentive** this is, effectively, a **discount**, which will be spread over the period of the operating lease in accordance with the accruals principle. For instance, if a company entered into a four-year operating lease, but was not required to make any payments until year two, the total payments to be made over years two to four should be charged evenly over years one to four.

Where a cashback incentive is received, the total amount payable over the lease term, less the cashback, should be charged evenly over the term of the lease. This can be done by crediting the cashback received to deferred income, and releasing it to profit or loss over the lease term.

Conversely, if a deposit is required at the start of the lease, the deposit is spread over the period of the operating lease. The total amount payable over the lease term, including the deposit, is charged evenly in each period as the operating lease charges, with the balancing figure being recorded as prepayments.

Example: Operating lease 2

Ginny Co enters into a non-cancellable three-year operating lease with the following terms:

Annual rental:	$6,000 per annum
Cashback incentive received at the start of the lease:	$1,500
Asset's useful life:	10 years

Required

How will the cashback incentive and the annual rentals be recorded in the financial statements of Ginny Co for each of the three years of the lease?

Solution

The total being paid over the three-year lease term is $16,500 ($6,000 × 3 – $1,500 cashback). This should be spread evenly over the three years to show an annual charge of $5,500.

	$	$
Year 1		
DEBIT Cash	1,500	
CREDIT Deferred income		1,500
DEBIT Operating lease charges	5,500	
DEBIT Deferred income ($1,500 ÷ 3)	500	
CREDIT Cash		6,000

Being operating lease charge for year 1

	$	$
Years 2 and 3		
DEBIT Operating lease charges	5,500	
DEBIT Deferred income	500	
CREDIT Cash		6,000

Being operating lease charge for years 2 and 3

Example: Operating lease 3

Ginny Co enters into the same lease as above, but now pays a deposit of $3,000 when the lease is signed followed by an annual charge of $5,000 each year for three years.

Required

How should the payments for each year of the lease be recorded?

Solution

The total being paid over the three-year lease term is $18,000 ($3,000 + [3 × $5,000]). This should be spread evenly over the three years to show an annual charge of $6,000.

		$	$
Year 1			
DEBIT	Operating lease charges	6,000	
DEBIT	Prepayments	2,000	
CREDIT	Cash ($3,000 + $5,000)		8,000
Year 2			
DEBIT	Operating lease charges	6,000	
CREDIT	Prepayments		1,000
CREDIT	Cash		5,000
Year 3			
DEBIT	Operating lease charges	6,000	
CREDIT	Prepayments		1,000
CREDIT	Cash		5,000

The prepayment established in year 1 is then released over years 2 and 3 to show a constant operating lease cost of $6,000 each year.

2.1.3 Operating lease disclosures

IAS 17 requires the following disclosures by lessees in respect of **operating leases**.

The total of future minimum lease payments under non-cancellable operating leases for each of the following periods:

- Not later than one year
- Later than one year and not later than five years
- Later than five years

This disclosure note is required because, although operating leases do not give rise to a liability on the statement of financial position, they are non-cancellable and so they do entail a future financial commitment, which should be disclosed.

IAS 17 also requires a general description of the entity's significant lease arrangements and the amount of lease payments recognised as an expense in the period.

2.2 Accounting for finance leases

2.2.1 Initial recognition

IAS 17 requires that, when an asset changes hands under a **finance lease, lessor and lessee should account for the transaction as though it were a credit sale**. In the lessee's books therefore:

DEBIT   Property, plant and equipment   **to capitalise the asset**
CREDIT   Finance lease liability   **to recognise the lease liability**

The amount to be recorded in this way is the **lower** of:

- The **fair value of the leased asset** and

- The **present value of the minimum lease payments** which will, generally, be the purchase price of the asset

The result of this double entry is that the lessee has recognised a liability which equates to the **capital cost of the asset**.

2.2.2 Subsequent measurement of the asset

The asset should be **depreciated** over the shorter of:

- The lease term
- The asset's useful life

If there is reasonable certainty of **eventual ownership** of the asset, then it should be depreciated over its **useful life**.

2.2.3 Subsequent measurement of the liability

The substance of a finance lease arrangement is that the lessee takes ownership of an asset and then pays for that asset in instalments. This same effect could have been achieved if the entity had taken a loan with a bank and used the loan to purchase the asset from the lessor. In effect then, the lease payments are similar to loan repayments and therefore they include an element of **interest** (also called **finance charge**) and an element of **capital repayment**.

The accounting problem is to decide what proportion of each instalment paid by the lessee represents interest, and what proportion represents a repayment of the capital. The finance charge is expensed as finance costs in the **statement of profit or loss**. The aim is that the finance charge should reduce over the lease term in line with the outstanding liability.

There are three apportionment methods you may encounter:

- The straight-line method
- The actuarial method
- The sum of the digits method

Exam skills

An examination question will always make it clear which method should be used. If you are given an interest rate, you will be expected to use the actuarial method. If not, use the sum of the digits method.

The **straight-line method** is simple, but does not provide a constant rate of interest. The interest amount is simply allocated equally over the lease periods. You are not likely to be asked to use this method in the exam, but you should know about it.

The **actuarial method** is the best and most scientific method. It derives from the common-sense assumption that the interest charged by a lessor company will equal the rate of return desired by the company, multiplied by the amount of capital it has invested.

BPP
LEARNING MEDIA

(a) At the beginning of the lease, the capital invested is equal to the fair value of the asset (less any initial deposit paid by the lessee).

(b) This amount reduces as each instalment is paid. It follows that the interest accruing is greatest in the early part of the lease term, and gradually reduces as capital is repaid.

Finance charge for the period = Interest rate implicit in lease x capital outstanding.

LEARN

Later in this section, we will look at a simple example of the actuarial method.

Exam skills

If you are required to use the actuarial method in the exam, you will be given the interest rate.

The **sum of the digits** method approximates to the actuarial method, splitting the total interest (without reference to a rate of interest) in such a way that the greater proportion falls in the earlier years. This method should only be used **when the implicit rate of interest in the lease is unavailable.**

The procedure is as follows.

 Assign a digit to each instalment. The digit 1 should be assigned to the final instalment, 2 to the penultimate instalment and so on.

 Add the digits. A quick method of adding the digits is to use the formula $\dfrac{n(n+1)}{2}$ where n is the number of instalments. For example, for a lease with five payments in arrears:

$$\text{Sum of digits} = \frac{n(n+1)}{2} = \frac{5(5+1)}{2} = 15$$

where n = number of interest bearing payments

 Calculate the finance charge included in each instalment. This is calculated as:

Sum of digits fraction × total finance charge

For a lease with five payments in arrears, the total finance charge would be allocated to the instalments as follows:

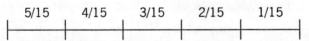

5/15   4/15   3/15   2/15   1/15

Later in this section, we will look at a simple example of the sum of the digits method.

2.2.4 Accounting entries

Once the interest has been calculated using one of these methods, the capital element of the lease repayment can be calculated (capital element = lease payment – interest element). The double entries to record the interest and the lease payment are as follows.

To record the interest:

DEBIT   Finance charge (with the calculated interest element)
CREDIT   Finance lease liability

To record the lease payment:

DEBIT   Finance lease liability
CREDIT   Cash

At the end of the year, the balance on the finance lease liability account will represent the outstanding capital liability. This liability should be split into current and non-current liabilities. Future interest/finance charges are not part of this figure because the capital could be paid off at any time, thus avoiding these charges.

The following example shows how to account for a finance lease using the actuarial and sum-of-the-digits methods of interest allocation described above.

Example: Finance lease accounting

On 1 January 20X0 Bacchus Co, wine merchants, bought a small bottling and labelling machine from Silenus Co under a finance lease. The cash price of the machine was $7,710 while the amount to be paid was $10,000. The agreement required the immediate payment of a $2,000 deposit with the balance being settled at $2,000 per annum **in arrears** commencing on 31 December 20X0. The charge of $2,290 represents interest of 15% per annum, calculated on the remaining balance of the liability during each accounting period. Depreciation on the plant is to be provided at the rate of 20% per annum on a straight-line basis assuming a residual value of nil. At the end of the lease, ownership will pass to Bacchus Co.

Required

Show the breakdown of each instalment between interest and capital, using the sum-of-the-digits method and the actuarial method.

Use the breakdown calculated for the **actuarial method** to give the following statement of financial position extracts relating to the machine as at 31 December each year from 20X0 to 20X3:

(a)   Non-current assets: machine at net book value
(b)   Current liabilities: obligations under finance lease
(c)   Non-current liabilities: obligations under finance lease

Solution

In this example, enough detail is given to use either the sum-of-the-digits method or the actuarial method. In an examination question, you would normally be directed to use one method specifically.

Sum-of-the-digits method

Each instalment is allocated a digit as follows.

Instalment	Digit
First (20X0)	4
Second (20X1)	3
Third (20X2)	2
Fourth (20X3)	1
	10

Or using the formula, $\dfrac{4 \times 5}{2} = 10$.

The $2,290 interest charges can then be apportioned.

		$
First instalment	$2,290 × 4/10	916
Second instalment	$2,290 × 3/10	687
Third instalment	$2,290 × 2/10	458
Fourth instalment	$2,290 × 1/10	229
		2,290

The breakdown is then as follows.

	First instalment $	Second instalment $	Third instalment $	Fourth Instalment $
Interest	916	687	458	229
Capital repayment (balance)	1,084	1,313	1,542	1,771
	2,000	2,000	2,000	2,000

The workings for the finance lease can then be calculated as follows.

	Balance $
Cash price of machine	7,710
Deposit	(2,000)
Capital balance at 1 January 20X0	5,710
Interest	916
First instalment	(2,000)
Capital balance at 31 December 20X0	4,626
Interest	687
Second instalment	(2,000)
Capital balance at 31 December 20X1	3,313
Interest	458
Third instalment	(2,000)
Capital balance at 31 December 20X2	1,771
Interest	229
Fourth instalment	(2,000)
Capital balance at 31 December 20X3	–

Actuarial method

The instalments in this example are paid in **arrears**, therefore interest is calculated as 15% of the outstanding balance at the beginning of each year ie **before** the lease payment has been made.

	Balance $
Cash price of machine	7,710
Deposit	(2,000)
Capital balance at 1 January 20X0	5,710
Interest (5,710 × 15%)	856
First instalment	(2,000)
Capital balance at 31 December 20X0	4,566
Interest (4,566 × 15%)	685
Second instalment	(2,000)
Capital balance at 31 December 20X1	3,251
Interest (3,251 × 15%)	488
Third instalment	(2,000)
Capital balance at 31 December 20X2	1,739
Interest (1,739 × 15%)	261
Fourth instalment	(2,000)
Capital balance at 31 December 20X3	–

The journal entries at 1 January 20X0 will be:

(i)   To record the asset and initial finance lease liability

DEBIT	Property, plant and equipment	$7,710	
CREDIT	Finance lease liability: Silenus		$7,710

(ii) To record the deposit payment

DEBIT	Finance lease liability: Silenus	$2,000	
CREDIT	Cash		$2,000

The journal entries at 31 December 20X0 will be:

(i) To record the interest element

DEBIT	Finance charge	$856	
CREDIT	Finance lease liability: Silenus		$856

(ii) To record the annual lease payment

DEBIT	Finance lease liability: Silenus	$2,000	
CREDIT	Cash		$2,000

The statement of financial position extracts are as follows.

(a) **Non-current assets: machine at net book value** (Note. Eventual ownership is certain.)

		$
At 31 December 20X0	Machine at cost	7,710
	Accumulated depreciation (7,710 × 1/5)	1,542
	Carrying amount	6,168
At 31 December 20X1	Machine at cost	7,710
	Accumulated depreciation (7,710 × 2/5)	3,084
	Carrying amount	4,626
At 31 December 20X2	Machine at cost	7,710
	Accumulated depreciation (7,710 × 3/5)	4,626
	Carrying amount	3,084
At 31 December 20X3	Machine at cost	7,710
	Accumulated depreciation (7,710 × 4/5)	6,168
	Carrying amount	1,542

(b) **Current liabilities: obligations under finance lease**

	$
At 31 December 20X0	1,315
At 31 December 20X1	1,512
At 31 December 20X2	1,739
At 31 December 20X3	–

Current liabilities represent the portion of the liability that is payable within one year. When lease payments are paid in arrears, the easiest way to calculate the current liabilities balance is to first identify the non-current liability, which is simply the capital balance outstanding in the following year, and deduct this from the capital balance outstanding at the current year end.

For example:

Current liability at 31 December 20X0 = total capital balance at 31 December 20X0 – total capital balance at 31 December 20X1

= $4,566 – $3,251

= $1,315

(c) **Non-current liabilities: obligations under finance lease**

	$
At 31 December 20X0	3,251
At 31 December 20X1	1,739
At 31 December 20X2	–
At 31 December 20X3	–

Notice that when lease payments are made in arrears, the year-end liability is **all capital**. Any interest which has accrued during the year has been settled by the instalment paid in that year, because the instalment is paid in arrears.

2.2.5 Payments in advance or in arrears

It is important to note whether payments are made **in advance** or **in arrears** because it has an effect on the mechanics of the calculation you will perform, and on the year-end liability.

In the sum-of-the-digits method of allocating interest, payments made in arrears mean that the number of finance periods is equal to the number of instalments paid. But if payments are made in advance, the number of finance periods is the number of instalments minus one. This is because the lease liability is extinguished one period earlier if repayments are made in advance as opposed to in arrears, and so it is not necessary to allocate interest to that final period.

When lease payments are made **in advance**, the first payment made repays capital only as no time has yet elapsed for interest to accrue. At the end of each accounting period, the year-end liability will include capital and interest that has accrued to date but which has not yet been paid.

Question 4.2	Sum-of-the-digits method

Learning outcome B1

Dundas Co purchased a machine under a finance lease on 1 January 20X6. The lease is for four years with instalments of $2,000 to be paid **in advance** on 1 January each year. The fair value of the machine was $6,500. Its useful life is six years, and its residual value is nil. Dundas will depreciate the machine on a straight-line basis.

In apportioning interest to respective accounting periods, the company uses the 'sum-of-the-digits method'.

Required

Show the following statement of financial position extracts relating to the machine as at each year end from 31 December 20X6 to 31 December 20X9.

(a)   Non-current assets: machine at net book value
(b)   Current liabilities: obligations under finance lease
(c)   Non-current liabilities: obligations under finance lease

Exam alert

When doing lease calculations, you must highlight the **answer** to the question. Many students can do the calculation correctly but struggle to select the correct answer to the question from their workings.

Section summary

You must learn (through repeated practice) how to apply the actuarial and sum-of-the-digits methods of interest allocation.

Chapter Summary

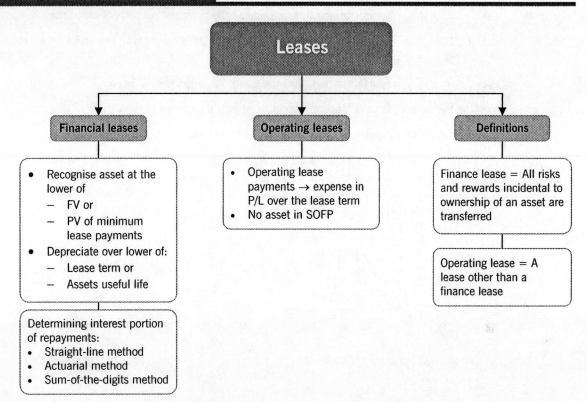

Leases

Financial leases

- Recognise asset at the lower of
  - FV or
  - PV of minimum lease payments
- Depreciate over lower of:
  - Lease term or
  - Assets useful life

Determining interest portion of repayments:
- Straight-line method
- Actuarial method
- Sum-of-the-digits method

Operating leases

- Operating lease payments → expense in P/L over the lease term
- No asset in SOFP

Definitions

Finance lease = All risks and rewards incidental to ownership of an asset are transferred

Operating lease = A lease other than a finance lease

Quick Quiz

1   (a)   .... leases transfer substantially all the risks and rewards of ownership.

    (b)   .... leases are usually short-term rental agreements with the lessor being responsible for the repairs and maintenance of the asset.

2   A business acquires an asset under a finance lease. What is the double entry?

3   What is the formula to calculate each period's interest using sum of the digits?

4   List the disclosures required under IAS 17 for lessees in respect of operating leases.

5   A lorry has an expected useful life of six years. It is acquired under a four-year finance lease and will probably be bought at the end of the lease. Over which period should it be depreciated?

Answers to Quick Quiz

1   (a)   Finance
     (b)   Operating

2   DEBIT   Asset account
     CREDIT   Finance lease liability account

3    $\dfrac{\text{Digit applicable to the instalment}}{\text{Sum of the digits}} \times$ Total interest charge

4   See Section 2.1.3 for operating leases and Section 2.2.4 for finance leases.

5   As eventual ownership of the lorry is reasonably certain, it should be depreciated over its six-year useful life.

Answers to Questions

4.1 Finance lease or operating lease?

This is a **finance lease** as the lessor **transfers** substantially all the **risks and rewards** to PH (the lessee). This is evidenced by:

*   The lease term (5 years) being for a major part of the asset's economic life (6 years)
*   The present value of the minimum lease payments being the same as the fair value of the asset ($24 million)
*   Ownership being transferred to the lessee (PH) at the end of the lease term

4.2 Sum-of-the-digits method

	$
Fair value of machine at 1 January 20X6	6,500
First instalment paid at 1 January 20X6	(2,000)
	4,500
Interest 20X6 (W)	750
Balance at 31 December 20X6	5,250
Second Instalment paid at 1 January 20X7	(2,000)
	3,250
Interest 20X7 (W)	500
Balance at 31 December 20X7	3,750
Third Instalment paid at 1 January 20X8	(2,000)
	1,750
Interest 20X8 (W)	250
Balance at 31 December 20X8	2,000
Fourth Instalment paid at 1 January 20X9	(2,000)
Balance at 31 December 20X9	–

Note that because the lease payments are made **in advance**, the lease payment for each year is deducted from the outstanding capital balance **before** the interest is added on. It is particularly important to set your calculation up this way when using the actuarial method of allocating interest, so that you calculate the interest on the correct capital balance.

Working

	$
Finance charge	
Total lease payments	8,000
Fair value of machine	(6,500)
Finance charge	1,500

Number of finance periods = total number of repayments − 1 = 3

	$
Sum of the digits = 3 + 2 + 1 = 6	
Interest charge 20X6 = $1,500 × $\frac{3}{6}$	750
Interest charge 20X7 = $1,500 × $\frac{2}{6}$	500
Interest charge 20X8 = $1,500 × $\frac{1}{6}$	250
	1,500

(a) **Non-current assets: machine at net book value**

		$
At 31 December 20X6	Machine at cost	6,500
	Accumulated depreciation (W)	(1,625)
	Carrying amount	4,875
At 31 December 20X7	Machine at cost	6,500
	Accumulated depreciation	(3,250)
	Carrying amount	3,250
At 31 December 20X8	Machine at cost	6,500
	Accumulated depreciation	(4,875)
	Carrying amount	1,625
At 31 December 20X9	Machine at cost	6,500
	Accumulated depreciation	(6,500)
	Carrying amount	–

Working

Annual depreciation charge on a straight-line basis = $\frac{\$6,500}{4}$ = $1,625 per year

(b) **Current liabilities: obligations under finance lease**

	$
At 31 December 20X6 (see **Note**)	2,000
At 31 December 20X7	2,000
At 31 December 20X8	2,000
At 31 December 20X9	–

Note. The interest element ($750) of the current liability could be shown separately as interest payable. Similarly for the following years.

Notice how the year-end liability includes capital **and interest** that has accrued to date but which has not yet been paid. This is because the lease payments are made **in advance**, so they are made before any interest has accrued. Look back at the example in the chapter and compare the two answers to make sure you see the difference between when payments are made in arrears and when they are made in advance.

(c)   **Non-current liabilities: obligations under finance lease**

	$
At 31 December 20X6 (5,250 – 2,000)	3,250
At 31 December 20X7 (3,750 – 2,000)	1,750
At 31 December 20X8 (2,000 – 2000)	–
At 31 December 20X9	–

	Number	Level	Marks	Time
Now try these questions from the Exam Question Bank	Q7	Introductory	N/A	13 mins

PROVISIONS, CONTINGENT LIABILITIES AND CONTINGENT ASSETS

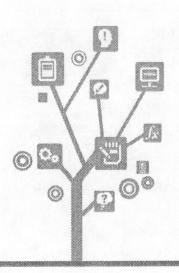

IAS 37 and IAS 10 are very important as they can affect many items in the financial statements. Students sometimes get them confused with each other, so make sure you learn all the relevant definitions and understand the standard accounting treatment.

Topic list	learning outcomes	syllabus references
1 IAS 37 *Provisions, contingent liabilities and contingent assets*	B1	B1(c)(d)
2 Contingent liabilities	B1	B1(c)(d)
3 Contingent assets	B1	B1(c)(d)
4 IAS 37 flowchart	B1	B1(c)(d)

Chapter Overview

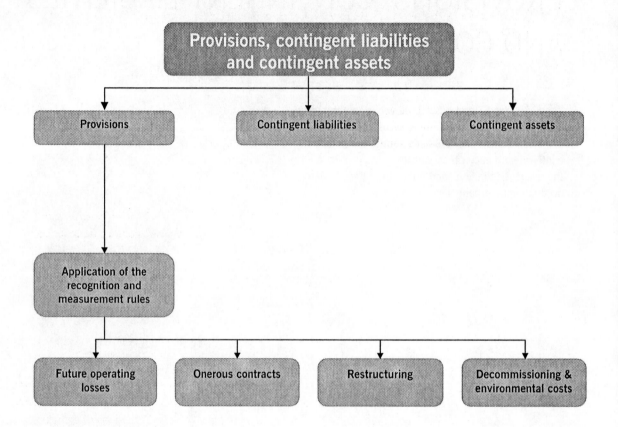

1   IAS 37 *Provisions,contingent liabilities and contingent assets*

Introduction

This section introduces provisions, contingent liabilities and contingent assets. You will need to be able to identify these in a given scenario.

1.1 Dealing with uncertainty

Financial statements must include **all the information necessary for an understanding of the entity's financial position**. Provisions, contingent liabilities and contingent assets are **uncertainties** that must be accounted for consistently if we are to achieve this understanding.

1.2 Objective

IAS 37 *Provisions, contingent liabilities and contingent assets* aims to ensure that appropriate **recognition criteria** and **measurement bases** are applied to provisions, contingent liabilities and contingent assets and that **sufficient information** is disclosed in the **notes** to the financial statements to enable users to understand their nature, timing and amount.

1.3 Provisions

You will be familiar with provisions (allowances) for depreciation and doubtful debts from your earlier studies. The provisions addressed by IAS 37 are, however, rather different.

Before IAS 37, there was no accounting standard dealing with provisions. Companies wanting to show their results in the most favourable light used to make large one-off provisions in years where a high level of underlying profit was generated. These provisions, often known as big bath provisions, were then available to shield expenditure in future years when perhaps the underlying profits were not as good.

In other words, provisions were used for **profit smoothing**. Profit smoothing is misleading.

KEY POINT

The key aim of IAS 37 is to ensure that provisions are made only where there are valid grounds for them. IAS 37 views a provision as a **liability**.

KEY TERMS

A PROVISION is a liability of uncertain timing or amount.

A LIABILITY is an obligation of an entity to transfer economic benefits as a result of past transactions or events.   (*IAS 37*)

IAS 37 distinguishes provisions from other liabilities such as trade payables and accruals. This is on the basis that, for a provision, there is **uncertainty** about the timing or amount of the future expenditure. While uncertainty is clearly present in the case of certain accruals, the uncertainty is, generally, much less than for provisions.

1.4 Recognition

IAS 37 states that a provision should be **recognised** as a liability in the financial statements when, and only when, **all three** of the following conditions are met:

*   An entity has a **present obligation** (legal or constructive) as a result of a past event

*   It is probable that a **transfer of economic benefits** will be required to settle the obligation

*   A **reliable estimate** can be made of the amount of the obligation

The process for adjusting a provision at the end of each reporting period is as follows:

 STEP 1 Calculate the provision required at the end of the period based on the information provided.

 STEP 2 Compare this to the provision brought forward as shown in the trial balance.

	$
Provision b/d	X
Movement (to P/L)	X/(X)
Provision c/d	X

STEP 3 Adjust the provision by a charge or a credit to the statement of profit or loss.

A provision is recognised, and adjusted, as follows:

For an **increase** in the provision

DEBIT   Expenses (statement of profit or loss)
CREDIT   Provisions (statement of financial position – liabilities)

For a **decrease** in the provision

DEBIT   Provisions (statement of financial position – liabilities)
CREDIT   Expenses (statement of profit or loss)

1.4.1 Meaning of obligation

An obligation can either be:

*   Legal or
*   Constructive

It is fairly clear what a **legal obligation** is: it is one which arises from a contract, legislation or from any other operation of law. However, you may not know what a **constructive obligation** is.

KEY TERM

IAS 37 defines a CONSTRUCTIVE OBLIGATION as:

An obligation that derives from an entity's actions where:

*   By an established pattern of past practice, published policies or in a sufficiently specific current statement the entity has indicated to other parties that it will accept certain responsibilities and

*   As a result, the entity has created a **valid expectation** on the part of those other parties that it will discharge those responsibilities

Question 5.1	Recognising a provision

Learning outcome B1

In which of the following circumstances shall a provision be recognised?

(a)   On 13 December 20X9 the board of an entity decided to close down a division. The accounting date of the company is 31 December. Before 31 December 20X9 the decision was not communicated to any of those affected and no other steps were taken to implement the decision.

(b)   The board agreed a detailed closure plan on 20 December 20X9 and details were given to customers and employees.

(c) A company is obliged to incur clean up costs for environmental damage (that has already been caused).

(d) A company intends to carry out future expenditure to operate in a particular way in the future.

1.4.2 Probable transfer of economic benefits

For the purposes of IAS 37, a transfer of economic benefits is regarded as **probable** if the event is **more likely than not** to occur. This appears to indicate a probability of more than 50%. However, the standard makes it clear that where there are a number of similar obligations the probability should be based on considering the population as a whole, rather than one single item. Often it will be a matter of judgement to determine the probability of an event occurring and hence its accounting treatment.

Example: Transfer of economic benefits

If a company has entered into a warranty obligation, then the probability of transfer of economic benefits may well be extremely small in respect of one specific item. However, when considering the population as a whole, the probability of some transfer of economic benefits is quite likely to be much higher. If there is a **greater than 50% probability** of some transfer of economic benefits, then a **provision** should be made for the **expected amount**.

1.5 Measurement of provisions

KEY POINT

The amount recognised as a provision should be the **best estimate** of the expenditure required to settle the present obligation at the end of the reporting period.

The estimates will be determined by the **judgement** of the entity's management supplemented by the experience of similar transactions. If the provision relates to just one item, the best estimate of the expenditure will be the **individual most likely outcome**.

When a provision is needed that involves a lot of items (for example, a warranty provision, where each item sold has a warranty attached to it), then the provision is calculated using the **expected value approach**. The expected value approach takes each expected outcome (ie the amount of money that will need to be paid under each circumstance) and weights it according to the probability of that outcome happening. This is illustrated in the following question.

Question 5.2   Warranty provision

Learning outcome B1

Parker Co sells goods with a warranty under which customers are covered for the cost of repairs of any manufacturing defect that becomes apparent within the first six months of purchase. The company's past experience and future expectations indicate the following pattern of likely repairs.

% of goods sold	Defects	Cost of repairs if all goods had this defect $m
75	None	–
20	Minor	1.0
5	Major	4.0

What provision should be made for warranty claims?

1.6 Provisions: other issues

1.6.1 Discounting

Where the effect of the **time value of money** is material, the amount of a provision should be the **present value** of the expenditure required to settle the obligation. An appropriate **discount** rate should be used.

The discount rate should be a **pre-tax rate** that reflects current market assessments of the time value of money. **The discount rate(s) should not reflect risks for which future cash flow estimates have been adjusted.**

We introduced the technique of discounting in Chapter 2.

1.6.2 Future events

Future events which are reasonably expected to occur (eg new legislation, changes in technology) may affect the amount required to settle the enterprise's obligation and should be taken into account.

1.6.3 Expected disposal of assets

Gains from the expected disposal of assets should not be taken into account in measuring a provision.

1.6.4 Reimbursements

Some or all of the expenditure needed to settle a provision may be expected to be recovered from a third party. If so, the **reimbursement should be recognised only when it is virtually certain that reimbursement will be received if the entity settles the obligation.**

(a)   The reimbursement should be treated as a **separate asset**, and the amount recognised should not be greater than the provision itself.

(b)   The provision and the amount recognised for reimbursement may be netted off in profit or loss.

1.6.5 Changes in provisions

Provisions should be reviewed at the end of each reporting period and adjusted to reflect the current best estimate. If it is no longer probable that a transfer of economic benefits will be required to settle the obligation, the provision should be reversed.

1.6.6 Use of provisions

A provision should be used only for expenditures for which the provision was originally recognised. Setting expenditures against a provision that was originally recognised for another purpose would conceal the impact of two different events.

1.6.7 Future operating losses

Provisions should not be recognised for future operating losses. They do not meet the definition of a liability or the *Conceptual Framework* recognition criteria.

1.7 Onerous contracts

If an entity has a contract that is onerous, the present obligation under the contract **should be recognised and measured** as a provision. An example might be vacant leasehold property.

KEY TERM

An ONEROUS CONTRACT is a contract entered into with another party under which the **unavoidable costs** of fulfilling the terms of the contract **exceed the benefits** expected to be received under it.

Where an entity has a contract that is onerous, a provision must be made for the net loss, which is the *lower* of:

* The net cost of **fulfilling** the contract and
* The penalties from the **failure to fulfil** the contract

Learning outcome B1

Peaches Co operates profitably from a factory that it has leased under an operating lease. During December 20X0 Peaches relocates its operations to a new factory. The lease on the old factory continues for the next four years, at a rental of $21,000 per annum. It can be sub-let for a rental of $5,000 per annum or cancelled for a penalty of $50,000.

Required

Explain the accounting treatment in respect of this contract in Peaches Co's financial statements.

1.8 Provisions for restructuring

One of the main purposes of IAS 37 was to target abuses of provisions for restructuring. Accordingly, IAS 37 lays down **strict criteria** to determine when such a provision can be made.

KEY TERM

IAS 37 defines a RESTRUCTURING as:

A programme that is planned and controlled by management and materially changes either:

* The scope of a business undertaken by an entity or
* The manner in which that business is conducted

IAS 37 gives the following **examples** of events that may fall under the definition of restructuring.

* The **sale or termination** of a line of business
* The **closure of business locations** in a country or region or the **relocation** of business activities from one country region to another
* **Changes in management structure**, for example the elimination of a layer of management
* **Fundamental reorganisations** that have a material effect on the **nature and focus** of the entity's operations

The question is whether or not an entity has an obligation at the end of the reporting period. Such an obligation only arises where an entity:

* Has a **detailed formal plan** for the restructuring, and
* Has **raised a valid expectation** in those affected that it will carry out the restructuring by starting to implement that plan or announcing its main features to those affected by it

Where the restructuring involves the **sale of an operation**, then IAS 37 states that no obligation arises until the entity has entered into a **binding sale agreement**. This is because until this has occurred, the entity will be able to change its mind and withdraw from the sale even if its intentions have been announced publicly.

1.8.1 Costs to be included within a restructuring provision

IAS 37 states that a restructuring provision should include only the **direct expenditures** arising from the restructuring, which are those that are both:

* **Necessarily entailed** by the restructuring and
* Not associated with the **ongoing activities** of the entity

The following costs should specifically **not** be included within a restructuring provision.

- **Retraining** or relocating continuing staff
- **Marketing**
- **Investment in new systems** and distribution networks

Question 5.4	Restructuring provision

Learning outcome B1

On 12 December 20X1 the board of Peaches Co decided to close down a division. The detailed plan was agreed by the board on 20 December 20X1, and letters sent to notify customers. By the year end of 31 December 20X1, the staff had received redundancy notices.

Required

Explain the appropriate accounting treatment for the closure for the year ended 31 December 20X1.

1.9 Decommissioning costs

When an oil company purchases an oilfield, it is often only granted licences to explore and extract raw materials provided that it makes good any damage made during the exploration and extraction process. Prior to IAS 37, most oil companies set up the provision gradually over the life of the field, so that no one year would be unduly burdened with the cost.

IAS 37, however, insists that a legal obligation exists on the initial expenditure on the field, and therefore a liability exists immediately. This would appear to result in a large charge to profit or loss in the first year of operation of the field. However, IAS 37 takes the view that the cost of purchasing the field in the first place is not only the cost of the field itself but also the costs of putting it right again. Thus all the costs of abandonment may be capitalised.

An entity should provide for decommissioning costs from the date on which the **obligating event occurs**. These costs will be added onto the cost of the non-current asset:

DEBIT   Property, plant and equipment
CREDIT   Provision

Question 5.5	Decommissioning costs

Learning outcome B1

Sesame Co built an oil rig at a cost of $80m. The oil rig came into operation on 1 January 20X2. The operating licence is for 20 years from 1 January 20X2, after which time the company is obliged to dismantle the oil rig and dispose of the parts in an environmentally friendly way. At 1 January 20X2, the cost of dismantling in 20 years' time was estimated at $10m.

An appropriate discount rate is 6%.

Required

(a)   What is the accounting entry to record the provision on 1 January 20X2?

(b)   What is the carrying amount of the oil rig at 31 December 20X2?

(c)   What is the carrying amount of the provision at 31 December 20X2?

(d)   Explain the treatment of any environmental damage arising through operating the oil rig (assuming the company is legally required to clean it up at the end of the rig's life).

Round your answers to the nearest $'000.

1.10 Warranty provision

Warranties are argued to be genuine provisions as on past experience it is probable (ie more likely than not) that some claims will emerge. The provision must be estimated, however, on the basis of the class as a whole and not on individual claims. There is a clear legal obligation in this case.

1.11 Other expenditures and IAS 37

IAS 37 can be applied to the following types of expenditure. Note the reasons why the first two examples do not constitute a provision, while the last one does.

(a)   **Major repairs**. In the past, it has been quite popular for companies to provide for expenditure on a major overhaul to be accrued gradually over the intervening years between overhauls. This is no longer possible as IAS 37 states that this is a mere *intention* to carry out repairs, not an *obligation*. The entity can always sell the asset in the meantime. The only solution is to treat major assets such as aircraft, ships, furnaces etc as a series of smaller assets, where each part is depreciated over different lives. Thus, any major overhaul may be argued to be replacement and therefore capital, rather than revenue, expenditure.

(b)   **Self insurance**. A number of companies have created a provision for self insurance based on the expected cost of making good the damage, instead of paying premiums to an insurance company. Under IAS 37, this provision is no longer justifiable as the entity has no obligation until a fire or another triggering event occurs. No obligation exists until that time.

(c)   **Environmental contamination**. If the company has an environmental policy such that other parties would expect the company to clean up any contamination or if the company has broken current environmental legislation, then a provision for environmental damage must be made.

KEY POINT

A mere management decision is not normally sufficient to trigger recognition of a provision. Management decisions may sometimes trigger recognition, but only if earlier events such as negotiations with employee representatives and other interested parties have been concluded, subject only to management approval.

2   Contingent liabilities

Now that you have covered provisions, it will be easier to understand contingent assets and liabilities.

KEY TERM

A CONTINGENT LIABILITY is:

- A **possible obligation** that arises from past events and whose existence will be confirmed only by the occurrence or non-occurrence of one or more uncertain future events not wholly within the entity's control or

- A **present obligation** that arises from past events, but is not recognised because:

  - It is **not probable** that a transfer of economic benefits will be required to settle the obligation or

  - The amount of the obligation **cannot be measured** with sufficient reliability

As a rule of thumb, probable means more than 50% likely. If an obligation is probable, it is not a contingent liability – instead, a provision is needed.

2.1 Treatment of contingent liabilities

KEY POINT

Contingent liabilities **should not be recognised** in financial statements but they **should be disclosed**, unless the possibility of an outflow of economic benefits is **remote**.

BPP

For each class of contingent liability, the entity should disclose all of the following at the reporting date:

*   A brief description of the **nature** of the contingent liability
*   An estimate of its **financial effect**
*   An indication of the **uncertainties** relating to the amount or timing of any outflow
*   The possibility of any **reimbursement**

Example: Contingent liability

Eggsellent Co sold eggs to Cuisine Co that they used in baking cakes. The cakes were then sold to the public. Unfortunately, five of Cuisine Co's customers are now in hospital suffering from food poisoning after eating the cakes, and Cuisine Co believe that it is due to the eggs.

Cuisine Co are now suing Eggsellent Co. Eggsellent's solicitor advises that there is a 35% chance that Eggsellent will lose the case. Should Eggsellent lose the case, it will be liable to pay a penalty of $100,000.

Required

(a)   What kind of obligation, if any, exists?
(b)   Does a contingent liability exist?

Solution

(a)   Possible obligation: the existence of the obligation will be decided by the outcome of the court case.

(b)   Yes, because there is a possible outflow of resources (35% chance of having to pay $100,000). The contingent liability will therefore need to be disclosed given that the possibility of outflow is not remote.

3 Contingent assets

KEY TERM

IAS 37 defines a CONTINGENT ASSET as:

A possible asset that arises from past events and whose existence will be confirmed by the occurrence of one or more uncertain future events not wholly within the entity's control.

3.1 Treatment of contingent assets

KEY POINT

A contingent asset **must not be recognised as an asset** in the statement of financial position. Instead it should be **disclosed in the notes to the accounts** if it is **probable** that the economic benefits associated with the asset will flow to the entity.

Contingent assets must only be disclosed in the notes if they are **probable**. In that case, the following should be disclosed:

*   A brief description of the nature of the contingent asset at the reporting date

*   An estimate of its likely financial effect

If the flow of economic benefits associated with the contingent asset becomes **virtually certain**, it should then be recognised as an asset in the statement of financial position as it is no longer a contingent asset.

Example: Contingent assets and contingent liabilities

A company is engaged in a legal dispute. The outcome is not yet known. A number of possibilities arise:

- It expects to have to pay about $100,000. **A provision is recognised**.

- Possible damages are $100,000 but it is not expected to have to pay them. **A contingent liability is disclosed**.

- The company expects to have to pay damages but is unable to estimate the amount. **A contingent liability is disclosed**.

- The company expects to receive damages of $100,000 and this is virtually certain. **An asset is recognised**.

- The company expects to probably receive damages of $100,000. **A contingent asset is disclosed**.

- The company thinks it may receive damages, but it is not probable. **No disclosure required**.

Question 5.6

Contingent assets

Learning outcome B1

DE sells electronic goods with a warranty. Shortly before the year end, DE discovered a serious fault with their goods and had to recall all items sold for repair or replacement. However, DE believed the fault was due to a defective component purchased from their manufacturers, FG.

DE have instructed their lawyers to sue FG for compensation. The lawyers believe that there is a 60% chance of success.

Required

How should DE account for this compensation?

A   Record an asset in the statement of financial position
B   Disclose a contingent asset in the financial statements
C   Disclose a contingent liability in the financial statements
D   Do nothing

4 IAS 37 flowchart

You must practise the questions below to get the hang of IAS 37. But first, study the flowchart, taken from IAS 37, which is a good summary of its requirements.

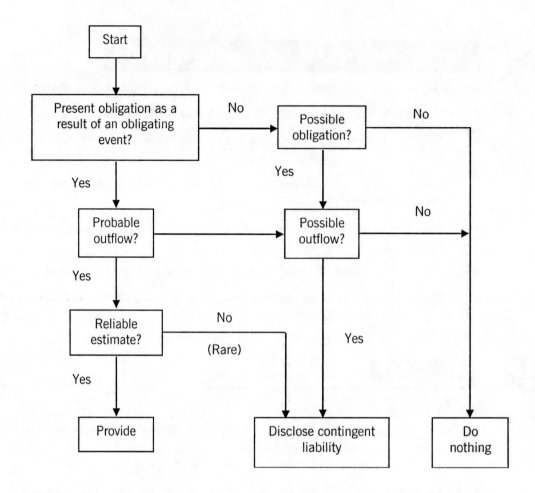

 Exam skills

If you learn this flowchart you should be able to deal with most questions you are likely to meet in an exam.

 Question 5.7   Provide or not? (I)

Learning outcome B1

During 20X0 Smack Co gives a guarantee of certain borrowings of Pony Co, whose financial condition at that time is sound. During 20X1, the financial condition of Pony Co deteriorates and at 30 June 20X1 Pony Co files for protection from its creditors.

What accounting treatment is required by Smack Co:

(a)   At 31 December 20X0?
(b)   At 31 December 20X1?

| Question 5.8 | Provide or not? (II) |

Learning outcome B1

Warren Co gives warranties at the time of sale to purchasers of its products. Under the terms of the warranty the manufacturer undertakes to make good, by repair or replacement, manufacturing defects that become apparent within a period of three years from the date of the sale. Should a provision be recognised?

| Question 5.9 | Provide or not? (III) |

Learning outcome B1

After a wedding in 20X0 ten people became seriously ill, possibly as a result of food poisoning from products sold by Callow Co. Legal proceedings are started seeking damages from Callow, but it disputes liability. Up to the date of approval of the financial statements for the year to 31 December 20X0, Callow's lawyers advise that it is probable that it will not be found liable. However, when Callow prepares the financial statements for the year to 31 December 20X1 its lawyers advise that, owing to developments in the case, it is probable that it will be found liable.

What is the required accounting treatment by Callow Co:

(a)   At 31 December 20X0?
(b)   At 31 December 20X1?

Section summary

- The objective of IAS 37 is to ensure that appropriate recognition criteria and measurement bases are applied to provisions and contingencies, and that sufficient information is disclosed.

- IAS 37 seeks to ensure that provisions are **only recognised** when a **measurable obligation** exists. It includes detailed rules that can be used to ascertain when an obligation exists and how to measure the obligation.

- IAS 37 aims to **eliminate profit smoothing**.

Chapter Summary

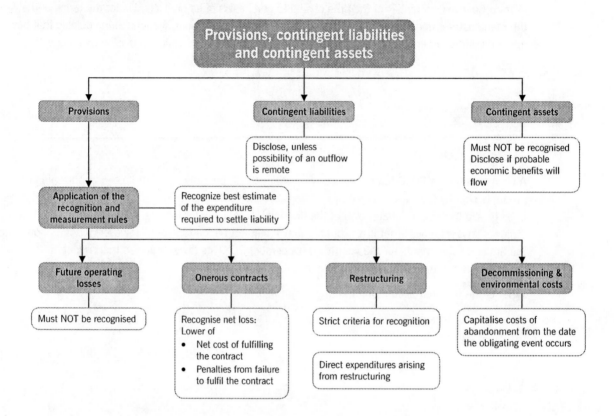

Quick Quiz

1 A provision is a .... of .... timing or amount.

2 A programme is undertaken by management which converts the previously wholly-owned chain of restaurants they ran into franchises. Is this restructuring?

3 Define contingent asset and contingent liability.

Answers to Quick Quiz

1   Liability, uncertain

2   Yes. The manner in which the business is conducted has changed.

3   Refer to Sections 2 and 3

Answers to Questions

5.1 Recognising a provision

(a)   No provision would be recognised at 31 December 20X9 as the decision has not been implemented.

(b)   A provision would be made in the 20X9 financial statements.

(c)   A provision for such costs is appropriate.

(d)   No present obligation exists and under IAS 37 no provision would be appropriate. This is because the entity could avoid the future expenditure by its future actions, maybe by changing its method of operation.

5.2 Warranty provision

Parker Co should use expected values to calculate the provision.

(75% × $nil) + (20% × $1.0m) + (5% × $4.0m) = $400,000.

5.3 Onerous contract

	Honour contract		*Cancel contract*
	$		
Cost of rentals (4 × $21,000)	84,000		Penalty $50,000
Income from sub-let (4 × $5,000)	(20,000)		
Net cost	64,000		

Therefore the unavoidable cost is $50,000.

This will be shown as a provision in the statement of financial position and as an expense in profit or loss.

5.4 Restructuring provision

The communication of the decision to the customers and employees gives rise to a constructive obligation because it creates a valid expectation that the division will be closed. The outflow of resources embodying economic benefits is probable so, at 31 December 20X1 a provision should be recognised for the best estimate of the costs of closing the division.

5.5 Decommissioning costs

(a)   The provision should be discounted to its present value as the time value of money is material = $10m × $1/1.06^{20}$ = $3,118,000 (rounded to nearest $'000)

     The entry would be:

     DEBIT   Non-current assets $3,118,000

     CREDIT   Provision $3,118,000

(b)   Carrying amount of oil rig

	$'000
Cost	80,000
Provision $(10,000 \times 1/1.06^{20})$	3,118
	83,118
Depreciation (83,118 / 20 years)	(4,156)
	78,962

(c)   Provision for dismantling costs

	$'000
At 1 January 20X2	3,118
Interest $(3,118 \times 6\%)$	187
C/d at 31 December 20X2	3,305

(d)   The obligation to rectify damage caused by extraction of the oil only arises as the extraction progresses.

Therefore the provision is increased year on year for the discounted expected future costs related to damage caused by extraction of the oil each year and the amount charged to profit or loss.

5.6 Contingent asset

B   Disclose a contingent asset in the financial statements because IAS 37 defines probable as more likely than not and therefore a 60% chance of success qualifies as probable. It is an asset rather than a liability as there is a probable inflow rather than outflow.

5.7 Provide or not? (I)

(a)   **At 31 December 20X0**: There is a present obligation as a result of a past obligating event. The obligating event is the giving of the guarantee, which gives rise to a legal obligation. However, at 31 December 20X0 no transfer of economic benefits is probable in settlement of the obligation.

No provision is recognised. The guarantee is disclosed as a contingent liability unless the probability of any transfer is regarded as remote.

(b)   **At 31 December 20X1**: As above, there is a present obligation as a result of a past obligating event, namely the giving of the guarantee. At 31 December 20X1 it is probable that a transfer of economic benefit will be required to settle the obligation. A provision is therefore recognised for the best estimate of the obligation.

5.8 Provide or not? (II)

Warren Co **cannot avoid** the cost of repairing or replacing all items of product that manifest manufacturing defects in respect of which warranties are given before the end of the reporting period, and a provision for the cost of this should therefore be made.

Warren Co is obliged to repair or replace items that fail within the entire warranty period. Therefore, in respect of **this year's sales**, the obligation provided for at the end of the reporting period, should be the cost of making good items for which defects have been notified but not yet processed, **plus** an estimate of costs in respect of the other items sold for which there is sufficient evidence that manufacturing defects **will** manifest themselves during their remaining periods of warranty cover.

5.9 Provide or not? (III)

(a)   At 31 December 20X0

On the basis of the evidence available when the financial statements were approved, there is no obligation as a result of past events. No provision is recognised. The matter is disclosed as a contingent liability unless the probability of any transfer is regarded as remote.

(b)   At 31 December 20X1

On the basis of the evidence available, there is a present obligation. A transfer of economic benefits in settlement is probable. A provision is recognised for the best estimate of the amount needed to settle the present obligation.

Now try these questions from the Practice Question Bank	Number	Level	Marks	Time
	Q8	Introductory	N/A	7mins

DEFERRED TAXATION

This chapter considers the accounting treatment and disclosure requirements contained in IAS 12 *Income taxes* for deferred tax in the financial statements.

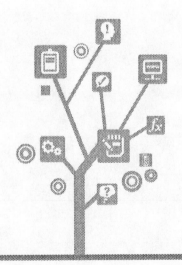

Topic list	learning outcomes	syllabus references
1 Deferred tax	B1	B1(c)
2 Deferred tax liabilities	B1	B1(d)
3 Deferred tax assets	B1	B1(d)
4 Measurement	B1	B1(d)

Chapter Overview

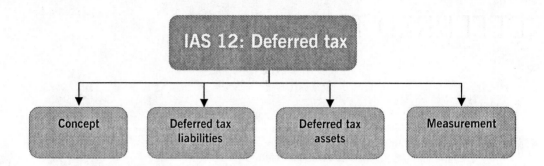

1   Deferred tax

Introduction

Deferred tax is an accounting measure used to match the tax effects of transactions with their accounting impact. It does **not** represent tax currently payable to the tax authorities. Deferred tax is quite complex so read this section carefully working through all the examples.

1.1 What is deferred tax?

Deferred tax is an **accounting adjustment**. It is not a tax which is currently payable to the tax authorities. Deferred tax arises because the accounting treatment of a transaction can be different from the tax treatment of the transaction.

Some of these differences are **permanent** and some of these differences are **temporary**. Permanent differences are expenses that are included in the statement of profit or loss (for example, client entertaining, donations to political parties in the UK), but which will **never be deductible for tax purposes**. Temporary differences arise because of timing differences between the tax treatment and the accounting treatment. These include items that are accounted for on an accruals basis for the financial statements, but are treated on a cash basis when calculating the tax due.

Deferred tax is the tax attributable to temporary differences.

1.2 Definitions

Here are the definitions relating to deferred tax given in IAS 12 *Income taxes*.

KEY TERMS

DEFERRED TAX LIABILITIES are the amounts of income taxes payable in future periods in respect of **taxable temporary differences**.

DEFERRED TAX ASSETS are the amounts of income taxes recoverable in future periods in respect of **deductible temporary differences**.

TEMPORARY DIFFERENCES are differences between the carrying amount of an asset or liability in the statement of financial position and its tax base. Temporary differences may be either:

- TAXABLE TEMPORARY DIFFERENCES, which are temporary differences that will result in taxable amounts in determining taxable profit (tax loss) of future periods when the carrying amount of the asset or liability is recovered or settled

- DEDUCTIBLE TEMPORARY DIFFERENCES, which are temporary differences that will result in amounts that are deductible in determining taxable profit (tax loss) of future periods when the carrying amount of the asset or liability is recovered or settled

The TAX BASE of an asset or liability is the amount attributed to that asset or liability for tax purposes.

(IAS 12)

So to summarise: deferred tax is the tax attributable to **temporary differences**.

Temporary differences are either:

- **Taxable temporary differences**: Amounts that are taxable in the future for example, accelerated tax depreciation, or

- **Deductible temporary differences**: Amounts that are tax deductible in the future for example, unutilised tax losses.

Taxable temporary differences give rise to **deferred tax liabilities**. Deductible temporary differences give rise to **deferred tax assets**.

The procedure to follow in calculating deferred tax is as follows:

 Identify situations where the tax treatment is **different** from the accounting treatment.

 Determine whether the differences caused by the tax treatment and the accounting treatment result in a **temporary or permanent difference**. If the difference is permanent, there will be no deferred tax.

 If the difference is **temporary**, calculate the tax base of the asset or liability (ie the carrying value according to the tax authorities) and compare it to the carrying value in the financial statements. This is the temporary difference.

 Calculate the deferred tax liability or asset = **temporary difference × tax rate %**.

The deferred tax liability/asset is calculated as follows:

	$
Carrying amount of asset/(liability) [in accounting statement of financial position]	X/(X)
Less tax base [value for tax purposes]	(X)/X
Temporary difference	X/(X)
Deferred tax (liability)/asset [always opposite sign to temporary difference] (temporary difference x tax rate %)	(X)/X

1.3 Links with the Conceptual Framework

You will remember that we discussed the International Accounting Standards Board's (IASB's) *Conceptual Framework* in Chapter 3. The principles of the *Conceptual Framework* help to explain why deferred tax exists, and why deferred tax assets and liabilities should be recorded in the financial statements.

1.3.1 Definition of asset and liability

As a result of a past transaction or event, the entity has an **obligation** to pay tax or a **right** to future tax relief. Therefore, the *Conceptual Framework* definition of a liability or asset has been met and if no current tax charge or credit has been recorded, a deferred tax liability or asset should be recognised.

1.3.2 The accruals concept

To achieve matching in the statement of profit or loss and other comprehensive income, the **tax should be recorded in the accounts in the same period in which the item that the tax relates to is recorded**. If the tax arises in a different period than the item is recorded in the financial statements, a deferred tax adjustment is required.

Now we need to look at some of the definitions in IAS 12 in more detail.

1.4 Tax base

1.4.1 Assets

The tax base of an asset is its value for tax purposes.

This is the amount that will be deductible for tax purposes against any taxable economic benefits when the entity recovers the carrying value of the asset. Where those economic benefits are not taxable, the tax base of the asset is the same as its carrying amount.

Question 6.1

Tax base (1)

Learning outcome B1

State the tax base of each of the following assets.

(a) A machine cost $10,000. For tax purposes, tax depreciation of $3,000 has already been deducted in the current and prior periods and the remaining cost will be deductible in future periods, either as depreciation or through a deduction on disposal. Revenue generated by using the machine is taxable, any gain on disposal of the machine will be taxable and any loss on disposal will be deductible for tax purposes.

(b) Interest receivable has a carrying amount of $1,000. The related interest revenue will be taxed on a cash basis (ie when it is received).

(c) Trade receivables have a carrying amount of $10,000. The related revenue has already been included in the current period's taxable profit (tax loss).

(d) A loan receivable has a carrying amount of $1m. The repayment of the loan will have no tax consequences.

1.4.2 Liabilities

In the case of a liability, the tax base will be its carrying amount less any amount that will be deducted for tax purposes in relation to the liability in future periods. For revenue received in advance, the tax base of the resulting liability is its carrying amount less any amount of the revenue that will not be taxable in future periods.

Question 6.2

Tax base (2)

Learning outcome B1

State the tax base of each of the following liabilities.

(a) Current liabilities include accrued expenses with a carrying amount of $1,000. The related expense will be deducted for tax purposes on a cash basis.

(b) Current liabilities include interest revenue received in advance, with a carrying amount of $10,000. The related interest revenue was taxed on a cash basis.

(c) Current liabilities include accrued expenses with a carrying amount of $2,000. The related expense has already been deducted for tax purposes.

(d) Current liabilities include accrued fines and penalties with a carrying amount of $100. Fines and penalties are not deductible for tax purposes.

(e) A loan payable has a carrying amount of $1m. The repayment of the loan will have no tax consequences.

1.5 Temporary differences

As we have seen above, the difference between the **accounting carrying amount** of an asset or liability and its **tax base** is called a **temporary difference**.

Some common types of temporary differences are summarised below.

Item	Carrying amount in the statement of financial position	Tax base in tax accounts
Non-current asset	**Net book value** Cost – accumulated depreciation	**Tax written down value** Cost – Tax depreciation Temporary difference is cumulative tax depreciation less cumulative financial statement depreciation.
Accrued income	Included in financial statements on an accruals basis ie when **RECEIVABLE**	If only included in tax accounts when **RECEIVED, tax base will be nil** at reporting date. The temporary difference is equal to the accrued income in the financial statements. If included in tax accounts on an accruals basis, the tax base is also the accrued income and there is no temporary difference so no deferred tax adjustment.
Accrued expenses and provisions	Included in financial statements on an accruals basis ie when **PAYABLE**	If included in tax accounts when **PAID, tax base will be nil** at reporting date. The temporary difference is equal to the accrual or provision in the financial statements. If included in tax accounts on an accruals basis, the tax base is also the accrual or provision and there is no temporary difference so no deferred tax adjustment.
Income received in advance	When the cash is received, it will be in the financial statements as deferred income ie a liability	If included in tax accounts when cash received the income will already have been taxed so **tax base is nil**. The temporary difference is equal to the liability.
Trading losses	Reported profit is negative	Taxable profit is nil. Temporary difference will equal cumulative losses.

IAS 12 gives the following examples of circumstances in which the carrying amount of an asset or liability will be **equal to its tax base** – ie the temporary difference is nil, and **no deferred tax arises**:

- **Accrued expenses** which have already been deducted in determining an entity's current tax liability for the current or earlier periods

- A **loan payable** which is measured at the amount originally received and this amount is the same as the amount repayable on final maturity of the loan

- **Accrued expenses** which will never be deductible for tax purposes

- **Accrued income** which will never be taxable

Section summary

- Deferred tax is an **accounting device**. It does not represent tax currently payable to the tax authorities.
- The **tax base** of an asset or liability is the value of that asset or liability for tax purposes.
- Deferred tax is the tax attributable to **temporary differences**.

2 Deferred tax liabilities

Introduction

In this section we will look at what taxable temporary differences are, and how they give rise to deferred tax liabilities.

2.1 Taxable temporary differences

KEY POINT

The rule to remember is that:

A taxable temporary difference gives rise to a deferred tax liability.

The following are examples of circumstances that give rise to taxable temporary differences.

(a) **Accelerated tax allowances**: For tax purposes, non-current assets are often depreciated at a different rate to the depreciation policy adopted by the company for accounting purposes. A taxable temporary difference arises where tax (or **capital**) allowances or tax depreciation rates are available **at a rate higher than the accounting depreciation rates** applied to the same assets.

(b) **Revaluations of assets**: A taxable temporary difference occurs when an asset is revalued and no equivalent adjustment is made for tax purposes. The gain arising on the increase in the value of the asset will be taxable on the use or sale of the asset and therefore a **deferred tax liability** is recognised because the gain itself has been recognised.

We will look in more detail at both of the above in the following sections.

2.2 Accounting entries

The double entry to create or increase a deferred tax provision is as follows:

DEBIT   Deferred tax expense (statement of profit or loss and comprehensive income)
CREDIT   Deferred tax liability (statement of financial position)

To reverse or decrease a deferred tax provision:

DEBIT   Deferred tax liability (statement of financial position)
CREDIT   Deferred tax expense (statement of profit or loss and other comprehensive income)

The deferred tax expense is reported in the **statement of profit or loss and other comprehensive income in the same place as the income or expense it relates to**. Normally this will be in profit or loss but for a revaluation of property, plant and equipment, it will be in **other comprehensive income**. We will revisit deferred tax on revaluation below.

2.3 Accelerated tax allowances

Depreciation is an area where deferred tax assets and liabilities often arise. This is because in many tax jurisdictions, accounting depreciation is deemed to be too subjective: each entity determines its own depreciation policy, so that the same asset may be depreciated over 10 years in one entity, and over 15 years in another. If tax deductions were granted based on accounting depreciation, this would too easily give rise to mismatches and the accounting policy over depreciation would be open to abuse.

The common solution to this is for a fixed rate of depreciation to be dictated by tax legislation. **Tax depreciation** (otherwise known as **writing down allowances** or, in the UK, **capital allowances**) could be set at a higher rate than the accounting depreciation rate applied by the company to any given asset. The asset then depreciates more quickly for tax purposes than it is depreciated in the company's financial statements. The temporary differences that arise are called **accelerated tax allowances**.

The reverse can also happen: the tax depreciation on an asset could be set at a lower rate than the accounting depreciation rate applied. The asset then depreciates more slowly for tax purposes than it is depreciated in the company's financial statements. We then have **decelerated tax allowances**, which give rise to deferred tax assets. We will look at deferred tax assets in the next section.

Example: Taxable temporary differences

Leisure Tours buys a coach on 1 January 20X1 for $60,000. The coach has a useful life of two years and will be scrapped at the end of its life. For tax purposes, a 100% capital allowance is granted in the first year.

The company operates in country X and has a profit before tax of $100,000 in each of the years 20X1 and 20X2. The rate of corporation tax in country X is 25%.

Scenario 1

If we ignore all tax adjustments, Leisure Tours would have the following financial results:

	20X1	20X2
	$	$
Profit before tax	100,000	100,000
Tax at 25%	(25,000)	(25,000)
Profit for the year	75,000	75,000

Scenario 2

If we adjust for tax depreciation but ignore deferred taxation, Leisure Tours would have the following financial statements:

	20X1	20X2
	$	$
Profit before tax	100,000	100,000
Add back accounting depreciation (W1)	30,000	30,000
Less tax depreciation	(60,000)	(-)
Taxable profit	70,000	130,000
Tax at 25%	17,500	32,500

(W1) Accounting depreciation
     $60,000 ÷ 2 years = $30,000 per annum

We can see that there is a **temporary difference** because by the end of 20X2, the full value of the asset ($60,000) has been deducted from both the accounting profit and the tax profit.

As a result of the temporary difference, there is a **mismatch between the tax charge and the accounting profit**. Not enough tax has been charged in 20X1 and too much tax charged in 20X2. A **deferred tax adjustment is required** to match the tax charge to the accounting profit.

Question 6.3   Accelerated tax allowances

Learning outcome B1

Required

(a) Using the information for Leisure Tours in the illustration above, prepare extracts from the financial statements to show how the company would account for deferred tax on the temporary difference.

(b) Prepare the accounting entries in respect of deferred tax for 20X1 and 20X2.

2.4 Revaluations of non-current assets

In many tax jurisdictions, the revaluation of non-current assets does not give rise to a tax charge in the year in which the revaluation takes place. However, the increase in the value of the asset will be taxed eventually – most probably, when the asset is sold.

A taxable temporary difference arises: an accounting gain has been recorded in the financial statements, but no gain is recognised for tax purposes. This results in a deferred tax liability.

IAS 12 requires deferred tax on revaluations to be charged to **other comprehensive income**. This is because the accounting gain is reported in other comprehensive income. The recording of the related deferred tax expense therefore matches the recognition of the accounting gain.

Question 6.4	Revaluation

Learning outcome B1

A company purchased some land on 1 January 20X7 for $400,000. On 31 December 20X8 the land was revalued to $500,000. In the tax regime in which the company operates revaluations do not affect either the tax base of the asset or taxable profits.

The income tax rate is 30%. Profit for the year was $850,000.

Required

Prepare the accounting entry to record the deferred tax in relation to this revaluation for the year ended 31 December 20X8.

Section summary

- Taxable temporary differences give rise to a **deferred tax liability**.

- Examples of situations where deferred tax liabilities can arise include accelerated tax allowances and revaluations of non-current assets.

3 Deferred tax assets

Introduction

In this section we look at what deductible temporary differences are, and how they can give rise to a deferred tax asset.

3.1 Deductible temporary differences

KEY POINT

The rule to remember is that:

A deductible temporary difference gives rise to a deferred tax asset.

However, the deferred tax asset must also satisfy the **recognition criteria** given in IAS 12. This states that a deferred tax asset should be recognised for deductible temporary differences to the extent that it is **probable that taxable profits will be available** against which it can be utilised.

Like all other assets, a deferred tax asset can only be recognised where there will be **an inflow of probable future economic benefits**.

The following are examples of circumstances that give rise to taxable temporary differences.

(a)   **Decelerated tax allowances**: For tax purposes, non-current assets are often depreciated at a different rate to the depreciation policy adopted by the company for accounting purposes. A deductible temporary difference arises where tax (or **capital**) allowances or tax depreciation rates are available **at a rate lower than the accounting depreciation rates** applied to the same assets.

(b)   **Unutilised tax losses**: Losses that can be carried forward to reduce the current tax on future profits represent a future tax saving. Therefore, a **deferred tax asset** is recognised in respect of tax losses to the extent that it is probable that the losses can be used before they expire.

3.2 Accounting entries

To double entry to create or increase a deferred tax asset is as follows:

DEBIT   Deferred tax asset (statement of financial position)
CREDIT   Deferred tax expense (statement of profit or loss and other comprehensive income)

To reverse or decrease a deferred tax asset:

DEBIT   Deferred tax expense (statement of profit or loss and other comprehensive income)
CREDIT   Deferred tax asset (statement of financial position)

Again, as we have seen for the deferred tax liability, the deferred tax expense is reported in the **statement of profit or loss and other comprehensive income, in the same place as the item it relates to**. Normally this will be in profit or loss, but for a revaluation of property, plant and equipment it will be in **other comprehensive income**.

Example: Deductible temporary differences

Pargatha Co recognises a liability of $10,000 for accrued product warranty costs on 31 December 20X7. These product warranty costs will not be deductible for tax purposes until the entity pays claims. The tax rate is 25%.

Required

State the deferred tax implications of this situation.

Solution

What is the tax base of the liability? It is nil (carrying amount of $10,000 less the amount that will be deductible for tax purposes in respect of the liability in future periods).

When the liability is settled for its carrying amount, the entity's future taxable profit will be reduced by $10,000 and, therefore, its future tax payments by $10,000 × 25% = $2,500.

The difference of $10,000 between the carrying amount ($10,000) and the tax base (nil) is a deductible temporary difference. The entity should therefore recognise a deferred tax asset of $10,000 × 25% = $2,500 **provided that** it is probable that the entity will earn sufficient taxable profits in future periods to benefit from a reduction in tax payments.

3.3 Tax losses

An entity may have tax losses that it can carry forward to deduct against **future** taxable profits. IAS 12 requires that these tax losses be recognised as deferred tax assets where it is probable that the entity will generate future taxable profits against which they can offset the losses.

Question 6.5

Tax losses

Learning outcome B1

BG incurs $80,000 of tax losses in the year ended 31 December 20X1 which it can carry forward for two accounting periods before they expire. The company expects to make a loss in 20X2 and to return to profitability in 20X3, expecting to make a profit of $50,000 in that year. The company pays tax at 20%.

Required

Calculate the amount of any deferred tax asset or liability at 31 December 20X1and show the accounting entry BG should make to provide for any deferred tax on the tax losses.

Section summary

- Deductible temporary differences give rise to a **deferred tax asset**.

- **Prudence** dictates that deferred tax assets can only be recognised when **sufficient future taxable profits** exist against which they can be utilised.

4 Measurement

Introduction

Now that you have learned the calculation of temporary differences, we will look at what determines the tax rate to be applied in calculating deferred tax.

Deferred tax assets and liabilities are measured at the tax rates expected to apply to the period when the asset is realised or the liability settled, based on tax rates (and tax laws) that have been **enacted** (or **substantively enacted**) by the end of the reporting period.

The definition of the point at which tax laws are enacted or substantively enacted varies from country to country. In the UK, substantive enactment occurs when the relevant legislation receives its third reading in the House of Commons. The tax legislation, thus substantively enacted, must then be applied in calculating the tax charge and balances – including deferred tax.

Changes in tax rates after the year end are therefore **non-adjusting events** after the reporting period.

An entity is likely to have a brought down deferred tax asset or liability from the previous year. Therefore, an accounting entry will only be required for the movement in the deferred tax asset or liability (rather than for the whole carried down balance):

	$
Deferred tax asset/liability b/d	X
Increases/decreases in deferred tax [accounting entry to statement of profit or loss and other comprehensive income]	X/(X)
Deferred tax asset/liability c/d	X

Example: Measurement of deferred tax

TF had a net deferred tax liability of $11,000 at 31 December 20X1. At 31 December 20X2, the following temporary differences exist:

*   TF made a provision for warranties of $30,000 on 31 December 20X2, but tax relief will not be granted until the costs are incurred.

*   TF purchased an item of equipment for $500,000 on 1 January 20X2. It has a useful life of ten years. Tax depreciation is charged on a 20% reducing balance basis.

The income tax rate is 30%.

Required

Prepare the accounting entry to record the movement in the net deferred tax asset or liability for the year ended 31 December 20X2.

Solution

DEBIT	Deferred tax liability	$5,000	
CREDIT	Deferred tax expense (in P/L)		$5,000

Being decrease in deferred tax liability at 31 December 20X2

Workings

1   *Movement in deferred tax liability*

	$
Deferred tax liability at 1 January 20X2	11,000
∴ Decrease in liability	(5,000)
Deferred tax liability at 31 December 20X2 (W2)	6,000

2   *Deferred tax liability at 31 December 20X2*

	Carrying amount $	Tax base $	Temporary difference $	Tax rate	Deferred tax liability $
Provision	(30,000)	-	(30,000)	× 30%	9,000
Equipment	500,000 × 9/10 = 450,000	500,000 × 80% = 400,000	50,000	× 30%	(15,000)
Net deferred tax liability					(6,000)

Section summary

Deferred tax assets and liabilities must be presented separately from other assets and liabilities in the statement of financial position, measured at the tax rate expected to apply when the asset is realised or the liability is settled.

Chapter Summary

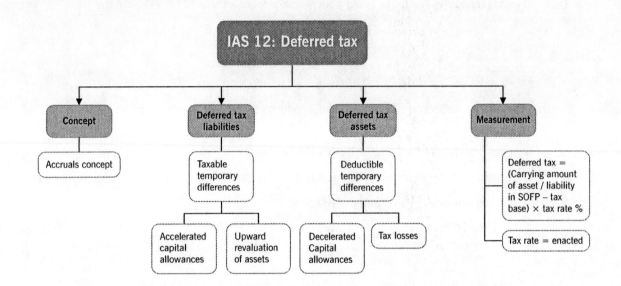

Quick Quiz

1   The tax expense related to the profit from ordinary activities should be shown in the statement of profit or loss.

    True ☐

    False ☐

2   Deferred tax liabilities are the amounts of income taxes payable in future periods in respect of

    ....

3   Give three examples of taxable temporary differences.

4   Current tax is the amount of income tax payable in respect of the .... for a period.

5   Deductible temporary differences give rise to a:

    A   Deferred tax asset
    B   Deferred tax liability

Answers to Quick Quiz

1   True

2   Taxable temporary differences

3   Examples are:

- Interest revenue
- Depreciation
- Development costs
- Prepayments
- Sale of goods revenue

4   Taxable profit

5   A

Answers to Questions

6.1 Tax base (1)

(a)   The tax base of the machine is $10,000 – $3,000 = $7,000.

(b)   The tax base of the interest receivable is $nil.

(c)   The tax base of the trade receivables is $10,000. The accounting treatment is the same as the tax treatment, so there is no temporary difference at the reporting date.

(d)   The tax base of the loan is $1m.

6.2 Tax base (2)

(a)   The tax base of the accrued expenses is nil.

(b)   The tax base of the interest received in advance is nil.

(c)   The tax base of the accrued expenses is $2,000.

(d)   The tax base of the accrued fines and penalties is $100.

(e)   The tax base of the loan is $1m.

6.3 Accelerated tax allowances

(a) **Extracts from financial statements**

Extract from statement of financial position

	20X1	20X2
	$	$
Deferred tax liability	7,500	–

Extract from statement of profit or loss

	20X1	20X2
	$	$
Profit before tax	100,000	100,000
Current tax (Scenario 2)	(17,500)	(32,500)
Deferred tax (W1)	(7,500)	7,500
Profit for the year	75,000	75,000

(b) **Accounting entries**

20X1:

DEBIT	Deferred tax expense (in P/L)	$7,500
CREDIT	Deferred tax liability	$7,500

Being recognition of a deferred tax liability in respect of accelerated tax allowances

20X2:

DEBIT	Deferred tax liability	$7,500
CREDIT	Deferred tax expense (in P/L)	$7,500

Being reversal of deferred tax liability on accelerated tax allowances

Workings

1   *Deferred tax*

	Carrying amount $	Tax written down value $	Difference $	Tax at 25% $
Cost at 1 January 20X1	60,000	60,000		
Accounting depreciation	(30,000)			
Tax depreciation (100%)		(60,000)		
At 31 December 20X1	30,000	–	30,000	7,500
Accounting depreciation	(30,000)			
Tax depreciation (25% × $30,000)		–		
At 31 December 20X2	–	–	–	–

6.4 Revaluation

DEBIT	Other comprehensive income (and revaluation surplus)	$30,000
CREDIT	Deferred tax liability (W1)	$30,000

Being deferred tax liability on revaluation surplus

Working

1   *Deferred tax*

	$
Carrying amount of asset	500,000
Less: Tax base	(400,000)
Temporary difference	100,000
Deferred tax (liability) (30% × 100,000)	(30,000)

6.5 Tax losses

A deferred tax asset is recognised in 20X1 for the portion of the losses for which relief is likely to be granted: $50,000 × 20% = $10,000:

DEBIT	Deferred tax asset (statement of financial position)	$10,000
CREDIT	Deferred tax (statement of profit or loss)	$10,000

In 20X3, the deferred tax asset is reversed resulting in a charge to profit or loss when the profits that the tax losses are used against are earned.

Now try these questions from the Practice Question Bank	Number	Level	Marks	Time
	Q9	Introductory	N/A	7 mins

SHARE-BASED PAYMENTS

 This chapter deals with IFRS 2 on share-based payment, a controversial area.

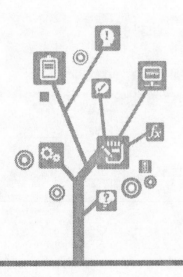

Topic list	learning outcomes	syllabus references
1 IFRS 2 *Share-based Payment*	B1	B1(c)(d)

Chapter Overview

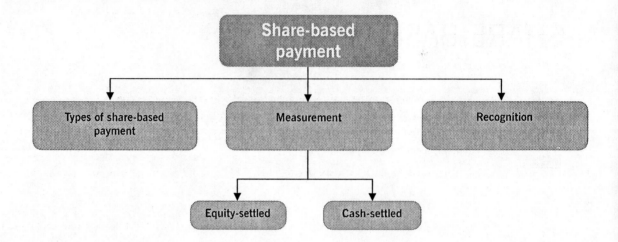

1 IFRS 2 *Share-based payment*

Introduction

Transactions whereby entities purchase goods or services from other parties, such as suppliers and employees, by **issuing shares or share options** to those other parties, are **increasingly common**.

1.1 Background

Share schemes are a common feature of employee and executive remuneration. In some countries, tax incentives are offered to encourage the use of share-based payment. Companies whose shares or share options are regarded as a valuable currency may also use share-based payment to obtain professional services.

The increasing use of share-based payment raised questions about the accounting treatment of such transactions in company financial statements. Because the granting of share options often involved no initial cash outflow, no expense would be recorded. This led to an **anomaly**: if a company paid its employees in cash, an expense would be recognised in profit or loss, but if the payment took the form of share options, no expense would be recognised. The omission also gave rise to corporate governance concerns.

IFRS 2 *Share-based payment* was issued to deal with this.

1.1.1 Arguments against recognition of share-based payment in financial statements

There were a number of arguments against recognition. The International Accounting Standards Board (IASB) has considered and rejected the arguments below.

(a) **No cost therefore no charge**

There is no cost to the entity because the granting of shares or options does not require the entity to sacrifice cash or other assets. Therefore, a charge should not be recognised.

This argument is unsound because it ignores the fact that a transaction has occurred. The employees have provided valuable services to the entity in return for valuable shares or options.

(b) **Earnings per share is hit twice**

It is argued that the charge to profit or loss for the employee services consumed reduces the entity's earnings, while at the same time there is an increase in the number of shares issued.

However, the dual impact on earnings per share simply reflects the two economic events that have occurred.

(i)   The entity has issued shares or options, thus increasing the denominator of the earnings per share calculation.

(ii) It has also consumed the resources it received for those shares or options, thus reducing the numerator.

(c) **Adverse economic consequences**

It could be argued that entities might be discouraged from introducing or continuing employee share plans if they were required to recognise them in the financial statements. However, if this happened, it might be because the requirement for entities to account properly for employee share plans would reveal the economic consequences of such plans.

A situation whereby entities are able to obtain and consume resources by issuing valuable shares or options without having to account for such transactions, could be perceived as a distortion.

1.2 Objective and scope

IFRS 2 requires an entity to **reflect the effects of share-based payment transactions** in its statement of profit or loss and statement of financial position.

The accounting requirements depend on how the share-based payment transaction is settled: by equity, by cash, or a choice between the two.

(a) **Equity-settled**: The entity receives goods or services in exchange for equity instruments of the entity (including shares or share options).

(b) **Cash-settled**: The entity receives goods or services in exchange for amounts of cash that are based on the price (or value) of the entity's shares or other equity instruments of the entity.

(c) **Equity or cash**: Either the entity or the supplier has a **choice** as to whether the entity settles the transaction in cash (or other assets) or by issuing equity instruments.

Exam alert

For the purposes of your exam, you only need to know about (a) and (b).

IFRS 2 only applies to share-based transactions for the acquisition of goods and services. It does not apply to other transactions with holders of equity instruments, such as share dividends, purchase of treasury shares, or the issue of additional shares in a rights issue.

Certain transactions are **outside the scope** of the IFRS, such as the issue of equity instruments in exchange for control of another entity in a business combination.

1.3 Definitions

Let us first look at the definitions of some key terms:

KEY TERMS

SHARE-BASED PAYMENT TRANSACTION. A transaction in which the entity receives or acquires goods or services either **as consideration** for its equity instruments or by **incurring liabilities** for amounts based on the price **of the entity's shares or other equity instruments** of the entity.

SHARE-BASED PAYMENT ARRANGEMENT. An agreement between the entity and another party (including an employee) to enter into a share-based payment transaction, which thereby entitles the other party to receive cash or other assets of the entity for amounts that are based on the price of the entity's shares or other equity instruments of the entity, or to receive equity instruments of the entity, provided the specified vesting conditions, if any, are met.

EQUITY INSTRUMENT. A contract that evidences a residual interest in the assets of an entity after deducting all of its liabilities.

EQUITY INSTRUMENT GRANTED The right (conditional or unconditional) to an equity instrument of the entity conferred by the entity on another party, under a share-based payment arrangement.

SHARE OPTION. A contract that gives the holder the right, but not the obligation, to subscribe to the entity's shares at a fixed or determinable price for a specified period of time.

FAIR VALUE. The amount for which an asset could be exchanged, a liability settled, or an equity instrument granted could be exchanged, between knowledgeable, willing parties in an arm's length transaction. (Note that this definition is different from that in IFRS 13 *Fair value measurement,* but the IFRS 2 definition applies.)

INTRINSIC VALUE .The difference between the fair value of the shares to which the counterparty has the (conditional or unconditional) right to subscribe or which it has the right to receive, and the price (if any) the other party is (or will be) required to pay for those shares. For example, a share option with an exercise price of $15 on a share with a fair value of $20, has an intrinsic value of $5.

MEASUREMENT DATE. The date at which the fair value of the equity instruments granted is measured. For transactions with employees and others providing similar services, the measurement date is grant date. For transactions with parties other than employees (and those providing similar services), the measurement date is the date the entity obtains the goods or the counterparty renders service.

To VEST means to become an entitlement. Under a share-based payment arrangement, a counterparty's right to receive cash, other assets or equity instruments of the entity vests upon satisfaction of any specified vesting conditions.

VESTING CONDITIONS. The conditions that must be satisfied for the counterparty to become entitled to receive cash, other assets or equity instruments of the entity, under a share-based payment arrangement. Vesting conditions may include service conditions, which require the other party to complete a specified period of service, and performance conditions, which require specified performance targets to be met (such as a specified increase in the entity's profit over a specified period of time).

1.4 Recognition: the basic principle

An entity should **recognise goods or services received or acquired in a share-based payment transaction when it obtains the goods or as the services are received.** Goods or services received or acquired in a share-based payment transaction **should be recognised as expenses** unless they qualify for recognition as **assets**. For example, services are normally recognised as expenses (because they are normally rendered immediately), while goods are recognised as assets.

If the goods or services were received or acquired in an **equity-settled** share-based payment transaction, the entity should recognise **a corresponding increase in equity** (reserves).

If the goods or services were received or acquired in a **cash-settled** share-based payment transaction, the entity should recognise a **liability**.

For example, where an entity grants share options to its employees for their services, the transaction should be recorded as follows:

DEBIT   Staff costs
CREDIT   Other reserves [within equity] (if equity-settled) OR
CREDIT   Liability (if cash-settled)

Where performance by the counterparty is not immediate, the expense is **spread** over the period until the counterparty becomes entitled to receive the share-based payment (the **vesting period**). For example, with employee services a minimum period of service may have to be completed before entitlement to the share-based payment.

VESTING PERIOD. The period during which all the specified vesting conditions of a share-based payment arrangement are to be satisfied.

KEY TERM

For example, for a share-based payment granted for employee services where a minimum period of service must be completed before entitlement to the share-based payment:

LEARN

> The equity/liability value at the period end
>
> > = Estimated number of employees entitled to the share-based payment
> >
> > × Number of equity instruments per employee
> >
> > × Fair value of each equity instrument
> >
> > × Proportion of vesting period elapsed at the period end

There are different methods for determining the fair value of the equity instrument. We will look at this in more detail in the next sections.

Where the share-based payment was in existence in the prior year, the accounting entry is made with the movement in the equity or liability:

Equity/liability:

B/d	X
Cash paid	(X)
(cash-settled only)	
Expense (balancing figure)	X
C/d	X

Exam alert

Most share-based payment questions in past exams have focused on share-based payment transactions for employee services, rather than those for the purchase of goods.

1.5 Equity-settled share-based payment transactions

1.5.1 Measurement

The issue here is how to measure the cost of the goods and services received and the equity instruments (eg the share options) granted in return.

The general principle in IFRS 2 is that when an entity recognises the goods or services received and the corresponding increase in equity, it should measure these at the **fair value of the goods or services received**. Where the transaction is with **parties other than employees**, there is a rebuttable presumption that the fair value of the goods or services received can be estimated reliably.

In such cases, the entity should measure the share-based payment **expense using the fair value of the goods or services received**. This is called the **direct method**.

Where the direct method is used, fair value should be measured at the date the entity obtains the goods or the counterparty renders service.

If the fair value of the goods or services received cannot be measured reliably, the entity should measure their value by reference to the **fair value of the equity instruments granted**. This is called the **indirect method**, and is the method often adopted for employee services.

Where the indirect method is used, the fair value of those equity instruments should be measured at **grant date**.

KEY TERM

GRANT DATE. The date at which the entity and another party (including an employee) agree to a share-based payment arrangement, being when the entity and the other party have a shared understanding of the terms and conditions of the arrangement. At grant date, the entity confers on the other party (the counterparty) the right to cash, other assets, or equity instruments of the entity, provided the specified vesting conditions, if any, are met. If that agreement is subject to an approval process (for example, by shareholders), grant date is the date when that approval is obtained.

1.5.2 Determining the fair value of equity instruments granted

Where the indirect method is used, the fair value of the equity instruments is based on **market prices**, if available, taking into account the terms and conditions upon which those equity instruments were granted.

If market prices are not available, the entity should estimate the fair value of the equity instruments granted using a **valuation technique**. (These are beyond the scope of this exam.)

1.5.3 Transactions in which services are received

If the equity instruments granted **vest immediately** (ie the counterparty is not required to complete a specified period of service before becoming unconditionally entitled to the equity instruments), it is presumed that the services have already been received. The entity should **recognise the services received in full**, with a corresponding increase in equity, **on grant date**.

If the equity instruments granted **do not vest until the counterparty completes a specified period of service**, the entity should account for those services **as they are rendered** by the counterparty during the vesting period.

For example, if an employee is granted share options on condition that he or she completes three years' service, then the fair value of the share-based payment, determined at grant date, should be expensed over that three-year vesting period.

Where the share-based payment is equity-settled, the fair value of each equity instrument should be based on the fair value at grant date. No adjustment should be made to this fair value in subsequent years.

The total fair value to be recognised should be based on the **best available estimate** of the **number of equity instruments expected to vest**. The entity should **revise** that estimate if subsequent information indicates that the number of equity instruments expected to vest differs from previous estimates. On **vesting date**, the entity should revise the estimate to **equal the number of equity instruments that actually vest**.

For example, for share options granted to employees, the entity will estimate the number of employees entitled to exercise their share options. Any changes in the number of employees expected to receive the share options is treated as a change in accounting estimate and is recognised in the period of the change.

Example: Equity-settled share-based payment transaction

On 1 January 20X1 an entity grants 100 share options to each of its 400 employees. Each grant is conditional upon the employee working for the entity until 31 December 20X3. The fair value of each share option is $20.

During 20X1 20 employees leave and the entity estimates that 20% of the employees (ie 80 employees) will leave during the three-year period.

During 20X2 a further 25 employees leave and the entity now estimates that 25% of its employees (ie 100 employees) will leave during the three-year period.

During 20X3 a further 10 employees leave. The share options granted to the remaining employees are vested at the end of 20X3.

Required

Calculate the remuneration expense that will be recognised in respect of the share-based payment transaction for each of the three years, and show the accounting entries required.

Solution

IFRS 2 requires the entity to recognise the remuneration expense, based on the fair value of the share options granted, as the services are received during the three-year vesting period.

In 20X1 and 20X2 the entity estimates the number of options expected to vest (by estimating the number of employees likely to leave) and bases the amount that it recognises for the year on this estimate.

In 20X3 it recognises an amount based on the number of options that actually vest. A total of 55 employees left during the three-year period and therefore 34,500 options (400 – 55 employees × 100 options) are vested.

The amount recognised as an expense for each of the three years is calculated as follows:

	Cumulative expense at year end $	Expense for year $
20X1 (400 − 80) × 100 × $20 × 1/3	213,333	213,333
20X2 (400 − 100) × 100 × $20 × 2/3	400,000	186,667
20X3 345 × 100 × $20	690,000	290,000

20X1

DEBIT	Staff costs	$213,333	
CREDIT	Other reserves (within equity)		$213,333

20X2

DEBIT	Staff costs	$186,667	
CREDIT	Other reserves (within equity)		$186,667

20X3

DEBIT	Staff costs	$290,000	
CREDIT	Other reserves (within equity)		$290,000

Question 7.1   Share-based payment

Learning outcomes

An entity grants 100 share options on its $1 shares to each of its 500 employees on 1 January 20X5. Each grant is conditional upon the employee working for the entity over the next three years. The fair value of each share option as at 1 January 20X5 is $15.

On the basis of a weighted average probability, the entity estimates on 1 January that 20% of employees will leave during the three-year period and therefore forfeit their rights to share options.

Required

Show the accounting entries which will be required over the three-year period in the event of the following:

(a)   20 employees leave during 20X5 and the estimate of total employee departures over the three-year period is revised to 15% (75 employees)

(b)   22 employees leave during 20X6 and the estimate of total employee departures over the three-year period is revised to 12% (60 employees)

(c)   15 employees leave during 20X7, so a total of 57 employees left and forfeited their rights to share options. A total of 44,300 share options (443 employees × 100 options) are vested at the end of 20X7.

1.6 Cash-settled share-based payment transactions

Examples of this type of transaction include:

(a) **Share appreciation rights (SARs)** granted to employees: the employees become entitled to a future cash payment (rather than an equity instrument), based on the increase in the entity's share price from a specified level over a specified period of time or

(b) An entity granting to its employees a right to receive a future cash payment by granting them a **right to shares that are redeemable**

Again, as we have seen for the equity-settled share-based payment transactions, the entity should measure the share-based payment expense using the method that provides the most reliable information.

(a) If the fair value of the goods or services received **can be measured** reliably, the **direct method** is used. The share-based payment is measured at the fair value of the goods or services received.

(b) If the fair value of the goods or services received **cannot be measured** reliably, the **indirect method** is used. The share-based payment is measured at the fair value of the equity instruments granted.

Note, however, **where the indirect method is used** in measuring cash-settled share-based payment transactions, the entity should **remeasure** the fair value of the liability **at each reporting date**, until the liability is settled. This differs from the treatment of equity-settled share-based payments which we saw above. Any changes in fair value are recognised in profit or loss, up to the date of settlement.

The entity should recognise the services received, and a liability to pay for those services, **as the employees render service**. For example, if SARs do not vest until the employees have completed a specified period of service the entity should recognise the services received and the related liability, over that period.

Example: Cash-settled share-based payment transaction

On 1 January 20X4 an entity grants 100 cash SARs to each of its 500 employees on condition that the employees remain in its employ for the next two years. The SARs vest on 31 December 20X5 and may be exercised at any time up to 31 December 20X6. The fair value of each SAR at grant date is $7.40.

Year ended	Leavers	No. of employees exercising rights	Outstanding SARs	Estimated further leavers	Fair value of SARs $	Intrinsic value (ie cash paid) $
31 December 20X4	50	–	450	60	8.00	
31 December 20X5	50	100	300	–	8.50	8.10
31 December 20X6	–	300	–	–	–	9.00

Required

Show the expense and liability which will appear in the financial statements in each of the three years.

Solution

For the three years to the vesting date of 31 December 20X6, the expense is based on the entity's estimate of the number of SARs that will actually vest (as for an equity-settled transaction). However, the fair value of the liability is **remeasured** at each year end.

	$
Year ended 31 December 20X4	
Liability c/d and P/L expense ((500 – 110) × 100 × $8.00 × ½)	<u>156,000</u>

	$
Year ended 31 December 20X5	
Liability b/d	156,000
∴ Profit or loss expense	180,000
Less cash paid on exercise of SARs by employees (100 × 100 × $8.10)	(81,000)
Liability c/d (300 × 100 × $8.50)	<u>255,000</u>

	$
Year ended 31 December 20X6	
Liability b/d	255,000
∴ Profit or loss expense	15,000
Less cash paid on exercise of SARs by employees (300 × 100 × $9.00)	(270,000)
Liability c/d	<u>-</u>

1.7 Choice between settling in cash or in equity

Where either the entity or the other party has a choice of settling in cash or by issuing equity instruments, the accounting treatment depends upon whether the entity has incurred a liability to settle in cash (or other assets).

If the entity has incurred a liability to settle in cash or other assets, it should account for the transaction as a cash-settled share-based payment transaction.

If no such liability has been incurred, the entity should account for the transaction as an equity-settled share-based payment transaction.

Section summary

Share-based payment transactions should be recognised in the financial statements. You need to understand and be able to advise on:

- Recognition
- Measurement
- Disclosure

of both equity-settled and cash-settled transactions.

Chapter Summary

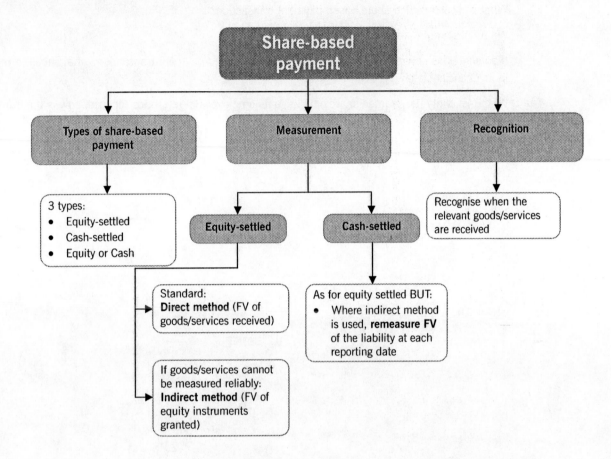

Quick Quiz

1   What is a cash-settled share-based payment transaction?

2   What does grant date mean?

3   If an entity has entered into an equity-settled share-based payment transaction, what should it recognise in its financial statements?

4   Where an entity has granted share options to its employees in return for services, how is the transaction measured?

Answers to Quick Quiz

1   A transaction in which the entity receives goods or services in exchange for amounts of cash that are based on the price (or value) of the entity's shares or other equity instruments of the entity.

2   The date at which the entity and another party (including an employee) agree to a share-based payment arrangement, being when the entity and the other party have a shared understanding of the terms and conditions of the arrangement.

3   The goods or services received and a corresponding increase in equity.

4   By reference to the fair value of the equity instruments granted, measured at grant date.

Answers to Questions

7.1   Share-based payment

(a)   *20X5* $

Equity c/d and P/L expense $((500 - 75) \times 100 \times \$15 \times 1/3)$ 212,500

| DEBIT | Staff costs | $212,500 | |
| CREDIT | Other reserves (within equity) | | $212,500 |

(b)   *20X6* $

Equity b/d   212,500

∴ Profit or loss expense   227,500

Equity c/d $((500 - 60) \times 100 \times \$15 \times 2/3) =$ 440,000

| DEBIT | Expenses | $227,500 | |
| CREDIT | Other reserves (within equity) | | $227,500 |

(c)   *20X7* $

Equity b/d   440,000

∴ Profit or loss expense   224,500

Equity c/d $(443 \times 100 \times \$15) =$ 664,500

| DEBIT | Expenses | $224,500 | |
| CREDIT | Other reserves (within equity) | | $224,500 |

Now try these questions from the Practice Question Bank	Number	Level	Marks	Time
	Q10	Introductory	N/A	5 mins
	Q11	Introductory	10	18 mins

REVENUE

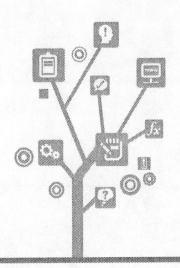

In determining the amount of revenue that should be recognised, the IASB Conceptual Framework comes to the fore again. Revenue is a very topical area and has been for some time.

Chapter Overview

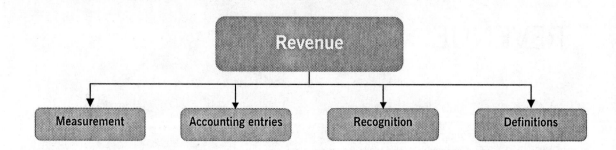

1 The IASB *Conceptual Framework*

Do you remember our discussions on the IASB"s *Conceptual Framework*, and the principle of substance over form, in Chapter 3?

The 1989 *Framework* included substance over form as a qualitative characteristic. The 2011 *Conceptual Framework* does not mention substance over form but the IASB considers it to be implied in the concept of faithful representation. To account for an item according to its legal form but not its economic substance would not be a faithful representation.

1.1 Basic principles

How does the *Conceptual Framework* enforce the substance over form principle? Its main method is to define the elements of financial statements and therefore to give rules for their recognition. The key considerations are whether a transaction has **given rise to new assets and liabilities**, and whether it has **changed any existing assets and liabilities**.

The characteristics of transactions whose substance is not readily apparent are as follows.

(a)   The **legal title** to an item is separated from the ability to enjoy the principal benefits, and the exposure to the main risks associated with it.

(b)   The transaction is **linked to one or more others** so that the commercial effect of the transaction cannot be understood without reference to the complete series.

(c)   The transaction includes **one or more options**, under such terms that it makes it highly likely that the option(s) will be exercised.

2 Definitions

We looked at the definition of an asset and a liability in Chapter 3.

KEY TERMS

- An ASSET is a resource controlled by the entity as a result of past events and from which future economic benefits are expected to flow to the entity.

- A LIABILITY is a present obligation of the entity arising from past events, the settlement of which is expected to result in an outflow from the entity of resources embodying economic benefits.

(Conceptual Framework)

Identifying **who has the risks** relating to an asset will, generally, indicate **who has the benefits** and hence **who has the asset**. If an entity is unable to avoid an **outflow of benefits**, this will provide evidence that it has a liability.

Now let us consider the IASB *Conceptual Framework* definitions of income and expenses. It is clearly linked with the definitions of assets and liabilities.

KEY TERM

INCOME is increases in economic benefits during the accounting period in the form of **inflows or enhancements of assets or decreases of liabilities** that result in increases in equity, other than those relating to contributions from equity participants.   *(Conceptual Framework)*

You will note that the definition of income above encompasses both **revenue** and **gains**. Revenue is the focus of this chapter.

Let's break down the three possible forms of income described above:

- Income in the form of **inflows** relates to **cash sales**

- Income in the form of **enhancements of assets** relates to **credit sales** (increase in trade receivable)

- Income in the form of **decreases of liabilities** relates to **deferred income**. When income is received in advance, it is recorded as a liability ie deferred income. Then when the income is earned, the

deferred income is reversed in the statement of financial position and income recorded in the statement of profit or loss.

The *Conceptual Framework* definition underlies the definition of revenue in IAS 18 *Revenue*.

KEY TERM

REVENUE is income that arises in the course of ordinary activities of an entity and includes income from:

- Sale of goods
- Rendering of services
- Interest
- Royalties and dividends

INTEREST is the charge for the use of cash or cash equivalents or amounts due to the entity.

ROYALTIES are charges for the use of non-current assets of the entity eg patents, computer software and trademarks.

DIVIDENDS are distributions of profit to holders of equity investments, in proportion to their holdings, of each relevant class of capital.

Revenue includes only those amounts receivable by an **entity on its own account**. Amounts collected on behalf of third parties eg **sales taxes**, **are excluded** from revenue as they are not economic benefits that flow to the entity.

It is not sufficient, however, that the asset or liability fulfils the above definitions; it must also satisfy **recognition criteria** in order to be shown in an entity's accounts.

Example: Types of revenue

Which of the following would qualify as revenue under IAS 18? Tick as appropriate.

	Revenue?
A share issue	
A car dealer selling a car to a customer	
Profit on disposal of a non-current asset	
Interest earned on an investment in a bond	
A fee received in return for provision of a training course	

Solution

	Revenue?
A share issue	X
A car dealer selling a car to a customer **(sale of goods)**	✓
Profit on disposal of a non-current asset	X
Interest earned on an investment in a bond **(interest)**	✓
A fee received in return for provision of a training course **(rendering of services)**	✓

A share issue qualifies as equity (not revenue). A profit on disposal of a non-current asset is outside the scope of IAS 18 and instead is covered by IAS 16 *Property, plant and equipment*.

2.1 Recognition

Accruals accounting is based on the **matching of costs with the revenue they generate**. It is crucially important under this convention that we can establish the point at which revenue may be recognised, so that the correct treatment can be applied to the related costs. For example, the costs of producing an item of finished goods should be carried as an asset in the statement of financial position until such time as it is sold; they should then be written off as a charge to the trading account. Which of these two treatments should be applied cannot be decided until it is clear at what moment the sale of the item takes place.

The decision has a **direct impact on profit**, since it would be unacceptable to recognise the profit on sale until a sale had taken place in accordance with the criteria of revenue recognition.

You should recall both of the recognition criteria required for assets and liabilities in the *Conceptual Framework*:

- It is **probable** that any future **economic benefit** associated with the item will flow to or from the entity.

- The item has a cost or value that can be **measured with reliability**.

IAS 18 governs the recognition of revenue. Revenue from the sale of goods is recognised as **earned at the point of sale**, because at that point all five criteria set out in IAS 18 will, generally, have been met.

(a)   The entity has transferred to the buyer the **significant risks and rewards** of ownership of the goods.

(b)   The entity retains **no continuing managerial involvement** or effective control over the goods sold.

(c)   The amount of revenue can be **measured reliably**.

(d)   It is **probable** that the **economic benefits** associated with the transaction will flow to the entity.

(e)   Costs incurred in the transaction can be **measured reliably**.

At earlier points in the business cycle there will not, in general, be **firm evidence** that the above criteria will be met. Until work on a product is complete, there is a risk that some flaw in the manufacturing process will necessitate its writing off; even when the product is complete, there is no guarantee that it will find a buyer.

At later points in the business cycle, for example when cash is received for the sale, the recognition of revenue would occur in a period later than that in which the related costs were charged. Revenue recognition would then depend on fortuitous circumstances, such as the cash flow of a company's customers, and might fluctuate misleadingly from one period to another.

Criteria (c), (d) and **(e)** above from IAS 18 are, effectively, the ***Conceptual Framework* recognition criteria**. Under the accruals concept, revenue and the related cost of sales should be recognised in the same period which is why the reliable measurement criterion applies to both revenue and costs.

The specific guidance for recognition of income in the *Conceptual Framework* is when an increase in future economic benefits related to an increase in an asset or a decrease in a liability has arisen that can be measured with reliability. Again, this is consistent with the IAS 18 rules.

The IAS 18 probable economic benefits criteria also ties in with the *Conceptual Framework* **definition of income** as increases in economic benefits.

Section summary

Important points to remember from the *Conceptual Framework* are:

- **Substance over form** as implied in faithful representation
- Definitions of **assets** and **liabilities**
- Definition of **recognition**
- **Criteria** for recognition

3 Revenue recognition

Introduction

Revenue recognition is straightforward in most business transactions, but some situations are more complicated and some give opportunities for manipulation.

3.1 IAS 18 *Revenue*

IAS 18 governs the recognition of revenue in specific (common) types of transaction. Generally, recognition should be when it is probable that **future economic benefits** will flow to the entity and when these benefits can be **measured reliably**.

Income, as defined by the *Conceptual Framework*, includes both revenue and gains. Revenue is income arising in the ordinary course of an entity's activities and it may be called different names, such as sales, fees, interest, dividends or royalties.

3.2 Measurement of revenue

When a transaction takes place, the amount of revenue is usually decided by the **agreement of the buyer and seller**. The revenue is actually measured, however, as the **fair value of the consideration received**, which will take account of any trade discounts and volume rebates. If the revenue is receivable more than 12 months after it has been earned it will usually be **discounted to present value**.

3.3 Identification of the transaction

Normally, each transaction can be looked at **as a whole**. Sometimes, however, transactions are more complicated, and it is necessary to break a transaction down into its **component parts**. For example, a sale may include the transfer of goods and the provision of future servicing, the revenue for which should be deferred over the period the service is performed.

At the other end of the scale, **seemingly separate transactions must be considered together** if apart they lose their commercial meaning. An example would be to sell an asset with an agreement to buy it back at a later date. The second transaction cancels the first and so both must be considered together.

3.4 Sale of goods

As introduced earlier, revenue from the sale of goods should only be recognised when all these conditions are satisfied.

(a)   The entity has transferred the **significant risks and rewards** of ownership of the goods to the buyer.

(b)   The entity has **no continuing managerial involvement** to the degree usually associated with ownership, and no longer has effective control over the goods sold.

(c)   The amount of revenue can be **measured reliably.**

(d)   It is probable that the **economic benefits** associated with the transaction will flow to the entity.

(e)   The **costs incurred** in respect of the transaction can be measured reliably.

The transfer of risks and rewards can only be decided by examining each transaction. Mainly, the transfer occurs at the same time as either the **transfer of legal title**, or the **passing of possession** to the buyer – this is what happens when you buy something in a shop.

If **significant risks and rewards remain with the seller**, then the transaction is **not** a sale and revenue cannot be recognised, for example if the receipt of the revenue from a particular sale depends on the buyer receiving revenue from his own sale of the goods.

It is possible for the seller to retain only an **insignificant risk of ownership** and for the sale and revenue to be recognised. The main example here is where the seller retains title only to ensure collection of what is owed on the goods. This is a common commercial situation and, when it arises, the revenue should be recognised on the date of sale.

The probability of the entity receiving the revenue arising from a transaction must be assessed. It may only become probable that the economic benefits will be received when an uncertainty is removed, for example government permission for funds to be received from another country. Only when the uncertainty is removed should the revenue be recognised. This is in contrast with the situation where revenue has already been recognised but where the **collectability of the cash** is brought into doubt. Where recovery has ceased to be probable, the amount should be recognised as an expense, **not** an adjustment of the revenue previously recognised. These points also refer to the rendering of services, interest, royalties and dividends discussed in Section 3.7 below.

Matching should take place ie the revenue and expenses relating to the same transaction should be recognised at the same time. It is usually easy to estimate expenses at the date of sale (eg warranty costs, shipment costs etc). Where they cannot be estimated reliably, then revenue cannot be recognised; any consideration which has already been received is treated as a liability.

3.5 Journal entries

The journal entries to record the sale of goods are as follows:

Cash sales

DEBIT   Cash
CREDIT   Revenue

Credit sales

DEBIT   Trade receivables
CREDIT   Revenue

Where revenue is **received in advance**, the journal entry upon the receipt of cash is as follows:

DEBIT   Cash
CREDIT   Deferred income

When the sale transaction actually occurs, the journal entry to reverse the deferred income is then made:

DEBIT   Deferred income
CREDIT   Revenue

Where revenue is accrued, the journal entry to record the transaction is as follows:

DEBIT   Accrued income
CREDIT   Revenue

Example: Revenue recognition journal entries 1

A washing machine sells for $500 with a one-year warranty. The dealer knows from experience that 15% of these machines develop a fault in the first year and that the average cost of repair is $100. He sells 200 machines on credit. How does he account for this sale?

Solution

He will recognise revenue of $100,000 ($500 × 200) and an associated provision of $3,000 ($100 × 200 × 15%).

The journal entries to record this transaction are as follows:

DEBIT	Trade receivables	$100,000	
CREDIT	Revenue		$100,000

Being credit sales revenue

DEBIT	Warranty expense	$3,000	
CREDIT	Warranty provision		$3,000

Being the recognition of warranty liability on sales

Example: Revenue recognition journal entries 2

GE is an investment property business. On 31 December 20X5, GE received rental income of $500,000 for the year ended 30 September 20X6.

Required

What is the accounting entry to record this receipt in GE's financial statements for the year ended 31 December 20X5 (tick as appropriate)?

(a)	DEBIT	Cash	$500,000	
	CREDIT	Revenue		$500,000
(b)	DEBIT	Trade receivables	$500,000	
	CREDIT	Revenue		$500,000
(c)	DEBIT	Cash	$500,000	
	CREDIT	Revenue		$125,000
	CREDIT	Deferred income		$375,000
(d)	DEBIT	Accrued income	$375,000	
	DEBIT	Revenue	$125,000	
	CREDIT	Cash		$500,000

Solution

The correct answer is (c):

DEBIT	Cash		$500,000
CREDIT	Revenue (3/12 x $500,000) [for 01.10.X5 – 31.12.X5)	$125,000	
CREDIT	Deferred income (9/12 x $500,000) [for 01.01.X6 – 30.9.X6]	$375,000	

3.6 Servicing fees included in the price

The sales price of a product may include an identifiable amount for subsequent servicing. In this case, that amount is deferred and recognised as revenue over the period during which the service is performed. The amount deferred must cover the cost of those services together with a reasonable profit on those services.

Example: Servicing fees included in the price

A computerised accountancy package is sold with one year's after-sales support. The cost of providing support to one customer for one year is calculated to be $50. The company has a mark-up on cost of 15%. The product is sold for $350. How is this sale accounted for?

Solution

$57.50 (50 + (50 × 15%)) will be treated as deferred income and recognised over the course of the year.

The remaining $292.50 will be treated as revenue and recognised immediately.

3.7 Rendering of services

Revenue from the rendering of services should be recognised as follows:

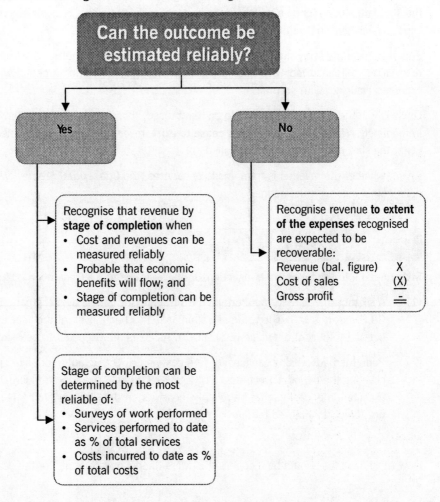

When the outcome of a transaction involving the rendering of services can be estimated reliably, the associated revenue should be recognised by reference to the **stage of completion of the transaction** at the end of the reporting period. The outcome of a transaction can be estimated reliably when **all** these conditions are satisfied.

(a)   The amount of revenue can be **measured reliably**.

(b)   It is probable that the **economic benefits** associated with the transaction will flow to the entity.

(c) The **stage of completion** of the transaction at the end of the reporting period can be measured reliably.

(d) The **costs incurred** for the transaction and the costs to complete the transaction can be measured reliably.

The parties to the transaction will normally have to agree the following before an entity can make reliable estimates.

(a) Each party's **enforceable rights** regarding the service to be provided and received by the parties

(b) The **consideration** to be exchanged

(c) The **manner and terms of settlement**

There are various methods of determining the stage of completion of a transaction, but for practical purposes, when services are performed by an indeterminate number of acts over a period of time, revenue should be recognised on a **straight-line basis** over the period unless there is evidence for the use of a more appropriate method. If one act is of more significance than the others, then the significant act should be carried out **before** revenue is recognised.

When the outcome of the transaction involving the rendering of services cannot be estimated reliably, the standard recommends a **no loss/no gain approach**. Revenue is recognised only to the extent of the expenses recognised that are recoverable.

This is particularly likely during the **early stages of a transaction**, but it is still probable that the entity will recover the costs incurred. Therefore, the revenue recognised in such a period will be equal to the expenses incurred, with no profit.

Obviously, if the costs are not likely to be reimbursed, then they must be recognised as an expense immediately. **When the uncertainties cease to exist**, revenue should be recognised when conditions (a) to (d) at the start of this section are satisfied.

Again, whether the revenue is from goods or services, the *Conceptual Framework* recognition criteria and definition of income must be met.

Example: Rendering of services

MN entered into the following transactions in the year ended 31 December 20X2:

(1) A six-month contract to undertake IFRS training for Louise over the period 1 September 20X2 to 28 February 20X3. The value of training she has been given at the year end amounts to $45,000 out of a total contract value of $60,000. All costs are expected to be recoverable.

(2) Performed advertising services for Ben costing $4,450 relating to a fixed price $20,000 contract covering the period 1 December 20X2 to 31 March 20X3. Due to fluctuating advertising costs, the expected total cost cannot be reliably measured at the year end, but MN is certain that Ben will pay the costs incurred to date.

Required

How much revenue should be recognised in MN's financial statements for the year ended 31 December 20X2?

Solution

	$
Training for Louise	45,000
Advertising for Ben	4,450
	49,450

Notes:

1   Item 1 is accrued based on the value of work performed rather than accrued on a time-apportioned basis in accordance with IAS 18.

2   For item 2, since the outcome of the service transaction cannot be reliably measured at the year end only $4,450 is recognised as revenue rather than on a time-apportioned basis. This matches with the costs recognised ensuring that no profit is recorded until the outcome can be reliably measured.

3.8 Interest, royalties and dividends

When others use the entity's assets yielding interest, royalties and dividends, the revenue should be recognised on the bases set out below when the *Conceptual Framework* recognition criteria are met.

(a)   It is probable that the **economic benefits** associated with the transaction will flow to the entity.

(b)   The amount of the revenue can be **measured reliably**.

The revenue is recognised on the following bases.

(a)   **Interest** is recognised on a time-apportioned basis that takes into account the **effective yield** on the asset.

(b)   **Royalties** are recognised on an accruals basis in accordance with the **substance** of the relevant agreement.

(c)   **Dividends** are recognised when the **shareholder's right to receive payment** is established.

It is unlikely that you would be asked about anything as complex as this in the exam, but you should be aware of the basic requirements of the Standard. The **effective yield** on an asset mentioned above is the rate of interest required to discount the stream of future cash receipts expected over the life of the asset, to equal the initial carrying amount of the asset.

For royalties, sometimes the true substance of the agreement may require some other systematic and rational method of recognition.

Once again, the points made above about **probability and collectability** on sale of goods also apply here.

Example: Interest income

MNB acquired an investment in a debt instrument on 1 January 20X0 at its par value of $3 million. Transaction costs relating to the acquisition were $200,000. The investment pays a fixed annual return of 6%, which is received in arrears. The principal amount will be repaid to MNB in 4 years' time at a premium of $400,000. The investment has been correctly classified as held to maturity. The investment has an effective interest rate of approximately 7.05%.

For the year ended 31 December 20X0, MNB has recorded interest received in profit or loss.

Required

(a)   What is the amount of interest income that should have been recorded in profit or loss?

(b)   What accounting entry is required to correct MNB's accounting treatment?

Solution

(a)   Interest income

	$
Investment at 1 January 20X0 (3,000,000 + 200,000)	3,200,000
Finance income (7.05% × 3,200,000)	225,600
Interest received (6% × 3,000,000)	(180,000)
Investment at 31 December 20X0	3,245,600

Therefore, interest income to report in profit or loss should be $225,600 (the effective interest).

(b)   Correcting accounting entry

DEBIT	Investment ($225,600 − $180,000)	$45,600	
CREDIT	Interest income		$45,600

Being correction of interest income on investment in debt

4 Measurement of revenue

The amount of revenue arising on a transaction is usually determined by agreement between the seller and the buyer (or user). It should be measured at the **fair value of the consideration received or receivable**, after adjusting for any trade discounts or volume rebates allowed. In most cases, the fair value of the consideration is simply the amount of cash or cash equivalents received, or to be received.

4.1 Deferred consideration

However, when the cash inflow is **deferred**, the fair value of the consideration may be less than the nominal amount of cash receivable. This would be the case where, for example, the seller grants a period of interest-free credit to the buyer for the purchase of the goods. If the arrangement effectively constitutes a **financing transaction**, it will be necessary to **discount** the deferred consideration to present value to determine the fair value of the revenue.

We looked at discounting in Chapter 2. When discounting deferred consideration, the fair value of the consideration is determined by discounting all future receipts using an **imputed rate of interest**. The imputed rate of interest will be given to you in the exam. According to IAS 18, the imputed rate of interest is either:

(a)   The prevailing rate for a similar instrument of an issuer with a similar credit rating **or**

(b)   A rate of interest that discounts the nominal amount of the instrument to the current cash sales price of the goods or services

whichever can be determined more clearly

For example,, if a company is due to receive deferred revenue of $1,000 in two years' time, the present value of the revenue receivable, based on an imputed rate of interest of 5%, is calculated as follows:

$$\$1,000 \times \frac{1}{(1.05)^2} = \$907.03$$

The difference between the fair value of the transaction and the nominal sales value is accounted for as interest revenue, and is accrued over the period until payment is due,

ie $907.03 × 5% = $45.35 in year 1

4.2 Exchange of goods or services

When **goods or services are exchanged** or swapped for goods or services which are of **a similar nature and value**, the exchange should **not** be accounted for as a transaction which generates revenue. IAS 18 gives the example of commodities like milk, where suppliers exchange inventories in various locations to fulfil demand on a timely basis in a particular location.

By contrast, when goods are sold or services are rendered in exchange for **dissimilar goods or services**, the exchange should be accounted for as a transaction which generates revenue. The revenue is **measured at the fair value of the goods or services received**, adjusted by the amount of any cash or cash equivalents transferred. When the fair value of the goods or services received cannot be measured reliably, the revenue is measured at the fair value of the goods or services given up, adjusted by the amount of any cash or cash equivalents transferred.

Chapter Summary

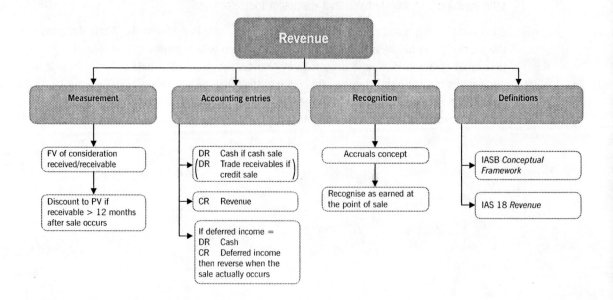

Quick Quiz

1   What is meant by the concept of substance over form?

2   What are the common features of transactions whose substance is not readily apparent?

3   When should the revenue from a sale of goods be recognised?

Answers to Quick Quiz

1   The principle is that transactions and other events must be accounted for and presented in accordance with their substance and economic reality rather than merely their legal form.

2   (a)   The legal title is separated from the ability to enjoy benefits.

     (b)   The transaction is linked to other(s) so that the substance cannot be understood without reference to the series as a whole.

3   When the following five conditions are satisfied:

     (a)   the seller has transferred the risks and rewards to the buyers

     (b)   the seller no longer has managerial involvement

     (c)   the amount of revenue can be measured reliably

     (d)   it is probable that economic benefits will flow to the seller

     (e)   the costs incurred can be measured reliably.

Now try these questions from the Practice Question Bank	Number	Level	Marks	Time
	Q12	Introductory	N/A	5 mins

SIMPLE GROUPS

Part C

BASIC GROUPS

Consolidation is an extremely important area of your Paper F2 syllabus.

The key to consolidation questions in the examination is to adopt a logical approach.

In this chapter, we will revise the definitions and basic consolidation techniques that you met in Paper F1. We will also look at IFRS 10 *Consolidated financial statements* in more detail.

This chapter introduces the idea of subsidiaries that are not fully owned by the parent company. Instead there are (outside) shareholders called **non-controlling interests (NCI)**.

We will see the effect of NCI on goodwill, reserves, dividends, intra-group trading and fair values.

A recent standard, IFRS 13 *Fair value measurement*, deals with fair value measurements. We will also see consolidations where the acquisition takes place part way through the accounting year.

In the exam, any consolidation is highly likely to involve NCI. Therefore you need to practice these techniques thoroughly. Make sure you work on *every* question in this chapter.

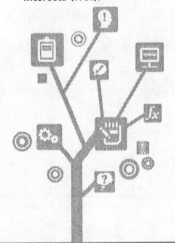

Topic list	learning outcomes	syllabus references
1 Group financial statements	B1	B1(a)
2 IFRS 10 *Consolidated financial statements*	B1	B1(a)
3 Consolidated statement of financial position	B1	B1(a)
4 Fair values in acquisition accounting	B1	B1(a)
5 Non-controlling interests	B1	B1(a)
6 Other adjustments to the statement of financial position	B1	B1(a)
7 Acquisition of a subsidiary during its accounting period	B1	B1(a)
8 Consolidated statement of profit or loss and other comprehensive income	B1	B1(a)
9 Subsidiaries acquired exclusively with a view to resale	B1	B1(a)

Chapter Overview

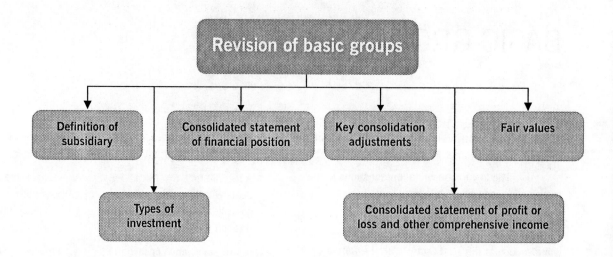

1 Group financial statements

Introduction

In this section we will deal with the concept of a group and start to see how groups are accounted for in accordance with International Financial Reporting Standards (IFRSs).

1.1 Why group financial statements?

There are many reasons for businesses to operate as groups; for the goodwill associated with the names of the subsidiaries, for tax or legal purposes and so forth. In many countries, company law requires that the results of a group should be presented as a whole. Unfortunately, it is not possible simply to add all the results together, and this chapter will teach you how to **consolidate** all the results of companies within a group.

In traditional accounting terminology, a **group of companies** consists of a **parent company** and one or more **subsidiary companies** which are controlled by the parent company.

1.2 Accounting standards

We will be looking at seven accounting standards in this and subsequent chapters.

- IFRS 3 *Business combinations*
- IFRS 10 *Consolidated financial statements*
- IAS 28 *Investments in associates and joint ventures*
- IAS 39 *Financial investments: recognition and measurement*
- IFRS 11 *Joint arrangements*
- IFRS 12 *Disclosure of interests in other entities*
- IFRS 13 *Fair value measurement*

These standards are all concerned with different aspects of group financial statements, but there is some overlap between them, particularly between IFRS 3 and IFRS 10.

In this chapter we will concentrate on IFRS 3 and IFRS 10, which cover the basic group definitions and consolidation procedures of a parent-subsidiary relationship. First of all, however, we will look at all the important definitions involved in group financial statements, which **determine how to account for each particular type of investment**.

1.3 Definitions   5/10

We will look at some of these definitions in more detail later, but they are useful here in that they give you an overview of all aspects of group financial statements.

Exam skills

All the definitions relating to group financial statements are extremely important. You must **learn them** and **understand** their meaning and application.

KEY TERMS

CONTROL. An investor controls an investee when the investor **is exposed**, or has **rights**, **to variable returns** from its involvement with the investee, and has the **ability to affect those returns** through **power** over the investee.   *(IFRS 10)*

POWER. Existing rights that give the current ability to direct the relevant activities of the investee.   *(IFRS 10)*

SUBSIDIARY. An entity that is **controlled** by another entity.   *(IFRS 10)*

PARENT. An entity that **controls** one or more subsidiaries.   *(IFRS 10)*

GROUP. A **parent** and all its **subsidiaries**.   *(IFRS 10)*

ASSOCIATE. An entity over which an investor has **significant influence**.   *(IAS 28)*

SIGNIFICANT INFLUENCE is the power to **participate in the financial and operating policy** decisions of an investee, but is not control or joint control over those policies.   *(IAS 28)*

JOINT ARRANGEMENT. An arrangement of which two or more parties have **joint control**.   *(IAS 28)*

JOINT CONTROL. The **contractually-agreed sharing of control** of an arrangement, which exists only when decisions about the relevant activities require the unanimous consent of the parties sharing control.

     (IAS 28)

JOINT VENTURE. A joint arrangement whereby the parties that have joint control (the joint venturers) of the arrangement have rights to the net assets of the arrangement.   *(IAS 28, IFRS 11)*

We can summarise the different types of investment and the required accounting for them as follows.

Investment	Criteria	Treatment in group financial statements
Subsidiary	Control	Full consolidation
Associate	Significant influence	Equity accounting (see Chapter 10)
Joint venture	Joint control with rights to net assets	Equity accounting (see Chapter 10)
Joint operation	Joint control with rights to individual assets and obligations for individual liabilities	Line by line (see Chapter 10)
Investment which is none of the above	Asset held for accretion of wealth	As for single company accounts per IAS 39 (see Chapter 3)

1.4 Investments in subsidiaries

When should an investment be treated as a subsidiary? The key here is **control**. In most cases, this will involve the holding company or parent owning a majority of the ordinary shares in the subsidiary (to which normal voting rights are attached). There are circumstances, however, when the parent may own only a minority of the voting power in the subsidiary, but the parent still has control.

IFRS 10 provides a definition of control and identifies three separate elements of control:

(a)   **Power** over the investee

(b)   Exposure to, or rights to, **variable returns** from its involvement with the investee and

(c)   The ability to use its power over the investee to affect the amount of the investor's returns

If there are changes to one or more of these three elements of control, then an investor should reassess whether it controls an investee.

1.4.1 Power

Power is defined as **existing rights that give the current ability to direct the relevant activities of the investee**. There is no requirement for that power to have been exercised.

Relevant activities may include:

(a)   Selling and purchasing goods or services
(b)   Managing financial assets

(c)   Selecting, acquiring and disposing of assets

(d)   Researching and developing new products and processes

(e)   Determining a funding structure or obtaining funding.

In some cases, assessing power is straightforward, for example, where power is obtained directly and solely from having the majority of voting rights or potential voting rights, and as a result the ability to direct relevant activities.

In other cases, assessment is more complex and more than one factor must be considered. IFRS 10 gives the following examples of **rights**, other than voting or potential voting rights, which individually, or alone, can give an investor power.

(a)   Rights to appoint, reassign or remove key management personnel who can direct the relevant activities

(b)   Rights to appoint or remove another entity that directs the relevant activities

(c)   Rights to direct the investee to enter into, or veto changes to, transactions for the benefit of the investor

(d)   Other rights, such as those specified in a management contract

IFRS 10 suggests that the **ability** rather than a contractual right to achieve the above may also indicate that an investor has power over an investee.

An investor can have power over an investee even where other entities have significant influence or other ability to participate in the direction of relevant activities.

1.4.2 Returns

An investor must have exposure, or rights, to **variable returns** from its involvement with the investee in order to establish control.

This is the case where the investor's returns from its involvement have the potential to vary as a result of the investee's performance.

Returns may include:

(a)   Dividends

(b)   Remuneration for servicing an investee's assets or liabilities

(c)   Fees and exposure to loss from providing credit support

(d)   Returns as a result of achieving synergies or economies of scale through an investor combining use of their assets with use of the investee's assets

1.4.3 Link between power and returns

In order to establish control, an investor must be able to use its power to affect its returns from its involvement with the investee. This is the case even where the investor delegates its decision-making powers to an agent.

Exam skills

You should learn the contents of the above paragraph as you may be asked to apply them in the exam, for example as at May 2010.

1.4.4 Potential voting rights

An entity may own share warrants, share call options or other similar instruments that are **convertible into ordinary shares** in another entity. If these are exercised or converted, they may give the entity voting power (or reduce another party's voting power) over the financial and operating policies of the other entity.

(These are known as potential voting rights.) The **existence and effect** of potential voting rights, including potential voting rights held by another entity, should be considered when assessing whether an entity has control over another entity (and therefore has a subsidiary). Potential voting rights are considered only if the rights are **substantive** (meaning that the holder must have the practical ability to exercise the right).

In assessing whether potential voting rights give rise to control, the investor should consider the **purpose and design of the instrument**. This includes an assessment of the various terms and conditions of the instrument as well as the investor's apparent expectations, motives and reasons for agreeing to those terms and conditions.

1.4.5 Structured entities

These are dealt with here because they are another example of the exercise of power and control.

A structured entity is defined by IFRS 12 as **an entity that has been designed so that voting or similar rights are not the dominant factor in deciding who controls the entity**, such as when any voting rights related to administrative tasks only and the relevant activities are directed by means of contractual arrangements.

A structured entity (sometimes referred to as a **special purpose entity**) may be created to accomplish a specific, defined objective. Examples include research and development, or securitisation of financial assets. Such special purpose entities may be incorporated or unincorporated. Often there are strict and permanent limits on the decision-making powers of their governing board or other management. They operate on autopilot ie the policy guiding their activities cannot be modified other than perhaps by their sponsor. The sponsor frequently transfers assets to the structured entity or performs services for it.

If the IFRS 10 **definition of control** above is met, structured entities must be **consolidated**. If the definition of control is not met, the entity is not consolidated, but significant disclosures are still required by IFRS 12.

1.4.6 Accounting treatment in group financial statements

IFRS 10 requires a parent to present consolidated financial statements in which the financial statements of the parent and subsidiary (or subsidiaries) are combined and presented **as a single entity**.

We will look at the process of preparing consolidated financial statements in the sections that follow.

1.5 Investments in associates

This type of investment is something less than a subsidiary, but more than a simple investment. The key criterion here is **significant influence**. This is defined as the **power to participate, but not to control** (which would make the investment a subsidiary).

Significant influence can be determined by the holding of voting rights (usually attached to shares) in the entity. IAS 28 states that if an investor holds **20% or more** of the voting power of the investee, it can be presumed that the investor has significant influence over the investee, *unless* it can be clearly shown that this is not the case.

Significant influence can be presumed *not* to exist if the investor holds **less than 20%** of the voting power of the investee, unless it can be demonstrated otherwise.

The **existence of significant influence** is evidenced in one or more of the following ways.

(a) Representation on the **board of directors** (or equivalent) of the investee
(b) Participation in the **policy-making process**
(c) **Material transactions** between investor and investee
(d) Interchange of management personnel
(e) Provision of essential technical information

1.5.1 Accounting treatment in group financial statements

IAS 28 requires the use of the **equity method** of accounting for investments in associates. This method will be explained in detail in Chapter 10.

1.6 Accounting for investments in joint arrangements

IFRS 11 classes joint arrangements as either **joint operations** or **joint ventures**. The classification of a joint arrangement as a joint operation or a joint venture depends upon the rights and obligations of the parties to the arrangement. The detail of how to distinguish between joint operations and joint ventures will be considered in Chapter 10.

1.6.1 Accounting treatment in group financial statements

IFRS 11 and IAS 28 require **joint ventures** to be accounted for using the **equity method** (as for associates).

IFRS 11 requires **joint operations** to be recognised on a **line by line** basis. We will look at the accounting treatment for both joint ventures and joint operations in Chapter 10.

1.7 Accounting for subsidiaries, associates and joint ventures in the parent's separate financial statements

Be it a subsidiary, an associate or a joint arrangement IAS 27 *Separate financial statements* permits the investment be carried in the investor's separate financial statements either:

(a)   At **cost** or

(b)   As an **available for sale** financial asset under IAS 39 *Financial instruments: recognition and measurement* (ie at fair value with gains and losses in other comprehensive income, as discussed in Chapter 3)

When consolidating the group financial statements, the investment must be cancelled out, as we will see in more detail in the sections below:

(a)   If the investment is held at **cost**, the cost of the investment must be cancelled.

(b)   If the investment is held as an **available for sale** financial asset, **both** the **investment** (at fair value) and the **revaluation gains or losses** on the investment (in other comprehensive income in the statement of profit or loss and other comprehensive income) must be cancelled.

Example: Structured entities

A company, XY, operates a payroll services division for itself and a number of external customers. It decides to transfer the business of the division to a new entity ABC set up by XY. The sales director of ABC owns 100% of the share capital of ABC. The operating and financial policies of ABC will be decided by the board of XY under a signed contract. ABC's profits and losses will flow to XY, and ABC has acquired a loan guaranteed by XY.

The directors of XY wish to avoid consolidating the results of ABC because the loan will adversely affect their gearing ratio.

Discuss how the relationship with ABC should be reflected in the financial statements of the XY group.

Solution

IFRS 10 *Consolidated financial statements* defines a **subsidiary** as **an entity that is controlled by another entity**. An investor controls an investee when the investor:

- Has power over the investee to direct relevant activities
- Is exposed, or has rights, to variable returns from its involvement with the investee and
- Has the ability to use its power to affect those returns

While control is presumed to exist when the parent owns more than half of the voting power, **control may exist when a parent owns less than half the voting power but exercises control over the entity** under a statute or agreement.

Here, on the face of it, ABC does not look like a subsidiary of XY because XY does not own any of the shares (it is 100% owned by ABC's sales director). However, XY has **power** over ABC to direct its relevant activities through the **contractual agreement** between ABC and XY, which states that the board of XY is to make the operating and financial policies of ABC.

XY is also **exposed to the variable returns** of ABC as the **profits and losses of ABC flow to XY**. Further exposure comes from **XY acting as guarantor** for ABC's loan as XY would become liable on default.

Finally, XY has the **ability to use their power** through the contractual agreement. Therefore, **the IFRS 10 definition of control has been met**.

XY should consolidate 100% of ABC's assets and loan liability. Non-consolidation just to avoid increasing gearing would result in non-compliance with IFRS 10, and therefore is not permitted.

Section summary

Many large businesses consist of several companies controlled by one central or administrative company. Together these companies are called a **group**. The controlling company, called the **parent** or **holding company**, will own some or all of the shares in the other companies, called subsidiaries.

2   IFRS 10 *Consolidated financial statements*

Introduction

There are a number of regulations governing the preparation of group financial statements.

2.1 Definitions

KEY TERM

CONSOLIDATED FINANCIAL STATEMENTS. The financial statements of a **group** presented as those of a **single** economic entity.   (*IFRS 10*)

When a parent company issues consolidated financial statements, it should consolidate **all subsidiaries**, both foreign and domestic. The first step in any consolidation is to identify the subsidiaries using the definition as set out in Section 1.3 above.

2.2 Exemption from preparing group financial statements

A parent company **need not present** consolidated financial statements if, and only if, all of the following hold:

(a)   The parent is itself a **wholly-owned subsidiary** or it is a **partially-owned subsidiary** of another entity and its other owners, including those not otherwise entitled to vote, have been informed about, and do not object to, the parent not presenting consolidated financial statements

(b)   Its securities are **not publicly traded**

(c)   It is **not in the process of issuing securities** in public securities markets and

(d)   The **ultimate or intermediate parent** publishes consolidated financial statements that comply with IFRSs

A parent that does not present consolidated financial statements must comply with the IAS 27 rules on separate financial statements.

2.3 Exclusion of a subsidiary from consolidation   11/11

Where a parent controls one or more subsidiaries, IFRS 10 requires that consolidated financial statements are prepared to include **all subsidiaries, both foreign and domestic** other than those held for sale in accordance with IFRS 5 *Non-current assets held for sale and discontinued operations*.

In this instance, the subsidiary will still be included in the consolidated financial statements but not on a line by line basis (see Section 9 for more detail).

The rules on exclusion of subsidiaries from consolidation are necessarily strict, because this is a common method used by entities to manipulate their results. If a subsidiary which carries a large amount of debt can be excluded, then the gearing of the group as a whole will be improved. In other words, this is a way of taking debt **out of the consolidated statement of financial position**.

2.4 Different reporting dates

In most cases, all group companies will prepare financial statements to the same reporting date. One or more subsidiaries may, however, prepare financial statements to a different reporting date from the parent and the bulk of other subsidiaries in the group.

In such cases, the subsidiary may prepare additional statements to the reporting date of the rest of the group, for consolidation purposes. If this is not possible, the subsidiary's accounts may still be used for the consolidation, provided that the gap between the reporting dates is **three months or less**.

Where a subsidiary's financial statements are drawn up to a different accounting date, **adjustments should be made** for the effects of significant transactions or other events that occur between that date and the parent's reporting date.

2.5 Uniform accounting policies

Consolidated financial statements should be prepared using **the same accounting policies** for like transactions and other events in similar circumstances.

Adjustments must be made where members of a group use different accounting policies, so that their financial statements are suitable for consolidation.

2.6 Date of inclusion/exclusion

IFRS 10 requires the results of subsidiary undertakings to be included in the consolidated financial statements from:

(a)   The date of acquisition ie the **date on which the investor obtains control of the investee** to

(b)   The date of disposal ie the **date the investor loses control of the investee**

Once an investment is no longer a subsidiary, it should be treated as an associate under IAS 28 (if applicable) or as an investment under IAS 39 (see Chapter 3).

We will look at changes in group structures in more detail in Chapter 11.

2.7 Main points

IFRS 10 covers the basic rules and definitions of the parent-subsidiary relationship. You should learn:

- **Definitions**
- Rules for **exemption** from preparing consolidated financial statements
- **Disclosure requirements**

Section summary

IFRS 10 requires a parent company to present **consolidated** financial statements.

3   Consolidated statement of financial position   9/11, 3/12

Introduction

We will now consider how the consolidated statement of financial position is prepared.

3.1 Basic procedure

The preparation of a consolidated statement of financial position, in a very simple form, consists of two procedures.

(a)   Take the individual financial statements of the parent company and each subsidiary and **cancel out items** which appear as an asset in one company and a liability in another

(b)   Add together all the uncancelled assets and liabilities throughout the group

Items requiring adjustment may include the following.

(a)   **Fair value adjustments** need to be made where the fair value of an asset/liability in the subsidiary is different from its carrying amount in the subsidiary's financial statements.

(b)   The asset **shares in subsidiary companies** which appears in the parent company's financial statements will be matched with the share capital in the subsidiaries' financial statements.

(c)   There may be **intragroup trading** within the group. For example, S Co may sell goods on credit to P Co. P Co would then be a receivable in the accounts of S Co, while S Co would be a payable in the accounts of P Co. These need to be cancelled out so that the consolidated statement of financial position shows amounts owing between the group as a single entity and the outside world, and **not** those due between members of the group.

(d)   There may be **intragroup balances**, either as a result of intragroup trading or financing (for example, the parent company lending to the subsidiary). Intragroup balances must also be eliminated in full.

(e)   **Property, plant and equipment** may have been transferred from one company to another. The unrealised profit on intragroup transfers of property, plant and equipment must be eliminated, and the associated depreciation adjusted down.

We will discuss each of the following adjustments in turn in the sections that follow in this chapter. First, let us look at a basic example of cancellation.

Example: Cancellation

P Co regularly sells goods to its wholly-owned subsidiary company, S Co, which it has owned since S Co's incorporation. The statements of financial position of the two companies on 31 December 20X6 are given below.

STATEMENT OF FINANCIAL POSITION AS AT 31 DECEMBER 20X6

	P Co $	S Co $
Assets		
Non-current assets		
Property, plant and equipment	35,000	45,000
Investment in 40,000 $1 shares in S Co at cost	40,000	
	75,000	
Current assets		
Inventories	16,000	12,000
Receivables: S Co	2,000	
Other	6,000	9,000
Cash at bank	1,000	
Total assets	100,000	66,000
Equity and liabilities		
Equity		
40,000 $1 ordinary shares		40,000
70,000 $1 ordinary shares	70,000	
Retained earnings	16,000	19,000
	86,000	59,000
Current liabilities		
Bank overdraft		3,000
Payables: P Co		2,000
Payables: Other	14,000	2,000
Total equity and liabilities	100,000	66,000

Required

Prepare the consolidated statement of financial position of P Co at 31 December 20X6.

Solution

The cancelling items are:

(a)   P Co's asset investment in shares of S Co ($40,000) cancels with S Co's share capital ($40,000)

(b)   P Co's asset receivables: S Co ($2,000) cancels with S Co's liability payables: P Co ($2,000)

The remaining assets and liabilities are added together to produce the following consolidated statement of financial position.

P CO
CONSOLIDATED STATEMENT OF FINANCIAL POSITION AS AT 31 DECEMBER 20X6

	$	$
Assets		
Non-current assets		
Property, plant and equipment (35,000 + 45,000)		80,000
Current assets		
Inventories (16,000 + 12,000)	28,000	
Receivables (6,000 + 9,000)	15,000	
Cash at bank	1,000	
		44,000
Total assets		124,000
Equity and liabilities		
Equity		
70,000 $1 ordinary shares	70,000	
Retained earnings (16,000 + 19,000)	35,000	
		105,000
Current liabilities		
Bank overdraft	3,000	
Payables (14,000 + 2,000)	16,000	
		19,000
Total equity and liabilities		124,000

(a)   P Co's bank balance is **not netted off** with S Co's bank overdraft, as this would be less informative and would conflict with the principle that assets and liabilities should not be netted off.

(b)   The share capital in the consolidated statement of financial position is the **share capital of the parent company alone**. This must *always* be the case, no matter how complex the consolidation, because the share capital of subsidiary companies must *always* be a wholly cancelling item.

(c)   The **retained earnings of P and S are aggregated** because S was **acquired on incorporation** so all of S's retained earnings are post-acquisition and have been generated under the control of P.

3.2 Complications with cancellation

An item may appear in the statements of financial position of a parent company and its subsidiary, but not at the same amounts.

(a)   The parent company may have acquired **shares in the subsidiary** at a price **greater or less than their par value**. The asset will appear in the parent company's accounts at cost, while the share capital will appear in the subsidiary's accounts at par value. This raises the issue of **goodwill**, which is dealt with in the next section.

(b)   The parent company **may not** have **acquired all the shares of the subsidiary** (so the subsidiary may be only partly owned). This raises the issue of **non-controlling interests**, which are dealt with later in this chapter.

(c)   The intragroup trading balances may be out of step because of **goods or cash in transit**.

(d)   One company may have **issued loan stock** of which a **proportion only** is taken up by the other company.

The following question illustrates the techniques needed to deal with items (c) and (d) above. The procedure is to **cancel as far as possible**.

(a)   **Uncancelled loan stock** will appear as a **liability of the group**.

(b)   **Differences in balances on intragroup accounts** represent **goods or cash in transit**, which will **need to be adjusted** so that they agree and can then be cancelled. The adjustment for goods or cash in transit is to **accelerate the transaction to its ultimate destination**.

Learning outcome B1

The statements of financial position of P Co and its subsidiary S Co have been made up to 30 June. P Co has owned all the ordinary shares and 40% of the loan stock of S Co since its incorporation.

P CO
STATEMENT OF FINANCIAL POSITION AS AT 30 JUNE

	$	$
Assets		
Non-current assets		
Property, plant and equipment	120,000	
Investment in S Co, at cost		
80,000 ordinary shares of $1 each	80,000	
$20,000 of 12% loan stock in S Co	20,000	
		220,000
Current assets		
Inventories	50,000	
Receivables	40,000	
Current account with S Co	18,000	
Cash	4,000	
		112,000
Total assets		332,000
Equity and liabilities		
Equity		
Ordinary shares of $1 each, fully paid	100,000	
Retained earnings	95,000	
		195,000
Non-current liabilities		
10% loan stock		75,000
Current liabilities		
Payables	47,000	
Taxation	15,000	
		62,000
Total equity and liabilities		332,000

S CO
STATEMENT OF FINANCIAL POSITION AS AT 30 JUNE

	$	$
Non-current assets		
Property, plant and equipment		100,000
Current assets		
Inventories	60,000	
Receivables	30,000	
Cash	6,000	
		96,000
Total assets		196,000
Equity and liabilities		
Equity		
80,000 ordinary shares of $1 each, fully paid	80,000	
Retained earnings	28,000	
		108,000
Non-current liabilities		
12% loan stock		50,000
Current liabilities		
Payables	16,000	
Taxation	10,000	
Current account with P Co	12,000	
		38,000
Total equity and liabilities		196,000

The difference on the current accounts arises because of goods in transit.

Required

Prepare the consolidated statement of financial position of P Co as at 30 June.

4   Fair values in acquisition accounting   3/11

Introduction

The use of fair values is key in acquisition accounting. At the date of acquisition, both the consideration transferred and the assets and liabilities acquired must be measured at fair value.

4.1 Fair value

As we have just seen in the section above, one of the adjustments which may be required in preparing a consolidated statement of financial position relates to fair value. We will now look at the nature of fair value in more detail.

4.1.1 What is fair value?

Fair value is defined as follows by IFRS 13 *Fair value measurement*. You have seen this several times now – it is an important definition.

KEY TERM

FAIR VALUE. The price that would be received to sell an asset or paid to transfer a liability in an orderly transaction between market participants at the measurement date.   *(IFRS 13)*

4.1.2 Why is fair value important?

Fair value is a crucial component in calculating the amount of goodwill that arises in a business combination, for example, when a parent company acquires a subsidiary.

KEY TERM

GOODWILL. Any excess of the consideration transferred over the acquirer's interest in the fair value of the identifiable assets and liabilities acquired as at the date of the exchange transaction.

The **statement of financial position of a subsidiary company** at the date it is acquired may not be a guide to the fair value of its net assets. For example, the market value of a freehold building may have risen greatly since it was acquired, but it may appear in the statement of financial position at historical cost less accumulated depreciation.

We will look at the requirements of IFRS 3 (Revised) and IFRS 13 regarding fair value in more detail below. First, let us look at some practical matters.

4.2 Fair value adjustment calculations

Goodwill may be described as the **difference** between the **cost** of the investment and the **book value** of net assets acquired by the group. If this calculation is to comply with the definition above, however, we must ensure that the book values of the subsidiary's net assets are the same as their **fair value**.

There are two possible ways of achieving this.

(a)   The **subsidiary company** might **incorporate any necessary revaluations** in its own books of account. In this case, we can proceed directly to the consolidation, taking asset values and reserves figures straight from the subsidiary company's statement of financial position.

(b)   The **revaluations** may be made as a **consolidation adjustment without being incorporated** in the subsidiary company's books. In this case, we must make the necessary adjustments to the subsidiary's statement of financial position as a working. Only then can we proceed to the consolidation.

Note. Remember that when depreciating assets are revalued, there may be a corresponding alteration in the amount of depreciation charged and accumulated.

The difference between the fair values and the book values is a consolidation adjustment made only for the purposes of the consolidated financial statements. The pro-forma working below shows how the fair value consolidation adjustments affect other consolidation workings (which we will look at in a full worked example later).

	At acq'n date	Movement	Year end
	$	$	$
Inventories	X	(X)	X
Depreciable non-current assets	X	(X)	X
Non-depreciable non-current assets	X	(X)	X
Other fair value adjustments	X	(X)	X
	X	(X)	X
	↓	↓	↓
	Goodwill	Ret'd earnings	SOFP

As you can see, the first column records the **difference between the fair value and the book value** of each type of asset at the acquisition date. The total of these differences must be taken into account in calculating goodwill (which we will look at later in this chapter), as an adjustment to the net fair value of identifiable assets acquired/liabilities assumed on acquisition.

The second column shows the amount of **movement on the fair value** of the relevant assets between the acquisition date and the current year end. One common type of movement, in the case of depreciable non-current assets, is the adjustment to accumulated depreciation arising from fair value adjustments. This adjustment must be reflected in the calculations for the subsidiary's post-acquisition retained earnings.

The final column shows the fair value adjustment which needs to be made in the **consolidated statement of financial position** in respect of each type of asset at the year end.

4.3 Example: Fair value adjustments

Wheat Co acquired 100% of the ordinary shares of Barley Co on 1 January 20X5. At that date, the fair value of Barley Co's non-current assets was $23,000 greater than their net book value. Barley Co has not incorporated any revaluation in its books of account.

It is now early 20X6 and Wheat Co is preparing the group consolidated financial statements for the year ended 31 December 20X5.

Barley Co's non-current asset balance is recorded in its individual statement of financial position at $28,000 at 31 December 20X5.

Wheat Co's own non-current assets are recorded in its individual financial statements for the year at a net book value of $63,000.

If Barley Co had revalued its non-current assets at 1 January 20X5, an addition of $3,000 would have been made to the depreciation charged to profit or loss for the year ended 31 December 20X5.

The fair value adjustment workings would be as follows:

	At acq'n date	Movement	Year end
	$	$	$
Property, plant and equipment	23,000	(3,000)	20,000
	23,000	(3,000)	20,000
	↓	↓	↓
	Goodwill	Ret'd earnings	SOFP

Based on the workings above, we can calculate the non-current asset balance in the consolidated statement of financial position as follows:

Consolidated non-current asset balance = Wheat Co $63,000 + unadjusted Barley Co $28,000 + fair value adjustment $20,000 = $111,000

We will look at the goodwill and retained earnings workings later in this chapter.

Question 9.2

Fair values

Learning outcome B1

An asset is recorded in S Co's books at its historical cost of $4,000. On 1 January 20X5 P Co bought 100% of S Co's equity. Its directors attributed a fair value of $3,000 to the asset as at that date. It had been depreciated for two years out of an expected life of four years on the straight-line basis. There was no expected residual value. On 30 June 20X5 the asset was sold for $2,600. What is the profit or loss on disposal of this asset to be recorded in S Co's accounts and in P Co's consolidated accounts for the year ended 31 December 20X5?

4.4 IFRS 3 (Revised) and IFRS 13

The general rule under IFRS 3 (Revised) is that the subsidiary's assets and liabilities **must be measured at fair value** at the **acquisition date** except in **limited, stated cases**. (We will look at the exceptions in Section 4.4.5 below.)

The assets and liabilities must:

(a) Meet the definitions of assets and liabilities in the *Conceptual Framework*.

(b) Be part of what the acquiree (or its former owners) exchanged in the business combination rather than the result of separate transactions

As we have seen in Chapter 3, IFRS 13 provides a hierarchy of inputs for arriving at fair value. Level 1 inputs should be used where possible:

Level 1 Quoted prices in active markets for identical assets that the entity can access at the measurement date

Level 2 Inputs other than quoted prices that are directly or indirectly observable for the asset

Level 3 Unobservable inputs for the asset

4.4.1 Examples of fair value and business combinations

For non-financial assets, fair value is decided based on the highest and best use of the asset as determined by a market participant. The following examples, adapted from the illustrative examples to IFRS 13, demonstrate what is meant by this.

Example: Land

Anscome Co has acquired land in a business combination. The land is currently developed for industrial use as a site for a factory. The current use of land is presumed to be its highest and best use unless market or other factors suggest a different use. Nearby sites have recently been developed for residential use as sites for high-rise apartment buildings. On the basis of that development and recent zoning and other changes to facilitate that development, Anscome determines that the land currently used as a site for a factory could be developed as a site for residential use (ie for high-rise apartment buildings) because market participants would take into account the potential to develop the site for residential use when pricing the land.

How would the highest and best use of the land be determined?

Solution

The highest and best use of the land would be determined by comparing both of the following:

(a) The value of the land as currently developed for industrial use (ie the land would be used in combination with other assets, such as the factory, or with other assets and liabilities)

(b) The value of the land as a vacant site for residential use, taking into account the costs of demolishing the factory and other costs (including the uncertainty about whether the entity would be able to convert the asset to the alternative use) necessary to convert the land to a vacant site (ie the land is to be used by market participants on a stand-alone basis)

The highest and best use of the land would be determined on the basis of the higher of those values.

Example: Research and development project

Searcher acquires a research and development (R & D) project in a business combination. Searcher does not intend to complete the project. If completed, the project would compete with one of its own projects (to provide the next generation of the entity's commercialised technology). Instead, the entity intends to hold (ie lock up) the project to prevent its competitors from obtaining access to the technology. In doing this, the project is expected to provide defensive value principally by improving the prospects for the entity's own competing technology.

If it could purchase the R & D project, Developer Co would continue to develop the project and that use would maximise the value of the group of assets or of assets and liabilities in which the project would be used (ie the asset would be used in combination with other assets or with other assets and liabilities). Developer Co does not have similar technology.

How would the fair value of the project be measured?

Solution

The fair value of the project would be measured on the basis of the price that would be received in a current transaction to sell the project, assuming that the R & D would be used with its complementary assets and the associated liabilities and that those assets and liabilities would be available to Developer Co.

4.4.2 Restructuring and future losses

An acquirer **should not recognise liabilities for future losses** or other costs expected to be incurred as a result of the business combination.

IFRS 3 (Revised) explains that a plan to restructure a subsidiary following an acquisition is not a present obligation of the acquiree at the acquisition date. Neither does it meet the definition of a contingent liability. Therefore, an acquirer **should not recognise a liability for** such **a restructuring plan** as part of allocating the cost of the combination unless the subsidiary was already committed to the plan before the acquisition.

This **prevents creative accounting**. An acquirer cannot set up a provision for restructuring or future losses of a subsidiary and then release this to profit or loss in subsequent periods in order to reduce losses or smooth profits.

4.4.3 Intangible assets

The acquiree may have **intangible assets**, such as development expenditure. These can be recognised separately from goodwill only if they are **identifiable**. An intangible asset is identifiable only if it:

(a)   Is **separable** ie capable of being separated or divided from the entity and sold, transferred, or exchanged, either individually or together with a related contract, asset or liability or

(b)   Arises from **contractual or other legal rights**

Remember, some intangible assets may not have been recognised in the subsidiary's separate financial statements before the acquisition: these could include brands, licences, trade names, domain names, customer relationships, and so on.

4.4.4 Contingent liabilities

Contingent liabilities of the acquiree are **recognised** if their **fair value can be measured reliably**. A **contingent liability** must be recognised even if the outflow is not probable, provided there is a **present obligation**.

This is a departure from the normal rules in IAS 37 *Provisions, contingent liabilities and contingent assets,* where contingent liabilities are not normally recognised, only disclosed.

After their initial recognition, the acquirer should measure contingent liabilities that are recognised separately at the higher of:

(a)   The amount that would be recognised in accordance with IAS 37

(b)   The amount initially recognised

4.4.5 Other exceptions to the recognition or measurement principles

(a)   **Deferred tax assets/liabilities**: use IAS 12 *Income taxes* values

(b)   **Employee benefit assets/liabilities**: use IAS 19 *Employee benefits* values

(c)   **Indemnification assets**: measurement should be consistent with the measurement of the indemnified item (for example, an employee benefit or a contingent liability) less an allowance for uncollectible amounts

(d)   **Reacquired rights** (ie licence granted to a subsidiary before it was acquired): fair value based on the remaining term, ignoring the likelihood of renewal

(e)   **Share-based payment**: use IFRS 2 *Share-based payment* values

(f)   **Assets held for sale**: use IFRS 5 *Non-current assets held for sale and discontinued operations* values – fair value less costs to sell

4.5 Goodwill arising on acquisition

Goodwill arising on consolidation is one form of **purchased goodwill**, and is governed by IFRS 3. IFRS 3 requires that goodwill arising on consolidation should **be capitalised in the consolidated statement of financial position** and **reviewed for impairment every year**.

As we have seen when we introduced the concept of fair value, goodwill arising on consolidation is the **difference** between the **cost** of an acquisition and the **value of the subsidiary's net assets** acquired.

In subsequent periods, goodwill should be carried in the statement of financial position at **cost less any accumulated impairment losses**.

Question 9.3	Fair values

Learning outcome B1

AB acquired all of CD's 400,000 ordinary shares for $2,000,000 on 28 February 20X5. CD was purchased from its directors who will remain directors of the business. AB incurred legal and professional fees as a result of the acquisition of $75,000.

The book values of the assets and liabilities of CD acquired, as extracted from the general ledger, were $1,300,000.

As at the date of acquisition:

- CD had a customer list which it had not recognised as an asset because it was internally generated. However, on acquisition, as customer lists are often leased or exchanged, external experts managed to establish a fair value for the list of $100,000.

- An item of equipment, with a book value of $440,000, was found to have a market value of $660,000.

- CD had a contingent liability in respect of a major warranty claim with a fair value of $30,000.

- AB intended to reorganise CD's operations following the acquisition at an approximate cost of $150,000.

Required

Calculate goodwill on the acquisition of CD, in accordance with the requirements of IFRS 3 *Business combinations*, explaining your treatment of the legal fees, the customer list, the contingent liability and the reorganisation costs.

4.5.1 Accounting

To begin with, **we will examine the entries made by the parent company in its own statement of financial position when it acquires shares**.

When a company, P Co, wishes to **purchase shares** in a company, S Co, it must pay the previous owners of those shares. The most obvious form of payment would be in **cash**. Suppose P Co purchases all 40,000 $1 shares in S Co and pays $60,000 cash to the previous shareholders in consideration. The entries in P Co's books would be:

DEBIT	Investment in S Co at cost	$60,000	
CREDIT	Bank		$60,000

However, the previous shareholders might be prepared to accept some other form of consideration. For example, they might accept an agreed number of **shares** in P Co. P Co would then issue new shares in the agreed number and allot them to the former shareholders of S Co. This kind of deal might be attractive to P Co since it avoids the need for a heavy cash outlay. The former shareholders of S Co would retain an indirect interest in that company's profitability via their new holding in its parent company.

Continuing this example, suppose the shareholders of S Co agreed to accept one $1 ordinary share in P Co for every two $1 ordinary shares in S Co. P Co would then need to issue and allot 20,000 new $1 shares. How would this transaction be recorded in the books of P Co?

The former shareholders of S Co have presumably agreed to accept 20,000 shares in P Co because they consider each of those shares to have a value of $3. This view of the matter suggests the following method of recording the transaction in P Co's books.

DEBIT	Investment in S Co $60,000	
CREDIT	Share capital	$20,000
CREDIT	Share premium account	$40,000

The amount which P Co records in its books as the cost of its investment in S Co may be more or less than the book value of the assets it acquires. Suppose that S Co in the previous example has nil reserves and nil liabilities, so that its share capital of $40,000 is balanced by net assets with a book value of $40,000. For simplicity, assume for now that the book value of S Co's assets is the same as their market or fair value.

Now when the directors of P Co agree to pay $60,000 for a 100% investment in S Co, they must believe that, in addition to its tangible assets of $40,000, S Co also has, say, a customer base worth $20,000. This amount of $20,000 paid over and above the value of the identifiable assets acquired is called **goodwill arising on consolidation** (sometimes **premium on acquisition**).

Following the normal cancellation procedure, the $40,000 share capital in S Co's statement of financial position could be cancelled against $40,000 of the 'investment in S Co' in the statement of financial position of P Co. This would leave a $20,000 debit uncancelled in the parent company's financial statements, and this $20,000 would appear in the consolidated statement of financial position under the caption '**Intangible non-current assets: goodwill arising on consolidation**'.

4.5.2 Bargain purchase

Note that goodwill can be **negative**: the aggregate of the fair values of the separable net assets acquired may **exceed** what the parent company paid for them. IFRS 3 refers to this as a **bargain purchase**. In this situation:

(a)   An entity should first **re-assess** the amounts at which it has measured both the cost of the combination and the acquiree's identifiable net assets. This exercise should identify any errors.

(b)   Any **excess remaining** should be recognised immediately in profit or loss.

4.5.3 Goodwill and pre-acquisition profits

Up to now, we have assumed that S Co had nil retained earnings when its shares were purchased by P Co. Assuming instead that S Co had earned profits of $8,000 in the period before acquisition, its statement of financial position just before the purchase would look as follows.

	$
Total assets	<u>48,000</u>
Share capital	40,000
Retained earnings	<u>8,000</u>
	<u>48,000</u>

If P Co now purchases all the shares in S Co, it will acquire total assets worth $48,000 at a cost of $60,000. Clearly, in this case, S Co's goodwill will now be valued at $12,000. It should be apparent that any earnings retained by the subsidiary **prior to its acquisition** by the parent company must be **incorporated in the cancellation process** so as to arrive at a figure for goodwill arising on consolidation. In other words, not only S Co's share capital, but also its **pre-acquisition** retained earnings, must be cancelled against the asset investment in S Co in the accounts of the parent company. The uncancelled balance of $12,000 appears in the consolidated statement of financial position.

The consequence of this is that **any pre-acquisition retained earnings of a subsidiary company are not aggregated with the parent company's retained earnings** in the consolidated statement of financial position. The figure of consolidated retained earnings comprises the retained earnings of the parent company plus the **post-acquisition retained earnings only of subsidiary companies**. The post-acquisition retained earnings are simply retained earnings now *less* retained earnings at acquisition.

4.5.4 Pro forma working

We will look at a worked example, below, which demonstrates how goodwill with pre-acquisition profits is calculated. Before we do so, however, it is time to introduce the pro forma working for goodwill.

You will see that, as well as some of the net assets at acquisition that we have just discussed, the working also incorporates non-controlling interests and impairment losses on goodwill. Don't worry about them for now. We will turn our attention to these items shortly as we work through this topic. Keep this pro forma flagged for your reference.

	$	$
Consideration transferred		X
Non-controlling interests		X
Less: Net assets at acquisition:		
Ordinary share capital	X	
Share premium	X	
Retained earnings on acquisition	X	
Other reserves at acquisition	X	
Fair value adjustments at acquisition	<u>X</u>	
		(X)
		X
Less: Impairment losses on goodwill to date		<u>(X)</u>
Goodwill		<u><u>X</u></u>

Example: Goodwill and pre-acquisition profits

Sing Co acquired 100% of the ordinary shares of Wing Co on 31 March 20X5 for $80,000. The draft statement of financial position of Wing Co at acquisition was as follows.

WING CO
STATEMENT OF FINANCIAL POSITION AS AT 31 MARCH 20X5

	$
Current assets	60,000
Equity	
50,000 ordinary shares of $1 each	50,000
Retained earnings	10,000
	60,000

Calculate the goodwill arising on acquisition.

Solution

Applying the pro-forma working, the goodwill can be calculated as follows.

	$	$
Consideration transferred		80,000
Less net assets at acquisition		
Ordinary share capital	50,000	
Pre-acquisition retained earnings	10,000	
		(60,000)
Goodwill		20,000

4.5.5 Fair value adjustments

If the book values of the net assets acquired in the subsidiary's financial statements do not reflect the assets' fair value, fair value adjustments must be made when calculating goodwill.

In the exam, the scenario will make clear whether or not any fair value adjustments should be made, usually by stating that the fair value of an asset or liability is greater or less than its current book value by $x.

Example: Goodwill with fair value adjustments

Let's revisit Wheat Co and Barley Co, which we looked at in Section 4.3 above.

Wheat Co purchased 100% of the 20,000 $1 ordinary shares of Barley Co on 1 January 20X5 for a consideration of $68,000. At that date, the balance of Barley Co's retained earnings was $21,000.

As we saw in Section 4.3, the fair value of Barley Co's non-current assets was $23,000 greater than their net book value at acquisition.

Required

Calculate the goodwill arising on the acquisition of Barley Co.

Solution

Goodwill

	$	$
Consideration transferred		68,000
Less: Net assets at acquisition		
Ordinary share capital	20,000	
Retained earnings	21,000	
Fair value adjustment	23,000	
		(64,000)
Goodwill		4,000

4.6 Forms of consideration

The consideration paid by the parent for the shares in the subsidiary can take different forms. IFRS 3 requires this consideration to be measured at fair value. This will affect the calculation of goodwill. Here are some examples.

4.6.1 Contingent consideration

Contingent consideration is where the acquirer has an obligation to transfer additional assets (eg cash) or equity interests (shares) to the former owners of the subsidiary as part of the exchange for control of the subsidiary if **specified future events occur or conditions are met**.

The parent should **measure** this contingent consideration at its **acquisition date fair value** and record it as part of the consideration transferred in the goodwill working. It should be classified as either a liability or equity on the basis of the definitions of an equity instrument and a financial liability in IAS 32 *Financial instruments: presentation*.

Subsequently, for changes in the fair value due to additional information about facts and circumstances that **existed at the acquisition date, goodwill should be adjusted** as long as it is within one year of the acquisition date.

For all other changes (eg targets met), contingent consideration classified as **equity** should **not be remeasured**. Contingent consideration classified as a **liability** should be **remeasured** with the subsequent **gain or loss** being recorded in **profit or loss**.

4.6.2 Deferred consideration

An agreement may be made that part of the consideration for the combination will be paid at a future date. This consideration will therefore be discounted to its present value using the acquiring entity's cost of capital.

Example: Contingent and deferred consideration

P acquired 75% of S's 80 million $1 shares on 1 January 20X6. Scheduled payments comprised:

- $3.50 per share payable immediately in cash

- $108 million payable on 1 January 20X7

- An amount equivalent to three times the profit after tax of S for the year ended 31 December 20X6, payable on 31 March 20X7.

- New shares issued in P on a 1 for 3 basis (the nominal value of P's shares is $1 and the market value of P's shares at 1 January 20X6 was $4.50)

On 1 January 20X6 the fair value attributed to the consideration based on profit was $50 million. By 31 December 20X6 the fair value was considered to be $55 million. The change arose as a result of a change in expected profits.

P's cost of capital is 8%.

How should the consideration transferred be treated in the financial statements of the P group for the year ended 31 December 20X6?

Solution

As at 1 January 20X6, the consideration transferred will be recorded at:

	$m
Cash consideration (80m shares × 75% × $3.50)	210
Deferred consideration ($108m × 1/1.08)	100
Contingent consideration	50
Shares (1/3 × 75% × 80m × $4.50)	90
Total consideration	450

At 31 December 20X6 $8m ($100m x 8%) will be charged to finance costs, being the **unwinding of the discount** on the deferred consideration. The deferred consideration was discounted by $8m to allow for the time value of money. At 1 January 20X7 the full amount becomes payable.

The **liability** relating to the **contingent consideration** must be **remeasured** to its revised fair value of $55 million at 31 December 20X6, and the **loss** of $5 million should be **recorded in profit or loss**. Goodwill should not be revised because the change in fair value relates to a post-acquisition event (change in expected profits) rather than additional information regarding facts at the acquisition date.

4.7 Adjustments after the initial accounting is complete

Sometimes the fair values of the acquiree's identifiable assets, liabilities or contingent liabilities or the consideration transferred can only be determined **provisionally** by the **end of the period in which the combination takes place**. In this situation, the acquirer **should account for the combination using those provisional values**. The acquirer should **recognise any adjustments** to those provisional values as a result of completing the initial accounting:

(a)   **Within twelve months** of the acquisition date and
(b)   **From** the acquisition date (ie retrospectively)

This means that:

(a)   The **carrying amount** of an item that is recognised or adjusted as a result of completing the initial accounting shall be calculated **as if its fair value** at the acquisition date **had been recognised from that date**.

(b)   **Goodwill should be adjusted** from the acquisition date by an amount equal to the adjustment to the fair value of the item being recognised or adjusted.

Any further adjustments after the initial accounting is complete should be **recognised only to correct an error** in accordance with IAS 8 *Accounting policies, changes in accounting estimates and errors*. Any subsequent changes in estimates are dealt with in accordance with IAS 8 (ie the effect is recognised in the current and future periods). IAS 8 requires an entity to account for an error correction retrospectively, and to present financial statements as if the error had never occurred by restating the comparative information for the prior period(s) in which the error occurred.

4.7.1 Impairment to goodwill

Goodwill should be **reviewed for impairment every year**. In the reporting periods subsequent to the acquisition, goodwill should be carried in the statement of financial position at **cost less any accumulated impairment losses**.

In the exam, impairment to goodwill could either be stated as an absolute amount (eg goodwill has been impaired by $x) or as a percentage.

Goodwill arising on consolidation is subjected to an annual impairment review and impairment may be expressed as an amount or as a percentage. The journal to record the impairment of goodwill is as follows:

DEBIT   Group retained earnings
CREDIT   Goodwill

Let us return to the Wheat Co acquisition of Barley Co.

Example: Goodwill impairment

On 31 December 20X5 an impairment review was conducted and it was decided that the goodwill on acquisition of Barley Co has been impaired by 10%.

Required

Taking the results of previous workings, calculate the goodwill arising on the acquisition of Barley Co following the impairment.

Solution

Goodwill

	$	$
Consideration transferred		68,000
Less: Net assets at acquisition		
Ordinary share capital	20,000	
Retained earnings	21,000	
Fair value adjustment	23,000	
		(64,000)
		4,000
Less: Impairment loss on goodwill (4,000 x 10%)		(400)
Goodwill		3,600

4.7.2 Reverse acquisitions

IFRS 3 (Revised) also addresses a certain type of acquisition, known as a **reverse acquisition or takeover**. This is where Company A acquires ownership of Company B through a share exchange. (For example, a private entity may arrange to have itself **acquired** by a smaller public entity as a means of obtaining a stock exchange listing.) The number of shares issued by Company A as consideration to the shareholders of Company B is so great that control of the combined entity after the transaction is with the shareholders of Company B.

In legal terms Company A may be regarded as the parent or continuing entity, but IFRS 3 (revised) states that, as it is the Company B shareholders who control the combined entity, **Company B should be treated as the acquirer**. Company B should apply the acquisition (or purchase) method to the assets and liabilities of Company A.

4.8 Calculating consolidated retained earnings

Retained earnings are reported as part of equity in P Co's consolidated statement of financial position. In consolidating S Co's retained earnings a crucial question to ask is, 'How much did S Co earn as part of the group? Only the retained earnings which arise in S Co **after the acquisition** should be consolidated as part of the group's retained earnings.

As we have mentioned above, fair value adjustments also affect group retained earnings. Also, as you would expect, would any impairment losses (for example, goodwill impairment).

The pro forma for the consolidated retained earnings working is as follows. Don't worry about the associate/joint venture column for now. We will look at this in Chapter 10. Make sure you flag this working for later reference.

	Parent	Subsidiary	Associate/ joint venture
Per question	X	X	X
Adjustments	X/(X)	X/(X)	X/(X)
Fair value adjustments movement		X/(X)	X/(X)
Pre-acquisition retained earnings		(X)	(X)
		Y	Z
Group share of post-acq'n ret'd earnings:			
Subsidiary (Y × %)	X		
Associate/joint venture (Z × %)	X		
Less: Group share of impairment losses to date	(X)		
	X		

Let's return to Wheat Co and Barley Co. We will first calculate the consolidated retained earnings, then pull together all the workings that we have seen previously in this section to prepare Wheat Co's consolidated statement of financial position.

Example: Consolidated retained earnings

Wheat Co and Barley Co's individual statements of financial position as at 31 December 20X5 are given below.

WHEAT CO
STATEMENT OF FINANCIAL POSITION AS AT 31 DECEMBER 20X5

	$	$
Assets		
Non-current assets		
Tangible assets	63,000	
Investment in S Co at cost	68,000	
		131,000
Current assets		65,000
Total assets		196,000
Equity and liabilities		
Equity		
Ordinary shares of $1 each	80,000	
Retained earnings	96,000	
		176,000
Current liabilities		20,000
Total equity and liabilities		196,000

BARLEY CO
STATEMENT OF FINANCIAL POSITION AS AT 31 DECEMBER 20X5

	$	$
Assets		
Tangible non-current assets		28,000
Current assets		43,000
Total assets		71,000
Equity and liabilities		
Equity		
Ordinary shares of $1 each	20,000	
Retained earnings	41,000	
		61,000
Current liabilities		10,000
Total equity and liabilities		71,000

Barley Co has not incorporated any revaluation in its books of account.

Required

(a)   Calculate Wheat Co's consolidated retained earnings as at 31 December 20X5.

(b)   Prepare Wheat Co's consolidated statement of financial position based on the above and previous workings, including:

–   The non-current asset fair value adjustment of $23,000
–   The 10% impairment on goodwill

Solution

(a)   **Consolidated retained earnings**

The individual statements of financial position provided give us Wheat Co and Barley Co's retained earnings at 31 December 20X5, one year after Barley Co was acquired.

	Wheat Co $	Barley Co $
Per question	96,000	41,000
Depreciation adjustment (Section 4.3)		(3,000)
Pre-acquisition retained earnings (Section 4.5.5)		(21,000)
Post-acquisition Barley Co		17,000
Group share in Barley Co		
(17,000 × 100%)	17,000	
	113,000	
Less: Group share of impairment losses to date (Section 4.7.1)	(400)	
Group retained earnings	112,600	

(b)   **Consolidated statement of financial position**

To prepare the consolidated statement of financial position, we need the three workings that we have already seen. They are provided again here to give you an idea of how the consolidation process, which we introduced in Section 4, works in practice:

(i)   Fair value adjustment (here, W4)
(ii)   Goodwill (here, W2) and
(iii)   Retained earnings (here, W3)

Once we have these supporting workings, we **add together each of the asset and liability balances** in each company's statement of financial position (**except for the ordinary shares**). Don't forget that in this case, a fair value adjustment must be made to the non-current assets balance.

Ready? Wheat Co's consolidated statement of financial position is as follows.

WHEAT CO CONSOLIDATED STATEMENT OF FINANCIAL POSITION AS AT 31 AUGUST 20X5

	$	$
Non-current assets		
Property, plant and equipment (63,000 + 28,000 + FV adj 20,000 (W4))	111,000	
Goodwill (W2)	3,600	
		114,600
Current assets (65,000 + 43,000)		108,000
		222,600
Equity and liabilities		
Equity		
Ordinary shares of $1 each	80,000	
Retained earnings (W3)	112,600	
		192,600
Current liabilities (20,000 + 10,000)		30,000
		222,600

Workings

1   *Group structure*

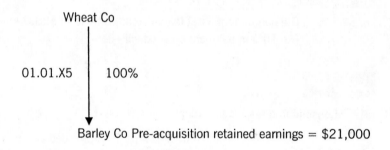

Wheat Co

01.01.X5   100%

Barley Co Pre-acquisition retained earnings = $21,000

2   *Goodwill*

	$	$
Consideration transferred		68,000
Net assets at acquisition as represented by		
Ordinary share capital	20,000	
Retained earnings (W1)	21,000	
Fair value adjustment (W4)	23,000	
		(64,000)
		4,000
		(400)
Goodwill		3,600

3   *Retained earnings*

	Wheat Co $	Barley Co $
Per question	96,000	41,000
Depreciation adjustment (W4)		(3,000)
Pre-acquisition retained earnings		(21,000)
Post-acquisition Barley Co		17,000
Group share in Barley Co		
(17,000 × 100%)	17,000	
	113,000	
Less: Group share of impairment losses to date	(400)	
Group retained earnings	112,600	

4 *Fair value adjustments*

	At acq'n date	Movement	Year end
	$	$	$
Property, plant and equipment	23,000	(3,000)	20,000
	23,000	(3,000)	20,000
	↓	↓	↓
	Goodwill	Ret'd earnings	SOFP

Note. Barley Co has not incorporated the revaluation in its draft statement of financial position. Before beginning the consolidation workings we must therefore adjust for the fair value uplift at the acquisition date, the additional depreciation charge that must be reflected in the subsidiary's post-acquisition retained earnings and the remaining uplift that must be reflected in the consolidated statement of financial position. The fair value table working is an efficient way of dealing with this, even where there are several fair value adjustments.

Section summary

Goodwill is calculated by comparing the fair value of the consideration with the fair value of the identifiable assets and liabilities acquired.

The accounting requirements and disclosures of the **fair value exercise** are covered by **IFRS 3 (revised)**. **IFRS 13** *Fair value measurement* gives extensive guidance on how the fair value of assets and liabilities should be established.

IFRS 3 does not allow combinations to be accounted for as a uniting of interests; all combinations must be treated as acquisitions.

5 Non-controlling interests

Introduction

A parent company does not have to **own** 100% of a subsidiary in order to **control it. Usually a holding of** more than 50% of the voting shares gives **control**. Where this is the case, the outside shareholders who own the smaller portion of the shares are known as **non-controlling interests (NCI)**.

5.1 Principles of the consolidated statement of financial position

As you have seen in the final example in Section 4 above, 100% of the assets and liabilities of subsidiary companies are included in the consolidated statement of financial position. This applies even in the case of subsidiaries which are only partly owned, as the consolidated statement of financial position shows all of the assets and liabilities that are **controlled** by the parent.

However, when the parent company does not own 100% of the shares, a proportion of the net assets of such subsidiaries in fact belongs to investors from outside the group (**non-controlling interests**, referred to as NCI below). This figure must be shown within the equity section of the statement of financial position.

NON-CONTROLLING INTERESTS. The equity in a subsidiary not attributable, directly or indirectly, to a parent. *(IFRS 3, IFRS 10)*

KEY TERM

Imagine a situation where Company A acquires 80% of Company B's shares. Company A gains over 50% of the voting power in Company B. Therefore, Company A controls Company B – Company B is Company A's subsidiary. Company B's assets and liabilities would therefore be 100% consolidated in the group consolidated statement of financial position.

However, 20% of Company B's shares and retained earnings are actually owned by other parties. These are referred to as non-controlling interests. In order to ensure that the statement of financial position reflects the fact that Company A has not acquired all of Company B's net assets, the value of non-controlling interests needs to be shown separately, and goodwill needs to be adjusted accordingly.

5.2 Accounting treatment in the group financial statements

Where there are non-controlling interests in a subsidiary, the subsidiary must still be **100% consolidated in the parent company's financial statements**.

However, the **group financial statements** need to show the **extent to which the subsidiary's net assets are owned by other parties** (ie the non-controlling interests). It is therefore necessary to calculate and disclose the value of non-controlling interests in the group financial statements.

IFRS 3 allows two alternative ways of calculating non-controlling interests in the group statement of financial position. Non-controlling interests **at the acquisition date** can be valued at:

(a)   Their **proportionate share** of the fair value of the subsidiary's net assets or
(b)   **Fair value** (usually based on the market value of the shares held by the non-controlling interests)

The diagram below summarises the differences between the two methods (using the example of an 80% subsidiary).

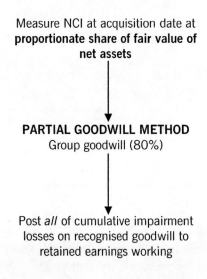

Measure NCI at acquisition date at **proportionate share of fair value of net assets**

PARTIAL GOODWILL METHOD
Group goodwill (80%)

Post *all* of cumulative impairment losses on recognised goodwill to retained earnings working

Measure NCI at acquisition date at **fair value** (ie how much it would cost the parent to buy the remaining shares)

FAIR VALUE METHOD

Group goodwill	80%
NCI goodwill	20%
	100%

Post *group share (80%)* of cumulative impairment losses on recognised goodwill to retained earnings working & NCI share of impairment losses (20%) to NCI working

You are required to be able to apply both of these methods in F2. The option to value non-controlling interests at fair value at acquisition was introduced by the revised IFRS 3, but it is just an option. Companies can choose to adopt it or to continue to value non-controlling interests using the proportionate method.

Exam skills

The exam question will tell you which method to use. If you are required to use the fair value method, then you will be given the share price or told what the fair value of the non-controlling interests is. In recent years, the fair value method has been more frequently examined in the F2 paper.

5.3 Attribution of losses

Under IFRS 10, non-controlling interests can be negative. This is consistent with the idea that non-controlling interests are part of the equity of the group.

Example: Non-controlling interests (1)

P buys 75% of S for $60m on 1 January 20X8. On 1 January 20X8 the share capital of S was $15m and the retained earnings of S were $25m. The fair values of S's net assets were equivalent to their book values at acquisition.

Required

(a)   Calculate goodwill on the assumption it is group policy to value non-controlling interests at the date of acquisition at the proportionate share of the fair value of the acquiree's identifiable assets acquired and liabilities assumed.

(b)   Calculate goodwill on the assumption it is group policy to value non-controlling interests at fair value at the date of acquisition which was $16m.

(c)   Demonstrate that the fair value goodwill method results in goodwill for the group and non-controlling interests.

Solution

(a)   *Partial goodwill method*

	$m	$m
Consideration transferred		60
NCI (at % FV of net assets) (25% × 40)		10
Fair value of net assets at acquisition		
Share capital	15	
Retained earnings	25	
		(40)
		30

(b)   *Fair value goodwill method*

	$m	$m
Consideration transferred		60
NCI (at full fair value)		16
Fair value of net assets at acquisition		
Share capital	15	
Retained earnings	25	
		(40)
		36

(c)   *Proof that fair value goodwill method results in goodwill for group and NCI*

		Group	NCI
	$m	$m	$m
Consideration transferred/FV of NCI		60	16
Fair value of net assets at acquisition			
Share capital	15		
Retained earnings	25		
	40		
Group share/NCI share	× 75%	(30)	× 25% (10)
		30	6

$36m

5.4 Calculating the value of non-controlling interests

As we stated above, non-controlling interests must be valued and shown on a separate line under 'Equity' in the consolidated statement of financial position.

5.4.1 Non-controlling interests' pro forma working

The value of non-controlling interests is calculated as follows:

NCI at acquisition (at % FV of net assets or at fair value)*	X
NCI share of post-acquisition retained earnings (from retained earnings working Y × NCI %)	X
Less NCI share of impairment losses (only if NCI at full FV at acquisition)	(X)
	X

* Where the non-controlling interests are measured at fair value at acquisition, this value will be provided in the question.

Where the non-controlling interests are measured at their proportionate share of the fair value of net assets, their value at acquisition is calculated as the total equity of the subsidiary at the date of acquisition x the NCI%.

5.4.2 Retained earnings

You will recall that the retained earnings pro forma working included the **group share** of the subsidiary's post-acquisition reserves. In the examples we have seen thus far, this is calculated as 100% of the subsidiary's post-acquisition earnings.

The existence of non-controlling interests means that not all of the post-acquisition earnings belong to the group. Therefore, in calculating the group's consolidated retained earnings, only the percentage owned by the group should be taken into account. For example, where P Co owns 60% of the shares in S Co, if the post-acquisition earnings of S Co are $100,000, the group's share of the post-acquisition reserves would be $60,000 (60% of $100,000).

What happens to the remaining portion of post-acquisition earnings? This is taken into account in calculating non-controlling interests, as shown in the pro forma above.

Below, the two methods are applied in an extended exam-standard example. The proportionate method and the fair value method are presented side by side for ease of comparison.

Example: Non-controlling interests (2)

The statements of financial position for two entities as at 31 December 20X9 are presented below:

STATEMENTS OF FINANCIAL POSITION AS AT 31 DECEMBER 20X9

	BC $'000	HJ $'000
Non-current assets		
Property, plant and equipment	2,300	1,900
Available for sale investment (note 1)	920	–
	3,220	1,900
Current assets	3,340	1,790
	6,560	3,690
Equity		
Share capital	1,000	500
Retained earnings	3,430	1,800
Other components of equity	200	–
	4,630	2,300
Non-current liabilities	350	290
Current liabilities	1,580	1,100
	6,560	3,690

Notes

(1)   BC acquired a 60% investment in HJ on 1 January 20X6 for $720,000 when the retained earnings of HJ were $300,000. The investment has been classified as available for sale in BC's individual financial statements, with any associated gains or losses recorded within other components of equity.

(2)   As at 1 January 20X6 the fair value of the net assets acquired was the same as the book value with the exception of an item of property, plant and equipment with a fair value of $800,000 and a carrying value of $600,000. This asset was assessed to have a remaining useful life of ten years from the date of acquisition.

(3)   An impairment review was conducted at 31 December 20X9 and it was decided that the goodwill on acquisition of HJ was impaired by 10%.

Required

Prepare the consolidated statement of financial position for the BC Group as at 31 December 20X9 under the following assumptions:

(a)   It is group policy to value non-controlling interests at fair value at the date of acquisition. The fair value of the non-controlling interests at 1 January 20X6 was $480,000.

(b)   It is group policy to value non-controlling interests at their proportionate share of the fair value of the net assets at acquisition.

Solution

BC GROUP
CONSOLIDATED STATEMENT OF FINANCIAL POSITION AS AT 31 DECEMBER 20X9

	(a) $'000	(b) $'000
Non-current assets		
Property, plant and equipment (2,300 + 1,900 + 120 (W5))	4,320	4,320
Goodwill (W2)	180	108
	4,500	4,428
Current assets (3,340 + 1,790)	5,130	5,130
	9,630	9,558
Equity attributable to owners of the parent		
Share capital	1,000	1,000
Retained earnings (W3)	4,270	4,270
	5,270	5,270
Non-controlling interests (W4)	1,040	968
	6,310	6,238
Non-current liabilities (350 + 290)	640	640
Current liabilities (1,580 + 1,100)	2,680	2,680
	9,630	9,558

Note. Other components of equity have been cancelled on consolidation, as they relate to the revaluation gains on the investment in HJ (which has been treated as available for sale). In order to cancel the cost of the investment of $720,000 in the goodwill working, both the investment at its fair value of $920,000 and the revaluation gains of $200,000 must be eliminated on consolidation.

Workings

1   *Group structure*

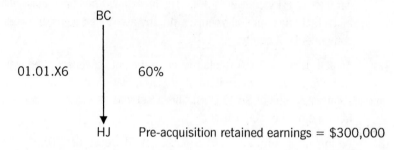

BC

01.01.X6   60%

HJ   Pre-acquisition retained earnings = $300,000

2   *Goodwill*

	Part (a)		Part (b)	
	$'000	$'000	$'000	$'000
Consideration transferred *		720		720
Non-controlling interests		480	(1,000 × 40%)**	400
Fair value of net assets at acquisition:				
Share capital	500		500	
Retained earnings (W1)	300		300	
Fair value adjustment (W5)	200		200	
		(1,000)		(1,000)
		200		120
Less impairment losses to date (10%)		(20)		(12)
		180		108

* This comprises the investment at its fair value of $920,000 less the revaluation gains of $200,000 in other components of equity.

** The $1,000,000 comprises HJ's equity of $500,000, retained earnings at acquisition of $300,000 and fair value adjustment relating to property, plant and equipment of $200,000.

3   *Retained earnings*

	BC $'000	HJ $'000
Per question	3,430	1,800
Fair value adjustment – extra depreciation (W5)		(80)
Pre-acquisition (W1)		(300)
		1,420
Group share of HJ's post-acquisition reserves:		
(1,420 × 60%)	852	
Less impairment loss on goodwill:		
Part (a) (20 (W2) × 60%)/*Part (b)* (12 (W2))	(12)	
	4,270	

4   *Non-controlling interests*

	Part (a) $'000	Part (b) $'000
NCI at acquisition (W2)	480	400
NCI share of post-acquisition reserves (1,420 (W3) × 40%)	568	568
NCI share of impairment losses (20 (W2) × 40%)	(8)	(–)
	1,040	968

5   *Fair value adjustment*

	At acquisition 01.01.X6 $'000	Movement X6, X7, X8, X9 $'000	Year end 31.12.X9 $'000
Property, plant and equipment (800 – 600)	200	(80)*	120
	Goodwill	Retained earnings	Property, plant and equipment

* Extra depreciation = 200 × 1/10 = 20 annual deprecation × 4 years = 80

Exam skills

In the exam, the **consolidation question** will tell you which method to use. It will state either:

It is the group policy to value the non-controlling interests at full (or fair) value or

It is the group policy to value the non-controlling interests at its proportionate share of the (fair value of the) subsidiary's identifiable net assets

5.5 Impairment of goodwill

We discussed the impairment of goodwill in Section 4 above.

When non-controlling interests are measured using the **proportionate method**, the double entry to write off the impairment is:

DEBIT   Group retained earnings
CREDIT   Goodwill

However, when non-controlling interests are valued **at fair value**, the goodwill in the statement of financial position includes goodwill attributable to the non-controlling interests. In this case, the double entry will reflect the non-controlling interests' proportion based on their shareholding as follows:

DEBIT   Group retained earnings
CREDIT   Goodwill

DEBIT   Non-controlling interests
CREDIT   Goodwill

In our solution to the example in Section 5.4 above, the non-controlling interests hold 40%. The double entry for the 10% impairment of goodwill using the proportionate method would be:

DEBIT   Retained earnings $12,000
CREDIT   Goodwill $12,000

The double entry for the impairment of goodwill using the fair value method would be:

DEBIT   Retained earnings $12,000
DEBIT   Non-controlling interests $8,000
CREDIT   Goodwill $20,000

Section summary

When there are non-controlling interests in a subsidiary the consolidated statement of financial position will include 100% of the subsidiary's assets and liabilities. This shows the assets and liabilities under group **control**.

The **ownership** of the net assets is shown by including **non-controlling interests** in the equity section of the statement of financial position.

There are **two methods** of calculating non-controlling interests at acquisition:

(a)   The NCI's proportionate share of the subsidiary's net assets (the partial goodwill method)
(b)   Fair value (the full goodwill method)

6   Other adjustments to the statement of financial position

Introduction

We will now consider how the consolidated financial statement of financial position is prepared.

6.1 Basic procedure

You will recall that a number of adjustments may be required to the consolidated statement of financial position.

(a)   **Fair value adjustments** need to be made where the fair value of an asset/liability in the subsidiary is different from its net book value in the subsidiary's accounts.

(b)   The asset **shares in subsidiary companies** which appears in the parent company's financial statements will be matched with the share capital in the subsidiaries' financial statements.

(c)   There may be **intragroup trading** within the group. For example, S Co may sell goods on credit to P Co. P Co would then be a receivable in the accounts of S Co, while S Co would be a payable in the accounts of P Co. These need to be cancelled out so that the consolidated statement of financial position shows amounts owing between the group as a single entity and the outside world, and **not** those due between members of the group.

(d)   There may be **intragroup balances**, either as a result of intragroup trading or financing (for example, the parent company lending to the subsidiary). Intragroup balances must also be eliminated in full.

(e)   **Property, plant and equipment** may have been transferred from one company to another. The unrealised profit on intragroup transfers of property, plant and equipment must be eliminated, and the associated depreciation adjusted down.

We have already worked through (a) and (b) in the sections above. Let's now turn our attention to the adjustments described in (c), (d) and (e).

6.2 Intragroup trading

6.2.1 Unrealised profit

Any receivable/payable balances outstanding between the companies are cancelled on consolidation. No further problem arises if all such intragroup transactions are **undertaken at cost**, without any mark-up for profit.

However, each company in a group is a separate trading entity and may wish to treat other group companies in the same way as any other customer. In this case, a company (say A Co) may buy goods at one price and sell them at a higher price to another group company (B Co). The accounts of A Co will quite properly include the profit earned on sales to B Co; and similarly B Co's statement of financial position will include inventories at their cost to B Co, ie at the amount at which they were purchased from A Co.

This gives rise to two problems.

(a)   Although A Co makes a profit as soon as it sells goods to B Co, the group does not make a sale or achieve a profit until an outside customer buys the goods from B Co.

(b)   Any purchases from A Co which remain unsold by B Co at the year end will be included in B Co's inventory. Their value in the statement of financial position will be their cost to B Co, which is not the same as their cost to the group.

The objective of consolidated accounts is to present the financial position of several connected companies as that of a single entity, the group. This means that **in a consolidated statement of financial position, the only profits recognised should be those earned by the group** in providing goods or services to outsiders; and similarly, inventory in the consolidated statement of financial position should be valued at cost to the group.

Suppose that a parent company P Co buys goods for $1,600 and sells them to a wholly-owned subsidiary S Co for $2,000. The goods are in S Co's inventory at the year end and appear in S Co's statement of financial position at $2,000. In this case, P Co will record a profit of $400 in its individual accounts, but from the group's point of view the figures are:

Cost	$1,600
External sales	nil
Closing inventory at cost	$1,600
Profit/loss	nil

If we add together the figures for retained earnings and inventory in the individual statements of financial position of P Co and S Co the resulting figures for consolidated retained earnings and consolidated inventory will each be overstated by $400. A **consolidation adjustment** is therefore necessary as follows.

DEBIT   Group retained earnings (adjust in the **seller's** column in the retained earnings working)

CREDIT   Group inventories (statement of financial position)

With the amount of **profit unrealised** by the group.

Question 9.4   Unrealised profit

Learning outcome B1

P Co acquired all the shares in S Co one year ago when the reserves (retained earnings) of S Co stood at $10,000. Draft statements of financial position for each company are as follows.

	P Co		S Co	
	$	$	$	$
Assets				
Non-current assets				
Property, plant and equipment	80,000			40,000
Investment in S Co at cost	46,000			
		126,000		
Current assets		40,000		30,000
Total assets		166,000		70,000
Equity and liabilities				
Equity				
Ordinary shares of $1 each	100,000		30,000	
Retained earnings	45,000		22,000	
		145,000		52,000
Current liabilities		21,000		18,000
Total equity and liabilities		166,000		70,000

During the year S Co sold goods to P Co for $50,000, the profit to S Co being 20% of selling price. At the end of the reporting period, $15,000 of these goods remained unsold in the inventories of P Co.
At the same date, P Co owed S Co $12,000 for goods bought and this debt is included in the trade payables of P Co and the receivables of S Co.

The goodwill arising on consolidation has been impaired. The amount of the impairment is $1,500.

Required

Prepare a draft consolidated statement of financial position for P Co.

6.2.2 Non-controlling interests and unrealised profits

If the **intragroup sale was made by the parent company**, there is no effect on the non-controlling interests.

However, if the **intragroup sale was made by the subsidiary** with non-controlling interests, we need to think about the impact this will have.

Consider this: A subsidiary S Co is 75% owned and sells goods to the parent company, P Co, for $16,000 cost plus $4,000 profit ie for $20,000. If these items remain in P Co's inventory at the end of the reporting period, the unrealised profit of $4,000 earned by S Co and charged to P Co will be partly owned by the non-controlling interests of S Co.

To do this, using the methods we have followed up to now, the adjustment for unrealised profits is:

Entries to learn

DEBIT   Retained earnings (of the company who made the sale)
CREDIT   Group inventories (statement of financial position)

The credit is made on the face of the group statement of financial position and the debit to the **appropriate column** of the retained reserves working. This will then split the unrealised profit between the group and the NCI if the subsidiary made the sale.

Example: Non-controlling interests and intra-group profits (1)

P Co has owned 75% of the shares of S Co since the incorporation of that company. During the year to 31 December 20X2, S Co sold goods costing $16,000 to P Co at a price of $20,000 and these goods were still unsold by P Co at the end of the year. Draft statements of financial position of each company at 31 December 20X2 were as follows.

	P Co		S Co	
	$	$	$	$
Assets				
Non-current assets				
Property, plant and equipment	125,000		120,000	
Investment: 75,000 shares in S Co at cost	75,000		–	
		200,000		120,000
Current assets				
Inventories	50,000		48,000	
Trade receivables	20,000		16,000	
		70,000		64,000
Total assets		270,000		184,000
Equity and liabilities				
Equity				
Ordinary shares of $1 each fully paid	80,000		100,000	
Retained earnings	150,000		60,000	
		230,000		160,000
Current liabilities		40,000		24,000
Total equity and liabilities		270,000		184,000

Required

Prepare the consolidated statement of financial position of P Co at 31 December 20X2. It is the group's policy to value non-controlling interests at acquisition at their proportionate share of the subsidiary's net assets.

Solution

P CO
CONSOLIDATED STATEMENT OF FINANCIAL POSITION AS AT 31 DECEMBER 20X2

	$	$
Assets		
Property, plant and equipment (125,000 + 120,000)		245,000
Current assets		
Inventories $(50,000 + 48,000 – 4,000 unrealised profit)	94,000	
Trade receivables (20,000 + 16,000)	36,000	
		130,000
Total assets		375,000
Equity and liabilities		
Equity		
Ordinary shares of $1 each	80,000	
Retained earnings (W2)	192,000	
		272,000
Non-controlling interests (W3)		39,000
		311,000
Current liabilities (40,000 + 24,000)		64,000
Total equity and liabilities		375,000

Workings

1   *Group structure*

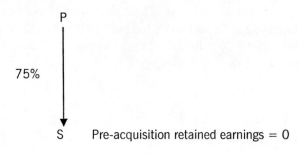

P

75%

S   Pre-acquisition retained earnings = 0

2   *Retained earnings*

	P Co $	S Co $
Per question	150,000	60,000
Less unrealised profit (20,000 – 16,000)		(4,000)
Pre-acquisition		–
		56,000
Share of S Co: $56,000 × 75%	42,000	
	192,000	

3   *Non-controlling interests*

	$
NCI at acquisition (25% × 100,000)	25,000
NCI share of post-acquisition retained earnings (25% × 56,000)	14,000
	39,000

Note. No goodwill working is necessary as the acquisition was at the date of incorporation. The profit earned by S Co but unrealised by the group is $4,000, of which $3,000 (75%) is attributable to the group and $1,000 (25%) to non-controlling interests. This is reflected in the working by making the **adjustment to profit in S's column** in the retained earnings working.

Example: Non-controlling interests and intra-group profits (2)

Explain how the answer to the above example would change if the facts remained the same except that the goods were sold by P Co to S Co.

Solution

Note. As above, no goodwill working is necessary as the acquisition was at the date of incorporation. The full unrealised profit is always deducted from group inventories but this time, as P made the sale, the debit is made against P Co's retained earnings $4,000. The full amount is charged to consolidated retained earnings and none to non-controlling interests.

	P Co $	S Co $
Retained earnings		
Per question	150,000	60,000
Less unrealised profit	(4,000)	
	146,000	
Pre-acquisition		60,000
Share of S Co: $60,000 × 75%	45,000	
	191,000	
Non-controlling interests		
NCI at acquisition (25% × 100,000)		25,000
NCI share of post-acquisition retained earnings (25% × 60,000)		15,000
		40,000

Section summary

Unrealised profit must be removed from the consolidated statement of financial position charged against the retained earnings of the company that **made the sale**.

6.3 Intragroup sales of non-current assets

The transfer of property, plant and equipment at a profit within the group gives rise to the same kind of issues as the transfer of inventories, namely that the property, plant and equipment should be stated at cost to the group and the profit on the sale is unrealised.

An additional issue is that the items of property, plant and equipment will subsequently be depreciated based on the new carrying value. This means that the unrealised profit on sale becomes realised through use, which therefore reduces the consolidation adjustment.

The adjustment should be made in the books of the company making the sale as follows:

(1) Calculate the unrealised profit:

Unrealised profit on transfer	X
Less proportion depreciated by year end	(X)
	X

(2) Adjust in the books of the company making the sale:

DEBIT (↓)   Retained earnings
CREDIT (↓) Property, plant and equipment

Example: Intragroup sales of non-current assets

P owns 100% of S. On 1 January 20X3 P transfers a machine with a NBV of $20,000 to S for $25,000. At that date, the asset has a remaining useful life of five years.

Required

What is the adjustment required in the consolidated statement of financial position of the P group as at 31 December 20X3 regarding the intragroup transfer of the machine?

Solution

(1) Calculate the unrealised profit:

	$
Unrealised profit on transfer ($25,000 – $20,000)	5,000
Less proportion depreciated by year end ($5,000/5 years)	(1,000)
	4,000

(2) Adjust in the books of the company making the sale:

DEBIT (↓)	Retained earnings of P	$4,000	
CREDIT (↓)	Property, plant and equipment		$4,000

6.3.1 Non-controlling interests and intragroup sales of non-current assets

We will now consider the effect of NCI on intragroup sales of non-current assets.

The principle is the same as when dealing with unrealised profits on intragroup trading, adjust the retained earnings of the company that made the sale. The effect of NCI is best dealt with by the following example.

Example: NCI and intragroup sale of non-current assets

P Co acquired 60% of S Co on incorporation. On 1 January 20X1 S Co sells plant with a net book value of $10,000 to P Co for $12,500. At 1 January 20X1 the plant had a remaining useful life of ten years. The companies make up financial statements to 31 December 20X1 and the balances on their retained earnings at that date are:

P Co	After charging depreciation of 10% on plant	$27,000
S Co	Including profit on sale of plant	$18,000

Required

Show the workings for consolidated retained earnings.

Solution

Retained earnings

	P Co $	S Co $
Per question	27,000	18,000
Unrealised profit on sale of plant (W1)		(2,250)
Pre-acquisition		–
		15,750
Share of S Co: $15,750 × 60%	9,450	
	36,450	

Workings

1 *Unrealised profit*

	$
Unrealised profit on transfer ($12,500 – $10,000)	2,500
Less proportion depreciated by year end ($2,500/10 years)	(250)
	2,250

Notes

1   Non-controlling interests in the retained earnings of S Co are 40% × $15,750 = $6,300.

2   The asset is written down to cost and depreciation on the profit element is removed. The group profit for the year is thus reduced by a net (($2,250) × 60%) = $1,350.

3   As shown above, the adjustment to retained earnings is made in the company that made the sale.

Section summary

The unrealised profits on the intragroup sale of non-current assets includes an adjustment for excess depreciation.

7 Acquisition of a subsidiary during its accounting period

Introduction

In paper F1, all acquisitions of subsidiaries took place at the end of the accounting period. In paper F2, you may be asked to deal with examples where the parent acquires a subsidiary during its accounting period.

7.1 Accounting problem

As we have already seen, at the end of the accounting year it will be necessary to prepare consolidated accounts.

The subsidiary company's statement of financial position to be consolidated will show the subsidiary's retained earnings as at the end of the period. For consolidation purposes, however, it is necessary to distinguish between:

(a)   Profits earned before acquisition

(b)   Profits earned after acquisition

In practice, a subsidiary company's profit may not accrue evenly over the year, for example, the subsidiary might be engaged in a trade, such as toy sales, with marked seasonal fluctuations. Nevertheless, in the exam the assumption can be made that **profits accrue evenly** whenever it is impracticable to arrive at an accurate split of pre- and post-acquisition profits. Questions will normally say to assume that profits accrue evenly over the period.

Once the amount of pre-acquisition profit has been established the appropriate consolidation workings (goodwill, retained earnings) can be produced.

Question 9.5   Mid-year acquisition

Learning outcome B1

Hinge Co acquired 80% of the ordinary shares of Singe Co on 1 April 20X5.

On 31 December 20X4 Singe Co's financial statements showed a share premium account of $4,000 and retained earnings of $15,000. The statements of financial position of the two companies at 31 December 20X5 are set out below. Neither company has paid any dividends during the year. Non-controlling interests at acquisition should be valued at fair value. The share price just prior to the acquisition was $3.10.

HINGE CO
STATEMENT OF FINANCIAL POSITION AS AT 31 DECEMBER 20X5

	$	$
Assets		
Non-current assets		
Property, plant and equipment	32,000	
16,000 ordinary shares of 50c each in Singe Co	50,000	
		82,000
Current assets		85,000
Total assets		167,000
Equity and liabilities		
Equity		
Ordinary share capital ($1 shares)	100,000	
Share premium account	7,000	
Retained earnings	40,000	
		147,000
Current liabilities		20,000
Total equity and liabilities		167,000

SINGE CO
STATEMENT OF FINANCIAL POSITION AS AT 31 DECEMBER 20X5

	$	$
Assets		
Property, plant and equipment		30,000
Current assets		43,000
Total assets		73,000
Equity and liabilities		
Ordinary share capital (20,000 shares of 50c each)	10,000	
Share premium account	4,000	
Retained earnings	39,000	
		53,000
Current liabilities		20,000
Total equity and liabilities		73,000

Required

Prepare the consolidated statement of financial position of Hinge Co at 31 December 20X5. You should assume that profits have accrued evenly over the year to 31 December 20X5. There has been no impairment of goodwill.

Example: Pre-acquisition losses of a subsidiary

As an illustration of the entries arising when a subsidiary has pre-acquisition losses, suppose P Co acquired all 50,000 $1 ordinary shares in S Co for $20,000 on 1 January 20X1 when there was a debit balance of $35,000 on S Co's retained earnings. In the years 20X1 to 20X4 S Co makes profits of $45,000 in total, leaving a credit balance of $10,000 on retained earnings at 31 December 20X4. P Co's retained earnings at the same date are $70,000.

Solution

The consolidation workings would appear as follows.

1   *Goodwill*

	$	$
Consideration transferred		20,000
Net assets at acquisition		
Ordinary share capital	50,000	
Retained earnings	(35,000)	
		(15,000)
Goodwill		5,000

2   *Retained earnings*

	P Co $	S Co $
At the end of the reporting period	70,000	10,000
Pre-acquisition loss		35,000
		45,000
S Co share of post-acquisition retained earnings		
(45,000 × 100%)	45,000	
	115,000	

Section summary

When a parent company acquires a subsidiary during its accounting period the profits for the period need to be apportioned between pre- and post-acquisition. **Only post-acquisition profits are included in group retained earnings.**

---

8 Consolidated statement of profit or loss and other comprehensive income

8.1 The consolidated statement of profit or loss

Introduction

The consolidated statement of profit or loss summarises the revenue and expenses of the group as a single entity.

We shall start by looking at the consolidated statement of profit or loss and other comprehensive income for 100% owned subsidiaries here.

8.1.1 Consolidation procedure

It is customary in practice to prepare a working paper (known as a **consolidation schedule**) on which the individual statements of profit or loss are set out side by side and totalled to form the basis of the consolidated statement of profit or loss.

Example: Consolidated statement of profit or loss

P Co acquired 100% of the ordinary shares of S Co on that company's incorporation in 20X3. The summarised statements of profit or loss of the two companies for the year ending 31 December 20X6 are set out below.

	P Co $	S Co $
Sales revenue	75,000	38,000
Cost of sales	(30,000)	(20,000)
Gross profit	45,000	18,000
Administrative expenses	(14,000)	(8,000)
Profit before tax	31,000	10,000
Income tax expense	(10,000)	(2,000)
Profit for the year	21,000	8,000

Required

Prepare the consolidated statement of profit or loss for P Co and its subsidiary for the year ended 31 December 20X6.

Solution

P CO
CONSOLIDATED STATEMENT OF PROFIT OR LOSS
FOR THE YEAR ENDED 31 DECEMBER 20X6

	$
Sales revenue (75,000 + 38,000)	113,000
Cost of sales (30,000 + 20,000)	(50,000)
Gross profit	63,000
Administrative expenses (14,000 + 8,000)	(22,000)
Profit before tax	41,000
Income tax expense (10,000 + 2,000)	(12,000)
Profit for the year	29,000

We will now look at the complications introduced by **intragroup trading** and **intragroup dividends**.

8.1.2 Intragroup trading

Like the consolidated statement of financial position, the consolidated statement of profit or loss should deal with the results of the group as those of a single entity. When one company in a group sells goods to another, an identical amount is included in the sales revenue of the first company and in the cost of sales of the second. Yet as far as the entity's dealings with outsiders are concerned, no sale has taken place.

The consolidated figures for sales revenue and cost of sales should represent **sales to** and **purchases from**, outsiders. An adjustment is therefore necessary to reduce the sales revenue and cost of sales figures by the value of intragroup sales during the year.

We have also seen earlier in this chapter that any unrealised profits on intragroup trading should be excluded from the figure for group profits. This will occur whenever goods sold at a profit within the group remain in the inventory of the purchasing company at the year end. The best way to deal with this is to **calculate the unrealised profit** on unsold inventories at the year end as we have already seen, and **reduce profit by adding it to the cost of sales.**

Example: Intragroup trading

Suppose in our earlier example that S Co had recorded sales of $5,000 to P Co during 20X6. S Co had purchased these goods from outside suppliers at a cost of $3,000. One half of the goods remained in P Co's inventory at 31 December 20X6. Prepare the revised consolidated statement of profit or loss.

Solution

The consolidated statement of profit or loss for the year ended 31 December 20X6 would now be as follows.

	$
Sales revenue (75,000 + 38,000 − 5,000)	108,000
Cost of sales (30,000 + 20,000 − 5,000 + 1,000*)	(46,000)
Gross profit	62,000
Administrative expenses	(22,000)
Profit before taxation	40,000
Income tax expense	(12,000)
Profit for the year	28,000

*Unrealised profit: ½ × ($5,000 − $3,000). An adjustment will be made for the unrealised profit against the inventory figure in the consolidated statement of financial position.

8.1.3 Intragroup dividends

In our example so far, we have assumed that S Co retains all of its after-tax profit. It may be, however, that S Co distributes some of its profits as dividends.

If the parent company has received dividends from the subsidiary during the year, these should be eliminated (cancelled) from the consolidated statement of profit or loss. The only investment income to appear in the consolidated statement of profit or loss is that received from outside the group.

8.1.4 Recap

The table below summarises the main points about the consolidated statement of profit or loss.

Purpose	To show the results of the group for an accounting period as if it were a single entity.
Sales revenue to profit for year	100% P + 100% S (excluding adjustments for intragroup transactions).
Reason	To show the results of the group which were controlled by the parent company.
Intragroup sales	Strip out intragroup activity from both sales revenue and cost of sales.
Unrealised profit on intragroup sales	Increase cost of sales by unrealised profit.
Depreciation	If the value of S's non-current assets has been subjected to a fair value uplift, then any additional depreciation for the year must be charged in the consolidated statement of profit or loss.
Transfer of non-current assets	The profit on transfer must be eliminated and expenses must be reduced by any additional depreciation arising from the increased carrying value of the asset.

8.2 The consolidated statement of profit or loss and other comprehensive income

Introduction

A consolidated statement of profit or loss and other comprehensive income will be easy to produce once you have done the statement of profit or loss. In this section, we take the last question and add an item of other comprehensive income to illustrate this.

Example: Consolidated statement of profit or loss and other comprehensive

Using the answer to the previous example, show the consolidated statement of profit or loss and other comprehensive income if P Co and S Co made a revaluation gain on their properties during the year of $15,000 and $5,000 respectively.

Solution

	$
Sales revenue	108,000
Cost of sales	(46,000)
Gross profit	62,000
Administrative expenses	(22,000)
Profit before taxation	40,000
Income tax expense	(12,000)
Profit for the year	28,000
Other comprehensive income:	
Gain on property revaluation (15,000 + 5,000)	20,000
Total comprehensive income for the year	48,000

IAS 1 *Presentation of financial statements* (Revised) also allows a two-statement format, where we would produce a separate statement of profit or loss and statement of other comprehensive income. The separate consolidated statement of other comprehensive income would be as follows.

CONSOLIDATED STATEMENT OF COMPREHENSIVE INCOME

	$
Profit for the year	28,000
Other comprehensive income:	
Gain on property revaluation	20,000
Total comprehensive income for the year	48,000

9 Subsidiaries acquired exclusively with a view to resale

Under IFRS 5 *Non-current assets held for sale and discontinued operations,* a subsidiary acquired exclusively with the intention of reselling it is likely to qualify as:

- A disposal group **held for sale** in the statement of financial position and
- A **discontinued operation** in the statement of profit or loss and other comprehensive income

if the held for sale criteria are met.

Let's first look at what the key terms mean.

9.1 Criteria for subsidiaries held for sale

KEY TERM

DISCONTINUED OPERATION. A component of an entity that either has been disposed of or is classified as held for sale and:

(a)   Represents a separate major line of business or geographical area of operations,

(b)   Is part of a single coordinated plan to dispose of a separate major line of business or geographical area of operations or

(c)   Is a subsidiary acquired exclusively with a view to resale   (*IFRS 5*)

A **component** of an entity is one that has operations and cash flows that can be clearly distinguished, operationally and for financial reporting purposes, from the rest of the entity.

To be classified as **held for sale**, all of the following criteria must be met:

(a)   The disposal group (ie the subsidiary) must be **available for immediate sale** in its present condition and

(b)   The sale must be **highly probable**. This means:

   (i)   **P**rice at which the disposal group (ie the subsidiary) is actively marketed for sale must be reasonable in relation to its current fair value

   (ii)   **U**nlikely that significant changes will be made to the plan or the plan withdrawn (indicated by actions required to complete the plan)

   (iii) **M**anagement (at the appropriate level) must be committed to a plan to sell

   (iv)   **A**ctive programme to locate a buyer and complete the plan must have been initiated

   (v)   **S**ale expected to qualify for recognition as a completed sale within one year from the date of classification as held for sale (subject to limited specified exceptions)

9.1.1 Statement of financial position

If the held for sale criteria are met, the disposal group (ie the subsidiary classified as held for sale) is measured at the lower of:

- Carrying amount,, and
- Fair value less costs to sell

Additionally, instead of consolidating the subsidiary's assets and liabilities line by line in the consolidated statement of financial position, its assets and liabilities should be disclosed:

(a)   As single amounts (of assets and liabilities)

(b)   On the face of the statement of financial position

(c)   Separately from other assets and liabilities and

(d)   Normally as current assets and liabilities (individually, not offset against each other as a net amount)

9.2 Statement of profit or loss and other comprehensive income

A subsidiary acquired exclusively with a view to resale is likely to meet the **discontinued operation** criteria and should be presented separately as follows in the consolidated statement of profit or loss and other comprehensive income:

On the face of the statement of profit or loss and other comprehensive income:

Single amount comprising the total of:

(a)   The **post-tax profit or loss** of discontinued operations and

(b)   The **post-tax gain or loss recognised on the remeasurement to fair value** less costs to sell or on the disposal of assets/disposal groups comprising the discontinued operation

On the face of the statement of profit or loss and other comprehensive income or in the notes:

(a)   Revenue

(b)   Expenses

(c)   Profit before tax

(d)   Income tax expense

(e)   Post-tax gain or loss on disposal of assets/disposal groups or on remeasurement to fair value less costs to sell

Chapter Summary

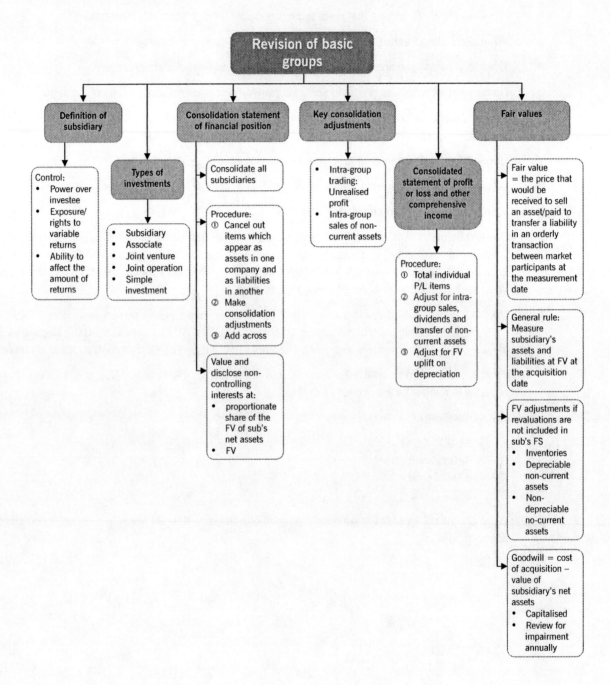

Quick Quiz

1   Define a subsidiary.

2   What are the three criteria that need to be met under IFRS 10 to determine control?

3   What accounting treatment does IFRS 10 require of a parent company?

4   When is a parent exempted from preparing consolidated financial statements?

5   Under what circumstances should subsidiary undertakings be excluded from consolidation?

6   How should an investment in a subsidiary be accounted for in the separate financial statements of the parent?

7   Under IFRS 13 *Fair value measurement* what is meant by Level 1 inputs?

8   Where does unrealised profit on intragroup trading appear in the statement of profit or loss?

9   What are non-controlling interests?

10   Chicken Co owns 80% of Egg Co. Egg Co sells goods to Chicken Co at cost plus 50%. The total invoiced sales to Chicken Co by Egg Co in the year ended 31 December 20X9 were $900,000 and, of these sales, goods which had been invoiced at $60,000 were held in inventory by Chicken Co at 31 December 20X9. What is the reduction in aggregate group gross profit?

11   Major Co, which makes up its accounts to 31 December, has an 80% owned subsidiary Minor Co. Minor Co sells goods to Major Co at a mark-up on cost of 33.33%. At 31 December 20X8, Major had $12,000 of such goods in its inventory and at 31 December 20X9 had $15,000 of such goods in its inventory.

       What is the amount by which the consolidated profit attributable to Major Co's shareholders should be adjusted in respect of the above?

       (Ignore taxation.)

       A $1,000 Debit
       B $800 Credit
       C $750 Credit
       D $600 Debit

12   What are the components making up the figure of non-controlling interests in a consolidated statement of financial position?

Answers to Quick Quiz

1   An entity that is controlled by another entity.

2   An investor (the parent) controls an investee (the subsidiary) if all of the following IFRS 10 criteria are met:

   –   Power over the investee
   –   Exposure or rights to variable returns from its involvement with the investee and
   –   The ability to use its power over the investee to affect the amount of the investor's return

3   The financial statements of parent and subsidiary are combined and presented as a single entity.

4   When the parent is itself a wholly-owned subsidiary, or a partially-owned subsidiary and the non-controlling interests do not object.

5   Very rarely, if at all. See Section 2.3.

6   (a)   At cost or
     (b)   In accordance with IAS 39

7   Quoted prices in active markets for identical assets or liabilities that the entity can access at the measurement date.

8   As an addition to cost of sales.

9   The equity in a subsidiary not attributable, directly or indirectly, to a parent.

10    $\dfrac{\$60,000 \times 50}{150} = \$20,000$

11   D $600 Debit

     $(15,000 - 12,000) \times 33.3/133.3 \times 80\%$

12   The non-controlling interests at acquisition (measured either at their proportionate share of the subsidiary's net assets or at fair value) plus their share of the subsidiary's post-acquisition retained reserves, less impairment of goodwill (if NCI measured at fair value at the date of acquisition)

Answers to Questions

9.1 Cancellation

P CO
CONSOLIDATED STATEMENT OF FINANCIAL POSITION AS AT 30 JUNE

	$	$
Assets		
Non-current assets		
Property, plant and equipment (120,000 + 100,000)		220,000
Current assets		
Inventories (50,000 + 60,000 + 6,000)	116,000	
Receivables (40,000 + 30,000)	70,000	
Cash (4,000 + 6,000)	10,000	
		196,000
Total assets		416,000
Equity and liabilities		
Equity		
Ordinary shares of $1 each, fully paid (parent)	100,000	
Retained earnings (95,000 + 28,000)	123,000	
		223,000
Non-current liabilities		
10% loan stock	75,000	
12% loan stock (50,000 × 60%)	30,000	
		105,000
Current liabilities		
Payables (47,000 + 16,000)	63,000	
Taxation (15,000 + 10,000)	25,000	
		88,000
Total equity and liabilities		416,000

Note especially how:

(a)   The uncancelled loan stock in S Co becomes a liability of the group.

(b)   Goods in transit is the difference between the current accounts ($18,000 – $12,000). The goods are in transit to S Co (as S's current account showing the amount payable to P Co is $6,000 less than the corresponding receivable shown by P Co).This is adjusted in S's books as:

DEBIT   Inventories $6,000
CREDIT   Current account with P Co $6,000

The current accounts then agree and cancel.

(c)   The investment in S Co's shares is cancelled against S Co's share capital.

9.2 Fair values

S Co's financial statements:

NBV at disposal (at historical cost) = cost $4,000 – accumulated depreciation $2,500 = $1,500
Accumulated depreciation = ($4,000/4) x 2½ = $2,500
∴ Profit on disposal = Sales proceeds $2,600 – NBV $1,500 = $1,100

P Co's consolidated financial statements:

NBV at disposal (at fair value) = fair value $3,000 – accumulated depreciation $750 = $2,250

Accumulated depreciation = ($3,000/2) x ½ = $750

∴ Profit on disposal for consolidation = Sales proceeds $2,600 – NBV $2,250 = $350

9.3 Fair values

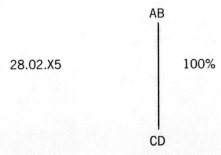

Goodwill

	$	$
Consideration transferred		2,000,000
Fair value of net assets at acquisition:		
Carrying value per question	1,300,000	
Fair value adjustments:		
Intangible asset	100,000	
Property, plant and equipment (660,000 – 440,000))	220,000	
Contingent liability	(30,000)	
		(1,590,000)
Goodwill		410,000

Explanation

1   The legal and professional fees of $75,000 should be recognised as an expense as they relate to a benefit (service) immediately consumed.

2   The customer list should be recognised as an intangible asset in the consolidated financial statements, as it is capable of being sold separately from the rest of the business ie identifiable.

3   Even though contingent liabilities are normally only disclosed under IAS 37 *Provisions, contingent liabilities and contingent assets,* IFRS 3 makes an exception and states that it should be recognised at acquisition at its fair value of $30,000 as there is a present legal obligation (the warranty contract) and it can be measured reliably.

4   The potential provision for reorganisation of $150,000 should not be recognised at acquisition because it is merely an intention not an obligation.

9.4 Unrealised profit

P CO
CONSOLIDATED STATEMENT OF FINANCIAL POSITION

	$	$
Assets		
Non-current assets		
Property, plant and equipment (80,000 + 40,000)	120,000	
Goodwill (W2)	4,500	
		124,500
Current assets (W4)		55,000
Total assets		179,500
Equity and liabilities		
Equity		
Ordinary shares of $1 each	100,000	
Retained earnings (W3)	52,500	
		152,500
Current liabilities (W5)		27,000
Total equity and liabilities		179,500

Workings

1   *Group structure*

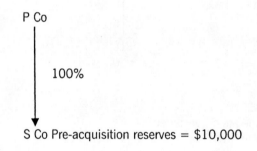

P Co

100%

S Co Pre-acquisition reserves = $10,000

2   *Goodwill*

	$	$
Consideration transferred		46,000
Net assets acquired as represented by		
Share capital	30,000	
Retained earnings (W1)	10,000	
		(40,000)
Goodwill		6,000
Impairment loss		(1,500)
		4,500

3   *Retained earnings*

	P Co $	S Co $
Retained earnings per question	45,000	22,000
Unrealised profit (20% × $15,000)		(3,000)
Pre-acquisition		(10,000)
		9,000
Share of S Co	9,000	
Goodwill impairment loss	(1,500)	
	52,500	

4   *Current assets*

	$	$
In P Co's statement of financial position		40,000
In S Co's statement of financial position	30,000	
Less: S Co's current account with P Co cancelled	(12,000)	
		18,000
		58,000
Less unrealised profit excluded from inventory valuation		(3,000)
		55,000

5   *Current liabilities*

	$
In P Co's statement of financial position	21,000
Less: P Co's current account with S Co cancelled	(12,000)
	9,000
In S Co's statement of financial position	18,000
	27,000

9.5 Mid-year acquisition

HINGE CO
CONSOLIDATED STATEMENT OF FINANCIAL POSITION AS AT 31 DECEMBER 20X5

	$	$
Assets		
Property, plant and equipment (32,000 + 30,000)		62,000
Goodwill (W2)		27,400
Current assets (85,000 + 43,000)		128,000
Total assets		217,400
Equity and liabilities		
Ordinary share capital	100,000	
Share premium account	7,000	
Retained earnings (W3)	54,400	
		161,400
Non-controlling interests (W4)		16,000
		177,400
Current liabilities (20,000 + 20,000)		40,000
Total equity and liabilities		217,400

Workings

1   *Group structure*

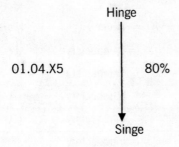

Hinge

01.04.X5   80%

Singe

Pre-acquisition retained earnings of Singe Co:

	$
Balance at 31 December 20X4	15,000
Profit for three months to 31 March 20X5 ($\frac{3}{12} \times 24,000^*$)	6,000
Pre-acquisition retained earnings	21,000

* Singe Co has made a profit of $24,000 ($39,000 – $15,000) for the year. This is assumed to have arisen evenly over the year, ie $6,000 in the three months to 31 March and $18,000 in the nine months after acquisition.

The balance of $4,000 on share premium account is all pre-acquisition.

The consolidation workings can now be drawn up.

2   *Goodwill*

	$	$
Consideration transferred		50,000
Non-controlling interests (20% × 20,000 shares × $3.10)		12,400
		62,400
Net assets at acquisition:		
Ordinary share capital	10,000	
Retained earnings (pre-acquisition) (W1)	21,000	
Share premium	4,000	
		(35,000)
Goodwill		27,400

3   *Retained earnings*

	Hinge Co $	Singe Co $
Per question	40,000	39,000
Pre-acquisition (W2)		(21,000)
		18,000
Share of Singe: $18,000 × 80%	14,400	
	54,400	

4   *Non-controlling interests at reporting date*

	$
NCI at acquisition (W1)	12,400
NCI share of Singe's post-acquisition retained earnings (20% × 18,000 (W2))	3,600
	16,000

Now try these questions from the Practice Question Bank

Number	Level	Marks	Time
Q13	Introductory	N/A	14 mins
Q14	Introductory	10	18 mins
Q15	Introductory	10	18 mins
Q16	Introductory	10	18 mins
Q17	Introductory	14	25 mins

ASSOCIATES AND JOINT ARRANGEMENTS

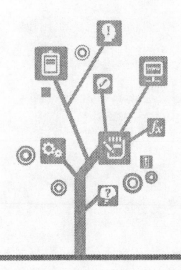

Some investments are not subsidiaries but they may be much more than simple trade investments. The most important of these are associates and joint arrangements, which are the subject of this chapter.

Associates and joint ventures have to be included in consolidated financial statements, according to the revised IAS 28, under the **equity method.** Section 1 shows how to do this. You have already studied associates in paper F1.

Joint arrangements can take a number of forms and Section 2 will look at the IFRS 11 provisions and the different forms of joint arrangement.

Section 3 deals with a new standard, IFRS 12, on the disclosures about interests in other entities needed in the financial statements.

Topic list	learning outcomes	syllabus references
1 IAS 28 *Investments in associates and joint ventures*	B1	B1(a)
2 IFRS 11 *Joint arrangements*	B1	B1(a)
3 IFRS 12 *Disclosure of interests in other entities*	B1	B1(a)

Chapter Overview

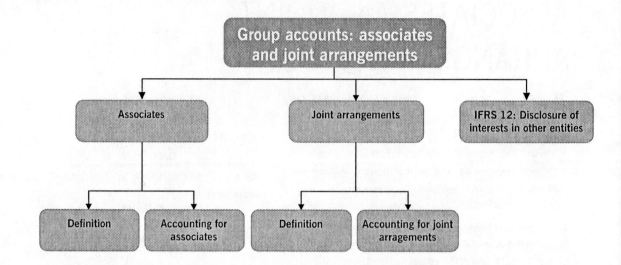

1 IAS 28 *Investments in associates and joint ventures*

11/10, 9/12

> **Introduction**
>
> We looked at investments in associates and joint ventures briefly in Chapter 9. IAS 28 *Investments in associates and joint ventures* covers this type of investment.

1.1 Definitions

In this section we will focus on **associates**. The criteria that exist to identify a **joint venture** will be covered in Section 2, although the method for accounting for a joint venture is identical to that used for associates.

Some of the important definitions in Chapter 9 are repeated here, with some additional important terms.

KEY TERMS

ASSOCIATE. An entity over which an investor has significant influence.

SIGNIFICANT INFLUENCE is the power to participate in the financial and operating policy decisions of an economic activity, but is not control or joint control over those policies.

JOINT CONTROL is the contractually-agreed sharing of control over an economic activity.

EQUITY METHOD. A method of accounting whereby the investment is initially recorded at cost and adjusted thereafter for the post-acquisition change in the investor's share of investee's net assets. The investor's profit or loss includes its share of the investee's profit or loss, and the investor's other comprehensive income includes its share of the investee's other comprehensive income.

We have already looked at how the **status** of an investment in an associate should be determined. Go back to Chapter 9 to revise it if necessary. (Note that, as with an investment in a subsidiary, any **potential voting rights** should be taken into account in assessing whether the investor has **significant influence** over the investee.)

IAS 28 requires all investments in associates and joint ventures to be accounted for using the equity method, unless the investment is classified as held for sale in accordance with IFRS 5 *Separate Financial Statements*, in which case it should be accounted for under IFRS 5.

An investor is exempt from applying the equity method if:

(a) It is a parent exempt from preparing consolidated financial statements under IAS 27 *Non-current Assets Held for Sale and Discontinued Operations* (revised) or

(b) All of the following apply:

   (i) The investor is a **wholly-owned subsidiary** or it is a **partially-owned subsidiary** of another entity and its other owners, including those not otherwise entitled to vote, have been informed about, and do not object to, the investor not applying the equity method

   (ii) Its securities are **not publicly traded**

   (iii) It is **not in the process of issuing securities** in public securities markets and

   (iv) The **ultimate or intermediate parent** publishes consolidated financial statements that comply with International Financial Reporting Standards (IFRSs)

IAS 28 **does not allow** an investment in an associate to be excluded from equity accounting when an investee operates under severe long-term restrictions that significantly impair its ability to transfer funds to the investor. Significant influence must be lost before the equity method ceases to be applicable.

The use of the equity method should be **discontinued** from the date that the investor **ceases to have significant influence**.

From that date, the investor shall account for the investment in accordance with IAS 39 *Financial instruments: recognition and measurement*. Under IAS 39, the fair value of the retained interest must be regarded as its fair value on initial recognition as a financial asset.

1.2 Separate financial statements of the investor

Note that in the separate financial statements of the investor, an interest in an associate is accounted for either:

(a) At **cost** or

(b) In accordance with **IAS 39**

1.3 Application of the equity method: consolidated accounts

KEY POINT

The **equity method** should be applied in the consolidated accounts:

- **Statement of financial position**: investments in associates at cost plus (or minus) the group's share of the associate's post-acquisition profits (or losses) less impairment losses on the investments in associates to date

- **Profit or loss (statement of profit or loss and other comprehensive income)**: group share of associate's profit after tax

- **Other comprehensive income (statement of profit or loss and other comprehensive income)**: group share of associate's other comprehensive income after tax

Many of the procedures required to apply the equity method are the same as are required for full consolidation. In particular, **fair value adjustments** are required, and the group share of **intragroup unrealised profits** must be excluded.

1.3.1 Consolidated statement of profit or loss and other comprehensive income

The basic principle is that the investing company (X Co) should take account of its **share of the earnings** of the associate, Y Co, whether or not Y Co distributes the earnings as dividends. X Co achieves this by adding to consolidated profit the group's share of Y Co's profit after tax.

Notice the difference between this treatment and the **consolidation** of a subsidiary company's results. If Y Co were a subsidiary, X Co would take credit for the whole of its sales revenue, cost of sales etc and would then prepare a reconciliation at the end of the statement showing how much of the group profit and total comprehensive income is owned by non-controlling interests.

Under equity accounting, the associate's sales revenue, cost of sales and so on are **not amalgamated** with those of the group. Instead, the **group share** only of the associate's **profit after tax** and **other comprehensive income** for the year is included in the relevant sections of the statement of profit or loss and other comprehensive income.

1.3.2 Consolidated statement of financial position

A figure for **investments in associates** is shown, which at the time of the acquisition must be stated at cost. This amount will increase or decrease each year by the amount of the group's share of the associate's total comprehensive income retained for the year. Any impairments to date of investments in associates are then deducted from both the investment and consolidated reserves.

The group share of the associate's reserves is also included within the group reserves figure in the equity section of the consolidated statement of financial position.

Example: Associate

P Co, a company with subsidiaries, acquires 25,000 of the 100,000 $1 ordinary shares in A Co for $60,000 on 1 January 20X8. In the year to 31 December 20X8, A Co earns a profit for the year of $24,000 from which it declares a dividend of $6,000.

How will A Co's results be accounted for in the individual and consolidated accounts of P Co for the year ended 31 December 20X8?

Solution

In the **individual accounts** of P Co, the investment will be recorded on 1 January 20X8 at cost. Unless there is an impairment in the value of the investment (see below), this amount will remain in the individual statement of financial position of P Co permanently. The only entry in P Co's statement of profit or loss and other comprehensive income will be to record dividends received (25% x $6,000 = $1,500). For the year ended 31 December 20X8, P Co will:

DEBIT	Cash	$1,500	
CREDIT	Income from shares in associates		$1,500

In the **consolidated accounts** of P Co equity accounting principles will be used to account for the investment in A Co. Consolidated profit for the year will include the group's share of A Co's profit after tax (25% × $24,000 = $6,000).

To the extent that this has been distributed as dividend, it is already included in P Co's individual accounts and will automatically be brought into the consolidated results. That part of the group's profit share which has not been distributed as dividend ($4,500) will be brought into consolidation by the following adjustment.

DEBIT	Investments in associates	$4,500	
CREDIT	Income from shares in associates		$4,500

The asset investments in associates is then stated at $64,500, being cost plus the group share of post-acquisition retained profits.

1.4 Consolidated statement of profit or loss and other comprehensive income

The treatment of associates' profits in the following proforma should be studied carefully.

1.4.1 Pro-forma consolidated statement of profit or loss and other comprehensive income

The following is a **suggested layout** (for a statement of profit or loss and other comprehensive income) for a company having subsidiaries as well as associates.

	$'000
Revenue	1,400
Cost of sales	(770)
Gross profit	630
Distribution costs and administrative expenses	(290)
	340
Interest and similar income receivable	30
	370
Finance costs	(20)
	350
Share of profit (after tax) of associate	17
Profit before taxation	367
Income tax expense (parent company and subsidiaries)	(145)
Profit for the year	222
Profit attributable to:	
Owners of the parent	200
Non-controlling interests	22
	222

1.5 Consolidated statement of financial position

As explained earlier, the consolidated statement of financial position will contain an asset, **investments in associates.** The amount at which this asset is stated will be its original cost plus the **group's share** of the associate's **total comprehensive income earned since acquisition** which has not been distributed as dividends. Any **impairment** of investments in associates to date must be **deducted.**

1.6 Other accounting considerations

The following points are also relevant and are similar to a parent-subsidiary consolidation situation.

(a)   Use financial statements drawn up to the **same reporting date.**

(b)   If this is impracticable, adjust the financial statements for **significant transactions/ events** in the intervening period. The difference between the reporting date of the associate and that of the investor must be no more than three months.

(c)   Use **uniform accounting policies** for like transactions and events in similar circumstances, adjusting the associate's statements to reflect group policies if necessary.

(d)   If an associate has **cumulative preference shares** held by outside interests, calculate the share of the investor's profits/losses after adjusting for the preference dividends (whether or not declared).

1.7 Upstream and downstream transactions

A group (made up of a parent and its consolidated subsidiaries) may trade with its associates. This introduces the possibility of unrealised profits if goods sold within the group are still in inventories at the year end. This is similar to unrealised profits arising on trading between a parent and a subsidiary. The important thing to remember is that when an **associate** is involved, **only the group's share is eliminated.**

The precise accounting entries depend on the direction of the transaction. **Upstream** transactions are sales of assets from an associate to the investor. **Downstream** transactions are sales of assets from the investor to an associate.

The double entry in the consolidated statement of financial position is as follows, where A% is the parent's holding in the associate, and PUP is the provision for unrealised profit.

DEBIT   Retained earnings of parent   PUP × A%
CREDIT   Group inventories   PUP × A%

For upstream transactions (associate sells to parent/subsidiary) where the parent holds the inventories.

Or

DEBIT   Retained earnings of parent /subsidiary   PUP × A%
CREDIT   Investments in associates   PUP × A%

For downstream transactions, (parent/subsidiary sells to associate) where the associate holds the inventory.

In the consolidated statement of profit or loss and other comprehensive income, for upstream transactions (associate sells to parent/subsidiary) the share of the associate's profit is reduced by the group share of the unrealised profit (resulting in the above debit to retained earnings). For downstream transactions (parent/subsidiary sells to associate), cost of sales is increased by the group share of the unrealised profit (resulting in the above debit to retained earnings).

Example: Downstream transaction

A Co, a parent with subsidiaries, holds 25% of the equity shares in B Co. During the year, A Co makes sales of $1,000,000 to B Co at cost plus a 25% mark-up. At the year end, B Co has all these goods still in inventories.

Solution

A Co has made an unrealised profit of $200,000 (1,000,000 × 25/125) on its sales to the associate (B Co). The group's share of this is 25% ie $50,000. This must be eliminated.

The double entry is:

DEBIT   A: Retained earnings $50,000
CREDIT   Investment in associate (B Co) $50,000

Because the sale was made to the associate, the group's share of the unsold inventories forms part of the investments in associates at the year end.

In the consolidated statement of profit or loss, the share of the profit of the associate would also be reduced by $50,000.

If the sale had been from the associate B to A ie an upstream transaction, the double entry would have been.

DEBIT   A: Retained earnings $50,000
CREDIT   A: Inventories $50,000

If preparing the consolidated statement of profit or loss and other comprehensive income, you would add the $50,000 to cost of sales, as the **parent** made the sales in this example.

1.8 Associate's losses

When the equity method is being used and the investor's share of losses of the associate equals or exceeds its interest in the associate, the investor should **discontinue** including its share of further losses. The investment is reported at nil value. The interest in the associate is normally the carrying amount of the investment in the associate, but it also includes any other long-term interests, for example preference shares or long-term receivables or loans.

After the investor's interest is reduced to nil, **additional losses** should only be recognised where the investor has incurred obligations or made payments on behalf of the associate (for example, if it has guaranteed amounts owed to third parties by the associate).

Should the associate return to profit, the parent may resume recognising its share of profits only after they equal the share of losses not recognised.

1.9 Impairment losses

IAS 39 sets out a list of indications that a financial asset (including an associate) may have become impaired. Any impairment loss is recognised in accordance with IAS 36 *Impairment of Assets* for each associate as a single asset. There is no separate testing for impairment of goodwill, as the goodwill that forms part of the carrying amount of an investment in an associate is not separately recognised. An impairment loss is not allocated to any asset, including goodwill, that forms part of the carrying amount of the investment in an associate. Accordingly, any reversal of that impairment loss is recognised in accordance with IAS 36 to the extent that the recoverable amount of the investment subsequently increases.

Exam alert

In the exam, impairment losses on the associate for the current year should be deducted from the share of the associate's profits.

1.10 Non-controlling interests/associate held by a subsidiary

Where the investment in an associate is held by a subsidiary in which there are non-controlling interests, the non-controlling interests shown in the consolidated financial statements of the group should include the **non-controlling interests of the subsidiary's interest** in the results and post-acquisition reserves of the associate.

This means that the group accounts must include the gross share of post-acquisition reserves and post-tax profits, and the **non-controlling interests** should be accounted **for separately**. For example, we will suppose that P Co owns 60% of S Co which owns 25% of A Co. A Co is then an indirect associate (or sub-associate) of P Co. The relevant amounts for inclusion in the consolidated financial statements of the P Co group would be as follows.

CONSOLIDATED STATEMENT OF PROFIT OR LOSS AND OTHER COMPREHENSIVE INCOME

Profit before interest and tax (P 100% + S 100%)
Share of profit after tax of associate (A 25%)
Tax (P 100% + S 100%)
Profit for the year attributable to:
Owners of the parent (P 100% + S 60% + A 15%*)
Non-controlling interests (S 40% + A 10%**)

CONSOLIDATED STATEMENT OF FINANCIAL POSITION
Investment in associate (figures based on 25% holding)
Non-controlling interests (NCI at acq'n + (40% × post-acq'n reserves of S) + (10%** × post-acq'n reserves of A))
Group reserves ((100% × P) + (60% × post-acquisition of S) + (15% * × post-acquisition of A))

Notes

* Share of A attributable to owners of the parent = 60% × 25% = 15%
** Share of A attributable to non-controlling interests of S = 40% × 25% = 10%

1.11 Comprehensive question

The following question provides comprehensive revision of the topics covered up to this point in the chapter. It is written in the style of an F2 question, but only includes issues that you should remember from your earlier studies. It is important that you are confident about these techniques before moving on to the new and more complicated group accounting topics that are tested in paper F2.

| Question 10.1 | Basic group accounting techniques |

Learning outcome B1

Otway, a public limited company, acquired a subsidiary, Holgarth, on 1 July 20X2 and an associate, Batterbee, on 1 July 20X5. The details of the acquisitions at the respective dates are as follows:

Investee	Ordinary share capital of $1	Share premium	Retained earnings	Revaluation surplus	Fair value of net assets at acquisition	Cost of investment	Ordinary share capital acquired
	$m	$m	$m	$m	$m	$m	$m
Holgarth	400	140	120	40	800	765	320
Batterbee	220	83	195	54	652	203	55

The draft financial statements for the year ended 30 June 20X6 are as follows.

STATEMENTS OF FINANCIAL POSITION AS AT 30 JUNE 20X6

	Otway $m	Holgarth $m	Batterbee $m
Non-current assets			
Property, plant and equipment	1,012	920	442
Intangible assets	–	350	27
Investment in Holgarth	765	–	–
Investment in Batterbee	203	–	–
	1,980	1,270	469
Current assets			
Inventories	620	1,460	214
Trade receivables	950	529	330
Cash and cash equivalents	900	510	45
	2,470	2,499	589
	4,450	3,769	1,058
Equity and liabilities			
Share capital	1,000	400	220
Share premium	200	140	83
Retained earnings	1,128	809	263
Revaluation surplus	142	70	62
	2,470	1,419	628
Non-current liabilities			
Deferred tax liability	100	50	36
Current liabilities			
Trade and other payables	1,880	2,300	394
	4,450	3,769	1,058

STATEMENTS OF PROFIT OR LOSS AND OTHER COMPREHENSIVE INCOME
FOR THE YEAR ENDED 30 JUNE 20X6

	Otway $m	Holgarth $m	Batterbee $m
Revenue	4,480	4,200	1,460
Cost of sales	(2,690)	(2,940)	(1,020)
Gross profit	1,790	1,260	440
Distribution costs and administrative expenses	(620)	(290)	(196)
Finance costs	(50)	(80)	(24)
Dividend income (from Holgarth and Batterbee)	260	-	-
Profit before tax	1,380	890	220
Income tax expense	(330)	(274)	(72)
Profit for the year	1,050	616	148
Other comprehensive income that will not be reclassified to profit or loss			
Gain on revaluation of property	30	7	12
Income tax expense relating to other comp income	(9)	(2)	(4)
Other comprehensive income, net of tax	21	5	8
Total comprehensive income for the year	1,071	621	156
Dividends paid in the year	250	300	80
Retained earnings brought forward	328	493	195

Additional information:

(a)   Neither Holgarth nor Batterbee had any reserves other than retained earnings and share premium at the date of acquisition. Neither has issued new shares since acquisition.

(b)   The fair value difference on the subsidiary relates to property, plant and equipment being depreciated through cost of sales over a remaining useful life of ten years from the acquisition date. The fair value difference on the associate relates to a piece of land (which has not been sold since acquisition).

(c)   Group policy is to measure non-controlling interests at acquisition at fair value. The fair value of the non-controlling interests on 1 July 20X2 was calculated as $188m.

(d)   During the year ended 30 June 20X6 Holgarth sold goods to Otway for $1,300 million. The company makes a profit of 30% on the selling price. $140 million of these goods were held by Otway on 30 June 20X6.

(e)   Annual impairment tests have indicated impairment losses of $100m relating to the recognised goodwill of Holgarth including $25m in the current year. The Otway Group recognises impairment losses on goodwill in administrative expenses. No impairment losses to date have been necessary for the investment in Batterbee.

Required

Prepare the statement of profit or loss and other comprehensive income for the year ended 30 June 20X6 for the Otway Group and a statement of financial position at that date.

Exam alert

It is not unusual in the exam to have both an associate and a subsidiary to account for in a consolidation.

1.12 Summary of entries

Consolidated statement of profit or loss and other comprehensive income	Profit after tax	Include group share of associate, disclosed separately
	Other comprehensive income	Include group share of associate, disclosed separately
Consolidated statement of financial position	Interests in associated companies should be stated at:	$
	(a) Cost	X
	(b) Share of post-acquisition retained earnings	X
	(c) Less impairment losses to date	(X)
		X
	Also disclose group's share of post-acquisition reserves of associates and movements therein.	

Section summary

IAS 28 deals with accounting for associates. The definitions are important as they govern the accounting treatment, particularly significant influence

The **equity method** should be applied in the consolidated accounts:

- **Statement of financial position:** investments in associates at cost plus (or minus) the group's share of the associate's post-acquisition profits (or losses) less impairment losses to date

- **Statement of profit or loss and other comprehensive income:**

    – Group share of profits of the associate (profit after tax)
    – Group share of other comprehensive income of the associate

2 IFRS 11 *Joint arrangements*

Introduction

IFRS 11 *Joint arrangements* classifies joint arrangements as either **joint operations** or **joint ventures**.

The classification of a joint arrangement as a joint operation or a joint venture depends upon the **rights and obligations** of the parties to the arrangement.

Joint arrangements are often found when each party can **contribute in different ways** to the activity. For example, one party may provide finance, another purchases or manufactures goods, while a third offers their marketing skills.

IFRS 11 *Joint arrangements* covers all types of joint arrangements. It is not concerned with the accounts of the joint arrangement itself (if separate accounts are maintained), but rather **how the interest in a joint arrangement is accounted for by each party**.

2.1 Definitions

IFRS 11 begins by listing some important definitions.

KEY TERMS

JOINT ARRANGEMENT. An arrangement in which two or more parties have **joint control**.

JOINT CONTROL. The contractually-agreed sharing of control of an arrangement, which exists only when decisions about the relevant activities require the **unanimous consent** of the parties sharing control.

JOINT OPERATION. A joint arrangement whereby the parties that have joint control of the arrangement have **rights to the assets and obligations for the liabilities** relating to the arrangement.

JOINT VENTURE. A joint arrangement whereby the parties that have joint control of the arrangement have **rights to the net assets** of the arrangement.   *(IFRS 11)*

2.2 Forms of joint arrangement

IFRS 11 classifies joint arrangements as either joint operations or joint ventures. The classification of a joint arrangement as a joint operation or a joint venture depends upon the rights and obligations of the parties to the arrangement.

A **joint operation** is a joint arrangement whereby the parties that have joint control (the joint operators) have rights to the assets and obligations for the liabilities of that joint arrangement. A joint arrangement that is **not structured through a separate entity** is always a joint operation.

A **joint venture** is a joint arrangement whereby the parties that have **joint control** (the joint venturers) of the arrangement have **rights to the net assets** of the arrangement.

A **joint arrangement** that is structured through a **separate entity** may be either a joint operation or a joint venture. In order to ascertain the classification, the parties to the arrangement should assess the terms of the contractual arrangement together with any other facts or circumstances to assess whether they have:

(a)   Rights to the assets, and obligations for the liabilities, in relation to the arrangement (indicating a joint operation)

(b)   Rights to the net assets of the arrangement (indicating a joint venture)

Detailed guidance is provided in the appendices to IFRS 11 in order to help this assessment, giving consideration to for example, the wording contained within contractual arrangements.

IFRS 11 summarises the basic issues that underlie the classifications in the following diagram:

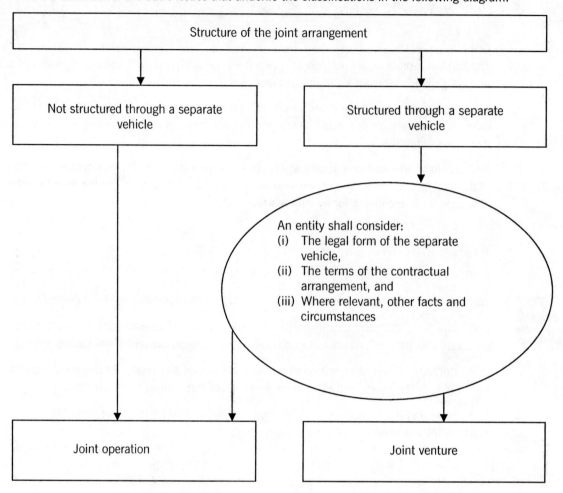

2.2.1 Contractual arrangement

The existence of a contractual agreement distinguishes a joint arrangement from an investment in an associate. **If there is no contractual arrangement, then a joint arrangement does not exist.**

Evidence of a contractual arrangement could be in one of several forms.

(a)   **Contract** between the parties
(b)   **Minutes** of discussions between the parties
(c)   Incorporation in the **articles or by-laws** of the joint venture

The contractual arrangement is usually **in writing**, whatever its form, and it will deal with the following issues surrounding the joint venture.

(a)   **Its purpose, activity and duration**

(b)   The appointment of its **board of directors** (or equivalent) and the **voting rights** of the parties

(c)   **Capital contributions** to it by the parties

(d)   How its output, income, expenses or results are **shared** between the parties

It is the contractual arrangement which establishes **joint control** over the joint venture, so that no single party can control the activity of the joint venture on its own.

The terms of the contractual arrangement are key in deciding whether the arrangement is a joint venture or joint operation. IFRS 11 includes a table of issues to consider, and explains the influence of a range of points that could be included in the contract .The table is summarised below.

	Joint operation	Joint venture
The terms of the contractual arrangement	The parties to the joint arrangement have rights to the assets and obligations for the liabilities relating to the arrangement.	The parties to the joint arrangement have rights to the net assets of the arrangement (ie it is the separate vehicle, not the parties, that has rights to the assets and obligations for the liabilities).
Rights to assets	The parties to the joint arrangement share all interests (eg rights, title or ownership) in the assets relating to the arrangement in a specified proportion (eg in proportion to the parties' ownership interest in the arrangement or in proportion to the activity carried out through the arrangement that is directly attributed to them).	The assets brought into the arrangement or subsequently acquired by the joint arrangement are the arrangement's assets. The parties have no interests (ie no rights, title or ownership) in the assets of the arrangement.
Obligations for liabilities	The parties share all liabilities, obligations, costs and expenses in a specified proportion (eg in proportion to their ownership interest in the arrangement or in proportion to the activity carried out through the arrangement that is directly attributed to them). The parties to the joint arrangement are liable for claims by third parties.	The joint arrangement is liable for the debts and obligations of the arrangement. The parties are liable to the arrangement only to the extent of their respective: • Investments in the arrangement or • Obligations to contribute any unpaid or additional capital to the arrangement or • Both Creditors of the joint arrangement do not have rights of recourse against any party.
Revenues, expenses, profit or loss	The contractual arrangement establishes the allocation of revenues and expenses on the basis of the relative performance of each party to the joint arrangement. For example, the contractual arrangement might establish that revenues and expenses are allocated on the basis of the capacity that each party uses in a plant operated jointly.	The contractual arrangement establishes each party's share in the profit or loss relating to the activities of the arrangement.
Guarantees	The provision of guarantees to third parties, or the commitment by the parties to provide them, does not, by itself, determine that the joint arrangement is a joint operation.	

Question 10.2 | Joint arrangements

Learning outcomes B1

This question is based on *Illustrative Example 2* from IFRS 11.

Two real estate companies (the parties) set up a separate vehicle (Supermall) for the purpose of acquiring and operating a shopping centre. The contractual arrangement between the parties establishes joint control of the activities that are conducted in Supermall. The main feature of Supermall's legal form is that the entity, not the parties, has rights to the assets, and obligations for the liabilities, relating to the arrangement. These activities include the rental of the retail units, managing the car park, maintaining the centre and its equipment – such as lifts – and building the reputation and customer base for the centre as a whole.

The terms of the contractual arrangement are such that:

(a)   Supermall owns the shopping centre. The contractual arrangement does not specify that the parties have rights to the shopping centre.

(b)   The parties are not liable in respect of the debts, liabilities or obligations of Supermall. If Supermall is unable to pay any of its debts or other liabilities or to discharge its obligations to third parties, the liability of each party to any third party will be limited to the unpaid amount of that party's capital contribution.

(c)   The parties have the right to sell or pledge their interests in Supermall.

(d)   Each party receives a share of the income from operating the shopping centre (which is the rental income net of the operating costs) in accordance with its interest in Supermall.

Required

Explain how Supermall should be classified in accordance with IFRS 11 *Joint arrangements*.

2.3 Accounting treatment

KEY POINT

The accounting treatment of joint arrangements depends on whether the arrangement is a joint venture or joint operation.

2.3.1 Accounting for joint operations

IFRS 11 requires that a joint operator recognises line by line the following in relation to its interest in a joint operation:

(a)   Its assets, including its share of any jointly-held assets
(b)   Its liabilities, including its share of any jointly-incurred liabilities
(c)   Its revenue from the sale of its share of the output arising from the joint operation
(d)   Its share of the revenue from the sale of the output by the joint operation and
(e)   Its expenses, including its share of any expenses incurred jointly

This treatment is applicable in both the separate and consolidated financial statements of the joint operator.

Question 10.3 | Joint operations

Learning outcome B1

Can you think of examples of situations where this type of joint venture might take place?

2.3.2 Joint ventures

KEY POINT

> IFRS 11 and IAS 28 require **joint ventures** to be accounted for using **the equity method**.

Prior to the new group accounting standards issued in 2011, the old standard on joint ventures (IAS 31) permitted either equity accounting or proportionate consolidation to be used for joint ventures. The choice has now been removed. (Proportionate consolidation meant including the investor's share of the assets, liabilities, income and expenses of the joint venture, line by line.)

The rules for equity accounting are included in IAS 28 *Investments in associates and joint ventures*. These have been covered in detail in Section 1 above.

2.3.3 Application of IAS 28 (2011) to joint ventures

The consolidated statement of financial position is prepared by:

(a) Including the interest in the joint venture at cost plus the share of post-acquisition reserves less impairment losses to date

(b) Including the group share of the post-acquisition total comprehensive income in group reserves

The consolidated statement of profit or loss and other comprehensive income will include:

(a) The group share of the joint venture's profit or loss
(b) The group share of the joint venture's other comprehensive income

The use of the equity method should be **discontinued** from the date on which the joint venturer ceases to have joint control over, or have significant influence on, a joint venture.

2.3.4 Transactions between a joint venturer and a joint venture

Upstream transactions

When a joint venture sells assets to the joint venturer, the joint venturer should not recognise its share of the profit made by the joint venture on the transaction in question until it resells the assets to an independent third party ie until the profit is realised.

Therefore, as for an associate, the **group share of the unrealised profit or loss** in year-end inventory or non-current assets must be **eliminated**.

Downstream transactions

When the joint venturer sells assets to the joint venture then, as above, the group **share of the unrealised profit or loss** in year-end inventory or non-current assets must be **eliminated** unless:

(a) There is a loss and

(b) The transaction provides evidence of a reduction in the net realisable value of the asset or of an impairment loss

In this instance, the **loss should be recognised in full** by the joint venturer.

Section summary

- There are two types of joint arrangement: joint operations and joint ventures

- A contractual arrangement must exist which establishes joint control

- Joint control is important: unanimous consent of the parties sharing control is required

- Joint operations are accounted for by including the investor's share of assets, liabilities, income and expenses as per the contractual arrangement

- Joint ventures are accounted for using the equity method as under IAS 28

3 IFRS 12 *Disclosure of interests in other entities*

IFRS 12 *Disclosure of interests in other entities* was issued in May 2011 as part of the package of five standards relating to consolidation. It removes all disclosure requirements from other standards relating to group accounting, and provides guidance applicable to consolidated financial statements.

The standard requires disclosure of:

(a) The significant judgements and assumptions made in determining the nature of an interest in another entity or arrangement, and in determining the type of joint arrangement in which an interest is held

(b) Information about interests in subsidiaries, associates, joint arrangements and structured entities that are not controlled by an investor

3.1 Disclosure for subsidiaries

The following disclosures are required in respect of subsidiaries:

(a) The interest that non-controlling interests have in the group's activities and cash flows, including the name of relevant subsidiaries, their principal place of business and the interest and voting rights of the non-controlling interests

(b) Nature and extent of significant restrictions on an investor's ability to use group assets and liabilities

(c) Nature of the risks associated with an entity's interests in consolidated structured entities, such as the provision of financial support

(d) Consequences of changes in ownership interest in a subsidiary (whether control is lost or not)

3.2 Disclosures for associates and joint arrangements

The following disclosures are required in respect of associates and joint arrangements:

(a) Nature, extent and financial effects of an entity's interests in associates or joint arrangements, including name of the investee, principal place of business, the investor's interest in the investee, method of accounting for the investee and restrictions on the investee's ability to transfer funds to the investor

(b) Risks associated with an interest in an associate or joint venture

(c) Summarised financial information, with more detail required for joint ventures than for associates

3.3 Disclosures for unconsolidated structured entities

IFRS 12 defines a structured entity as an entity that has been designed so that voting or similar rights are not the dominant factor in deciding who controls the entity, such as when any voting rights relate to administrative tasks only and the relevant activities are directed by means of contractual arrangements.

If these structured entities are not consolidated in the group accounts, the following disclosures are required:

(a) Nature and extent of interests in unconsolidated structured entities including nature, purpose, size and activities of the structured entity and how the structured entity is financed

(b) Risks associated with the unconsolidated structured entity including the assets and liabilities in its financial statements relating to unconsolidated structured entities, the entity's maximum exposure to loss from its interests in unconsolidated structured entities, and details of any financial support the entity has provided or intends to provide to unconsolidated structured entities

Section summary

IFRS 12 deals with the disclosures required for each type of investment.

Chapter Summary

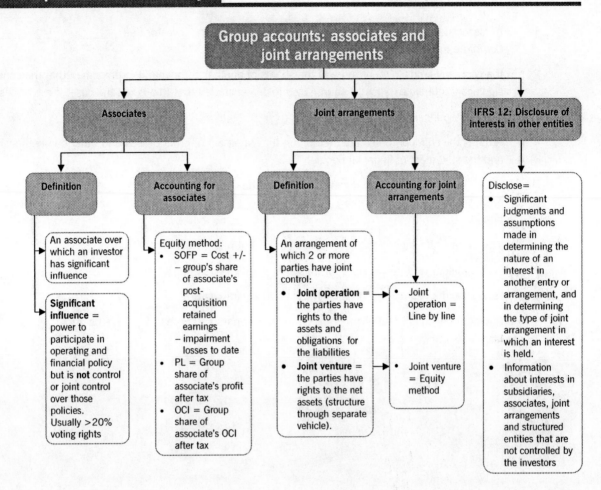

Group accounts: associates and joint arrangements

Associates

Joint arrangements

IFRS 12: Disclosure of interests in other entities

Definition

An associate over which an investor has significant influence

Significant influence = power to participate in operating and financial policy but is **not** control or joint control over those policies. Usually >20% voting rights

Accounting for associates

Equity method:
- SOFP = Cost +/-
  – group's share of associate's post-acquisition retained earnings
  – impairment losses to date
- PL = Group share of associate's profit after tax
- OCI = Group share of associate's OCI after tax

Definition

An arrangement of which 2 or more parties have joint control:
- **Joint operation** = the parties have rights to the assets and obligations for the liabilities
- **Joint venture** = the parties have rights to the net assets (structure through separate vehicle).

Accounting for joint arrangements

- Joint operation = Line by line
- Joint venture = Equity method

Disclose=
- Significant judgments and assumptions made in determining the nature of an interest in another entry or arrangement, and in determining the type of joint arrangement in which an interest is held.
- Information about interests in subsidiaries, associates, joint arrangements and structured entities that are not controlled by the investors

Quick Quiz

1   An associate is an _____ over which the investor has _____ .
     Complete the blanks.

2   If a company holds 20% or more of the shares of another company, it is presumed that the company has
     significant influence (unless it can be clearly demonstrated that this is not the case). True or false?

3   What is significant influence?

4   What is the effect of the equity method on the statement of profit or loss and other comprehensive income
     and the statement of financial position?

5   A joint venture is a joint arrangement whereby the parties that have_____ of the
     arrangement have rights to the_____of the arrangement. *Complete the
     blanks.*

6   What forms of evidence of a contractual agreement might exist?

7   How should a venturer account for its share of a joint operation?

8   How should a venturer account for its share of a joint venture?

9   A joint arrangement that is structured through a separate vehicle will always be a joint venture. True or
     false?

Answers to Quick Quiz

1   An associate is an **entity** over which the investor has a **significant influence**.

2   True.

3   The power to participate in the financial and operating decisions of the investee but not control or joint control.

4   (a)   Statement of profit or loss and other comprehensive income – investing entity includes its share of the profit for the year of the associate or joint venture

     (b)   Statement of financial position – the investments in associates or joint ventures is initially recorded at cost. This will then increase each year by the group share of the associate/joint venture's post-acquisition reserves. Any impairment losses in the investments in associates to date should be deducted

5   A joint venture is a joint arrangement whereby the parties that have **joint control** of the arrangement have rights to the **net assets** of the arrangement.

6   **Evidence** of a contractual arrangement could be in one of several forms.

     •   **Contract** between the parties
     •   **Minutes** of discussion between the parties
     •   Incorporation in the **articles or by-laws** of the joint venture

7   IFRS 11 requires that a joint operator recognises line by line the following in relation to its interest in a joint operation:

     (a)   Its assets, including its share of any jointly-held assets
     (b)   Its liabilities, including its share of any jointly-incurred liabilities
     (c)   Its revenue from the sale of its share of the output arising from the joint operation
     (d)   Its share of the revenue from the sale of the output by the joint operation and
     (e)   Its expenses, including its share of any expenses incurred jointly

8   A joint venture is accounted for using the equity method as required by IAS 28 *Investments in associates and joint ventures*.

9   False. Joint arrangements that are structured through a separate vehicle may be either joint ventures or joint operations. The classification will depend on whether the venturer has **rights to the net assets** of the arrangement (joint venture) or **rights to the assets and obligations for the liabilities** (joint operation). This will depend on the terms of the contractual arrangement.

Answers to Questions

10.1 Basic group accounting techniques

OTWAY GROUP
CONSOLIDATED STATEMENT OF FINANCIAL POSITION AS AT 30 JUNE 20X6

	$m
Non-current assets	
Property, plant and equipment (1,012 + 920 + (W9) 60)	1,992
Goodwill (W2)	53
Other intangible assets	350
Investments in associates(W3)	222
	2,617
Current assets	
Inventories (620 + 1,460 – (W8) 42)	2,038
Trade receivables (950 + 529)	1,479
Cash and cash equivalents (900 + 510)	1,410
	4,927
	7,544
Equity attributable to owners of the parent	
Share capital	1,000
Share premium	200
Retained earnings (W4)	1,551
Revaluation surplus (W5)	168
	2,919
Non-controlling interests (W6)	295
	3,214
Non-current liabilities	
Deferred tax liability (100 + 50)	150
Current liabilities	
Trade and other payables (1,880 + 2,300)	4,180
	7,544

OTWAY GROUP
CONSOLIDATED STATEMENT OF PROFIT OR LOSS AND OTHER COMPREHENSIVE INCOME
FOR THE YEAR ENDED 30 JUNE 20X6

	$m
Revenue (4,480 + 4,200 − (W8) 1,300)	7,380
Cost of sales (2,690 + 2,940 − (W8) 1,300 + (W8) 42 + (W9) 10)	(4,382)
Gross profit	2,998
Distribution costs and administrative expenses (620 + 290 + 25 impairment)	(935)
Finance costs (50 + 80)	(130)
Share of profit of associate (148 × 25%)	37
Profit before tax	1,970
Income tax expense (330 + 274)	(604)
Profit for the year	1,366
Other comprehensive income that will not be reclassified to profit or loss:	
Gain on revaluation of property (30 + 7)	37
Share of other comprehensive income of associate (8 × 25%)	2
Income tax expense relating to other comprehensive income (9 + 2)	(11)
Other comprehensive income for the year, net of tax	28
Total comprehensive income for the year	1,394
Profit attributable to:	
Owners of the parent (1,297 − 94)	1,258
Non-controlling interests (W7)	108
	1,366
Total comprehensive income attributable to:	
Owners of the parent (1,325 − 95)	1,285
Non-controlling interests (W7)	109
	1,394

Workings

1   *Group structure*

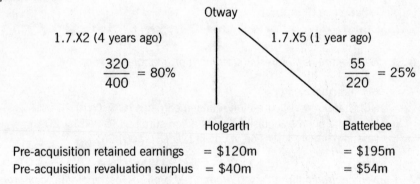

	Holgarth	Batterbee
Pre-acquisition retained earnings	= $120m	= $195m
Pre-acquisition revaluation surplus	= $40m	= $54m

2   *Goodwill*

	Holgarth	
	$m	$m
Consideration transferred		765
Non-controlling interests (fair value (FV))		188
FV of net assets acquired:		
Share capital	400	
Share premium	140	
Retained earnings at acq'n (W1)	120	
Revaluation surplus at acq'n (W1)	40	
∴ Fair value adjustment	100	
Total FV of net assets		(800)
		153
Less cumulative impairment losses		(100)
		53

3   *Investments in associates*

	$m
Cost of associate	203
Share of post-acquisition retained earnings (W4)	17
Share of post-acquisition revaluation surplus (W5)	2
Less impairment losses on associate to date	(0)
	222

4   *Consolidated retained earnings c/f*

	Otway $m	Holgarth $m	Batterbee $m
Per question	1,128	809	263
Provision for unrealised profit (PUP) (W8)		(42)	
Depreciation on FV adjustment (W9)		(40)	(0)
Less pre-acquisition (W1)		(120)	(195)
		607	68

Group share:

Holgarth [607 × 80%]	486
Batterbee [68 × 25%]	17
Less impairment losses on goodwill	
Holgarth [80% × 100] (W2)	(80)
Less impairment losses on associate	
Batterbee	(0)
	1,551

5   *Consolidated revaluation surplus c/f*

	Otway $m	Holgarth $m	Batterbee $m
Per question	142	70	62
Less: Pre-acquisition		(40)	(54)
		30	8

Group share:

Holgarth [30 × 80%]	24
Batterbee [8 × 25%]	2
	168

6   *Non-controlling interests (statement of financial position)*

	$m
NCI at acquisition (W2)	188
NCI share of post-acquisition retained earnings [607 (W4) × 20%]	121
NCI share of post-acquisition revaluation surplus [30 (W5) × 20%]	6
Less impairment losses on goodwill [20% × 100] (W2)	(20)
	295

7   *Non-controlling interests (statement of profit or loss and other comprehensive income)*

	Profit for year $m	Total comprehensive income $m
Holgarth's PFY/TCI per question	616	621
Less: impairment losses	(25)	(25)
Less: PUP (W8)	(42)	(42)
Less: FV depreciation (W9)	(10)	(10)
	539	544
× NCI share 20% =	108	109

8   *Intragroup trading*

Cancel intragroup sales and purchases:

DEBIT	Revenue	$1,300m	
CREDIT	Cost of sales		$1,300m

Unrealised profit (Holgarth to Otway):
= $140m in inventories × 30/100 margin = $42m

DEBIT	Cost of sales/Retained earnings of Holgarth	$42m	
CREDIT	Inventories		$42m

9   *Fair value adjustment – Holgarth*

	At acquisition $m	Additional depreciation* $m	At year end $m
Property, plant and equipment (800 – 400 – 140 –120 – 40)	100	(40)	60
	$\overline{100}$	$\overline{(40)}$	$\overline{60}$

* Additional depreciation = $^{100}\!/_{10}$ = 10 per annum to cost of sales × 4 years = 40

10.2 Joint arrangements

Supermall has been set up as a **separate vehicle**. As such, it could be either a joint operation or joint venture, so other facts must be considered.

There are no facts that suggest that the two real estate companies have rights to substantially all the benefits of the assets of Supermall, or an obligation for its liabilities. Therefore, it appears that Supermall (the joint arrangement) rather than the two real estate companies has rights to the assets and obligations for the liabilities of the joint arrangement.

The real estate companies' liability is limited to any unpaid capital contribution.

As a result, each party has an interest in the **net assets** of Supermall and should account for it as a **joint venture** using the **equity method**.

IFRS 11 contains many examples illustrating the principles of how to classify joint arrangements. You can find them at www.iasb.org.

10.3 Joint operations

IFRS 11 gives examples in the oil, gas and mineral extraction industries. In such industries companies may, say, jointly control and operate an oil or gas pipeline. Each company transports its own products down the pipeline and pays an agreed proportion of the expenses of operating the pipeline (perhaps based on volume). In this case, the parties have rights to assets (such as exploration permits and the oil or gas produced by the activities).

A further example is a property which is jointly controlled, each venturer taking a share of the rental income and bearing a portion of the expense.

Now try these questions from the Practice Question Bank	Number	Level	Marks	Time
	Q18	Introductory	N/A	11 mins
	Q19	Introductory	10	18 mins
	Q20	Introductory	10	18 mins

ADVANCED GROUPS

Part D

CHANGES IN GROUP STRUCTURES

Changes in group structures appear regularly in consolidation questions in both sections of the F2 exam paper. Your approach should be the same as for more simple consolidation questions: *methodical and logical*. As long as you can identify the basic elements of the consolidation there will be plenty of marks available even if you cannot deal with the more complicated aspects.

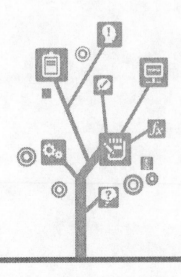

Topic list	learning outcomes	syllabus references
1 Business combinations achieved in stages	B2	B2(a)
2 Disposals where control is retained	B2	B2(a)
3 Disposals where control/significant influence is lost	B2	B2(a)
4 Business reorganisations	B2	B2(a)

Chapter Overview

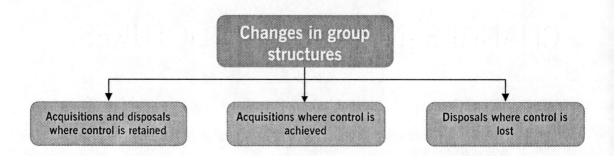

1   Business combinations achieved in stages   11/10, 5/12

Introduction

A parent company may acquire a controlling interest in the shares of a subsidiary as a result of **several successive share purchases**, rather than by purchasing the shares all on the same day. Business combinations achieved in stages may also be known as **step acquisitions** or **piecemeal acquisitions**. We will use this term step acquisitions throughout this chapter.

1.1 Types of step acquisitions

Step acquisitions can lead to a holding in another entity progressing from an investment to a subsidiary.

There are three possible types of step acquisitions:

(a)   A previously-held **interest**, say 10%, with **no significant influence** (accounted for under IAS 39) is **increased to a controlling interest** of 50% or more

(b)   A **previously-held equity interest**, say 35%, accounted for as an **associate** under IAS 28, is increased to a controlling interest of 50% or more

(c)   A **controlling interest** in a subsidiary is **increased**, say from 60% to 80%

The first two transactions are treated in the same way, but the third is not. There is a reason for this.

Exam alert

At this level, you will only be examined on step acquisitions involving a simple investment with no significant influence becoming a subsidiary, or an increase in the controlling interest in a subsidiary. Step acquisitions involving an associate becoming a subsidiary will not be examined.

1.2 General principle: crossing an accounting boundary

Under the revised IFRS 3 *Business combinations* a business combination occurs only when one entity **obtains control over another**, which is generally when 50% or more has been acquired. The Deloitte guide *Business Combinations and Changes in Ownership Interests* calls this **crossing an accounting boundary**.

When this happens, the original investment is treated as if it were **disposed of at fair value and re-acquired at fair value**. This **previously-held interest** at fair value, together with any consideration transferred is the **cost of the combination** used in calculating the goodwill. A gain or loss on de-recognition of the original investment is recognised in profit or loss.

If the 50% **boundary is not crossed**, as when the interest in a subsidiary is increased, the event is treated as a **transaction between owners**.

Whenever you cross the 50% boundary, you revalue and a gain or loss is reported in profit or loss for the year. If you do not cross the 50% boundary, no gain or loss is reported; instead there is an adjustment to the parent's equity.

The following diagram, from the *Deloitte* guide, may help you visualise the boundary.

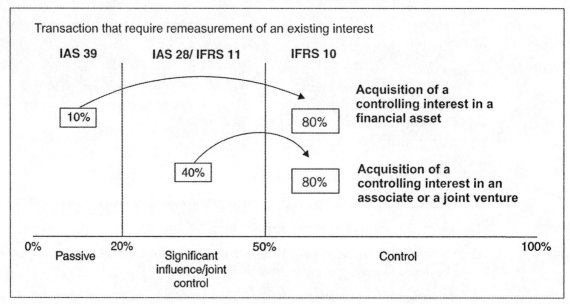

As you will see from the diagram, the third situation in paragraph 1.1 where an interest in a subsidiary is increased from say, 60% to 80%, does not involve crossing that all-important 50% threshold. Likewise, purchases of stakes of up to 50% do not involve crossing the control boundary, and therefore do not trigger a calculation of goodwill.

In the Deloitte diagram above, in substance, the parent has:

- Sold a 10% investment – so we need to remeasure the investment to fair value and record a gain or loss on derecognition in profit or loss

- Purchased an 80% subsidiary – so we need to calculate goodwill including the consideration transferred for the 70% acquired and the fair value of the previously-held 10% at the date control is achieved

Exam alert

In an exam, if the control boundary is crossed, this triggers two events:

- Revalue the previously-held investment to fair value and recognise a gain or loss on derecognition

- Calculate goodwill on the whole shareholding (including the previously-held investment at fair value)

Remember that the examiner may include a consolidated statement of changes in equity as well as a statement of profit or loss and other comprehensive income or a statement of financial position.

1.3 Investment becoming a subsidiary: calculation of goodwill

The previously-held investment is remeasured to fair value, with any gain being reported in profit or loss, and the goodwill calculated as follows:

	$
Consideration transferred	X
Non-controlling interests (at %FV of new assets or full FV)	X
Fair value of acquirer's previously-held equity interest	X
Less: net fair value of identifiable assets	
acquired and liabilities assumed	(X)
	X

1.3.1 Analogy: trading in a small car for a larger one

It may seem counter-intuitive that the previous investment is now part of the cost for the purposes of calculating the goodwill. One way of looking at it is to imagine that you are part-exchanging a small car for a larger one. The value of the car you trade in is put towards the cost of the new vehicle, together with your cash (the consideration transferred). Likewise, the company making the acquisition has part-exchanged its smaller investment – at fair value – for a larger one, and must naturally pay on top of that to obtain the larger investment.

This analogy is not exact, but may help.

Try the following question to get the hang of the calculation of goodwill and profit on derecognition of the investment.

Question 11.1	Step acquisition

Learning outcome B2

Good, whose year end is 30 June 20X9, has a subsidiary, Will, which it acquired in stages. The details of the acquisition are as follows:

		Retained earnings	
Date of acquisition	Holding acquired %	at acquisition $m	Purchase consideration $m
1 July 20X7	10	270	60
1 July 20X8	60	400	480

The share capital of Will has remained unchanged since its incorporation at $300m. The fair values of the net assets of Will were the same as their carrying amounts at the date of the acquisition. Good did not have significant influence over Will at any time before gaining control of Will. At 1 July 20X8, the fair value of Good's 10% holding in Will was $80m. The group policy is to measure non-controlling interests at acquisition at their proportionate share of the fair value of the subsidiary's identifiable net assets.

Required

(a) Calculate the goodwill on the acquisition of Will that will appear in the consolidated statement of financial position at 30 June 20X9.

(b) Calculate the profit on the derecognition of any previously-held investment in Will to be reported in group profit or loss for the year ended 30 June 20X9.

1.4 Increase in previously-held controlling interest: adjustment to parent's equity   5/11

An example of this would be where an investment goes from a 60% subsidiary to an 80% subsidiary. In substance, there has been no acquisition as the entity is still a subsidiary. The 50% threshold has not been crossed, so there is no remeasurement to fair value and no gain or loss to profit or loss for the year. Instead, in substance, there has been a **transaction between owners** ie the parent has purchased a 20% shareholding from the non-controlling interests. This should be recorded in the equity section of the consolidated statement of financial position as follows:

(a) A decrease in non-controlling interests (in the above example from 40% to 20%)

(b) An adjustment to the parents equity (the consideration paid less the decrease in NCI)

Both of these movements in equity need to be recorded in a separate line in the consolidated statement of changes in equity.

The pro-forma for **the calculation of the adjustment to the parent's equity** is as follows:

	$
Fair value of consideration paid	(X)
Decrease in NCI in net assets and goodwill* at date of transaction	X
Adjustment to parent's equity	(X̄)

*__Note__. There will only be a decrease in the NCI share in goodwill where non-controlling interests are measured at fair value at the date of acquisition. If non-controlling interests are measured at the proportionate share of the net assets at acquisition, there is no goodwill for NCI.

If you are wondering why the increase in shareholding is treated as a transaction between owners, the revised IFRS 3 views **the group as an economic entity**, and **views all providers of equity**, including non-controlling interests, as **owners of the group**.

You can practise this adjustment in the example below.

Example: Step or piecemeal acquisition of a subsidiary

Peace acquired 60% of Miel's shares on 1 January 20X2 for $6,960,000 (equivalent to the fair value of $14.50 per share acquired on that date). On acquisition, Miel's reserves were standing at $7,800,000.

At 31 December 20X2 Miel's reserves stood at $7,900,000. Peace's reserves stood at $40,800,000.

On 1 January 20X3 Peace acquired an additional 10% interest in Miel for $1,200,000.

Group policy is to measure non-controlling interests at the date of acquisition at fair value.

No impairment losses on recognised goodwill have been necessary to date.

Required

Show the consolidated non-controlling interests and reserves figures when Peace acquires the additional 10% interest in Miel on 1 January 20X3.

Solution

Non-controlling interests

	$'000
NCI at acquisition (800 × 40% × $14.50)	4,640
NCI share of retained earnings since acquisition (W1)	40
	4,680
Decrease in NCI (4,680 × 10%/40%)	(1,170)
	3,510

Consolidated reserves

	$'000
Consolidated reserves at 31 December 20X2 (W1)	40,860
Adjustment to parent's equity on acq'n of 10% (W2)	(30)
	40,830

Note. No other figures in the statement of financial position are affected.

A journal entry may help you to understand the effect of this adjustment:

		$'000	$'000
DEBIT	Consolidated reserves	30	
DEBIT	NCI	1,170	
CREDIT	Cash (consideration paid)		1,200

Workings

1   *Consolidated reserves*

	Peace	Miel 60%
	$'000	$'000
Per question	40,800	7,900
Reserves at acquisition		(7,800)
		100
Share of post-acquisition reserves		
Miel 60% (100 × 60%)	60	
	40,860	

NCI share of retained earnings since acquisition = 40% x $100,000 = $40,000

2   *Adjustment to parent's equity on acquisition of additional 10% of Miel*

	$'000
Fair value of consideration paid	(1,200)
Decrease in NCI in net assets at acq'n (from NCI working)	1,170
	(30)

Section summary

Transactions of the type described in this chapter can be very complicated and certainly look rather daunting. Remember and apply the **basic techniques** and you should find such questions easier than you expected.

Step acquisitions (piecemeal acquisitions) can lead to a company becoming an investment and then a subsidiary over time. Make sure you can deal with each of these situations.

Where control is achieved in stages:

- Remeasure any previously-held equity interest to fair value at the date control is achieved (and include this amount in the goodwill calculation)

- Report any gain or loss on derecognition in profit or loss

- Where a controlling interest is increased, treat as a transaction between owners by decreasing non-controlling interests and recording an adjustment in the parent's equity

2   Disposals where control is retained   3/12

Introduction

Disposals of shares in a subsidiary may or may not result in a loss of control. In this section, we will consider what happens when control is retained.

Disposals are, in many ways, a mirror image of step acquisitions. The same principles underlie both.

KEY POINT

2.1 Types of disposal

2.1.1 Disposals where control is lost

There are three main types of disposals in which control is lost.

(a)   Full disposal: all the holding is sold (say, 80% to nil)
(b)   Subsidiary to associate (say, 80% to 30%)
(c)   Subsidiary to trade investment (say, 80% to 10%)

In your exam you are most likely to meet a partial disposal, from either subsidiary to associate or subsidiary to trade investment.

2.1.2 Disposals where control is retained

There is only one kind of disposal where control is retained: **subsidiary to subsidiary**, for example an 80% holding to a 60% holding.

Disposals where control is lost are treated differently from disposals where control is retained. There is a reason for this.

2.2 General principle: crossing an accounting boundary

Under the revised IFRS 3 disposal occurs only when one entity loses control over another, which is generally when its holding is decreased to less than 50%. The *Deloitte* guide *Business Combinations and Changes in Ownership Interests* calls this crossing an accounting boundary.

On disposal of a controlling interest, any retained interest (an associate or trade investment) is measured at fair value on the date that control is lost. This fair value is used in the calculation of the gain or loss on disposal and also becomes the carrying amount for subsequent accounting for the retained interest.

If the **50%** boundary is **not crossed**, as when the interest in a subsidiary is reduced, the event is treated as a **transaction between owners**.

Whenever you cross the 50% boundary, you revalue the remaining shareholding, and a gain or loss is reported in profit or loss for the year. If you do not cross the 50% boundary, no gain or loss is reported; instead there is an adjustment to the parent's equity.

The following diagram, from the *Deloittes* guide may help you visualise the boundary:

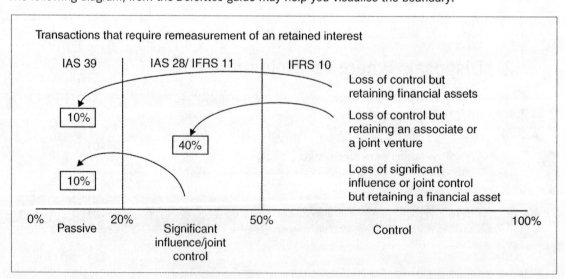

As you will see from the diagram, the situation in paragraph 2.1.2 where an interest in a subsidiary is reduced from say 80% to 60% would not involve crossing that all-important 50% threshold.

2.3 Effective date of disposal

The effective date of disposal is **when control passes**: the date for accounting for an entity ceasing to be a subsidiary is the date on which its former parent relinquishes its control over that undertaking. The consolidated statement of profit or loss (statement of profit or loss and other comprehensive income) should include the results of a subsidiary up to the date of its disposal. IAS 37 and IFRS 5 will have an impact here.

2.4 Disposals where control is retained

Control is retained where the disposal is from **subsidiary to subsidiary**. In substance, there has been no disposal as the entity is still a subsidiary. Instead, it is treated as a transaction been group shareholders ie the parent is selling shares to the non-controlling interests. Therefore, the following two steps must be taken:

- Record an increase in non-controlling interests in the NCI working for the consolidated statement of financial position.

- Record an adjustment to the parent's equity (consideration received less increase in NCI).

The detail of the accounting treatment in the consolidated financial statements is shown below.

2.4.1 Statement of profit or loss and other comprehensive income

(a)   The subsidiary is **consolidated in full** for the whole period.

(b)   The **non-controlling interests in the statement of profit or loss** will be based on the percentage before and after disposal ie time-apportioned.

(c)   There is no profit or loss on disposal.

2.4.2 Statement of financial position

(a)   The increase in the non-controlling interests on disposal must be shown in the non-controlling interests working (the end result being the year-end NCI based on the year-end percentage).

(b)   The consideration received less the increase in non-controlling interests is shown as an adjustment to the parent's equity.

(c)   Goodwill on acquisition is unchanged in the consolidated statement of financial position.

2.4.3 Adjustment to the parent's equity

This reflects the fact that the non-controlling share has increased (as the parent's share has reduced). A subsidiary to subsidiary disposal is, in effect, **a transaction between owners**. Specifically, it is a reallocation of ownership between parent and non-controlling equity holders. **The goodwill is unchanged**, because it is a historical figure, unaffected by the reallocation. The adjustment to the parent's equity is calculated as follows:

	$
Fair value of consideration received	X
Increase in NCI in net assets and goodwill* at disposal	(X)
Adjustment to parent's equity	X

* **Note**. A change in NCI's share of goodwill only occurs where non-controlling interests are measured at fair value at the date of acquisition (ie when there is an increase in the NCI share of goodwill already recognised). If non-controlling interests are measured at the proportionate share of net assets, there is no goodwill for NCI.

If you are wondering why the decrease in shareholding is treated as a transaction between owners, the revised IFRS 3 views **the group as an economic entity**, and views **all providers of equity**, including non-

controlling interests, as **owners of the group**. Non-controlling shareholders are not outsiders; they are owners of the group just like the parent.

You can practise the adjustment to parent's equity in the example and in requirement (b) of Question 11.2 later in this chapter.

Exam alert

Exam questions with a disposal where control is not lost could require a statement of changes in equity to be prepared, as this is where the increase in non-controlling interests and the adjustment to parent's equity will be shown in a separate line.

2.4.4 Gain in the parent's separate financial statements

This calculation is more straightforward: the proceeds are compared with the carrying value of the investment sold. The investment will be held at cost or at fair value if held as an available for sale financial asset:

	$
Fair value of consideration received	X
Less carrying value of investment disposed	(X)
Profit/(loss) on disposal	X/(X)

The profit on disposal is generally taxable, and the **tax based on the parent's gain** rather than the group's will also need to be recognised in the consolidated financial statements.

Section summary

Disposals do not always result in a loss of control. Remember particularly how to deal with **goodwill**.

3   Disposals where control/significant influence is lost   3/12

Introduction

Disposals of shares in a subsidiary may or may not result in a loss of control. If control is lost, then any remaining investment will need to be recategorised as an associate or a trade investment.

3.1 Control lost: calculation of group gain on disposal

A pro-forma calculation is shown below. This needs to be adapted for the circumstances in the question, in particular whether it is a full or partial disposal:

	$	$
Fair value of consideration received		X
Fair value of any investment retained		X
Less: share of consolidated carrying amount at date control lost		
Net assets	X	
Goodwill	X	
Less non-controlling interests	(X)	
		(X)
Group profit/(loss)		X/(X)

Following IAS 1 *Presentation of financial statements*, this gain may need to be disclosed separately if it is material.

3.1.1 Analogy: trading in a large car for a smaller one

It may seem counter-intuitive that the investment retained is now part of the proceeds for the purposes of calculating the gain. One way of looking at it is to imagine that you are selling a larger car and putting part of the proceeds towards a smaller one. If the larger car you are selling cost you less than the smaller car and cash combined, you have made a profit. Likewise, the company making the disposal sold a larger stake to gain, at fair value, a smaller stake and some cash on top, which is the consideration received.

This analogy is not exact, but may help.

3.2 Control lost: calculation of gain in parent's separate financial statements

This is calculated as for disposals where control is retained: see paragraph 2.4.4 above.

3.3 Disposals where control is lost: accounting treatment

For a **full disposal**, apply the following treatment.

(a)   **Statement of profit or loss and other comprehensive income**

   (i)   Consolidate results and non-controlling interests to the date of disposal.

   (ii)   Show the group profit or loss on disposal.

(b)   **Statement of financial position**

There will be no non-controlling interests and no consolidation as there is no subsidiary at the date the statement of financial position is being prepared.

A full disposal is illustrated in requirement (a) of Question 11.2 later in this chapter.

For **partial disposals**, use the following treatments.

(a)   **Subsidiary to associate**

   (i)   **Statement of profit or loss and other comprehensive income**

      (1)   Treat the undertaking as a subsidiary up to the date of disposal ie consolidate for the correct number of months and show the non-controlling interests in that amount.

      (2)   Show the profit or loss on disposal.

      (3)   Treat as an associate thereafter ie equity account by including the group share of the associate's profit and the group share of the associate's other comprehensive income pro-rated for the number of months the investment was an associate.

   (ii)   **Statement of financial position**

      (1)   The investment remaining is at its fair value at the date of disposal (to calculate the gain).

      (2)   Equity account (as an associate) thereafter, using the fair value as the new cost. (Post-acquisition retained earnings are added to this cost in future years to arrive at the carrying value of the investment in the associate in the statement of financial position.)

A part disposal where a subsidiary becomes an associate is illustrated in the next example and in requirement (c) of Question 11.2 later in this chapter.

(b) **Subsidiary to simple investment**

    (i) **Statement of profit or loss and other comprehensive income**

        (1) Treat the undertaking as a subsidiary up to the date of disposal ie consolidate.

        (2) Show the profit or loss on disposal.

        (3) Show dividend income and revaluation gains/losses on the investment only thereafter.

    (ii) **Statement of financial position**

        (1) The investment remaining is at its fair value at the date of disposal (to calculate the gain).

        (2) Thereafter, treat as an available for sale financial asset under IAS 39.

A part disposal where a subsidiary becomes an available for sale financial asset is illustrated in requirement (d) of Question 11.2 later in this chapter.

Example: Partial disposal

Chalk Co bought 100% of the voting share capital of Cheese Co on its incorporation on 1 January 20X2 for $160,000. Cheese Co earned and retained $240,000 from that date until 31 December 20X7. At that date the statements of financial position of the company and the group were as follows.

	Chalk Co $'000	Cheese Co $'000	Consolidated $'000
Investment in Cheese	160	–	–
Other assets	1,000	500	1,500
	1,160	500	1,500
Share capital	400	160	400
Retained earnings	560	240	800
	960	400	1,200
Current liabilities	200	100	300
	1,160	500	1,500

It is the group's policy to value the non-controlling interests at their proportionate share of the fair value of the subsidiary's identifiable net assets.

On 1 January 20X8 Chalk Co sold 40% of its shareholding in Cheese Co for $280,000. The profit on disposal (ignoring tax) in the financial statements of the parent company is calculated as follows.

	Chalk $'000
Fair value of consideration received	280
Carrying value of investment (40% × 160)	(64
Profit on sale	216

We now move on to calculate the adjustment to equity for the group financial statements.

Because only 40% of the 100% subsidiary has been sold, leaving a 60% subsidiary, **control is retained**. This means that there is **no group profit on disposal in profit or loss for the year**. Instead, there is an **adjustment to the parent's equity**, which affects group retained earnings.

KEY POINT

Remember that when control is retained, the disposal is just a transaction between owners. The non-controlling shareholders are owners of the group, just like the parent.

The adjustment to parent's equity is calculated as follows:

	$'000
Fair value of consideration received	280
Increase in non-controlling interests in net assets at the date of disposal (40% × 400)	(160)
Adjustment to parent's equity	120

This increases group retained earnings and does not go through group profit or loss for the year. (Note that there is no goodwill in this example, as the subsidiary was acquired on incorporation.)

Solution

Subsidiary status

The statements of financial position immediately after the sale will appear as follows.

	Chalk Co $'000	Cheese Co $'000	Consolidated $'000
Investment in Cheese (160-64)	96	–	–
Other assets	1,280	500	1,780
	1,376	500	1,780
Share capital	400	160	400
Retained earnings*	776	240	920
Current liabilities	200	100	300
	1,376	500	1,620
Non-controlling interests			160
			1,780

*Chalk's retained earnings are $560,000 + $216,000 profit on disposal. Group retained earnings are increased by the adjustment above: $800,000 + $120,000 = $920,000. Non-controlling interests are measured at the proportionate share of the net assets ie $400,000 × 40% = $160,000.

Solution

Associate status

Using the above example, assume that Chalk Co sold 60% of its holding in Cheese Co for $440,000. The fair value of the 40% holding retained was $200,000. The gain or loss on disposal in the books of the parent company would be calculated as follows.

	Parent company $'000
Fair value of consideration received	440
Carrying value of investment (60% × 160)	(96)
Profit on sale	344

This time control is lost, so there will be a gain in group profit or loss, calculated as follows:

	$'000
Fair value of consideration received	440
Fair value of investment retained	200
Less Chalk's share of consolidated carrying value at date control lost (100% × 400)	(400)
Group profit on sale	240

Note that there was no goodwill arising on the acquisition of Cheese (as Cheese was acquired on incorporation), otherwise this too would be deducted in the calculation.

The statements of financial position would now appear as follows.

	Chalk Co $'000	Cheese Co $'000	Consolidated $'000
Investment in Cheese (Note 1)	64		200
Other assets	1,440	500	1,440
	1,504	500	1,640
Share capital	400	160	400
Retained earnings (Note 2)	904	240	1,040
Current liabilities	200	100	200
	1,504	500	1,640

Notes

1   The investment in Cheese is at fair value in the group statement of financial position. In fact it is equity accounted at fair value at the date when control was lost plus a share of post-acquisition retained earnings. However, there are no retained earnings yet because control has only just been lost.

2   Chalk's retained earnings are $560,000 (per question) plus the parent's profit on disposal of $344,000. Group retained earnings are $800,000 (per the original consolidated statement of financial position in the question) plus group profit on the sale of $240,000 ie $1,040,000.

Exam alert

Questions may involve part-disposals, leaving investments with both subsidiary and associate status. Disposals are likely to come up regularly at F2, since you have not covered them before.

The following comprehensive question should help you get to grips with disposal problems. **Give yourself at least two hours**. This is a difficult question.

Question 11.2   Disposal

Learning outcome B2

Smith Co bought 80% of the share capital of Jones Co for $324,000 on 1 October 20X5. At that date, Jones Co's retained earnings balance stood at $180,000. The statements of financial position at 30 September 20X8 and the summarised statements of profit or loss and other comprehensive income to that date are given below.

	Smith Co $'000	Jones Co $'000
Non-current assets	360	270
Investment in Jones Co	324	–
Current assets	370	370
	1,054	640
Equity		
$1 ordinary shares	540	180
Retained earnings	414	360
	954	540
Current liabilities	100	100
	1,054	640
Profit before tax	153	126
Tax	(45)	(36)
Profit for the year	108	90

No entries have been made in the financial statements for any of the following transactions.

Assume that profits accrue evenly throughout the year. Neither entity has any other comprehensive income.

It is the group's policy to value the non-controlling interests at fair value at the date of acquisition. The fair value of the non-controlling interests in Jones Co on 1 October 20X5 was $81,000.

Ignore taxation.

Required

Prepare the consolidated statement of financial position and statement of profit or loss at 30 September 20X8 in each of the following circumstances. (Assume no impairment of goodwill.)

(a)   Smith Co sells its entire holding in Jones Co for $650,000 on 30 September 20X8.

(b)   Smith Co sells 25% of its holding in Jones Co for $162,500 on 30 June 20X8. For part (b) only, prepare the consolidated statement of changes in equity, as well as the statement of financial position and statement of profit or loss. The total group equity as at 30 September 20X7 was $1,017,000, which included $99,000 attributable to the non-controlling interests.

(c)   Smith Co sells 50% of its holding in Jones Co for $325,000 on 30 June 20X8, and the remaining holding (fair value $325,000) is to be dealt with as an associate.

(d)   Smith Co sells 50% of its holding in Jones Co for $325,000 on 30 June 20X8, and the remaining holding (fair value $325,000) is to be dealt with as an available for sale financial asset. There was no increase in the fair value of the remaining holding between 30 June 20X8 and 30 September 20X8.

Section summary

Disposals may occur in consolidation questions.

* The effective date of disposal is when **control passes**.

* Treatment of **goodwill** is according to IFRS 3.

* Disposals may be **full** or **partial**, to subsidiary, associate or investment status.

    – If **control is lost**, the interest retained is **fair valued** and becomes part of the calculation of the gain on disposal.

    – If **control is retained**, the change in non-controlling interests is shown as **an adjustment to parent's equity**.

* **Gain or loss** on disposal is calculated for the parent company and the group.

4 Business reorganisations

Introduction

Business reorganisations (ie internal group reorganisations) can take many forms. Apart from divisionalisation, all other internal reorganisations will not affect the consolidated financial statements, but they will affect the accounts of individual companies within the group.

Groups will reorganise on occasions for a variety of reasons.

(a)   A group may want to **float** a business to **reduce the gearing** of the group. The holding company will initially transfer the business into a separate company.

(b)   Companies may be transferred to another business during a **divisionalisation** process.

(c)   The group may reverse into another company to obtain a **stock exchange quotation**.

(d)   Internal reorganisations may create efficiencies of group structure for **tax purposes**.

Such reorganisations involve a restructuring of the relationships within a group. Companies may be transferred to another business during a divisionalisation process. There is generally no effect on the consolidated financial statements, provided that no non-controlling interests are affected, because such reorganisations are only internal. The impact on the individual companies within the group, however, can be substantial. Various different transactions are described here, **only involving 100% subsidiaries**.

4.1 New top parent company

A new top holding company might be needed as a vehicle for flotation or to improve the co-ordination of a diverse business. The new company, P, will issue its own shares to the holders of the shares in S.

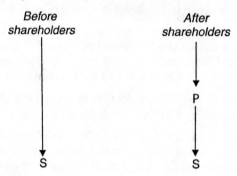

4.2 Subsidiary moved up

This transaction is shown in the diagram below. It might be carried out to allow S_1 to be **sold** while S_2 is retained, or to **split diverse businesses**.

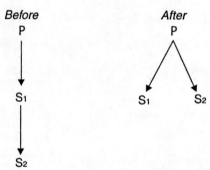

S_1 could transfer its investment in S_2 to P as a dividend *in specie* or by P paying cash. A share for share exchange is not possible because an allotment by P to S_1 is void. A **dividend in specie** is simply a dividend paid other than in cash.

S_1 must have sufficient **distributable profits** for a dividend *in specie*. If the investment in S_2 has been revalued then that can be treated as a realised profit for the purposes of determining the legality of the distribution. For example, suppose the statement of financial position of S_1 is as follows.

	$m
Investment in S_2 (cost $100m)	900
Other net assets	100
	1,000
Share capital	100
Revaluation surplus	800
Retained earnings	100
	1,000

It appears that S_1 cannot make a distribution of more than $100m. If, however, S_1 makes a distribution in kind of its investment in S_2, then the **revaluation surplus** can be treated as realised.

It is not clear how P should account for the transaction. The carrying value of S_2 might be used, but there may be **no legal rule**. P will need to write down its investment in S_1 at the same time. A transfer for cash is probably easiest, but there are still legal pitfalls as to what is distributable, depending on how the transfer is recorded.

There will be **no effect** on the group financial statements as the group has stayed the same: it has made no acquisitions or disposals.

4.3 Subsidiary moved along

This is a transaction which is treated in a very similar manner to that described above.

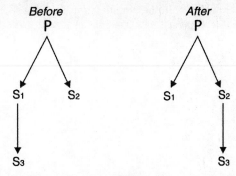

The problem of an effective distribution does not arise here because the holding company did not buy the subsidiary. There may be problems with **financial assistance** if S_2 pays less than the fair value to purchase S_3 as a prelude to S_1 leaving the group.

4.4 Subsidiary moved down

This situation could arise if P is in one country and S_1 and S_2 are in another. A **tax group** can be formed out of such a restructuring.

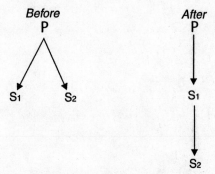

If S_1 paid cash for S_2, the transaction would be straightforward (as described above). It is unclear whether P should recognise a gain or loss on the sale if S_2 is sold for more or less than carrying value. S_1 would be deemed to have made a distribution (avoiding any advance tax payable) only if the **price was excessive**.

Section summary

Reasons for business reorganisations include:

- Stock exchange flotation
- Divisionalisation
- Potential tax advantages

There is usually no effect on the consolidated financial statements provided the non-controlling interests are unchanged. However, a gain or loss may arise in the individual financial statements of the subsidiaries, which will need to be eliminated in the consolidated financial statements.

Chapter Summary

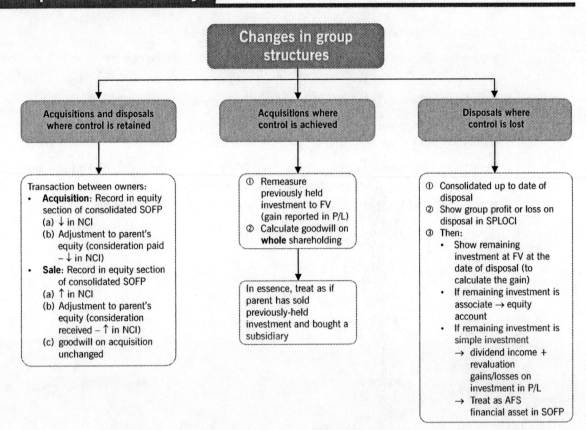

Changes in group structures

Acquisitions and disposals where control is retained

Transaction between owners:
- **Acquisition**: Record in equity section of consolidated SOFP
  - (a) ↓ in NCI
  - (b) Adjustment to parent's equity (consideration paid − ↓ in NCI)
- **Sale**: Record in equity section of consolidated SOFP
  - (a) ↑ in NCI
  - (b) Adjustment to parent's equity (consideration received − ↑ in NCI)
  - (c) goodwill on acquisition unchanged

Acquisitions where control is achieved

① Remeasure previously held investment to FV (gain reported in P/L)
② Calculate goodwill on **whole** shareholding

In essence, treat as if parent has sold previously-held investment and bought a subsidiary

Disposals where control is lost

① Consolidated up to date of disposal
② Show group profit or loss on disposal in SPLOCI
③ Then:
  - Show remaining investment at FV at the date of disposal (to calculate the gain)
  - If remaining investment is associate → equity account
  - If remaining investment is simple investment
    - → dividend income + revaluation gains/losses on investment in P/L
    - → Treat as AFS financial asset in SOFP

Quick Quiz

1   Control is always lost when there is a disposal. True or false?

2   Why is the fair value of the interest retained used in the calculation of a gain on disposal where control is lost?

3   When is the effective date of disposal of shares in an investment?

4   Subside owns 60% of Diary at 31 December 20X8. On 1 July 20X9 it buys a further 20% of Diary. How should this transaction be treated in the group financial statements at 31 December 20X9?

5   Ditch had a 75% subsidiary, Dodge, at 30 June 20X8. On 1 January 20X9 it sold two-thirds of this investment, leaving it with a 25% holding, over which it retained significant influence. How will the remaining investment in Dodge appear in the group financial statements for the year ended 30 June 20X9?

Answers to Quick Quiz

1   False. Control may be retained if the disposal is from subsidiary to subsidiary, even though the parent owns less and the non-controlling interests own more.

2   It may be viewed as part of the consideration received.

3   When control passes.

4   As a transaction between owners, with a decrease in non-controlling interests (from 40% to 20%) and an adjustment to the parent's equity to reflect the difference between the consideration paid and the decrease in non-controlling interests.

5   It will be equity accounted as an associate. In the consolidated statement of financial position, an investment in associate will be recorded taking its fair value at the date of disposal plus a 25% share of the profits accrued between the date of disposal and the year end, less any impairment at the year end. In the consolidated statement of profit or loss and other comprehensive income, Dodge will be consolidated for the first six months and equity accounted for the remaining six months.

Answers to Questions

11.1   Step acquisition

(a)   *Goodwill (at date control obtained)*

	$m	$m
Consideration transferred		480
NCI (30% × 700)		210
Fair value of previously-held equity interest		80
Fair value of identifiable assets acquired and liabilities assumed		
Share capital	300	
Retained earnings	400	
		(700)
		70

(b)   *Profit on derecognition of investment*

	$m
Fair value at date control obtained (see part (a))	80
Cost	(60)
	20

11.2   Disposal

(a)   *Complete disposal at year end (80% to 0%)*

CONSOLIDATED STATEMENT OF FINANCIAL POSITION AS AT 30 SEPTEMBER 20X8

	$'000
Non-current assets	360
Current assets (370 + 650)	1,020
	1,380
Equity	
$1 ordinary shares	540
Retained earnings (W3)	740
Current liabilities	100
	1,380

CONSOLIDATED STATEMENT OF PROFIT OR LOSS FOR THE YEAR ENDED 30 SEPTEMBER 20X8

	$'000
Profit before tax (153 + 126)	279
Profit on disposal (W4)	182
Tax (45 + 36)	(81)
Profit for the year	380
Profit attributable to:	
Owners of the parent	362
Non-controlling interests (20% × 90)	18
	380

Workings

1   *Group structure and timeline*

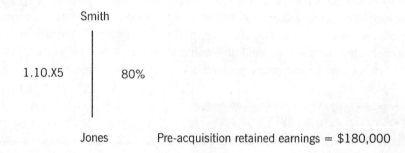

2   *Goodwill (for group profit on disposal calculation)*

	$'000	$'000
Consideration transferred		324
Non-controlling interests		81
Less net assets at acquisition		
Share capital	180	
Retained earnings (W1)	180	
		(360)
		45

3   *Retained earnings carried forward*

	Smith	Jones
	$'000	$'000
Per question/date of disposal	414	360
Add group gain on disposal (W4)	182	–
Pre-acquisition (W1)	–	(180)
		180
Share of post-acquisition reserves up to the disposal (80% × 180)	144	
	740	

4   *Profit on disposal of Jones Co*

	$'000	$'000
Fair value of consideration received		650
Less share of consolidated carrying value when control lost:		
Net assets (540 × 80%)	432	
Goodwill (45 (W2) × 80%)	36	
		(468)
		182

(b)   *Partial disposal: subsidiary to subsidiary (80% to 60%)*

CONSOLIDATED STATEMENT OF FINANCIAL POSITION AS AT 30 SEPTEMBER 20X8

	$'000
Non-current assets (360 + 270)	630.0
Goodwill (part (a)(W2))	45.0
Current assets (370 + 370 + 162.5)	902.5
	1,577.5
Equity	
$1 ordinary shares	540.0
Retained earnings (W2)	603.5
	1,143.5
Non-controlling interests (W3)	234.0
Current liabilities (100 + 100)	200.0
	1,577.5

CONSOLIDATED STATEMENT OF PROFIT OR LOSS FOR THE YEAR ENDED 30 SEPTEMBER 20X8

	$'000	$'000
Profit before tax (153 +126)		279.0
Tax (45 + 36)		(81.0)
Profit for the period		198.0
Profit attributable to:		
Owners of the parent		175.5
Non-controlling interests		
20% × 90 × 9/12	13.5	
40% × 90 × 3/12	9.0	
		22.5
		198.0

CONSOLIDATED STATEMENT OF CHANGES IN EQUITY
FOR THE YEAR TO 30 SEPTEMBER 20X8

	Equity attributable to owners of the parent	Non-controlling interests	Total
	$'000	$'000	$'000
Balance at 1 October 20X7 (per question)	918.0	99.0	1,017.0
Total comprehensive income for the year (per SPL)	175.5	22.5	198.0
Adjustment to parent's equity (W4)	50.0	112.5	162.5
Balance at 30 September 20X8 (per SOFP)	1,143.5	234.0	1,377.5

Workings

1   *Timeline*

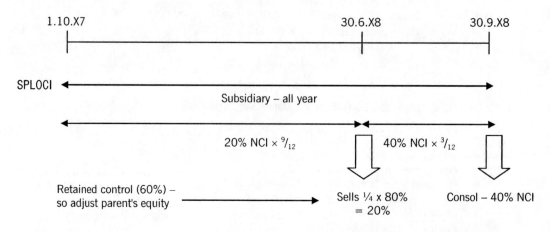

2   *Group retained earnings*

	Smith	Jones 80%	Jones 60% retained
	$'000	$'000	$'000
Per question/at date of disposal			
$(360 - (90 \times \frac{3}{12}))$	414.0	337.5	360.0
Adjustment to parent's equity on disposal (W4)	50.0		
Retained earnings at acquisition		(180.0)	(337.5)
		157.5	22.5
Jones share of post-acq'n earnings			
(157.5 × 80%)	126.0		
Jones share of post-acq'n earnings			
(22.5 × 60%)	13.5		
	603.5		

3   *Non-controlling interests (SOFP)*

	$'000
NCI at acquisition (part (a)(W2))	81.0
NCI share of post-acq'n reserves to disposal (W2) (157.5 × 20%)	31.5
NCI at disposal	112.5
Increase in NCI on disposal (112.5 × 20%/20%)	112.5
NCI share of post-acq'n reserves to year end (W2) (22.5 × 40%)	9.0
	234.0

4   *Adjustment to parent's equity on disposal of 20% of Jones*

	$'000
Fair value of consideration received	162.5
Less increase in NCI in net assets and goodwill at disposal (W3)	(112.5)
	50.0

Note. A journal entry will explain how this is treated in the consolidated financial statements:

	$'000	$'000
DEBIT Cash (added to Smith's current assets on SOFP)	160.0	
CREDIT NCI		112.5
CREDIT Equity attributable to owners of the parent		47.5

(c)   *Partial disposal: subsidiary to associate (80% to 40%)*

CONSOLIDATED STATEMENT OF FINANCIAL POSITION AS AT 30 SEPTEMBER 20X8

	$'000
Non-current assets	360
Investment in associate (W2)	334
Current assets (370 + 325)	695
	1,389
Equity	
$1 ordinary shares	540
Retained earnings (W3)	749
Current liabilities	100
	1,389

CONSOLIDATED STATEMENT OF PROFIT OR LOSS FOR THE YEAR ENDED 30 SEPTEMBER 20X8

	$'000
Profit before tax (153 + (9/12 × 126))	247.5
Profit on disposal (W4)	200.0
Share of profit of associate (90 × 3/12× 40%)	9.0
Tax (45 + (9/12 × 36))	(72.0)
Profit for the period	384.5
Profit attributable to:	
Owners of the parent	371.0
Non-controlling interests (20% × 90 × 9/12)	13.5
	384.5

Workings

1   *Timeline*

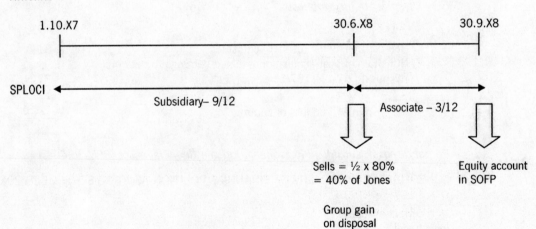

2   *Investment in associate*

	$'000
Fair value at date control lost (new cost)	325
Share of post-acq'n retained reserves (90 × 3/12 × 40%) (W3)	9
	334

3 *Group retained earnings*

	Smith	Jones 80% (subsidiary)	Jones 40% retained (associate)
	$'000	$'000	$'000
Per question/at date of disposal (360 – (90 × 3/12))	414	337.5	360
Group profit on disposal (W4)	200		
Retained earnings at acquisition/date control lost		(180)	(337.5)
		157.5	22.5
Jones share of post-acq'n earnings (157.5 × 80%)	126		
Jones share of post-acq'n earnings (22.5 × 40%)	9		
	749		

4 *Profit on disposal in Smith Co*

	$'000	$'000
Fair value of consideration received		325
Fair value of 40% investment retained		325
Less share of consolidated carrying value when control lost		
Net assets (540 – (90 × 3/12)	517.5	
Goodwill (Part (a)(W2))	45.0	
Less non-controlling interests (W5)	(112.5)	
		(450)
		200

5 *Non-controlling interests*

	$'000
Non-controlling interests at acquisition	81.0
NCI share of post-acquisition retained earnings to date of disposal (20% × 157.5)	31.5
	112.5
Decrease in NCI on loss of control	(112.5)
	0.0

(d) *Partial disposal: subsidiary to available for sale financial asset (80% to 40%)*

CONSOLIDATED STATEMENT OF FINANCIAL POSITION AS AT 30 SEPTEMBER 20X8

	$'000
Non-current assets	360
Investment	325
Current assets (370 + 325)	695
	1,380
Equity	
$1 ordinary shares	540
Retained earnings (W2)	740
Current liabilities	100
	1,380

CONSOLIDATED STATEMENT OF PROFIT OR LOSS FOR THE YEAR ENDED 30 SEPTEMBER 20X8

	$'000
Profit before tax (153 + (9/12 × 126))	247.5
Profit on disposal (Part (c)(W4))	200.0
Tax (45 + (9/12 × 36))	(72.0)
Profit for the period	375.5
Profit attributable to:	
Owners of the parent	362.0
Non-controlling interests (20% × 90 × 9/12)	13.5
	375.5

Workings

1   *Timeline*

(AFSFA = available for sale financial asset)

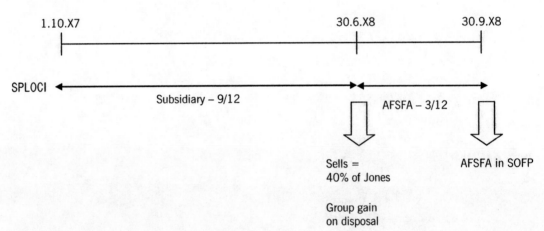

2   *Retained earnings*

	Smith $'000	Jones $'000
Per question/at date of disposal (360 – (90 × 3/12))	414	337.5
Group profit on disposal (Part (c)(W4))	200	
Retained earnings at acquisition		(180.0)
		157.5
Jones share of post-acq'n earnings (157.5 × 80%)	126	
	740	

Now try these questions from the Practice Question Bank	**Number**	**Level**	**Marks**	**Time**
	Q21	Introductory	N/A	5 mins

INDIRECT CONTROL OF SUBSIDIARIES

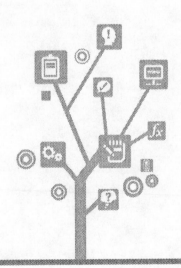

This chapter introduces the second of several more complicated consolidation topics. The best way to tackle these questions is to be logical and to carry out the consolidation on a **step by step** basis.

In questions of this nature, it is very helpful to sketch a **diagram of the group structure**, as we have done. This clarifies the situation and it should point you in the right direction: always sketch the group structure as your first working and double check it against the information in the question.

Topic list	learning outcomes	syllabus references
1 Complex groups	B2	B2(c)
2 Consolidating sub-subsidiaries	B2	B2(c)
3 Direct holdings in sub-subsidiaries	B2	B2(c)
4 Indirect associates	B2	B2(c)

Chapter Overview

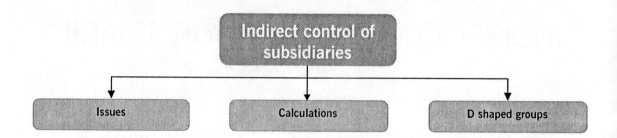

1 Complex groups

Introduction

In this section we shall consider how the principles of statement of financial position consolidation may be applied to more complex structures of companies within a group.

1.1 Types of complex group

(a) **Several subsidiary companies**

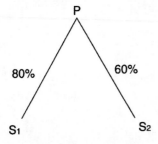

You have already seen this type of structure in your previous studies.

(b) **Sub-subsidiaries**

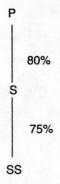

P holds a controlling interest in S which in turn holds a controlling interest in SS. SS is therefore a subsidiary of a subsidiary of P, in other words a **sub-subsidiary** of P.

(c) **Direct holdings in sub-subsidiaries: D-shaped groups**

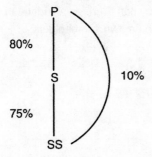

In this example, SS is a sub-subsidiary of P with additional shares held directly by P.

In practice, groups are usually larger, and therefore more complex, but the procedures for consolidation of large groups will not differ from those we shall now describe for smaller ones.

1.2 A parent company which has several subsidiaries

Where a company P has several subsidiaries S_1, S_2, S_3 and so on, the technique for consolidation is exactly as previously described. **Cancellation** is from the parent company, which has assets of investments in subsidiaries S_1, S_2, S_3, to each of the several subsidiaries.

The consolidated statement of financial position will show:

(a)   A single figure for **non-controlling interests** and
(b)   A single figure for **goodwill** arising

A single working should be used for each of the constituents of the consolidated statement of financial position: one working for goodwill, one for non-controlling interests, one for retained earnings (reserves), and so on.

1.3 Sub-subsidiaries

A slightly different problem arises when there are sub-subsidiaries in the group, which is how should we **identify the non-controlling interests** in the retained earnings of the group? Suppose P owns 80% of the equity of S, and that S in turn owns 60% of the equity of SS.

It would appear that in this situation:

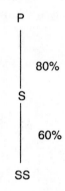

(a)   P owns 80% of 60% = 48% of SS
(b)   The non-controlling interests in S own 20% of 60% = 12% of SS
(c)   The non-controlling interests in SS itself own the remaining 40% of the SS equity

SS is nevertheless a **sub-subsidiary** of P, because it is a subsidiary of S which in turn is a subsidiary of P. The chain of control thus makes SS a sub-subsidiary of P which owns only 48% of its equity.

The total non-controlling interests in SS may be checked by considering a **dividend** of $100 paid by SS where S then distributes its share of this dividend in full to its own shareholders.

		$
S will receive	$60	
P will receive	80% × $60 =	48
Leaving for the total NCI in SS		52
		100

Effective interest

Learning outcome B2

Top Co owns 60% of the equity of Middle Co, which owns 75% of the equity of Bottom Co. What is Top Co's effective holding in Bottom Co?

1.4 Date of effective control

The date the sub-subsidiary comes under the **control of the parent company** is either:

(a)   The date P acquired S if S already holds shares in SS or
(b)   If S acquires shares in SS later, then that later date

You need to think about the dates of acquisition and the order in which the group is built up when you identify which balances to select as the **pre-acquisition** reserves of the sub-subsidiary.

Section summary

When a parent company has **several subsidiaries**, the consolidated statement of financial position shows a single figure for non-controlling interests and for goodwill arising on consolidation. Analysing the group structure, calculating the effective ownership and identifying the dates of control are the key issues in questions on this area.

2   Consolidating sub-subsidiaries

2.1 Consolidated statement of financial position

Introduction

The basic consolidation method in the statement of financial position is as follows.

(a)   **Net assets** show what the group controls (P + 100% S + 100% SS).

(b)   **Equity (capital and reserves)**: show who owns the net assets included elsewhere in the statement of financial position. Reserves (retained earnings), therefore, are based on **effective holdings**.

The basic steps are exactly as you have seen in simpler group structures. As you will see in the examples in this chapter, there are some new complications to be aware of in the workings for **goodwill** and **non-controlling interests**.

Exam alert

Don't panic if a question seems very complicated – sketch the group structure and analyse the information in the question methodically.

Example: Subsidiary acquired first

The draft statements of financial position of P Co, S Co and SS Co on 30 June 20X7 were as follows.

	P Co $	S Co $	SS Co $
Assets			
Non-current assets			
Tangible assets	105,000	125,000	180,000
Investments, at cost			
80,000 shares in S Co	120,000	–	–
60,000 shares in SS Co	–	110,000	–
Current assets	80,000	70,000	60,000
	305,000	305,000	240,000
Equity and liabilities			
Equity			
Ordinary shares of $1 each	80,000	100,000	100,000
Retained earnings	195,000	170,000	115,000
	275,000	270,000	215,000
Payables	30,000	35,000	25,000
	305,000	305,000	240,000

P Co acquired its shares in S Co on 1 July 20X4 when the reserves of S Co stood at $40,000.

S Co acquired its shares in SS Co on 1 July 20X5 when the reserves of SS Co stood at $50,000.

It is the group's policy to measure the non-controlling interests at acquisition at their proportionate share of the fair value of the subsidiary's net assets.

Required

Prepare the draft consolidated statement of financial position as at 30 June 20X7.

Note. Assume no impairment of goodwill.

Solution

This is **two acquisitions** from the point of view of the P group. In 20X4 the group buys 80% of S. Then in 20X5 S (which is now part of the P group) buys 60% of SS.

P buys 80% of S, and then S (80% of S from the group's point of view) buys 60% of SS.

Having calculated the non-controlling interests and the P group interest (see working 1 below), the workings can be constructed. You should, however, note the following.

(a) Group structure working (see working 1)

(b) **Goodwill working**: compare the costs of investments and the non-controlling interests (at proportionate share of net assets, based on effective interest for SS) with the net assets. You should set this out in two columns. In SS Co's goodwill working, as the investment in SS Co is in S Co's books, you need to multiply the investment by P Co's share in S Co. The share of the investment in SS Co belonging to the non-controlling interests of S Co is cancelled in the non-controlling interests working for S Co.

(c) **Retained earnings working**: bring in the share of S Co's and SS Co's post-acquisition retained earnings in the normal way (using the effective percentage for SS).

(d) **Non-controlling interests working**: calculate non-controlling interests in the usual way, using a 20% NCI in S Co's post-acquisition retained earnings and a 52% non-controlling interests in SS Co's post-acquisition retained earnings. In S Co's NCI working, you will need to deduct the NCI's share of the investment in SS Co – this is because we always cancel 100% of the investment on

consolidation and P Co's share is cancelled in the goodwill working so we need to cancel the NCI in S Co's share in S Co's NCI working.

Workings

1   *Group structure*

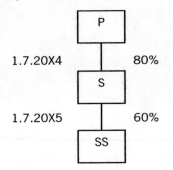

1.7.20X4	80%
1.7.20X5	60%

Effective interests in SS:
P Group (80% × 60%)   = 48%
NCI   = 52%

2   *Goodwill*

	S		SS	
	$	$	$	$
Consideration transferred		120,000	(80% × 110,000)	88,000
Non-controlling interests	(20% × 140,000)	28,000	(52% × 150,000)	78,000
Fair value of identifiable NA acquired:				
Share capital	100,000		100,000	
Retained earnings	40,000		50,000	
		(140,000)		(150,000)
		8,000		16,000
			$24,000	

3   *Retained earnings*

	P Co	S Co	SS Co
	$	$	$
Per question	195,000	170,000	115,000
Pre-acquisition		(40,000)	(50,000)
Post-acquisition		130,000	65,000
Group share:			
In S Co ($130,000 × 80%)	104,000		
In SS Co ($65,000 × 48%)	31,200		
Group retained earnings	330,200		

4   *Non-controlling interests*

	S	SS
	$	$
NCI at acquisition (W2)	28,000	78,000
NCI share of post-acquisition retained earnings		
($130,000 (W3) × 20%)/ ($65,000 (W3) × 52%)	26,000	33,800
Less NCI in investment in SS ($110,000 × 20%)	(22,000)	–
	32,000	111,800
		$143,800

P CO
CONSOLIDATED STATEMENT OF FINANCIAL POSITION AT 30 JUNE 20X7

	$
Assets	
Non-current assets	
Tangible assets (105,000 + 125,000 + 180,000)	410,000
Goodwill (W2)	24,000
Current assets (80,000 + 70,000 + 60,000)	210,000
	644,000
Equity	
Ordinary shares of $1 each fully paid	80,000
Retained earnings (W3)	330,200
	410,200
Non-controlling interests (W4)	143,800
	554,000
Payables (30,000 + 35,000 + 25,000)	90,000
	644,000

2.2 Date of acquisition

Care must be taken when consolidating sub-subsidiaries, because (usually) either:

(a)   The parent company acquired the subsidiary **before** the subsidiary bought the sub-subsidiary (as in the example above); *OR*

(b)   The parent company acquired the subsidiary **after** the subsidiary bought the sub-subsidiary

Depending on whether (a) or (b) is the case, the retained earnings of the sub-subsidiary held at acquisition will be different.

The rule to remember here, when considering pre- and post-acquisition profits, is that we are only interested in the consolidated results of the **parent company**. We will use the example above to demonstrate the required approach. Therefore, the pre-acquisition reserves should be at the date the **parent** obtains control of the sub-subsidiary. If the parent company acquires the subsidiary before the subsidiary acquires the sub-subsidiary, this will be the date that the subsidiary acquires the sub-subsidiary. However, if the parent company acquires the subsidiary after the subsidiary has acquired the sub-subsidiary, this will be the date the parent buys the subsidiary (rather than when the subsidiary acquired the sub-subsidiary).

Example: Sub-subsidiary acquired first

Again using the figures in Example: subsidiary acquired first, assume that:

(a)   S Co purchased its holding in SS Co on 1 July 20X4
(b)   P Co purchased its holding in S Co on 1 July 20X5

The retained earnings figures on the respective dates of acquisition are the same, but on 1 July 20X5 when P Co purchased its holding in S Co, the retained earnings of SS Co were $60,000.

It is the group's policy to measure the non-controlling interests at their proportionate share of the fair value of the subsidiary's net assets.

Solution

The point here is that SS Co only became part of the P group on 1 July 20X5, not on 1 July 20X4. This means that only the retained earnings of SS Co arising after 1 July 20X5 can be included in the post-acquisition reserves of P Co group. Goodwill arising on the acquisition will be calculated by comparing P's share of the cost of the SS investment by S in SS and the non-controlling interests in SS (using the

effective %), to the net assets at acquisition represented by the share capital of SS and its retained earnings **at the date P acquired S** (here $60,000).

P CO
CONSOLIDATED STATEMENT OF FINANCIAL POSITION AS AT 30 JUNE 20X7

	$
Assets	
Non-current assets	
Tangible assets (105,000 + 125,000 + 180,000)	410,000
Goodwill (W2)	19,200
	429,200
Current assets (80,000 + 70,000 + 60,000)	210,000
	639,200
Equity and liabilities	
Ordinary shares $1 each, fully paid	80,000
Retained earnings (W3)	325,400
	405,400
Non-controlling interests (W4)	143,800
	549,200
Payables	90,000
	639,200

Workings

1   *Group structure*

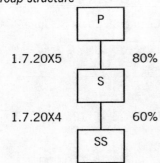

P owns an effective interest of 48% in SS. NCI in SS is 52%.

2   *Goodwill*

The working should be set out as:

	S		SS	
	$	$	$	$
Consideration transferred		120,000	(80% × 110,000)	88,000
Non-controlling interests	(20% × 140,000)	28,000	(52% × 160,000)	83,200
Fair value of net assets at acquisition:				
Share capital	100,000		100,000	
Retained earnings	40,000		60,000	
		(140,000)		(160,000)
		8,000		11,200
			$19,200	

Note. Retained earnings of SS are as at 1 July 20X5 when P acquired control of S.

3   *Retained earnings*

	P Co	S Co	SS Co
	$	$	$
Per question		170,000	115,000
Pre-acquisition		(40,000)	(60,000)
Post-acquisition		130,000	55,000

Group share:	
In S Co ($130,000 × 80%)	104,000
In SS Co ($55,000 × 48%)	26,400
Group retained earnings	325,400

4   Non-controlling interests

The cost of investment in SS is again deducted as 100% of the investment in SS must be cancelled and only 80% was cancelled in SS's goodwill working.

	S $	SS $
NCI at acquisition (W2)	28,000	83,200
NCI share of post-acquisition retained earnings	26,000	28,600
($130,000 (W3) × 20%)/ ($55,000 (W3) × 52%)		
Less NCI in investment in SS ($110,000 × 20%)	(22,000)	–
	32,000	111,800

$143,800

Example: Subsidiary acquired first: non-controlling interests at fair value

The draft statements of financial position of P Co, S Co and SS Co on 30 June 20X7 were as follows.

	P Co $	S Co $	SS Co $
Assets			
Non-current assets			
Tangible assets	105,000	125,000	180,000
Investments at cost			
80,000 shares in S Co	120,000	–	–
60,000 shares in SS Co	–	110,000	–
Current assets	80,000	70,000	60,000
	305,000	305,000	240,000
Equity and liabilities			
Equity			
Ordinary shares of $1 each	80,000	100,000	100,000
Retained earnings	195,000	170,000	115,000
	275,000	270,000	215,000
Payables	30,000	35,000	25,000
	305,000	305,000	240,000

P Co acquired its shares in S Co on 1 July 20X4 when the reserves of S Co stood at $40,000 and S Co acquired its shares in SS Co on 1 July 20X5 when the reserves of SS Co stood at $50,000.

It is the group's policy to measure the non-controlling interests at **fair value** at the date of acquisition. The fair value of the non-controlling interests in S on 1 July 20X4 was $30,000. The fair value of the 52% non-controlling interests on 1 July 20X5 was $95,160.

Required

Prepare the draft consolidated statement of financial position of P Group at 30 June 20X7.

Note. Assume no impairment of goodwill

Solution

As we have seen in earlier chapters, the group's policy on measurement of the non-controlling interests at acquisition does not change the steps we follow in the consolidation.

P CO
CONSOLIDATED STATEMENT OF FINANCIAL POSITION AT 30 JUNE 20X7

	$
Assets	
Non-current assets	
Tangible assets	410,000
Goodwill (W2)	43,160
Current assets	210,000
	663,160
Equity	
Ordinary shares of $1 each fully paid	80,000
Retained earnings (W3)	330,200
	410,200
Non-controlling interests (W4)	162,960
	573,160
Payables	90,000
	663,160

Workings

1   *Group structure*

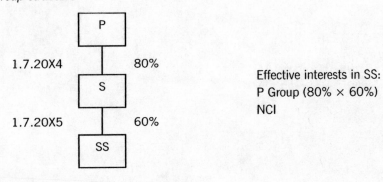

Effective interests in SS:
P Group (80% × 60%)   = 48%
NCI   = 52%

2   *Goodwill*

		S		SS	
	$	$		$	$
Consideration transferred		120,000	($110,000 × 80%)	88,000	
Non-controlling interests (at FV)		30,000		95,160	
Fair value of identifiable net assets acquired					
Share capital	100,000			100,000	
Retained earnings	40,000			50,000	
		(140,000)			(150,000)
		10,000			33,160

$43,160

3   *Retained earnings*

	P Co $	S Co $	SS Co $
Per question	195,000	170,000	115,000
Pre-acquisition		(40,000)	(50,000)
Post-acquisition		130,000	65,000
Group share:			
In S Co ($130,000 × 80%)	104,000		
In SS Co ($65,000 × 48%)	31,200		
Group retained earnings	330,200		

4   *Non-controlling interests*

	S $	SS $
NCI at acquisition (W2)	30,000	95,160
NCI share of post-acquisition retained earnings ($130,000 (W3) × 20%)/ ($65,000 (W3) × 52%)	26,000	33,800
Less NCI in investment in SS ($110,000 × 20%)	(22,000)	–
	34,000	128,960

$162,960

Question 12.2

Learning outcome B2

The statements of financial position of Antelope Co, Yak Co and Zebra Co at 31 March 20X4 are summarised as follows.

	Antelope Co		Yak Co		Zebra Co	
	$	$	$	$	$	$
Assets						
Non-current assets						
Freehold property		100,000		100,000		–
Plant and machinery		210,000		80,000		3,000
		310,000		180,000		3,000
Investments in subsidiaries						
Shares, at cost	110,000		6,200			–
Loan account	–		13,200			–
		110,000		19,400		3,000
Current assets						
Inventories	170,000		20,500		15,000	
Receivables	140,000		50,000		1,000	
Due from Yak Co	10,000		–			
Cash at bank	60,000		16,500		4,000	
		380,000		87,000		20,000
		800,000		286,400		23,000
Equity and liabilities						
Equity						
Ordinary share capital	200,000		100,000		10,000	
Retained earnings	379,600		129,200		(1,000)	
		579,600		229,200		9,000
Non-current liabilities						
Loan from Yak Co		–		–		13,200
Current liabilities						
Trade payables	160,400		40,200		800	
Due to Yak Co	–		10,000		–	
Taxation	60,000		7,000		–	
		220,400		57,200		800
		800,000		286,400		23,000

Notes

1. Antelope Co acquired 75% of the shares of Yak Co on 1 April 20X1 when the credit balance on the retained earnings of that company was $40,000. No dividends have been paid since that date.

2. Yak Co acquired 80% of the shares in Zebra Co on 1 January 20X3 when there was a debit balance on the retained earnings of that company of $3,000.

3. During the year to 31 March 20X4 Antelope Co sold inventory to Yak Co for $20,000. At 31 March 20X4 50% of this amount was still held in the inventories of Yak Co. Antelope earns a mark-up of 25% on all sales.

4. It is the group's policy to measure the non-controlling interests at fair value at the date of acquisition. The fair value of the non-controlling interests in Yak Co at 1 April 20X1 was $36,000. The fair value of the 40% non-controlling interests in Antelope Co at 1 January 20X3 was $3,100.

Required

Prepare the draft consolidated statement of financial position of Antelope Co at 31 March 20X4. (Assume no impairment of goodwill.)

2.3 Consolidated statement of profit or loss and other comprehensive income

The basic consolidation method in the statement of profit or loss and other comprehensive income is as follows.

(a) **Income, expenses, other comprehensive income:** show what the group controls line by line (P + 100% S + 100% SS).

(b) **Non-controlling interests:** show the non-controlling interests' share of S and SS's profit and total comprehensive income. The NCI in SS should be based on the **effective holding**.

The basic steps are exactly as you have seen in simpler group structures.

Example: Consolidated statement of profit or loss and other comprehensive income

The statements of profit or loss and other comprehensive income of A, B and C for the year ended 31 December 20X2 are provided below:

	A $m	B $m	C $m
Revenue	2,000	1,200	800
Cost of sales	(1,400)	(800)	(400)
Gross profit	600	400	400
Operating expenses	(240)	(160)	(200)
	360	240	200
Investment income (Note 3)	100	30	–
Profit before tax	460	270	200
Income tax expense	(140)	(90)	(60)
Profit for the year	320	180	140
Other comprehensive income	80	50	10
Total comprehensive income for the year	400	230	150

Notes:

1   A acquired 80% of the ordinary share capital of B on 1 January 20X0 and B acquired 75% of the ordinary share capital of C on 1 January 20X1.

2   There has been no impairment to goodwill since the acquisition date.

3   In the year ended 31 December 20X2 all three entities paid a dividend to their ordinary shareholders. A paid a dividend of $160 million, B paid a dividend of $100 million and C paid a dividend of $40 million.

Required

Prepare the consolidated statement of profit or loss and other comprehensive income for the A Group for the year ended 31 December 20X2.

Solution

As we have seen in earlier chapters, the group's policy on measurement of the non-controlling interests at acquisition does not change the steps we follow in the consolidation.

	$m
Revenue (2,000 + 1,200 + 800)	4,000
Cost of sales (1,400 + 800 + 400)	(2,600)
Gross profit	1,400
Operating expenses (240 + 160 + 200)	(600)
	800
Investment income (100 + 30 – 80 (W3) – 30 (W3))	20
Profit before tax	820
Income tax expense (140 + 90 + 60)	(290)
Profit for the year	530
Other comprehensive income (80 + 50 + 10)	140
Total comprehensive income for the year	670
Profit attributable to:	
Owners of the parent (530 – 92)	438
Non-controlling interests (W2)	92
	530
Total comprehensive income attributable to:	
Owners of the parent (670 – 106)	564
Non-controlling interests (W2)	106
	670

1   *Group structure*

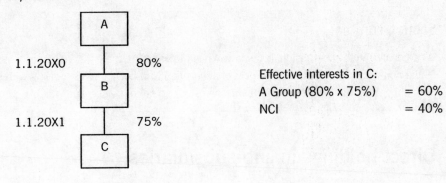

Effective interests in C:
A Group (80% x 75%)   = 60%
NCI   = 40%

2   *Non-controlling interests*

	$m
In profit for the year:	
B (180 × 20%)	36
C (140 × 40%)	56
	92
In total comprehensive income:	
B (230 × 20%)	46
C (150 × 40%)	60
Group retained earnings	106

3   *Intragroup dividend income*

Dividends paid by B to A = $100m × 80% = $80m (cancel out of investment income)
Dividends paid by C to B = $40m × 75% = $30m (cancel out of investment income)

You should follow this **step by step approach** in all questions. This applies to Section 3 below as well.

 STEP 1   Sketch the **group structure** and check it against the question.

 STEP 2   Add details to the sketch of dates of acquisition, holdings acquired (percentage and nominal values) and cost.

 STEP 3   Draw up a proforma for the statement of financial position.

 STEP 4   Work methodically down the statements of financial position, transferring figures to proforma or workings.

 STEP 5   Use the notes in the question to make adjustments such as eliminating intragroup balances and unrealised profits.

 STEP 6   **Goodwill working**: compare costs of investment with the **effective** group interests acquired.

 STEP 7   **Reserves working**: include the group share of subsidiary and sub-subsidiary post-acquisition retained earnings (effective holdings again).

 STEP 8   **Non-controlling interests working**: total NCI in subsidiary plus total NCI in sub-subsidiary.

 STEP 9   Prepare the **consolidated statement of financial position** (and statement of profit or loss and other comprehensive income if required).

Section summary

When dealing with **sub-subsidiaries**, you will need to calculate the effective interests owned by the group and by the non-controlling interests. The date of acquisition is important when dealing with sub-subsidiaries. Remember that it is the post-acquisition reserves from a group perspective which are important.

3 Direct holdings in sub-subsidiaries

Introduction

Consider the following structure, sometimes called a **D-shaped group**.

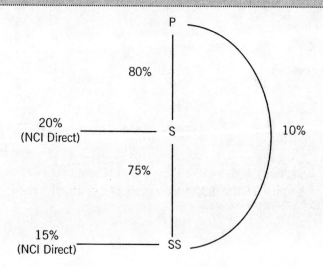

In the structure above, there is:

(a) A **direct** non-controlling share in S of   20%
(b) A **direct** non-controlling share in SS of   15%
(c) An **indirect** non-controlling share in SS of 20% × 75% =   15%
                                                                30%

The effective interest in SS is:

Indirect group interest 80% × 75%   =   60% interest
Direct group interest   10%
                                            70%
∴ NCI   30%
                                           100%

Having ascertained the structure and non-controlling interests, proceed as for a typical sub-subsidiary situation.

Question 12.3	D-shaped group

Learning outcome B2

The draft statements of financial position of Hulk Co, Molehill Co and Pimple Co as at 31 May 20X5 are as follows.

	Hulk Co		Molehill Co		Pimple Co	
	$	$	$	$	$	$
Assets						
Non-current assets						
Tangible assets		90,000		60,000		60,000
Investments in						
Subsidiaries at cost						
Shares in Molehill Co	90,000		–		–	
Shares in Pimple Co	25,000		42,000		–	
		115,000		42,000		–
		205,000		102,000		60,000
Current assets		40,000		50,000		40,000
		245,000		152,000		100,000
Equity and liabilities						
Equity						
Ordinary shares $1	100,000		50,000		50,000	
Revaluation surplus	50,000		20,000		–	
Retained earnings	45,000		32,000		25,000	
		195,000		102,000		75,000
Non-current liabilities						
12% loan		–		10,000		–
		195,000		112,000		75,000
Current liabilities						
Payables		50,000		40,000		25,000
		245,000		152,000		100,000

(a) Hulk Co acquired 60% of the shares in Molehill on 1 January 20X3 when the balance on that company's retained earnings was $8,000 (credit) and there was no revaluation surplus.

(b) Hulk acquired 20% of the shares of Pimple Co and Molehill acquired 60% of the shares of Pimple Co on 1 January 20X4 when that company's retained earnings stood at $15,000.

(c) There has been no payment of dividends by either Molehill or Pimple since they became subsidiaries.

(d) There was no impairment of goodwill.

(e) It is the group's policy to measure the non-controlling interests at acquisition at its proportionate share of the fair value of the subsidiary's net assets.

Required

Prepare the consolidated statement of financial position of Hulk Co as at 31 May 20X5.

Section summary

D-shaped groups are consolidated in the same way as a typical sub-subsidiary situation. It is the structure and non-controlling interests' calculations that are important.

4 Indirect associates

A group may have an indirect associate as illustrated in the following diagram.

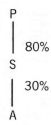

P

| 80%

S

| 30%

A

Notes

1   P **controls** a 30% investment in A, so A is an associate. This is the percentage we use for the investment in associate working in the consolidated statement of financial position and for the share of the associate's profit and other comprehensive income in the consolidated statement of profit or loss and other comprehensive income.

2   P **owns** 80% × 30% = 24% in A. This is the percentage we use in the consolidated retained earnings working.

3   The **non-controlling interests in S** own 20% × 30% = 6% in A.

4.1 Treatment in the consolidated financial statements

The principles are very similar to those seen earlier in the context of indirect subsidiaries.

*   In the statement of financial position the investment is based on **control**, while retained earnings and non-controlling interests are based on **ownership**.

*   In the statement of profit or loss and other comprehensive income the profit/other comprehensive income is based on **control**, with **ownership** being shown in the analysis of profits/total comprehensive income at the end of the statement.

STATEMENT OF FINANCIAL POSITION

Investment in associate	
Cost of investment (per S's SOFP)	X
S's share (30%) of A's post-acquisition earnings	X
	X̄

Retained earnings	P	S	A
Per question	X	X	X
Less pre-acq'n reserves		(X)	(X)
		$\overline{Y}$	$\overline{Z}$
P's share of S's post-acq'n earnings (Y × 80%)	X		
P's share of A's post-acq'n earnings (Z × 24%)	X		
	$\overline{X}$		
Non-controlling interests			
NCI at acq'n		X	
Add NCI in S's post-acq'n earnings (Y × 20%)		X	
Add NCI in A's post-acq'n earnings (Z × 6%)		X	
		$\overline{X}$	

STATEMENT OF PROFIT OR LOSS AND OTHER COMPREHENSIVE INCOME

Share of associate's profit for the year	30% × A's PFY
Share of associate's other comprehensive income for the year	30% × A's OCI
Profit attributable to:	
Owners of the parent	X
Non-controlling interests [(20% × S's PFY) + (**6%** × A's PFY)]	X
	X
Total comprehensive income attributable to:	
Owners of the parent	X
Non-controlling interests [(20% × S's TCI) + (**6%** × A's TCI)]	X
	X

Section summary

- A group may have an indirect associate.

- The equity accounted investment in the statement of financial position and the share of the associate's profit in the statement of profit or loss and other comprehensive income should be based on the proportion **owned by the subsidiary** (and **controlled by the group**).

- Effective ownership percentages are used to calculate group retained earnings and the NCI in the indirect associate.

Chapter Summary

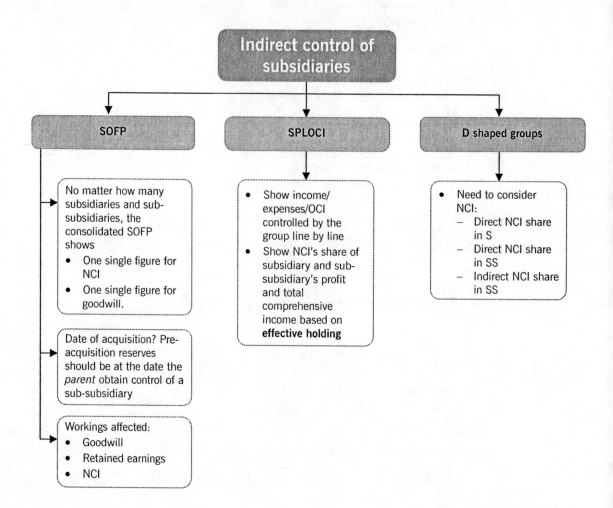

Indirect control of subsidiaries

SOFP

No matter how many subsidiaries and sub-subsidiaries, the consolidated SOFP shows
- One single figure for NCI
- One single figure for goodwill.

Date of acquisition? Pre-acquisition reserves should be at the date the *parent* obtain control of a sub-subsidiary

Workings affected:
- Goodwill
- Retained earnings
- NCI

SPLOCI

- Show income/expenses/OCI controlled by the group line by line
- Show NCI's share of subsidiary and sub-subsidiary's profit and total comprehensive income based on **effective holding**

D shaped groups

- Need to consider NCI:
  - Direct NCI share in S
  - Direct NCI share in SS
  - Indirect NCI share in SS

Quick Quiz

1   B Co owns 60% of the equity of C Co which owns 75% of the equity of D Co. What is the total non-controlling interests' percentage ownership in D Co?

2   What is the basic consolidation method for sub-subsidiaries in the consolidated statement of financial position?

3   P Co owns 25% of R Co's equity and 75% of Q Co's equity. Q Co owns 40% of R Co's equity. What is the total non-controlling interests' percentage ownership in R Co?

Answers to Quick Quiz

1 B

  | 60%

  C

  | 75%

  D

Effective interest in D = 60% x 75%   = 45%
Therefore, non-controlling interests   = 55%
                                       100%

(Alternatively, you could calculate it as 25% + (40% of 75%) = 55%)

2 • Net assets: show what the group controls
   • Equity (capital and reserves): show who owns the net assets

3

                        P

              75% |
                   |
    25%   ———— Q   25%
  (NCI direct)
                   |
              40% |
                   |
    35%   ———— R
  (NCI direct)

Effective interest in R: Direct   25%
                            Indirect (75% × 40%)   30%
                                                    55%
                            Non-controlling interests 45%
                                                   100%

(Alternatively, you could calculate non-controlling interests as 35% + (25% × 40%) = 45%)

Answers to Questions

12.1 Effective interest

Top owns 60% of 75% of Bottom Co = 45%.

12.2 Sub-subsidiary

ANTELOPE CO
CONSOLIDATED STATEMENT OF FINANCIAL POSITION AS AT 31 MARCH 20X4

	$	$
Assets		
Non-current assets		
Freehold property (100,000 + 100,000)		200,000
Plant and machinery (210,000 + 80,000 + 3,000)		293,000
		493,000
Goodwill (W2)		6,750
Current assets		499,750
Inventories (170,000 + 20,500 + 15,000 – 2,000 (W5))	203,500	
Receivables (140,000 + 50,000 + 1,000)	191,000	
Cash at bank (60,000 + 16,500 + 4,000)	80,500	
		475,000
		974,750
Equity and liabilities		
Equity		
Ordinary share capital		200,000
Retained earnings (W3)		445,700
		645,700
Non-controlling interests (W4)		60,650
		706,350
Current liabilities		
Trade payables (160,400 + 40,200 + 800)	201,400	
Taxation (60,000 + 7,000)	67,000	
		268,400
		974,750

Workings

1 *Group structure*

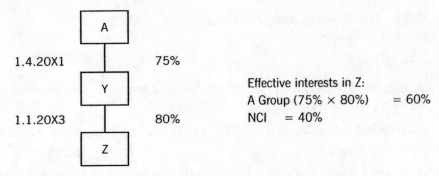

Effective interests in Z:
A Group (75% × 80%) = 60%
NCI = 40%

2 *Goodwill*

		Y		Z	
	$	$		$	$
Consideration transferred		110,000	(75% × 6,200)		4,650
Non-controlling interests (at fair value)		36,000			3,100
Fair value of identifiable NA acquired:					
Share capital	100,000			10,000	
Retained earnings	40,000			(3,000)	
		(140,000)			(7,000)
		6,000			750

$$\underbrace{}$$

$6,750

3 *Retained earnings*

	Antelope	Yak	Zebra
	$	$	$
Per question	379,600	129,200	(1,000)
Unrealised profit in inventories (W5)	(2,000)		
Pre-acquisition profit/losses		(40,000)	3,000
Post-acquisition profits		89,200	2,000
Group share			
In Yak ($89,200 × 75%)	66,900		
In Zebra ($2,000 × 60%)	1,200		
Group retained earnings	445,700		

4 *Non-controlling interests*

	Yak	Zebra
	$	$
NCI at acquisition (W2)	36,000	3,100
NCI in post-acquisition retained earnings	22,300	800
($89,200 (W3) × 25%)/($2,000 (W3) × 40%)		
Less NCI share of investment in Zebra ($6,200 × 25%)	(1,550)	–
	56,750	3,900

$$\underbrace{}$$

$60,650

5 *Unrealised profit*

Antelope (parent) sells to Yak (subsidiary)

PUP = $20,000 × ½ in inventory × 25/125 mark-up = $2,000

DEBIT	Retained earnings of Antelope	$2,000	
CREDIT	Inventories		$2,000

6 *Intragroup balances*

The intragroup receivable of $10,000 in Antelope's books cancels with the intragroup payable of $10,000 in Yak's books.

The intragroup loan receivable of $13,200 in Yak's books cancels with the intragroup loan payable in Zebra's books of $13,200.

The end result is that all intragroup payables and receivables are eliminated in the consolidated statement of financial position.

12.3 'D' -shaped group

HULK CO
CONSOLIDATED STATEMENT OF FINANCIAL POSITION AS AT 31 MAY 20X5

	$	$
Assets		
Non-current assets		
Tangible assets (90,000 + 60,000 + 60,000)	210,000	
Goodwill (W2)	69,000	
		279,000
Current assets (40,000 + 50,000 + 40,000)		130,000
		409,000
Equity and liabilities		
Equity		
Ordinary shares $1	100,000	
Revaluation surplus (W4)	62,000	
Retained earnings (W3)	65,000	
	227,000	
Non-controlling interests (W5)	57,000	
		284,000
Non-current liabilities		
12% loan		10,000
		294,000
Current liabilities		
Payables (50,000 + 40,000 + 25,000)		115,000
		409,000

Workings

1   *Group structure*

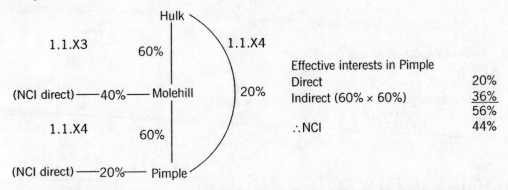

Note. Pimple comes into Hulk's control on 1 January 20X4. As the investments in Pimple by Hulk and Molehill both happened on the same date, only one goodwill calculation is needed in respect of Pimple.

The direct non-controlling interests in Molehill Co is		40%
The direct non-controlling interests in Pimple Co is	20%	
The indirect non-controlling interests in Pimple Co is (40% of 60%)	24%	
The total non-controlling interests in Pimple Co is		44%
The group share of Molehill Co is 60% and of Pimple Co is 56%		

2 *Goodwill*

	Hulk in Molehill $	$	Hulk and Molehill in Pimple $	$
Consideration transferred – direct		90,000		25,000
– indirect			(60% × 42,000)	25,200
Non-controlling interests ($58,000 × 40%)/ ($65,000 × 44%)		23,200		28,600
Fair value of net assets at acquisition:				
Share capital	50,000		50,000	
Retained earnings	8,000		15,000	
		(58,000)		(65,000)
		55,200		13,800
			$69,000	

3 *Retained earnings*

	Hulk $	Molehill $	Pimple $
Per question	45,000	32,000	25,000
Pre-acquisition profits		(8,000)	(15,000)
Post-acquisition retained earnings		24,000	10,000
Group share:			
In Molehill ($24,000 × 60%)	14,400		
In Pimple ($10,000 × 56%)	5,600		
Group retained earnings	65,000		

4 *Revaluation surplus*

	$
Hulk Co	50,000
Molehill Co all post-acquisition ($20,000 × 60%)	12,000
	62,000

Note. Pimple does not have any revaluation surplus.

5 *Non-controlling interests*

	Molehill $	Pimple $
NCI at acquisition (W2)	23,200	28,600
NCI share of post-acquisition retained earnings ($24,000 (W3) × 40%)/ ($10,000 (W3) × 44%)	9,600	4,400
NCI share of post-acquisition revaluation surplus ($20,000 (W4) × 40%)	8,000	–
Less NCI share of investment in Pimple ($42,000 × 40%)	(16,800)	–
	24,000	33,000
		$57,000

	Number	Level	Marks	Time
Now try these questions from the Practice Question Bank	Q22	Introductory	N/A	5 mins

FOREIGN SUBSIDIARIES

Many of the largest companies in any country, while based there, have subsidiaries and other interests all over the world: they are truly **global companies** and so foreign currency consolidations take place frequently in practice. Make sure you understand this topic, as it is likely to be examined.

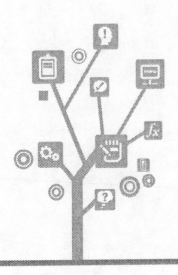

Topic list	learning outcomes	syllabus references
1 Foreign currency translation	B2	B2(b)
2 IAS 21 Individual company stage	B2	B2(b)
3 IAS 21 Consolidated financial statements stage	B2	B2(b)

Chapter Overview

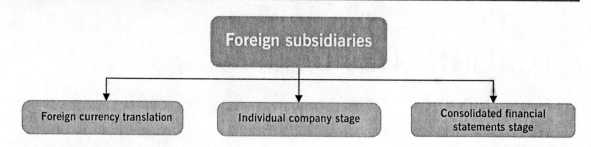

1   Foreign currency translation

Introduction

If a company trades overseas, it will buy or sell assets in foreign currencies. For example, an Indian company might buy materials from Canada, pay for them in US dollars, and then sell its finished goods in Germany, receiving payment in euros. The purchase and sale must be translated into the company's local currency (here the Indian rupee) to record the double entry in the nominal ledger. If the company owes money in a foreign currency at the end of the accounting year, or holds monetary assets which were bought in a foreign currency, those liabilities or assets must be also translated into the local currency.

A company might have a subsidiary abroad (ie a foreign entity that it owns), and the subsidiary will trade in its own local currency. The subsidiary will keep its nominal ledger and prepare its annual financial statements in its own currency. However, at the year end the parent company must consolidate the results of the overseas subsidiary into its group financial statements, so that the assets and liabilities and the annual profits of the subsidiary are translated into the parent company's currency.

If foreign currency exchange rates remained constant, there would be no accounting problem. As you will be aware, however, foreign exchange rates are continually changing. It is not inconceivable, for example, that the rate of exchange between the Polish zloty and British sterling might be Z6.2 to £1 at the start of the accounting year, and Z5.6 to £1 at the end of the year (in this example, a 10% increase in the relative strength of the zloty).

There are two distinct types of foreign currency transaction, conversion and translation.

1.1 Conversion gains and losses   3/12

Conversion is the process of exchanging amounts of one foreign currency for another.

For example, suppose a US company buys a large consignment of goods from a supplier in Germany. The order is placed on 1 May and the agreed price is €124,250. At the time of delivery, the rate of foreign exchange was €2 to $1. The local company would record the amount owed in its books as follows.

DEBIT   Purchases (€124,250 ÷ 2) $62,125
CREDIT   Payables $62,125

When the local company comes to pay the supplier, it needs to obtain some foreign currency. By this time, however, if the rate of exchange has altered to €2.05 to $1, the cost of raising €124,250 would be (÷ 2.05) $60,610. The company would need to spend only $60,610 to settle a debt for inventories costing $62,125. As the payable is settled for less than the company originally thought it would have to pay, a profit on conversion or exchange gain of $1,515 ($62,125 − $60,610) has arisen.

DEBIT   Payables account $62,125
CREDIT   Cash $60,610
CREDIT   Profit on conversion (exchange gain) $1,515

Profits (or losses) on conversion would be included in profit or loss for the year in which conversion (whether payment or receipt) takes place.

Suppose that another US company sells goods to a Chinese company, and it is agreed that payment should be made in Chinese yuan at a price of Y116,000. We will further assume that the exchange rate at the time of sale is Y10.75 to $1, but when the debt is eventually paid, the rate has altered to Y10.8 to $1. The company would record the sale as follows.

DEBIT   Receivables (116,000 ÷ 10.75) $10,791
CREDIT   Revenue $10,791

When the Y116,000 are paid, the local company will convert them into \$, to obtain ($\div$ 10.8) \$10,741. In this example, there has been a loss on conversion of \$50 which will be written off to profit or loss for the year:

DEBIT	Cash	\$10,741	
DEBIT	Loss on conversion (exchange loss)	\$50	
CREDIT	Receivables account		\$10,791

There are **no accounting difficulties** concerned with foreign currency conversion gains or losses, and the procedures described above are uncontroversial.

1.2 Translation

Foreign currency translation, as distinct from conversion, does not involve the act of exchanging one currency for another. **Translation is required at the end of an accounting period when a company still holds assets or liabilities in its statement of financial position, which were obtained or incurred in a foreign currency.**

These assets or liabilities might consist of any of the following:

(a) An individual home company holding individual **assets** or **liabilities** originating in a foreign currency deal

(b) An individual home company with a separate **branch** of the business operating abroad which keeps its own books of account in the local currency

(c) A home company which wishes to consolidate the **results of a foreign subsidiary**

There has been great **uncertainty** about the method which should be used to translate the following:

- Value of assets and liabilities from a foreign currency into \$ for the year-end statement of financial position

- Profits of an independent foreign branch or subsidiary into \$ for the annual statement of profit or loss and other comprehensive income

Suppose, for example, that an Indian subsidiary purchases a piece of property for 2,100,000 rupees on 31 December 20X7. The rate of exchange at this time was 70 rupees to \$1. During 20X8, the subsidiary charged depreciation on the building of 16,800 rupees, so that at 31 December 20X8, the subsidiary recorded the asset as follows.

	Rupees
Property at cost	2,100,000
Less accumulated depreciation	16,800
Net book value	2,083,200

At this date, the rate of exchange has changed to 60 rupees to \$1.

The parent company must translate the subsidiary and this particular asset's value into \$, but there is a **choice of exchange rates**.

(a) Should the rate of exchange for translation be the rate which existed at the date of purchase, which would give a net book value of 2,083,200 $\div$ 70 = \$29,760?

(b) Should the rate of exchange for translation be the rate existing at the end of 20X8 (the closing rate of 60 rupees to \$1)? This would give a net book value of \$34,720.

Similarly, should depreciation be charged to group profit or loss at the rate of 70 rupees to \$1 (the historical rate), 60 rupees to \$1 (the closing rate), or at an average rate for the year (say, 64 rupees to \$1)?

1.3 Consolidated financial statements

If a parent has a subsidiary whose financial statements are presented in a foreign currency, those financial statements must be translated into the local currency before they can be included in the consolidated financial statements.

The **closing rate** is used for most items in the **statement of financial position** and the statement of financial position is prepared as at the year end. The **statement of profit or loss and other comprehensive income** is translated at the actual rate or **average rate** if a close approximation. **Exchange differences** are recognised in **other comprehensive income**.

We will look at the consolidation of foreign subsidiaries in much more detail in Section 3 of this chapter.

Section summary

Questions on foreign currency translation have always been popular with examiners. In general, you are required to prepare **consolidated financial statements** for a group which includes a foreign subsidiary.

2 IAS: Individual company stage

Introduction

The questions discussed above are addressed by IAS 21 *The effects of changes in foreign exchange rates*. We will examine those matters which affect single company accounts here.

2.1 Definitions

These are some of the definitions given by IAS 21.

KEY TERMS

FOREIGN CURRENCY. A currency other than the functional currency of the entity.

FUNCTIONAL CURRENCY. The currency of the primary economic environment in which the entity operates.

PRESENTATION CURRENCY. The currency in which the financial statements are presented.

EXCHANGE RATE. The ratio of exchange between two currencies.

EXCHANGE DIFFERENCE. The difference resulting from translating a given number of units of one currency into another currency at different exchange rates.

CLOSING RATE. The spot exchange rate at the year-end date.

SPOT EXCHANGE RATE. The exchange rate for immediate delivery.

MONETARY ITEMS. Units of currency held, and assets and liabilities to be received or paid in a fixed or determinable number of units of currency. *(IAS 21)*

Each entity – whether an individual company, a parent of a group, or an operation within a group (such as a subsidiary, associate or branch) – should determine its **functional currency** and **measure its results and financial position in that currency**.

For most individual companies the functional currency will be the currency of the country in which they are located and in which they carry out most of their transactions. Determining the functional currency is much more likely to be an issue where an entity operates as part of a group. IAS 21 contains detailed guidance on how to determine an entity's functional currency and we will look at this in more detail in Section 3.

An entity can **present** its financial statements in any currency (or currencies) it chooses: in other words, it can have a **presentation currency** that is different from its functional currency. IAS 21 deals with the situation in which financial statements are presented in a currency other than the functional currency.

Again, this is unlikely to be an issue for most individual companies. Their presentation currency will normally be the same as their functional currency (the currency of the country in which they operate).

A company's presentation currency may be different from its functional currency if it is listed on a foreign stock exchange or operates within a group, and we will look at this in Section 3.

2.2 Determining functional currency

IAS 21 states that an entity should consider the following factors in determining its functional currency:

(a) The currency that mainly **influences sales prices** for goods and services (often the currency in which prices are denominated and settled)

(b) The currency of the **country whose competitive forces and regulations** mainly determine the sales prices of its goods and services

(c) The currency that mainly **influences labour, material and other costs** of providing goods or services (often the currency in which prices are denominated and settled)

Sometimes the functional currency of an entity is not immediately obvious. Management must then exercise judgement and may also need to consider:

(a) The currency in which **funds from financing activities** (raising loans and issuing equity) are generated

(b) The currency in which **receipts from operating activities** are usually retained

2.3 Foreign currency transactions: initial recognition

IAS 21 states that a foreign currency transaction should be recorded, on initial recognition in the functional currency, by applying the exchange rate between the reporting currency and the foreign currency **at the date of the transaction** to the foreign currency amount.

An **average rate** for a period may be used if exchange rates do not fluctuate significantly.

2.4 Reporting at subsequent year ends

The following rules apply at each subsequent year end.

(a) Report foreign currency **monetary items** (eg receivables, payables, cash, loans) using the **closing rate**

(b) Report **non-monetary items** (eg non-current assets, inventories) which are carried at **historical cost** in a foreign currency using the **exchange rate at the date of the transaction** (historical rate)

(c) Report **non-monetary items** which are carried at **fair value** in a foreign currency using the exchange rates that existed **when the values were measured**

2.5 Recognition of exchange differences

Exchange differences occur when there is a **change in the exchange rate** between the transaction date and the date of settlement of monetary items arising from a foreign currency transaction.

Exchange differences arising on the settlement of monetary items (receivables, payables, loans, cash in a foreign currency) or on translating an entity's monetary items at rates different from those at which they were translated initially, or reported in previous financial statements, should be **recognised in profit or loss** in the period in which they arise.

There are two situations to consider.

(a) The transaction is **settled in the same period** as that in which it occurred: all the exchange difference is recognised in that period.

(b) The transaction is **settled in a subsequent accounting period**: the exchange difference recognised in each intervening period up to the period of settlement is determined by the change in exchange rates during that period.

In other words, where a monetary item has not been settled at the end of a period, it should be **restated using the closing exchange rate** and any gain or loss taken to the statement of profit or loss.

For **non-monetary items carried at fair value** which are retranslated at the date of remeasurement, exchange differences should be **recognised in the same place as the revaluation gain or loss**. If a gain or loss on a non-monetary item is recognised in other comprehensive income (eg revaluation of a property), any exchange component of that gain or loss shall be recognised in other comprehensive income. Where a gain or loss is recognised in profit or loss, any exchange component of that gain or loss shall be recognised in profit or loss.

Question 13.1

Entries

Learning outcome B2

White Cliffs Co, whose year end is 31 December, buys some goods from Rinka SA of France on 30 September 20X1. The invoice value is €40,000 and is due for settlement in equal instalments on 30 November 20X1 and 31 January 20X2. The exchange rate moved as follows.

	€= $1
30 September 20X1	1.60
30 November 20X1	1.80
31 December 20X1	1.90
31 January 20X2	1.85

Required

State the accounting entries in the books of White Cliffs Co.

Section summary

Foreign transactions are initially translated at the **exchange rate at the date of the transaction**. At the year end, **monetary** assets and liabilities are translated at the **closing rate. Exchange differences** are recognised in **profit or loss**.

Non-monetary assets and liabilities are only **retranslated if they are carried at fair value**. The exchange gain or loss is recognised in the same place as the revaluation gain or loss (either profit or loss or other comprehensive income).

3 IAS 21: Consolidated financial statements stage 5/11, 11/11

Introduction

We will now look at the effect on consolidated financial statements.

3.1 Definitions

The following definitions are relevant here.

KEY TERMS

FOREIGN OPERATION. A subsidiary, associate, joint arrangement or branch of a reporting entity, the activities of which are based or conducted in a country or currency other than those of the reporting entity.

NET INVESTMENT IN A FOREIGN OPERATION. The amount of the reporting entity's interest in the net assets of that operation.

(IAS 21)

In consolidated financial statements, **the presentation currency used is the functional currency of the parent company**.

Therefore, a holding or parent company with foreign operations must translate the financial statements of those operations into its own reporting currency before they can be consolidated into the group financial statements. Whether or not the subsidiary needs translating depends on whether the functional currency of the subsidiary is the same as or different to the parent's functional currency. If the subsidiary's functional currency is the same as the parent's, it won't need translating for the group financial statements. However, if the subsidiary's functional currency is different to the parent's, it will need translation for the group financial statements.

To determine the functional currency of the foreign operation, the factors in Section 2.2 must be considered, but, in addition, the following factors should be considered in determining whether its functional currency is the same as that of the reporting entity:

(a)   Whether the activities of the foreign operation are carried out as an **extension of the parent**, rather than being carried out with a **significant degree of autonomy**

(b)   Whether **transactions with the parent** are a high or a low proportion of the foreign operation's activities

(c)   Whether **cash flows** from the activities of the foreign operation **directly affect the cash flows of the parent** and are readily available for remittance to it

(d)   Whether **cash flows** from the activities of the foreign operation are **sufficient to service** existing and normally expected **debt** obligations without funds being made available by the reporting entity

Exam alert

A question involving foreign currency is almost certain to consist of a foreign operation consolidation.

To sum up: in order to determine the functional currency of a foreign operation it is necessary to consider the **relationship** between the foreign operation and its parent.

- If the foreign operation carries out its business as though it were an **extension of the parent's operations**, it almost certainly has the **same functional currency** as the parent.

- If the foreign operation is **semi-autonomous**, it almost certainly has a **different functional currency** from the parent.

The translation method used has to reflect the economic reality of the relationship between the reporting entity (the parent) and the foreign operation.

3.1.1 Same functional currency as the reporting entity

In this situation, the foreign operation normally carries on its business as though it were an **extension of the reporting entity's operations**. For example, it may only sell goods imported from, and remit the proceeds directly to, the reporting entity.

Any **movement in the exchange rate** between the reporting currency and the foreign operation's currency will have an **immediate impact** on the reporting entity's cash flows from the foreign operations. In other words, changes in the exchange rate affect the **individual monetary items** held by the foreign operation, *not* the reporting entity's net investment in that operation.

In this instance, the foreign operation will maintain its nominal ledger in the parent's currency, so there will be **no need to translate** the subsidiary's financial statements for consolidation purposes.

3.1.2 Different functional currency from the reporting entity

In this situation, although the reporting entity may be able to exercise control, the foreign operation normally operates in a **semi-autonomous** way. It accumulates cash and other monetary items, generates income and incurs expenses, and may also arrange borrowings, all **in its own local currency**.

A change in the exchange rate will produce **little or no direct effect on the present and future cash flows** from operations of either the foreign operation or the reporting entity. Rather, the change in exchange rate affects the reporting entity's **net investment** in the foreign operation, not the individual monetary and non-monetary items held by the foreign operation.

In this instance, the foreign operation will maintain its nominal ledger in its own local currency, so its financial statements will **need to be translated** into the parent's currency for consolidation purposes.

Exam alert

Where the foreign operation's functional currency is different from the parent's, the financial statements need to be translated before consolidation.

3.2 Accounting treatment: different functional currency from the reporting entity

The financial statements of the foreign operation must be translated to the functional currency of the parent. Different procedures must be followed here, because the functional currency of the parent is the **presentation currency** of the foreign operation.

(a) The **assets and liabilities** shown in the foreign operation's statement of financial position are translated at the **closing rate** at the year end, regardless of the date on which those items originated.

(b) Amounts in the **statement of profit or loss and other comprehensive income** should be translated at the rate ruling at the date of the transaction (an **average rate** will usually be used for practical purposes if exchange rates do not fluctuate significantly).

(c) **Exchange differences** arising from the retranslation at the end of each year of the parent's net investment should be **recognised in other comprehensive income**, not through the profit or loss for the year, until the disposal of the net investment. On disposal, the gains or losses recognised to date will be reclassified to profit or loss.

Any **goodwill and fair value adjustments** are treated as assets and liabilities of the foreign operation and are translated at the **closing rate**.

3.3 Practical approach in the exam

You will find it helpful to adopt the following approach when translating the functional currency of foreign operations in the exam:

(a) **Statement of financial position**

All assets and liabilities – at the closing rate

Share capital and pre-acquisition reserves – at the rate at the date of acquisition of the subsidiary

Post-acquisition reserves – balancing figure

(b) **Statement of profit or loss and other comprehensive income**

All items – at the actual rate or average rate as an approximation

Example: Different functional currency from the reporting entity

A dollar-based company, Stone Co, set up a foreign subsidiary on 30 June 20X7. Stone subscribed €24,000 for share capital when the exchange rate was €2 = $1. The subsidiary, Brick Inc, borrowed €72,000 and bought a non-monetary asset for €96,000. Stone Co prepared its accounts on 31 December 20X7, and by that time the exchange rate had moved to €3 = $1. As a result of highly unusual circumstances, Brick Inc sold its asset early in 20X8 for €96,000. It repaid its loan and was liquidated. Stone's capital of €24,000 was repaid in February 20X8 when the exchange rate was €3 = $1.

Required

Account for the above transactions as if the entity has a different functional currency from the parent.

Solution

From the above it can be seen that Stone Co will record its initial investment at $12,000 (€24,000/2) which is the starting cost of its shares. The statement of financial position of Brick Inc at 31 December 20X7 is summarised below.

	€'000
Non-monetary asset	96
Share capital	24
Loan	72
	96

This may be translated as follows.

	$'000
Non-monetary asset (€96,000/3)	32
Share capital and reserves (retained earnings) (balancing figure)	8
Loan (€72,000/3)	24
	32
Exchange gain/(loss) for 20X7	(4)

The exchange gain and loss are the differences between the value of the original investment ($12,000) and the total of share capital and reserves (retained earnings) as disclosed by the above statement of financial position.

On liquidation, Stone Co will receive $8,000 (€24,000 converted at €3 = $1). No gain or loss will arise in 20X8.

3.4 Some practical points

The following points apply.

(a)   For consolidation purposes calculations are simpler if a subsidiary's share capital and pre-acquisition reserves are translated at the **historical rate** (the rate when the investing company acquired its interest) and post-acquisition reserves are found as a balancing figure.

(b)   IAS 21 requires that the accumulated exchange differences should be shown as a separate component of equity but for exam purposes, these can be merged with retained earnings.

3.5 Summary of method

A summary of the translation method is given below, which shows the main steps to follow in the consolidation process.

Step	Method
Translate the **closing statement of financial position** and use this for preparing the consolidated statement of financial position in the normal way.	Use the following rates: • Assets and liabilities at closing rate • Share capital + pre-acquisition reserves at historical rate (at date of acquisition of subsidiary) • Post-acquisition reserves as a balancing figure (includes exchange differences)
Translate the **statement of profit or loss/statement of profit or loss and other comprehensive income**. (In all cases, dividends should be translated at the rate ruling when the dividend was paid).	Use the **average rate** for the year for all items (but see comment on dividends). The figures obtained can then be used in preparing the consolidated statement of profit or loss but the statement of profit or loss and other comprehensive income cannot be completed until the exchange difference has been calculated.
Translate **net assets** (equity) at the **beginning of the year**. (Only do this if you are preparing a consolidated statement of profit or loss and other comprehensive income and need to find exchange differences for the year.)	Calculate opening net assets (equity) in the foreign currency as: Closing net assets (equity) X Less total comprehensive income for yr (X) Opening net assets (equity) X Then divide opening net assets by the opening rate (ie the exchange rate as at the previous year end).

STEP 4 Calculate the **total exchange difference** for the year as follows.

	$
Closing net assets at closing rate (Step 1)	X
Less opening net assets at opening rate (Step 3)	(X)
	X
Less retained profit as translated (Step 2 less any dividends)	(X)
Exchange differences on net assets	X

It may be necessary to adjust for any profits or losses taken direct to reserves during the year.

You will also need to add on any exchange differences arising on goodwill in the year (see Section 3.2).

This stage will be **unnecessary** if you are only required to prepare the statement of financial position. If you are asked to state the total exchange differences or are asked to prepare a statement of profit or loss and other comprehensive income, then the exchange difference will be shown.

For **exam purposes**, you can translate the closing shareholders' funds as follows.

(a)   Share capital + pre-acquisition reserves at historical rate

(b)   Post-acquisition reserves as a balancing figure

Exam alert

You should learn this summary.

Question 13.2   Consolidated financial statements

Learning outcome B2

The abridged statements of financial position and statements of profit or loss of Darius Co and its foreign subsidiary, Xerxes Inc, appear below.

STATEMENTS OF FINANCIAL POSITION AS AT 31 DECEMBER 20X9

	Darius Co		Xerxes Inc	
	$'000	$'000	€'000	€'000
Assets				
Non-current assets				
Plant at cost	600		500	
Less depreciation	(250)		(200)	
		350		300
Investment in Xerxes (100,000 €1 shares)		25		–
		375		300
Current assets				
Inventories	225		200	
Receivables	150		100	
		375		300
		750		600

	Darius Co		Xerxes Inc	
	$'000	$'000	€'000	€'000
Equity and liabilities				
Equity				
Ordinary $1/€1 shares	300		100	
Retained earnings	300		280	
		600		380
Loans		50		110
Current liabilities		100		110
		750		600

STATEMENTS OF PROFIT OR LOSS AND COMPREHENSIVE INCOME
FOR THE YEAR ENDED 31 DECEMBER 20X9

	Darius Co	Xerxes Inc
	$'000	€'000
Profit before tax	200	160
Tax	100	80
Profit for the year, retained	100	80

The following further information is given.

(a) Darius Co has had its interest in Xerxes Inc since the incorporation of the company. Neither company paid dividends during the year to 31 December 20X9 and neither company had any other comprehensive income in their separate financial statements.

(b) Depreciation is 8% per annum on cost.

(c) There have been no loan repayments or movements in non-current assets during the year. The opening inventory of Xerxes Inc was €120,000. Assume that inventory turnover times are very short. Opening receivables were €80,000 and opening current liabilities €130,000.

(d) Exchange rates: €4 to $1 when Xerxes Inc was incorporated
€2 to $1 on 31 December 20X8
€1.6 to $1 average rate of exchange year ended 31 December 20X9
€1 to $1 on 31 December 20X9

Required

Prepare the summarised consolidated financial statements of Darius Co for the year ended 31 December 20X9.

3.6 Analysis of exchange differences

The exchange differences in the above exercise could be reconciled by splitting them into their component parts.

Exam alert

Such a split is not required by IAS 21, nor is it required in your exam but it may help your understanding of the subject.

The exchange difference consists of those exchange gains/losses arising from:

- Translating **income/expense items** at the exchange rates at the dates of transactions (or **average rate** as a close approximation), whereas **assets/liabilities** are translated at the **closing rate**

- Translating the **opening net investment** (opening net assets) in the foreign entity at a closing rate different from the closing rate at which it was previously reported

This can be demonstrated using the above question.

The opening statement of financial position of Xerxes Inc in € is:

	€'000
Non-current assets (300 NBV c/f + [500 × 8%] depreciation for year)	340
Inventories (given in question)	120
Receivables (given in question)	80
	540
Equity (380 c/f – 80 profit for year)	300
Loans (question says no repayments)	110
Current liabilities (given in question)	130
	540

Using the opening statement of financial position and translating at €2 = $1 (the opening rate) and €1 = $1 (the closing rate) gives the following.

	€2 = $1 $'000	€1 = $1 $'000	Difference $'000
Non-current assets	170	340	170
Inventories	60	120	60
Receivables	40	80	40
	270	540	270
Shareholders' funds	150	300	150
Loans	55	110	55
	205	410	205
Current liabilities	65	130	65
	270	540	270

Translating the statement of profit or loss using €1.60 = $1 and €1 = $1 gives the following results.

	€1.60 = $1 $'000	€1 = $1 $'000	Difference $'000
Profit before tax, depreciation and increase in inventory values (balancing figure)	75	120	45
Increase in inventory values (200 – 120)	50	80	30
	125	200	75
Depreciation (500 x 8%)	(25)	(40)	(15)
	100	160	60
Tax	(50)	(80)	(30)
Profit for the year, retained	50	80	30

The overall position is then:

	$'000	$'000
Gain on non-current assets (170 – 15)		155
Loss on loan		(55)
Gain on inventories (60 + 30)	90	
Loss on net monetary current assets/liabilities (all other differences)		
(40 receivables – 65 current liabilities + 45 profit - 30 tax)	(10)	
		80
Net exchange gain (as above)		180

3.7 Non-controlling interests

In problems involving non-controlling interests, the following points should be noted.

(a)   The figure for **non-controlling interests in the statement of financial position** will be calculated in $ using the method seen earlier in Chapter 9.

	$
NCI at acquisition (either at fair value or NCI % of net assets) [from goodwill working]	X
NCI share of post-acquisition reserves	X
Less: impairment losses to date	(X)
	X

(b)   The **non-controlling interests in the reconciliation following the statement of profit or loss/statement of profit or loss and other comprehensive income** will be the appropriate proportion of dollar profits and other comprehensive income. The non-controlling interests in other comprehensive income will include their share of exchange differences on translating the subsidiary, but will exclude exchange differences arising on retranslating goodwill (see below) if the group measures non-controlling interests at acquisition using the proportionate method.

3.8 Goodwill and fair value adjustments

Goodwill and fair value adjustments arising on the acquisition of a foreign operation should be treated as assets and liabilities of the acquired entity. This means that they should be expressed in the functional currency of the foreign operation and translated at the **closing rate**.

First, goodwill needs to be calculated using the foreign currency then translated using each year-end's closing rate. IAS 21 allows impairment losses to either be translated at the average or closing rate. As the examiner uses the average rate in her answers, the average rate should be used.

Here is a layout for calculating goodwill and the exchange gain or loss.

FC = foreign currency
HR = historic rate
OR = opening rate
CR = closing rate
β   = balancing figure

Goodwill

	FC'000	FC'000	*Rate*	$'000	
Consideration transferred		X	HR		
Non-controlling interests		X	HR		
Share capital	X				
Retained earnings	X				
		(X)	HR		
At acquisition (01.01.X1)		X	HR	X	
Impairment losses 20X1		(X)	OR	(X)	
Exchange differences 20X1		–	–	β	Cumulative exchange
At 31.12.X1		X	OR	X	differences (post to
Impairment losses 20X2		(X)	CR	(X)	reserves & NCI working
Exchange differences 20X2 (to OCI)		–	–	β	[if NCI at fair value at acq'n])
At 31.12.X2		X	CR	X	

Exchange differences for the year calculated for the consolidated statement of profit or loss will now need to include the exchange differences arising on goodwill in the current year. The complete proforma for the exchange differences arising in the year is shown below.

	$'000
On translation of financial statements	
Closing net assets as translated	X
Less opening net assets as translated at the time	(X)
	X
Less retained profit as translated at the time	(X)
	X/(X)
On goodwill (see above)	X/(X)
	X/(X)

Example: Including goodwill and non-controlling interests

Bennie, a public limited company, acquired 80% of Jennie, a limited company, for $993,000 on 1 January 20X1. Jennie is a foreign operation whose functional currency is the Jen.

STATEMENTS OF FINANCIAL POSITION AT 31 DECEMBER 20X2

	Bennie $'000	Jennie J'000
Property, plant and equipment	5,705	7,280
Cost of investment in Jennie	993	–
	6,698	7,280
Current assets	2,222	5,600
	8,920	12,880
Share capital	1,700	1,200
Pre-acquisition reserves	=	5,280
Post-acquisition reserves	5,185	2,400
	6,885	8,880
Current liabilities	2,035	4,000
	8,920	12,880

STATEMENTS OF PROFIT OR LOSS AND OTHER COMPREHENSIVE INCOME
FOR THE YEAR ENDED 31 DECEMBER 20X2

	Bennie $'000	Jennie J'000
Revenue	9,840	14,620
Cost of sales	(5,870)	(8,160)
Gross profit	3,970	6,460
Operating expenses	(2,380)	(3,570)
Dividend from Jennie	112	–
Profit before tax	1,702	2,890
Income tax expense	(530)	(850)
Profit/total comprehensive income for the year	1,172	2,040

STATEMENTS OF CHANGES IN EQUITY FOR THE YEAR (EXTRACT FROM RETAINED RESERVES)

	Bennie $'000	Jennie J'000
Balance at 1 January 20X2	4,623	6,760
Dividends paid	(610)	(1,120)
Total profit/comprehensive income for the year	1,172	2,040
Balance at 31 December 20X2	5,185	7,680

Jennie pays its dividends on 31 December. A dividend of 1,160,000 Jens was paid on 31 December 20X1.

Jennie's statements of financial position at acquisition and at 31 December 20X1 were as follows:

	01.01.X1 J'000	31.12.X1 J'000
Property, plant and equipment	5,710	6,800
Current assets	3,360	5,040
	9,070	11,840
Share capital	1,200	1,200
Retained reserves	5,280	6,760
	6,480	7,960
Current liabilities	2,590	3,880
	9,070	11,840

Exchange rates were as follows

1 January 20X1	$1: 12 Jens
31 December 20X1	$1: 10 Jens
31 December 20X2	$1: 8 Jens
Weighted average rate for 20X1	$1: 11 Jens
Weighted average rate for 20X2	$1: 8.5 Jens

The fair values of the identifiable net assets of Jennie were equivalent to their book values at the acquisition date. Bennie chose to measure the non-controlling interests in Jennie at fair value at the date of acquisition. The fair value of the non-controlling interests in Jennie was measured at 2,676,000 Jens on 1 January 20X1.

An impairment test conducted at the year end revealed impairment losses of 1,870,000 Jens on recognised goodwill. No impairment losses were necessary in the year ended 31 December 20X1.

Required

Prepare the consolidated statement of financial position as at 31 December 20X2 and consolidated statement of profit or loss and other comprehensive income for the Bennie Group for the year then ended. (Round to nearest $'000.)

Solution

BENNIE GROUP CONSOLIDATED STATEMENT OF FINANCIAL POSITION AT 31 DECEMBER 20X2

	$'000
Property, plant and equipment (5,705 + (W2) 910)	6,615
Goodwill (W4)	780
	7,395
Current assets (2,222 + (W2) 700)	2,922
	10,317
Share capital	1,700
Retained reserves (W5)	5,724
	7,424
Non-controlling interests (W6)	358
	7,782
Current liabilities (2,035 + (W2) 500)	2,535
	10,317

CONSOLIDATED STATEMENT OF PROFIT OR LOSS AND OTHER COMPREHENSIVE INCOME
FOR YEAR ENDED 31 DECEMBER 20X2

	$'000
Revenue (9,840 + (W3) 1,720)	11,560
Cost of sales (5,870 + (W3) 960)	(6,830)
Gross profit	4,730
Operating expenses (2,380 + (W3) 420)	(2,800)
Goodwill impairment loss (W4)	(220)
Profit before tax	1,710
Income tax expense (530 + (W3) 100)	(630)
Profit for the year	1,080
Other comprehensive income	
Items that may subsequently be reclassified to profit or loss	
Exchange differences on translating foreign operations (W8)	403
Total comprehensive income for the year	1,483
Profit attributable to:	
Owners of the parent (balancing figure)	1,076
Non-controlling interests (W7)	4
	1,080
Total comprehensive income attributable to:	
Owners of the parent (balancing figure)	1,398
Non-controlling interests (W7)	85
	1,483

Workings

1   *Group structure*

Bennie

01.01.X1 | 80%

Jennie   Pre-acquisition ret'd reserves 5,280,000 Jens

2   *Translation of Jennie – Statement of financial position*

	J'000	@	$'000
Property, plant and equipment	7,280	8	910
Current assets	5,600	8	700
	12,880		1,610
Share capital	1,200	12	100
Pre-acquisition reserves	5,280	12	440 ⎫ 1,01
Post-acquisition reserves	2,400	Bal	570 ⎭
	8,880		1,110
Current liabilities	4,000	8	500
	12,880		1,610

3   *Translation of Jennie – Statement of profit or loss and other comprehensive income*

	J'000	@	$'000
Revenue	14,620	8.5	1,720
Cost of sales	(8,160)	8.5	(960)
Gross profit	6,460		760
Operating expenses	(3,570)	8.5	(420)
Profit before tax	2,890		340
Income tax expense	(850)	8.5	(100)
Profit for the year	2,040		240

4 *Goodwill*

	J'000	J'000	Rate	$'000
Consideration transferred (993 × 12)		11,916	12	993
Non-controlling interests (at fair value)		2,676	12	223
Less fair value of net assets at acquisition				
Share capital	1,200			
Retained reserves	5,280			
		(6,480)	12	(540)
Goodwill at acquisition		8,112	12	676
Impairment losses 20X1		(0)		(0)
Exchange gain/(loss) 20X1		-	Bal	135
Goodwill at 31 December 20X1		8,112	10	811
Impairment losses 20X2		(1,870)	8.5	(220)
Exchange gain/(loss) 20X2		-	Bal	189
Goodwill at year end		6,242	8	780

Note. Goodwill is initially measured in the **subsidiary's currency**, and then retranslated at each year end so that we can identify the cumulative exchange differences. In the consolidated statement of financial position these are taken to reserves and non-controlling interests as NCI is measured at fair value at acquisition (see Workings 6 and 7).

5 *Consolidated retained reserves carried forward*

	Bennie $'000	Jennie $'000
Per question/(W2)	5,185	1,010
Reserves at acquisition (W2)		(440)
		570
Group share of post-acquisition retained reserves:		
Jennie (570 × 80%)	456	
Less group share of impairment losses to date ((W4) 220 x 80%)	(176)	
Group share of exchange differences on goodwill [((W4) 135 + 189) × 80%]	259	
	5,724	

6 *Non-controlling interests (SOFP)*

	$'000
NCI at acquisition (W4)	223
Add NCI share of post-acquisition retained reserves of Jennie ((W2) 570 × 20%)	114
Less NCI share of impairment losses (W4) (220 × 20%)	(44)
NCI share of exchange differences on goodwill [((W4) 135 + 189) × 20%]	65
	358

Note. NCI are only given their share of the impairment losses and exchange differences on goodwill because NCI is measured at fair value at acquisition (full goodwill method). If NCI had been measured at the proportionate share of net assets at acquisition, the NCI would not be allocated any impairment losses or exchange differences on goodwill (they would have been posted to reserves in full).

7   *Non-controlling interests (SPLOCI)*

	Profit for year $'000	Total comp. income $'000
Profit for the year (W3)	240	240
Impairment losses (W4)	(220)	(220)
Other comprehensive income: exchange differences (W8)	–	403
	20	423
× 20%	4	85

Note. NCI are only given their share of impairment losses because NCI is measured at fair value at acquisition (full goodwill method).

8   *Exchange differences arising during the year*

	SPLOCI $'000
On translation of net assets (NA) of Jennie:	
Closing NA at CR (W2)	1,110
Opening NA @ OR (7,960/10)	(796)
	314
Less: retained profit as translated ((W3) 240 – J1,120/8)	(100)
	214
On goodwill (W4)	189
	403

Note. To arrive at retained profit, dividends must be deducted (copied from Jennie's statement of changes in equity given in the question) translated at the exchange rate at the date they were paid (here at the year-end date). These exchange differences only need to be calculated if you are preparing a consolidated statement of profit or loss and other comprehensive income.

3.9 Further matters relating to foreign operations

3.9.1 Consolidation procedures

Follow normal consolidation procedures, except that where an exchange difference arises on **long- or short-term intragroup monetary items**, these cannot be offset against other intragroup balances. This is because these are commitments to convert one currency into another, thus exposing the reporting entity to a gain or loss through currency fluctuations. This type of exchange difference should be recognised in profit or loss unless it relates to a long-term receivable or loan for which settlement is neither planned nor likely to occur in the foreseeable future. This is because, in substance, it is part of the entity's net investment in the foreign operation. In this case, in the consolidated financial statements, these exchange differences should initially be recognised in other comprehensive income and reclassified to profit or loss on disposal of the net investment.

If the foreign operation's **reporting date** is different from that of the parent, it is acceptable to use the accounts made up to that date for consolidation as long as adjustments are made for any significant changes in rates in the interim.

3.9.2 Hyperinflationary economies

The financial statements of a foreign operation operating in a hyperinflationary economy must be adjusted under IAS 29 *Financial reporting in hyperinflationary economies* before they are translated into the parent's reporting currency and then consolidated. When the economy **ceases to be hyperinflationary**, and the foreign operation ceases to apply IAS 29, the amounts restated to the price level at the date the

entity ceased to restate its financial statements should be used as the historical costs for translation purposes.

3.9.3 Disposal of foreign entity

When a parent disposes of a foreign entity, the cumulative amount of deemed exchange differences relating to that foreign entity should be **recognised as an income or expense** in the same period in which the gain or loss on disposal is recognised. Effectively, this means that these exchange differences are recognised once by taking them to other comprehensive income and reserves, and then are recognised for a second time (**recycled or reclassified**) by transferring them from other comprehensive income and reserves to the statement of profit or loss and other comprehensive income on disposal of the foreign operation.

3.9.4 In the parent's financial statements

In the parent company's own financial statements exchange differences arising on a **monetary item** that is effectively part of the parent's net investment in the foreign entity should be recognised **in profit or loss** in the separate financial statements of the reporting entity or the individual financial statements of the foreign operation, as appropriate.

3.10 Change in functional currency

The functional currency of an entity can be changed only if there is a change to the underlying transactions, events and conditions that are relevant to the entity. For example, an entity's functional currency may change if there is a change in the currency that mainly influences the sales price of goods and services.

Where there is a change in an entity's functional currency, the entity translates all items into the new functional currency **prospectively** (ie from the date of the change) using the exchange rate at the date of the change.

3.11 Tax effects of exchange differences

IAS 12 *Income taxes* should be applied when there are tax effects arising from gains or losses on foreign currency transactions and exchange differences arising on the translation of the financial statements of foreign operations.

Section summary

You may have to make the decision yourself as to whether the subsidiary has the same functional currency as the parent or a different functional currency from the parent. This determines whether you need to translate the subsidiary for consolidation purposes.

You must be able to calculate **exchange differences**.

Practising examination questions is the best way of learning this topic.

Where the functional currency of a foreign operation is **different** from that of the parent/reporting entity, the results need to be translated before consolidation.

- Operation is semi-autonomous
- Translate assets and liabilities at closing rate
- Translate share capital and pre-acquisition reserves at acquisition date rate
- Find post-acquisition reserves as a balancing figure
- Translate statement of profit or loss and other comprehensive income at average rate
- Exchange differences through other comprehensive income

Chapter Summary

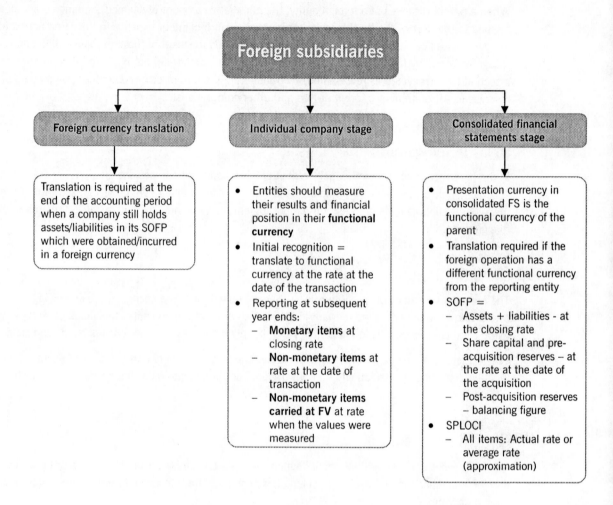

Foreign subsidiaries

Foreign currency translation

Translation is required at the end of the accounting period when a company still holds assets/liabilities in its SOFP which were obtained/incurred in a foreign currency

Individual company stage

- Entities should measure their results and financial position in their **functional currency**
- Initial recognition = translate to functional currency at the rate at the date of the transaction
- Reporting at subsequent year ends:
  - **Monetary items** at closing rate
  - **Non-monetary items** at rate at the date of transaction
  - **Non-monetary items carried at FV** at rate when the values were measured

Consolidated financial statements stage

- Presentation currency in consolidated FS is the functional currency of the parent
- Translation required if the foreign operation has a different functional currency from the reporting entity
- SOFP =
  - Assets + liabilities - at the closing rate
  - Share capital and pre-acquisition reserves – at the rate at the date of the acquisition
  - Post-acquisition reserves – balancing figure
- SPLOCI
  - All items: Actual rate or average rate (approximation)

Quick Quiz

1   What is the difference between conversion and translation?

2   Define monetary items according to IAS 21.

3   How should foreign currency transactions be recognised initially in an individual enterprise's accounts?

4   What factors must management take into account when determining the functional currency of a foreign operation?

5   How should goodwill and fair value adjustments be treated on consolidation of a foreign operation?

6   When can an entity's functional currency be changed?

Answers to Quick Quiz

1   (a)   Conversion is the process of exchanging one currency for another.
    (b)   Translation is the restatement of the value of one currency in another currency.

2   Units of currency held and assets and liabilities to be received or paid in a fixed or determinable number of units of currency (eg cash, receivables, payables, loans).

3   Use the exchange rate at the date of the transaction. An average rate for a period can be used if the exchange rates did not fluctuate significantly.

4   See Section 3.1.

5   Treat as assets/liabilities of the foreign operation and translate at the closing rate.

6   Only if there is a change to the underlying transactions relevant to the entity.

Answers to Questions

13.1   Entries

The purchase will be recorded in the books of White Cliffs Co using the rate of exchange ruling on 30 September.

DEBIT	Purchases	$25,000
CREDIT	Trade payables	$25,000

Being the $ cost of goods purchased for €40,000 (€40,000 ÷ €1.60)

On 30 November 20X1, White Cliffs must pay €20,000. This will cost €20,000 ÷ €1.80 = $11,111 and the company has therefore made an exchange gain of $12,500 – $11,111 = $1,389.

DEBIT	Trade payables	$12,500
CREDIT	Exchange gains: Profit or loss	$1,389
CREDIT	Cash	$11,111

On 31 December 20X1, the year end, the outstanding liability will be recalculated using the rate applicable to that date: €20,000 ÷ €1.90 = $10,526. A further exchange gain of $1,974 has been made and will be recorded as follows.

DEBIT	Trade payables	$1,974
CREDIT	Exchange gains: Profit or loss	$1,974

The total exchange gain of $3,363 will be included in the operating profit for the year ended 31 December.

On 31 January 20X2, White Cliffs must pay the second instalment of €20,000. This will cost them $10,811 (€20,000 ÷ €1.85).

DEBIT	Trade payables	$10,526
DEBIT	Exchange losses: Profit or loss	$285
CREDIT	Cash	$10,811

13.2 Consolidated financial statements

The statement of financial position of Xerxes Inc at 31 December 20X9 should be translated – the assets and liabilities at the closing rate of €1 = $1; the share capital and pre-acquisition reserves at the historic rate at the date of acquisition of the subsidiary of €4 = $1; pre-acquisition reserves should be found as a balancing figure (as they will include exchange differences).

SUMMARISED TRANSLATED STATEMENT OF FINANCIAL POSITION OF XERXES INC AT 31 DECEMBER 20X9

	$'000	$'000
Non-current assets (NBV) (€300,000/1 CR)		300
Current assets		
Inventories (€200,000/1 CR)	200	
Receivables (€100,000/1 CR)	100	
		300
		600
Equity		
Share capital (€100,000/4 HR)		25
Pre-acquisition retained earnings (nil as acquired on incorporation)		–
Post-acquisition retained earnings (balancing figure – includes exchange differences)		355
		380
Non-current liabilities (€110,000/1 CR)		110
Current liabilities (€110,000/1 CR)		110
		600

SUMMARISED CONSOLIDATED STATEMENT OF FINANCIAL POSITION AS AT 31 DECEMBER 20X9

		$'000	$'000
Assets			
Non-current assets (NBV)	(350 + 300)		650
Current assets			
Inventories	(225 + 200)	425	
Receivables	(150 + 100)	250	
			675
			1,325
Equity and liabilities			
Equity			
Ordinary $1 shares (Darius only)			300
Retained earnings	(300 + 355)		655
			955
Non-current liabilities: loans	(50 + 110)		160
Current liabilities	(100 + 110)		210
			1,325

Note. It is quite unnecessary to know the amount of the exchange differences when preparing the consolidated statement of financial position.

The statement of profit or loss and other comprehensive income should be translated at average rate (€1.6 = $1).

SUMMARISED TRANSLATED STATEMENT OF PROFIT OR LOSS AND OTHER COMPREHENSIVE INCOME OF XERXES INC FOR THE YEAR ENDED 31 DECEMBER 20X9

	$'000
Profit before tax (€160,000/1.6 AR)	100
Tax (€80,000/1.6 AR)	(50)
Profit for the year	50

SUMMARISED CONSOLIDATED STATEMENT OF PROFIT OR LOSS AND OTHER COMPREHENSIVE INCOME FOR THE YEAR ENDED 31 DECEMBER 20X9

		$'000
Profit before tax	(200 + 100)	300
Tax	(100 + 50)	(150)
Profit for the year	(100 + 50)	150

The statement of profit or loss and other comprehensive income cannot be completed until the exchange difference has been calculated.

 STEP 3   Net assets (equity) at the beginning of the year can be found as follows.

	€'000
Net assets (equity) at 31 December 20X9	380
Retained profit for year	(80)
Net assets (equity) at 31 December 20X8	300
Translated at €2 = $1 gives	150

 STEP 4   The exchange difference can now be calculated and the statement of profit or loss and other comprehensive income completed.

	$'000
Closing net assets at closing rate (step 1)	380
Opening net assets at opening rate (step 3)	(150)
	230
Less retained profit (step 2)	(50)
Exchange gain	180

SUMMARISED CONSOLIDATED STATEMENT OF PROFIT OR LOSS AND OTHER COMPREHENSIVE INCOME FOR THE YEAR ENDED 31 DECEMBER 20X9

		$'000
Profit before tax	(200 + 100)	300
Tax	(100 + 50)	150
Profit for the year	(100 + 50)	150
Other comprehensive income		
Exchange difference on translating foreign operations		180
Total comprehensive income		330

CONSOLIDATED STATEMENT OF CHANGES IN EQUITY (EXTRACT FOR RESERVES) FOR THE YEAR ENDED 31 DECEMBER 20X9

	$'000
Consolidated reserves at 31 December 20X8	325
Total comprehensive income for the year	330
Consolidated reserves at 31 December 20X9	655

Note. The post-acquisition reserves of Xerxes Inc at the beginning of the year must have been $150,000 (opening net assets) – $25,000 (share capital) = $125,000, and the reserves of Darius Co must have been $300,000 (reserves at 31 December 20X9) – $100,000 (profit for the year) = $200,000. The consolidated reserves must therefore have been $325,000.

Now try this question from
the Practice Question Bank

Number	Level	Marks	Time
Q23	Introductory	N/A	4 mins

CONSOLIDATED STATEMENTS OF PROFIT OR LOSS AND OTHER COMPREHENSIVE INCOME AND STATEMENTS OF CHANGES IN EQUITY

 This chapter deals with the consolidated statement of profit or loss and other comprehensive income, a topic that is examined frequently.

In addition, you need to be able to prepare the consolidated statement of changes in equity.

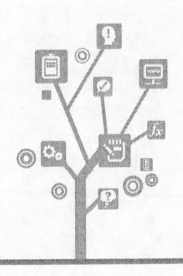

Topic list	learning outcomes	syllabus references
1 Non-controlling interests and the consolidated statement of profit or loss and other comprehensive income	B1	B1(a)
2 The consolidated statement of changes in equity	B1	B1(a)

338   14: The consolidated statement of profit or loss and other
       comprehensive income and the statement of changes in equity

PART D ADVANCED GROUPS

Chapter Overview

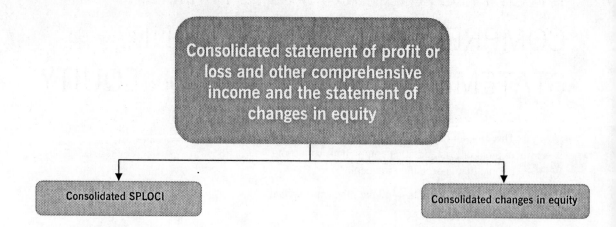

1 Non-controlling interests and the consolidated statement of profit or loss and other comprehensive income

Introduction

The statement of profit or loss and other comprehensive income must show the profit or loss and other comprehensive income **controlled** by the group. It must also identify the **ownership** of the profit and total comprehensive income, splitting these amounts into the portions owned by the parent and the non-controlling interests.

We will now look at the effect of non-controlling interests on the statement of profit or loss and other comprehensive income. You will recognise that this section applies the same principles that we have already covered in relation to the statement of financial position.

1.1 Other comprehensive income

Exam alert

At F2, items of **other comprehensive income** are more likely to be tested in a consolidation question than at F1. This is because new accounting standards are examinable at F2 which result in items being recorded in other comprehensive income (such as revaluation gains on available for sale financial assets).

We will now consider how to deal with non-controlling interests in questions where you are required to prepare a consolidated statement of profit or loss and other comprehensive income.

The difference between a statement of profit or loss and a statement of profit or loss and other comprehensive income (SPLOCI) is other comprehensive income (gains/losses posted to reserves in the year), which is included in the statement of profit or loss and other comprehensive income but not in the statement of profit or loss.

We add across the parent's and 100% of the subsidiary's other comprehensive income line by line (in the same way as we add across revenue to profit for year line by line) to show control.

As well as revaluation gains, the elements of other comprehensive income include the following items, taken from IAS 1 *Presentation of Financial Statements* (revised).

Other comprehensive income	*Chapter*	*20X7*	*20X6*
Exchange differences on translating foreign operations (may be reclassified to P/L)	13	X	X
Available for sale financial assets (may be reclassified to P/L)	3	X	X
Gains on property revaluation (not reclassified)	–	X	X
Gains (losses) on remeasurement of defined benefit pension plans (not reclassified)	3	(X)	X
Share of other comprehensive income of associates (not reclassified)	10	X	(X)
Income tax relating to components of other comprehensive income	8	X	(X)
		X̲	X̲

The chapter references given above show the chapter in this Study Text where you will find further information on these elements. Gains on property revaluation were dealt with at F1 and should be revision. IAS 1 was revised in 2011 and these changes are dealt with in Chapter 17.

340   14: The consolidated statement of profit or loss and other
comprehensive income and the statement of changes in equity

PART D ADVANCED GROUPS

Exam alert

Exam questions often cover a wide range of topics from across the syllabus, so you should be prepared to encounter issues like accounting for pensions or financial instruments within consolidation questions.

1.2 Preparing the consolidated statement of profit or loss and other comprehensive income   11/10, 3/11, 11/11, 3/12, 5/12

Adding the parent's and 100% of the subsidiary's income, expenses and other comprehensive income line by line denotes **control**. However, we also need to reflect **ownership** in the consolidated statement of profit or loss and other comprehensive income. This is reflected in a new reconciliation presented at the foot of the consolidated statement of profit or loss and other comprehensive income, which shows ownership of the profit and total comprehensive income for the year.

The diagram below illustrates the method to be followed.

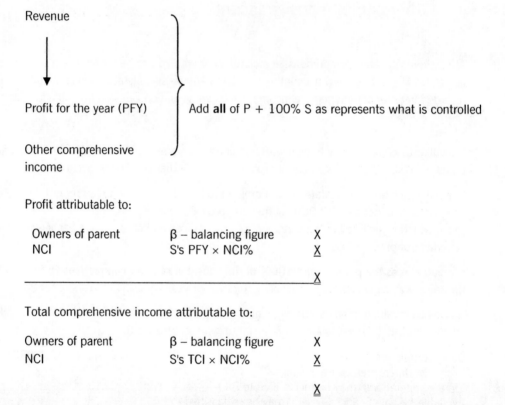

Note. You should always add **all** of the impairment loss on recognised goodwill for the year to expenses (regardless of whether the full or partial goodwill method is used).

Using the same information from Chapter 9 Section 8, the following examples will introduce the most important points about consolidating a subsidiary with non-controlling interests in the statement of profit or loss. We will still consolidate 100% of the subsidiary's results to show the results arising under group control, but we also need to show how much is owned by the non-controlling interests.

Example

P Co acquired 75% of the ordinary shares of S Co on that company's incorporation on 1 January 20X3. The summarised statements of profit or loss of the two companies for the year ended 31 December 20X6 are set out below.

	P Co $	S Co $
Revenue	75,000	38,000
Cost of sales	(30,000)	(20,000)
Gross profit	45,000	18,000
Distribution and administrative expenses	(14,000)	(8,000)
Profit before tax	31,000	10,000
Income tax expense	(10,000)	(2,000)
Profit for the year	21,000	8,000

Required

Prepare the consolidated statement of profit or loss for the year ending 31 December 20X6.

Solution

P CO
CONSOLIDATED STATEMENT OF PROFIT OR LOSS
FOR THE YEAR ENDED 31 DECEMBER 20X6

	$
Sales revenue ($75,000 + $38,000)	113,000
Cost of sales ($30,000 + $20,000)	(50,000)
Gross profit	63,000
Administrative expenses ($14,000 + $8,000)	(22,000)
Profit before tax	41,000
Income tax expense ($10,000 + $2,000)	(12,000)
Profit for the year	29,000
Profit attributable to:	
Owners of the parent (balancing figure)	27,000
Non-controlling interests (W2)	2,000
	29,000

Workings

1   *Group structure*

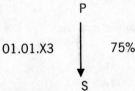

01.01.X3   75%

2   *Non-controlling interests*

	$
Profit for the year – per question	8,000
NCI share (25%) =	2,000

Notice how the non-controlling interests are dealt with.

(a)   Down to the line **profit for the year**, the **whole** of S Co's results is included without reference to group share or non-controlling interests. A **reconciliation** is then inserted to show the ownership of the profits.

(b)   Complete the reconciliation in this order:

(i)   Fill in the total profit for the year

(ii)   Calculate the NCI share of profit (NCI % × subsidiary's profit after tax)

(iii) Deduce the amount attributable to the members of the parent as a balancing figure

342   14: The consolidated statement of profit or loss and other
comprehensive income and the statement of changes in equity

PART D ADVANCED GROUPS

We will now look at the complications introduced by **intragroup trading, intragroup dividends** and **mid-year acquisitions** of subsidiaries.

1.2.1 Non-controlling interests and intragroup trading

In Chapter 9 we revised the basic issues relating to intragroup trading.

The consolidated figures for sales revenue and cost of sales should represent **sales to, and purchases from, outsiders**. An adjustment is therefore necessary to reduce the sales revenue and cost of sales figures by the value of **intragroup sales** during the year.

We have also seen that any **unrealised profits** on intragroup trading should be excluded from the figure for group profits. This will occur whenever goods sold at a profit within the group remain in the inventory of the purchasing company at the year end.

If there are non-controlling interests in the subsidiary, the impact of intragroup trading on the non-controlling interests depends on whether the parent, or the subsidiary, made the sale.

(a)   If the **parent** is the seller, there will be no **effect on the non-controlling interests**

(b)   If the **subsidiary** is the seller, then any adjustment that results in a change to the subsidiary's profit in the consolidated financial statements will require an adjustment to non-controlling interests.

   (i)   The **intragroup sale** will be eliminated in full – no further effect on non-controlling interests

   (ii)   Any **unrealised profit** will be eliminated

   (iii)   The figure for the subsidiary's **profit after tax** used to calculate the **non-controlling interests** must be adjusted for the unrealised profit

   (iv)   **Fair value adjustments** may be necessary for intragroup sales of non-current assets

   (v)   **Impairment of goodwill** for the year (only if using the full goodwill method)

Example: intragroup trading

Suppose in our earlier example that S Co had recorded sales of $5,000 to P Co during 20X6. S Co had purchased these goods from outside suppliers at a cost of $3,000. One half of the goods remained in P Co's inventory at 31 December 20X6. Prepare the revised consolidated statement of profit or loss.

Solution

The consolidated statement of profit or loss for the year ended 31 December 20X6 would now be as follows.

	$
Sales revenue ($75,000 + $38,000 − $5,000 (W3))	108,000
Cost of sales ($30,000 + $20,000 − $5,000 + $1,000 (W3))	(46,000)
Gross profit	62,000
Administrative expenses	(22,000)
Profit before taxation	40,000
Income tax expense	(12,000)
Profit for the year	28,000
Profit attributable to:	
Owners of the parent	26,250
Non-controlling interests (W2)	1,750
	28,000

Workings

1   *Group structure*

P

01.01.X3   75%

S

2   *Non-controlling interests*

	$
Profit for the year – per question	8,000
Provision for unrealised profit (PUP) (W3)	(1,000)
	7,000
NCI share	× 25%
	= 1,750

3   *Intragroup trading*

S → P

- Intragroup revenue and cost of sales:

    Cancel $5,000 out of revenue and cost of sales

- PUP = 1/2 in inventories × ($5,000 – $3,000) mark-up = $1,000

    Increase cost of sales by $1,000 and reduce profit for the year in non-controlling interests working (as subsidiary is the seller)

Note. In this example, the unrealised profit arose on sales made by the subsidiary. This means that it has to be eliminated from the subsidiary's profit before non-controlling interests are calculated.

Question 14.1

Non-controlling interests

Learning outcome B1

The statements of profit or loss and other comprehensive income for two entities for the year ended 30 September 20X5 are presented below.

STATEMENTS OF PROFIT OR LOSS AND OTHER COMPREHENSIVE INCOME
FOR THE YEAR ENDED 30 SEPTEMBER 20X5

	CV $'000	SG $'000
Revenue	5,000	4,200
Cost of sales	(4,100)	(3,500)
Gross profit	900	700
Distribution and administrative expenses	(320)	(180)
Investment income	50	–
Profit before tax	630	520
Income tax expense	(240)	(170)
Profit for the year	390	350
Other comprehensive income:		
Gain on revaluation of property (net of deferred tax)	60	20
Total comprehensive income for the year	450	370

344   14: The consolidated statement of profit or loss and other
          comprehensive income and the statement of changes in equity

PART D ADVANCED GROUPS

Notes

1   CV acquired a 75% investment in SG on 1 October 20X2. It is group policy to measure non-controlling interests at fair value at acquisition. Goodwill of $250,000 arose on acquisition. The fair value of the net assets was deemed to be the same as the carrying value of net assets.

2   No impairment of goodwill had been necessary up to 1 October 20X4. However, the directors conducted an impairment review at 30 September 20X5 and decided that goodwill on acquisition was impaired by 20%.

3   During the year ended 30 September 20X5, SG sold goods to CV for $300,000. Two-thirds of these goods remain in CV's inventories at the year end. SG charges a mark-up of 25% on cost.

4   SG paid a dividend of $60,000 to its equity shareholders on 30 September 20X5.CV has included its share of the dividend in investment income.

Required

(a)   Prepare the consolidated statement of profit or loss and other comprehensive income for the CV group for the year ended 30 September 20X5.

(b)   How would non-controlling interests differ if non-controlling interests at acquisition had been measured at the proportionate share of the net assets, and if CV had sold the goods to SG in note (3)?

1.2.2 Mid-year acquisitions

We have seen in the previous chapters that retained earnings in the consolidated statement of financial position include the group's share of the **post-acquisition** retained earnings of the subsidiary. We only consolidate what the subsidiary has earned since it came under the parent's control.

A **similar principle** is followed in the **consolidated statement of profit or loss/consolidated statement of profit or loss and other comprehensive income**.

If the subsidiary is **acquired during the accounting year**, only the post-acquisition results are included in the consolidated statement of profit or loss. In the exam, you may have to **time-apportion** the income and expenses of the subsidiary to calculate the post-acquisition elements. You may find it helpful to draw a timeline. Assume revenue, expenses and other comprehensive income accrue evenly, unless told otherwise.

1.2.3 Intragroup dividends

If the subsidiary has paid a dividend during the year, the parent will have recognised their share of this in profit or loss. In the consolidated statement of profit or loss and other comprehensive income, this must be cancelled out.

This follows the same principle that we saw in connection with the statement of financial position. In the statement of financial position, the investment that appears in the parent's separate financial statements is cancelled out, and the subsidiary's assets and liabilities are included instead. In the consolidated statement of profit or loss and other comprehensive income, the dividend income recognised by the parent is **cancelled out** and we show the subsidiary's income and expenses instead.

| Question 14.2 | Mid-year acquisition |

Learning outcome B1

JT acquired 90% of the issued share capital of MB on 1 April 20X7.

At the year end 31 December 20X7 the two companies have the following statements of financial position:

	JT		MB	
	$'000	$'000	$'000	$'000
Investment in MB		4,000		–
Other assets		10,500		6,000
		14,500		6,000
Share capital ($1 shares)		6,000		1,000
Share premium		–		500
Retained earnings				
1 January 20X7	4,000		1,500	
Profit for 20X7	2,000		1,000	
		6,000		2,500
		12,000		4,000
Liabilities		2,500		2,000
		14,500		6,000

The statements of profit or loss for the two companies for the year ended 31 December 20X7 are as follows.

	JT	MB
	$'000	$'000
Revenue	10,000	4,000
Cost of sales and expenses	(6,000)	(2,100)
Profit before tax	4,000	1,900
Income tax expense	(1,400)	(900)
Profit for the year	2,600	1,000

Notes

1   On 14 November 20X7 JT sold inventories to MB at a transfer price of $200,000, which included a profit on transfer of $30,000. Half of these inventories had been sold by MB by the year end.

2   An impairment test carried out at the year end revealed impairment losses of $20,000 relating to recognised goodwill. The group measures non-controlling interests at fair value at the date of acquisition. The share price just prior to the acquisition was $4.50.

3   On 1 April 20X7 MB owned some items of equipment with a fair value that was $100,000 in excess of its book value. Additional depreciation on fair value adjustments amounted to $10,000 in the post-acquisition period.

Required

(a)   Calculate the goodwill figure that would appear in the consolidated statement of financial position as at 31 December 20X7.

(b)   Prepare the consolidated statement of profit or loss for the JT Group for the year ended 31 December 20X7.

1.3 Income tax relating to components of other comprehensive income

You will not be expected to calculate the income tax effects. In the pilot paper, you were given the figures for tax effects and asked to prepare a consolidated statement of profit or loss and other comprehensive income. All that was needed was to include the figure in other comprehensive income, as shown above.

1.4 Technique summary

Purpose	To show the results of the group for an accounting period as if it were a single entity
Sales revenue to profit for year, and other comprehensive income	100% P + 100% S (excluding adjustments for intercompany transactions) Time-apportioned to include only **post-acquisition** results if subsidiary was acquired part way through the year
Reason	To show the results of the group which were controlled by the parent company
Intragroup sales	Strip out intercompany activity from both sales revenue and cost of sales
Unrealised profit on intragroup sales	(a) Goods sold by parent: increase cost of sales by unrealised profit (b) Goods sold by subsidiary: increase cost of sales by full amount of unrealised profit and decrease non-controlling interests by their share of unrealised profit
Depreciation	If the value of subsidiary's non-current assets has been subjected to a fair value uplift then any additional depreciation must be charged in the consolidated statement of profit or loss (see Chapter 9). The non-controlling interests will need to be adjusted for their share
Transfer of non-current assets	The profit on transfer must be eliminated and expenses must be reduced by any additional depreciation arising from the increased carrying value of the asset (see Chapter 9). Non-controlling interests are adjusted if the asset was sold by the subsidiary
Non-controlling interests in profit	Subsidiary's profit after tax X Less: Impairment loss for the year (X) * Unrealised profit (X) Additional depreciation following FV uplift (X) ** Unrealised profit net of additional depreciation following disposal of non-current assets (X) Y × NCI% X NCI profit X * Only applicable if sales of goods made by subsidiary ** Only applicable if sale of non-current assets made by subsidiary
Non-controlling interests in total comprehensive income	Apply adjustments to total comprehensive income, as applied above to profit after tax
Reason	To show the extent to which income generated through parent's control is in fact owned by other parties

Section summary

The consolidated statement of profit or loss and other comprehensive income is produced using the same principles as the consolidated statement of profit or loss.

2   The consolidated statement of changes in equity   5/11, 5/12

Introduction

A consolidated statement of changes in equity (SOCIE) presents movements in the period of a group's share capital, reserves and non-controlling interests.

2.1 Purpose of the consolidated statement of changes in equity

The consolidated statement of changes in equity (SOCIE) simply reconciles the movement in equity in the consolidated statement of financial position at the beginning and end of the period.

The calculation of the component figures is therefore the same as for the consolidated statement of financial position (SOFP).

2.2 Consolidated statement of changes in equity

The IAS 1 (revised) proforma is as follows:

	Share capital	Retained earnings	Translation of foreign operations	Available for sale financial assets	Re-valuation surplus	Total	NCI	Total
Bal at 1 Jan 20X6	X	X	X	X	X	X	X	X
Issue of share cap	X	–	–	–	–	X	–	X
Dividends	–	(X)	–	–	–	(X)	(X)	(X)
Total comprehensive income for year	–	X	X	X	X	X	X	X
Transfer to retained earnings	–	X	–	–	(X)	X	–	X
Bal at 31 Dec 20X6	X	X	X	X	X	X	X	X

Exam alert

In the F2 exam, you will not be expected to prepare such a detailed statement as the example above.

You could be expected to prepare a more summarised version, where share capital and reserves are combined into one column, headed **Equity attributable to owners of the parent**.

The exam question in May 2011 combined this topic with a step acquisition (covered in Chapter 11).

A consolidated statement of changes in equity in the F2 exam would look like this:

	Equity attributable to owners of the parent $'000	Non-controlling interests $'000	Total $'000	
Balance at 31.12.X1	X	X	X	(Parent share capital (SC)/Share premium (SP) + Group reserves)/ NCI
Share issue	X	–	X	Given in question (see **Note**)
Total comprehensive income for the year	X	X	X	From SPLOCI
Dividends	(X)	(X)	(X)	Parent/(Subsidiary × NCI%)
Adjustments to equity	X/(X)	X/(X)	X/(X)	See Chapter 11
Balance at 31.12.X2	X	X	X	(P SC/SP + Group reserves)/ NCI

Note. No balance in NCI column as share issue by subsidiary in the year not examinable in F2

The figures in the statement involve no new calculations. They are worked out as follows:

Read the question and draw up the group structure (W1), highlighting useful information:

- The % owned
- Acquisition date
- Pre-acquisition reserves

Draw up a proforma

Complete the dividends line:

- parent's dividend in **equity attributable to owners of the parent** column
- subsidiary's dividend multiplied by NCI % in **non-controlling interests** column

Copy total comprehensive income (TCI) attributable to owners of parent and to NCI from consolidated SPLOCI if given. If not given, calculate as follows:

- Work out consolidated TCI by adding the parent's TCI, the subsidiary's TCI, the group share of the associate's TCI and deducting any intragroup adjustments that affect profit (eg PUP, fair value adjustments)

- Calculate NCI in TCI as per standard consolidated SPLOCI working and post to NCI column in the consolidated SOCIE:

	$
Subsidiary's TCI	X
Adjustments that affect subsidiary's profit/OCI (eg PUP, fair value adj, impairment if full goodwill method)	(X)
	X
NCI share	×%
	= X

- Calculate TCI attributable to the owners of the parent as consolidated TCI less NCI (as if preparing the ownership reconciliation at the foot of the consolidated SPLOCI). Post this figure to the **attributable to the owners of the parent** column in the consolidated SOCIE.

STEP 5

Calculate equity and NCI at the end of the period as follows:

- Equity = parent's share capital + consolidated reserves (from standard reserves working from consolidated SOFP – see below)

	Parent	Subsidiary	Assoc/JV
Per question	X	X	X
Adjustments	X(X)	X(X)	X(X)
Fair value adjustments movement		X/(X)	X/(X)
Pre-acquisition retained earnings		(X)	(X)
		A	B

Group share of post-acq'n ret'd earnings:	
Subsidiary (A × %)	X
Associate/Joint venture (B × %)	X
Less group share of impairment losses to date	(X)
	X

- NCI – complete standard NCI working for consolidated SOFP:

NCI at acquisition (NCI % of net assets OR fair value)	X
NCI share of post-acquisition reserves	X
NCI share of impairment losses (only if using full goodwill method)	(X)
	X

STEP 6

Find equity and NCI at beginning of the period as a balancing figure

Example: Consolidated statement of changes in equity

The summarised consolidated financial statements of the P Group for the year ended 31 December 20X4 are as follows:

P GROUP

CONSOLIDATED STATEMENT OF FINANCIAL POSITION AS AT 31 DECEMBER 20X4

	$'000
Non-current assets	36,900
Current assets	28,200
	65,100
Equity attributable to owners of the parent	
Share capital	12,300
Share premium	5,800
Revaluation surplus	350
Retained earnings	32,100
	50,550
Non-controlling interests	1,750
	52,300
Non-current liabilities	5,200
Current liabilities	7,600
	65,100

CONSOLIDATED STATEMENT OF PROFIT OR LOSS AND OTHER COMPREHENSIVE INCOME
FOR THE YEAR ENDED 31 DECEMBER 20X4

	$'000
Profit before tax	16,500
Income tax expense	(5,200)
Profit for the year	11,300
Other comprehensive income	500
Total comprehensive income for the year	11,800
Profit attributable to:	
Owners of the parent	11,100
Non-controlling interests	200
	11,300
Total comprehensive income for the year attributable to	
Owners of the parent	11,450
Non-controlling interests	350
	11,800

Note. The P group is made up of the parent P and a 70% owned subsidiary S. The dividends paid for the year ended 31 December 20X4 by P and S were $800,000 and $500,000 respectively.

Required

Prepare the consolidated statement of changes in equity for the P group for the year ended 31 December 20X4.

Solution

P GROUP – CONSOLIDATED STATEMENT OF CHANGES IN EQUITY

	Equity attributable to owners of the parent	Non-controlling interests	Total
	$'000	$'000	$'000
Balance at 1 January 20X4 *(balancing figure)*	39,900	1,550	41,450
Total comprehensive income for the year *(consol SPLOCI)*	11,450	350	11,800
Dividends			
(Parent)/(NCI % of subsidiary's ie 30% × $500,000)	(800)	(150)	(950)
Balance at 31 December 20X4 *(consol SOFP)*	50,550	1,750	52,300

Workings

1   *Group structure*

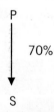

P

70%

S

2.2.1 Necessary workings

If a consolidated statement of financial position and consolidated statement of profit or loss and other comprehensive income are not given in the question, the figures needed for the consolidated statement of changes in equity must be recreated with a series of workings:

- Cancellation of intragroup items affecting profit

- Ownership reconciliation from consolidated statement of profit or loss and other comprehensive income

- Equity carried forward (similar to retained earnings working for consolidated statement of financial position)

- Non-controlling interests carried forward (same as non-controlling interests working for consolidated statement of financial position)

Question 14.3	Consolidated statement of changes in equity

Learning outcome B1

Summarised statements of changes in equity for the year ended 30 June 20X5 for SM and its only subsidiary CE are shown below.

STATEMENTS OF CHANGES IN EQUITY FOR THE YEAR ENDED 30 JUNE 20X5

	SM	CE
	$'000	$'000
Balance at 1 July 20X4	500,000	130,000
Issue of shares	25,000	–
Total comprehensive income for the year	75,000	40,000
Dividends	(16,000)	(10,000)
Balance at 30 June 20X5	584,000	160,000

Notes

1   SM acquired 37.5m of CE's 50m $1 ordinary shares on 1 July 20X2, when CE's total equity was $80m. The first dividend CE has paid since acquisition is the amount of $10m shown in the summarised statement above. The total comprehensive income for the year in SM's summarised statement of changes in equity includes its share of the dividend paid by CE.

2   During the year ended 30 June 20X5, CE sold some goods to SM for $15m at a mark-up of 25% on cost. At the year end two-thirds of these goods had been sold on to third parties.

3   It is group accounting policy to measure non-controlling interests at acquisition at the proportionate share of the fair value of net assets. There has been no impairment of recognised goodwill in CE to date.

Required

Prepare the consolidated statement of changes in equity for the year ended 30 June 20X5.

Section summary

The consolidated statement of changes in equity reconciles the movement in equity over the year, with the results recognised in the consolidated statement of profit or loss and other comprehensive income and dividends paid out of the group. It links the consolidated statement of financial position with the consolidated statement of profit or loss and other comprehensive income.

352 | 14: The consolidated statement of profit or loss and other
comprehensive income and the statement of changes in equity

PART D ADVANCED GROUPS

Chapter Summary

Consolidated statement of profit or loss and other comprehensive income and the statement of changes in equity

Consolidated SPLOCI

- **Sales revenue to profit** for the year, and **OCI**: 100% consolidate (time apportion to include only post-acquisition results if mid-way acquisition
- **Intra-group sales:** Cancel out
- **Unrealised profit** on intra-group sales: If goods sold by parent, increase COS by unrealised profit; if goods sold by subsidiary, increase COS by full amount of unrealised profit and decrease NCI by NCI share of unrealised profit
- **Depreciation:** Consider need for FV adjustment
- **Transfer of non-current assets:** Eliminate profit on transfer and reduce expenses by any additional depreciation arising from increased carrying value of the asset. Adjust for NCI if asset was transferred from subsidiary

Consolidated changes in equity

- **Dividends:** Apportion between parent's share of dividend and NCI's share (S x NCI%)
- **Total comprehensive income:** From SPLOCI, calculate NCI share. Parent's share is the balancing figure.
- **Equity and NCI:** Calculate the amounts at the end of the period. The equity and NCI at the beginning of the period is a balancing figure.

Quick Quiz

1 Where does unrealised profit on intragroup trading appear in the consolidated statement of profit or loss and other comprehensive income?

2 At the beginning of the year a 75% subsidiary transfers a non-current asset to the parent for $500,000. Its carrying value was $400,000 and it has four years of useful life left. How is this accounted for at the end of the year in the consolidated statement of profit or loss and other comprehensive income? (See coverage of this type of transaction in Chapter 9).

354   14: The consolidated statement of profit or loss and other
comprehensive income and the statement of changes in equity

PART D ADVANCED GROUPS

Answers to Quick Quiz

1   As an addition to consolidated cost of sales (reducing the group profit)

2

	$
Unrealised profit	100,000
Additional depreciation (100 ÷ 4)	(25,000)
Net charge to statement of profit or loss	75,000

		$	$
DEBIT	Additional depreciation	25,000	
DEBIT	Group profit (75%)	56,250	
DEBIT	Non-controlling interests (25%)	18,750	
CREDIT	Non-current asset		100,000
		100,000	100,000

Answers to Questions

14.1   Non-controlling interests

(a)   CV GROUP

CONSOLIDATED STATEMENT OF PROFIT OR LOSS AND OTHER COMPREHENSIVE INCOME FOR THE
YEAR ENDED 30 SEPTEMBER 20X5

	$'000
Revenue (5,000 + 4,200 – 300 (W4))	8,900
Cost of sales (4,100 + 3,500 – 300 (W4) + 40 (W4))	(7,340)
Gross profit	1,560
Distribution and administration expenses (320 + 180 + 50 (W3))	(550)
Investment income (50 – 45 (W5))	5
Profit before tax	1,015
Income tax expense (240 + 170)	(410)
Profit for the year	605
Other comprehensive income:	
Gains on property revaluation (net of tax) (60 + 20)	80
Total comprehensive income for the year	685

Profit attributable to:	
Owners of the parent (615 – 65)	540
Non-controlling interests (W2)	65
	605
Total comprehensive income attributable to:	
Owners of the parent (695 – 70)	615
Non-controlling interests (W2)	70
	685

Workings

1   Group structure

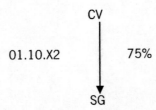

01.10.X2   75%

2   Non-controlling interests

	PFY	TCI
	$'000	$'000
Per question	350	370
Impairment loss for year (W3)	(50)	(50)
PUP (W4)	(40)	(40)
	260	280
NCI share	× 25%	× 25%
	= 65	= 70

3   Impairment of goodwill

Impairment of goodwill for the year = $250,000 goodwill × 20% impairment = $50,000

Add $50,000 to administration expenses and deduct from PFY/TCI in NCI working (as full goodwill method adopted here)

4   Intragroup trading

SG → CV

- Intragroup revenue and cost of sales:

  Cancel $300,000 out of revenue and cost of sales

- PUP = $300,000 × 2/3 in inventories × 25/125 mark-up = $40,000

  Increase cost of sales by $40,000 and reduce PFY/TCI in NCI working (as subsidiary is the seller)

5   Intragroup dividend

CV's share of SG's dividend = $60,000 x 75% = $45,000

Cancel $45,000 out of investment income

(b)   **Non-controlling interests (under partial goodwill method and if parent sells to subsidiary for intragroup trading)**

Non-controlling interests

	PFY	TCI
	$'000	$'000
Per question	350	370
NCI share	× 25%	× 25%
	= 87.5	= 92.5

Note. PUP is only deducted when the subsidiary is the seller and the parent is the seller here. Impairment loss for the year is only deducted under the full goodwill method and the partial goodwill method is used in part (b).

356 | 14: The consolidated statement of profit or loss and other comprehensive income and the statement of changes in equity

PART D ADVANCED GROUPS

14.2 Mid-year acquisition

(a) **Goodwill**

	$'000	$'000
Consideration transferred		4,000
Non-controlling interests (1,000 × 10% × $4.50)		450
Net assets at acquisition as represented by:		
Share capital	1,000	
Share premium	500	
Retained earnings (W1)	1,750	
Fair value adjustment	100	
		(3,350)
		1,100
Impairment losses to date		(20)
Goodwill at 31 December 20X7		1,080

Workings

1 *Group structure*

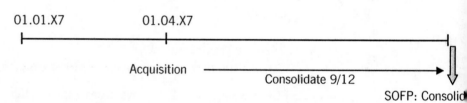

MB – pre-acq'n reserves (01.04.X7)

	$'000
Retained earnings at 01.0.X7	1,500
For the 3 months to 01.04.X7 (1000 x 3/12)	250
Retained earnings at 01.04.X7	1,750

(b) JT GROUP – CONSOLIDATED STATEMENT OF PROFIT OR LOSS
FOR THE YEAR ENDED 31 DECEMBER 20X7

	$'000
Revenue $(10,000 + (4,000 \times \frac{9}{12}) - 200)$	12,800
Cost of sales and expenses $(6,000 + (2,100 \times \frac{9}{12}) - 200 + 15 + 20 + 10))$	(7,420)
Profit before tax	5,380
Income tax expense $(1,400 + (900 \times \frac{9}{12}))$	(2,075)
Profit for the year	3,305
Attributable to:	
Equity holders of the parent	3,233
Non-controlling interests $[((1,000 \times \frac{9}{12}) - 20 - 10) \times 10\%]$	72
	3,305

14.3 Consolidated statement of changes in equity

SM GROUP – CONSOLIDATED STATEMENT OF CHANGES IN EQUITY

	Equity attributable to owners of the parent	Non-controlling interests	Total
	$'000	$'000	$'000
Balance at 1 July 20X4 (balancing figure)	537,500	32,500	570,000
Issue of shares	25,000	–	25,000
Total comprehensive income for the year (W4)	96,750	9,750	106,500
Dividends (25% × $10m)	(16,000)	(2,500)	(18,500)
Balance at 30 June 20X5 (W5)/(W6)	643,250	39,750	683,000

Workings

1   *Group structure*

SM

01.07.X2   37.5m/50m = 75%

CE

Pre-acq'n reserves = $80m – $50m = $30m

2   *Unrealised profit*

CE →SM

PUP = $15m × 1/3 in inventory x 25/125 mark-up = $1m
DEBIT   CE's cost of sales (and CE's retained earnings) $1m
CREDIT   Inventories $1m

3   *Intragroup dividend*

Intragroup dividend income = 75% × $10m = $7.5m → Cancel out of SM's profit/total comprehensive income

4   *Consolidated total comprehensive income for the year*

	$'000
Consolidated TCI [($75m – $7.5m (W3)] + [$40m – $1m (W2))]	106,500
Total comprehensive income attributable to:	
Owners of parent (balancing figure)	96,750
Non-controlling interests ($40m – $1m (W2)) × 25%	9,750
	106,500

5   *Consolidated equity at 30 June 20X5*

	SM	CE
	$'000	$'000
Per question	584,000	160,000
PUP (W2)		(1,000)
Pre-acquisition equity		(80,000)
		79,000
Share of CE post-acquisition reserves (75% × $79m)	59,250	
	643,250	

6   *Non-controlling interests at 30 June 20X5*

	$'000
NCI at acquisition (25% × $80m)	20,000
NCI share of post-acquisition reserves ($79m (W5) × 25%)	19,750
	39,750

7   *Proof of consolidated equity at 1 July 20X4*

	SM	CE
	$'000	$'000
Per question	500,000	130,000
Pre-acquisition equity		(80,000)
		50,000
Share of CE post-acquisition (75% × $50m)	37,500	
	537,500	

8   *Proof of non-controlling interests at 1 July 20X4*

	$'000
NCI at acquisition (W6)	20,000
NCI share of post-acquisition reserves ($50m (W7) x 25%)	12,500
	32,500

Now try these questions from the Practice Question Bank

Number	Level	Marks	Time
Q24	Introductory	N/A	5 mins
Q25	Introductory	12	22 mins
Q26	Introductory	15	27 mins
Q27	Introductory	25	45 mins
Q28	Introductory	17	31 mins
Q29	Introductory	18	32 mins

CONSOLIDATED STATEMENTS OF CASH FLOWS

A statement of cash flows is an additional primary statement of **great value** to users of financial statements for the extra information it provides.

You should be familiar with the basic principles, techniques and definitions relating to statements of cash flows from your earlier studies. This chapter develops the principles and preparation techniques to include **consolidated financial statements**.

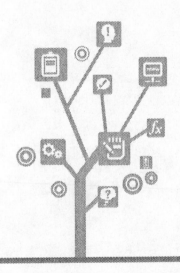

Topic list	learning outcomes	syllabus references
1 Cash flows	B1	B1(a)
2 IAS 7 *Statement of Cash Flows*: single company	B1	B1(a)
3 Consolidated statement of cash flows	B1	B1(a)
4 Foreign exchange and statement of cash flows	B1	B1(a)

Chapter Overview

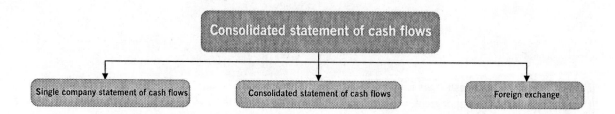

1   Cash flows

Introduction

Cash flows are much easier than profit to understand as a concept.

1.1 Cash flow accounting: advantages

The main advantages of using cash flow accounting (including both historical and forecast cash flows) are as follows.

(a)   The **survival** of a company depends on its ability to generate cash. Cash flow accounting directs attention towards this critical issue.

(b)   Cash flow is more **comprehensive** than profit which is dependent on accounting conventions and concepts.

(c)   Creditors (long- and short-term) are more interested in an entity's **ability to repay** them than in its profitability. While profits might indicate that cash is likely to be available, cash flow accounting is more direct with its message.

(d)   Cash flow reporting provides a better means of **comparing** the results of different companies than traditional profit reporting.

(e)   Cash flow reporting satisfies the **needs of all users** better.

   (i)   For **management**. It provides the sort of information on which decisions should be taken (in management accounting, 'relevant costs' to a decision are future cash flows). Traditional profit accounting does not help with decision-making.

   (ii)   For **shareholders and auditors**. Cash flow accounting can provide a satisfactory basis for stewardship accounting.

   (iii)   For **creditors and employees**. Their information needs will be better served by cash flow accounting.

(f)   **Cash flow forecasts** are easier to prepare, as well as more useful, than profit forecasts.

(g)   Cash flow statements are more easily understood, and can be **audited more easily** than financial statements based on the accruals concept.

(h)   Cash flow accounting can be both **retrospective**, and also include a **forecast** for the future. This is of great information value to all users of accounting information.

(i)   Forecasts can subsequently be monitored by the use of **variance statements** which compare actual cash flows against the forecast.

Looking at the same question from a different angle, readers of financial statements can be **misled** by the profit figure.

(a)   Shareholders might believe that if a company makes a profit after tax of, say $100,000, then this is the amount which it could afford to pay as a **dividend**. Unless the company has sufficient cash available to stay in business and also to pay a dividend, the shareholders' expectations would be wrong.

(b)   Employees might believe that if a company makes profits, it can afford to pay **higher wages** next year. This opinion may not be correct: the ability to pay wages depends on the availability of cash.

(c)   Creditors might consider that a profitable company is a **going concern**.

   (i)   If a company builds up large amounts of **unsold inventories** of goods, their cost would not be chargeable against profits, but cash would have been used up in making them, thus weakening the company's liquid resources.

(ii) A company might **capitalise** large development costs, having spent considerable amounts of money on R & D, but only charge small amounts against current profits. As a result, the company might show reasonable profits, but get into severe difficulties with its liquidity position.

(d) Management might suppose that if their company makes a historical cost profit and reinvests some of those profits, then the company must be **expanding**. This is not the case: in a period of inflation, a company might have a historical cost profit but a current cost accounting loss, which means that the operating capability of the firm will be declining.

(e) The **survival** of a business entity depends not so much on profits as on its ability to pay its debts when they fall due. Such payments might include statement of profit or loss and other comprehensive income items such as material purchases, wages, interest and taxation etc but also capital payments for new fixed assets and the repayment of loan capital when this falls due (eg on the redemption of debentures).

Exam alert

The March 2011 resit paper included a question where a statement of cash flows had to be **analysed,** rather than prepared.

Section summary

Statements of cash flows are a useful addition to the financial statements of companies because it is recognised that accounting profit is not the only indicator of a company's performance.

Statements of cash flows concentrate on the sources and uses of cash and are a useful indicator of a company's **liquidity and solvency.**

2 IAS 7 *Statement of cash flows*: single company

Introduction

The aim of IAS 7 is to provide information to users of financial statements about the cash flows of an entity's **ability to generate cash and cash equivalents**, as well as indicating the cash needs of the entity. The statement of cash flows provides **historical** information about cash and cash equivalents, classifying cash flows between operating, investing and financing activities. It is worth revising the basic principles in the context of a single company before moving on to the extra considerations when preparing the statement of cash flows for a group.

2.1 Scope

A statement of cash flows should be presented as an **integral part** of an entity's financial statements. All types of entity can provide useful information about cash flows, as the need for cash is universal, whatever the nature of their revenue-producing activities. Therefore, **all entities are required by the standard to produce a statement of cash flows.**

2.2 Benefits of cash flow information

The use of statements of cash flows is very much **in conjunction** with the rest of the financial statements. Users can gain further appreciation of the change in net assets, of the entity's financial position (liquidity and solvency) and the entity's ability to adapt to changing circumstances by affecting the amount and timing of cash flows. Statements of cash flows **enhance comparability,** as they are not affected by differing accounting policies used for the same type of transactions or events.

Cash flow information of a historical nature can be used as an indicator of the amount, timing and certainty of **future cash flows**. Past forecast cash flow information can be **checked for accuracy** as actual figures emerge. The relationship between profit and cash flows can be analysed, as can changes in prices over time.

2.3 Definitions

The standard gives the following definitions, the most important of which are **cash** and **cash equivalents**.

KEY TERMS

CASH comprises cash on hand and demand deposits.

CASH EQUIVALENTS are short-term, highly liquid investments that are readily convertible to known amounts of cash, and which are subject to an insignificant risk of changes in value.

CASH FLOWS are inflows and outflows of cash and cash equivalents.

OPERATING ACTIVITIES are the principal revenue-producing activities of the entity and other activities that are not investing or financing activities.

INVESTING ACTIVITIES are the acquisition and disposal of long-term assets and other investments not included in cash equivalents.

FINANCING ACTIVITIES are activities that result in changes in the size and composition of the contributed equity and borrowings of the entity.   *(IAS 7)*

2.4 Cash and cash equivalents

The standard expands on the definition of cash equivalents: they are not held for investment or other long-term purposes, rather to meet short-term cash commitments. To fulfil the above definition, an investment's **maturity date should normally be three months from its acquisition date**. It would usually be the case then that equity investments (ie shares in other companies) are **not** cash equivalents. An exception would be where preferred shares were acquired with a very close maturity date.

Loans and other borrowings from banks are classified as investing activities. In some countries, however, **bank overdrafts** are repayable on demand and are treated as part of an entity's total cash management system. In these circumstances, an overdrawn balance will be included in cash and cash equivalents. Such banking arrangements are characterised by a balance which fluctuates between overdrawn and credit.

Movements between different types of cash and cash equivalent are not included in cash flows. The investment of surplus cash in cash equivalents is part of cash management, not part of operating, investing or financing activities.

2.5 Presentation of a statement of cash flows

IAS 7 requires statements of cash flows to report cash flows during the period classified by **operating, investing** and **financing activities**.

The manner of presentation of cash flows from operating, investing and financing activities **depends on the nature of the entity**. By classifying cash flows between different activities in this way, users can see the impact on cash and cash equivalents of each one, and their relationships with each other. We can look at each in more detail.

2.5.1 Operating activities

This is perhaps the key part of the statement of cash flows, because it shows whether, and to what extent, companies can **generate cash from their operations**. It is these operating cash flows which must,

in the end, pay for all cash outflows relating to other activities, such as paying loan interest, dividends and so on. Most of the components of cash flows from operating activities will be those items which **determine the net profit or loss of the entity**, ie they relate to the main revenue-producing activities of the entity. The standard gives the following as examples of cash flows from operating activities.

- Cash receipts from the sale of goods and the rendering of services

- Cash receipts from royalties, fees, commissions and other revenue

- Cash payments to suppliers for goods and services

- Cash payments to and on behalf of employees

- Cash payments/refunds of income taxes unless they can be specifically identified with financing or investing activities

- Cash receipts and payments from contracts held for dealing or trading purposes

Certain items may be included in the net profit or loss for the period which do **not** relate to operational cash flows, for example, the profit or loss on the sale of a piece of plant will be included in net profit or loss, but the cash flows will be classed as **financing**.

2.5.2 Investing activities

The cash flows classified under this heading show the extent of new investment in **assets which will generate future profit and cash flows**. Only expenditures which result in a recognised asset in the statement of financial position should be classified as investing activities. The standard gives the following examples of cash flows arising from investing activities.

- Cash payments to acquire property, plant and equipment, intangibles and other long-term assets, including those relating to capitalised development costs and self-constructed property, plant and equipment

- Cash receipts from sales of property, plant and equipment, intangibles and other long-term assets

- Cash payments to acquire equity or debt instruments in other entities, and interests in joint ventures

- Cash receipts from sales of equity or debt instruments in other entities, and interests in joint ventures

- Cash advances and loans made to other parties

- Cash receipts from the repayment of advances and loans made to other parties

- Cash payments for, or receipts from, futures/forward/option/swap contracts except where the contracts are held for dealing purposes or the payments/receipts are classified as financing activities

2.5.3 Financing activities

This section of the statement of cash flows shows the share of cash which the entity's capital providers have claimed during the period. This is an indicator of the likely **claims on future cash flows** from the providers of capital (ie interest and dividend payments). The standard gives the following examples of cash flows which might arise under these headings.

- Cash proceeds from issuing shares

- Cash payments to owners to acquire or redeem the entity's shares

- Cash proceeds from issuing debentures, loans, notes, bonds, mortgages and other short or long-term borrowings

- Cash repayments of amounts borrowed

- Cash payments by a lessee for the reduction of the outstanding liability relating to a finance lease

2.6 Reporting cash flows from operating activities

The standard offers a choice of method for this part of the statement of cash flows.

(a)   **Direct method**: disclose major classes of gross cash receipts and gross cash payments

(b)   **Indirect method**: net profit or loss is adjusted for:

  (i)   Changes during the period in inventories and operating payables and receivables

  (ii)   Non-cash items (such as depreciation, provisions, deferred taxes, unrealised foreign exchanges gains and losses, and undistributed profits of associates)

  (iii)   All other items for which the cash effects are investing or financing cash flows

Proformas for both methods are shown in Section 2.11.

2.6.1 Using the direct method

There are different ways in which the **information about gross cash receipts and payments** can be obtained. The most obvious way is simply to extract the information from the accounting records. This may be a laborious task, however, and the indirect method below may be easier.

2.6.2 Using the indirect method

This method is undoubtedly **easier** from the point of view of the preparer of the statement of cash flows. As we have mentioned above, the net profit or loss for the period is adjusted for the following.

(a)   Changes during the period in inventories, operating receivables and payables

(b)   Non-cash items, and

(c)   Other items, the cash flows from which should be classified under investing or financing activities

It is important to understand why **certain items are added and others subtracted**. Note the following points.

(a)   Depreciation is not a cash expense, but is deducted in arriving at the profit figure in the statement of profit or loss and other comprehensive income. It makes sense, therefore, to eliminate it by adding it back.

(b)   By the same logic, a loss on a disposal of a non-current asset (arising through underprovision of depreciation) needs to be added back and a profit deducted.

(c)   An increase in inventories means less cash – you have spent cash on buying inventory.

(d)   An increase in receivables means the company's debtors have not paid as much and therefore there is less cash.

(e)   If we pay off payables, causing the figure to decrease, again we have less cash.

2.6.3 Indirect versus direct

The direct method is encouraged where the necessary information is not too costly to obtain, but IAS 7 does not require it. The reason why the direct method is preferred is that it provides information not available elsewhere in the financial statements.

Exam alert

For the purposes of your F2 exam, the indirect method is more often used.

2.7 Interest and dividends

Cash flows from interest and dividends received and paid should each be **disclosed separately**. Each should be classified in a consistent manner from period to period as either operating,, investing or financing activities.

Dividends paid by the entity can be classified in **one of two ways**.

(a) As a **financing cash flow**, showing the cost of obtaining financial resources

(b) As a component of **cash flows from operating activities** so that users can assess the entity's ability to pay dividends out of operating cash flows

2.8 Taxes on income

Cash flows arising from taxes on income should be **separately disclosed** and should be classified as cash flows from operating activities *unless* they can be specifically identified with financing and investing activities.

Taxation cash flows are often **difficult to match** to the originating underlying transaction, so most of the time all tax cash flows are classified as arising from operating activities.

2.9 Components of cash and cash equivalents

The components of cash and cash equivalents should be disclosed and a **reconciliation** should be presented, showing the amounts in the statement of cash flows reconciled with the equivalent items reported in the statement of financial position.

It is also necessary to disclose the **accounting policy** used in deciding the items included in cash and cash equivalents, in accordance with IAS 1 *Presentation of financial statements*, but also because of the wide range of cash management practices worldwide.

2.10 Other disclosures

All entities should disclose, together with a **commentary by management**, the amount of cash or cash equivalent balances held by the entity that are not available for use by the group.

IAS 7 encourages the disclosure of other information relevant to users in understanding the financial position and liquidity of the entity, including:

(a) The amount of undrawn borrowing facilities which are available, and any restrictions on the use of these facilities

(b) The aggregate amount of cash flows that represent **increases in operating capacity**, separately from cash flows that are required to maintain operating capacity

(c) The amount of cash flows arising from the operating, investing and financing activities of each reporting **segment**

2.11 Pro-forma statements of cash flows

In the next section, we will look at the procedures for preparing a statement of cash flows. First, the example below, adapted from the example given in the standard, shows pro-forma statements of cash flows under the direct and indirect methods.

2.11.1 Direct method

STATEMENT OF CASH FLOWS (DIRECT METHOD)
YEAR ENDED 31 DECEMBER 20X7

	$m	$m
Cash flows from operating activities		
Cash receipts from customers	30,150	
Cash paid to suppliers and employees	(27,600)	
Cash generated from operations	2,550	
Interest paid	(270)	
Income taxes paid	(900)	
Net cash from operating activities		1,380
Cash flows from investing activities		
Acquisition of subsidiary net of cash acquired (see **Note** below)	(550	
Purchase of property, plant and equipment	(350)	
Proceeds from sale of equipment	20	
Interest received	200	
Dividends received	200	
Net cash used in investing activities		(480)
Cash flows from financing activities		
Proceeds from issue of share capital	250	
Proceeds from long-term borrowings	250	
Payment of finance lease liabilities	(90)	
Dividends paid*	(1,200)	
Net cash used in financing activities		(790)
Net increase in cash and cash equivalents		110
Cash and cash equivalents at beginning of period (Note A)		120
Cash and cash equivalents at end of period (Note A)		230

* This could also be shown as an operating cash flow

2.11.2 Indirect method

STATEMENT OF CASH FLOWS (INDIRECT METHOD)
YEAR ENDED 31 DECEMBER 20X7

	$m	$m
Cash flows from operating activities		
Profit before taxation	3,350	
Adjustments for:		
Depreciation	450	
Foreign exchange loss (see **Note** below)	40	
Investment income	(500)	
Interest expense	400	
	3,740	
Increase in trade and other receivables	(500)	
Decrease in inventories	1,050	
Decrease in trade payables	(1,740)	
Cash generated from operations	2,550	
Interest paid	(270)	
Income taxes paid	(900)	
Net cash from operating activities		1,380
Cash flows from investing activities		
Acquisition of subsidiary net of cash acquired (see **Note** below)	(550)	
Purchase of property, plant and equipment	(350)	
Proceeds from sale of equipment	20	
Interest received	200	
Dividends received	200	
Net cash used in investing activities		(480)
Cash flows from financing activities		
Proceeds from issue of share capital	250	
Proceeds from long-term borrowings	250	
Payment of finance lease liabilities	(90)	
Dividends paid*	(1,200)	
Net cash used in financing activities		(790)
Net increase in cash and cash equivalents		110
Cash and cash equivalents at beginning of period (Note A)		120
Cash and cash equivalents at end of period (Note A)		230

* This could also be shown as an operating cash flow

Note A

Cash and cash equivalents

	20X7	20X6
	$m	$m
Cash on hand and balances with banks	40	25
Short-term investments	190	135
Cash and cash equivalents as previously reported	230	160
Effect of exchange rate changes	–	(40)
Cash and cash equivalents as restated	230	120

Note. While foreign exchange losses and the acquisition of subsidiaries are less relevant to single company, statements of cash flows they are likely to appear in group consolidated statements of cash flows, which we will look at later in this chapter. They have therefore been included here for completeness.

2.12 Step procedure

Remember the steps involved in the preparation of a statement of cash flows.

 Read the question and set up a pro-forma statement of cash flows.

 Transfer the statement of financial position figures to the face of the statement of cash flows or workings. Work methodically, line by line, down the statement of financial position.

 Transfer the statement of profit or loss and other comprehensive income figures to the face of the statement of cash flows or workings.

 Deal with additional information.

 Finish off workings and transfer figures to answer.

 Do additional workings for the direct method (if required).

 Finish off statement of cash flows.

Question 15.1	Single company

Learning outcome B1

Kane Co's statement of profit or loss for the year ended 31 December 20X8 and statements of financial position at 31 December 20X7 and 31 December 20X8 were as follows.

KANE CO
STATEMENT OF PROFIT OR LOSS FOR THE YEAR ENDED 31 DECEMBER 20X8

	$'000	$'000
Sales		720
Raw materials consumed	70	
Staff costs	94	
Depreciation	118	
Loss on disposal of long-term asset	18	
		300
		420
Interest payable		28
Profit before tax		392
Income tax expense		124
Profit for the year		268

KANE CO
STATEMENT OF FINANCIAL POSITION AS AT 31 DECEMBER 20X8

	20X8		20X7	
	$'000	$'000	$'000	$'000
Assets				
Non-current assets				
Cost	1,596		1,560	
Depreciation	318		224	
		1,278		1,336
Current assets				
Inventory	24		20	
Trade receivables	76		58	
Bank	48		56	
		148		134
Total assets		1,426		1,470
Equity and liabilities				
Equity				
Share capital	360		340	
Share premium	36		24	
Retained earnings	686		490	
		1,082		854
Non-current liabilities				
Long-term loans		200		500
Current liabilities				
Trade payables	42		30	
Taxation	102		86	
		144		116
Total equity and liabilities		1,426		1,470

During the year, the company paid $90,000 for a new piece of machinery.

Required

Prepare a statement of cash flows for Kane Co for the year ended 31 December 20X8 in accordance with the requirements of IAS 7, using the indirect method.

Section summary

Remember the **step by step preparation procedure** and use it for all the questions you practise.

You need to be aware of the **format** of the statement as laid out in **IAS 7**. Setting out the format is an essential first stage in preparing the statement, so this format must be learnt.

3 Consolidated statement of cash flows   11/11, 5/12

Introduction

Consolidated statements of cash flows follow the same principles as for single company statements, with some additional complications.

A group's statement of cash flows should only show flows of cash **external** to the group. This follows the same principle that you have already met in the context of the group statement of financial position and statement of profit or loss and other comprehensive income.

Exam questions usually provide the opening and closing **consolidated statement of financial position** and the **consolidated statement of profit or loss and other comprehensive income** for the year. This means

that you can apply the same techniques that you have used for single company statements of cash flows, without the need to eliminate intragroup items, as the intragroup transactions and balances will have been eliminated already in the consolidated financial statements given in the question.

The extra issues that you will have to deal with in consolidated statements of cash flows are:

(a) Cash paid to non-controlling interests
(b) Cash received from associates
(c) Payments to acquire subsidiaries
(d) Receipts from sales of subsidiaries.

3.1 Non-controlling interests

The group statement of cash flows shows movements in group cash. In earlier chapters, you have seen that the cash shown on the consolidated statement of financial position includes 100% of the cash balance of any subsidiaries, irrespective of whether there are non-controlling interests in the subsidiaries.

The only item you will have to calculate is the actual amount of cash paid out by the group to the non-controlling interests ie any dividends paid to the non-controlling interests. **Dividends paid to non-controlling interests** should be included under the heading **'cash flow from financing'** and disclosed separately.

You will need to set up a working in the same style as the example below. This will reconcile the opening and closing balances on the non-controlling interests account from the consolidated statement of financial position, and the amount of **total comprehensive income** attributed to the non-controlling interests, to identify the cash paid out as dividends as a balancing item.

Example: Non-controlling interests

The following are extracts of the consolidated results for Jarvis Co for the year ended 31 December 20X8.

CONSOLIDATED STATEMENT OF PROFIT OR LOSS (EXTRACT)

	$'000
Group profit before tax	90
Income tax expense	(30)
Profit for the year	60
Profit attributable to:	
Owners of the parent	45
Non-controlling interests	15
	60

CONSOLIDATED STATEMENT OF FINANCIAL POSITION (EXTRACT)

	20X1	20X2
	$'000	$'000
Non-controlling interests	300	306

Required

Calculate the dividends paid to the non-controlling interests during the year.

Solution

Dividends paid to non-controlling interests

	$'000
B/d	300
TCI attributable to NCI	15
	315
Dividends paid to NCI (balancing figure)	(9)
C/d	306

Notes

1   In this example, there is no other comprehensive income so the total comprehensive income here is equal to the profit for the year.

2   On the statement of financial position, the NCI balance includes the NCI share of **retained earnings** (ie **after** deduction of dividends). Dividends are not deducted in the statement of profit or loss and other comprehensive income so the NCI share of total comprehensive income is stated **before** deduction of dividends. Therefore, the balancing figure in this working must be the dividends paid to the NCI.

3.2 Associates and joint ventures

An entity which reports its interest in an associate or a joint venture using the equity method includes in its statement of cash flows the cash flows in respect of its investments in the associate or joint venture, and distributions and other payments or receipts between it and the associate or joint venture.

Dividends from associates are normally included as a separate item in '**cash flows from investing activities.**'

In the following example, you will see that the method used to calculate the dividend received from an associate is very similar to the method used to calculate the dividend paid to non-controlling interests.

Example: Associate

CONSOLIDATED STATEMENT OF PROFIT OR LOSS AND OTHER COMPREHENSIVE INCOME FOR THE YEAR ENDED 31 DECEMBER 20X2

	$'000
Profit before interest and tax	60
Share of profit of associates	9
Profit before tax	69
Income tax expense	(20)
Profit for the year	49
Other comprehensive income:	
Gains on property revaluation	15
Share of other comprehensive income of associates	3
Exchange loss on translating foreign associate	(2)
Income tax relating to components of other comprehensive income	(5)
Other comprehensive income for the year, net of tax	11
Total comprehensive income for the year	60

CONSOLIDATED STATEMENTS OF FINANCIAL POSITION AS AT 31 DECEMBER

	20X2	20X1
	$'000	$'000
Investments in associates	94	88

Required

Calculate the dividend received from associates.

Solution

Investments in associates

	$'000
B/d	88
SPLOCI – share of profit	9
SPLOCI – share of OCI	3
Exchange loss on translating foreign associate	(2)
	98
Dividends received from associate (balancing figure)	(4)
C/d	94

Note. In the statement of financial position, the investment in associate balance includes the group share of the associate's **retained earnings** (ie **after** deduction of dividends). Dividends are not deducted in the statement of comprehensive income so the group share of the associate's profit and other comprehensive income (if any) is stated **before** deduction of dividends. Therefore, the balancing figure in this working must be the dividends received from the associate.

3.3 Acquisitions and disposals of subsidiaries and other business units

An entity should present separately the aggregate cash flows arising from acquisitions and from disposals of subsidiaries or other business units, and classify them as **investing activities**.

When a group **acquires** a new subsidiary, there are **two** effects on group cash:

(a) A **decrease in group cash** to the extent that **consideration is paid in cash** by the parent, and

(b) An **increase** in group cash as the cash held by the new subsidiary at acquisition will be consolidated within group cash from that date.

When a group **disposes of** a subsidiary, the **two** effects are:

(a) An **increase** in group cash if cash proceeds are received by the parent, and

(b) A **decrease** in group cash as the cash held by the subsidiary at the dates of its disposal will cease to be consolidated from that date.

Disclosure is required of the following, in aggregate, in respect of both acquisitions and disposals of subsidiaries or other business units during the period.

(a) Total purchase/disposal consideration

(b) Portion of purchase/disposal consideration discharged by means of cash/cash equivalents

(c) Amount of cash/cash equivalents in the subsidiary or business unit disposed of

(d) Amount of assets and liabilities other than cash/cash equivalents in the subsidiary or business unit acquired or disposed of, summarised by major category

The acquisition or disposal of a subsidiary should be included under the heading '**cash flows from investing activities**' and show the cash flow **net** of cash/cash equivalents acquired or disposed of.

3.4 Finance lease transactions

When rentals under a finance lease are paid, the **interest and capital elements are split out** and included under the net cash from '**operations (interest paid)**' and '**financing activities**' headings respectively.

3.5 Recap

The preparation of consolidated statements of cash flows will be, in many respects, the same as those for single companies, with the following **additional complications**.

- Acquisitions and disposals of subsidiary undertakings
- Cancellation of intragroup transactions
- Non-controlling interests
- Associates and joint ventures
- Finance leases

Exam alert

Various complications may arise in a consolidated statement of cash flows in the exam, the most important of which are covered above. Question 15.2, given below, is comprehensive. The Pilot Paper asked for the preparation of a consolidated statement of cash flows and a report on the usefulness of group statements of cash flows, generally and specifically to the entity in the question.

Exam skills

Your priority must be to **show the cash flow** relating to an acquisition or disposal on the statement of cash flows. This is straightforward, as you simply need to identify the relevant cash inflows and outflows.

On the group statement of cash flows, the acquisition or disposal is shown as a one-line item. The complication is that you will be working from consolidated statements of financial position where the subsidiary's assets and liabilities will have been added in line by line. You must **adjust for the assets and liabilities acquired (or disposed of)** in the relevant workings, otherwise you will double-count the acquisition or disposal.

Question 15.2	Consolidated cash flow

Learning outcome B1

Topiary Co is a 40 year old company producing garden statues carved from marble. Twenty-two years ago it acquired a 100% interest in a marble importing company, Hardstuff Co. In 20W9 it acquired a 40% interest in a competitor, Landscapes Co, and on 1 January 20X7 it acquired a 75% interest in Garden Furniture Designs. The draft consolidated financial statements for the Topiary Group are as follows.

DRAFT CONSOLIDATED STATEMENT OF PROFIT OR LOSS
FOR THE YEAR ENDED 31 DECEMBER 20X7

	$'000	$'000
Operating profit		4,455
Share of profits after tax of associates		1,050
Income from long-term investments		465
Interest payable		(450)
Profit before taxation		5,520
Tax on profit		
Income tax	1,173	
Deferred taxation	312	
		(1,485)
Profit for the year		4,035
Attributable to: owners of the parent		3,735
non-controlling interests		300
		4,035

DRAFT CONSOLIDATED STATEMENT OF FINANCIAL POSITION
AS AT 31 DECEMBER 20X7

	20X6		20X7	
	$'000	$'000	$'000	$'000
Non-current assets				
Buildings at net book value		6,600		6,225
Plant and machinery at cost	4,200		9,000	
Aggregate depreciation	(3,300)		(3,600)	
Net book value		900		5,400
		7,500		11,625
Goodwill				300
Investments in associates		3,000		3,300
Long-term investments		1,230		1,230
		11,730		16,455
Current assets				
Inventories	3,000		5,925	
Receivables	3,825		5,550	
Cash	5,460		13,545	
		12,285		25,020
		24,015		41,475
Equity attributable to owners of the parent				
Share capital (25c shares)	6,000		11,820	
Share premium account	6,285		8,649	
Retained earnings	7,500		10,335	
	19,785		30,804	
Non-controlling interests	–		345	
		19,785		31,149
Non-current liabilities				
Obligations under finance leases	510		2,130	
Loans	1,500		4,380	
Deferred tax	39		90	
		2,049		6,600
Current liabilities				
Trade payables	840		1,500	
Obligations under finance leases	600		720	
Income tax	651		1,386	
Accrued interest and finance charges	90		120	
		2,181		3,726
		24,015		41,475

Notes

1 There had been no acquisitions or disposals of buildings during the year.

Machinery costing $1.5m was sold for $1.5m resulting in a profit of $300,000. New machinery was acquired in 20X7 including additions of $2.55m acquired under finance leases.

2 *Information relating to the acquisition of Garden Furniture Designs*

	$'000
Machinery	495
Inventories	96
Trade receivables	84
Cash	336
Trade payables	(204)
Income tax	(51)
	756
Non-controlling interests	(189)
	567
Goodwill	300
	867

2,640,000 shares issued as part consideration	825
Balance of consideration paid in cash	42
	867

3   Loans were issued at a discount in 20X7 and the carrying amount of the loans at 31 December 20X7 included $120,000, representing the finance cost attributable to the discount and allocated in respect of the current reporting period.

Required

Prepare a consolidated statement of cash flows for the Topiary Group for the year ended 31 December 20X7 as required by IAS 7, using the indirect method. There is no need to provide notes to the statement of cash flows.

Section summary

A **consolidated statement of cash flows** should not present a great problem if you understand how to deal with acquisitions and disposals of subsidiaries, non-controlling interests and dividends.

4   Foreign exchange and statements of cash flows

Introduction

An additional complication would involve translating foreign currencies prior to preparing a statement of cash flows.

Exam alert

Complications like foreign currencies in cash flow are unlikely to come up, so skim read this section if you're in a hurry.

4.1 Individual companies

Receipts and payments should be translated into the reporting currency at the **rate ruling** at the date on which the receipt or payment is made.

Exchange differences **do not give rise to cash flows** and therefore they would not be reflected in the statement of cash flows.

4.2 Group companies

The main problems relating to foreign exchange differences are when dealing with the cash flows of an overseas subsidiary. IAS 7 requires that all cash flows relating to an overseas subsidiary be translated at the exchange rates between the functional currency and the foreign currency at the date of the cash flows. Where the presentation currency method has been used to consolidate the subsidiary's results (as will be the case most of the time) then the subsidiary's cash flows will be translated using the average rate (because this is the rate used to translate the subsidiary's statement of comprehensive income).

If the **average rate** is used, then merely using the statements of financial position to derive the figures would not be appropriate as the resulting statement of cash flows would not comply with IAS 7, some items being translated at the closing rate. The practical answer to this problem is to use the following method (which would be time-consuming in practice).

Produce a statement of cash flows for each subsidiary.

 Translate each into the parent's currency using the average rate.

 Consolidate them into the group statement of cash flows (after eliminating intragroup items).

The other main point to note is that the exchange differences on translation must be **analysed into their constituent parts**, namely long-term assets, receivables, cash, payables and non-controlling interests and so forth. You may be asked to perform this exercise in the examination, although in the example shown below the split is given.

Example: foreign currency translation

Acquisitions

On 1 October 20X8, P, a public limited company, acquired 90% of S, a limited company, by issuing 100,000 shares at an agreed value of $1.60 per share and $140,000 in cash.

At that time the statement of financial position of S (equivalent to the fair value of the assets and liabilities) was as follows:

	$'000
Property, plant and equipment	190
Inventories	70
Trade receivables	30
Cash and cash equivalents	10
Trade payables	(40)
	260

Group policy is to value non-controlling interests at the date of acquisition at the proportionate share of the fair value of the acquiree's identifiable assets acquired and liabilities assumed.

The consolidated statements of financial position of P as at 31 December were as follows:

	20X8	20X7
	$'000	$'000
Non-current assets		
Property, plant and equipment	2,642	2,300
Goodwill	66	–
	2,708	2,300
Current assets		
Inventories	1,450	1,200
Trade receivables	1,370	1,100
Cash and cash equivalents	2	50
	2,822	2,350
	5,530	4,650
Equity attributable to owners of the parent		
Share capital ($1 ordinary shares)	1,150	1,000
Share premium account	590	500
Retained earnings	1,784	1,530
Revaluation surplus	74	–
	3,598	3,030
Non-controlling interests	32	–
	3,630	3,030

Non-current liabilities
Deferred tax	80	40
Current liabilities		
Trade payables	1,710	1,520
Current tax	110	60
	1,820	1,580
	5,530	4,650

The consolidated statement of profit or loss and other comprehensive income for the year ended 31 December 20X8 was as follows:

	$'000
Revenue	10,000
Cost of sales	(7,500)
Gross profit	2,500
Administrative expenses	(2,077)
Profit before tax	423
Income tax expense	(150)
Profit for the year	273
Other comprehensive income:	
Items that will not be reclassified to profit or loss	
Gains on property revaluation	115
Income tax relating to items that will not be reclassified	(40)
Other comprehensive income for the year, net of tax	75
Total comprehensive income for the year	348

Profit attributable to:	
Owners of the parent	264
Non-controlling interests	9
	273
Total comprehensive income attributable to:	
Owners of the parent	338
Non-controlling interests	10
	348

You are also given the following information.

1   All other subsidiaries are wholly owned.

2   Depreciation charged to the consolidated profit or loss amounted to $210,000.

3   Part of the additions to property, plant and equipment during the year was imports made by P, from a foreign supplier on 30 September 20X8 for 108,000 corona. This was paid in full on 30 November 20X8.

      Exchange gains and losses are included in administrative expenses. Relevant exchange rates were as follows:

	Corona to $1
30 September 20X8	4.0
30 November 20X8	4.5

4   There were no disposals of property, plant and equipment during the year.

Required

Prepare a consolidated statement of cash flows for the year ended 31 December 20X8 under the indirect method in accordance with IAS 7.

Solution

P GROUP

CONSOLIDATED STATEMENT OF CASH FLOWS FOR THE YEAR ENDED 31 DECEMBER 20X8

	$'000	$'000
Cash flows from operating activities		
Profit before taxation	423	
Adjustments for:		
Depreciation	210	
Foreign exchange gain (W8)	(3)	
	630	
Increase in trade receivables (W3)	(240)	
Increase in inventories (W3)	(180)	
Increase in trade payables (W3)	150	
Cash generated from operations	360	
Income taxes paid (W7)	(100)	
Net cash from operating activities		260
Cash flows from investing activities		
Acquisition of subsidiary net of cash acquired (140 – 10)	(130)	
Foreign purchase of property, plant and equipment (W8)	(24)	
Purchase of property, plant and equipment (W1)	(220)	
Net cash used in investing activities		(374)
Cash flows from financing activities		
Proceeds from issue of share capital (W4)	80	
Dividends paid to owners of the parent (W5)	(10)	
Dividends paid to non-controlling interests (W6)	(4)	
Net cash from financing activities		66
Net decrease in cash and cash equivalents		(48)
Cash and cash equivalents at the beginning of the year		50
Cash and cash equivalents at the end of the year		2

Workings

1	*Property, plant and equipment*	
		$'000
	B/d	2,300
	Revaluation	115
	Depreciation	(210)
	Foreign purchase (W8)	27
	Acquisition of subsidiary	190
		2,422
	Additions (in $) (balancing figure)	220
	C/d	2,642

2	*Goodwill*	
		$'000
	B/d	-
	Acquisition of subsidiary*	66
		66
	Impairment loss (balancing figure)	(-)
	C/d	66

	* Goodwill on acquisition of subsidiary:	
		$'000
	Consideration transferred (140 + (100 × $1.60))	300
	NCI (260 × 10%)	26
	Less: Net assets at acquisition	(260)
		66

3 *Inventories, trade receivables and trade payables*

	Inventories	Trade receivables	Trade payables
	$'000	$'000	$'000
B/d	1,200	1,100	1,520
Acquisition of subsidiary	70	30	40
	1,270	1,130	1,560
Increase (balancing figure)	180	240	150
C/d	1,450	1,370	1,710

4 *Share capital and share premium*

	$'000
B/d (1,000 + 500)	1,500
Acquisition of subsidiary (100 × $1.60)	160
	1,660
Issue for cash (balancing figure)	80
C/d (1,150 + 590)	1,740

5 *Retained earnings (to find dividends paid to owners of the parent)*

	$'000
B/d	1,530
SPLOCI – profit attributable to owners of parent	264
	1,794
Dividends paid to owners of the parent (balancing figure)	(10)
C/d	1,784

6 *Non-controlling interests*

	$'000
B/d	-
SPLOCI – TCI	10
Acquisition of subsidiary (W2)	26
	36
Dividends paid (balancing figure)	(4)
C/d	32

7 *Current and deferred tax*

	$'000
B/d (40 + 60)	100
SPLOCI – P/L	150
SPLOCI – OCI	40
	290
Tax paid (balancing figure)	(100)
C/d (80 + 110)	190

8 *Foreign transaction*

Transactions recorded on:	$'000	$'000
(a) 30 Sep DR Property, plant & equipment (108/4)	27 (to (W1))	
CR Payables		27
(b) 30 Nov DR Payables (to clear)	27	
CR Cash (108/4.5)		24 (to CF investing)
CR P/L (Admin expenses)		3 (to CF operating adj)

Section summary

A **foreign exchange difference** in a group statement of cash flows must be analysed into its constituent parts.

Chapter Summary

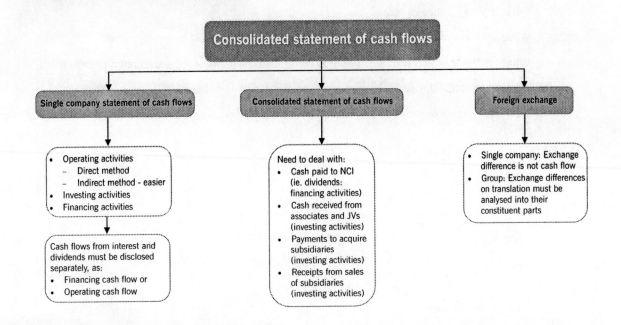

Consolidated statement of cash flows

Single company statement of cash flows

- Operating activities
  - Direct method
  - Indirect method - easier
- Investing activities
- Financing activities

Cash flows from interest and dividends must be disclosed separately, as:
- Financing cash flow or
- Operating cash flow

Consolidated statement of cash flows

Need to deal with:
- Cash paid to NCI (ie. dividends: financing activities)
- Cash received from associates and JVs (investing activities)
- Payments to acquire subsidiaries (investing activities)
- Receipts from sales of subsidiaries (investing activities)

Foreign exchange

- Single company: Exchange difference is not cash flow
- Group: Exchange differences on translation must be analysed into their constituent parts

Quick Quiz

1   What is the objective of IAS 7?

2   What are the benefits of cash flow information according to IAS 7?

3   What are the standard headings required by IAS 7 to be included in a statement of cash flows?

4   What is the indirect method of preparing a statement of cash flows?

5   How should an acquisition or disposal of a subsidiary be shown in the consolidated statement of cash flows?

Answers to Quick Quiz

1   To provide users of financial statements with information about the entity's ability to generate cash and cash equivalents, and the entity's cash needs.

2   See Paragraph 2.2.

3   Operating, investing and financing activities.

4   To determine the cash flow from operating activities, the net profit or loss for the period is adjusted for non-cash items; changes in inventories, receivables and payables from operations; and other items resulting from investing or financing activities.

5   Cash flows from acquisitions and disposals are presented separately under investing activities.

Answers to Questions

15.1 Single company

KANE CO
STATEMENT OF CASH FLOWS FOR THE YEAR ENDED 31 DECEMBER 20X8

	$'000	$'000
Cash flows from operating activities		
Operating profit	420	
Depreciation charges	118	
Loss on sale of tangible non-current assets	18	
Increase in inventories	(4)	
Increase in receivables	(18)	
Increase in payables	12	
Cash generated from operations	546	
Interest paid	(28)	
Dividends paid (W2)	(72)	
Tax paid (W3)	(108)	
Net cash from operating activities		338
Cash flows from investing activities		
Payments to acquire tangible non-current assets	(90)	
Receipts from sales of tangible non-current assets (W1)	12	
Net cash used in investing activities		(78)
Cash flows from financing activities		
Issues of share capital (W4)	32	
Long-term loans repaid (500 – 200)	(300)	
Net cash used in financing activities		(268)
Decrease in cash and cash equivalents		(8)
Cash and cash equivalents at 1 January 20X8		56
Cash and cash equivalents at 31 December 20X8		48

Note. The workings in this example have been set out as T-accounts (as you may have seen in your earlier studies) and also as simple schedules. As the other areas of the F2 syllabus do not require the use of T-accounts, we use the simpler working format in the later examples in this chapter. Of course, you only need to produce one version of each working in exam questions.

Workings

1   *Non-current asset disposals*

COST

	$'000		$'000
At 1 January 20X8	1,560	At 31 December 20X8	1,596
Purchases	90	Disposals (balance)	54
	1,650		1,650

	$'000
Non-current assets cost c/d	1,560
Purchases	90
Disposals (balancing figure)	(54)
Non-current assets cost c/d	1,596

ACCUMULATED DEPRECIATION

	$'000		$'000
At 31 December 20X8	318	At 1 January 20X8	224
Depreciation on disposals (balance)	24	Charge for year	118
	342		342

	$'000
Non-current assets depreciation b/d	224
Depreciation charge for year	118
Depreciation on disposals (balancing figure)	(24)
Non-current assets depreciation c/d	318
NBV of disposals (54 – 24)	30
Net loss reported	(18)
Proceeds of disposals	12

2   *Dividends paid to owners of the parent*

RETAINED EARNINGS

	$'000		$'000
At 31 December 20X8	686	At 1 January 20X8	490
Dividends paid		Profit for the year	268
(balance)	72		
	758		758

	$'000
Retained earnings b/d	490
Profit for the year	268
Dividends paid (balance)	(72)
Retained earnings c/d	686

3   *Tax paid*

TAXATION LIABILITY

	$'000		$'000
At 31 December 20X8	102	At 1 January 20X8	86
Tax paid		Income tax expense	124
(balance)	108		
	210		210

	$'000
B/d	86
Income tax expense	124
Tax paid (balance)	(108)
C/d	102

4   *Proceeds of issues of shares*

SHARE CAPITAL (INCLUDING SHARE PREMIUM)

	$'000		$'000
		At 1 January 20X8 share capital	340
At 31 December 20X8 share capital	360	At 1 January 20X8 share premium	24
At 31 December 20X8 share premium	36	Cash received (balance)	32
	396		396

	$'000
B/d (340 + 24)	364
Cash received (balance)	32
C/d (360 + 36)	396

15.2 Consolidated cash flow

TOPIARY CO
CONSOLIDATED STATEMENT OF CASH FLOWS
FOR THE YEAR ENDED 31 DECEMBER 20X7

	$'000	$'000
Cash flows from operating activities		
Profit before taxation	5,520	
Adjustments for:		
Depreciation (W3)	975	
Profit on sale of plant	(300)	
Share of associate's profits (see note on (W5))	(1,050)	
Investment income	(465)	
Interest payable	450	
Operating profit before working capital changes	5,130	
Increase in trade and other receivables (W6)	(1,641)	
Increase in inventories (W6)	(2,829)	
Increase in trade payables (W6)	456	
Cash generated from operations	1,116	
Interest paid (W13)	(300)	
Income taxes paid (W12)	(750)	
Net cash from operating activities		66
Cash flows from investing activities		
Acquisition of subsidiary net of cash required (W14)	294	
Purchase of property, plant and equipment (W2)	(3,255)	
Proceeds from sale of plant	1,500	
Dividends from investment	465	
Dividends from associate (W5)	750	
Net cash used in investing activities		(246)
Cash flows from financing activities		
Issue of ordinary share capital (W7)	7,359	
Issue of loan notes (W11)	2,760	
Capital payments under finance leases (W10)	(810)	
Dividends paid (W8)	(900)	
Dividends paid to non-controlling interests (W9)	(144)	
Net cash flows from financing activities		8,265
Net increase in cash and cash equivalents		8,085
Cash and cash equivalents at 1 January 20X7		5,460
Cash and cash equivalents at 31 December 20X7		13,545

Workings

1   *Buildings*

	$'000
Net book value b/d	6,600
Depreciation charge (balancing figure)	(375)
Net book value c/d	6,225

2   *Purchase of plant and machinery*

	$'000
Cost b/d	4,200
Disposal	(1,500)
Additions under finance leases	2,550
Acquisition of subsidiary	495
	5,745
Additions (balancing figure)	3,255
Cost c/d	9,000

3   *Depreciation charges*

	$'000
Accumulated depreciation b/d	3,300
Depreciation on disposal (1,500 – 1,200*)	(300)
Depreciation charge (balancing figure)	600
Accumulated depreciation c/d	3,600

*Disposal	$'000
Proceeds	1,500
Net book value (balancing figure)	(1,200)
Profit on disposal	300

Total depreciation charge: ($375,000 (W1) + $600,000) = $975,000

4   *Goodwill*

	$'000
Balance b/d	–
Impairment in year	–
Acquisition of subsidiary	300
Balance c/d	300

Note. This working shows that there has been no impairment of goodwill in the year.

5   *Dividends from associate*

Investment in associate

	$'000
Balance b/d	3,000
SPLOCI – share of profit after tax	1,050
Dividends received from associate (balancing figure)	(750)
Balance c/d	3,300

Note. The share of the associate's profit, recognised in the consolidated statement of profit or loss and other comprehensive income, is not a cash item so is added back on the face of the statement of cash flows in the section that calculates the cash generated from operations. The **dividend received** from the associate is the cash item and appears in the investing activities section.

6 *Inventories, trade receivables and trade payables*

	Inventories	Receivables	Payables
	$'000	$'000	$'000
Balance b/d	3,000	3,825	840
Acquisition of subsidiary	96	84	204
	3,096	3,909	1,044
Increase/(decrease) (balancing figure)	2,829	1,641	456
Balance c/d	5,925	5,550	1,500

7 *Issue of ordinary share capital*

Share capital (including share premium)

	$'000
Balance b/d (6,000 + 6,285)	12,285
Acquisition of subsidiary	825
Issue for cash (balancing figure)	7,359
Balance c/d (11,820 + 8,649)	20,469

8 *Dividends paid to owners of the parent*

	$'000
Retained earnings b/d	7,500
Profit attributable to owners of the parent	3,735
Dividends paid (balancing figure)	(900)
Retained earnings c/d	10,335

9 *Dividends paid to non-controlling interests*

	$'000
Non-controlling interests b/d	–
Acquisition of subsidiary	189
Profit attributable to NCI	300
Dividends paid (balancing figure)	(144)
Non-controlling interests c/d	345

10 *Capital payments under leases*

	$'000	$'000
Balance b/d		
Current	600	
Long-term	510	
		1,110
New lease commitment (machinery)		2,550
Cash outflow (balancing figure)		(810)
Balance c/d		
Current	720	
Long-term	2,130	
		2,850

11 *Issue of loan notes*

	$'000
Balance b/d	1,500
Finance cost	120
Cash inflow (balancing figure)	2,760
Balance c/d	4,380

12 *Taxation*

	$'000	$'000
Balance b/d		
Income tax	651	
Deferred tax	39	
		690
SPLOCI – P/L (1,173 + 312)		1,485
On acquisition of subsidiary		51
Tax paid (balancing figure)		(750)
Balance c/d		
Income tax	1,386	
Deferred tax	90	
		1,476

13 *Interest*

	$'000
Balance b/d	90
SPLOCI (450 – 120) (excluding the discount credited to the carrying value of loans)	330
Interest paid in cash (balancing figure)	(300)
Balance c/d	120

14 *Purchase of subsidiary*

	$'000
Cash received on acquisition of subsidiary	336
Less cash consideration	(42)
Cash inflow	294

Note. Only the **cash** consideration is included in the figure reported in the statement of cash flows. The **shares** issued as part of the consideration are reflected in the share capital working (W7) above.

Now try these questions from the Practice Question Bank

Number	Level	Marks	Time
Q30	Introductory	N/A	7 mins
Q31	Introductory	25	45 mins

DISCLOSURES AND ETHICS

Part E

RELATED PARTIES

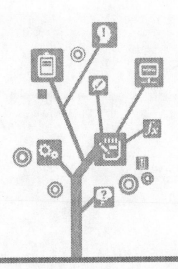

Transparency over the nature and amount of related party transactions are crucial information to the users of the financial statements. Because of the risks of distortion associated with this area, IAS 24 sets out disclosure requirements specific to related parties.

Chapter Overview

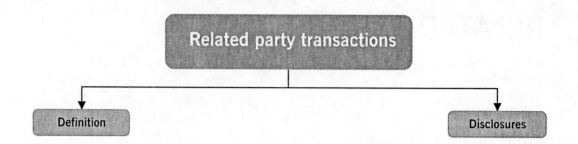

1   IAS 24 *Related party disclosures*   **6/11**

Introduction

IAS 24 is primarily a disclosure standard. It is concerned with improving the quality of information provided by published accounts and also with strengthening their stewardship roles.

In the absence of information to the contrary, it is assumed that a reporting entity has **independent discretionary power** over its resources and transactions, and pursues its activities independently of the interests of its individual owners, managers and others. Transactions are presumed to have been undertaken on an **arm's length basis** ie on terms such as could have been obtained in a transaction with an external party, in which each side bargained knowledgeably and freely, unaffected by any relationship between them.

These assumptions may not be justified when **related party relationships** exist, because the requisite conditions for competitive, free market dealings may not be present. While the parties may endeavour to achieve arm's length bargaining, the very nature of the relationship may preclude this occurring.

1.1 Objective

This is the related parties issue, and IAS 24 tackles it by ensuring that financial statements contain the disclosures necessary to draw attention to the possibility that the reported financial position and results may have been affected by the existence of related parties and by material transactions with them. In other words, this is a standard which is primarily concerned with **disclosure**.

1.2 Scope

The standard requires disclosure of related party transactions and outstanding balances in the **separate financial statements** of a parent, venturer or investor presented in accordance with IAS 27 *Separate financial statements*, as well as in consolidated financial statements.

An entity's financial statements disclose related party transactions and outstanding balances with other entities in a group. **Intragroup** transactions and balances are **eliminated** in the preparation of consolidated financial statements.

1.3 Definitions

The following important definitions are given by the standard. Note that the definitions of **control** and **significant influence** are now the same as those given in IFRS 10 *Consolidated financial statements*, IAS 28 *Investments in associates and joint ventures* and IFRS 11 *Joint arrangements*. The definitions of related parties were revised in 2009.

KEY TERMS

RELATED PARTY. A related party is a person or entity that is related to the entity that is preparing its financial statements.

(a)   A **person** or a close member of that person's family is **related** to a reporting entity if that person:

    (i)   Has control or joint control over the reporting entity

    (ii)   Has significant influence over the reporting entity or

    (iii) Is a member of the key management personnel of the reporting entity or of a parent of the reporting entity

(b)   An **entity** is related to a reporting entity if any of the following conditions applies:

    (i)   The entity and the reporting entity are members of the same group (which means that each parent, subsidiary and fellow subsidiary is related to the others)

(ii)   One entity is an associate or joint venture of the other entity (or an associate or joint venture of a member of a group of which the other entity is a member)

(iii)   Both entities are joint ventures of the same third party

(iv)   One entity is a joint venture of a third entity and the other entity is an associate of the third entity

(v)   The entity is a post-employment defined benefit plan for the benefit of employees of either the reporting entity or an entity related to the reporting entity. If the reporting entity is itself such a plan, the sponsoring employers are also related to the reporting entity

(vi)   The entity is controlled or jointly controlled by a person identified in (a)

(vii)   A person identified in (a)(i) has significant influence over the entity or is a member of the key management personnel of the entity (or of a parent of the entity)

RELATED PARTY TRANSACTION. A transfer of resources, services or obligations between related parties, regardless of whether a price is charged.

CONTROL is the power to govern the financial and operating policies of an entity so as to obtain benefits from its activities.

SIGNIFICANT INFLUENCE is the power to participate in the financial and operating policy decisions of an entity, but is not control over these policies. Significant ownership may be gained by share ownership, statute or agreement.

JOINT CONTROL is the contractually agreed sharing of control over an economic activity.

KEY MANAGEMENT PERSONNEL are those persons having authority and responsibility for planning, directing and controlling the activities of the entity, directly or indirectly, including any director (whether executive or otherwise) of that entity.

CLOSE MEMBERS OF THE FAMILY OF AN INDIVIDUAL are those family members who may be expected to influence, or be influenced by, that individual in their dealings with the entity. They may include:

(a)   The individual's domestic partner and children
(b)   Children of the domestic partner
(c)   Dependants of the individual or the domestic partner   (IAS 24)

The most important point to remember here is that, when considering each possible related party relationship, attention must be paid to the **substance of the relationship, not merely the legal form.**

IAS 24 lists the following which are **not necessarily related parties.**

(a)   **Two entities simply because they have a director or other key management in common** (notwithstanding the definition of related party above, although it is necessary to consider how that director would affect both entities)

(b)   **Two venturers simply because they share joint control over a joint venture**

(c)   Certain other bodies, simply as a result of their **role in normal business dealings** with the entity:

     (i)   Providers of finance
     (ii)   Trade unions
     (iii)   Public utilities
     (iv)   Government departments and agencies

(d)   **Any single customer, supplier, franchisor, distributor or general agent** with whom the entity transacts a significant amount of business, simply by virtue of the resulting economic dependence

1.4 Exemption for government-related entities

Before the 2009 revision of IAS 24, if a government controlled or significantly influenced an entity, the entity was required to disclose information about all transactions with other entities controlled, or significantly influenced, by the same government. The revised standard still requires disclosures that are significant to users of the financial statements, but **eliminates the need to disclose information that is costly to gather, and of less value to users**. It achieves this by limiting the disclosure required to transactions that are individually or collectively significant.

1.5 Disclosure

As noted above, IAS 24 is almost entirely concerned with disclosure and its provisions are meant to **supplement** those disclosure requirements required by national company legislation and other IFRSs (particularly IAS 1,,IFRS 10, IFRS 11 and IFRS 12).

The standard lists some **examples** of transactions that are disclosed if they are with a related party:

- Purchases or sales of goods (finished or unfinished)
- Purchases or sales of property and other assets
- Rendering or receiving of services
- Leases
- Transfer of research and development
- Transfers under licence agreements
- Provision of finance (including loans and equity contributions in cash or in kind)
- Provision of guarantees and collateral security
- Settlement of liabilities on behalf of the entity or by the entity on behalf of another party.

Relationships between **parents and subsidiaries** must be **disclosed irrespective** of **whether** any **transactions** have **taken place between** the related parties. An entity must disclose the **name** of its **parent** and, if different, the **ultimate controlling party**. This will enable a reader of the financial statements to be able to form a view about the effects of a related party relationship on the reporting entity.

If neither the parent nor the ultimate controlling party produces financial statements available for public use, the name of the next most senior parent that does so shall also be disclosed.

An entity should disclose key management personnel compensation in total for various categories.

(a)   Items of a similar nature may be **disclosed in aggregate** *unless* separate disclosure is necessary for an understanding of the effect on the financial statements.

(b)   Disclosures that related party transactions were made on terms equivalent to those that prevail in arm's length transactions are made only if such disclosures can be substantiated.

1.6 Section summary

IAS 24 is primarily concerned with **disclosure**. You should learn the following.

- **Definitions**: these are very important
- Relationships covered
- Relationships that **may not** necessarily be between related parties
- **Disclosures**: again, very important, representing the whole purpose of the standard

Question 16.1   Related parties

Learning outcome B3

Fancy Feet Co is a UK company which supplies handmade leather shoes to a chain of high street shoe shops. The company is also the sole importer of some famous high quality Greek stoneware which is supplied to an upmarket shop in London's West End.

Fancy Feet Co was set up some years ago by Georgios Kostades who left Greece when he fell out with the military government. The company is owned and run by Mr Kostades and his three children.

The shoes are purchased from a French company, the shares of which are owned by the Kostades Family Trust (Monaco).

Required

Identify the financial accounting issues arising out of the above scenario.

2 Question

Try this longer question on related parties.

Question 16.2   RP Group

Discuss whether the following events would require disclosure in the financial statements of the RP Group, a public limited group, under IAS 24 *Related party disclosures*.

The RP Group, merchant bankers, has a number of subsidiaries, associates and joint ventures in its group structure. During the financial year to 31 October 20X9 the following events occurred.

(a)   The company agreed to finance a management buyout of a group company, AB, a limited company. In addition to providing loan finance, the company has retained a 25% equity holding in the company and has a main board director on the board of AB. RP received management fees, interest payments and dividends from AB.

(b)   On 1 July 20X9 RP sold a wholly-owned subsidiary, X, a limited company, to Z, a public limited company. During the year RP supplied X with second-hand office equipment and X leased its factory from RP. The transactions were all contracted for at market rates.

(c)   The retirement benefit scheme of the group is managed by another merchant bank. An investment manager of the group retirement benefit scheme is also a non-executive director of the RP Group and received an annual fee for his services of $25,000, which is not material in the group context. The company pays $16m per annum into the scheme and occasionally transfers assets into the scheme. In 20X9, property, plant and equipment of $10m were transferred into the scheme and a recharge of administrative costs of $3m was made.

Chapter Summary

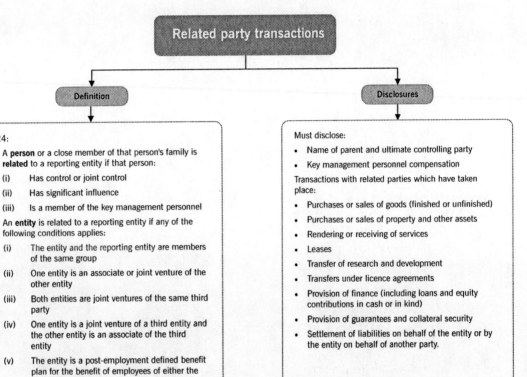

Related party transactions

Definition

IFRS 24:

(a) A **person** or a close member of that person's family is **related** to a reporting entity if that person:

    (i) Has control or joint control

    (ii) Has significant influence

    (iii) Is a member of the key management personnel

(b) An **entity** is related to a reporting entity if any of the following conditions applies:

    (i) The entity and the reporting entity are members of the same group

    (ii) One entity is an associate or joint venture of the other entity

    (iii) Both entities are joint ventures of the same third party

    (iv) One entity is a joint venture of a third entity and the other entity is an associate of the third entity

    (v) The entity is a post-employment defined benefit plan for the benefit of employees of either the reporting entity or an entity related to the reporting entity.

    (vi) The entity is controlled or jointly controlled by a person identified in (a)

    (vii) A person identified in (a)(i) has significant influence over the entity or is a member of the key management personnel of the entity (or of a parent of the entity)

Disclosures

Must disclose:

- Name of parent and ultimate controlling party
- Key management personnel compensation

Transactions with related parties which have taken place:

- Purchases or sales of goods (finished or unfinished)
- Purchases or sales of property and other assets
- Rendering or receiving of services
- Leases
- Transfer of research and development
- Transfers under licence agreements
- Provision of finance (including loans and equity contributions in cash or in kind)
- Provision of guarantees and collateral security
- Settlement of liabilities on behalf of the entity or by the entity on behalf of another party.

Quick Quiz

1   What is a related party transaction?

2   A managing director of a company is a related party of that company. *True/False?*

Answers to Quick Quiz

1   A transfer of resources, services or obligations between related parties, regardless of whether a price is charged.

2   True. A member of the key management personnel of an entity is a related party of that entity.

Answers to Questions

16.1 Related parties

Issues

(a)   The basis on which Fancy Feet trades with the Greek supplier and the French company owned by the Kostades Family Trust.

(b)   Whether the overseas companies trade on commercial terms with the UK company or do the foreign entities control the UK company.

(c)   Who owns the Greek company: is this a related party under the provisions of IAS 24?

(d)   Should the nature of trade suggest a related party controls Fancy Feet Co? Detailed disclosures will be required in the accounts.

16.2 RP Group

(a)   IAS 24 does not require disclosure of transactions between companies and providers of finance in the ordinary course of business. As RP is a merchant bank, no disclosure is needed between RP and AB. However, RP owns 25% of the equity of AB and it would seem significant influence exists (in IAS 28, **greater than 20% existing holding means significant influence is presumed**) and therefore AB could be an associate of RP. IAS 24 regards associates as related parties.

The decision as to associate status depends upon the ability of RP to exercise significant influence, especially as the other 75% of votes are owned by the management of AB.

Merchant banks tend to regard companies which would qualify for associate status as trade investments since the relationship is designed to provide finance.

IAS 28 presumes that a party owning or able to exercise control over 20% of voting rights is a related party. So an investor with a 25% holding and a director on the board would be expected to have significant influence over operating and financial policies in such a way as to inhibit the pursuit of separate interests. If it can be shown that this is not the case, there is no related party relationship.

If it is decided that there is a related party situation then **all material transactions** should be disclosed including **management fees, interest, dividends and the terms of the loan**.

(b)   **IAS 24 does *not* require intragroup transactions and balances eliminated on consolidation to be disclosed**. IAS 24 does not deal with the situation where an undertaking becomes, or ceases to be, a subsidiary during the year.

Best practice indicates that related party transactions should be disclosed for the period when X was not part of the group. Transactions between RP and X should be disclosed between 1 July 20X9 and 31 October 20X9, but transactions prior to 1 July 20X9 will have been eliminated on consolidation.

There is no related party relationship between RP and Z since it is a normal business transaction unless either party's interests have been influenced or controlled in some way by the other party.

(c)   **Employee retirement benefit schemes** of the reporting entity are included in the IAS 24 definition of **related parties**.

The contributions paid, the non-current asset transfer ($10m) and the charge of administrative costs ($3m) must be disclosed.

The pension investment manager would not normally be considered a related party. However, the manager is key management personnel by virtue of his non-executive directorship.

Directors are deemed to be related parties by IAS 24, and the manager receives a $25,000 fee. IAS 24 requires the disclosure of **compensation paid to key management personnel** and the fee falls within the definition of compensation. Therefore, it must be disclosed.

Now try these questions from the Practice Question Bank

Number	Level	Marks	Time
Q32	Introductory	N/A	7 mins

EARNINGS PER SHARE

 Earnings per share is important: it is used internationally as a comparative performance figure.

As a result, there is an accounting standard that sets out detailed rules on how it must be calculated.

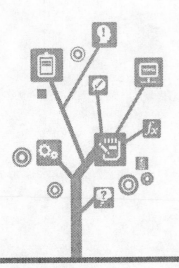

Topic list	learning outcomes	syllabus references
1 IAS 33 *Earnings per share*	B4	B4(a)

Chapter Overview

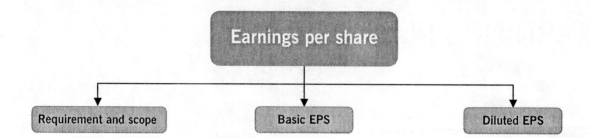

1 IAS 33 *Earnings per share*

Introduction

The objective of IAS 33 is to improve the comparability of the performance of different entities in the same period and of the same entity in different accounting periods.

1.1 Definitions

The following definitions are given in IAS 33.

KEY TERMS

ORDINARY SHARE. an equity instrument that is subordinate to all other classes of equity instruments.

POTENTIAL ORDINARY SHARE. A financial instrument or other contract that may entitle its holder to ordinary shares.

OPTIONS, WARRANTS AND THEIR EQUIVALENTS. Financial instruments that give the holder the right to purchase ordinary shares.

DILUTION. A reduction in earnings per share or an increase in loss per share resulting from the assumption that convertible instruments are converted, that options or warrants are exercised, or that ordinary shares are issued upon the satisfaction of certain conditions.

ANTIDILUTION. An increase in earnings per share or a reduction in loss per share resulting from the assumption that convertible instruments are converted, that options or warrants are exercised, or that ordinary shares are issued upon the satisfaction of certain conditions. *(IAS 33)*

1.1.1 Ordinary shares

There may be more than one class of ordinary share, but ordinary shares of the same class will have the same rights to receive dividends. Ordinary shares participate in the net profit for the period **only after other types of shares** eg preference shares.

1.1.2 Potential ordinary shares

IAS 33 identifies the following examples of financial instrument and other contracts generating potential ordinary shares.

(a) **Debts** (financial liabilities) **or equity instruments**, including preference shares, that are convertible into ordinary shares

(b) **Share warrants and options**

(c) Shares that would be issued upon the satisfaction of **certain conditions** resulting from contractual arrangements, such as the purchase of a business or other assets

1.2 Scope

IAS 33 has the following **scope restrictions**.

(a) Only companies with (potential) ordinary shares which are **publicly traded** need to present EPS (including companies in the process of being listed).

(b) EPS need only be presented on the basis of **consolidated results** where the parent's results are shown as well.

(c) Where companies **choose** to present EPS, even when they have no (potential) ordinary shares which are traded, they must do so according to IAS 33.

Exam alert

The May 2010 exam included a question on EPS, including basic and diluted EPS with an issue of shares at full market price and a bonus issue during the year.

1.3 Basic EPS   9/11, 11/11

Basic EPS should be calculated for **profit or loss attributable to ordinary equity holders** of the parent entity and **profit or loss from continuing operations** attributable to those equity holders (if this is presented).

Basic EPS should be calculated by dividing the **net profit** or loss for the period attributable to ordinary equity holders by the **weighted average number of ordinary shares** outstanding during the period.

$$\text{Basic EPS} = \frac{\text{Net profit/(loss) attributable to ordinary shareholders}}{\text{Weighted average number of ordinary shares outstanding during the period}}$$

1.3.1 Earnings

Earnings includes **all items of income and expense** (including tax) attributable to ordinary equity holders of the parent that are recognised in the period, including tax expense and dividends on preference shares classified as liabilities. Preference dividends on preference shares classified as equity should also be deducted.

In **group** financial statements, the earnings figure used to calculate EPS is the **profit attributable to the owners of the parent** ie the profit or loss of the consolidated entity after adjusting for non-controlling interests.

1.3.2 Per share

The number of ordinary shares used should be the weighted average number of ordinary shares during the period. This figure (for all periods presented) should be **adjusted for events**, other than the conversion of potential ordinary shares, which have changed the number of shares outstanding without a corresponding change in resources.

The **time-weighting factor** is the number of days the shares were outstanding compared with the total number of days in the period. A reasonable approximation is usually adequate. In the exam, time-weighting can normally be performed based on the number of months the shares were in issue.

Shares are usually included in the weighted average number of shares from the **date consideration is receivable**, which is usually the date of issue. In other cases consider the specific terms attached to their issue (consider the substance of any contract). Ordinary shares issued as **purchase consideration** in an acquisition should be included as of the date of acquisition because the acquired entity's results will also be included from that date.

Ordinary shares that will be issued on the **conversion** of a mandatorily convertible instrument are included in the calculation from the **date the contract is entered into**.

If ordinary shares are **partly paid**, they are treated as a fraction of an ordinary share to the extent they are entitled to dividends relative to fully-paid ordinary shares.

1.4 Effect on basic EPS of changes in capital structure   5/10

1.4.1 New issues/buy-backs

When there has been an issue of new shares or a buy-back of shares at full market price, the corresponding figures for EPS for the previous year will be comparable with the current year because, as the weighted average number of shares has risen or fallen, there has been a **corresponding increase or decrease in resources**. Nothing has affected the value or the earnings capacity of the remaining shares.

If the issue occurred part way through the year, this needs to be **time-apportioned** to reflect the fact that the extra funds could only be employed by the company to generate extra earnings for part of the year.

There are other events, however, which change the number of shares outstanding, **without a corresponding change in resources**. In these circumstances, (four of which are considered by IAS 33), it is necessary to make adjustments so that the current and prior period EPS figures are comparable.

Example: New issues

Alpha Co has earnings of $300,000 for the year ended 31 December 20X7. The company had 3 million shares in issue on 1 January 20X7. On 1 September 20X7 the company issued 900,000 shares at full market price.

The weighted average number of shares to use in the EPS calculation can be worked out by keeping track of the number of shares in issue over the year, and working out the appropriate time fractions:

Date	Narrative	No. of shares	Time period	Weighted average
01.01.X7	B/d	3,000,000	$\times \dfrac{8}{12}$	2,000,000
01.09.X7	Issue at full market price	900,000	$\times \dfrac{4}{12}$	1,300,000
		3,900,000		3,300,000

The EPS for the year would be:

$$\frac{\$300,000}{3,300,000} = 9.1 \text{ c}$$

1.4.2 Capitalisation/bonus issue

In a capitalisation or bonus issue, ordinary shares are issued to existing shareholders for **no additional consideration**. The number of ordinary shares has increased without an increase in resources, so the company cannot be expected to generate the same return after a bonus issue.

This problem is solved by **adjusting the number of ordinary shares outstanding before the event** for the proportionate change in the number of shares outstanding as if the event had occurred at the beginning of the earliest period reported. This is referred to as applying the bonus fraction **retrospectively**. The **prior year's EPS**, shown as a comparative in the financial statements must also be restated for the effect of the bonus issue otherwise the year on year comparison would be misleading.

Example: Bonus issue

Following on from the previous example, Alpha Co has earnings of $300,000 for the year ended 31 December 20X8. On 1 June 20X8 the company has a bonus issue of 1 share for every 3 shares held.

In the calculation of EPS for the year ended 31 December 20X8, the bonus issue is treated as if it had taken place on the first day of the year.

	20X8	20X7 (as previously stated)
Earnings	$300,000	$300,000
Shares (3,300,000 $\times \dfrac{4}{3}$)	4,400,000	3,300,000
EPS	6.8 c	9.1 c

Retrospective application of the effect of the bonus issue means that the 20X7 figure must be restated as if the bonus issue had taken place at the start of that year. This could be done by recalculating the number of shares used in the EPS calculation:

$$\frac{\$300,000}{3,300,000\,(4/3)} = 6.8\,c$$

The number of shares has been increased by the **bonus fraction** (calculated as the number of shares after the bonus issue divided by the number of shares before the bonus issue).

There is an alternative and simpler way to do the restatement. Rather than reworking the EPS calculation with a changed number of shares, multiply the prior year EPS figure by the **reciprocal** of the bonus fraction ie:

$$9.1\,c \times \frac{3}{4} = 6.8c$$

1.4.3 Rights issue

A rights issue of shares is an issue of new shares to existing shareholders **at a price below the current market value**. The offer of new shares is made on the basis of x new shares for every y shares currently held eg a 1 for 3 rights issue is an offer of 1 new share at the offer price for every 3 shares currently held.

In this situation, the company does receive new funds to invest and, to this extent, the issue is similar to an issue at full market price, so the shares must be **time-weighted**. The new resources received for each new share are less than the value of each existing share, so there is also a **bonus element** included in a rights issue.

A bonus fraction must be calculated as follows:

$$\frac{\text{Fair value per share immediately before the exercise of rights}}{\text{Theoretical ex - rights price}}$$

Exam questions normally state the market value of the shares before the rights issue. The calculation of the theoretical ex rights price (TERP) and the bonus fraction can be illustrated as follows:

- Assume a rights issue on the basis of 1 for 5
- The share price immediately before the rights issue was $4.00
- The rights price was $3.40

	$
5 shares @ $4	20.00
1 share @ $3.40	3.40
6 shares	23.40

TERP = $23.40 ÷ 6 = $3.90

The bonus fraction is $\dfrac{4}{3.9}$

Once the bonus element of the rights issue has been calculated, it is used in exactly the same way as the bonus fraction in a bonus issue:

(a) In the weighted average number of shares calculation, apply the fraction to all periods (ie months) prior to the issue

(b) Restate the prior year comparative EPS by the reciprocal of the fraction

This technique will be illustrated in the numerical question below.

Question 17.1

Learning outcome B4

Give the formula for the bonus element of a rights issue.

Basic EPS

Question 17.2

Learning outcome B4

Macarone Co prepares financial statements to 31 December. It has produced the following net profit figures.

	$m
20X6	1.1
20X7	1.5

On 1 January 20X6 the number of shares outstanding was 500,000. During 20X7 the company announced a rights issue with the following details.

Rights:	1 new share for each 5 outstanding (100,000 new shares in total)
Exercise price:	$5.00
Last date to exercise rights:	1 March 20X7

The market (fair) value of one share in Macarone immediately prior to exercise on 1 March 20X7 = $11.00.

Required

Calculate the EPS for 20X6 and 20X7.

Smith Co

Question 17.3

On 1 January 20X1 Smith Co had 4,000,000 ordinary shares in issue.

On 30 April 20X1 the company issued, at full market price, 540,000 ordinary shares.

On 31 July 20X1 the company made a rights issue of 1 for 10 @ $4.00. The fair value of the shares on the last day before the issue of shares from the rights issue was $6.20.

Finally, on 30 September 20X1 the company made a 1 for 20 bonus issue.

Profit for the year ended 31 December 20X1 was $800,000.

The reported EPS for the year ended 31 December 20X0 was 18.6c.

Required

Calculate the EPS for the year ended 31 December 20X1 and the restated EPS for the year ended 31 December 20X0.

1.5 Diluted EPS   11/11

At the end of an accounting period, a company may have in issue some **securities** which do not (at present) have any claim to a share of equity earnings, but **may give rise to such a claim in the future**. These are the potential ordinary shares that were mentioned earlier in the chapter. Examples include:

(a)   **Debts (financial liabilities) or equity instruments**, including **preference shares**, that are **convertible into ordinary shares**

(b)   **Share warrants and options**

(c)   Shares that would be issued upon the satisfaction of **certain conditions** resulting from contractual arrangements, such as the purchase of a business or other assets

In such circumstances, the future number of equity shares in issue might increase, which in turn results in a fall in EPS. In other words, a **future increase** in the **number of equity shares will cause a dilution or watering down of equity**, and it is possible to calculate a **diluted EPS** (ie the EPS that would have been obtained during the financial period if the dilution had already taken place).

This will indicate to investors the possible effects of a future dilution.

1.5.1 Earnings to calculate the diluted EPS

The earnings calculated for basic EPS should be adjusted by the **post-tax** (including deferred tax) effect of the following.

(a)   Any **dividends** on dilutive potential ordinary shares that were deducted to arrive at earnings for basic EPS

(b)   **Interest recognised** in the period for the dilutive potential ordinary shares

(c)   Any **other changes in income or expenses** (fees and discount, premium accounted for as yield adjustments) that would result from the conversion of the dilutive potential ordinary shares

The conversion of some potential ordinary shares may lead to changes in **other income or expenses**. For example, the reduction of interest expense related to potential ordinary shares and the resulting increase in net profit for the period may lead to an increase in the expense relating to a non-discretionary employee profit-sharing plan. When calculating diluted EPS, the net profit or loss for the period is adjusted for any such consequential changes in income or expense.

1.5.2 Number of shares to calculate the diluted EPS

The number of ordinary shares is the weighted average number of ordinary shares calculated for basic EPS plus the weighted average number of ordinary shares that would be issued on the conversion of **all** the **dilutive potential ordinary shares** into ordinary shares.

It should be assumed that dilutive ordinary shares were converted into ordinary shares at the **beginning of the period** or, if later, at the actual date of issue. There are two other points.

(a)   The computation assumes the most **advantageous conversion rate** or exercise rate from the standpoint of the holder of the potential ordinary shares.

(b)   A **subsidiary, joint venture or associate** may issue potential ordinary shares that are convertible into either ordinary shares of the subsidiary, joint venture or associate, or ordinary shares of the reporting entity. If these potential ordinary shares have a dilutive effect on the consolidated basic EPS of the reporting entity, they are included in the calculation of diluted EPS.

Example: Diluted EPS

For the year ended 31 December 20X7 Farrah Co had a basic EPS of 105c based on earnings of $105,000 and 100,000 ordinary $1 shares. On 1 January 20X7 Farrah Co issued convertible loan stock. Assuming the conversion is fully subscribed, there would be an increase of 32,000 shares. The liability element of the loan stock at 1 January 20X7 is $50,000 and the effective interest is 6%. The rate of tax is 30%.

Required

Calculate the diluted EPS.

Solution

Diluted EPS is calculated as follows.

 Number of shares: add the additional shares that would be issued on conversion of the loan stock to the weighted average number used in the basic EPS calculation.

	No of shares
Basic weighted average	100,000
Add: additional shares on conversion	32,000
Diluted number	132,000

 Earnings: Farrah Co will save effective interest on the liability component of $3,000 ($50,000 × 6%) but this increase in profits will be taxed. Hence the earnings figure may be recalculated:

	$
Basic earnings	105,000
Add back loan stock interest net of tax saved	
($3,000 × 70%)	2,100
	107,100

 Calculation: Diluted EPS

$107,100/132,000 = 81.1 c

1.5.3 Treatment of options

It should be assumed that options are exercised, and that the assumed proceeds would have been received from the issue of shares at **fair value**. Fair value for this purpose is calculated on the basis of the average price of the ordinary shares during the period.

Options and other share purchase arrangements are dilutive when they would result in the issue of ordinary shares for **less than fair value**. In order to calculate diluted EPS, each transaction of this type is treated as consisting of two parts.

(a)   A contract to issue a certain number of ordinary shares at their **average market price** during the period. These shares are fairly priced and are assumed to be neither dilutive nor antidilutive. They are ignored in the computation of diluted EPS.

(b)   A contract to issue the remaining ordinary shares for **no consideration**. Such ordinary shares generate no proceeds and have no effect on the net profit attributable to ordinary shares outstanding. Therefore, such shares are dilutive and they are added to the number of ordinary shares outstanding in the computation of diluted EPS.

Pro-forma calculation

Number of shares under option	X
Number that would have been issued at average market price (AMP)	
[(no. of options × exercise price)/AMP]	(X)
Number of shares treated as issued for nil consideration	X

Question 17.4   EPS 1

Learning outcome B4

Brand Co has the following results for the year ended 31 December 20X7.

Net profit for year	$1,200,000
Weighted average number of ordinary shares outstanding during year	500,000 shares
Average fair value of one ordinary share during year	$20.00
Weighted average number of shares under option during year	100,000 shares
Exercise price for shares under option during year	$15.00

Required

Calculate both basic and diluted EPS.

1.6 Presentation

An entity should present on the **face of the statement of profit or loss and other comprehensive income** basic and diluted EPS for:

(a) Profit or loss from continuing operations and

(b) Profit or loss for the period for each class of ordinary share that has a different right to share in the net profit for the period.

The basic and diluted EPS should be presented with **equal prominence** for all periods presented.

Basic and diluted EPS for any **discontinued operations** must also be presented.

Disclosure must still be made where the EPS figures (basic and/or diluted) are **negative** (ie a loss per share).

1.7 Disclosure

An entity should disclose the following.

(a) The amounts used as the **numerators** in calculating basic and diluted EPS, and a **reconciliation** of those amounts to the profit or loss attributable to the parent entity for the period

(b) The weighted average number of ordinary shares used as the **denominator** in calculating basic and diluted EPS, and a **reconciliation** of these denominators to each other

(c) Instruments that could potentially dilute basic EPS, but which were **not included** in the calculation because they were **antidilutive** for the period presented

An entity should also disclose a description of ordinary share transactions or potential ordinary share transactions, other than capitalisation or bonus issues and share splits, which occur **after the reporting date** when they are of such importance that non-disclosure would affect the ability of the users of the financial statements to make proper evaluations and decisions (see IAS 10 *Events after the reporting date*). Examples of such transactions include the following.

- Issue of shares for cash

- Issue of shares when the proceeds are used to repay debt or preferred shares outstanding at the reporting date

- Redemption of ordinary shares outstanding

- Conversion or exercise of potential ordinary shares, outstanding at the reporting date, into ordinary shares

- Issue of warrants, options or convertible securities

- Achievement of conditions that would result in the issue of contingently issuable shares

EPS amounts are not adjusted for such transactions occurring after the reporting date because such transactions **do not affect the amount of capital used** to produce the net profit or loss for the period.

1.8 Alternative EPS figures

An entity may present **alternative EPS figures if it wishes**. However, IAS 33 lays out certain rules where this takes place.

(a)   The weighted average number of shares as calculated under IAS 33 **must** be used.

(b)   A **reconciliation** must be given between the component of profit used in the alternative EPS (if it is not a line item in the statement of profit or loss and other comprehensive income) and the line item for profit reported in the statement of profit or loss and other comprehensive income.

(c)   The entity must indicate the basis on which the **numerator** is determined.

(d)   Basic and diluted EPS must be shown with **equal prominence**.

1.9 Significance of earnings per share

EPS is one of the most frequently quoted statistics in financial analysis. Because of the widespread use of the **Price/Earnings (P/E) ratio** as a yardstick for investment decisions, it became increasingly important.

It seems that reported and forecast EPS can, through the P/E ratio, have a **significant effect on a company's share price**. Thus, a share price might fall if it looks as if EPS is going to be low. This is not very rational as EPS can depend on many, often subjective, assumptions used in preparing a historical statement, namely the statement of profit or loss and other comprehensive income. It does not necessarily bear any relation to the value of a company and its shares. Nevertheless, the market is sensitive to EPS.

EPS has also served as a means of assessing the **stewardship and management** role performed by company directors and managers. Remuneration packages might be linked to EPS growth, thereby increasing the pressure on management to improve EPS. The danger of this, however, is that management effort may go into distorting results to produce a favourable EPS.

Section summary

Earnings per share is a measure of the amount of profits earned by a company for each ordinary share. Earnings are profits after tax, preference dividends and non-controlling interests.

Basic EPS is calculated by dividing the net profit or loss for the period attributable to ordinary shareholders by the weighted average number of ordinary shares outstanding during the period.

You should know how to calculate **basic EPS** and how to deal with related complications (issue of shares for cash, bonus issue, rights issue).

Diluted EPS is calculated by adjusting the net profit attributable to ordinary shareholders and the weighted average number of shares outstanding for the effects of all dilutive potential ordinary shares.

You must be able to deal with **convertible debt** and **options**.

EPS is an important measure for investors.

Chapter Summary

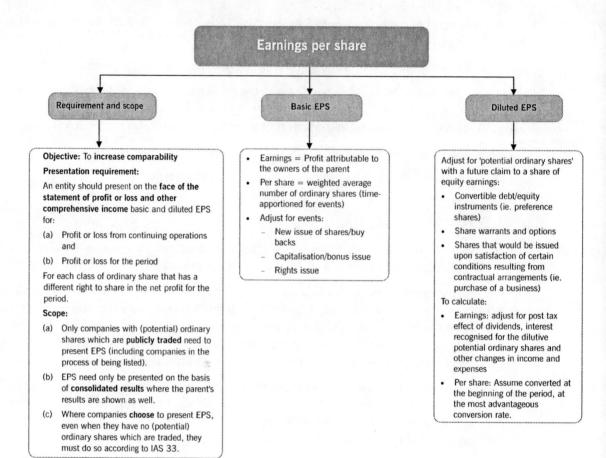

Earnings per share

Requirement and scope

Objective: To **increase comparability**

Presentation requirement:

An entity should present on the **face of the statement of profit or loss and other comprehensive income** basic and diluted EPS for:

(a) Profit or loss from continuing operations and

(b) Profit or loss for the period

For each class of ordinary share that has a different right to share in the net profit for the period.

Scope:

(a) Only companies with (potential) ordinary shares which are **publicly traded** need to present EPS (including companies in the process of being listed).

(b) EPS need only be presented on the basis of **consolidated results** where the parent's results are shown as well.

(c) Where companies **choose** to present EPS, even when they have no (potential) ordinary shares which are traded, they must do so according to IAS 33.

Basic EPS

- Earnings = Profit attributable to the owners of the parent
- Per share = weighted average number of ordinary shares (time-apportioned for events)
- Adjust for events:
  - New issue of shares/buy backs
  - Capitalisation/bonus issue
  - Rights issue

Diluted EPS

Adjust for 'potential ordinary shares' with a future claim to a share of equity earnings:

- Convertible debt/equity instruments (ie. preference shares)
- Share warrants and options
- Shares that would be issued upon satisfaction of certain conditions resulting from contractual arrangements (ie. purchase of a business)

To calculate:

- Earnings: adjust for post tax effect of dividends, interest recognised for the dilutive potential ordinary shares and other changes in income and expenses
- Per share: Assume converted at the beginning of the period, at the most advantageous conversion rate.

Quick Quiz

1   All entities must disclose EPS. True or false?

2   Why is the numerator adjusted for convertible bonds when calculating diluted EPS?

Answers to Quick Quiz

1   False. Only entities whose ordinary shares are publicly traded need to disclose EPS.

2   Because the conversion of bonds into shares will affect earnings by the interest saving (net of tax).

Answers to Questions

17.1 Were you awake?

$$\text{Bonus element} = \frac{\text{Fair value per share immediately before exercise of rights}}{\text{Theoretical ex-rights price}}$$

17.2 Basic EPS

Computation of EPS

		20X6 $	20X7 $
20X6	EPS as originally reported $\dfrac{\$1,100,000}{500,000}$	2.20	
20X6	EPS restated for rights issue = $2.2 \times \dfrac{10}{11}$ (W2)	2.00	
20X7	EPS $\dfrac{\$1,500,000}{591,666\,(W1)}$		2.53

Workings

1   *Weighted average number of shares*

Date	Narrative	No. of shares	Time period	Bonus fraction	Weighted average
01.01.X7	b/d	500,000	$\times \dfrac{2}{12}$	$\times \dfrac{11}{10}$	91,666
01.03.X7	Rights issue 1 for 5	100,000			
		600,000	$\times \dfrac{10}{12}$		500,000
					591,666

2   *Bonus element of rights issue*

	$
5 shares @ $11	55
1 share @ $5	5
6 shares	60

TERP = 60 ÷ 6 = $10

The bonus fraction is 11/10

17.3 Smith Co

EPS for year ended 31.12.X1 $\dfrac{\$800,000}{4,860,767(W1)}$ = 16.5c

Restated EPS for year ended 31.12.X0

$18.6c \times \dfrac{6.00}{6.20} \times 20/21 = 17.1c$

Workings

1 *Weighted average number of shares*

Date	Narrative	Shares	Time	Bonus fraction	Weighted average
01.01.X1		4,000,000	$\times \dfrac{4}{12}$	$\times \dfrac{6.20}{6.00 \,(W2)} \times \dfrac{21}{20}$	1,446,667
30.04.X1	Full market price	540,000			
		4,540,000	$\times \dfrac{3}{12}$	$\times \dfrac{6.20}{6.00 \,(W2)} \times \dfrac{21}{20}$	1,231,475
31.07.X1	Rights issue (1/10)	454,000			
		4,994,000	$\times \dfrac{2}{12}$	$\times \dfrac{21}{20}$	873,950
30.9.X1	Bonus issue (1/20)	249,700			
		5,234,700	$\times \dfrac{3}{12}$		1,308,675
					4,860,767

2 *TERP*

	$
10 shares @ $6.20	62.00
1 share @ $4.00	4.00
11 shares	66.00

∴ TERP = $66/11 shares = $6.00

17.4 EPS 1

Basic EPS $= \dfrac{\$1,200,000}{500,000} = \$2.40$

Diluted EPS $= \dfrac{\$1,200,000\,*}{500,000 + 25,000\,(W1)} = \$2.29$

Workings

1 *Number of shares issued for nil consideration*

Number of shares under option	100,000
Number that would have been issued at average market price (AMP) [(100,000 x $15)/$20]	(75,000)
Number of shares treated as issued for nil consideration	25,000

* The earnings have not been increased as the total number of shares has been increased only by the number of shares (25,000) deemed for the purpose of the computation to have been issued for nil consideration.

Now try these questions from the Practice Question Bank	Number	Level	Marks	Time
	Q33	Introductory	N/A	7 mins
	Q34	Introductory	14	25 mins

ETHICS IN FINANCIAL REPORTING

Ethics need to be applied in all aspects of managerial behaviour. An attempt to manipulate profit figures, or non-disclosure of a close relationship may amount to unethical behaviour.

Ethics are most likely to be considered in the context of possible dilemmas faced by the accountant in business. A scenario question at the end of this Study Text asks for a discussion of why directors might have acted unethically in adopting accounting policies to boost earnings.

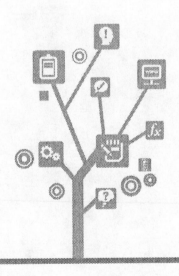

Topic list	learning outcomes	syllabus references
1 Ethical theory	B1	B1(e)
2 Influences on ethics	B1	B1(e)
3 Ethics in organisations	B1	B1(e)
4 Principles and guidance on professional ethics	B1	B1(e)
5 Ethical compliance problems	B1	B1(e)

Chapter Overview

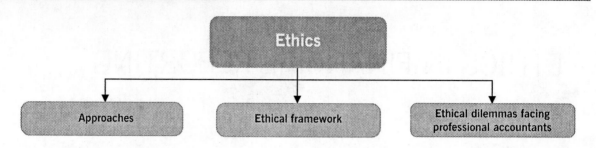

1 Ethical theory

Introduction

A key debate in ethical theory is whether ethics can be determined by **objective, universal principles.** How important the **consequences of actions** should be in determining an ethical position is also a significant issue.

1.1 Do ethics change over time and place?

One viewpoint is that ethics do vary between time and place. Slavery, for example, is now regarded as wrong, whereas in Roman times slavery was acceptable. The view that ethics vary between different ages and different communities is known as **ethical relativism.**

The opposing view is that ethics are unchanging over time and place; some courses of action are always right, others are always wrong. A simple example would be saying that it is always wrong to steal. The view that there are certain unchanging ethical rules is known as **ethical absolutism.**

1.2 Should you consider the consequences of your actions when making ethical decisions?

One view is that society is best served by everyone following certain ethical rules, and obeying them no matter what the results are. The argument is that people will undermine society if they disobey the ethical rules, even if they do so with the intention of avoiding adverse consequences. This viewpoint, known as **deontological ethics,** was developed by Kant.

The opposing viewpoint is that you cannot divorce an action from its consequences, and when taking ethical decisions you must take account of what the consequences will be. This viewpoint is known as **teleological ethics.** If you take this viewpoint, that implies that you have to define what the best possible consequences are.

1.3 What thought processes do people use when making ethical decisions?

What the theories are aiming to do is to complete the following sentence:

You should act ethically because ...

There are three possible options:

- You should act ethically because you'll be punished if you don't.

- You should act ethically because your country's laws say you should.

- You should act ethically because it's always right to do so, no matter what the consequences and costs are to you personally.

Question 18.1	Ethical issues

Learning outcome B1

Briefly explain the main ethical issues that are involved in the following situations.

(a) Dealing with a repressive authoritarian government abroad

(b) An aggressive advertising campaign

(c)   Employee redundancies

(d)   Payments or gifts to officials who have the power to help or hinder the payees' operations

1.4 Role of ethical theory

Ethics is concerned with right and wrong, and how conduct should be judged to be good or bad. It is about how we should live our lives and, in particular, how we should **behave towards other people**. It is therefore relevant to all forms of human activity.

It is important to understand that if ethics is applicable to corporate behaviour at all, it must therefore be a fundamental aspect of the company's **mission**, since everything the organisation does flows from that. Managers responsible for strategic decision-making cannot avoid responsibility for their organisation's ethical standing. They should consciously apply ethical rules to all of their decisions in order to filter out potentially undesirable developments. The question is, however, what ethical rules should be obeyed – those that always apply or those that hold only in certain circumstances?

Accountancy is not a value-neutral profession. It establishes and follows rules for the protection of shareholder wealth and the reporting of the performance of capital investment. Business life is a fruitful source of ethical dilemmas because its whole purpose is **material gain**, the making of profit. Accountants in business have a responsibility to act in the public interest. How to reconcile the competitive profit-making motive of business with the public interest is a legitimate question to explore.

2   Influences on ethics

Introduction

Firms have to ensure they obey the law; but they also face **ethical concerns**, because their reputations depend on a good image.

KEY TERM

ETHICS. A set of moral principles to guide behaviour.

Social attitudes, such as a belief in the merits of education, progress through science and technology, and fair competition, are significant for the management of a business organisation. Other beliefs have either gained strength or been eroded in recent years:

(a)   There is a growing belief in preserving and improving the quality of life by reducing working hours, reversing the spread of pollution, developing leisure activities and so on. Pressures on organisations to consider the environment are particularly strong because most environmental damage is irreversible and some is fatal to humans and wildlife.

(b)   Many pressure groups have been organised in recent years to protect social minorities and underprivileged groups. Legislation has been passed in an attempt to prevent discrimination on grounds of race, sex, disability, age and sexual orientation.

(c)   Issues relating to the environmental consequences of corporate activities are currently debated, and respect for the environment has come to be regarded as an unquestionable good.

The ethical environment refers to justice, respect for the law and a moral code. The conduct of an organisation, its management and employees will be measured against ethical standards by the customers, suppliers and other members of the public with whom they deal.

2.1 Ethical problems facing managers

Managers have a duty (in most entities) to aim for profit. At the same time, modern ethical standards impose a duty to guard, preserve and enhance the value of the entity for the good of all touched by it, including the general public.

In the area of **products and production**, managers have responsibility to ensure that the public and their own employees are protected from danger. Attempts to increase profitability by cutting costs may lead to dangerous working conditions or to inadequate safety standards in products. In the US, product liability litigation is so common that this legal threat may be a more effective deterrent than general ethical standards. The Consumer Protection Act 1987 and EU legislation generally, is beginning to ensure that ethical standards are similarly enforced in the UK.

Another ethical problem concerns **payments by companies to government or municipal officials** who have power to help or hinder the payers' operations.

Business ethics are also relevant to **competitive behaviour**. This is because a market can only be free if competition is, in some basic respects, fair. There is a distinction between competing aggressively and competing unethically.

3 Ethics in organisations

Companies have to follow legal standards, or else they will be subject to fines and their officers might face similar charges. Ethics in organisations relates to **social responsibility** and **business practice**.

People who work for organisations bring their own values into work with them. Organisations contain a variety of ethical systems.

(a)   **Personal ethics** (eg deriving from a person's upbringing, religious or non-religious beliefs, political opinions, personality). People have different ethical viewpoints at different stages in their lives. Some will judge situations on 'gut feel'. Some will consciously or unconsciously adopt a general approach to ethical dilemmas, such as **the end justifies the means**.

(b)   **Professional ethics** (eg CIMA's *Code of Ethics for Professional Accountants* (*Code of Ethics*)).

(c)   **Organisation cultures** (eg customer first). Culture, in denoting what is normal behaviour, also denotes what is the right behaviour in many cases.

(d)   **Organisation systems**. Ethics might be contained in a formal code, reinforced by the overall statement of values. A problem might be that ethics does not always save money, and there is a real cost to ethical decisions. Besides, the organisation has different ethical duties to different stakeholders. Who sets priorities?

CASE STUDY

Organisation systems and targets do have ethical implications. The *Harvard Business Review* reported that the US retailer, Sears Roebuck & Company was deluged with complaints that customers of its car service centre were being charged for unnecessary work: apparently this was because mechanics had been given targets of the number of car spare parts they should sell.

3.1 Two approaches to managing ethics

Introduction

Inside the organisation, a **compliance-based approach** highlights conformity with the law. An **integrity-based approach** suggests a wider remit, incorporating ethics in the organisation's values and culture.

Organisations sometimes issue **codes of conduct** to employees. Many employees are bound by professional codes of conduct.

Lynne Paine (*Harvard Business Review*, March–April 1994) suggests that ethical decisions are becoming more important as penalties for companies that break the law become tougher. Paine suggests that there are two approaches to the management of ethics in organisations.

- Compliance-based
- Integrity-based

3.1.1 Compliance-based approach

A compliance-based approach is primarily designed to ensure that the company acts within the letter of the law, and that violations are prevented, detected and punished. Some organisations, faced with the legal consequences of unethical behaviour, take legal precautions such as those below.

- Compliance procedures

- Audits of contracts

- Systems for employees to inform superiors about criminal misconduct without fear of retribution

- Disciplinary procedures

Corporate compliance is limited in that it refers only to the law, but legal compliance is **not an adequate means for addressing the full range of ethical issues that arise every day**. This is especially the case in the UK, where **voluntary** codes of conduct and self-regulation are perhaps more prevalent than in the US.

The compliance approach also emphasises the threat of detection and punishment in order to channel appropriate behaviour. Arguably, some employers view compliance programmes as an insurance policy for senior management who can cover the tracks of their arbitrary management practices. After all, some performance targets are impossible to achieve without cutting corners: managers can escape responsibility by blaming the employee for not following the compliance programme, when to do so would have meant a failure to reach target.

Furthermore, mere compliance with the law is no guide to **exemplary** behaviour.

3.1.2 Integrity-based programmes

'*An integrity-based approach combines a concern for the law with an **emphasis on managerial responsibility** for ethical behaviour. Integrity strategies strive to define companies' guiding values, aspirations and patterns of thought and conduct. When integrated into the day-to-day operations of an organisation, such strategies can help prevent damaging ethical lapses, while tapping into powerful human impulses for moral thought and action.*'

It should be clear to you from this quotation that an integrity-based approach to ethics treats ethics as an issue of organisation culture.

Ethics management has several tasks.

- To define and give life to an organisation's defining values
- To create an environment that supports ethically sound behaviour
- To instil a sense of shared accountability amongst employees

The table below indicates some of the differences between the two main approaches.

	Compliance	Integrity
Ethos	Comply with external standards	Choose ethical standards
Objective	Keep to the law	Enable legal and responsible conduct
Originators	Lawyers	Management, with lawyers, HR specialists etc
Methods (both include education, and audits, controls, penalties)	Reduced employee discretion	Leadership, organisation systems
Behavioural assumptions	People are solitary self-interested beings	People are social beings with values
Standards	The law	Company values, aspirations (including law)
Staffing	Lawyers	Managers and lawyers
Education	The law, compliance systems	Values, the law, compliance systems
Activities	Develop standards, train and communicate, handle reports of misconduct, investigate, enforce, oversee compliance	Integrate values into company systems, provide guidance and consultation, identify and resolve problems, oversee compliance

In other words, an integrity-based approach **incorporates** ethics into corporate culture and systems.

It has also been suggested that the following institutions can be established.

- An **ethics committee** is a group of executives (perhaps including non-executive directors) appointed to oversee company ethics. It rules on misconduct. It may seek advice from specialists in business ethics.

- An **ethics ombudsman** is a manager who acts as the corporate conscience.

Accountants can also appeal to their professional body for ethical guidance.

Whistle-blowing is the disclosure by an employee of illegal, immoral or illegitimate practices on the part of the organisation. The whistle-blower often has to make a difficult choice between acting in the public interest, and maintaining confidentiality – an important aspect of the accountant's *Code of Ethics*.

4 Principles and guidance on professional ethics

Introduction

CIMA's *Code of Ethics for Professional Accountants* (*Code of Ethics*) is based on the International Federation of Accountants' (IFAC's) *Code of Ethics for Professional Accountants*.

4.1 The public interest

Introduction

Organisations sometimes issue **codes of conduct** to employees. Many employees are bound by professional codes of conduct.

The International Federation of Accountants' (IFAC's) *Code of Ethics for Professional Accountants* gives the key reason why accountancy bodies produce ethical guidance: the public interest.

A distinguishing mark of the accountancy profession is its acceptance of the responsibility to act in the public interest. Therefore, a professional accountant's responsibility is not exclusively to satisfy the needs of an individual client or employer.

The public interest is considered to be the collective well-being of the community of people and institutions the professional accountant serves, including clients, lenders, governments, employers, employees, investors, the business and financial community and others who rely on the work of professional accountants.

The **key reason** that **accountants need** to have an **ethical code** is that **people rely on them and their expertise**.

Accountants deal with a range of issues on behalf of clients. They often have access to confidential and sensitive information. It is therefore critical that accountants are, and are seen to be, independent.

CIMA publishes guidance for its members in its *Code of Ethics*. This guidance is given in the form of fundamental principles, specific guidance and explanatory notes. CIMA's *Code of Ethics* is based closely upon IFAC's *Code of Ethics for Professional Accountants*.

4.2 CIMA fundamental principles

- **Integrity** – to be **straightforward** and **honest** in all professional and business relationships.

- **Objectivity** – **not to allow bias**, **conflict of interest** or **undue influence** of others to override professional or business judgements.

- **Professional competence and due care** – to maintain **professional knowledge** and skill at a level required to ensure that a client or employer receives the advantage of competent professional service based on current developments in practice, legislation and techniques. To act **diligently** and in accordance with **applicable technical and professional standards**.

- **Confidentiality** – to respect the confidentiality of information acquired as a result of professional or business relationships **and not disclose** any such information to third parties without proper and specific authority, **unless there is a legal or professional right or duty to disclose**. Not to use information for the personal advantage of the professional accountant or third parties.

- **Professional behaviour** – to **comply with relevant laws and regulations** and avoid any action that discredits the profession.

4.3 A framework rather than a rules-based system

CIMA's ethical guidance takes a conceptual framework approach. It contains some rules, for example, the prohibition of making loans to clients, but in the main, it is flexible guidance. It can be seen as being a **framework rather than a set of rules**. There are a number of advantages of a framework over a system of ethical rules. These are outlined in the table below.

Advantages of an ethical framework over a rules-based system
A framework of guidance places the onus on the accountant to **actively consider** independence for every given situation rather than just agreeing a checklist of forbidden items. It also requires the accountant to **demonstrate** that a responsible conclusion has been reached about ethical issues.
The framework **prevents accountants interpreting legalistic requirements narrowly** to get around the ethical requirements. There is an extent to which rules engender deception, whereas principles encourage compliance.
A framework **allows for** the variations that are found in every **individual situation**. Each situation is likely to be different.
A framework can accommodate a **rapidly changing environment**, such as the one that accountants are constantly working in.
However, a **framework can contain prohibitions** (as noted above) where these are necessary, for example where safeguards are not feasible.

4.4 Ethical framework

CIMA's *Code of Ethics* provides the professional accountant with the following framework to deal with ethical issues:

Evaluate any **threats** to compliance with the fundamental principles (discussed in Section 4.2 above) and determine whether they are at an acceptable level.

Where the threats are not at an acceptable level, use professional judgement to determine whether appropriate **safeguards** can be applied to eliminate or reduce the threats.

Where no safeguard can eliminate or reduce the threats, decline or discontinue the specific professional service involved. (Or, if necessary, resign from the engagement or from the employing organisation.)

In determining the appropriate safeguards to apply, the professional accountant must consider whether a reasonable and informed third party, weighing all the specific facts and circumstances available at the time, would conclude that the threats would be eliminated or reduced to an acceptable level by the safeguards.

It is possible, on rare occasions, for the application of the CIMA *Code of Ethics* to result in a disproportionate outcome or an outcome that may not be in the public interest. In such cases, the professional accountant should consult with CIMA or the relevant regulator.

4.5 Threats

The CIMA *Code of Ethics* identifies five main types of threat to ethical compliance. These are:

(a)   **Self-interest threat:** the threat that a financial or other interest will inappropriately influence the professional accountant's judgement or behaviour.

(b)   **Self-review threat:** the threat that when relying on a previous judgement as part of providing a current service, a professional accountant will not appropriately evaluate the results of that judgement made by him/herself (or another individual within the professional accountant's firm/employing organisation).

(c)   **Advocacy threat:** the threat that a professional accountant will promote a client's or employer's position to the point that the professional accountant's objectivity is compromised.

(d) **Familiarity threat**: the threat that due to a long or close relationship with the client or employer, a professional accountant will be too sympathetic to their interests or too accepting of their work., and

(e) **Intimidation threat**: the threat that a professional accountant will be deterred from acting objectively because of actual or perceived pressures, including attempts to exercise undue influence over the professional accountant.

The table below provides examples of each of these types of threat.

Threat	Examples in business	Examples in public practice
Self-interest	• Holding a financial interest in the employing organisation • Concern over employment security	• A member of the audit team having a direct financial interest in the audit client • The audit firm earning a large proportion of its revenue from one single assurance client
Self-review	• Determining the accounting treatment of a business combination after performing the feasibility study that supported the acquisition decision	• The audit firm providing accounting advice to an audit client, and then auditing the resulting financial statements • A member of the audit team having recently been a director of the audit client
Advocacy	• Promoting the employing organisation's position	• The firm promoting shares in an audit client • A professional accountant acting as an advocate on behalf of the client in a litigation
Familiarity	• Being responsible for the organisation's financial reporting when a close family member makes decisions that affect the entity's financial reporting • Long association with business contacts influencing business decisions	• A member of the audit team having a close family member who is a director of the client • An audit partner who has worked on engagements for the same audit client for many years
Intimidation	• Threat of dismissal or replacement • A dominant personality attempting to influence the decision-making process (eg in respect of the application of an accounting principle)	• A firm being threatened with dismissal from an audit client • A firm being pressured to reduce the extent of audit work in order to reduce fees

4.6 Safeguards

Faced with the threats to ethical compliance discussed above, the professional accountant should consider the available safeguards to mitigate such threats.

The CIMA *Code of Ethics* sets out two categories of safeguards:

* Safeguards created by the profession, legislation or regulation; and
* Safeguards in the work environment.

The safeguards created by the profession, legislation or regulation include:

- Educational, training and experience requirements for entry into the profession

- Continuing professional development requirements

- Corporate governance regulations

- Professional standards (such as the *Code of Ethics*)

- Professional or regulatory monitoring and disciplinary procedures

- External review by a legally empowered third party of the reports, returns, communications or information produced by a professional accountant

The safeguards in the work environment, for an accountant in business, include:

- The employing organisation's systems of corporate oversight

- The employing organisation's ethics and conduct programmes

- Recruitment procedures focused on employing high calibre, competent staff

- Strong internal controls

- Appropriate disciplinary processes

- Leadership that stresses the importance of ethical behaviour

- Policies and procedures to implement and monitor the quality of employee performance

- Timely communication of the employing organisation's policies and procedures

- Policies and procedures to empower and encourage employees to communicate to senior management any ethical issues that concern them without fear of retribution

- Consultation with another appropriate professional accountant

For the professional accountant in public practice, the safeguards in the work environment include in addition to the above:

- Documented policies and procedures to identify threats to compliance, evaluate the significance of those threats and apply safeguards

- Policies and procedures to monitor and, if necessary, manage the reliance on revenue received from a single client

- Using different partners and engagement teams with separate reporting lines for the provision of non-assurance services to an assurance client

- Policies and procedures to prohibit individuals who are not members of an engagement team from inappropriately influencing the outcome of the engagement

- Engagement specific safeguards, such as:

  - Having a professional accountant who was not involved with the service provided review the work performed, or otherwise advise as necessary

  - Consulting an independent third party, such as a committee of independent directors, a professional regulatory body or another professional accountant

  - Discussing ethical issues with those charged with governance of the client

  - Disclosing to those charged with governance of the client the nature of services provided and the extent of fees charged

5 Ethical compliance problems

Introduction

Exam questions may ask you to think about what should be done if breaches of laws, regulations or ethical guidelines occur. In financial reporting, **professional competence** and **objectivity** are the key issues.

5.1 Ethics in financial reporting

CIMA's *Code of Ethics* identifies that accountants may be pressurised, either externally or by the possibility of personal gain, to become associated with misleading information. The *Code of Ethics* clearly states that members should not be associated with reports, returns, communications or other information where they believe that the information:

- Contains a **materially false** or **misleading** statement

- Contains statements or information furnished **recklessly**

- **Omits or obscures** information required to be included where such omission or obscurity would be misleading

5.2 Professional competence and due care

Professional competence is clearly a key issue when decisions are made about accounting treatments and disclosures. The CIMA *Code of Ethics* requires professional accountants to:

- Maintain professional knowledge and skill at the level required to ensure that clients or employers receive competent, professional service

- Act diligently in accordance with applicable technical and professional standards

This includes a duty to keep up to date with developments in IFRSs and other relevant regulations.

Circumstances that may threaten the ability of accountants in these roles to perform their duties with the appropriate degree of professional competence and due care include:

- Insufficient time for properly performing or completing the relevant duties

- Incomplete, restricted or otherwise inadequate information for performing the duties properly

- Insufficient experience, training and/or education

- Inadequate resources for the proper performance of the duties

Safeguards that may be considered include:

- Obtaining additional advice or training

- Ensuring that there is adequate time available for performing the relevant duties

- Obtaining assistance from someone with the necessary expertise

- Consulting where appropriate with:

    - Superiors within the employing organisation
    - Independent experts, or
    - CIMA

5.3 Objectivity and integrity

Objectivity and integrity may be threatened in a number of ways:

- Financial interests, such as profit-related bonuses or share options
- Inducements to encourage unethical behaviour

Let's look at each of the above in more detail. The table below summarises the circumstances that would give rise to threats to objectivity, and the possible safeguards recommended by the *Code of Ethics*.

	Circumstances	Safeguards
Financial interests	Accountant/immediate or close family member holds the following, the value of which could be directly affected by decisions made by the accountant: • A **direct or indirect financial interest** in the employing organisation • Eligibility for a **profit-related bonus** • **Share options** in the employing organisation (directly or indirectly) Accountant/immediate or close family member: • Holds, directly or indirectly, share options in the employing organisation which are, or will soon be, **eligible for conversion** • May qualify for share options in the employing organisation or **performance-related bonuses** if certain targets are achieved	• Policies and procedures for a **committee independent of management** to determine the level or form of **remuneration** of senior management • **Disclosure** of all relevant interests and of any plans to trade in relevant shares to those charged with the governance of the employing organisation, in accordance with any internal policies • **Consultation with superiors** within the employing organisation • **Consultation** with **those charged with the governance** of the employing organisation or **relevant professional bodies** • Internal and external **audit** procedures • Up to date **education** on ethical issues and the legal restrictions and other regulations surrounding potential insider trading

	Circumstances	Safeguards
Inducements	• Gifts • Hospitality • Preferential treatment • Inappropriate appeals to friendship or loyalty	• Evaluate threats associated with such offers • Immediately **inform higher levels of management** or those charged with governance of the employing organisation • **Inform** third parties of the offer (for example, **a professional body** or the employer of the individual who made the offer), or seek **legal advice** • **Advise immediate or close family members** of relevant threats and safeguards where they are potentially in positions that might result in offers of inducements (for example, as a result of their employment situation) • Inform higher levels of management or those charged with governance of the employing organisation where **immediate or close family members are employed by competitors** or potential suppliers of that organisation

5.4 Practical significance

Accountants working within a financial reporting environment can come under pressure to improve the financial performance or financial position of their employer. Finance managers who are part of the team putting together the results for publication must be careful to withstand pressures from their non-finance colleagues to indulge in reporting practices which dress up short-term performance and position. Financial managers must be conscious of their professional obligations and seek appropriate assistance from colleagues, peers or independent sources.

Chapter Summary

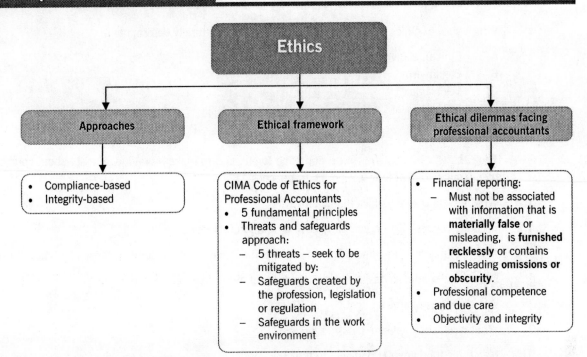

Ethics

Approaches
- Compliance-based
- Integrity-based

Ethical framework

CIMA Code of Ethics for
Professional Accountants
- 5 fundamental principles
- Threats and safeguards
  approach:
  - 5 threats – seek to be
    mitigated by:
  - Safeguards created by
    the profession, legislation
    or regulation
  - Safeguards in the work
    environment

**Ethical dilemmas facing
professional accountants**
- Financial reporting:
  - Must not be associated
    with information that is
    materially false or
    misleading, is **furnished
    recklessly** or contains
    misleading **omissions or
    obscurity**.
- Professional competence
  and due care
- Objectivity and integrity

Quick Quiz

1   Which view of ethics states that right and wrong are culturally determined?

    A   Ethical relativism

    B   Cognitivism

    C   Teleological

    D   Deontological

2   Fill in the blank.

The .... approach to ethics is to make moral judgements about courses of action by reference to their outcomes or consequences.

3   What ethical problems face management?

4   What objectives might a company have in relation to wider society?

5   To whom might management have responsibilities, and what are some of these responsibilities?

6   Describe two approaches to the management of ethics in an organisation.

7   What systems of ethics might you find in an organisation?

8   What is whistle-blowing?

9   Match the fundamental principle to the characteristic.

    (a)   Integrity

    (b)   Objectivity

    (i)   Members should be straightforward and honest in all professional and business relationships.

    (ii)   Members should not allow bias, conflict of interest or undue influence of others to override professional or business judgements.

Answers to Quick Quiz

1   A   Ethical relativism

2   Teleological or consequentialist

3   There is a constant tension between the need to achieve current profitability, the need to safeguard the stakeholders' long-term investment and the expectations of wider society.

4   Protection of the environment, support for good causes, a responsible attitude to product safety.

5   Managers of businesses are responsible to the owners for economic performance and to wider society for the externalities related to their business operations.

6   A compliance-based approach aims to remain within the letter of the law by establishing systems of audit and review so that transgressions may be detected and punished. An integrity-based approach tries to promote an ethical culture in which individuals will do the right thing.

7   Personal ethics, professional ethics, organisation culture, organisation systems.

8   Informing outside regulatory agencies about transgressions by one's organisation.

9   (a) (i)
    (b) (ii)

Answers to Questions

18.1 Ethical issues

(a)   Dealing with authoritarian governments can be supported on the grounds that it **contributes to economic growth and prosperity**, and all the benefits they bring to society in both countries concerned. However, it can also be opposed on consequentialist grounds as **contributing to the continuation of the regime**, and on deontological grounds as **fundamentally repugnant**.

(b)   Honesty in advertising is an important problem. Many products are promoted exclusively on image. Deliberately creating the impression that purchasing a particular product will enhance the happiness, success and sex appeal of the buyer can be attacked as **dishonest**. It can be defended on the grounds that the supplier is actually **selling a fantasy or dream** rather than a physical article.

(c)   Dealings with employees are coloured by the **opposing views of corporate responsibility and individual rights**. The idea of a job as property to be defended has now disappeared from labour relations in many countries, but corporate decisions that lead to redundancies are still deplored. This is because of the obvious **impact of sudden unemployment on aspirations and living standards**, even when the employment market is buoyant. Nevertheless, businesses have to consider the cost of employing labour as well as its productive capacity.

(d)   The main problem with payments or gifts to officials is making the distinction between those that should never be made, and those that can be made in certain cultural circumstances.

   (i)   **Extortion.** Foreign officials have been known to threaten companies with the complete closure of their local operations unless suitable payments are made.

   (ii) **Bribery.** This is payment for services to which a company is not legally entitled. There are some fine distinctions to be drawn, for example, some managers regard political contributions as bribery.

(iii)   **Grease money**. Multinational companies are sometimes unable to obtain services to which they are legally entitled because of deliberate stalling by local officials. Cash payments to the right people may then be enough to oil the machinery of bureaucracy.

(iv)   **Gifts**. In some cultures, gifts are regarded as an essential part of civilised negotiation, even in circumstances where to Western eyes they might appear ethically dubious. Managers operating in such a culture may feel pressurised to adopt the local customs.

Now try these questions from the Practice Question Bank	Number	Level	Marks	Time
	Q35	Introductory	N/A	9 mins

INTERPRETATION OF ACCOUNTS

Part F

ANALYSIS OF FINANCIAL PERFORMANCE AND POSITION

You must be able to **comment** on the ratios as well as calculate them and give suggested reasons for trends and differences. Pay close attention to Section 8 on report writing, as this will help you to improve your exam technique.

CIMA have stated that this syllabus places considerable emphasis on interpretation.

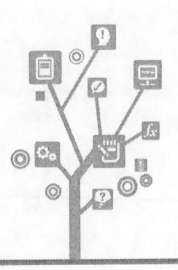

Topic list	learning outcomes	syllabus references
1 Sources of information and the role of regulation	C1	C1(a)(b)
2 The broad categories of ratios	C1	C1(a)(b)(c)
3 Profitability and return on capital	C1	C1(a)(b)(c)
4 Liquidity, gearing/leverage and working capital	C1	C1(a)(b)(c)
5 Investor ratios	C1	C1(a)(b)(c)
6 The nature of profit	C2	C2(a)
7 Other problems with financial analysis	C2	C2(a)

Chapter Overview

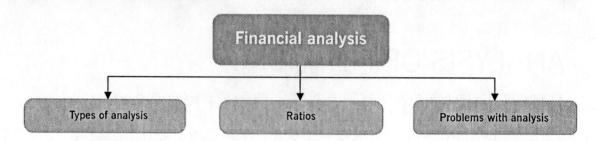

1 Sources of information and the role of regulation 11/12

Introduction

The accounts of a business are designed to provide users with information about its performance and financial position. The bare figures, however, are not particularly useful and it is only through **comparisons** (usually in ratios) that their significance can be established. Comparisons may be made with previous financial periods, with other similar businesses or with averages for the particular industry. The choice will depend on the purpose for which the comparison is being made and the information that is available.

1.1 User groups

Various groups are interested in the performance and financial position of a company.

(a) **Management** will use comparisons to ensure that the business is performing efficiently and according to plan.

(b) **Employees** and trade unions may use the information as a basis of wage negotiation.

(c) **Government** may use financial statements to prepare statistics or for assessing the worthiness of a government grant.

(d) Present and potential **investors** will assess the company with a view to judging whether it is a sound investment.

(e) **Lenders** and **suppliers** will want to judge its creditworthiness.

This text is concerned with financial rather than management accounting, and the ratios discussed here are therefore likely to be calculated by external users. The following sources of information are readily available to external users.

- Published financial statements and interim financial statements
- Documents filed as required by company legislation
- Statistics published by the government
- Other published sources eg *Investors Chronicle, The Economist, Wall Street Journal*

1.2 Financial analysis

The **lack of detailed information** available to the outsider is a considerable disadvantage in undertaking ratio analysis. The first difficulty is that there may simply be insufficient data to calculate all of the required ratios. A second concerns the availability of a suitable yardstick with which the calculated ratios may be compared.

1.2.1 Inter-temporal analysis

Looking first at inter-temporal or trend analysis (comparisons for the same business over time), some of the **problems** include the following.

- Changes in the nature of the business
- Unrealistic depreciation rates under historical cost accounting
- The changing value of the currency unit being reported
- Changes in accounting policies

Other factors will include changes in government incentive packages and changes from purchasing equipment to leasing.

1.2.2 Cross-sectional analysis

When undertaking cross-sectional analysis (making comparisons with other companies) the position is even more difficult because of the problem of identifying companies that are comparable. **Comparability** between companies may be impaired due to the following reasons.

(a)   Different degrees of diversification

(b)   Different production and purchasing policies (if an investor was analysing the smaller car manufacturers, he would find that some of them buy in engines from one of the 'majors' while others develop and manufacture their own)

(c)   Different financing policies (eg leasing as opposed to buying)

(d)   Different accounting policies (one of the most serious problems particularly in relation to non-current assets and inventory valuation)

(e)   Different effects of government incentives

The major **intragroup comparison organisations** (whose results are intended for the use of participating companies and are not generally available) go to considerable lengths to adjust accounts to comparable bases. The external user will rarely be in a position to make such adjustments. Although the position is improved by increases in disclosure requirements, direct comparisons between companies will inevitably, on occasion, continue to give rise to misleading results.

1.3 Social and political considerations

In recent years, the **social aspect** much in evidence has been that of **environmental issues**. Presenting a sustainable, environmentally-responsible image is now increasingly important for a company's reputation. Sometimes the public perception of how well a company is doing in environmental terms can even affect the company's financial profits (for example, increased margins on organic foods, or fines for environmental breaches).

Political considerations may also be far reaching. The regulatory regime may be instituted by statutes, but often self-regulation is encouraged through bodies such as the London Stock Exchange.

1.4 Multinational companies

Multinational companies have great difficulties sometimes because of the need to comply with **legislation** in a large number of countries. As well as different reporting requirements, different rules of incorporation exist, as well as different directors' rules and tax legislation. Sometimes the local rules can be so harsh that companies will avoid them altogether.

Different local reporting requirements will also make **consolidation** more difficult. The results of subsidiaries must be translated not only into the parent company's base currency but also using the accounting rules used by head office. This is a requirement of IFRSs because uniform accounting policies are called for.

1.5 The efficient market hypothesis and stock exchanges

It has been argued that stock markets in the most sophisticated economies eg the US, are **efficient capital markets.**

(a)   The prices of securities bought and sold reflect all the relevant information which is available to the buyers and sellers. In other words, share prices change quickly to reflect all new information about future prospects.

(b)   No individual dominates the market.

(c)   Transaction costs are not so high as to discourage trading significantly.

If the stock market is efficient, share prices should vary in a **rational way**, ie reflecting the known profits or losses of a company and the rate of return required based on interest rates.

Research in both Britain and the US has suggested that market prices anticipate mergers several months before they are formally announced, and the conclusion drawn is that the stock markets in these countries do exhibit **semi-strong efficiency**. It has also been argued that the market displays sufficient efficiency for investors to see through any window dressing of accounts by companies that use accounting conventions to overstate profits (ie creative accounting).

Evidence suggests that stock markets show efficiency that is **at least weak form**, but tending more towards a semi strong form. In other words, current share prices reflect all or most publicly available information about companies and their securities. However, it is very difficult to assess the market's efficiency in relation to shares which are not usually actively traded.

Fundamental analysis and **technical analysis** carried out by analysts and investment managers play an important role in creating an efficient stock market. This is because an efficient market depends on the widespread availability of cheap information about companies, their shares and market conditions, and this is what the firms of market makers and other financial institutions *do* provide for their clients and for the general investing public. In a market which demonstrates strong-form efficiency, such analysis would not identify profitable opportunities, ie where shares are undervalued, because such information would already be known and reflected in the share price.

On the other hand, stock market crashes raise serious questions about the validity of the **fundamental theory of share values** and the efficient market hypothesis. If these theories are correct, how can shares that were valued at one level on one day suddenly be worth 40% less the next day, without any change in expectations of corporate profits and dividends? On the other hand, a widely feared crash may fail to happen, suggesting that stock markets may not be altogether out of touch with the underlying values of companies.

Section summary

Keep the various **sources of financial information** in mind and the effects of insider dealing, the efficient market hypothesis and Stock Exchange regulations.

2   The broad categories of ratios   11/10, 3/11, 11/11, 9/12

Introduction

If you were to look at a statement of financial position or statement of profit or loss and other comprehensive income, how would you decide whether the company was doing well or badly? Or whether it was financially strong or financially vulnerable? And what would you be looking at in the figures to help you to make your judgement?

Ratio analysis involves **comparing one figure against another** to produce a ratio, and assessing whether the ratio indicates a weakness or strength in the company's affairs.

2.1 The broad categories of ratios

Broadly speaking, basic ratios can be grouped into five categories.

- Profitability and return
- Long-term solvency and stability
- Short-term solvency and liquidity
- Efficiency (turnover ratios)
- Investor ratios

Within each heading we will identify a number of standard measures or ratios that are normally calculated and generally accepted as meaningful indicators. One must stress, however, that each

individual business must be considered separately, and a ratio that is meaningful for a manufacturing company may be completely meaningless for a financial institution. When working out ratios, you should constantly think about what you are trying to achieve.

The key to obtaining meaningful information from ratio analysis is **comparison**. This may involve comparing ratios over time within the same business to establish whether things are improving or declining, and comparing ratios between similar businesses to see whether the company you are analysing is better or worse than average within its specific business sector.

It must be stressed that ratio analysis on its own is not sufficient for interpreting company accounts, and that there are **other items of information** which should be looked at, for example:

(a)　The content of any **accompanying commentary** on the accounts and other statements

(b)　The age and nature of the **company's assets**

(c)　**Current and future developments** in the company's markets, at home and overseas, recent acquisitions or disposals of a subsidiary by the company

(d)　**Unusual** items separately disclosed in the statement of profit or loss and other comprehensive income

(e)　Any other **noticeable features** of the report and accounts, such as events after the reporting date, contingent liabilities, a qualified auditors' report and the company's taxation position

Further reading

The March 2013 edition of *Financial Management* contains an article by Jayne Howson, a marker for this paper, about how ratio analysis is tested in the CIMA F2 exams. Make sure you read this article, as it contains some very helpful explanations about how you should calculate and analyse ratios in the exam.

The article can be accessed via this link: http://www.fm-magazine.com/study-centre/course-notes/financial-management-3 (Valid as of 18 April 2013).

Exam skills

In the exam, you must relate the analysis to the scenario given in the question.

Make sure that you use the formulae provided below when you calculate your ratios. If you do not use the exam-specified formula, you will not get any marks. Be warned!

Example: Calculating ratios

To illustrate the calculation of ratios, the following **draft** statement of financial position and statement of profit or loss figures will be used.

FURLONG CO
STATEMENT OF PROFIT OR LOSS FOR THE YEAR ENDED 31 DECEMBER 20X8

	Notes	20X8 $	20X7 $
Revenue		3,095,576	1,909,051
Cost of sales		(2,402,609)	(1,441,950)
Gross profit		692,967	467,101
Administrative expenses		(333,466)	(222,872)
Share of profit of associate		10,000	8,500
Interest	1	(17,371)	(19,127)
Profit before taxation		352,130	233,602
Taxation		(74,200)	(31,272)
Profit for the year		277,930	202,330
Dividend		(41,000)	(16,800)
Earnings per share		13.2c	9.6c

FURLONG CO
STATEMENT OF FINANCIAL POSITION AS AT 31 DECEMBER 20X8

	Notes	20X8 $	20X8 $	20X7 $	20X7 $
Assets					
Non-current assets					
Property, plant and equipment		712,180		576,071	
Investments in associates		90,000		80,000	
			802,180		656,071
Current assets					
Inventory		64,422		86,550	
Receivables	2	1,002,701		853,441	
Cash and cash equivalents		1,327		68,363	
			1,068,450		1,008,354
Total assets			1,870,630		1,664,425
Equity and liabilities					
Equity					
Ordinary shares 10c each	4	210,000		210,000	
Share premium account		48,178		48,178	
Retained earnings		630,721		393,791	
			888,899		651,969
Non-current liabilities					
10% loan stock 20X4/20Y0			100,000		100,000
Current liabilities	3		881,731		912,456
Total equity and liabilities			1,870,630		1,664,425

Notes

		20X8 $	20X7 $
1	*Interest*		
	Payable on bank overdrafts and other loans	8,115	11,909
	Payable on loan stock	10,000	10,000
		18,115	21,909
	Receivable on short-term deposits	(744)	(2,782)
	Net payable	17,371	19,127
2	*Receivables*		
	Amounts falling due within one year		
	Trade receivables	884,559	760,252
	Prepayments and accrued income	97,022	45,729
		981,581	805,981
	Amounts falling due after more than one year		
	Trade receivables	21,120	47,460
	Total receivables	1,002,701	853,441
3	*Current liabilities*		
	Trade payables	627,018	545,340
	Accruals and deferred income	81,279	280,464
	Corporate taxes	108,000	37,200
	Other taxes	44,434	32,652
	Dividend	21,000	16,800
		881,731	912,456
4	*Called-up share capital*		
	Authorised ordinary shares of 10c each	1,000,000	1,000,000
	Issued and fully paid ordinary shares of 10c each	210,000	210,000

Section summary

Your syllabus requires you to **appraise and communicate** the position and prospects of a business based on given and prepared statements and ratios.

Much of the material here on **basic ratios** should be revision for you.

Make sure that you can **define** all the ratios. Look out for variations in definitions of ratios which might appear in questions.

3 Profitability and return on capital

Introduction

In our example, the company made a profit in both 20X8 and 20X7, and there was an increase in profit between one year and the next:

(a)   Of 51% before taxation   (b)   Of 37% after taxation

Profit before taxation is generally thought to be a better figure to use than profit after taxation, because there might be unusual variations in the tax charge from year to year which would not affect the underlying profitability of the company's operations.

Another profit figure that should be calculated is **Profit before interest and taxation (PBIT)**. This is the amount of profit which the company earned before having to pay interest to the providers of loan capital. By providers of loan capital, we usually mean longer-term loan capital, such as debentures and

medium-term bank loans, which will be shown in the statement of financial position as non-current liabilities.

Profit before interest and tax (PBIT) is therefore:

(a)   The profit on ordinary activities before taxation **plus**

(b)   Interest payable shown in the statement of profit or loss

The PBIT **must not** include any profits or losses from **investments in associates**.

PBIT in our example is therefore:

	20X8	20X7
	$	$
Profit before tax	352,130	233,602
Less share of profit of associate	(10,000)	(8,500)
Add back interest payable	18,115	21,909
Profit before interest and tax	360,245	247,011

This shows a 45% growth between 20X7 and 20X8.

3.1 Return on capital employed (ROCE)

It is impossible to assess profits or profit growth properly without relating them to the **amount of funds (capital) that were employed in making the profits**. The most important profitability ratio is therefore return on capital employed (ROCE), which states the profit as a percentage of the amount of capital employed.

$$ROCE = \frac{\text{Profit before interest and taxation}}{\text{Capital employed}} \times 100\%$$

Capital employed = Shareholders' equity plus non-current liabilities* less investments in associates

* Also include overdraft if the company is using it as a long-term source of finance

The underlying principle is that we must **compare like with like**, and so if capital means share capital and reserves plus non-current liabilities less investments in associates, profit must also exclude the associates (share of associates' profit or loss) and mean the profit earned by all this capital together.

In our example, capital employed =   20X8 $888,899 + $100,000 – $90,000= $898,899

                                          20X7 $651,969 + $100,000 – $80,000= $671,969

	20X8	20X7
ROCE =	$\dfrac{\$360,245}{\$898,899}$	$\dfrac{\$247,011}{\$671,969}$
=	40.1%	36.8%

What does a company's ROCE tell us? What should we be looking for? There are three comparisons that can be made.

(a)   The **change in ROCE from one year to the next** can be examined. In this example, there has been an increase in ROCE by just over 3 percentage points from its 20X7 level.

(b)   The **ROCE being earned by other companies**, if this information is available, can be compared with the ROCE of this company. Here the information is not available.

(c)   A comparison of the ROCE with **current market borrowing rates** may be made.

(i)   What would be the cost of extra borrowing to the company if it needed more loans, and is it earning an ROCE that suggests it could make profits to make such borrowing worthwhile?

(ii)   Is the company making an ROCE which suggests that it is getting value for money from its current borrowing?

(iii)   Companies are in a risk business and commercial borrowing rates are a good independent yardstick against which company performance can be judged.

In this example, if we suppose that current market interest rates, say, for medium-term borrowing from banks, are around 10%, then the company's actual ROCE of 40.1% in 20X8 would not seem low. On the contrary, it might seem high.

However, it is easier to spot a low ROCE than a high one, because there is always a chance that the company's non-current assets, especially property, are **undervalued** in its statement of financial position, and so the capital employed figure might be unrealistically low. If the company had earned an ROCE, not of 40.1%, but of, say only 6%, then its return would have been below current borrowing rates and so disappointingly low.

3.2 Return on equity (ROE)

Return on equity gives a more restricted view of capital than ROCE, but it is based on the same principles.

$$ROE = \frac{\text{Profit after tax and preferred dividend}}{\text{Ordinary share capital and other equity}} \times 100\%$$

In our example, ROE is calculated as follows.

$$ROE = \underset{20X8}{\frac{\$277,930}{\$888,899}} = 31.3\% \qquad \underset{20X7}{\frac{\$202,330}{\$651,969}} = 31.0\%$$

ROE is **not a widely-used ratio**, however, because there are more useful ratios that give an indication of the return to shareholders, such as earnings per share, dividend per share, dividend yield and earnings yield, which are described later.

3.3 Analysing profitability and return in more detail: the secondary ratios

We often sub-analyse ROCE to find out more about why the ROCE is high or low, or better or worse than last year. There are two factors that contribute towards ROCE, both related to revenue.

(a)   **Operating profit margin.** A company might make a high or low operating profit margin on its sales. For example, a company that makes a profit of 25c per $1 of sales is making a bigger return on its revenue than another company making a profit of only 10c per $1 of sales.

(b)   **Asset turnover.** Asset turnover is a measure of how well the assets of a business are being used to generate sales. For example, if two companies each have capital employed of $100,000 and Company A makes sales of $400,000 per annum whereas Company B makes sales of only $200,000 per annum, Company A is making a higher revenue from the same amount of assets (twice as much asset turnover as Company B) and this will help A to make a higher ROCE than B. Asset turnover is expressed in terms of **x times** so that assets generate x times their value in annual sales. Here, Company A's asset turnover is 4 times and B's is 2 times.

Operating profit margin and asset turnover together explain the ROCE and if the ROCE is the primary profitability ratio, these other two are the secondary ratios. The relationship between the three ratios can be shown mathematically.

Operating profit margin × Asset turnover = ROCE

$$\therefore \quad \frac{PBIT}{Revenue} \quad \times \quad \frac{Revenue}{Capital\ employed} \quad = \quad \frac{PBIT}{Capital\ employed}$$

Where capital employed is as defined for ROCE

In our example:

		Operating profit margin		*Asset turnover*		*ROCE*
(a)	20X8	$\dfrac{\$360{,}245}{\$3{,}095{,}576}$	×	$\dfrac{\$3{,}095{,}576}{\$898{,}899}$	=	$\dfrac{\$360{,}245}{\$898{,}899}$
		11.64%	×	3.44 times	=	40.1%
(b)	20X7	$\dfrac{\$247{,}011}{\$1{,}909{,}051}$	×	$\dfrac{\$1{,}909{,}051}{\$671{,}969}$	=	$\dfrac{\$247{,}011}{\$671{,}969}$
		12.94%	×	2.84 times	=	36.8%

In this example, the company's improvement in ROCE between 20X7 and 20X8 is attributable to a higher asset turnover. Indeed the operating profit margin has fallen a little, but the higher asset turnover has more than compensated for this.

It is also worth commenting on the change in revenue from one year to the next. You may already have noticed that Furlong achieved sales growth of over 60% from $1.9m to $3.1m between 20X7 and 20X8. This is very strong growth, and this is certainly one of the most significant items in the statement of profit or loss and other comprehensive income.

There are two other asset turnover ratios that you may meet in the exam. Again, remember that your total assets and non-current assets figures must exclude any investments in associates as the revenue figure does not incorporate the associates and you need to compare like with like.

Total asset turnover = Revenue/Total assets

Non-current asset turnover = Revenue/ Non-current assets

3.3.1 A warning about comments on profit margin and asset turnover

It might be tempting to think that a high profit margin is good, and a low asset turnover means sluggish trading. In broad terms, this is so. However, there is a trade-off between operating profit margin and asset turnover, and you cannot look at one without allowing for the other.

(a) A **high operating profit margin** means a high profit per $1 of sales, but if this also means that sales prices are high there is a strong possibility that sales revenue will be depressed and so asset turnover lower.

(b) A **high asset turnover** means that the company is generating a lot of sales, but to do this it might have to keep its prices down and so accept a lower profit margin per $1 of sales.

Consider the following.

Company A
Revenue	$1,000,000
Capital employed	$1,000,000
PBIT	$200,000

Company B
Revenue	$4,000,000
Capital employed	$1,000,000
PBIT	$200,000

These figures would give the following ratios.

ROCE $= \dfrac{\$200,000}{\$1,000,000} = 20\%$ ROCE $= \dfrac{\$200,000}{\$1,000,000} = 20\%$

Profit margin $= \dfrac{\$200,000}{\$1,000,000} = 20\%$ Profit margin $= \dfrac{\$200,000}{\$4,000,000} = 5\%$

Asset turnover $= \dfrac{\$1,000,000}{\$1,000,000} = 1$ Asset turnover $= \dfrac{\$4,000,000}{\$1,000,000} = 4$

The companies have the same ROCE, but it is arrived at in a very different fashion. Company A operates with a low asset turnover and a comparatively high profit margin, whereas company B carries out much more business but on a lower profit margin. Company A could be operating at the luxury end of the market, while company B is operating at the popular end of the market.

3.4 Gross profit margin, operating profit margin, net profit margin and profit analysis

There are three possible profit margin figures that you can calculate:

$$\text{Gross profit margin} = \frac{\text{Gross profit}}{\text{Revenue}} \times 100\%$$

The gross profit margin measures how well a company is running its core operations.

$$\text{Operating profit margin} = \frac{\text{PBIT}}{\text{Revenue}} \times 100\%$$

PBIT is used because it avoids distortion when comparisons are made between two different companies where one is heavily financed by means of loans, and the other is financed entirely by ordinary share capital. The extra consideration for the operating margin over the gross margin is how well the company is controlling its overheads.

$$\text{Net profit margin} = \frac{\text{Profit for the year}}{\text{Revenue}} \times 100\%$$

The extra considerations for the net margin over the operating margin are interest and tax.

Looking at the three together can be quite informative.

For example, suppose that a company has the following summarised statement of profit or loss for two consecutive years.

	Year 1 $	Year 2 $
Revenue	70,000	100,000
Cost of sales	(42,000)	(55,000)
Gross profit	28,000	45,000
Distribution and administrative expenses	(16,000)	(29,000)
Finance costs	(2,000)	(2,000)
Profit before tax	10,000	14,000
Income tax expense	(3,000)	(4,000)
Profit for the year	7,000	10,000

Although the net profit margin is the same for both years at 10%, the gross profit margin is not.

In Year 1 it is: $\dfrac{\$28,000}{\$70,000}$ =   40%

And in Year 2 it is: $\dfrac{\$45,000}{\$100,000}$ =   45%

The improved gross profit margin has not led to an improvement in the net profit margin. We can see that this is largely due to poor cost control of operating overheads, since the operating margin has deteriorated despite the improvement in the gross margin:

In Year 1 it is: $\dfrac{\$10,000 + \$2,000}{\$70,000}$ =   17%

In Year 2 it is: $\dfrac{\$14,000 + \$2,000}{\$100,000}$ =   16%

Finance costs, and presumably borrowings and the rate of interest, have remained constant so this is not the reason for the difference in gross and net margins.

Section summary

Make sure you learn the ratios given.

---

4 Liquidity, gearing/leverage and working capital   11/12

Introduction

Debt ratios are concerned with **how much the company owes in relation to its size**, whether it is getting into heavier debt or improving its situation, and whether its debt burden seems heavy or light.

(a)   When a company is heavily in debt, banks and other potential lenders may be unwilling to advance further funds.

(b)   When a company is earning only a modest PBIT, and has a heavy debt burden, there will be very little profit left over for shareholders after the interest charges have been paid. Therefore if interest rates were to go up (on bank overdrafts for example), or the company were to borrow even more, it might soon be incurring interest charges in excess of PBIT. This might eventually lead to the liquidation of the company.

4.1 Long-term solvency: gearing and interest cover ratios

Points (a) and (b) above are two big reasons why companies should keep their debt burden under control. There are two ratios that are particularly worth looking at: the gearing ratio and interest cover.

4.2 Gearing

Gearing is concerned with a company's **long-term capital structure**. We can think of a company as consisting of non-current assets and net current assets (ie working capital, which is current assets minus current liabilities). These assets must be financed by long-term capital of the company, which is one of two things.

(a)   Equity, which can be divided into:
    (i)   Ordinary share capital and share premium
    (ii)   Cumulative irredeemable preference share capital and share premium (see Chapter 2)
    (iii)   Reserves (eg retained earnings, revaluation reserve)

(b)   Long-term debt, including:

(i)   Pension liabilities

(ii)   Overdraft, but only if it is used as a **long-term source of finance**

(iii)   Redeemable or cumulative irredeemable preference shares (see Chapter 2)

There are two possible ways of calculating the capital gearing ratio, as follows.

LEARN

$$\text{Gearing} = \frac{\text{Long}-\text{term debt}}{\text{Long}-\text{term debt}+\text{Equity}} \times 100\%$$

LEARN

$$\text{Gearing} = \frac{\text{Long}-\text{term debt}}{\text{Equity}} \times 100\%$$

Exam alert

Unless specified in the question, you can use either method in the exam, as long as you are consistent and set out the basis of your workings accordingly.

If you are not certain whether an overdraft should be included as prior charge capital, set out your reasons for including or excluding it in your answer.

There is **no absolute limit** to what a gearing ratio ought to be. A company with a gearing ratio of more than 50% is said to be highly geared (whereas low gearing means a gearing ratio of less than 50%). Many companies are highly geared, but if a highly geared company is becoming increasingly highly geared, it is likely to have difficulty in the future when it wants to borrow even more, unless it can also boost its shareholders' capital, either with retained profits or by a new share issue.

4.3 The implications of high or low gearing

We mentioned earlier that **gearing or leverage** is, among other things, an attempt to **quantify the degree of risk involved in holding equity shares in a company**, risk both in terms of the company's ability to remain in business and in terms of expected ordinary dividends from the company. The problem with a highly geared company is that by definition there is a lot of debt. Debt generally carries a fixed rate of interest (or fixed rate of dividend if in the form of preferred shares); hence there is a given (and large) amount to be paid out from profits to holders of debt before arriving at a residue available for distribution to the holders of equity. The level of risk will perhaps become clearer with the aid of an example.

	Company A $'000	Company B $'000	Company C $'000
Ordinary shares	600	400	300
Retained earnings	200	200	200
Revaluation reserve	100	100	100
	900	700	600
5% cumulative redeemable preference shares	–	–	100
10% loan stock	100	300	300
Capital employed	1,000	1,000	1,000
Gearing ratio	10%	30%	40%
Equity to assets ratio	90%	70%	60%

Now suppose that each company makes a PBIT of $50,000, and the rate of tax on company profits is 30%. Amounts available for distribution to equity shareholders will be as follows.

	Company A $'000	Company B $'000	Company C $'000
Profit before interest and tax	50	50	50.0
Interest	(10)	(30)	(35.0)
Taxable profit	40	20	15.0
Taxation at 30%	(12)	(6)	(4.5)
Profit after tax available for ordinary shareholders	28	14	10.5

If in the subsequent year PBIT falls to $40,000, the amounts available to ordinary shareholders will become as follows.

	Company A $'000	Company B $'000	Company C $'000
Profit before interest and tax	40	40	40.0
Interest	(10)	(30)	(35.0)
Taxable profit	30	10	5.0
Taxation at 30%	(9)	(3)	(1.5)
Profit after tax available for ordinary shareholders	21	7	3.5

Note the following (assuming that all profit is paid out as dividends so equity is unchanged).

Gearing ratio	10%	30%	40%
Equity to assets ratio	90%	70%	60%
Change in PBIT	– 20%	– 20%	– 20%
Change in profit available for ordinary shareholders	– 25%	– 50%	– 67%

The more highly geared the company, the greater the risk that little (if anything) will be available to distribute by way of dividend to the ordinary shareholders. The example clearly displays this fact in so far as the more highly geared the company, the greater the percentage change in profit available for ordinary shareholders for any given percentage change in PBIT. The relationship similarly holds when profits increase, and if PBIT had risen by 20% rather than fallen, you would find that once again the largest percentage change in profit available for ordinary shareholders (this means an increase) will be for the highly geared company. This means that where a company is highly geared there will be greater **volatility** of amounts available for ordinary shareholders, and presumably, therefore, greater volatility in dividends paid to those shareholders. That is the risk: you may do extremely well or extremely badly without a particularly large movement in the PBIT of the company.

The risk of a company's ability to remain in business was referred to earlier. Gearing is relevant to this. A highly geared company has a large amount of interest to pay annually. If those borrowings are **secured** in any way (and debentures in particular are secured), then the **holders of the debt are perfectly entitled to force the company** to **realise assets to pay their interest** if funds are not available from other sources. Clearly the more highly geared a company, the more likely this is to occur when and if profits fall.

4.4 Interest cover

The interest cover ratio shows whether a company is earning enough profits before interest and tax to pay its interest costs comfortably, or whether its interest costs are high in relation to the size of its profits, so that a fall in PBIT would then have a significant effect on profits available for ordinary shareholders.

$$\text{Interest cover} = \frac{\text{Profit before interest and tax}}{\text{Interest charges}}$$

Ideally interest cover should be at least one. Some consider an interest cover of two times or less to be low, and believe that it should really exceed three times before the company's interest costs are considered to be within acceptable limits. However, the level of acceptable interest cover varies depending on the industry in which the company operates.

Exam alert

As mentioned above, make sure you exclude any profit or loss from investments in associates when calculating the PBIT figure.

Returning to the example of Companies A, B and C, the interest cover was as follows.

		Company A	Company B	Company C
(a)	When PBIT was $50,000 =	$50,000	$50,000	$50,000
		$10,000	$30,000	$35,000
		5 times	1.67 times	1.43 times
(b)	When PBIT was $40,000 =	$40,000	$40,000	$40,000
		$10,000	$30,000	$35,000
		4 times	1.33 times	1.14 times

Note. We look at all interest payments, even interest charges on short-term debt, and so interest cover and gearing do not quite look at the same thing.

Both B and C have a low interest cover, which is a warning to ordinary shareholders that their profits are highly vulnerable, in percentage terms, to even small changes in PBIT.

Question 19.1   Interest cover

Learning outcome C1

Returning to the example of Furlong in Paragraph 2.1, what is the company's interest cover?

4.5 Short-term solvency and liquidity

Profitability is, of course, an important aspect of a company's performance, and gearing or leverage is another. Neither, however, addresses directly the key issue of **liquidity**.

KEY TERM

LIQUIDITY is the amount of cash a company can put its hands on quickly to settle its debts (and possibly to meet other unforeseen demands for cash payments too).

Liquid funds consist of:

(a)   Cash

(b)   Short-term investments for which there is a ready market

(c)   Fixed-term deposits with a bank or other financial institution, for example, a six-month high-interest deposit with a bank

(d)   Trade receivables (because they will pay what they owe within a reasonably short period of time)

(e)   Bills of exchange receivable (because like ordinary trade receivables, these represent amounts of cash due to be received within a relatively short period of time)

In summary, **liquid assets are current asset items that will or could soon be converted into cash, and cash itself.** Two common definitions of liquid assets are:

- All current assets without exception
- All current assets with the exception of inventories

A company can obtain liquid assets from sources other than sales of goods and services, such as the issue of shares for cash, a new loan or the sale of non-current assets. However, a company cannot rely on these at all times and, in general, obtaining liquid funds depends on making sales revenue and profits. Even so, profits do not always lead to increases in liquidity. This is mainly because funds generated from trading may be immediately invested in non-current assets or paid out as dividends. You should refer back to Chapter 15 on statement of cash flows to examine this issue.

The reason why a company needs liquid assets is so that it can meet its debts when they fall due. Payments are continually made for operating expenses and other costs, and so there is a **cash cycle** from trading activities of cash coming in from sales and cash going out for expenses.

4.6 The cash cycle

To help you to understand liquidity ratios, it is useful to begin with a brief explanation of the cash cycle or working capital cycle. The cash cycle describes **the flow of cash out of a business and back into it again as a result of normal trading operations**.

Cash goes out to pay for supplies, wages and salaries and other expenses, although payments can be delayed by taking some credit. A business might hold inventory for a while and then sell it. Cash will come back into the business from the sales, although customers might delay payment by themselves taking some credit.

The main points about the cash cycle are as follows.

(a) The timing of cash flows in and out of a business does not coincide with the time when sales and costs of sales occur. **Cash flows out can be postponed by taking credit. Cash flows in can be delayed by having receivables.**

(b) **The time between making a purchase and making a sale also affects cash flows.** If inventories are held for a long time, the delay between the cash payment for inventory and cash receipts from selling it will also be a long one.

(c) **Holding inventories and having receivables can therefore be seen as two reasons why cash receipts are delayed.** Another way of saying this is that if a company invests in working capital, its cash position will show a corresponding decrease.

(d) Similarly, **taking credit from creditors can be seen as a reason why cash payments are delayed.** The company's liquidity position will worsen when it has to pay the suppliers, unless it can get more cash in from sales and receivables in the meantime.

The liquidity ratios and working capital turnover ratios are used to test a company's liquidity, length of cash cycle, and investment in working capital.

4.7 Liquidity ratios: current ratio and quick ratio

The standard test of liquidity is the **current ratio**. It can be obtained from the statement of financial position.

$$\text{Current ratio} = \frac{\text{Current assets}}{\text{Current liabilities}}$$

The idea behind this is that a company should have enough current assets that give a promise of cash to come to meet its future commitments to pay off its current liabilities. Obviously, a **ratio in excess of one should be expected**. Otherwise, there would be the prospect that the company might be unable to pay its debts on time. In practice, a ratio comfortably in excess of one should be expected, but what is comfortable varies between different types of businesses.

Companies are not able to convert all their current assets into cash very quickly. In particular, some manufacturing companies might hold large quantities of raw material inventories, which must be used in production to create finished goods inventory. These might be warehoused for a long time, or sold on lengthy credit. In such businesses, where inventory turnover is slow, most inventories are not very liquid assets, because the cash cycle is so long. For these reasons, we calculate an additional liquidity ratio, known as the quick ratio or acid test ratio.

The **quick ratio**, or **acid test ratio**, is calculated as follows.

$$\text{Quick ratio} = \frac{\text{Current assets less inventory}}{\text{Current liabilities}}$$

This ratio should ideally be **at least one** for companies with a slow inventory turnover. For companies with a fast inventory turnover, a quick ratio can be comfortably less than one without suggesting that the company could be in cash flow trouble.

Both the current ratio and the quick ratio offer an indication of the company's liquidity position, but the absolute figures **should not be interpreted too literally**. It is often theorised that an acceptable current ratio is 1.5 and an acceptable quick ratio is 0.8, but these should only be used as a guide. Different businesses operate in very different ways. A supermarket group for example might have a current ratio of 0.52 and a quick ratio of 0.17. Supermarkets have low receivables (people do not buy groceries on credit), low cash (good cash management), medium inventories (high inventories but quick turnover, particularly in view of perishability) and very high payables.

Compare this with a manufacturing and retail organisation, with a current ratio of 1.44 and a quick ratio of 1.03. Such businesses operate with liquidity ratios closer to the standard.

What is important is the **trend** of these ratios. From this, one can easily ascertain whether liquidity is improving or deteriorating. If a supermarket has traded for the last 10 years (very successfully) with current ratios of 0.52 and quick ratios of 0.17 then it should be supposed that the company can continue in business with those levels of liquidity. If in the following year the current ratio were to fall to 0.38 and the quick ratio to 0.09, then further investigation into the liquidity situation would be appropriate. It is the relative position that is far more important than the absolute figures.

Don't forget the other side of the coin either. A current ratio and a quick ratio can get **bigger than they need to be**. A company that has large volumes of inventories and receivables might be over-investing in working capital, and so tying up more funds in the business than it needs to. This would suggest poor management of receivables (credit) or inventories by the company.

4.8 Efficiency ratios: control of receivables and inventories

A rough measure of the average length of time it takes for a company's customers to pay what they owe is the accounts receivable collection period, known as receivables days.

The estimated average receivables days is calculated as:

$$\frac{\text{Trade receivables}}{\text{Revenue}} \times 365 \text{ days}$$

The figure for sales should be taken as the sales revenue figure in the statement of profit or loss and other comprehensive income. The trade receivables figure is not the total figure for receivables in the statement

of financial position, which includes prepayments and non-trade receivables. The trade receivables figure will be itemised in an analysis of the receivable total, in a note to the accounts.

The estimate of the receivables days is **only approximate**.

(a)   The statement of financial position value of receivables might be abnormally high or low compared with the normal level the company usually has.

(b)   Revenue in the statement of profit or loss and other comprehensive income is exclusive of sales taxes, but receivables in the statement of financial position are inclusive of sales tax. We are not strictly comparing like with like.

Sales are usually made on normal credit terms of payment within 30 days. A collection period significantly in excess of this might be representative of poor management of funds of a business. However, some companies must allow generous credit terms to win customers. Exporting companies in particular may have to carry large amounts of receivables, and so their average collection period might be well in excess of 30 days. Equally, if the majority of an entity's sales are cash sales (eg for a retailer), receivables days will be very low.

The **trend of the collection period over time** is probably the best guide. If the collection period is increasing year on year, this is indicative of a poorly managed credit control function (and potentially therefore a poorly-managed company).

Examples: Receivables days

The collection period for various types of companies might be as follows.

Company	Trade receivables sales		Receivables days ($\times 365$)	Previous year		Receivables days ($\times 365$)
Supermarket	$\dfrac{\$5,016,000}{\$284,986,000}$	$=$	6.4 days	$\dfrac{\$3,977,000}{\$290,668,000}$	$=$	5.0 days
Manufacturer	$\dfrac{£458.3m}{£2,059.5m}=$	$=$	81.2 days	$\dfrac{\$272.4m}{\$1,274.2m}$	$=$	78.0 days
Sugar refiner and seller	$\dfrac{£306.4m}{£3,817m}=$	$=$	29.1 days	$\dfrac{\$287.0m}{\$3,366.3m}$	$=$	31.1 days

The differences in collection period reflect the differences between the types of business. Supermarkets have hardly any trade receivables at all, whereas the manufacturing companies have far more. The collection periods are fairly constant from the previous year for all three companies.

4.9 Inventory days

Another ratio worth calculating is the inventory turnover period or inventory days. This is another estimated figure, obtainable from published accounts, which indicates the average number of days that items of inventory are held for. As with receivables days, however, it is only an estimated figure, but one which should be reliable enough for comparing changes year on year.

LEARN

The inventory days is calculated as:

$$\frac{\text{Inventory}}{\text{Cost of sales}} \times 365 \text{ days}$$

This is another measure of how vigorously a business is trading. Increasing inventory days from one year to the next indicates:

(a)   A slowdown in trading or

(b)   A build-up in inventory levels, perhaps suggesting that the investment in inventories is becoming excessive

Generally, the **lower the inventory days the better** but several aspects of inventory-holding policy have to be balanced.

(a)   Lead times
(b)   Seasonal fluctuations in orders
(c)   Alternative uses of warehouse space
(d)   Bulk-buying discounts
(e)   Likelihood of inventory perishing or becoming obsolete

Presumably, if we add together the inventory days and receivables days this should give us an indication of how soon inventory is converted into cash. Both receivables days and inventory days therefore give us a further indication of the company's liquidity.

Example: Inventory days

The estimated inventory days for a supermarket are as follows.

Company	$\dfrac{Inventory}{Cost\ of\ sales}$	Inventory days (days × 365)	Previous year
Supermarket	$\dfrac{\$15,554,000}{\$254,571,000}$	22.3 days	$\dfrac{\$14,094,000}{\$261,368,000} \times 365 = 19.7$ days

4.10 Payables days

LEARN

Payables days is ideally calculated by the formula:

$$\frac{Trade\ accounts\ payable}{Purchases} \times 365\ days$$

It is rare to find purchases disclosed in published accounts and so **cost of sales serves as an approximation**. Payable days often help to assess a company's liquidity; an increase is often a sign of lack of long-term finance or poor management of current assets, resulting in the use of extended credit from suppliers, increased bank overdraft and so on.

Learning outcome C1

Calculate liquidity and working capital ratios from the accounts of TEB Co, a business which provides service support (cleaning etc) to customers worldwide. Comment on the results of your calculations.

	20X7 $m	20X6 $m
Revenue	2,176.2	2,344.8
Cost of sales	(1,659.0)	(1,731.5)
Gross profit	517.2	613.3
Current assets		
Inventories	42.7	78.0
Receivables (note 1)	378.9	431.4
Cash and cash equivalents	205.2	145.0
	626.8	654.4
Current liabilities		
Loans and overdrafts	32.4	81.1
Tax payable	67.8	76.7
Dividend	11.7	17.2
Payables (note 2)	487.2	467.2
	599.1	642.2
Net current assets	27.7	12.2

Notes

1	Trade receivables	295.2	335.5
2	Trade payables	190.8	188.1

The company in the exercise is a service company and hence it would be expected to have very low inventory and a very short inventory days. The similarity of receivables days and payables days means that the company is passing on most of the delay in receiving payment to its suppliers.

Learning outcome C1

(a) Calculate the operating cycle for Moribund plc for 20X2 on the basis of the following information.

		$
Inventory:	raw materials	150,000
	work in progress	60,000
	finished goods	200,000
Purchases		500,000
Trade receivables		230,000
Trade payables		120,000
Revenue		900,000
Cost of sales		750,000

Note. You will need to calculate inventory days, receivables days and payables days.

(b) List the steps which might be taken in order to improve the operating cycle.

Section summary

Make sure you understand and can define the ratios given.

5 Investor ratios   9/12

Introduction

The value of an investment in ordinary shares in a company **listed on a stock exchange** is its market value, and so investor ratios must have regard not only to information in the company's published financial statements but also to the current price. Several investor ratios involve using the share price.

5.1 Earnings per share (EPS)

It is possible to calculate the return on each ordinary share in the year. This is the earnings per share (EPS). EPS is the amount of net profit for the period that is attributable to each ordinary share which is outstanding during all or part of the period.

EPS: $\dfrac{\text{Profit available to ordinary shareholders}}{\text{Number of ordinary shares in issue}}$

Profit available to ordinary shareholders = Profit after tax and preference dividends

We looked at EPS in more detail in Chapter 17.

5.2 Dividend per share and dividend cover

The **dividend per share** in cents is self-explanatory, and clearly an item of some interest to shareholders.

Dividend cover is a ratio of: $\dfrac{\text{Earnings per share}}{\text{Dividend per (ordinary) share}}$

It shows the **proportion of profit for the year that is available for distribution to shareholders that has been paid (or proposed) and what proportion will be retained in the business to finance future growth**. A dividend cover of two times would indicate that the company had paid 50% of its distributable profits as dividends, and retained 50% in the business to help to finance future operations. Retained profits are an important source of funds for most companies, and so the dividend cover can in some cases be quite high.

A **significant change** in the dividend cover from one year to the next would be worth looking at closely. For example, if a company's dividend cover were to fall sharply between one year and the next, it could be that its profits had fallen, but the directors wished to pay at least the same amount as in the previous year, so as to keep shareholder expectations satisfied.

5.3 Price/Earnings (P/E) ratio

The **Price/Earnings (P/E) ratio** is the ratio of a company's current share price to the EPS.

A high P/E ratio indicates strong shareholder **confidence** in the company and its future eg in profit growth, and a lower P/E ratio indicates lower confidence.

The P/E ratio of one company can be compared with the P/E ratios of:

- Other companies in the same business sector
- Other companies generally

It is often used in **stock exchange reporting** where prices are readily available.

5.4 Profit retention ratio

LEARN

Profit retention ratio = Profit after dividends/Profit before dividends x 100%.

As you know, shareholders invest in companies for their ability to generate future wealth. Some shareholders seek high capital growth, while others prefer the lower-risk dividend income.

The profit retention ratio shows the portion of the profit to be reinvested into the business for future growth (rather than being paid out as dividends). Whether a high profit retention ratio is favourable, therefore, depends on which form of future wealth the shareholder prefers.

5.5 Dividend yield

Dividend yield is the return a shareholder is currently expecting on the shares of a company.

LEARN

$$\text{Dividend yield} = \frac{\text{Dividend on the share for the year}}{\text{Current market value of the share (ex - div)}} \times 100\%$$

(a)   The dividend per share is taken as the dividend for the previous year.

(b)   Ex div means that the share price does not include the right to the most recent dividend.

Shareholders look for **both dividend yield and capital growth**. Obviously, dividend yield is therefore an important aspect of a share's performance.

Question 19.4	Dividend yield

Learning outcome C1

In the year to 30 September 20X8, an advertising agency declares an interim ordinary dividend of 7.4c per share and a final ordinary dividend of 8.6c per share. Assuming an ex div share price of 315 cents, what is the dividend yield?

Question 19.5	Ratio analysis report: 1

Learning outcome C1

RST Co is considering purchasing an interest in its competitor XYZ Co. Both RST Co and XYZ Co operate in the clothes manufacturing industry. The managing director of RST Co has obtained the three most recent statements of profit or loss and statements of financial position of XYZ Co, as shown below.

XYZ CO
STATEMENTS OF PROFIT OR LOSS FOR YEARS ENDED 31 DECEMBER

	20X6 $'000	20X7 $'000	20X8 $'000
Revenue	18,000	18,900	19,845
Cost of sales	(10,440)	(10,340)	(11,890)
Gross profit	7,560	8,560	7,955
Distribution costs	(1,565)	(1,670)	(1,405)
Administrative expenses	(1,409)	(1,503)	(1,591)
Operating profit	4,586	5,387	4,959
Interest payable on bank overdraft	(104)	(215)	(450)
Interest payable on 12% debentures	(600)	(600)	(600)
Profit before taxation	3,882	4,572	3,909
Income tax	(1,380)	(2,000)	(1,838)
Profit for the year	2,502	2,572	2,071

XYZ CO
STATEMENTS OF FINANCIAL POSITION AS AT 31 DECEMBER

	20X6 $'000	20X6 $'000	20X7 $'000	20X7 $'000	20X8 $'000	20X8 $'000
Assets						
Non-current assets						
Land and buildings	11,460		12,121		11,081	
Plant and machinery	8,896		9,020		9,130	
		20,356		21,141		20,211
Current assets						
Inventory	1,775		2,663		3,995	
Trade receivables	1,440		2,260		3,164	
Cash	50		53		55	
		3,265		4,976		7,214
		23,621		26,117		27,425
Equity and liabilities						
Equity						
Share capital	8,000		8,000		8,000	
Retained earnings	6,434		7,313		7,584	
		14,434		15,313		15,584
Non-current liabilities						
12% debentures 20Y1 – 20Y4		5,000		5,000		5,000
Current liabilities						
Trade payables	1,990		2,254		2,246	
Bank	1,300		2,300		3,400	
Taxation	897		1,250		1,195	
		4,187		5,804		6,841
		23,621		26,117		27,425

XYZ Co paid dividends of $1.6m, $1.693m and $1.8m in the years ended 31 December 20X6, 20X7 and 20X8 respectively.

During 20X7, XYZ Co managed to negotiate a bulk-buying discount with its suppliers. However, in 20X8, due to XYZ regularly exceeding agreed credit terms, the suppliers withdrew the discount.

Required

Prepare a report for the managing director of RST Co commenting on the financial performance and position of XYZ Co, and highlighting any areas that require further investigation.

(Include ratios and other financial statistics where appropriate.)

| Question 19.6 | Ratio analysis report: 2 |

Learning outcome C1

GD is an entity that operates in the packaging industry across a number of different markets and activities. GD has applied to the financial institution where you are employed for a long-term loan of $150m. Your immediate supervisor was working on the report and recommendation in response to GD's request, but has fallen ill and you have been asked to complete the analysis and prepare the supporting documentation for the next management meeting to discuss applications for lending.

Extracts from the consolidated financial statements of GD are provided below:

STATEMENT OF FINANCIAL POSITION AS AT 30 JUNE

	20X8 $m	20X7 $m
Assets		
Non-current assets		
Property, plant and equipment	548	465
Goodwill	29	24
	577	489
Current assets		
Inventories	146	120
Receivables	115	125
Held for trading investments	31	18
Cash and cash equivalents	–	41
	292	304
Total assets	869	793
Equity and liabilities		
Equity attributable to owners of the parent		
Share capital ($1 shares)	120	120
Revaluation reserve	18	–
Retained earnings	293	183
	431	303
Non-controlling interests	65	61
Total equity	496	364
Non-current liabilities		
Long-term loans	90	180
Current liabilities		
Payables	185	160
Bank overdraft	50	–
Income tax payable	48	89
	283	249
Total liabilities	373	429
Total equity and liabilities	869	793

STATEMENT OF COMPREHENSIVE INCOME FOR THE YEAR ENDED 30 JUNE

	20X8 $m	20X7 $m
Revenue	1,200	1,400
Cost of sales	(840)	(930)
Gross profit	360	470
Distribution costs	(40)	(45)
Administrative expenses	(130)	(120)
Finance costs	(11)	(15)
Profit before tax	179	290
Income tax expense	(50)	(85)
Profit for the year	129	205
Other comprehensive income		
Revaluation of property	18	–
Total comprehensive income (net of tax)	147	205
Profit for the year attributable to:		
Owners of the parent	121	195
Non-controlling interests	8	10
	129	205
Total comprehensive income attributable to:		
Owners of the parent	139	195
Non-controlling interests	8	10
	147	205

Notes

1   In August 20X7 a new competitor entered one of GD's markets and pursued an aggressive strategy of increasing market share by undercutting GD's prices and prioritising volume sales. The directors had not anticipated this as GD had been the market leader in this area for the past few years.

2   The minutes from the most recent meeting of the Board of Directors state that the directors believe they can implement a new strategy to regain GD's market position in this segment, provided long-term funding can be secured. GD acquired a subsidiary during the year as part of the new strategy and revenue is forecast to increase by the second quarter of 20X9.

3   A meeting is scheduled with GD's main suppliers to discuss a reduction in costs for bulk orders.

4   The existing long-term loan is due to be repaid on 1 August 20X9.

5   Gains of $9m generated by the held for trading investments have been offset against administrative expenses.

Required

(a)   **Analyse** the financial performance and financial position of GD and recommend whether or not GD's application for borrowing should be considered further.
       Note. 8 marks are available for the calculation of relevant ratios.   **(21 marks)**

(b)   **Explain** what further information might be useful in assessing the future prospects of GD and its ability to service a new long-term loan.   **(4 marks)**

(Total = 25 marks)

Section summary

The ratios which help equity shareholders and other investors to assess the value and quality of an investment in the ordinary shares of a company are:

- EPS
- Dividend per share
- Dividend cover
- P/E ratio
- Dividend yield
- Profit retention ratio

6 The nature of profit

Introduction

We have seen throughout this text that accounting profit is an arbitrary figure, subject to the whims and biases of accountants and the variety of treatments in accounting standards. Go back to the contents page and pick out all the topics which demonstrate or indicate how company results are manipulated. Isn't it nearly all of them? Let us briefly mention some of them again.

6.1 IAS 20 *Accounting for Government Grants*

IAS 20 *Accounting for Government Grants* allows capital grants to be credited to revenue over the expected life of the asset in two ways.

(a)   By reducing the acquisition cost of the non-current asset by the amount of the grant and charging depreciation on the reduced amount

(b)   By treating the amount of the grant as a deferred credit and transferring a portion of it to revenue annually

The final profit figure is the same under both methods but the depreciation charge disclosed will be different, as will the carrying value of the asset.

6.2 IAS 2 *Inventories*

Entities are allowed to use different methods of valuing inventory under IAS 2 *Inventories*, which means that the final inventory figure in the statement of financial position will be different under each method. Profit will be affected by the closing inventory valuation, particularly where the level of inventory fluctuates to a great extent.

6.3 IAS 16 *Property, Plant and Equipment*

As with IAS 2, IAS 16 *Property, Plant and Equipment* allows different accounting bases for depreciation. Choosing to use the reducing balance method rather than the straight-line method can front-load the depreciation charge for assets. It is also the case that the subjectivity surrounding the estimated economic lives of assets can lead to manipulation of profits. (**Note**. Remember that some entities refuse to depreciate certain assets at all – mainly freehold property.)

6.4 IAS 38 *Intangible Assets*

Development costs must be capitalised under IAS 38 *Intangible Assets* if certain criteria are met, whereas all research costs should be written off. Although the criteria for capitalisation are quite strict, there is room for manipulation.

Section summary

You should note that the International Accounting Standards Board (IASB) is trying to stop abuses such as those described here by forcing entities to follow general tenets (*Conceptual Framework*) and also by restricting abusive practice.

7   Other problems with financial analysis   11/10, 3/11, 5/12

Introduction

Two frequent problems affecting financial analysis are discussed here.

- Seasonal fluctuations
- Window dressing

7.1 Seasonal fluctuations

Many entities are located in industries where trade is **seasonal**. For example:

- Firework manufacturers
- Swimwear manufacturers
- Ice cream makers
- Umbrella manufacturers

- Gas utilities
- Travel agents
- Flower suppliers and deliverers
- Football clubs

Year on year the seasonal fluctuations affecting such entities do not matter; a year end has to be chosen and as long as the fluctuations are at roughly the same time every year, then there should be no problem. Occasionally a perverse sense of humour will cause an entity to choose an accounting period ending in the middle of the busy season: this may affect the cut off because the busy season might be slightly early or late.

A **major difficulty** can arise if entities affected by seasonal fluctuations **change their accounting date**. A shorter period (normally) may encompass part, all or none of the busy season. Whatever happens, the figures will be distorted and the comparatives will be meaningless. Analysts would not know how to extrapolate the figures from the shorter period to produce a comparison for the previous year. Weightings could be used, but these are likely to be inaccurate.

CASE STUDY

Case Study

An example of the problems this can cause occurred when British Gas plc changed its accounting period to 31 December from 31 March. The entity published two sets of figures:

- For the year to 31 March 1991
- For the year to 31 December 1991

Thus including the first three months of the calendar year in both reports. As a note to the later accounts, the entity produced a statement of profit or loss and other comprehensive income for the last nine months of the calendar year.

Although the British Gas auditors did not qualify the audit report, the Review Panel was not very happy about this double counting of results. The nine-month profit and loss account did not meet the legal provisions of the Companies Act 1985 **either as to its location or its contents, nor did it contain the relevant EPS figure**. British Gas had to promise that in their 1992 results, the 1991 comparative would be for the nine-month period only.

The effect here is obvious. The first three months of the calendar year are when British Gas earns a high proportion of its profits (winter!). If the 1991 results had covered the period from 1 April only, then the profits would have been reduced by more than an average loss of three months' profit. By using a twelve-month period, British Gas avoided the risk of the period's results looking too bad.

7.2 Creative accounting

While still following IFRSs, there is scope for a company to manipulate its accounting policy to its advantage, so that the financial statements are presented in the best light.

- **Timing** of transactions may be delayed/speeded up to improve results

- **Profit smoothing** through choice of accounting policy eg inventory valuation

- **Distortion** when using **year-end figures**, particularly in seasonal industries or two entities with different year ends

- **Classification** of items eg expenses versus non-current assets

- **Off balance sheet financing** to improve gearing and ROCE eg operating leases

- **Revenue recognition policies** eg through adopting an aggressive accounting policy of early recognition

IAS 10 *Events after the reporting period* targets creative accounting policies focused around the timing of transactions and cut off. IAS 10 requires companies to disclose the reversal or maturity after the reporting date of transactions, the substance of which was primarily to alter the appearance of the statement of financial position. Note that creative accounting was not outlawed, but full disclosure would render such transactions useless.

In the exam, you should be aware of accounts and circumstances which may provide opportunities for creative accounting.

7.3 Other useful information

The information provided by the statements of financial position and profit or loss and other comprehensive income is limited. This restricts the conclusions that can be made. Useful information can be drawn from other sources as follows:

Financial

- Statement of cash flows
- Notes to the financial statements eg segment reporting
- Budgeted figures and forecasts
- Management accounts
- Industry averages
- Figures for a competitor
- Figures over a longer period eg five years

Non-financial

- Management commentary
- Market share
- Key employee information
- Sales mix
- Product range
- Pricing information
- State of order book
- Long-term plans of management

7.4 Summary of limitations of ratio analysis   11/11

Besides calculating and interpreting the ratios, you may be asked in the F2 exam to discuss the limitations of ratio analysis. Some of these limitations are summarised below.

(a)   **Information problems**

(i)   The base information is often out of date because the financial statements are filed months after the reporting date. This lack of timely information leads to problems of interpretation.

(ii)   Historic cost information may not be the most appropriate information for the decision for which the analysis is being undertaken.

(iii)   Information in published financial statements is generally summarised information and detailed information may be needed.

(iv)   Analysis of accounting information only identifies symptoms, not causes, and thus is of limited use.

(v)   Year-end figures are not representative, because they include year-end accounting adjustments.

(b)   **Comparison problems: trend analysis**

(i)   Effects of price changes make comparisons difficult unless adjustments are made.

(ii)   The impact of changes in technology on the price of assets, the likely return and the future markets make comparisons difficult.

(iii)   Impacts of a changing environment on the results are reflected in the accounting information.

(iv)   The potential effects of changes in accounting policies on the reported results may make comparisons difficult.

(v)   There may be problems associated with establishing a normal base year with which to compare other years.

(vi)   New companies do not have prior year comparatives.

(c)   **Comparison problems: across companies**

(i)   Different firms have different financial and business risk profiles and these may impact analysis.

(ii)   Different firms use different accounting policies.

(iii)   The sizes of the business and its comparators may impact on risk, structure and returns.

(iv)   Companies within the same industry may still engage in different business activities.

(v)   Related party transactions make the ratios incomparable, because these transactions may not have been at arm's length.

(vi)   The selection of industry norms, and the usefulness of those norms that are based on averages.

(d)   **Comparison problems: across industries**

(i)   Different industries are subject to different financial and business risk profiles, which may impact analysis.

(ii)   Certain industries may have industry-specific accounting policies.

(iii)   Different industries are subject to industry-specific legislation, taxation and regulations.

(e)   **Comparison problems: across countries**

(i)   The impacts of different environments on results, for example different countries or domestic versus multinational firms, may give rise to comparison problems.

(ii)   Firms operating or reporting in different countries may be subject to country-specific accounting policies (for example, US GAAP vs IFRS).

(iii)   Firms operating in different countries are subject to different legislations, taxation and regulations.

(iv)   The performance of firms operating in different countries is affected by different economies and currencies, giving rise to different business risks and financing structures.

You should use this summary as a type of checklist.

Section summary

Financial analysis is a vital tool for **many users of the financial statements**, especially investors.

Financial analysis is not a precise science. The nature of accounting information means that distortions and differences will always exist between sets of accounts not only from entity to entity but also over time.

Always remember that **profit** and **net assets** are fairly **arbitrary figures**, affected by different accounting policies and manipulation.

Seasonal fluctuations and window dressing arise quite often in practice. You must be on your guard to spot them.

Chapter Summary

Financial analysis

Types of analysis

Ratios

Problems with analysis

Sources of information:
- Published financial statements/interim FS
- Documents filed under company legislation
- Government statistics
- Other media

Types of analysis:
- Inter-temporal analysis
- Cross-sectional analysis

Profitability and return
- ROCE
- ROE
- Operating profit margin, asset turnover
- Gross profit margin, operating profit margin, net profit margin

Long-term solvency and stability
- Gearing
- Interest cover

Short-term solvency and liquidity
- Current ratio
- Quick ratio

Efficiency
- Receivable, inventory and payable days

Investor ratios
- EPS
- Dividend cover
- P/E ratio
- Profit retention ratio
- Dividend yield

- Different accounting treatments permitted by accounting standards:
  - Government grants
  - Inventories
  - Property, plant and equipment
  - Intangible assets
- Seasonal fluctions
- Creative accounting

Information problems
- Lack of timely information
- Lack of sufficiently detailed information in the financial statements

Trend analysis problems
- Effects of price changes
- Impacts of external factors (technology, economic environment)
- Effects of changes in accounting policies
- Difficulty in establish a benchmark

Problems re comparisons across companies
- Different risk profiles
- Different accounting policies
- Different business activities
- Distortions caused by related party transactions
- Effect of different environments where companies operate in different countries
- Effect of different legislations, taxations and regulations
- Different financing structures and business risks

Quick Quiz

1   What are the main sources of financial information available to external users?

2   What is the efficient market hypothesis?

3   Apart from ratio analysis, what other information might be helpful in interpreting a company's accounts?

4   In a period when profits are fluctuating, what effect does a company's level of gearing have on the profits available for ordinary shareholders?

5   Name some accounting standards which allow a choice of accounting policies.

6   The acid test or quick ratio should include:

A	Inventory of finished goods	C	Long-term loans
B	Raw materials and consumables	D	Trade receivables

7   The asset turnover of Taplow Co is 110% that of Stoke Co.

The ROCE of Taplow Co is 80% that of Stoke Co.

Calculate Taplow Co's operating profit margin expressed as a percentage of Stoke Co's.

8   Deal Co has the following capital structure:

	$'000
$1 ordinary shares	55,000
Retained earnings	12,000
	67,000
6% $1 cumulative redeemable preference shares	15,000
8% loan notes	30,000
	112,000

What is the most appropriate measure of the debt/equity ratio for a potential equity investor?

Answers to Quick Quiz

1   Published interim financial statements, filed documents, government statistics

2   See Section 1.5

3
- Other comments in the accounts eg Directors' Report
- Age and nature of the assets
- Current and future market developments
- Recent acquisition or disposal of subsidiaries
- Notes to the accounts, auditors' report, post-reporting date events etc

4   Profits available for the shareholders will be highly volatile and some years there may not be an ordinary dividend paid.

5   IASs 2, 16, 20 and 38

6   D   Acid test ratio $= \dfrac{CA - \text{Inventory}}{CL}$

7     $\dfrac{80}{110} = 73\%$

8   Debt $=$ $15 + 30 = 45$
       Equity $=$ $55 + 12 = 67$
       $\therefore 45/67 \times 100 = 67.2\%$

Answers to Questions

19.1   Interest cover

Interest payments should be taken gross from the note to the accounts, and not net of interest receipts as shown in the statement of profit or loss and other comprehensive income.

	20X8	20X7
PBIT	360,245	247,011
Interest payable	18,115	21,909
	= 20 times	= 11 times

Furlong has more than sufficient interest cover. In view of the company's low gearing, this is not too surprising.

19.2 Liquidity and working capital

	20X7	20X6
Current ratio	$\frac{626.8}{599.1} = 1.05$	$\frac{654.4}{642.2} = 1.02$
Quick ratio	$\frac{584.1}{599.1} = 0.97$	$\frac{576.4}{642.2} = 0.90$
Receivables days	$\frac{295.2}{2,176.2} \times 365 = 49.5$ days	$\frac{335.5}{2,344.8} \times 365 = 52.2$ days
Inventory days	$\frac{42.7}{1,659.0} \times 365 = 9.4$ days	$\frac{78.0}{1,731.5} \times 365 = 16.4$ days
Payables days	$\frac{190.8}{1,659.0} \times 365 = 42.0$ days	$\frac{188.1}{1,731.5} \times 365 = 39.7$ days

Both the current and quick ratios have improved year on year. This is because TEB is collecting its debts more quickly from its customers (evidenced by a decrease in receivables days from 52.2 days to 49.5 days) and selling its inventory more quickly (evidenced by a decrease in inventory days from 16.4 days to 9.4 days). Paying its suppliers more slowly (taking an average of 42 days as opposed to 40 days in the prior year) has also improved short-term liquidity. However, payables are being paid more quickly than money is collected from customers which is not a good strategy from a cash flow perspective.

The reason for inventory days being so low is because TEB is a services company and therefore holds very low levels of inventories.

19.3 Operating cycle

(a)   The operating cycle can be found as follows.

Inventory days: $\dfrac{\text{Total closing inventory}}{\text{Cost of goods sold}} \times 365$

plus

Receivables days: $\dfrac{\text{Closing trade receivables}}{\text{Sales}}$

less

Payables days: $\dfrac{\text{Closing trade payables}}{\text{Purchases}} \times 365$

	20X2
Total closing inventory ($)	410,000
Cost of goods sold ($)	750,000
Inventory days (410,000/750,000 × 365)	199.5 days
Closing receivables ($)	230,000
Sales ($)	900,000
Receivables days (230,000/900,000 × 365)	93.3 days
Closing payables ($)	120,000
Purchases ($)	500,000
Payables days (120,000/500,000 × 365)	(87.6 days)
Length of operating cycle (199.5 + 93.3 – 87.6)	205.2 days

(b)   The steps that could be taken to reduce the operating cycle include the following.

   (i)   Reducing the raw material inventory days by using inventory more quickly in the production process.

   (ii)   Reducing the time taken to produce goods. However, the company must ensure that quality is not sacrificed as a result of speeding up the production process.

   (iii) Increasing the period of credit taken from suppliers. The credit period already seems very long – if the company is allowed three months' credit by its suppliers, this could probably not be increased. If the credit period is extended then the company may lose discounts for prompt payment.

   (iv)   Reducing the finished goods inventory days by holding lower levels of finished goods.

   (v)   Reducing the receivables days. The administrative costs of speeding up debt collection and the effect on sales of reducing the credit period allowed must be evaluated. However, the credit period does already seem very long by the standards of most industries. It may be that generous terms have been allowed to secure large contracts and little will be able to be done about this in the short term.

19.4 Dividend yield

The total dividend per share is (7.4 + 8.6) = 16 cents

$$\text{Dividend yield} = \frac{16}{315} \times 100 = 5.1\%$$

19.5 Ratio analysis report: 1

REPORT

To: MD of RST Co
From: An Accountant   Date:
Subject: Financial performance and position of XYZ Co

Introduction

This report analyses the financial performance and position of a key competitor, XYZ Co, as a potential acquisition target.

Financial performance

Revenue has increased at a steady 5% per annum over the three-year period, showing a healthy growth.

In contrast, the gross profit margin has increased from 42% in 20X6 to 45% in 20X7 before dropping back to 40% in 20X8. The improvement in gross margin in 20X7 appears to be due to cheaper purchasing prices of raw materials from suppliers as a result of the negotiation of a new bulk discount. However, due to consistently exceeding credit terms, this bulk discount was lost in 20X8 which would have resulted in a return to the original higher purchasing price and partly explains the fall in gross margin. The fall in 20X8 below the 20X6 level suggests that there might also have been some manufacturing inefficiencies.

Similarly, the operating profit margin followed a similar trend moving from 26% in 20X6 to 29% in 20X7 and 25% in 20X8. Operating margin did not improve as much as the gross margin in 20X7, suggesting some cost inefficiencies. However, this trend was reversed in 20X8 where operating margin did not fall as much as gross margin and, in fact, distribution costs fell by almost 16% showing improved cost control in this area.

Growing interest on an increasing overdraft has had an adverse impact on net profit. Relying on an overdraft as a long-term source of finance is both expensive and risky as the bank could withdraw the facility at any time. Investment by RST Co would help with the long-term financing of XYZ Co and potentially allow the overdraft to be repaid. However, XYZ Co would need to improve their working capital management (see below) to avoid returning to an overdraft.

Return on capital employed (ROCE), as one would expect, has shown a similar pattern with an increase in 20X7 and a subsequent fall in 20X8 to a level below that of 20X6. The overdraft has been treated as debt when calculating ROCE as XYZ Co appears to be using the overdraft as a long-term source of finance given that the overdraft balance is significant and increasing year on year.

Financial position

Solvency

Gearing has increased year on year (20X6: 43.6%; 20X7: 47.7%; 20X8: 53.9%). The overdraft has been included as debt because XYZ Co seems to be using it as a source of long-term finance. The reason for the increase in gearing is the growing overdraft rather than the debentures, which have remained stable. Refinancing will be necessary to replace the overdraft with long-term finance. Also the debentures will need repaying in the next three to five years. As the overall gearing level is not excessive, XYZ Co may be able to raise further debt. If RST Co were to invest in debt or equity, it would help the long-term funding of XYZ Co.

Liquidity

At first glance it appears that XYZ Co's liquidity situation has improved over the period as the current ratio has increased from 0.78 in 20X6 to 0.86 in 20X7 and 1.05 in 20X8. However, the current ratio measures a company's ability to meet its current liabilities out of current assets. In most industries, a ratio of at least one would be ideal but XYZ Co did not meet this expectation in 20X6 and 20X7. Furthermore, this ratio is misleading as the largest asset in the form of inventory is the least liquid asset. This is especially the case for XYZ Co, a clothes manufacturer, as fashions change rapidly and inventory can easily become obsolete.

Therefore, the quick ratio which excludes inventory should be considered. XYZ Co's quick ratio, although improving, is low and this shows that current liabilities cannot be met from current assets if inventory is excluded. The only reason that the quick ratio has improved is because the overdraft has increased at a faster rate than inventory. As a major part of current liabilities is the bank overdraft, the company is obviously relying on the overdraft as a long-term source of finance. It would be useful to find out the terms of the bank funding and the projected cash flow requirements for future funding.

Working capital management

Inventory days have increased year on year (62 days in 20X6, 94 days in 20X7 and 123 days in 20X8). The increase in 20X7 can partly be explained by bulk buying to take advantage of the discount negotiated with suppliers. However, as the discount was lost in 20X8, this does not explain the further increase in 20X8. Given that XYZ Co operates in the fast-moving fashion industry, there is a high risk of inventory obsolescence.

As can be seen from the appendix, the receivables days have increased over the three years from 29 days to 58 days. This appears to be an indication of poor credit control or perhaps XYZ Co has given increased credit terms to some or all of its customers.

The increase in payable days from 70 days in 20X6 to 80 days in 20X7 has led to the suppliers withdrawing their bulk discount. This in turn has had an adverse effect on profitability. Payable days did fall again in 20X8 back down to 69 days so it is possible that XYZ Co may be able to renegotiate the discount again in the future. While taking advantage of free credit from suppliers helps improve liquidity, XYZ Co need to be careful not to exceed the credit terms too much as there is a risk of withdrawal of credit or even supplies.

Conclusion

XYZ Co is growing steadily and is profitable, although profitability has been fluctuating. If working capital management could be improved, on initial analysis, it appears that it is worth considering the possibility of investing in XYZ Co further.

Signed:

Management Accountant

APPENDIX TO REPORT

	20X6	20X7	20X8
% sales increase		5%	5%
Gross profit margin			
$= \dfrac{\text{Gross profit}}{\text{Revenue}}$	$\dfrac{7,560}{18,000}$	$\dfrac{8,560}{18,900}$	$\dfrac{7,955}{19,845}$
	= 42%	= 45%	= 40%
Operating profit margin			
$= \dfrac{\text{Profit before interest and tax}}{\text{Revenue}}$	$\dfrac{4,586}{18,000}$	$\dfrac{5,387}{18,900}$	$\dfrac{4,959}{19,845}$
	= 25.5%	= 28.5%	= 25%
ROCE			
$= \dfrac{\text{Profit before interest and tax}}{\text{Capital employed}}$	$\dfrac{4,586}{14,434+6,300}$	$\dfrac{5,387}{15,313+7,300}$	$\dfrac{4,959}{15,584+8,400}$
$\times 100\%$	= 22.1%	= 23.8%	= 20.7%
Gearing ratio			
$= \dfrac{\text{Debt}}{\text{Equity}} \times 100\%$	$\dfrac{5,000+1,300}{14,434}$	$\dfrac{5,000+2,300}{15,313}$	$\dfrac{5,000+3,400}{15,584}$
	= 43.6%	= 47.7%	= 53.9%
Current ratio			
$= \dfrac{\text{Current assets}}{\text{Current liabilities}}$	$\dfrac{3,265}{4,187}$	$\dfrac{4,976}{5,804}$	$\dfrac{7,214}{6,841}$
	= 0.78	= 0.86	= 1.05
Quick ratio			
$= \dfrac{\text{Current assets} - \text{inventory}}{\text{Current liabilities}}$	$\dfrac{3,265-1,775}{4,187}$	$\dfrac{4,976-2,663}{5,804}$	$\dfrac{7,214-3,995}{6,841}$
	= 0.36	= 0.40	= 0.47
Receivables days			
$= \dfrac{\text{Trade receivables}}{\text{Revenue}} \times 365 \text{ days}$	$\dfrac{1,440}{18,000}$	$\dfrac{2,260}{18,900}$	$\dfrac{3,164}{19,845}$
	= 29 days	= 44 days	= 58 days
Inventory days			
$= \dfrac{\text{Inventory}}{\text{Cost of sales}} \times 365 \text{ days}$	$\dfrac{1,775}{10,440}$	$\dfrac{2,663}{10,340}$	$\dfrac{3,995}{11,890}$
	= 62 days	= 94 days	= 123 days
Payable days			
$= \dfrac{\text{Trade payables}}{\text{Cost of sales}} \times 365 \text{ days}$	$\dfrac{1,990}{10,440}$	$\dfrac{2,254}{10,340}$	$\dfrac{2,246}{11,890}$
	= 70 days	= 80 days	= 69 days

19.6 Ratio analysis report: 2

(a) Analysis

Financial performance

Revenue trend

The new competitor in one of GD's markets appears to have stolen market share from GD with its aggressive pricing strategy. This has resulted in a year on year reduction in revenue of 14%.

Even the acquisition of a new subsidiary during the year has not been enough to counteract this effect. If it was acquired towards the end of the year, the full impact of the acquisition may not yet have been seen and the subsidiary may contribute more to group revenue in future years.

Profitability

GD's gross profit margin has **deteriorated**, so as well as a decline in volume, there has been a decline in the profitability.

This could be due to increases in the purchase prices of inventories, and profitability may improve in future if GD is successful in its negotiations over bulk-buying discounts with its suppliers. Although this may improve the gross margin, there is a risk that carrying excessive levels of inventory could place further stress on GD's cashflow and incur increased holding costs.

The **operating margin has also decreased** mainly due to an 8% increase in administration costs (a 15% increase if the gains on held for trading investments are ignored) despite the 14% decline in sales.

This may indicate that GD is not controlling costs effectively, but part of the increase may be due to higher depreciation charges as a result of the revaluation during the year.

Financial position

Liquidity

GD's liquidity has deteriorated during the year, as illustrated by the current ratio falling from 1.22 to 1.03 and the quick ratio falling from 0.74 to 0.52.

GD's cash position has deteriorated, going from a cash balance of $41m in 20X7 to an overdraft of $50m in 20X8. An overdraft is an expensive and risky form of finance as it can be recalled at any time.

The reasons for the decline in liquidity are:

- Purchases of property, plant and equipment during the year
- Acquisition of a subsidiary during the year
- Repayment of long-term loans
- Poor working capital management (see below)

Working capital management

There has been a **significant increase in inventory days** (from 47 to 63) which is tying up cash. This may be a result of GD selling lower volumes as a result of the competition in one of its markets. This could mean that they are holding unsaleable inventories, although this is unlikely to be a major risk with non-perishable packaging products.

Part of GD's new strategy is to negotiate a discount for bulk buying, but this could result in even longer holding periods with the related adverse effect on liquidity.

GD appears to **have reasonably efficient credit control** procedures as there is only a slight increase in receivables days from 33 to 35.

However, there has been a worrying increase in the time taken to settle payables. Payables days have increased from 63 to 80 days. Along with the overdraft, this suggests that GD **is struggling to pay its liabilities as they fall due**. This may put the company at a disadvantage in its negotiations for discounts from these suppliers, and could result in the suppliers withdrawing credit or even refusing to supply GD.

GD also appears to be **trading in investments**. This has generated some gains in the current year but is a risky activity, and in the company's current situation the $31m could be more effectively applied to the overdue payables or to reducing the overdraft.

Solvency

The low levels of the gearing ratio and the substantial margin of safety shown by the interest cover ratio (17.2 in 20X8 and 20.3 in 20X7) would appear to indicate that GD can easily afford to pay its interest as it falls due.

However, this does not allow us to conclude that GD's solvency is not at risk. As at the date of its last statement of financial position, if the overdraft were to be called in and suppliers to demand payment of all overdue balances, it looks as if GD would not be in a position to pay this.

Recommendation

The financial institution should have **serious reservations** about granting GD a loan because:

(i)   The company has been losing market share to the new competitor.

(ii)   There has been a decline in profit margins.

(iii)   GD's poor working capital management has led to deteriorating liquidity.

(iv)   It appears that the loan of $150m would have to be applied to clearing the overdraft, paying the existing loan due for repayment in 20X9 and paying overdue trade payables accounts, rather than in investing in new assets or further acquisitions that would improve the company's future trading prospects.

Lending to GD **should not be ruled out entirely** because:

(i)   GD is still profitable.

(ii)   GD has low gearing and can easily afford to pay increased amounts of interest.

(iii)   GD has significant assets to offer as security for loans.

(iv)   GD has a new subsidiary that may well contribute increasing revenue and profits in future.

<u>Ratios</u>

Note. Only 8 ratios would be required to achieve 8 marks. Any 8 from the following would be relevant to the analysis in this question.

			20X8		20X7
ROCE =	$\dfrac{\text{PBIT}}{\text{Equity} + \text{Debt}}$	=	$\dfrac{179+11}{496+90}$	=	$\dfrac{290+15}{364+180}$
		=	32.4%	=	56%
Gross Margin =	$\dfrac{\text{Gross Profit}}{\text{Revenue}}$	=	$\dfrac{360}{1,200}$	=	$\dfrac{470}{1,400}$
		=	30%	=	33.6%
Operating Margin =	$\dfrac{\text{PBIT}}{\text{Revenue}}$	=	$\dfrac{179+11}{1,200}$	=	$\dfrac{290+15}{1,400}$
		=	15.8%	=	21.8%
Current Ratio =	$\dfrac{\text{CA}}{\text{CL}}$ =	=	$\dfrac{292}{283}$	=	$\dfrac{304}{249}$
		=	1.03	=	1.22
Quick Ratio =	$\dfrac{\text{CA} - \text{Inventories}}{\text{CL}}$	=	$\dfrac{292-146}{283}$	=	$\dfrac{304-120}{249}$
		=	0.52	=	0.74
Inventory Days =	$\dfrac{\text{Inventory}}{\text{Cost of sales}} \times 365$ =		$\dfrac{146}{840} \times 365$	=	$\dfrac{120}{930} \times 365$
		=	63 Days	=	47 Days
Receivables Days =	$\dfrac{\text{Receivables}}{\text{Revenue}} \times 365$	=	$\dfrac{115}{1,200} \times 365$	=	$\dfrac{125}{1,400} \times 365$

| | | | = | 35 Days | = | 33 Days |

Payables Days $= \dfrac{\text{Payables}}{\text{Cost of sales}} \times 365 = \dfrac{185}{840} \times 365 = \dfrac{160}{930} \times 365$

| | | | = | 80 Days | = | 63 Days |

Gearing $= \dfrac{\text{Debt}}{\text{Equity}} \times 100\% = \dfrac{90}{496} = \dfrac{180}{364}$

| | | | = | 18% | = | 49% |

Interest cover $= \dfrac{\text{PBIT}}{\text{Interest}} = \dfrac{179+11}{11} = \dfrac{290+15}{15}$

| | | | = | 17.2 times | = | 20.3 times |

(b) **Further information required**

Note. Four points would be sufficient here. Our answer shows a wider range of points that would be relevant.

(i) Details about when the new subsidiary was acquired and forecasts of how much revenue and profit it is likely to contribute to the group in future years

(ii) Details of any security over the existing loans and which assets are involved

(iii) The limit of the overdraft facility and when it is due for renegotiation

(iv) A consolidated statement of cash flows for the year

(v) Profit and loss and cash flow forecasts indicating how GD intends to repay the loan due in August 20X9

(vi) Segmental information allowing analysis of trends in GD's different markets and activities

(vii) More details of the directors' new strategy to assess the reasonableness of any estimates and assumptions

---

Now try these questions from the Practice Question Bank

Number	Level	Marks	Time
Q36	Introductory	N/A	9 mins
Q37	Introductory	25	45 mins

MATHEMATICAL TABLES & EXAM FORMULAE

NOTE: At the time of printing the final Mathematical Tables and Formulae sheet had not been confirmed by CIMA. Please check the CIMA website for the latest information on what information will be provided in the exams.

Present value table

Present value of £1 = $(1+r)^{-n}$ where r = interest rate, n = number of periods until payment or receipt.

Periods (n)	1%	2%	3%	4%	5%	6%	7%	8%	9%	10%
1	0.990	0.980	0.971	0.962	0.952	0.943	0.935	0.926	0.917	0.909
2	0.980	0.961	0.943	0.925	0.907	0.890	0.873	0.857	0.842	0.826
3	0.971	0.942	0.915	0.889	0.864	0.840	0.816	0.794	0.772	0.751
4	0.961	0.924	0.888	0.855	0.823	0.792	0.763	0.735	0.708	0.683
5	0.951	0.906	0.863	0.822	0.784	0.747	0.713	0.681	0.650	0.621
6	0.942	0.888	0.837	0.790	0.746	0.705	0.666	0.630	0.596	0.564
7	0.933	0.871	0.813	0.760	0.711	0.665	0.623	0.583	0.547	0.513
8	0.923	0.853	0.789	0.731	0.677	0.627	0.582	0.540	0.502	0.467
9	0.914	0.837	0.766	0.703	0.645	0.592	0.544	0.500	0.460	0.424
10	0.905	0.820	0.744	0.676	0.614	0.558	0.508	0.463	0.422	0.386
11	0.896	0.804	0.722	0.650	0.585	0.527	0.475	0.429	0.388	0.350
12	0.887	0.788	0.701	0.625	0.557	0.497	0.444	0.397	0.356	0.319
13	0.879	0.773	0.681	0.601	0.530	0.469	0.415	0.368	0.326	0.290
14	0.870	0.758	0.661	0.577	0.505	0.442	0.388	0.340	0.299	0.263
15	0.861	0.743	0.642	0.555	0.481	0.417	0.362	0.315	0.275	0.239
16	0.853	0.728	0.623	0.534	0.458	0.394	0.339	0.292	0.252	0.218
17	0.844	0.714	0.605	0.513	0.436	0.371	0.317	0.270	0.231	0.198
18	0.836	0.700	0.587	0.494	0.416	0.350	0.296	0.250	0.212	0.180
19	0.828	0.686	0.570	0.475	0.396	0.331	0.277	0.232	0.194	0.164
20	0.820	0.673	0.554	0.456	0.377	0.312	0.258	0.215	0.178	0.149

Periods (n)	11%	12%	13%	14%	15%	16%	17%	18%	19%	20%
1	0.901	0.893	0.885	0.877	0.870	0.862	0.855	0.847	0.840	0.833
2	0.812	0.797	0.783	0.769	0.756	0.743	0.731	0.718	0.706	0.694
3	0.731	0.712	0.693	0.675	0.658	0.641	0.624	0.609	0.593	0.579
4	0.659	0.636	0.613	0.592	0.572	0.552	0.534	0.516	0.499	0.482
5	0.593	0.567	0.543	0.519	0.497	0.476	0.456	0.437	0.419	0.402
6	0.535	0.507	0.480	0.456	0.432	0.410	0.390	0.370	0.352	0.335
7	0.482	0.452	0.425	0.400	0.376	0.354	0.333	0.314	0.296	0.279
8	0.434	0.404	0.376	0.351	0.327	0.305	0.285	0.266	0.249	0.233
9	0.391	0.361	0.333	0.308	0.284	0.263	0.243	0.225	0.209	0.194
10	0.352	0.322	0.295	0.270	0.247	0.227	0.208	0.191	0.176	0.162
11	0.317	0.287	0.261	0.237	0.215	0.195	0.178	0.162	0.148	0.135
12	0.286	0.257	0.231	0.208	0.187	0.168	0.152	0.137	0.124	0.112
13	0.258	0.229	0.204	0.182	0.163	0.145	0.130	0.116	0.104	0.093
14	0.232	0.205	0.181	0.160	0.141	0.125	0.111	0.099	0.088	0.078
15	0.209	0.183	0.160	0.140	0.123	0.108	0.095	0.084	0.074	0.065
16	0.188	0.163	0.141	0.123	0.107	0.093	0.081	0.071	0.062	0.054
17	0.170	0.146	0.125	0.108	0.093	0.080	0.069	0.060	0.052	0.045
18	0.153	0.130	0.111	0.095	0.081	0.069	0.059	0.051	0.044	0.038
19	0.138	0.116	0.098	0.083	0.070	0.060	0.051	0.043	0.037	0.031
20	0.124	0.104	0.087	0.073	0.061	0.051	0.043	0.037	0.031	0.026

Cumulative present value table

This table shows the present value of £1 per annum, receivable or payable at the end of each year for *n* years.

Periods (n)	Discount rates (r)									
	1%	2%	3%	4%	5%	6%	7%	8%	9%	10%
1	0.990	0.980	0.971	0.962	0.952	0.943	0.935	0.926	0.917	0.909
2	1.970	1.942	1.913	1.886	1.859	1.833	1.808	1.783	1.759	1.736
3	2.941	2.884	2.829	2.775	2.723	2.673	2.624	2.577	2.531	2.487
4	3.902	3.808	3.717	3.630	3.546	3.465	3.387	3.312	3.240	3.170
5	4.853	4.713	4.580	4.452	4.329	4.212	4.100	3.993	3.890	3.791
6	5.795	5.601	5.417	5.242	5.076	4.917	4.767	4.623	4.486	4.355
7	6.728	6.472	6.230	6.002	5.786	5.582	5.389	5.206	5.033	4.868
8	7.652	7.325	7.020	6.733	6.463	6.210	5.971	5.747	5.535	5.335
9	8.566	8.162	7.786	7.435	7.108	6.802	6.515	6.247	5.995	5.759
10	9.471	8.983	8.530	8.111	7.722	7.360	7.024	6.710	6.418	6.145
11	10.37	9.787	9.253	8.760	8.306	7.887	7.499	7.139	6.805	6.495
12	11.26	10.58	9.954	9.385	8.863	8.384	7.943	7.536	7.161	6.814
13	12.13	11.35	10.63	9.986	9.394	8.853	8.358	7.904	7.487	7.103
14	13.00	12.11	11.30	10.56	9.899	9.295	8.745	8.244	7.786	7.367
15	13.87	12.85	11.94	11.12	10.38	9.712	9.108	8.559	8.061	7.606
16	14.718	13.578	12.561	11.652	10.838	10.106	9.447	8.851	8.313	7.824
17	15.562	14.292	13.166	12.166	11.274	10.477	9.763	9.122	8.544	8.022
18	16.398	14.992	13.754	12.659	11.690	10.828	10.059	9.372	8.756	8.201
19	17.226	15.678	14.324	13.134	12.085	11.158	10.336	9.604	8.950	8.365
20	18.046	16.351	14.877	13.590	12.462	11.470	10.594	9.818	9.129	8.514

Periods (n)	Discount rates (r)									
	11%	12%	13%	14%	15%	16%	17%	18%	19%	20%
1	0.901	0.893	0.885	0.877	0.870	0.862	0.855	0.847	0.840	0.833
2	1.713	1.690	1.668	1.647	1.626	1.605	1.585	1.566	1.547	1.528
3	2.444	2.402	2.361	2.322	2.283	2.246	2.210	2.174	2.140	2.106
4	3.102	3.037	2.974	2.914	2.855	2.798	2.743	2.690	2.639	2.589
5	3.696	3.605	3.517	3.433	3.352	3.274	3.199	3.127	3.058	2.991
6	4.231	4.111	3.998	3.889	3.784	3.685	3.589	3.498	3.410	3.326
7	4.712	4.564	4.423	4.288	4.160	4.039	3.922	3.812	3.706	3.605
8	5.146	4.968	4.799	4.639	4.487	4.344	4.207	4.078	3.954	3.837
9	5.537	5.328	5.132	4.946	4.772	4.607	4.451	4.303	4.163	4.031
10	5.889	5.650	5.426	5.216	5.019	4.833	4.659	4.494	4.339	4.192
11	6.207	5.938	5.687	5.453	5.234	5.029	4.836	4.656	4.486	4.327
12	6.492	6.194	5.918	5.660	5.421	5.197	4.988	4.793	4.611	4.439
13	6.750	6.424	6.122	5.842	5.583	5.342	5.118	4.910	4.715	4.533
14	6.982	6.628	6.302	6.002	5.724	5.468	5.229	5.008	4.802	4.611
15	7.191	6.811	6.462	6.142	5.847	5.575	5.324	5.092	4.876	4.675
16	7.379	6.974	6.604	6.265	5.954	5.668	5.405	5.162	4.938	4.730
17	7.549	7.120	6.729	6.373	6.047	5.749	5.475	5.222	4.990	4.775
18	7.702	7.250	6.840	6.467	6.128	5.818	5.534	5.273	5.033	4.812
19	7.839	7.366	6.938	6.550	6.198	5.877	5.584	5.316	5.070	4.843
20	7.963	7.469	7.025	6.623	6.259	5.929	5.628	5.353	5.101	4.870

Formulae

Annuity

Present value of an annuity of $1 per annum receivable or payable for n years, commencing in one year, discounted at r% per annum:

$$PV = \frac{1}{r}\left[1 - \frac{1}{[1+r]^n}\right]$$

Perpetuity

Present value of $1 per annum receivable or payable in perpetuity, commencing in one year, discounted at r% per annum:

$$PV = \frac{1}{r}$$

Growing perpetuity

Present value of $1 per annum, receivable or payable, commencing in one year, growing in perpetuity at a constant rate of g% per annum, discounted at r% per annum:

$$PV = \frac{1}{r-g}$$

Dividend growth model

Cost of ordinary (equity) share capital, having a current ex div price, P0, having just paid a dividend, d0, with the dividend growing in perpetuity by a constant g% per annum:

$$k_e = \frac{d_1}{P_0} + g$$

Gordon's growth approximation: $g = br$

Weighted average cost of capital

Weighted average cost of capital, given cost of equity of k_e, cost of debt of k_d, market value of equity in the firm of V_e, market value of debt in the firm of V_d and a rate of company tax of T.

$$WACC = \left[\frac{V_e}{V_e + V_d}\right]k_e + \left[\frac{V_d}{V_e + V_d}\right]k_d(1-T)$$

PRACTICE QUESTION AND ANSWER BANK

What the examiner means

The very important table below has been prepared by CIMA to help you interpret exam questions.

Learning objectives	Verbs used	Definition
1 Knowledge What are you expected to know	• List • State • Define	• Make a list of • Express, fully or clearly, the details of/facts of • Give the exact meaning of
2 Comprehension What you are expected to understand	• Describe • Distinguish • Explain • Identify • Illustrate	• Communicate the key features of • Highlight the differences between • Make clear or intelligible/state the meaning of • Recognise, establish or select after consideration • Use an example to describe or explain something
3 Application How you are expected to apply your knowledge	• Apply • Calculate/ compute • Demonstrate • Prepare • Reconcile • Solve • Tabulate	• Put to practical use • Ascertain or reckon mathematically • Prove with certainty or to exhibit by practical means • Make or get ready for use • Make or prove consistent/compatible • Find an answer to • Arrange in a table
4 Analysis How you are expected to analyse the detail of what you have learned	• Analyse • Categorise • Compare and contrast • Construct • Discuss • Interpret • Prioritise • Produce	• Examine in detail the structure of • Place into a defined class or division • Show the similarities and/or differences between • Build up or compile • Examine in detail by argument • Translate into intelligible or familiar terms • Place in order of priority or sequence for action • Create or bring into existence
5 Evaluation How you are expected to use your learning to evaluate, make decisions or recommendations	• Advise • Evaluate • Recommend	• Counsel, inform or notify • Appraise or assess the value of • Propose a course of action

Guidance in our Practice and Revision Kit focuses on how the verbs are used in questions.

1 Objective test questions: sources of long-term finance

14 mins

1.1 Which of the following is not a benefit, to the borrower, of an overdraft as opposed to a short-term loan?

    A   Flexible repayment schedule
    B   Only charged for the amount drawn down
    C   Easy to arrange
    D   Lower interest rates

1.2 According to the creditor hierarchy, list the following from high risk to low risk:

    1   Ordinary share capital
    2   Preference share capital
    3   Trade payables
    4   Bank loan with fixed and floating charges

    A   1,2,3,4
    B   1,3,2,4
    C   4,3,2,1
    D   4,2,3,1

1.3 Which one of the following is issued at a discount to its redemption value and pays its holder no interest during its life?

    A   A deep discount bond
    B   A gilt-edged security
    C   An unsecured loan note
    D   A zero coupon bond

1.4 Which of the following is NOT a function that financial intermediaries fulfil for customers and borrowers?

    A   Maturity transformation
    B   Fund aggregation
    C   Dividend creation
    D   Pooling of losses

1.5 Which of the following are money market instruments?

    1   Certificate of deposit
    2   Corporate bond
    3   Commercial paper
    4   Treasury bill

    A   1, 2 and 4 only
    B   1 and 3 only
    C   1, 3 and 4 only
    D   1, 2, 3 and 4

1.6   Which of the following statements about obtaining a full stock market listing is NOT correct?

A   Compliance costs are likely to increase, but better public profile and access to funds benefit the business.

B   All else being equal the value of the business is likely to be unaffected.

C   It allows owners to realise their investment.

D   It increases the liquidity of the shares for shareholders.

1.7   Rank the following from highest risk to lowest risk from the investor's perspective.

1   Preference share
2   Treasury bill
3   Corporate bond
4   Ordinary share

A   1, 4, 3, 2
B   1, 4, 2, 3
C   4, 2, 1, 3
D   4, 1, 3, 2

1.8   Which one of the following statements is incorrect?

A   Money markets are markets for long-term capital

B   Money markets are operated by banks and other financial institutions

C   Money market instruments include interest-bearing instruments, discount instruments and derivatives

D   Money market instruments are traded over the counter between institutional investors

2 Panda   27 mins

Panda is a large fashion retailer that opened stores in South East Asia three years ago. This has proved to be less successful than expected and so the directors of the company have decided to withdraw from the overseas market and to concentrate on the home market. To raise the finance necessary to close the overseas stores, the directors have also decided to make a one-for-five rights issue at a discount of 30% on the current market value. The most recent statement of profit or loss of the business is as follows.

STATEMENT OF PROFIT OR LOSS FOR THE YEAR ENDED 31 MAY 20X4

	$m
Sales	1,400.00
Net profit before interest and taxation	52.0
Interest payable	24.0
Net profit before taxation	28.0
Company tax	7.0
Net profit after taxation	21.0

Dividends paid are $14 million.

The capital and reserves of the business as at 31 May 20X4 are as follows.

	$m
$0.25 ordinary shares	60.0
Accumulated profits	320.0
	380.0

The shares of the business are currently traded on the Stock Exchange at a P/E ratio of 16 times. An investor owning 10,000 ordinary shares in the business has received information of the forthcoming rights issue but cannot decide whether to take up the rights issue, sell the rights or allow the rights offer to lapse.

Required

(a)   Calculate the theoretical ex-rights price of an ordinary share in Panda.   **(3 marks)**

(b)   Calculate the price at which the rights in Panda are likely to be traded.   **(3 marks)**

(c)   Evaluate each of the options available to the investor with 10,000 ordinary shares.   **(4 marks)**

(d)   Discuss, from the viewpoint of the business, how critical the pricing of a rights issue is likely to be.
                                                                                          (5 marks)

                                                                       (Total = 15 marks)

3 Objective test questions: cost of capital   16 mins

3.1   GG Co has a cost of equity of 25%. It has 4 million shares in issue, and has had for many years.

Its dividend payments in the years 20X9 to 20Y3 were as follows.

End of year	Dividends
	$'000
20X9	220
20Y0	257
20Y1	310
20Y2	356
20Y3	423

Dividends are expected to continue to grow at the same average rate into the future.

According to the dividend valuation model, what should be the share price at the start of 20Y4?

A $0.96
B $1.10
C $1.47
D $1.73

3.2   IPA Co is about to pay a $0.50 dividend on each ordinary share. Its earnings per share was $1.50.

Net assets per share is $6. Current share price is $4.50 per share.

What is the cost of equity?

A   31%
B   30%
C   22%
D   21%

3.3   HB Co has in issue 10% irredeemable loan notes, currently traded at 95% cum-interest.

If the tax rate changes from 30% to 20% for the company, the cost of irredeemable debt:

A   Increases to 9.4%
B   Increases to 8.4%
C   Decreases to 9.4%
D   Decreases to 8.4%

3.4   BRW Co has 10% redeemable loan notes in issue trading at $90. The loan notes are redeemable at a 10% premium in 5 years time, or convertible at that point into 20 ordinary shares. The current share price is $2.50 and is expected to grow at 10% per annum for the foreseeable future. BRW Co pays 30% corporation tax.

What is the best estimate of the cost of these loan notes?

A   9.8%
B   7.9%
C   11.5%
D   15.2%

3.5   IDO Co has a capital structure as follows:

	£m
10m $0.50 ordinary shares	5
Reserves	20
13% Irredeemable loan notes	7
	32

The ordinary shares are currently quoted at $3.00, and the loan notes at $90. IDO Co has a cost of equity of 12% and pays corporation tax at a rate of 30%.

What is IDO Co's weighted average cost of capital?

A   10.4%
B   11.1%
C   11.7%
D   11.8%

3.6   An 8% irredeemable $0.50 preference share is being traded for $0.30 cum-div currently in a company that pays corporation tax at a rate of 30%.

What is the cost of capital for these preference shares?

A   10.8%
B   15.4%
C   26.7%
D   18.7%

3.7   ELW Co recently paid a dividend of $0.50 a share. This is $0.10 more than 3 years ago. Shareholders have a required rate of return of 10%.

Using the dividend valuation model and assuming recent dividend growth is expected to continue, what is the current value of a share?

A $23.41
B $5
C $38.48
D $10.48

3.8   Which of the following need to be assumed when using the dividend valuation formula to estimate a share value?

1   The recent dividend, 'D_0', is typical ie doesn't vary significantly from historical trends
2   Growth will be constant
3   The cost of equity will remain constant
4   A majority shareholding is being purchased

A   1, 2 and 3 only
B   3 and 4 only
C   1 and 2 only
D   1, 2, 3 and 4

3.9   A 9% redeemable loan note in ATV Co is due to mature in 3 years time at a premium of 15%, or convertible into 25 ordinary shares at that point. The current share price is $4, expected to grow at 10% per annum. ATV pays corporation tax at a rate of 30%.

What is the current market value of the loan note if loan note holders require a 10% return?

A $108.75
B $115.63
C $102.03
D $122.34

4 Objective test questions: Financial instruments   11 mins

4.1   Which of the following are **not** classified as financial instruments under IAS 32 *Financial Instruments: Presentation* ?

A   Share options
B   Intangible assets
C   Trade receivables
D   Redeemable preference shares

4.2   An 8% $30 million convertible loan note was issued on 1 April 20X5 at par. Interest is payable in arrears on 31 March each year. The loan note is redeemable at par on 31 March 20X8 or convertible into equity shares at the option of the loan note holders on the basis of 30 shares for each $100 of loan. A similar instrument without the conversion option would have an interest rate of 10% per annum.

The present values of $1 receivable at the end of each year based on discount rates of 8% and 10% are:

		8%	10%
End of year	1	0.93	0.91
	2	0.86	0.83
	3	0.79	0.75

What amount will be credited to equity on 1 April 20X5 in respect of this financial instrument?

A $5,976,000
B $1,524,000
C $324,000
D $9,000,000

4.3 A 5% loan note was issued on 1 April 20X0 at its face value of $20 million. Direct costs of the issue were $500,000. The loan note will be redeemed on 31 March 20X3 at a substantial premium. The effective interest rate applicable is 10% per annum.

At what amount will the loan note appear in the statement of financial position as at 31 March 20x2?

A $21,000,000
B $20,450,000
C $22,100,000
D $21,495,000

4.4 How does the *Conceptual Framework* define an asset?

A   A resource owned by an entity as a result of past events and from which future economic benefits are expected to flow to the entity

B   A resource over which an entity has legal rights as a result of past events and from which economic benefits are expected to flow to the entity

C   A resource controlled by an entity as a result of past events and from which future economic benefits are expected to flow to the entity

D   A resource to which an entity has a future commitment as a result of past events and from which future economic benefits are expected to flow from the entity

4.5 Which one of the following would be classified as a liability?

A   Dexter's business manufactures a product under licence. In 12 months' time the licence expires and Dexter will have to pay $50,000 for it to be renewed.

B   Reckless purchased an investment 9 months ago for $120,000. The market for these investments has now fallen and Reckless's investment is valued at $90,000.

C   Carter has estimated the tax charge on its profits for the year just ended as $165,000.

D   Expansion is planning to invest in new machinery and has been quoted a price of $570,000.

4.6 The *Conceptual Framework* identifies four enhancing qualitative characteristics of financial information. For which of these characteristics is **disclosure of accounting policies** particularly important?

A   Verifiability
B   Timeliness
C   Comparability
D   Understandability

5 Amps   **18 mins**

Learning outcome: B1

Amps is a highly acquisitive company operating in the leisure industry. In order to finance acquisitions, the company has issued a number of financial instruments, both debt and equity, the details of which are given below.

(a) $1 million redeemable bonds were issued on 1 January 20X0, redeemable ten years later for the same amount. The interest rate attached to the bonds is 4% for years 1 to 3, 7% for years 4 to 7 and 10% for the final period. This gives a constant rate of return of 7.5%.

Amps has accounted for 20X0 interest by charging $40,000 to the statement of profit or loss and other comprehensive income.

(b)   Also during 20X0, the company issued $2m convertible debentures carrying interest at 7%. The debentures are convertible into ordinary shares in December 20X1 at the option of the holders.

Amps believe the conversion rights will be exercised and as a result has treated the debentures as part of equity. The annual return to the holders has been treated as a distribution.

Required

Explain how the above matters should be dealt with in the financial statements of Amps for the year ending 31 December 20X0.   **(10 marks)**

6 JKA   **18 mins**

Learning outcome: B1

JKA entered into the following transactions in the year ended 31 May 20X3:

1   JKA held a portfolio of trade receivables with a carrying amount of $4 million at 31 May 20X3. At that date, the entity entered into a factoring agreement with a bank, whereby it transfers the receivables in exchange for $3.6 million in cash. JKA has agreed to reimburse the factor for any shortfall between the amount collected and $3.6 million. Once the receivables have been collected, any amounts above $3.6 million, less interest on this amount, will be repaid to JKA. JKA has derecognised the receivables and charged $0.4 million as a loss to statement of profit or loss.

2   On 31 May 20X3, JKA sold a piece of land to DEX Finance for $500,000 when the carrying value of the land was $520,000 (the original cost of the asset). Under the terms of the sale agreement JKA has the option to repurchase the land within the next three years for between $560,000 and $600,000 depending on the date of the repurchase. The land must be repurchased for $600,000 at the end of the three year period if the option is not exercised before that time. JKA has derecognised the land and recorded the subsequent loss within profit for the year ended 31 May 20X3.

Required

(a)   **Explain** how the transfer of the receivables and the sale of the land should be accounted for in accordance with principles of the *Framework for Preparation and Presentation of Financial Statements*.   **(6 marks)**

(b)   **Prepare** any journal entries required to correct the accounting treatment for the year to 31 May 20X3.   **(4 marks)**

                                                            (Total: 10 marks)

7 Objective test questions: Leases

5 mins

7.1 A company leases some plant on 1 January 20X4. The cash price of the plant is $9,000, and the company leases it for four years, paying four annual instalments of $3,000 beginning on 31 December 20X4.

The company uses the sum of the digits method to allocate interest.

What is the interest charge for the year ended 31 December 20X5?

A $900
B $600
C $1,000
D $750

7.2 Which of the following statements defines a finance lease?

A A short term hire agreement

B A long term hire agreement where the legal title in the asset passes on the final payment

C A long term hire agreement where substantially all the risks and rewards of ownership are transferred

D A long term hire agreement where the hirer is responsible for maintenance of the asset

7.3 An asset is hired under a finance lease with a deposit of $30,000 on 1 January 20X1 plus 8 six monthly payments in arrears of $20,000 each. The fair value of the asset is $154,000. The finance charge is to be allocated using the sum of the digits method.

What is the finance charge for the year ending 31 December 20X3?

A $7,000
B $8,000
C $10,000
D $11,000

8 Objective test questions: Provisions, contingent liabilities and contingent assets   **7 mins**

8.1   Wick is being sued by a customer for $2 million for breach of contract over a cancelled order. Wick has obtained legal opinion that there is a 20% chance that Wick will lose the case. Accordingly, Wick has provided $400,000 ($2 million × 20%) in respect of the claim. The unrecoverable legal costs of defending the action are estimated at $100,000. These have not been provided for as the case will not go to court until next year.

What is the amount of the provision that should be made by Wick in accordance with IAS 37 *Provisions, Contingent Liabilities and Contingent Assets* ?

A $2,000,000
B $2,100,000
C $500,000
D $100,000

8.2   During the year Peterlee acquired an iron ore mine at a cost of $6 million. In addition, when all the ore has been extracted (estimated 10 years' time) the company will face estimated costs for landscaping the area affected by the mining that have a present value of $2 million. These costs would still have to be incurred even if no further ore was extracted.

How should this $2 million future cost be recognised in the financial statements?

A   Provision $2 million and $2 million capitalised as part of cost of mine.
B   Provision $2 million and $2 million charged to operating costs
C   Accrual $200,000 per annum for next 10 years
D   Should not be recognised as no cost has yet arisen

8.3   Hopewell sells a line of goods under a six-month warranty. Any defect arising during that period is repaired free of charge. Hopewell has calculated that if all the goods sold in the last six months of the year required repairs the cost would be $2 million. If all of these goods had more serious faults and had to be replaced the cost would be $6 million.

The normal pattern is that 80% of goods sold will be fault-free, 15% will require repairs and 5% will have to be replaced.

What is the amount of the provision required?

A $2 million
B $1.6 million
C $6 million
D $0.6 million

8.4   Which one of the following would **not** be valid grounds for a provision?

A   A company has a policy of cleaning up any environmental contamination caused by its operations, but is not legally obliged to do so.

B   A company is leasing an office building for which it has no further use. However, it is tied into the lease for another year.

C   A company is closing down a division. The Board has prepared detailed closure plans which have been communicated to customers and employees.

D   A company has acquired a machine which requires a major overhaul every three years. The cost of the first overhaul is reliably estimated at $120,000.

9 Objective test questions: Deferred tax

7 mins

9.1 In accounting for deferred tax, which of the following items can give rise to temporary differences?

1   Differences between accounting depreciation and tax allowances for capital expenditure
2   Expenses charged in the statement of profir or loss but disallowed for tax
3   Revaluation of a non-current asset
4   Unrelieved tax losses

A   1, 3 and 4 only
B   1 and 2 only
C   3 and 4 only
D   All four items

9.2 Which of the following are examples of assets or liabilities whose carrying amount is always equal to their tax base?

1   Accrued expenses that will never be deductible for tax purposes

2   Accrued expenses that have already been deducted in determining the current tax liability for current or earlier periods

3   Accrued income that will never be taxable

4   A loan payable in the statement of financial position at the amount originally received, which is also the amount eventually repayable

A   1 and 3 only
B   1 and 2 only
C   2 and 4 only
D   All four items

9.3 Which of the following statements about IAS 12 *Income taxes* are correct?

1   Companies may discount deferred tax assets and liabilities if the effect would be material.

2   The financial statements must disclose an explanation of the relationship between tax expense and accounting profit.

3   Deferred tax may not be recognised in respect of goodwill unless any impairment of that goodwill is deductible for tax purposes.

4   The tax base of an asset or liability is the amount attributed to that asset or liability for tax purposes.

A   All the statements are correct
B   2, 3 and 4 only are correct
C   1 and 4 only are correct
D   None of the statements is correct.

9.4 The following information relates to an entity.

- At 1 January 20X8, the net book value of non-current assets exceeded their tax written down value by $850,000.

- For the year ended 31 December 20X8, the entity claimed depreciation for tax purposes of $500,000 and charged depreciation of $450,000 in the financial statements.

- During the year ended 31 December 20X8, the entity revalued a freehold property. The revaluation surplus was $250,000.

- The tax rate was 30% throughout the year.

What is the provision for deferred tax required by IAS 12 *Income taxes* at 31 December 20X8?

A $240,000

B $270,000

C $315,000

D $345,000

10 Objective test questions: Share based payments   5 mins

10.1 A company grants 500 cash share appreciation rights to each of its 800 employees on 1 January 20X5, vesting on 31 December 20X7, on condition that they remain in its employ until that date. The fair value of each share appreciation right is $4.20 on 1 January 20X5 and $4.30 on 31 December 20X5. At 1 January 20X5 the company estimated that 620 employees would remain employed until the vesting date, adjusted to 610 at 31 December 20X5 as more employees had left than anticipated.

How much should be recognised as an expense in respect of the share appreciation rights for the year ended 31 December 20X5?

A $427,000
B $437,167
C $1,281,000
D $1,311,501

10.2 ABC Plc grants 500 share options to each of its 8 directors on 1 April 20X7, which will vest on 31 March 20X9. The fair value of each option at 1 April 20X7 is $12, and all the options are anticipated to vest on 31 March 20X9.

What is the accounting entry in the financial statements for the year ended 31 March 20X8?

A   Dr Staff expense $24,000 / Cr Other reserves (within equity) $24,000
B   Dr Staff expense $48,000 / Cr Other reserves (within equity) $48,000
C   Dr Asset $24,000 / Cr Liability $24,000
D   Dr Asset $48,000 / Cr Liability $48,000

10.3 On 1 May 20X6, More Shares Plc grants 25 share appreciation rights to each of its 3,500 employees, on the condition that each employee remains in service until 30 April 20X9. 55% of the rights are expected to vest on 30 April 20X9. The fair value of each right on 30 April 20X7 is $18, and their intrinsic value on that date is $12.

What is the accounting entry in the financial statements for the year ended 30 April 20X7?

A   Dr Assets $866,250 / Cr Liability $866,250
B   Dr Staff expense $288,750 / Cr Liability $288,750
C   Dr Staff expense $288,750 / Cr Other reserves (within equity) $288,750
D   Dr Staff expense $433,125 / Cr Liability $433,125

11 Share-based payment   18 mins

Learning outcome: A1

J&B granted 200 options on its $1 ordinary shares to each of its 800 employees on 1 January 20X1. Each grant is conditional upon the employee being employed by J&B until 31 December 20X3.

J&B estimated at 1 January 20X1 that:

(i)   The fair value of each option was $4 (before adjustment for the possibility of forfeiture).

(ii)   Approximately 50 employees would leave during 20X1, 40 during 20X2 and 30 during 20X3 thereby forfeiting their rights to receive the options. The departures were expected to be evenly spread within each year.

The exercise price of the options was $1.50 and the market value of a J&B share on 1 January 20X1 was $3.

In the event, only 40 employees left during 20X1 (and the estimate of total departures was revised down to 95 at 31 December 20X1), 20 during 20X2 (and the estimate of total departures was revised to 70 at 31 December 20X2) and none during 20X3, spread evenly during each year.

Required

The directors of J&B have asked you to illustrate how the scheme is accounted for under IFRS 2 *Share-based Payment*.

(a)   **Prepare** the double entries for the charge to statement of profit or loss for employee services over the three years and for the share issue, assuming all employees entitled to benefit from the scheme exercised their rights and the shares were issued on 31 December 20X3.   **(7 marks)**

(b)   **Explain** how your solution would differ had J&B offered its employees cash based options on the share value rather than share options.   **(3 marks)**

(Total: 10 marks)

12 Objective test questions: Revenue

5 mins

12.1 On 1 October 20X2 Most Co entered into a contract to construct a bridge over a river. The agreed price was $50 million and construction is expected to be completed on 30 September 20X4. Costs to date are:

	$m
Materials, labour and overheads	12
Specialist plant acquired 1 October 20X2	8

The sales value of the work done at 31 March 20X3 has been agreed at $22 million and the estimated cost to complete (excluding plant depreciation) is $10 million. The specialist plant will have no residual value at the end of the contract and should be depreciated on a monthly basis. Most recognises profits on uncompleted contracts on the percentage of completion basis as determined by the agreed work to date compared to the total contract price.

What is the profit to date on the contract at 31 March 20X3?

A $8,800,000
B $13,200,000
C $11,440,000
D $10,000,000

12.2 The following details apply to a construction contract at 31 December 20X5.

	$
Contract value	120,000
Costs to date	48,000
Estimated costs to completion	48,000
Progress billings	50,400

The contract is agreed to be 45% complete at 31 December 20X5.

What amount should appear in the statement of financial as at 31 December 20X5 as due from customers?

A $8,400
B $48,000
C $6,000
D $50,400

12.3 Sale and leaseback or sale and repurchase arrangements can be used to disguise the substance of loan transactions by taking them 'off balance sheet'. In this case the legal position is that the asset has been sold but the substance is that the seller still retains the benefits of ownership.

Which one of the following is **not** a feature which suggests that the substance of a transaction differs from its legal form?

A The seller of an asset retains the ability to use the asset.
B The seller has no further exposure to the risks of ownership
C The asset has been transferred at a price substantially above or below its fair value.
D The 'sold' asset remains on the sellers premises.

13 Objective test questions: Basic groups

14 mins

13.1 On what basis may a subsidiary be excluded from consolidation?

A   The activities of the subsidiary are dissimilar to the activities of the rest of the group

B   The subsidiary was acquired with the intention of reselling it after a short period of time

C   The subsidiary is based in a country with strict exchange controls which make it difficult for it to transfer funds to the parent

D   There is no basis on which a subsidiary may be excluded from consolidation

13.2 Which of the following is the criterion for treatment of an investment as an associate?

A   Ownership of a majority of the equity shares
B   Ability to exercise control
C   Existence of significant influence
D   Exposure to variable returns from involvement with the investee

13.3 Which of the following statements are correct when preparing consolidated financial statements?

1   A subsidiary cannot be consolidated unless it prepares financial statements to the same reporting date as the parent.

2   A subsidiary with a different reporting date may prepare additional statements up to the group reporting date for consolidation purposes.

3   A subsidiary's financial statements can be included in the consolidation if the gap between the parent and subsidiary reporting dates is five months or less.

4   Where a subsidiary's financial statements are drawn up to a different reporting date from those of the parent, adjustments should be made for significant transactions or events occurring between the two reporting dates.

A   1 only
B   2 and 3
C   2 and 4
D   3 and 4

13.4 IFRS 3 requires an acquirer to measure the assets and liabilities of the acquiree at the date of consolidation at fair value. IFRS 13 *Fair Value Measurement* provides guidance on how fair value should be established.

Which of the following is **not** one of the issues to be considered according to IFRS 13 when arriving at the fair value of a non-financial asset?

A   The characteristics of the asset

B   The present value of the future cash flows that the asset is expected to generate during its remaining life

C   The principal or most advantageous market for the asset

D   The highest and best use of the asset

13.5 Witch acquired 70% of the 200,000 equity shares of Wizard, its only subsidiary, on 1 April 20X8 when the retained earnings of Wizard were $450,000. The carrying amounts of Wizard's net assets at the date of acquisition were equal to their fair values apart from a building which had a carrying amount of $600,000 and a fair value of $850,000. The remaining useful life of the building at the acquisition date was 40 years.

Witch measures non-controlling interest at fair value, based on share price. The market value of Wizard shares at the date of acquisition was $1.75.

At 31 March 20X9 the retained earnings of Wizard were $750,000. At what amount should the non-controlling interest appear in the consolidated statement of financial position of Witch at 31 March 20X9?

A $195,000
B $193,125
C $135,000
D $188,750

13.6 On 1 June 20X1 Strawberry acquired 80% of the equity share capital of Raspberry. At the date of acquisition the fair values of Raspberry's net assets were equal to their carrying amounts with the exception of its property. This had a fair value of $1.2 million **below** its carrying amount. The property had a remaining useful life of 8 years.

What effect will any adjustment required in respect of the property have on group retained earnings at 30 September 20X1?

A   Increase $50,000
B   Decrease $50,000
C   Increase $40,000
D   Decrease $40,000

13.7 On 1 August 20X7, Orange purchased 18 million of the 24 million $1 equity shares of Banana. The acquisition was through a share exchange of two shares in Orange for every three shares in Banana. The market price of a share in Orange at 1 August 20X7 was $5.75. Orange will also pay in cash on 31 July 20X9 (two years after acquisition) $2.42 per acquired share of Banana. Orange's cost of capital is 10% per annum.

What is the amount of the consideration attributable to Orange for the acquisition of Banana?

A $105 million

B $139.5 million

C $108.2 million

D $103.8 million

13.8 Crash acquired 70% of Bang's 100,000 $1 ordinary shares for $800,000 when the retained earnings of Bang were $570,000 and the balance in its revaluation surplus was $150,000. Bang also has an internally-developed customer list which has been independently valued at $90,000. The non-controlling interest in Bang was judged to have a fair value of $220,000 at the date of acquisition.

What was the goodwill arising on acquisition?

A $200,000
B $163,000
C $226,000
D $110,000

14 Group financial statements
18 mins

In many countries, companies with subsidiaries have been required to publish group financial statements, usually in the form of consolidated financial statements. You are required to **state** why you feel the preparation of group financial statements is necessary and to **outline** their limitations, if any.

(10 marks)

15 Putney and Wandsworth
18 mins

Putney acquired 90% of the share capital of Wandsworth on 1 January 20X1 when Wandsworth's retained earnings stood at $10,000 and there was no balance on the revaluation surplus.

Their respective statements of financial position as at 31 December 20X5 are as follows.

	Putney $	Wandsworth $
Non-current assets		
Property, plant & equipment	135,000	60,000
Investment in Wandsworth	25,000	–
	160,000	60,000
Current assets	62,000	46,000
	222,000	106,000
Equity		
Share capital ($1 ordinary shares)	50,000	15,000
Revaluation surplus	50,000	15,000
Retained earnings	90,000	50,000
	190,000	80,000
Non-current liabilities	14,000	12,000
Current liabilities	18,000	14,000
	222,000	106,000

The group policy is to measure non-controlling interests at acquisition at their proportionate share of the fair value of the identifiable net assets. Impairment losses on goodwill to date have amounted to $1,250.

Required

Prepare the consolidated statement of financial position of Putney and its subsidiary as at 31 December 20X5.

(10 marks)

16 Balmes and Aribau

18 mins

Balmes Balmes acquired 80% of Aribau's ordinary share capital on 1 July 20X1 for $28.5 million. The balance on Aribau's retained earnings at that date was $24m and $2m on the general reserve.

Their respective statements of financial position as at 30 June 20X3 are as follows.

	Balmes $'000	Aribau $'000
Non-current assets		
Property, plant & equipment	97,300	34,400
Intangible assets	5,100	1,200
Investment in Aribau (note 1)	35,500	–
	137,900	35,600
Current assets		
Inventories	43,400	14,300
Trade and other receivables	36,800	17,400
Cash and cash equivalents	700	-
	80,900	31,700
	218,800	67,300
Equity		
Share capital ($1 ordinary shares)	50,000	5,000
General reserve	4,300	3,000
Retained earnings	118,800	37,100
	173,100	45,100
Non-current liabilities		
Loan notes	10,000	4,000
Current liabilities		
Trade payables	28,400	15,700
Income tax payable	7,300	2,400
Bank overdraft	-	100
	35,700	18,200
	218,800	67,300

Additional information

(a) Balmes' investment in Aribau has been classified as available for sale and is held at fair value. The gains earned on it have been recorded within the retained earnings of Balmes.

(b) At the date of acquisition, Aribau's property, plant and equipment included land and buildings at a carrying value of $12.5m (of which $4.5m related to the land). The fair value of the land and buildings was $14m (of which $5m related to the land). The buildings had an average remaining useful life of 20 years at that date.

(c) The group policy is to value non-controlling interests at acquisition at fair value. The fair value of the non-controlling interests in Aribau on 1 July 20X1 was $7 million.

(d) During June 20X3, Balmes conducted an impairment review of its investment in Aribau in the consolidated financial statements. This revealed impairment losses relating to recognised goodwill of $200,000. No impairment losses had previously been recognised.

Required

Prepare the consolidated statement of financial position for the Balmes Group as at 30 June 20X3.

(10 marks)

17 Reprise   25 mins

Reprise purchased 75% of Encore for $2,000,000 10 years ago when the balance on its retained earnings was $1,044,000. The statements of financial position of the two companies as at 31 March 20X4 are as follows:

	Reprise $'000	Encore $'000
Non-current assets		
Investment in Encore	2,000	–
Land and buildings	3,350	–
Plant and equipment	1,010	2,210
Motor vehicles	510	345
	6,870	2,555
Current assets		
Inventories	890	352
Trade receivables	1,372	514
Cash and cash equivalents	89	51
	2,351	917
	9,221	3,472
Equity		
Share capital - $1 ordinary shares	1,000	500
Retained earnings	4,225	2,610
Revaluation surplus	2,500	–
	7,725	3,110
Non-current liabilities		
10% debentures	500	–
Current liabilities		
Trade payables	996	362
	9,221	3,472

The following additional information is available:

(a)   Included in trade receivables of Reprise are amounts owed by Encore of $75,000. The current accounts do not at present balance due to a payment for $39,000 being in transit at the year end from Encore.

(b)   Included in the inventories of Encore are items purchased from Reprise during the year for $31,200. Reprise marks up its goods by 30% to achieve its selling price.

(c) $180,000 of the recognised goodwill arising is to be written off due to impairment losses.

(d)   Encore shares were trading at $4.40 just prior to acquisition by Reprise.

Required

Prepare the consolidated statement of financial position for the Reprise group of companies as at 31 March 20X4. It is the group policy to value the non-controlling interests at fair value at acquisition.

(14 marks)

18 Objective test questions: Associates and joint arrangements

11 mins

18.1 On 1 October 20X8 Viardot acquired 30 million of Pauline's 100 million shares in exchange for 75 million of its own shares. The stock market value of Viardot's shares at the date of this share exchange was $1.60 each.

Pauline's profit is subject to seasonal variation. Its profit for the year ended 31 March 20X9 was $100 million. $20 million of this profit was made from 1 April 20X8 to 30 September 20X8.

Viardot has one subsidiary and no other investments apart from Pauline.

What amount will be shown as 'investment in associate' in the consolidated statement of financial position of Viardot as at 31 March 20X9?

A $144 million
B $150 million
C $78 million
D $126 million

18.2 How should an associate be accounted for in the consolidated statement of profit or loss?

A   The associate's income and expenses are added to those of the group on a line-by-line basis.

B   The group share of the associate's income and expenses is added to the group figures on a line-by-line basis.

C   The group share of the associate's profit after tax is recorded as a one-line entry.

D   Only dividends received from the associate are recorded in the group statement of profit or loss.

18.3 Wellington owns 30% of Boot, which it purchased on 1 May 20X7 for $2.5 million. At that date Boot had retained earnings of $5.3 million. At the year end date of 31 October 20X7 Boot had retained earnings of $6.4 million after paying out a dividend of $1 million. On 30 September 20X7 Wellington sold $700,000 of goods to Boot, on which it made 30% profit. Boot had resold none of these goods by 31 October.

At what amount will Wellington record its investment in Boot in its consolidated statement of financial position at 31 October 20X7?

A $2,767,000
B $2,900,000
C $2,830,000
D $2,620,000

18.4 On 1 February 20X1 Picardy acquired 35% of the equity shares of Avignon, its only associate, for $10 million in cash. The post-tax profit of Avignon for the year to 30 September 20X1 was $3 million. Profits accrued evenly throughout the year. Avignon made a dividend payment of $1 million on 1 September 20X1. At 30 September 20X1 Picardy decided that an impairment loss of $500,000 should be recognised on its investment in Avignon.

What amount will be shown as 'investment in associate' in the statement of financial position of Picardy as at 30 September 20X1?

A $9,967,000
B $9,850,000
C $9,200,000
D $10,200,000

18.5 Which of the following statements are true with regards to group financial statements?

1   Under IFRS 11, joint operations are to be accounted for the same way as joint ventures.

2   Goodwill arising on consolidation may be capitalised and amortised, or capitalised and reviewed annually for impairment.

3   Under IFRS 11 joint ventures are to be accounted for using the equity method.

4   Goodwill must always be capitalised and reviewed for impairment annually.

A   Statements 1 and 2
B   Statements 1 and 4
C   Statements 2 and 3
D   Statements 3 and 4

18.6 What, according to IFRS 11, are the characteristics of a joint operation?

1   The parties with joint control have rights to the assets and obligations for the liabilities of the arrangement.

2   The parties with joint control have rights to the net assets of the arrangement.

3   The arrangement is never structured through a separate entity.

4   The arrangement is contractual.

A   1 and 3
B   1 and 4
C   2 and 3
D   2 and 4

19 Hever

36 mins

Hever has held shares in two companies, Spiro and Aldridge, for a number of years. As at 31 December 20X4 they have the following statements of financial position:

	Hever $'000	Spiro $'000	Aldridge $'000
Non-current assets			
Property, plant & equipment	370	190	260
Investments	218	–	–
	588	190	260
Current assets			
Inventories	160	100	180
Trade receivables	170	90	100
Cash	50	40	10
	380	230	290
	968	420	550
Equity			
Share capital ($1 ords)	200	80	50
Share premium	100	80	30
Retained earnings	568	200	400
	868	360	480
Current liabilities			
Trade payables	100	60	70
	968	420	550

You ascertain the following additional information:

(a)   The 'investments' in the statement of financial position comprise solely Hever's investment in Spiro ($128,000) and in Aldridge ($90,000).

(b)   The 48,000 shares in Spiro were acquired when Spiro's retained earnings balance stood at $20,000.

The 15,000 shares in Aldridge were acquired when that company had a retained earnings balance of $150,000.

(c)   When Hever acquired its shares in Spiro the fair value of Spiro's net assets equalled their book values with the following exceptions:

	$'000
Property, plant and equipment	50 higher
Inventories	20 lower (sold during 20X4)

Depreciation arising on the fair value adjustment to non-current assets since this date is $5,000.

(d)   During the year, Hever sold inventories to Spiro for $16,000, which originally cost Hever $10,000. Three-quarters of these inventories have subsequently been sold by Spiro.

(e)   No impairment losses on goodwill had been necessary by 31 December 20X4.

(f)   It is group policy to value non-controlling interests at fair value. The fair value of the non-controlling interests at acquisition was $90,000.

Required

Prepare the consolidated statement of financial position for the Hever group (incorporating the associate).

(20 marks)

20 Bayonet

18 mins

Learning outcome: A1

Bayonet, a public limited company, purchased 6m shares in Rifle, a public limited company, on 1 January 20X5 for $10m. Rifle had purchased 4m shares in Pistol, a public limited company for $9m on 31 December 20X2 when its retained earnings stood at $5m. The balances on retained earnings of the acquired companies were $8m and $6.5m respectively at 1 January 20X5. The fair value of the identifiable assets and liabilities of Rifle and Pistol was equivalent to their book values at the acquisition dates.

The statements of financial position of the three companies as at 31 December 20X9 are as follows:

	Bayonet $'000	Rifle $'000	Pistol $'000
Non-current assets			
Property, plant and equipment	14,500	12,140	17,500
Investment in Rifle	10,000		
Investment in Pistol	–	9,000	–
	24,500	21,140	17,500
Current assets			
Inventories	6,300	2,100	450
Trade receivables	4,900	2,000	2,320
Cash	500	1,440	515
	11,700	5,540	3,285
	36,200	26,680	20,785
Equity			
50c ordinary shares	5,000	4,000	2,500
Retained earnings	25,500	20,400	16,300
	30,500	24,400	18,800
Current liabilities	5,700	2,280	1,985
	36,200	26,680	20,785

Group policy is to value non-controlling interests at fair value at acquisition. The fair value of the non-controlling interests in Rifle was calculated as $3,230,000 on 1 January 20X5. The fair value of the 40% non-controlling interests in Pistol on 1 January 20X5 was $4.6m.

Impairment tests in current and previous years did not reveal any impairment losses.

Required

Prepare the consolidated statement of financial position of Bayonet as at 31 December 20X9.

(10 marks)

21 Objective test questions: Changes to group structures

5 mins

21.1 Jalfresi acquired 8 million of the 10 million issued share capital of Dopiaza on 1 October 20X1 for $14.8 million, when the balance on retained earnings was $6 million. On 30 September 20X8 Jalfresi sold 25% of its holding for $4.4 million. It is the group's policy to measure NCI at the proportionate share of the subsidiary's net assets.

Extracts from the statement of financial position of Dopiaza as at 30 September 20X8 is as follows:

	$'000
Share capital	10,000
Retained earnings	8,900
	18,900

What is the gain or loss on disposal/adjustment to parent's equity to be included in the financial statements for the year ended 30 September 20X8?

A $620,000 adjustment to parent's equity.

B $470,000 gain to statement of profit or loss for the year.

C $500,000 adjustment to parent's equity.

D $20,000 gain to statement of profit or loss for the year.

21.2 On 1 September 20X6, BLT held 60% of the ordinary share capital of its only subsidiary CMU. The consolidated equity of the group at that date was $576,600, of which $127,000 was attributable to the non-controlling interest. BLT measures non-controlling interests at acquisition at their proportionate share of the subsidiary's net assets.

On 28 February 20X7, exactly halfway through the financial year, BLT paid $135,000 to buy a further 20% of the ordinary share capital of CMU. In the year ended 31 August 20X7 BLT's profits for the period were $98,970 and CMU's were $30,000. It can be assumed that profits accrue evenly throughout the year.

What is the adjustment to parent's equity as a result of BLT's acquisition of further shares in CMU?

A $68,500 debit

B $68,500 credit

C $2,000 debit

D $2,000 credit

21.3 Bad, whose year end is 30 June 20X9 has a subsidiary, Conscience, which it acquired in stages. The details of the acquisition are as follows:

Date of acquisition	Holding acquired %	Retained earnings at acquisition $m	Purchase consideration $m
1 July 20X7	10	540	120
1 July 20X8	60	800	960

The share capital of Conscience has remained unchanged since its incorporation at $600m. The fair values of the net assets of Conscience were the same as their carrying amounts at the date of the acquisition. Bad did not have significant influence over Conscience at any time before gaining control of Conscience. At 1 July 20X8, the fair value of Bad's 10% holding in Conscience was $160m and the fair value of non-controlling interests was $420m. The group policy is to measure non-controlling interests at acquisition at their fair value.

What is the goodwill on the acquisition of Conscience that will appear in the consolidated statement of financial position at 30 June 20X9?

A $80,000,000
B $140,000,000
C $240,000,000
D $665,000,000

22 Objective test questions: Indirect control of subsidiaries

5 mins

22.1   Rag owns 75% of Tag and Tag owns 40% of Bobtail. Both companies were acquired 4 years ago. The profit before tax for the year of each company is as follows: Rag $6,000, Tag $5,000 and Bobtail $4,000. Each company has a $1,000 tax expense.

Rag measures non-controlling interests at acquisition at their proportionate share of the subsidiary's net assets.

Goodwill at acquisition of Tag was $1,000 and Bobtail $300. At the date of acquisition the fair value of Bobtail's buildings were $1,000 greater than their book value. The buildings are being depreciated over a remaining useful life of 20 years.

It is estimated that the goodwill at acquisition has suffered impairment losses in the year of $400 for Tag. Goodwill impairments are treated as an operating expense.

What is the figure in the consolidated statement of profit or loss for the non-controlling interests?

A $1,000
B $1,195
C $1,200
D $1,295

22.2   Apricot holds 75% of the issued share capital of Blackcurrant and 40% of the issued share capital of Cranberry.

Blackcurrant holds 60% of the issued share capital of Date.

The receivables balances of the four companies at the statement of financial position date are as follows:

	$'000
Apricot	120
Blackcurrent	110
Cranberry	100
Date	90

What will be the receivables figure to be included in the consolidated statement of financial position of Apricot?

A $230,000
B $320,000
C $340,000
D $420,000

22.3 The following diagram shows the structure of a group:

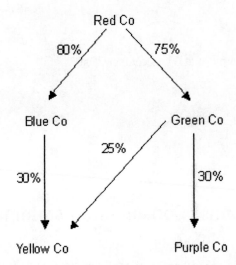

Which of the following are subsidiary undertakings of Red Co?

A   Blue Co and Green Co
B   Blue Co, Green Co and Yellow Co
C   Blue Co, Green Co, Yellow Co and Purple Co

23 Objective test questions: Foreign subsidiaries   4 mins

23.1 Parent has three overseas subsidiaries.

(1)   A is 80% owned. A does not normally enter into transactions with Parent, other than to pay dividends. It operates as a fairly autonomous entity on a day to day basis although Parent controls its long term strategy.

(2)   B is 100% owned and has been set up in order to assemble machines from materials provided by Parent. These are then sent to the UK where Parent sells them to third parties.

(3)   C is 75% owned and is located in France. It manufactures and sells its own range of products locally. It negotiates its own day to day financing needs with French banks.

Which of the subsidiaries are likely to have a different functional currency from Parent?

A   A and B
B   A and C
C   B and C
D   all three subsidiaries

23.2 Rat acquired 75% of the equity share capital of Mole, a foreign operation, on 1 January 20X5, when its net assets were Units 720,000. Summarised statements of financial position of the two entities at 31 December 20X6 are shown below:

	Rat	Mole
	$'000	Unit'000
Investment in Mole	350	–
Other net assets	2,550	960
	2,900	960
Share capital ($1/Unit1 ordinary shares)	1,000	500
Retained earnings	1,900	460
	2,900	960

Exchange rates were as follows:

	Unit=$1
1 January 20X5	2.0
31 December 20X6	2.5

What are consolidated retained earnings at 31 December 20X6?

A $1,902,000
B $1,918,000
C $1,972,000
D $2,084,000

24 Objective test questions: Consolidated statements of changes in equity

5 mins

24.1   Profits or losses attributable to non-controlling interests should be disclosed in the consolidated statement of profit or loss.

Which of the following statements concerning the presentation of non-controlling interest in the consolidated statement of profit or loss is correct?

A   The non-controlling interest share of revenue is deducted on the face of the statement of profit or loss.

B   The non-controlling interest share of operating profit before tax and the related taxation charge are separately disclosed.

C   The non-controlling interest share of after tax profits in subsidiaries is shown on the face of the statement of profit or loss.

D   Only profits attributable to the group appear in the statement of profit or loss.

24.2   B bought 83% of C on 1 July 20X1. C made a profit after tax of $330,880 for the year ended 31 December 20X1. Profits accrued evenly throughout the year.

What is the profit attributable to non-controlling interests in B's consolidated statement of profit or loss for the year ended 31 December 20X1?

A $18,749
B $28,125
C $56,250
D $66,273

24.3   Which of the following might appear as a separate item in the 'other comprehensive income' section of the statement of profit or loss and other comprehensive income?

A   A material irrecoverable debt arising in the year.
B   A share issue in the year.
C   An impairment loss on assets carried at depreciated historical cost.
D   An upward revaluation of the company's assets.

25 Fallowfield and Rusholme

22 mins

Fallowfield acquired a 60% holding in Rusholme three years ago when Rusholme's equity was $56,000 (share capital $40,000 plus reserves $16,000). Both businesses have been very successful since the acquisition and their respective statements of profit or loss and other comprehensive income for the year ended 30 June 20X8 and extracts from their statements of changes in equity are shown below.

	Fallowfield $	Rusholme $
Revenue	403,400	193,000
Cost of sales	(201,400)	(92,600)
Gross profit	202,000	100,400
Distribution costs	(16,000)	(14,600)
Administrative expenses	(24,250)	(17,800)
Dividends from Rusholme	15,000	
Profit before tax	176,750	68,000
Income tax expense	(61,750)	(22,000)
Profit for the year	115,000	46,000
Other comprehensive income (net of tax)	20,000	5,000
Total comprehensive income	135,000	51,000

STATEMENT OF CHANGES IN EQUITY (EXTRACT)

	Fallowfield Total equity $	Rusholme Total equity $
Balance at 30 June 20X7	243,000	101,000
Total comprehensive income for the year	135,000	51,000
Dividends	(40,000)	(25,000)
Balance at 30 June 20X8	338,000	127,000

Additional information

(a) During the year Rusholme sold some goods to Fallowfield for $40,000, including 25% mark-up. Half of these items were still in inventories at the year-end.

(b) Group policy is to measure non-controlling interests at acquisition at fair value. The fair value of Rusholme's non-controlling interest at acquisition was $30,000. There has been no impairment in goodwill since acquisition.

Required

Prepare the consolidated statement of profit or loss and other comprehensive income and statement of changes in equity (showing parent and non-controlling interest shares) of Fallowfield Co and its subsidiary for the year ended 30 June 20X8.
(12 marks)

26 Panther Group   27 mins

Panther operated as a single company, but in 20X4 decided to expand its operations. On 1 July 20X4, Panther paid $2,000,000 to acquire a 60% interest in Sabre, a company to which Panther had advanced a loan of $800,000 at an interest rate of 5% on 1 January 20X4.

The statements of profit or loss and other comprehensive income of Panther and Sabre for the year ended 31 December 20X4 are as follows:

	Panther $'000	Sabre $'000
Revenue	22,800	4,300
Cost of sales	(13,600)	(2,600)
Gross profit	9,200	1,700
Distribution costs	(2,900)	(500)
Administrative expenses	(1,800)	(300)
Finance costs	(200)	(40)
Finance income	50	–
Profit before tax	4,350	860
Income tax expense	(1,300)	(220)
Profit for the year	3,050	640
Other comprehensive income for the year, net of tax	1,600	180
Total comprehensive income for the year	4,650	820

Since acquisition, Sabre purchased $320,000 of goods from Panther. Of these, $60,000 remained in inventories at the year end. Sabre makes a mark-up on cost of 20% under the transfer pricing agreement between the two companies. The fair value of the identifiable net assets of Sabre on purchase were $200,000 greater than their book value. The difference relates to properties with a remaining useful life of 20 years.

Statement of changes in equity (extracts) for the two companies:

	Panther Reserves $'000	Sabre Reserves $'000
Balance at 1 January 20X4	12,750	2,480
Dividend paid	(900)	–
Total comprehensive income for the year	4,650	820
Balance at 31 December 20X4	16,500	3,300

Panther and Sabre had $400,000 and $150,000 of share capital in issue throughout the period respectively.

Required

Prepare the consolidated statement of profit or loss and other comprehensive income and statement of changes in equity (extract for reserves) for the Panther Group for the year ended 31 December 20X4.

No adjustments for impairment losses were necessary in the group financial statements.

Assume income and expenses (other than intragroup items) accrue evenly.   **(15 marks)**

27 CVB

45 mins

The statements of financial position for CVB and FG as at 30 September 20X5 are provided below:

	CVB $'000	FG $'000
Non-current assets		
Property, plant and equipment	22,000	5,000
Available for sale investment (note 1)	4,000	–
	26,000	5,000
Current assets		
Inventories	6,200	800
Trade receivables	6,600	1,900
Cash and cash equivalents	1,200	300
	14,000	3,000
Total assets	40,000	8,000
Equity		
Share capital - $1 ordinary shares	20,000	1,000
Retained earnings	7,500	5,000
Other components of equity	500	–
	28,000	6,000
Non-current liabilities		
5% bonds 2013 (note 2)	3,900	–
Current liabilities	8,100	2,000
Total liabilities	12,000	2,000
	40,000	8,000

Additional information

(a)   CVB acquired a 15% investment in FG on 1 May 20X3 for $600,000. The investment was classified as available for sale and the gains earned on it have been recorded within 'other components of equity' in CVB's individual financial statements. The fair value of the 15% investment at 1 April 20X5 was $800,000. On 1 April 20X5, CVB acquired an additional 60% of the equity share capital of FG at a cost of $2,900,000. In its own financial statements, CVB has kept its investment in FG as an available for sale financial asset recorded at its fair value of $4,000,000 as at 30 September 20X5.

(b)   CVB issued 4 million $1 5% redeemable bonds on 1 October 20X4 at par. The associated costs of issue were $100,000 and the net proceeds of $3.9 million have been recorded within non-current liabilities. The bonds are redeemable at $4.5 million on 30 September 20X8 and the effective interest associated with them is approximately 8.5%. The interest on the bonds is payable annually in arrears. The amount due has been paid in the year to 30 September 20X5 and charged to the statement of profit or loss.

(c)   An impairment review was conducted at the year end and it was decided that the goodwill on acquisition of FG was impaired by 10%.

(d)   It is the group policy to value non-controlling interest at fair value at the date of acquisition. The fair value of the non-controlling interest at 1 April 20X5 was $1.25 million.

(e)   The profit of FG for the year was $3 million, and the profits were assumed to accrue evenly throughout the year.

(f)   FG sold goods to CVB for $400,000. Half of these goods remained in inventories at 30 September 20X5. FG makes a 20% margin on all sales.

(g)   No dividends were paid by either entity in the year to 30 September 20X5.

Required

(a)   **Explain** how the investment in FG should be accounted for in the consolidated financial statements of CVB following the acquisition of the additional 60%.   **(5 marks)**

(b)   **Prepare** the consolidated statement of financial position as at 30 September 20X5 for the CVB Group.   **(20 marks)**

(Total: 25 marks)

28 Holmes and Deakin   31 mins

Holmes Co has owned 85% of the ordinary share capital of Deakin Co for some years. The shares were bought for $255,000 and Deakin Co's reserves at the time of purchase were $20,000. The group policy is to value non-controlling interests at fair value at the date of acquisition. The fair value of the non-controlling interests in Deakin at acquisition was $45,000.

On 28.2.X3 Holmes Co sold 40,000 of the Deakin shares for $160,000. The only entry made in respect of this transaction has been the receipt of the cash, which was credited to the 'investment in subsidiary' account. No dividends were paid by either entity in the period.

The following draft summarised financial statements are available.

STATEMENTS OF PROFIT OR LOSS AND OTHER COMPREHENSIVE INCOME FOR THE YEAR TO 31 MAY 20X3

	Holmes Co $'000	Deakin Co $'000
Revenue	1,000	540
Cost of sales and operating expenses	(800)	(430)
Profit before tax	200	110
Income tax expense	(90)	(60)
Profit for the year	110	50
Other comprehensive income (net of tax)	20	10
Total comprehensive income for the year	130	60

STATEMENTS OF FINANCIAL POSITION AS AT 31 May 20X3

	$'000	$'000
Non-current assets		
Property, plant and equipment (NBV)	535	178
Investment in Deakin Co	95	–
	630	178
Current assets		
Inventories	320	190
Trade receivables	250	175
Cash	80	89
	650	454
	1,280	632
Equity		
Share capital ($1 ordinary shares)	500	200
Reserves	310	170
	810	370

	$'000	$'000
Current liabilities		
Trade payables	295	171
Income tax payable	80	60
Provisions	95	31
	470	262
	1,280	632

No impairment losses have been necessary in the group financial statements to date.

Assume that the capital gain will be subject to corporate income tax at 30%.

Required

Prepare:

(a) The consolidated statement of profit or loss and other comprehensive income for Holmes for the year to 31 May 20X3   **(6 marks)**

(b) A consolidated statement of financial position as at 31 May 20X3; and   **(9 marks)**

(c) A consolidated statement of changes in equity extract (attributable to owners of the parent *only*) for the year ended 31 May 20X3.   **(2 marks)**

(Total: 17 marks)

29 Harvard   32 mins

The draft financial statements of Harvard and its subsidiary, Krakow sp. z o.o. are set out below.

STATEMENTS OF FINANCIAL POSITION AT 31 DECEMBER 20X5

	Harvard $ '000	Krakow PLN '000
Non-current assets		
Property, plant and equipment	2,870	4,860
Investment in Krakow	840	–
	3,710	4,860
Current assets		
Inventories	1,990	8,316
Trade receivables	1,630	4,572
Cash	240	2,016
	3,860	14,904
	7,570	19,764
Equity		
Share capital ($1/PLN1)	118	1,348
Retained reserves	502	14,060
	620	15,408
Non-current liabilities		
Loans	1,920	–
Current liabilities		
Trade payables	5,030	4,356
	7,570	19,764

STATEMENTS OF PROFIT OR LOSS AND OTHER COMPREHENSIVE INCOME FOR THE YEAR
ENDED 31 DECEMBER 20X5

Revenue	40,425	97,125
Cost of sales	(35,500)	(77,550)
Gross profit	4,925	19,575
Distribution and administrative expenses	(4,400)	(5,850)
Investment income	720	–
Profit before tax	1,245	13,725
Income tax expense	(300)	(4,725)
Profit/total comprehensive income for the year	945	9,000
Dividends paid during the period	700	3,744

The following additional information is given:

(a)   Exchange rates

	Zloty (PLN) to $
31 December 20X2	4.40
31 December 20X3	4.16
31 December 20X4	4.00
15 May 20X5	3.90
31 December 20X5	3.60
Average for 20X5	3.75

(b)   Harvard acquired 1,011,000 shares in Krakow for $840,000 on 31 December 20X2 when
Krakow's retained earnings stood at PLN 2,876,000. Krakow operates as an autonomous
subsidiary. Its functional currency is the Polish zloty.

The fair value of the identifiable net assets of Krakow were equivalent to their book values at the
acquisition date. Group policy is to measure non-controlling interests at acquisition at their
proportionate share of the fair value of the identifiable net assets.

(c)   Krakow paid an interim dividend of PLN 3,744,000 on 15 May 20X5. No other dividends were
paid or declared by Krakow in the period.

(d)   No impairment losses were necessary in the consolidated financial statements by 31 December
20X5.

Required

(a)   **Prepare** the consolidated statement of financial position at 31 December 20X5.   **(6 marks)**

(b)   **Prepare** the consolidated statement of profit or loss and other comprehensive income and
statement of changes in equity (attributable to owners of the parent *only*) for the year ended 31
December 20X5.   **(12 marks)**

(Total = 18 marks)

30 Objective test questions: Consolidated statements of cash flows

7 mins

30.1 The carrying amount of property, plant and equipment was $410 million at 31 March 20X1 and $680 million at 31 March 20X2. During the year, property with a carrying amount of $210 million was revalued to $290 million. The depreciation charge for the year was $115 million. There were no disposals.

What amount will appear on the statement of cash flows for the year ended 31 March 20X2 in respect of purchases of property, plant and equipment?

    A $270 million
    B $225 million
    C $235 million
    D $305 million

30.2 The statement of financial position of Beans at 31 March 20X7 showed property, plant and equipment with a carrying amount of $1,860,000. At 31 March 20X8 it had increased to $2,880,000.

During the year to 31 March 20X8 plant with a carrying amount of $240,000 was sold at a loss of $90,000, depreciation of $280,000 was charged and $100,000 was added to the revaluation surplus in respect of property, plant and equipment.

What amount should appear under 'investing activities' in the statement of cash flows of Beans for the year ended 31 March 20X8 as cash paid to acquire property, plant and equipment?

    A $1,640,000
    B $1,440,000
    C $1,260,000
    D $1,350,000

30.3 Extracts from Lazarin's statements of financial position are as follows:

Statement of financial position as at 31 March:

	20X1 $'000	20X0 $'000
Non-current assets		
Property, plant and equipment		
Leased plant	6,500	2,500
Non-current liabilities		
Finance lease obligations	4,800	2,000
Current liabilities		
Finance lease obligations	1,700	800

During the year to 31 March 20X1 depreciation charged on leased plant was $1,800,000.

What amount will be shown in the statement of cash flows of Lazarin for the year ended 31 March 20X1 in respect of payments made under finance leases?

    A $300,000
    B $7,100,000
    C $2,100,000
    D $5,800,000

30.4 On March 20X4, NS acquired 30% of the shares of TP. The investment was accounted for as an associate in NS's consolidated financial statements. Both NS and TP have an accounting year end of 31 October. NS has no other investments in associates.

Net profit for the year in TP's statement of profit or loss for the year ended 31 October 20X4 was $230,000. It declared and paid a dividend of $100,000 on 1 July 20X4. No other dividends were paid in the year.

What amount will be shown as an inflow in respect of earnings from the associate in the consolidated cash flow statement of NS for the year ended 31 October 20X4?

A $20,000
B $26,000
C $30,000
D $46,000

31 AH Group   45 mins

Learning outcome: A1

Extracts from the consolidated financial statements of the AH group for the year ended 30 June 20X5 are given below.

AH GROUP CONSOLIDATED STATEMENT OF PROFIT OR LOSS FOR THE YEAR
ENDED 30 JUNE 20X5

	20X5 $'000
Revenue	85,000
Cost of sales	59,750
Gross profit	25,250
Operating expenses	5,650
Finance cost	1,400
Disposal of property (note 2)	1,250
Profit before tax	19,450
Income tax	6,250
Profit/total comprehensive income for the year for the year	13,200
Profit/total comprehensive income attributable to:	
Owners of the parent	12,545
Non-controlling interest	655
	13,200

AH GROUP: EXTRACTS FROM STATEMENT OF CHANGES IN EQUITY FOR THE YEAR
ENDED 30 JUNE 20X5

	Share capital $'000	Share premium $'000	Consolidated retained earnings $'000
Opening balance	18,000	10,000	18,340
Issue of share capital	2,000	2,000	
Profit for year			12,545
Dividends			(6,000)
Closing balance	20,000	12,000	24,885

AH GROUP STATEMENT OF FINANCIAL POSITION AT 30 JUNE 20X5

	20X5		20X4	
	$'000	$'000	$'000	$'000
ASSETS				
Non current assets				
Property, plant and equipment	50,600		44,050	
Intangible assets (note 3)	6,410		4,160	
		57,010		48,210
Current assets				
Inventories	33,500		28,750	
Trade receivables	27,130		26,300	
Cash	1,870		3,900	
		62,500		58,950
		119,510		107,160
EQUITY AND LIABILITIES				
Equity				
Share capital	20,000		18,000	
Share premium	12,000		10,000	
Consolidated retained earnings	24,885		18,340	
		56,885		46,340
Non-controlling interest		3,625		1,920
Non current liabilities				
Interest-bearing borrowings		18,200		19,200
Current liabilities				
Trade payables	33,340		32,810	
Interest payable	1,360		1,440	
Tax	6,100		5,450	
		40,800		39,700
		119,510		107,160

Notes

(a)   Several years ago, AH acquired 80% of the issued ordinary shares of its subsidiary, BI. On 1 January 20X5, AH acquired 75% of the issued ordinary shares of CJ in exchange for a fresh issue of 2 million of its own $1 ordinary shares (issued at a premium of $1 each) and $2 million in cash. The net assets of CJ at the date of acquisition were assessed as having the following fair values.

	$'000
Property, plant and equipment	4,200
Inventories	1,650
Receivables	1,300
Cash	50
Trade payables	(1,950)
Tax	(250)
	5,000

(b)   During the year, AH disposed of a non-current asset of property for proceeds of $2,250,000. The carrying value of the asset at the date of disposal was $1,000,000. There were no other disposals of non-current assets. Depreciation of $7,950,000 was charged against consolidated profits for the year.

(c)   Intangible assets comprise goodwill on acquisition of BI and CJ (20X4: BI only). Goodwill has remained unimpaired since acquisition. Group policy is to measure non-controlling interests at acquisition at their proportionate share of the fair value of the identifiable net assets.

Required

Prepare the consolidated statement of cash flows of the AH Group for the financial year ended 30 June 20X5 in the form required by IAS 7 *Statement of cash flows*, and using the indirect method. Notes to the statement of cash flows are **not** required, but full workings should be shown.

(25 marks)

32 Objective test questions: Related parties

7 mins

32.1 Linney Co is a company specialised in luxury blinds. The majority of Linney Co's long term finance is provided by KPG Bank.

Linney Co is 90% owned by Corti, a listed entity. Corti is a long-established company controlled by the Benedetti family through an agreement which pools their voting rights.

Linney regularly provides blinds to Venetia Hotels, a company in which Laura McRae has a minority (10%) holding. Laura McRae is the wife of Francesco Benedetti, one of the key Benedetti family shareholders that controls Corti.

30% of Linney's revenue comes from transactions with a major supplier, Dreich.

Which of the following are NOT related parties of LM in accordance with IAS 24?

A   KPG Bank only
B   Dreich only
C   KPG Bank and Dreich
D   KPG Bank, Dreich and Laura McRae

32.2 Figleaf operates an international restaurant chain. It charges its subsidiaries an annual management services fee of 20% of profit before tax (before accounting for the fee). Figleaf is 100% owned by a holding company, Tree, which in turn is majority owned by a wealthy investor, Mr Chan.

Figleaf provides interest free loans to its junior employees and also a defined benefit pension plan. Figleaf made contributions of $3 million to the pension plan for the year ended 31 December 20X1. In the same year, Mr Chan made a loan of $5 million to Figleaf for the acquisition of new restaurants, at an interest of 2%.

Which of the following should be disclosed in the consolidated financial statements of the Figleaf Group under IAS 24?

1   The management fee from Figleaf's subsidiaries
2   The name of Figleaf's ultimate controlling party, Mr Chan
3   Details of the interest free loans to junior employees
4   Details of the pension plan
5   Details of the $5 million loan from Mr Chan

A   1, 2, 4 and 5 only
B   1, 2, 3 and 4 only
C   1, 2 and 4 only
D   All of the items should be disclosed

32.3 No disclosure is required of intragroup related party transactions in the consolidated financial statements.

Is this statement true or false?

A   True
B   False

32.4 Which of the following statements is/are CORRECT in relation to IAS 24 Related Party Disclosures?

1   A transaction with a related party only requires disclosure if it is at below market value

2   The aim of IAS 24 is to make users of financial statements aware of the potential impact of related party transactions on an entity's financial position and profit or loss

3   Two associates in the same group are related parties

4   If an entity has a joint venture and the joint venture has a subsidiary, both the joint venture and its subsidiary are related to the entity

A   1 and 3
B   2 and 4
C   3 and 4
D   All of the above

33 Objective test questions: Earnings per share   7 mins

33.1 Barwell had 10 million ordinary shares in issue throughout the year ended 30 June 20X3. On 1 July 20X2 it had issued $2 million of 6% convertible loan stock, each $5 of loan stock convertible into 4 ordinary shares on 1 July 20X6 at the option of the holder.

Barwell had profit after tax for the year ended 30 June 20X3 of $1,850,000. It pays tax on profits at 30%.

What was diluted EPS for the year?

A   16.7c
B   18.5c
C   16.1c

33.2 At 1 January 20X8 Artichoke had 5 million $1 equity shares in issue. On 1 June 20X8 it made a 1 for 5 rights issue at a price of $1.50. The market price of the shares on the last day of quotation with rights was $1.80.

Total earnings for the year ended 31 December 20X8 was $7.6 million.

What was EPS for the year?

A $1.35
B $1.36
C $1.27
D $1.06

33.3 Waffle had share capital of $7.5 million in 50c equity shares at 1 October 20X6. On 1 January 20X7 it made an issue of 4 million shares at full market price immediately followed by a 1 for 3 bonus issue.

The financial statements at 30 September 20X7 showed profit for the year of $12 million.

What was EPS for the year?

A   53c
B   73c
C   48c
D   50c

33.4 Plumstead had 4 million equity shares in issue throughout the year ended 31 March 20X7. On 30 September 20X7 it made a 1 for 4 bonus issue. Profit after tax for the year ended 31 March 20X8 was $3.6 million, out of which an equity dividend of 20c per share was paid. The financial statements for the year ended 31 March 20X7 showed EPS of 70c.

What is the EPS for the year ended 31 March 20X8 and the restated EPS for the year ended 31 March 20X7?

	20X8	20X7
A	72c	87.5c
B	52c	56c
C	80c	87.5c
D	72c	56c

34 Pilum

25 mins

A statement showing the retained profit of Pilum Co for the year ended 31 December 20X4 is set out below.

	$	$
Profit before tax		2,530,000
Income tax expense		(1,127,000)
		1,403,000
Transfer to reserves		(230,000)
Dividends paid in the period:		
Preference share dividends	276,000	
Ordinary share dividends	414,000	
		(690,000)
Retained profit		483,000

On 1 January 20X4 the issued share capital of Pilum Co was 4,600,000 6% irredeemable non-cumulative preference shares of $1 each and 4,120,000 ordinary shares of $1 each.

Required

Calculate the earnings per share (on basic and diluted basis) in respect of the year ended 31 December 20X4 for each of the following circumstances. (Each of the three circumstances (a) to (c) is to be dealt with separately.)

(a) On the basis that there was no change in the issued share capital of the company during the year ended 31 December 20X4. **(3 marks)**

(b) On the basis that the company made a rights issue of $1 ordinary shares on 1 October 20X4 in the proportion of 1 for every 5 shares held, at a price of $1.20. The market price for the shares at close of trade on the last day of quotation cum rights was $1.78 per share. **(5 marks)**

(c) On the basis that the company made no new issue of shares during the year ended 31 December 20X4 but on 1 January 20X4 issued $1,500,000 5% convertible loan stock with a five year term. The liability component of the loan stock at 1 January 20X4 was calculated as $1,320,975 using an effective interest rate of 8%. The loan stock may be converted into $1 ordinary shares as follows:

20X5 90 $1 shares for $100 nominal value loan stock

20X6 85 $1 shares for $100 nominal value loan stock

20X7 80 $1 shares for $100 nominal value loan stock

20X8 75 $1 shares for $100 nominal value loan stock **(6 marks)**

Assume where appropriate that the income tax rate is 30%.

(Total = 14 marks)

35 Objective test questions: Ethics in financial reporting

35.1 You are employed in the Finance department of Furlong Co. The company is involved in a court case that is on-going at the year end, which the lawyers believe it is going to lose. The lawyers estimate that there is a 20% of Furlong being ordered to pay a $60,000 fine, a 30% chance of it being ordered to pay a $80,000 fine and a 50% chance of it being ordered to pay a $150,000 fine. The directors propose to make a provision of $75,000.

Would adopting the proposed course of action comply with the CIMA *Code of Ethics*?

A Yes

B No

35.2   You are employed in the Finance department of Fathom Co. On 1 January 20X2, Fathom Co purchased 100,000 $1 ordinary shares of Guess Co for $2.30 each, incurring transaction costs $10,000. The intention is to hold the investment for the long term. At the year end, the directors intend to value the investment at its year end share price of $1.80 per share recognising a loss of $60,000 in other comprehensive income.

Would adopting the proposed course of action comply with the principle of professional competence in the CIMA *Code of Ethics*?

A   Yes
B   No

35.3   Which of the following most accurately describes what principle of confidentiality means for a professional accountant?

A   A professional accountant must never, in any circumstance, disclose any information acquired as a result of professional or business relationships to third parties.

B   A professional accountant must never disclose any information acquired as a result of professional or business relationships to third parties, except when requested by the police or tax authorities.

C   A professional accountant may only disclose information acquired as a result of professional or business relationships to third parties with the consent of the parties involved.

D   A professional accountant should not disclose any information acquired as a result of professional or business relationships to third parties without proper and specific authority, unless there is a legal or professional right or duty to disclose.

35.4   John, a professional accountant in business, is asked by the Financial Director of the company he is working for to determine the appropriate accounting treatment for a business combination. Five months previously, he had performed the feasibility study that supported the acquisition decision.

Which of the following ethical threat, if any, does John currently face?

A   Self-interest threat.
B   Self-review threat.
C   Advocacy threat.
D   No ethical threat arises.

35.5   The directors of TF receive a bonus if the operating cash flow exceeds a predetermined target for the year. In prior periods, the accounting policy has been to record dividends paid as an operating cash flow. The directors are proposing to change the accounting policy and record dividends paid as a financing cash flow.

When applying the CIMA *Code of Ethics* which of the following statements are appropriate in relation to this scenario?

1.   This accounting treatment is not permitted by IAS 7 and if adopted by the directors, they are not complying with the fundamental principle of professional competence.

2.   The accounting treatment is permitted by IAS 7 but the change in accounting policy should only be adopted if it results in information that is more reliable and relevant to the decisions of the users of financial statements.

3.   There is a self-interest threat as the directors are proposing an accounting treatment which will result in their own personal gain and might not be in the best interests of the entity and its stakeholders.

4.   The directors must contact the CIMA Ethics Helpline before taking any action.

A   1 and 4
B   2 and 3
C   1 and 3
D   2, 3 and 4

36 Objective test questions: Analysis of financial performance and position

9 mins

36.1   An entity has an average operating profit margin of 23% and an average asset turnover of 0.8, which is similar to the averages for the industry.

The entity is likely to be:

A   An architectural practice
B   A supermarket
C   An estate agent
D   A manufacturer

36.2   Extracts from the financial statements of Persimmon are as follows:

Statement of profit or loss		Statement of financial position	
	$'000		$'000
Operating profit	230	Ordinary shares	2,000
Finance costs	(15)	Revaluation surplus	300
Profit before tax	215	Retained earnings	1,200
Income tax	(15)		3,500
Profit for the year	200	10% loan notes	1,000
		Current liabilities	100
		Total equity and liabilities	4,600

What is the return on capital employed?

A   5.1%
B   4.7%
C   6.6%
D   6%

36.3   Which of the following will increase the length of a company's operating cycle?

A   Reducing the receivables collection period`
B   Reducing the inventory holding period
C   Reducing the payables payment period
D   Reducing time taken to produce goods

36.4   In the year to 31 December 20X9 Weston pays an interim equity dividend of 3.4c per share and declares a final equity dividend of 11.1c. It has 5 million $1 shares in issue and the ex div share price is $3.50.

What is the dividend yield?

A   4%
B   24%
C   3.2%
D   4.1%

36.5   Camargue is a listed company with four million 50c ordinary shares in issue. The following extract is from its financial statements for the year ended 30 September 20X4:

Statement of profit or loss

	$'000
Profit before tax	900
Income tax expense	(100)
Profit for the year	800

At 30 September 20X4 the market price of Camargue's shares was $1.50. What was the P/E ratio on that date?

A   6.6
B   7.5
C   3.75
D   3.3

37 DM   45 mins

DM, a listed entity, has just published its financial statements for the year ended 31 December 20X4. DM operates a chain of 42 supermarkets in one of the six major provinces of its country of operation. During 20X4, there has been speculation in the financial press that the entity was likely to be a takeover target for one of the larger national chains of supermarkets that is currently under-represented in DM's province. A recent newspaper report has suggested that DM's directors are unlikely to resist a takeover. The six board members are all nearing retirement, and all own significant non-controlling shareholdings in the business.

You have been approached by a private shareholder in DM. She is concerned that the directors have a conflict of interests and that the financial statements for 20X4 may have been manipulated.

The statement of profit or loss and other comprehensive income and summarised statement of changes in equity of DM, with comparatives, for the year ended 31 December 20X4, and a statement of financial position with comparatives at that date are as follows:

DM STATEMENT OF PROFIT OR LOSS AND OTHER COMPREHENSIVE INCOME FOR THE YEAR ENDED 31 DECEMBER 20X4

	20X4 $m	20X3 $m
Revenue, net of sales tax	1,255	1,220
Cost of sales	(1,177)	(1,145)
Gross profit	78	75
Operating expenses	(21)	(29)
Finance cost	(10)	(10)
Profit before tax	47	36
Income tax expense	(14)	(13)
Profit/total comprehensive income for the year	33	23

DM SUMMARISED STATEMENT OF CHANGES IN EQUITY FOR THE YEAR ENDED
31 DECEMBER 20X4

	20X4 $m	20X3 $m
Opening balance	276	261
Profit/total comprehensive income for the year	33	23
Dividends	(8)	(8)
Closing balance	301	276

DM STATEMENT OF FINANCIAL POSITION AT 31 DECEMBER 20X4

	20X4		20X3	
	$m	$m	$m	$m
Non-current assets				
Property, plant and equipment	580		575	
Goodwill	100		100	
		680		675
Current assets				
Inventories	47		46	
Trade receivables	12		13	
Cash	46		12	
		105		71
		785		746
Equity				
Share capital	150		150	
Retained earnings	151		126	
		301		276
Non-current liabilities				
Interest-bearing borrowings	142		140	
Deferred tax	25		21	
		167		161
Current liabilities				
Trade and other payables	297		273	
Short-term borrowings	20		36	
		317		309
		785		746

Notes

(a)   DM's directors have undertaken a reassessment of the useful lives of property, plant and equipment during the year. In most cases, they estimate that the useful lives have increased and the depreciation charges in 20X4 have been adjusted accordingly.

(b)   Six new stores have been opened during 20X4, bringing the total to 42.

(c)   Four key ratios for the supermarket sector (based on the latest available financial statements of twelve listed entities in the sector) are as follows:

(i)   Annual sales per store: $27.6m
(ii)   Gross profit margin: 5.9%
(iii)   Net profit margin: 3.9%
(iv)   Non-current asset turnover (including both tangible and intangible non-current assets): 1.93

Required

(a)   **Prepare** a report, addressed to the investor, analysing the performance and position of DM based on the financial statements and supplementary information provided above. The report should also include comparisons with the key sector ratios, and it should address the investor's concerns about the possible manipulation of the 20X4 financial statements.   **(20 marks)**

(b)   **Explain** the limitations of the use of sector comparatives in financial analysis.   **(5 marks)**

(Total: 25 marks)

1 Objective test questions: sources of long-term finance

1.1 **D** Short-term loans are subject to a loan agreement giving the bank security and a definite repayment schedule. This lowers the risk from their perspective, hence the interest rate charged is lower.

1.2 **A** Ordinary shares are most risky from the debt holder's perspective – the company can decide whether and how much of a dividend to pay.

Preference shares are next most risky – dividends are only payable if profit is available to pay dividends from.

Trade payables are next because they have to be paid before shareholders but are typically unsecured.

Finally, banks with fixed and floating charges face least risk.

1.3 **D** Zero coupon bonds are issued at a discount to their redemption value and do not pay any interest.

1.4 **C** Dividend creation benefits the intermediaries' investors, not their customers/borrowers.

1.5 **C** Money markets focus on short-term financial instruments. A corporate bond is a long-term source of finance, hence is a capital market instrument. Certificates of deposit and commercial paper are short-term private sector lending/borrowing. A treasury bill is short-term government borrowing.

1.6 **B** Increased regulation and transparency reduce the actual and perceived risk from the point of view of shareholders, making the shares more attractive and hence more valuable. In addition listed company shares are naturally more liquid than an equivalent unlisted company, again adding to their value. The process of listing is therefore likely to create value.

1.7 **D** Ordinary shares are riskiest as all other investors are preferential to ordinary shareholders. Preference shares are riskier than corporate bonds as preference shares are paid after corporate bonds – bonds imply a contractual right to receive a pre-defined level of return. Treasury bills are short-term government borrowing hence are the lowest risk of all.

1.8 **A** Money markets are markets for short-term capital, not long-term capital.

2 Panda

> **Top tips.** Remember in (b) that the value of rights is **not** the cost of the rights share. (c) emphasises that taking up and selling the rights should have identical effects.

(a) Current total market value = $21m × 16
$$= \$336m$$

Market value per share = $336m/(60m × 4)
$$= \$1.40$$

Rights issue price = $1.40 × 0.70
$$= \$0.98$$

Theoretical ex-rights price

	$
5 shares @ $1.40	7.00
1 share @ $0.98	0.98
6 shares	7.98

Theoretical ex-rights price   = $7.98/6
                              = $1.33

(b) **Rights price**

	$
Theoretical ex-rights price	1.33
Cost of rights share	0.98
Value of rights	0.35

(c) **Take up rights issue**

	$
Value of shares after rights issue (10,000 × 6/5 × $1.33)	15,960
Cost of rights (2,000 × $0.98)	(1,960)
	14,000

Sell rights

	$
Value of shares (10,000 × $1.33)	13,300
Sale of rights (2,000 × $0.35)	700
	14,000

Allow rights offer to lapse

	$
Value of shares (10,000 × $1.33)	13,300

If the investor either takes up the rights issue or sells his rights then his wealth will remain the same. The difference is that if he takes up the rights issue he will maintain his relative shareholding but if he sells his rights his percentage shareholding will fall, although he will gain $700 in cash.

However if the investor allows the rights to lapse his wealth will decrease by $700.

(d) Panda clearly needs to raise $47.04 million which is why it was decided to make a 1 for 5 rights issue of 48 million additional shares at a price of $0.98. Provided that this amount is raised it could have been done (for example) by issuing 96 million new shares as a two for five rights issue with the issue price at $0.49 per share.

The **price of the issue** and the **number of shares should not be important** in a competitive market as the value of the business will not change and nor will the shareholders' percentage shareholding.

However the critical factor about the **price of the rights issue** is that it **must be below the market value** at the time of the rights issue. If the rights issue price is higher than the market value then there is no incentive to shareholders to purchase the additional shares and the rights issue will fail. As far as the business is concerned the details of the rights issue including the price must be determined a considerable time before the rights issue actually takes place, therefore there is always the risk that the share price might fall in the intervening period.

3 Objective test questions: cost of capital

3.1   **D**   20X9 to 20Y3 covers 4 years of growth,

so the average annual growth rate $= \sqrt[4]{(423/220)} - 1 = 0.178 = 17.8\%$

$$K_e = \frac{d_0(1+g)}{P_0} + g$$

$$K_e - g = \frac{d_0(1+g)}{P_0}$$

$$P_0 = \frac{d_0(1+g)}{K_e - g}$$

= (423,000 × 1.178) / (0.25 – 0.178) = $6,920,750 for 4 million shares = $1.73 per share

3.2 **A**   g = retention rate × return on investment.

Retention rate = proportion of earnings retained = ($1.50 - $0.5)/$1.50 = 66.7%

Return on new investment = EPS / net assets per share = $1.5 / $6 = 0.25 so 25%

g = 66.7% × 25% = 16.7%

$$K_e = \frac{d_0(1+g)}{P_0} + g$$

$$= \frac{(\$0.50 \times 1.167)}{(\$4.50 - \$0.50)} + 0.167$$ Note: Share price given is cum div

= 31%

3.3 **A** $K_d = I(1-t) / P_o$

The loan note pays interest of $100 nominal × 10% = 10%. Ex-interest market price is $95 – $10 = $85.

Before the tax cut K_d = 10(1 – 0.3) / 85 = 8.2%

After the tax cut K_d = 10(1 – 0.2) / 85 = 9.4%

Decreasing tax reduces tax saved therefore increases the cost of debt.

3.4 **C**   Conversion value: Future share price = $2.50 × (1.1)^5 = $4.03;

so conversion value = 20 × $4.03 = $80.60. The cash alternative = 100 × 1.1 = $110 therefore investors would not convert and redemption value = $110.

Kd = IRR of the after tax cash flows as follows:

Time	$	DF 10%	Present value 10% ($)	DF 15%	Present value 15% ($)
0	(90)	1	(90)	1	(90)
1-5	10(1 – 0.3) = 7	3.791	26.54	3.352	23.46
5	110	0.621	68.31	0.497	54.67
			4.85		(11.87)

$$IRR = a + \frac{NPV_a}{NPV_a - NPV_b}(b - a)$$

$$= 10\% + \frac{4.85}{(4.85 + 11.87)}(15\% - 10\%)$$

= 11.5%

3.5 **C** $K_d = I(1 - T) / P_0 = 13(1 - 0.3) / 90 = 10.11\%$

$V_d = \$7m \times (90/100) = \$6.3m$

$K_e = 12\%$ (given)

$V_e = \$3 \times 10m$ shares $= \$30m$ Note: reserves are included as part of
share price

$V_e + V_d = \$6.3m + \$30m = \$36.3m$

$$\text{WACC} = \left[\frac{V_e}{V_e + V_d}\right]k_e + \left[\frac{V_d}{V_e + V_d}\right]k_d$$

$$= [30/36.3]12\% \quad + \quad (6.3/36.3)10.11\% \quad = 11.7\%$$

3.6 **B** ex-div share price $= \$0.30 - (8\% \times \$0.50) = \$0.26$

$K_p = \$0.50 \times 8\% / \$0.26 = 15.4\%$

Note: dividends are not tax deductible hence no adjustment for corporation tax is required.

3.7 **A** $$P_0 = \frac{D_0(1+g)}{(r_e - g)}$$ Given on the formula sheet

Growth 'g' – Dividends grew from ($\$0.50-\$0.10=$) $\$0.40$ to $\$0.50$ in 3 years. This is an
average annual growth rate of:

$\$0.40 (1+g)^3 = \$0.50$

$(1+g) = \sqrt[3]{(0.5/0.4)}$

$g = 0.077 = 7.7\%$

$$P_0 = \frac{\$0.50(1+0.077)}{(0.10-0.077)} = \$23.41$$

3.8 **A** Statement 1 needs to be assumed: If D_0 is not typical, a better valuation would include the
dividend that would have been paid if D_0 were in line with historical trends.

Statement 2 needs to be assumed: Only one rate for growth is included in the formula.

Statement 3 needs to be assumed: Only one cost of equity is included in the formula.

Statement 4 does not need to be assumed: Minority shareholders are entitled to dividends
only, hence this valuation technique is in fact best suited to a minority shareholding.

3.9 **D** Corporation tax is not relevant as investors pay market price and they receive the gross
dividend.

Redemption value $= (\$100 \times 1.15=) \$115$ cash or conversion value $= P_0(1+g)R = (4
\times 1.1^3 \times 25=) \$133.10$ worth of shares.

Investors would opt to convert, hence the redemption value built into market price will be
$\$133.10$.

Time		$	Discount factor 10%	Present value $
1-3	Interest	9	2.487	22.383
3	Redemption	133.10	0.751	99.9581
				122.3411

So current market value = $\$122.34$

4 Objective test questions: Financial instruments

4.1 **B**   Intangible assets. These do not give rise to a present right to receive cash or other financial assets. The other options are financial instruments.

4.2 **B**

	$'000
Interest years 1-3 (30m × 8% × (0.91 + 0.83 + 0.75)	5,976
Repayment year 3 (30m × 0.75)	22,500
Debt component	28,476
Equity option (β)	1,524
	30,000

4.3 **D**

	$'000
Proceeds (20m – 0.5m)	19,500
Interest 10%	1,950
Interest paid (20m × 5%)	(1,000)
Balance 30 March 20X1	20,450
Interest 10%	2,045
Interest paid	(1,000)
	21,495

4.4 **C**   A resource controlled by an entity as a result of past events and from which future economic benefits are expected to flow to the entity

4.5 **C**   This is a valid liability.

The licence payment could be avoided by ceasing manufacture.

The fall in value of the investment is a loss chargeable to the statement of profit or loss.

Planned expenditure does not constitute an obligation.

4.6 **C**   Disclosure of accounting policies is particularly important when comparing the results and performance of one entity against another which may be applying different policies.

5 Amps

(a)   **Redeemable bonds**

The current treatment accounts for interest on a cash basis. IAS 32 classifies these bonds as financial liabilities since they are not derivatives and they are not held for trading purposes. IAS 39 states that they should be held at amortised cost using their effective interest rate which means that the finance charge in any one year is equal to a constant rate based on the carrying amount. This applies the matching concept. Based upon an effective constant rate of interest of 7½% the charge in 20X0 should be $75,000. The difference between the revised charge of $75,000 and the amount paid to debt holders of $40,000 (ie $35,000) should be added to the statement of financial position liability, giving a total liability at 31 December 20X0 of $1,035,000.

(b)   **Convertible debentures**

The convertible debentures are compound instruments, as they have characteristics of both debt (the obligation to pay interest and to repay capital) and equity instruments (the right for the holder to have a share). The debt and equity elements should be classified separately as liability and equity as required by IAS 32. The split is based on measuring the debt element using market rates of return at inception for non-convertible debt of the same maturity date and value and treating the equity element as a balancing figure.

Consequently, the debt element of the convertible debentures should be reallocated as a current liability in this case. The annual return would be treated as finance costs until conversion/redemption.

6 JKA

(a)   **Factoring of receivables**

The *Framework* principles include a requirement that financial statements should reflect the substance of transactions. To determine whether the trade receivables should be recognised in JKA's or the factor's financial statements, it needs to be established which entity has the risks and benefits associated with the receivables, ie. which can demonstrate that they meet the *Framework*'s definition of an asset.

JKA retains the bad debt risk of the receivables because JKA has to reimburse the factor for any shortfall between the amounts collected and the $3.6 million transferred by the factor to JKA. JKA also has slow movement risk as under the terms of the agreement, JKA pays interest to the factor on outstanding balances.

JKA also retains some of the benefits associated with the $4 million receivables as the factor has to pay JKA any amounts received in excess of $3.6 million less any interest.

Therefore, JKA should not have derecognised the $4 million receivables and recorded a loss of $0.4 million in the statement of profit or loss. As they retain the most significant risks and benefits associated with the trade receivables, they need to reinstate the $4 million receivables in their statement of financial position, reverse the $0.4 million loss and record the proceeds of $3.6 million from the factor as a liability. In substance, JKA has received a loan, secured on its trade receivables.

Sale of land

There are features of this sale of land that suggest that its true substance is not a sale. The land is being sold to a finance company (DEX Finance), at less than its carrying value in JKA's statement of financial position. There is also an agreement giving JKA an option to repurchase the land within three years and requiring the entity to repurchase the land by the end of that period. This means that if the land increases in value, JKA can repurchase it at the agreed price and benefit from the increase in value but if the value of the land decreases, JKA will still be obliged to repurchase it and will suffer a loss.

The risks and benefit of owning the land remain with JKA, so in substance the transaction is a refinancing exercise. The land should be reinstated in the statement of financial position, the "loss" on the disposal should be reversed and the proceeds of the sale should be treated as a loan.

As the repurchase price is higher than the sales proceeds (from $60,000 to $100,000 higher depending on the price at the date of repurchase), in substance the excess represents interest payable on the loan. However, as the sale took place on the final day of the accounting period, no interest should be recognised in the current year.

(b) **Factoring of receivables**

DEBIT	Trade receivables	$4,000,000		
CREDIT	Liabilities		$3,600,000	
CREDIT	Profit or loss		$400,000	

Being correction of accounting treatment for factored receivables.

Sale of land

DEBIT	Property, plant and equipment	$520,000		
CREDIT	Liabilities		$500,000	
CREDIT	Profit or loss		$20,000	

Being correction of accounting treatment for sale of land.

7 Objective test questions: Leases

7.1 **A** $^3/_{10} \times \$3,000 = \$900$

7.2 **C** In a finance lease, the risks and rewards of ownership are transferred.

7.3 **A**

	$
Deposit	30,000
Instalments (8 × $20,000)	160,000
	190,000
Fair value	154,000
Interest	36,000

Sum of the digits $= \dfrac{8 \times 9}{2} = 36$

6 months to	June X1	$^8/_{36} \times \$36,000$		
	Dec X1	$^7/_{36} \times \$36,000$		
	June X2	$^6/_{36} \times \$36,000$		
	Dec X2	$^5/_{36} \times \$36,000$		
	June X3	$^4/_{36} \times \$36,000$	=	$4,000
	Dec X3	$^3/_{36} \times \$36,000$	=	$3,000
				$7,000

8 Objective test questions: Provisions, contingent liabilities and contingent assets

8.1 **D** Loss of the case is not 'probable' , so no provision is made, but the legal costs will have to be paid so should be provided for.

8.2 **A** $2 million should be provided for and capitalised as part of the cost of the mine. It will then be depreciated over the useful life.

8.3 **D**

	$m
$2 million × 15%	0.3
$6 million × 5%	0.3
	0.6

8.4 **D** The cost of the overhaul will be capitalised when it takes place. No obligation exists before the overhaul is carried out. The other options would all give rise to valid provisions.

9 Objective test questions: Deferred tax

9.1 **A** Item 2 consists of permanent differences, all the rest are temporary differences.

9.2 **D** All four items have a carrying amount equal to their tax base.

9.3 **B** IAS 12 states that deferred tax assets and liabilities should not be discounted.

9.4 **D**

	$
Taxable temporary differences b/f	850,000
Depreciation for tax purposes	500,000
Depreciation charged in the financial statements	(450,000)
Revaluation surplus	250,000
Taxable temporary differences c/f	1,150,000
Deferred tax at 30%	345,000

10 Objective test questions: Share based payment

10.1 **B** Expense recognised at 31 December 20X5 = (610 x 500 x $4.30 x 1/3) = $437,167. The granting of share appreciation rights represent a cash-settled share based payment transaction, so the fair value of liability must be remeasured at each reporting date.

10.2 **A** Share options are equity-settled, so credit goes to other reserves within equity. The directors' services do not qualify as assets, so the debit is taken to staff costs within statement of profit or loss. The amount recognised is calculated as 500 options x 8 directors x $12 x 1/2 years = $24,000.

10.3 **B** As this is a cash-settled payment, we credit liability, not equity. Since the payment relates to the employees' service, it is an expense, not an asset. Only the fair value of the share appreciation right is relevant, and the total cost must be spread over the 3 years of service to which the expense relates.

25 shares x 3,500 employees x 55% x $18 x 1/3 = $288,750

11 Share-based payment

(a) **Accounting entries**

31.12.X1 $

DEBIT   Staff costs   188,000
CREDIT   Other reserves (within equity)   188,000
         ((800 – 95) × 200 × $4 × 1/3)
Being share-based payment expense for the year ended 31 December 20X1

31.12.X2

DEBIT   Staff costs (W1)   201,333
CREDIT   Other reserves (within equity)   201,333
Being share-based payment expense for the year ended 31 December 20X2

31.12.X3

DEBIT   Staff costs (W2)   202,667
CREDIT   Other reserves (within equity)   202,667
Being share-based payment expense for the year ended 31 December 20X3

Issue of shares:

DEBIT   Cash (740 × 200 × $1.50)   222,000
DEBIT   Other reserves (within equity)   592,000

CREDIT   Share capital (740 × 200 × $1)   148,000
CREDIT   Share premium (balancing figure)   666,000
Being share issue

Workings

1   *Equity at 31.12.X2*

Equity b/d   188,000
∴ P/L charge   201,333
Equity c/d ((800 – 70) × 200 × $4 × 2/3)   389,333

2   *Equity at 31.12.X3*

Equity b/d   389,333
∴ P/L charge   202,667
Equity c/d ((800 – 40 – 20) × 200 × $4 × 3/3)   592,000

(b)   **Cash-settled share-based payment**

If J&B had offered cash payments based on the value of the shares at vesting date rather than options, the key differences would be recognising a liability in the statement of financial position rather than equity (reflecting the obligation to employees) and measuring it at the fair value at the year end date rather than the grant date (to reflect the best estimate of what will be paid).

In each of the three years a liability would be shown in the statement of financial position representing the expected amount payable based on the following:

No of employees estimated at the year end to be entitled to rights at the vesting date	×	Number of rights each	×	Fair value of each right at year end	×	Cumulative proportion of vesting period elapsed

The movement in the liability would be charged to the statement of profit or loss representing further entitlements received during the year and adjustments to expectations accrued in previous years.

The liability would continue to be adjusted (resulting in a statement of profit or loss charge) for changes in the fair value of the right over the period between when the rights become fully vested and are subsequently exercised. It would then be reduced for cash payments as the rights are exercised.

12 Objective test questions: Revenue

12.1   **A**

	$'000
Contract price	50,000
Costs to date	(12,000)
Specialist plant	(8,000)
Costs to complete	(10,000)
Total profit on contract	20,000

Profit to date = $20m × 22/50 = $8,800,000

12.2   **A**

	$
Costs incurred to date	48,000
Recognised profits (W)	10,800
Progress billings	(50,400)
Due from customers	8,400

Working	
Total contract revenue	120,000
Costs to date	(48,000)
Costs to complete	(48,000)
Total expected profit	24,000
Profit to date (24,000 × 45%)	10,800

12.3 **B**   This feature suggests that the transaction is a genuine sale.

If the seller retains the right to use the asset or it remains on his premises, then the risks and rewards have not been transferred. If the sale price does not equal market value, then the transaction is likely to be a secured loan.

13 Objective test questions: Basic groups

13.1 **D**   There is now no basis on which a subsidiary may be excluded from consolidation.

13.2 **C**   A and B give rise to a subsidiary relationship, D is part of the definition of control.

13.3 **B**   A subsidiary may prepare additional statements up to the group reporting date and, where statements for a different date are used, adjustments should be made for significant transactions. The allowable gap between reporting dates is three months, not five.

13.4 **B**   The present value of the future cash flows that the asset is expected to generate measures present value, not fair value. The other items would be considered in determining fair value.

13.5 **B**

	$
Fair value at acquisition (200,000 × 30% × $1.75)	105,000
Share of post-acquisition retained earnings ((750 – 450) × 30%)	90,000
Depreciation on fair value adjustment ((250/40) × 30%)	(1,875)
	193,125

13.6 **C**   ($1.2 million / 8 × 4/12) × 80% = $40,000

The adjustment will reduce depreciation over the next 8 years, so it will *increase* retained earnings.

13.7 **A**

	$'000
Shares (18m × 2/3 × $5.75)	69,000
Deferred consideration (18m × $2.42 × $1/1.1^2$)	36,000
	105,000

13.8 **D**

	$	$
Consideration transferred		800,000
Fair value of non-controlling interest		220,000
		1,020,000
Fair value of net assets:		
Shares	100,000	
Retained earnings	570,000	
Revaluation surplus	150,000	
Intangible	90,000	
		(910,000)
		110,000

14 Group financial statements

Tutorial note. This is a general question to get you thinking about the nature of a group. The question strongly hints that there *are* limitations to group financial statements.

The objective of annual financial statements is to help shareholders exercise control over their company by providing information about how its affairs have been conducted. The shareholders of a parent company would not be given sufficient information from the financial statements of the parent company on its own, because not enough would be known about the nature of the assets, income and profits of all the subsidiary companies in which the parent company has invested. The primary purpose of group financial statements is to provide a true and fair view of the position and earnings of the parent company group as a whole, from the standpoint of the shareholders in the parent company.

However, group financial statements can be argued to have certain limitations.

(a)   Group financial statements may be misleading.

    (i)   The solvency (liquidity) of one company may hide the insolvency of another.

    (ii)   The profit of one company may conceal the losses of another.

    (iii)   They imply that group companies will meet each others' debts (this is certainly not true: a parent company may watch creditors of an insolvent subsidiary go unpaid without having to step in).

(b)   There may be some difficulties in defining the group or 'entity' of companies, although company law and accounting standards have removed many of the grey areas here.

(c)   Where a group consists of widely diverse companies in different lines of business, a set of group financial statements may obscure much important detail unless supplementary information about each part of the group's business is provided.

15 Putney and Wandsworth

CONSOLIDATED STATEMENT OF FINANCIAL POSITION AS AT 31 DECEMBER 20X5

	$
Non-current assets	
Property, plant & equipment (135,000 + 60,000)	195,000
Goodwill (W2)	1,250
	196,250
Current assets (62,000 + 46,000)	108,000
	304,250
Equity attributable to the owners of the parent	
Share capital	50,000
Revaluation surplus (W3)	63,500
Retained earnings (W4)	124,750
	238,250
Non-controlling interests (W5)	8,000
	246,250
Non-current liabilities (14,000 + 12,000)	26,000
Current liabilities (18,000 + 14,000)	32,000
	304,250

Workings

1   *Group structure*

Putney

|
| 1.1.X1
|

Wandsworth Pre-acq'n ret'd earnings $10,000

2   *Goodwill*

	$	$
Consideration transferred		25,000
Non-controlling interest at acquisition (25,000 × 10%)		2,500
Net assets at acquisition:		
Share capital	15,000	
Retained earnings at acquisition	10,000	
		(25,000)
Goodwill at acquisition		2,500
Impairment losses to date		(1,250)
Goodwill at 31.12.X5		1,250

3   *Revaluation surplus*

	Putney	*Wandsworth*
Per question	50,000	15,000
Pre-acquisition	–	(0)
	50,000	15,000
Wandsworth – share of post acquisition revaluation surplus		
(15,000 × 90%)	13,500	
	63,500	

4   *Retained earnings*

	Putney	*Wandsworth*
Per question	90,000	50,000
Pre-acquisition	–	(10,000)
	90,000	40,000
Wandsworth – share of post acquisition earnings		
(40,000 × 90%)	36,000	
Less: goodwill impairment losses to date	(1,250)	
	124,750	

5   *Non-controlling interests*

NCI at acquisition (W2)	2,500
Share of post acquisition revaluation surplus (15,000(W3) × 10%)	1,500
Share of post acquisition earnings (40,000(W3) × 10%)	4,000
	8,000

16 Balmes and Aribau

BALMES GROUP
CONSOLIDATED STATEMENT OF FINANCIAL POSITION AS AT 30 JUNE 20X3

	$'000
Non-current assets	
Property, plant & equipment (97,300 + 34,400 + (W6) 1,400)	133,100
Goodwill (W2)	2,800
Other intangible assets (5,100 + 1,200)	6,300
	142,200
Current assets	
Inventories (43,400 + 14,300)	57,700
Trade and other receivables (36,800 + 17,400)	54,200
Cash and cash equivalents	700
	112,600
	254,800
Equity attributable to the owners of the parent	
Share capital	50,000
General reserve (W3)	5,100
Retained earnings (W4)	122,040
	177,140
Non-controlling interests (W5)	9,760
	186,900
Non-current liabilities	
Loan notes (10,000 + 4,000)	14,000
Current liabilities	
Trade payables (28,400 + 15,700)	44,100
Income tax payable (7,300 + 2,400)	9,700
Bank overdraft	100
	53,900
	254,800

Workings

1   *Group structure*

Balmes

1.7.X1   80%

Aribau   Pre-acquisition retained earnings = $25m
                Pre-acquisition general reserve = $2m

2   *Goodwill*

	$'000	$'000
Consideration transferred		28,500
Non-controlling interests at acquisition (fair value)		7,000
Net fair value of identifiable assets acquired:		
Share capital	5,000	
General reserve	2,000	
Retained earnings	24,000	
Fair value adjustments (W6)	1,500	
		(32,500)
		3,000
Impairment losses to date		(200)
		2,800

3 *General reserve*

	Balmes $'000	Aribau $'000
Per question	4,300	3,000
Pre-acquisition		(2,000)
		1,000
Aribau – post acquisition general reserve (1,000 × 80%)	800	
	5,100	

4 *Retained earnings*

	Balmes $'000	Aribau $'000
Per question	118,800	37,100
Revaluation gain on investment in Aribau cancelled on consolidation (35,500 – 28,500)	(7,000)	
Fair value adjustments movement (W6)		(100)
Pre-acquisition retained earnings		(24,000)
		13,000
Aribau – share of post-acquisition earnings (13,000 × 80%)	10,400	
Less: Group share of goodwill impairment losses to date (80% x 200 (W2))	(160)	
	122,040	

5 *Non-controlling interest*

	$'000
Non-controlling interests at acquisition (W2)	7,000
Share of post-acquisition general reserve (1,000 (W3) × 20%)	200
Share of post-acquisition earnings (13,000(W4) × 20%)	2,600
NCI share of impairment losses on goodwill (200 (W2) x 20%)	(40)
	9,760

6 *Fair value adjustments*

	At acquisition date $'000	Movement $'000	At y/e date $'000
Land (5,000 – 4,500)	500		500
Buildings ((14,000 – 5,000) – (12,500 – 4,500))	1,000	(100)*	900
	1,500	(100)	1,400

*Extra depreciation ($1,000,000 × 2/20)

17 Reprise

REPRISE GROUP – CONSOLIDATED STATEMENT OF FINANCIAL POSITION AS AT 31 MARCH 20X4

	$'000
Non-current assets	
Land and buildings	3,350.0
Plant and equipment (1,010 + 2,210)	3,220.0
Motor vehicles (510 + 345)	855.0
Goodwill (W2)	826.0
	8,251.0
Current assets	
Inventories (890 + 352 – (W5) 7.2)	1,234.8
Trade receivables (1,372 + 514 – 39 – (W6) 36)	1,811.0
Cash and cash equivalents (89 + 51 + 39)	179.0
	3,224.8
	11,475.8
Equity attributable to owners of the parent	
Share capital	1,000.0
Retained earnings (W3)	5,257.3
Revaluation surplus	2,500.0
	8,757.3
Non-controlling interests (W4)	896.5
	9,653.8
Non-current liabilities	
10% debentures	500.0
Current liabilities	
Trade payables (996 + 362 – (W6) 36)	1,322.0
	11,475.8

Workings

1   Group structure

     R

     | 75%   ∴ non-controlling interests = 25%

     E   Pre-acquisition retained earnings = $1,044,000

2   Goodwill

	$'000	$'000
Consideration transferred		2,000
Non-controlling interests (at fair value)		
(125,000 shares × $4.40)		550
Net assets at acquisition as represented by:		
Share capital	500	
Retained earnings	1,044	
		(1,544)
		1,006
Impairment losses to date		(180)
		826

3   *Consolidated retained earnings*

	Reprise $'000	Encore $'000
Per question	4,225	2,610
PUP (W5)	(7.2)	
Pre-acquisition retained earnings		(1,044)
		1,566
Group share of post-acquisition retained earnings:		
Encore (1,566 × 75%)	1,174.5	
Group share of impairment losses (180 (W2) × 75%)	(135)	
	5,257.3	

4   *Non-controlling interests*

	$'000
NCI at acquisition (W2)	550
NCI share of post-acquisition retained earnings ((W3) 1,566 × 25%)	391.5
NCI share of impairment losses (180 (W2) × 25%)	(45)
	896.5

5   *Unrealised profit on inventories*

Reprise ⟶ Encore

Unrealised profit included in inventories is:

$$\$31,200 \times \frac{30}{130} = \$7,200$$

DEBIT (↓) Retained earnings of Reprise $7,200

CREIT (↓) Inventories $7,200

6   *Trade receivables/trade payables*

Intragroup balance of $75,000 is reduced to $36,000 once cash-in-transit of $39,000 is followed through to its ultimate destination.

18 Objective test questions: Associates and joint arrangements

18.1 **A**

	$m
Cost (75m × $1.60)	120
Share of post-acquisition retained earnings (100 – 20) × 30%	24
	144

18.2 **C**   The group's share of the associate's profit after tax is recorded as a one-line entry. Option A would be correct for a subsidiary, not an associate. The dividends received from the associate are all that is recorded in the individual entity financial statements of the parent, but in the consolidated financial statements this is replaced by the group share of profit after tax.

18.3 **A**

	$'000
Cost of investment	2,500
Share of post-acquisition profit (6,400 – 5,300) × 30%)	330
PURP (700 × 30% ×30%)	(63)
	2,767

18.4 **B**

	$'000
Cost of investment	10,000
Share of post-acquisition profit (3,000 × 8/12) – 1,000) × 35%	350
Impairment	(500)
	9,850

18.5 **D** Joint ventures, like associates, are accounted for using the equity method. Joint operations are accounted for by including the investor's share of assets, liabilities, income and expenses as per the contractual arrangement. Goodwill must always be capitalised and reviewed for impairment annually.

18.6 **B** If the parties with joint control have rights to the net assets of the arrangement, then the arrangement is a joint venture. A joint operation may, in certain cases, be structured through a separate entity.

19 Hever

CONSOLIDATED STATEMENT OF FINANCIAL POSITION AS AT 31 DECEMBER 20X4

	$'000
Non-current assets	
Property, plant & equipment (370 + 190 + (W7) 45)	605
Goodwill (W2)	8
Investment in associate (W3)	165
	778
Current assets	
Inventories (160 + 100 – (W6) 1.5)	258.5
Trade receivables (170 + 90)	260
Cash (50 + 40)	90
	608.5
	1,386.5
Equity attributable to owners of the parent	
Share capital	200
Share premium reserve	100
Retained earnings (W4)	758.5
	1,058.5
Non-controlling interests (W5)	168
	1,226.5
Current liabilities	
Trade payables (100 + 60)	160
	1,386.5

Workings

1 Group structure

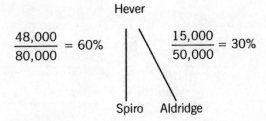

Hever

$\dfrac{48,000}{80,000} = 60\%$ $\dfrac{15,000}{50,000} = 30\%$

Spiro   Aldridge

Pre-acq'n reserves = $20k   = $150k

∴ In the absence of information to the contrary, Spiro is a subsidiary, and Aldridge an associate of Hever.

2   *Goodwill on consolidation – Spiro*

	$'000	$'000
Consideration transferred		128
Non-controlling interests (at 'full' fair value)		90
Net assets at acquisition:		
Share capital	80	
Share premium	80	
Retained earnings	20	
Fair value adjustments (W7)	30	
		(210)
Goodwill arising on consolidation		8

3   *Investment in associate*

	$'000
Cost of associate	90
Share of post-acquisition retained reserves (W4)	75
	165

4   *Retained earnings*

	Hever $'000	Spiro $'000	Aldridge $'000
Per question	568	200	400
PUP (W6)	(1.5)	–	–
Fair value movement (W7)		15	
Pre-acquisition retained earnings		(20)	(150)
		195	250

Group share of post acquisition ret'd earnings:	
Spiro (195 × 60%)	117
Aldridge (250 × 30%)	75
	758.5

5   *Non-controlling interests*

	$'000
NCI at acquisition (W2)	90
NCI share of post acquisition ret'd earnings ((W4) 195 × 40%)	78
	168

6   *Unrealised profit on inventories*

Hever ⟶ Spiro

Mark-up: $16,000 – $10,000 = $6,000 ∴ PUP = ¼ in inventory × $6,000 = $1,500

↓ Hever's retained earnings $1,500

↓ Inventories $1,500

7   *Fair values – adjustment to net assets*

	At acquisition	Movement	At year end
Property, plant and equipment	50	(5)	45
Inventories	(20)	20	0
	30	15	45

20 Bayonet

BAYONET GROUP
CONSOLIDATED STATEMENT OF FINANCIAL POSITION AS AT 31 DECEMBER 20X9

	$'000
Non-current assets	
Property, plant and equipment (14,500 + 12,140 + 17,500)	44,140
Goodwill (W2)	3,580
	47,720
Current assets	
Inventories (6,300 + 2,100 + 450)	8,850
Trade receivables (4,900 + 2,000 + 2,320)	9,220
Cash (500 + 1,440 + 515)	2,455
	20,525
	68,245
Equity attributable to owners of the parent	
Share capital – 50c ordinary shares	5,000
Retained earnings (W3)	40,680
	45,680
Non-controlling interests (W4)	12,600
	58,280
Current liabilities (5,700 + 2,280 + 1,985)	9,965
	68,245

Workings

1   Group structure

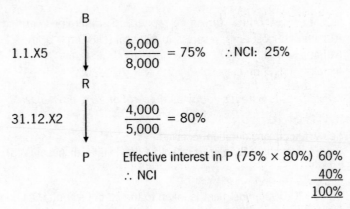

B

1.1.X5 $\frac{6,000}{8,000}$ = 75%   ∴NCI: 25%

R

31.12.X2 $\frac{4,000}{5,000}$ = 80%

P   Effective interest in P (75% × 80%) 60%
    ∴ NCI   40%
    100%

2   Goodwill

	Rifle		Pistol	
	$'000	$'000	$'000	$'000
Consideration transferred		10,000	(9,000 × 75%)	6,750
Non-controlling interests (at fair value)		3,230		4,600
Fair value of identifiable net assets at acq'n:				
Share capital	4,000		2,500	
Pre-acquisition retained earnings	8,000		6,500	
		(12,000)		(9,000)
		1,230		2,350
			3,580	

3   *Retained earnings*

	Bayonet $'000	Rifle $'000	Pistol $'000
Per question	25,500	20,400	16,300
Retained earnings at acquisition		(8,000)	(6,500)
		12,400	9,800
Group share of post acquisition ret'd earnings:			
Rifle (12,400 × 75%)	9,300		
Pistol (9,800 × 60%)	5,880		
	40,680		

4   *Non-controlling interests*

	Rifle $'000	Pistol $'000
NCI at acquisition (W2)	3,230	4,600
NCI share of post acquisition ret'd earnings:		
Rifle ((W3) 12,400 × 25%)	3,100	
Pistol ((W3) 9,800 × 40%)		3,920
Less: NCI share of investment in Pistol (9,000 × 25%)	(2,250)	
	4,080	8,520
	12,600	

21 Objective test questions: Changes in group structure

21.1 A

Non-controlling interests

	$'000
NCI at acquisition (($10m share capital + $6m retained earnings) × 20%)	3,200
NCI share of post acq'n reserves to disposal (($8.9m − $6m) × 20%)	580
NCI at disposal	3,780
Increase in NCI on disposal ($3,780k × 20%/20%)	3,780

Adjustment to parent's equity on disposal of 20% of Dopiaza

	$'000
Fair value of consideration received	4,400
Less increase in NCI in net assets and goodwill at disposal (W3)	(3,780)
	620

The $620,000 adjustment is taken to the parent's equity. As control has not been lost, no profit or loss on disposal will be recognised.

21.2 A

	$
Fair value of consideration paid	(135,000)
Decrease in NCI in net assets on acquisition (20/40 x 133,000(W))	66,500
	(68,500)

	$
Workings: NCI at 28.2.20X7	
NCI b/fwd at 1.8.20X6	127,000
Profits attributable to NCI to 28.2.20X7 (30,000 x 6/12 x 40%)	6,000
	133,000

The complete journal to reflect the transaction would be:

DR Non-controlling interests $66,500
DR Parent's equity $68,500
CR Cash $135,000

21.3 **B**

	$m	$m
Consideration transferred		960
NCI (per question)		420
Fair value of previously held equity interest		160
Fair value of identifiable assets acquired and liabilities assumed		
Share capital	600	
Retained earnings	800	
		(1,400)
		140

22 Objective test questions: Indirect control of subsidiaries

22.1 **D** NCI share of the profit after tax of Tag ((5,000 – 1,000) × 25% Plus share of indirect associate's profit after tax (4000 – 1000 – 50 depreciation) × 40% = 1,180 × 25% Note that Rag controls Tag's investment of 40% of Bobtail.

However, it only owns 30% (75% × 40%) in this indirect associate.

The non-controlling interests in Tag own 10% (25% × 40%). As non-controlling interests are measured using the proportionate method, no goodwill or impairments are allocated to the NCI.

22.2 **B**

	$'000
Apricot	120
Blackcurrent	110
Date	90
	320

Apricot does not control Cranberry. Cranberry's assets should therefore not be consolidated in the group financial statements.

22.3 **B** Blue Co and Green Co are clearly both subsidiaries. Because Red Co controls Blue Co and Green Co, it also controls 55% of the shares in Yellow Co (30% through Blue Co and 25% through Green Co).

23 Objective test questions: Foreign subsidiaries

23.1 **B** Subsidiary B is clearly an extension of Parent's own activities and therefore it almost certainly has the same functional currency as the parent.

23.2 **A** $1,902,000

	$'000	$'000
Rat		1,900
Mole: closing net assets (960 @ 2.5)	384	
opening net assets (720 @ 2.0)	(360)	
	24	
Group share (75%)		18
Retranslation of goodwill (160 @ 2 – 160 @ 2.5)		(16)
		1,902

	U"000
Goodwill	
Cost of investment (350 × 2)	700
Net assets acquired (75% × 720)	(540)
	160

24 Objective test questions: Consolidated statements of changes in equity

24.1 **C**   The non-controlling interest share of after tax profits in subsidiaries is shown on the face of the statement of profit or loss. Down to profit after tax, all of the results of the subsidiary are included, in order to show the results arising under group control. Then the non-controlling interest is deducted at that point to leave the profits which are owned by the group.

24.2 **B**   The profits attributable to non-controlling interests, adjusted for mid-year acquisition, is calculated as 17% x 6/12 x $330,880 = $28,125

24.3 **D**   It is the only one of the four options that is a gain or loss accounted for as 'other comprehensive income'.

25 Fallowfield and Rusholme

CONSOLIDATED STATEMENT OF PROFIT OR LOSS AND OTHER COMPREHENSIVE INCOME FOR THE YEAR ENDED 30 JUNE 20X8

	$
Revenue (403,400 + 193,000 – 40,000)	556,400
Cost of sales (201,400 + 92,600 – 40,000 + (W7) 4,000)	(258,000)
Gross profit	298,400
Distribution costs (16,000 + 14,600)	(30,600)
Administrative expenses (24,250 + 17,800)	(42,050)
Profit before tax	225,750
Income tax expense (61,750 + 22,000)	(83,750)
Profit for the year	142,000
Other comprehensive income (net of tax) (20,000 + 5,000)	25,000
Total comprehensive income for the year	167,000
Profit attributable to:	
Owners of the parent	125,200
Non-controlling interests (W2)	16,800
	142,000
Total comprehensive income attributable to:	
Owners of the parent	148,200
Non-controlling interests (W2)	18,800
	167,000

Tutorial note: Intragroup dividend income from Rusholme has been cancelled out on consolidation.

STATEMENT OF CHANGES IN EQUITY

	Equity attributable to owners of the parent $	Non-controlling interests (W4/W6) $	Total equity $
Balance at 30 June 20X7	270,000 (W3)	48,000	318,000
Total comprehensive income for the year	148,200	18,800	167,000
Dividends (NCI: 25,000 × 40%)	(40,000)	(10,000)	(50,000)
Balance at 30 June 20X8	378,200 (W5)	56,800	435,000

Workings

1　*Group structure*

Fallowfield

|　60%　3 years ago

Rusholme　Pre-acquisition reserves: $16,000

2　*Non-controlling interests (SPLOCI)*

	Profit for the year $	Total comprehensive income $
Per question	46,000	51,000
Less: PUP (W7)	(4,000)	(4,000)
	42,000	47,000
NCI share 40%	16,800	18,800

3　*Equity brought forward*

	Fallowfield $	Rusholme $
Per question	243,000	101,000
Pre-acquisition equity (SC 40,000 + Res 16,000)	–	(56,000)
	243,000	45,000
Rusholme – share of post acquisition (45,000 × 60%)	27,000	
	270,000	

4　*Non-controlling interest brought forward (SOFP)*

	$
NCI at acquisition (at fair value)	30,000
Share of post-acquisition retained earnings (b/f) (45,000(W3) × 40%)	18,000
	48,000

5　*Equity carried forward*

	Fallowfield $	Rusholme $
Per question	338,000	127,000
PUP (W7)	–	(4,000)
Pre-acquisition equity (SC 40,000 + Res 16,000)		(56,000)
	338,000	67,000
Rusholme – share of post-acquisition retained earnings (67,000 × 60%)	40,200	
	378,200	

6　*Non-controlling interest carried forward (SOFP)*

	$
NCI at acquisition (at fair value)	30,000
Share of post-acquisition retained earnings (c/f) (67,000(W5) × 40%)	26,800
	56,800

7   *Provision for unrealised profit*

Rusholme → Fallowfield

PUP = $40,000 × ½ in inventories × 25/125 mark up = $4,000

↑ Rusholme's cost of sales (& adjust NCI [SPLOCI] in (W2))

↓ Rusholme's retained earnings (in (W5))

↓ Group inventories (in SOFP)

26 Panther Group

PANTHER GROUP
CONSOLIDATED STATEMENT OF PROFIT OR LOSS AND OTHER COMPREHENSIVE INCOME
FOR THE YEAR ENDED 31 DECEMBER 20X4

	$'000
Revenue [22,800 + (4,300 × 6/12) – 320]	24,630
Cost of sales [13,600 + (2,600 × 6/12) – 320 + (W3) 10 + (W5) 5]	(14,595)
Gross profit	10,035
Distribution costs (2,900 + (500 × 6/12))	(3,150)
Administrative expenses (1,800 + (300 × 6/12))	(1,950)
Finance costs [200 + (40 × 6/12) – (W4) 20 cancellation]	(200)
Finance income (50 – (W4) 20 cancellation)	30
Profit before tax	4,765
Income tax expense [1,300 + (220 × 6/12)]	(1,410)
Profit for the year	3,355
Other comprehensive income for the year, net of tax [1,600 + (180 × 6/12)]	1,690
Total comprehensive income for the year	5,045
Profit attributable to:	
Owners of the parent (3,355 – 112)	3,229
Non-controlling interests (W2)	126
	3,355
Total comprehensive income attributable to:	
Owners of the parent (5,045 – 162)	4,883
Non-controlling interests (W2)	162
	5,045

CONSOLIDATED STATEMENT OF CHANGES IN EQUITY
FOR THE YEAR ENDED 31 DECEMBER 20X4 (EXTRACT)

	$'000
	Reserves
Balance at 1 January 20X4 (Panther only)	12,750
Dividend paid	(900)
Total comprehensive income for the year	4,883
Balance at 31 December 20X4 (W6)	16,733

Workings

1   *Group structure and timeline*

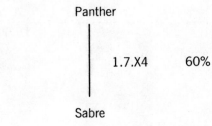

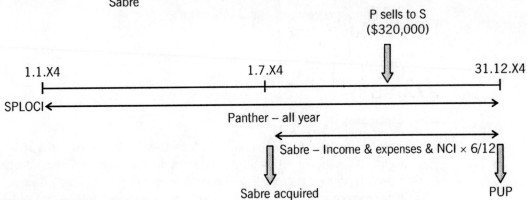

2   *Non-controlling interests*

	PFY $'000	TCI $'000
Per Q (640 × 6/12)/(820 × 6/12)	320	410
Additional depreciation on fair value adjustment (W5)	(5)	(5)
	315	405
NCI share	× 40%	× 40%
	= 126	= 162

3   *Unrealised profit on intragroup trading*

$$\text{Panther to Sabre} = \$60,000 \times \frac{20\%}{120\%} = \$10,000$$

Adjust cost of sales in books of seller (Panther).

4   *Interest on intragroup loan*

$800,000 × 5% × 6/12 = $20,000

Cancel in books of Panther and Sabre.

5   *Fair value adjustments*

	At acq'n 1.7.X4 $'000	Movement $'000	At year end 31.12.X4 $'000
Property	200	(200/20 × 6/12) (5)	195

6   Group reserves carried forward (proof)

	Panther $'000	Sabre $'000
Reserves per question	16,500	3,300
PUP (W3)	(10)	
Fair value movement (W5)		(5)
Pre-acquisition reserves [2,480 + (820 x 6/12)]		(2,890)
		405
Group share of post-acquisition reserves:		
Sabre (405 × 60%)	243	
	16,733	

27 CVB

(a)   **Explanation**

Prior to the acquisition of the 60% of FG on 1 April 20X5, CVB had a 15% shareholding in FG. As this did not give CVB significant influence or control over the relevant activities of FG, the 15% shareholding represented a financial asset under IAS 39 *Financial instruments: recognition and measurement* and CVB correctly treated it as available for sale i.e. at fair value with gains or losses recorded in other comprehensive income OCI.

On acquisition of the 60% on 1 April 20X5, CVB has a total shareholding of 75% and control of FG. Therefore FG should be treated as a subsidiary and consolidated in accordance with IFRS 10 *Consolidated financial statements*. At the acquisition is mid-year, the income, expenses and OCI would be pro-rated for six months in the consolidated statement of profit or loss and other comprehensive income.

In substance, on 1 April 20X5 CVB has 'sold' a 15% financial asset and therefore the financial asset should be derecognised with a profit or loss on derecognition recorded in the statement of profit or loss (and previous revaluation gains reclassified from OCI to statement of profit or loss).

In substance, CVB has then 'acquired' a 75% subsidiary. IFRS 3 *Business combinations* requires goodwill on acquisition to be calculated at the date control is obtained i.e. on 1 April 20X5. Therefore goodwill should be calculated on the full 75% shareholding (with consideration being the cost of the 60% acquired plus the fair value of the previously held interest of 15%).

(b)   CVB – CONSOLIDATED STATEMENT OF FINANCIAL POSITION AS AT 30 SEPTEMBER 20X5

	$'000
Non-current assets	
Property, plant and equipment (22,000 + 5,000)	27,000
Goodwill (W2)	405
	27,405
Current assets	
Inventories (6,200 + 800 – 40 (W7))	6,960
Receivables (6,600 + 1,900)	8,500
Cash and cash equivalents (1,200 + 300)	1,500
	16,960
Total assets	44,365

	$'000
EQUITY AND LIABILITIES	
Equity attributable to owners of the parent	
Share capital	20,000
Retained earnings (W3)	8,629
	28,629
Non-controlling interests (W4)	1,604
	30,233
Non-current liabilities	
5% Bonds 2013 (3,900 + 132 (W6))	4,032
Current liabilities (8,100 + 2,000)	10,100
Total liabilities	14,132
Total equity and liabilities	44,365

Workings

1   *Group structure*

CVB

15% (1.5.X3) + 60% (1.4.X5) = 75%

FG   PAR:

	$000
30.9.X5	5,000
Profits 1.4.X5 – 30.9.X5	
(3,000 × 6/12)	(1,500)
PAR at 1.4.X5	3,500

2   *Goodwill*

	$'000	$'000
Consideration transferred for the 60%		2,900
Non-controlling interests (at fair value)		1,250
Fair value of 15% holding at 1 April 20X5		800
Net assets at acquisition as represented by:		
Share capital	1,000	
Pre-acquisition retained earnings (W1)	3,500	
		(4,500)
		450
Impairment losses to date (10%)		(45)
		405

3   *Consolidated retained earnings*

	CVB $'000	RG $'000
Per question	7,500	5,000
Profit on derecognition of available for sale investment (W5)	200	
Additional finance cost on bonds (W6)	(132)	
PUP (W7)		(40)
Pre-acquisition retained earnings (W1)		(3,500)
		1,460
Group share of post acquisition retained earnings:		
RG (1,460 × 75%)	1,095	
Group share of impairment losses (45 (W2) × 75%)	(34)	
	8,629	

4   *Non-controlling interests*

	$'000
NCI at acquisition (1 April 20X5) (W2)	1,250
NCI share of post acquisition retained earnings (1,460 (W3) × 25%)	365
NCI share of impairment losses (45 (W2) × 25%)	(11)
	1,604

5   *Profit on derecognition of financial asset*

	$'000
Fair value of 15% investment in FG at 1 April 20X5	800
Cost of 15% investment in FG	(600)
	200

6   *Bonds*

	$'000
At 1 October 20X4 (4,000 – 100)	3,900
Finance cost (8.5% effective interest × 3,900 b/f)	332
Interest paid (5% coupon × 4,000 par value)	(200)
At 30 September 20X5	4,032

Adjustment required:

↑ Finance costs (and ↓ CVB's retained earnings) [$332,000 – $200,000] $132,000

↑ Bonds (within non-current liabilities) [$4,032,000 – $3,900,000] $132,000

7   *Provision for unrealised profit*

FG ⟶ CVB

PUP = $400,000 × ½ in inventories × 20/100 margin = $40,000

↓ FG's (seller's) retained earnings $40,000

↓ Inventories $40,000

28 Holmes and Deakin

(a)   HOLMES CO
CONSOLIDATED STATEMENT OF PROFIT OR LOSS AND OTHER COMPREHENSIVE INCOME
FOR THE YEAR ENDED 31 MAY 20X3

	$'000
Revenue (1,000 + 540)	1,540
Cost of sales and operating expenses (800 + 430)	(1,230)
Profit before tax	310
Income tax expense (90 + 60)	(150)
Profit for the year	160
Other comprehensive income (net of tax) (20 + 10)	30
Total comprehensive income for the year	190

Profit attributable to:

Owners of the parent β	150
Non-controlling interest $(50 \times \dfrac{9}{12} \times 15\%) + (50 \times \dfrac{3}{12} \times 35\%)$	10
	160

	$'000
Total comprehensive income attributable to:	
Owners of the parent β	178
Non-controlling interest $(60 \times \frac{9}{12} \times 15\%) + (60 \times \frac{3}{12} \times 35\%)$	12
	190

(b) HOLMES CO

CONSOLIDATED STATEMENT OF FINANCIAL POSITION AS AT 31 May 20X3

	$'000
Non-current assets	
Property, plant and equipment (535 + 178)	713
Goodwill (W2)	80
	793
Current assets	
Inventories (320 + 190)	510
Trade receivables (250 + 175)	425
Cash (80 + 89)	169
	1,104
	1,897
Equity attributable to owners of the parent	
Share capital $1 ordinary shares	500
Retained earnings (W3)	507.5
	1,007.5
Non-controlling interest (W4)	157.5
	1,165
Current liabilities	
Trade payables (295 + 171)	466
Income tax payable (80 + 60)	140
Provisions (95 + 31)	126
	732
	1,897

(c) STATEMENT OF CHANGES IN EQUITY (ATTRIBUTABLE TO OWNERS OF THE PARENT) AT 31 MAY 20X3

	$'000
Balance at 31.5.20X2 (500 + (W6) 256.5)	756.5
Total comprehensive income for the year	178
Adjustment to parent's equity on disposal (W5)	73
Balance at 31.5.20X3 (500 + (W3) 507.5)	1,007.5

Workings

1   Group structure and timeline

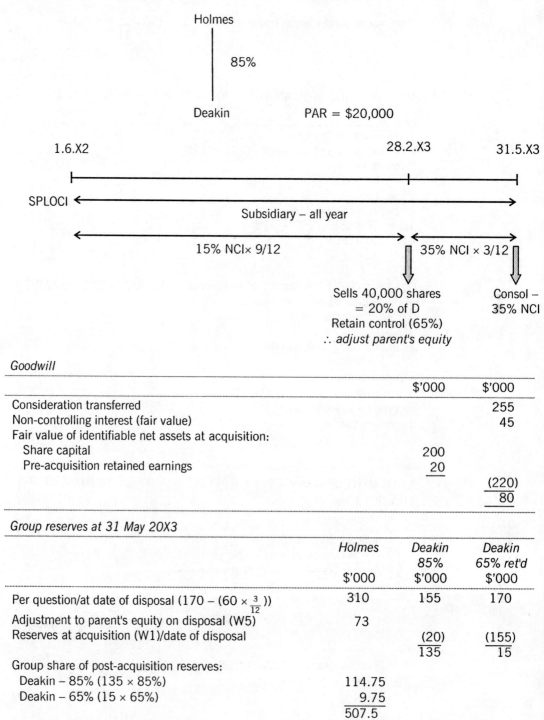

2   *Goodwill*

	$'000	$'000
Consideration transferred		255
Non-controlling interest (fair value)		45
Fair value of identifiable net assets at acquisition:		
Share capital	200	
Pre-acquisition retained earnings	20	
		(220)
		80

3   *Group reserves at 31 May 20X3*

	Holmes	Deakin 85%	Deakin 65% ret'd
	$'000	$'000	$'000
Per question/at date of disposal $(170 - (60 \times \frac{3}{12}))$	310	155	170
Adjustment to parent's equity on disposal (W5)	73		
Reserves at acquisition (W1)/date of disposal		(20)	(155)
		135	15
Group share of post-acquisition reserves:			
Deakin – 85% (135 × 85%)	114.75		
Deakin – 65% (15 × 65%)	9.75		
	507.5		

4   *Non-controlling interests (SOFP)*

	$'000
NCI at acquisition (W2)	45
NCI share of post-acquisition reserves to disposal (135 (W3) × 15%)	20.25
	65.25
Increase in NCI on disposal (65.25 × 20%/15%)	87
NCI share of post-acquisition reserves to year end (15 (W3)× 35%)	5.25
	157.5

5   *Adjustment to parent's equity on disposal of shares in group financial statements*

	$'000
Fair value of consideration received	160
Increase in NCI in net assets at disposal (W4) (87)	
	73

6   *Reserves brought forward*

	Holmes $'000	Deakin $'000
Per question (31.5.X3)	310	170
Less: Total comprehensive income for the year	(130)	(60)
Reserves at acquisition		(20)
	180	90
Deakin – share of post-acquisition earnings (90 × 85%)	76.5	
	256.5	

29 Harvard

(a)   HARVARD GROUP
CONSOLIDATED STATEMENT OF FINANCIAL POSITION AT 31 DECEMBER 20X5

	$'000
Non-current assets	
Property, plant and equipment (2,870 + (W2) 1,350)	4,220
Goodwill (W4)	146.7
	4,366.7
Current assets	
Inventories (1,990 + (W2) 2,310)	4,300
Trade receivables (1,630 + (W2) 1,270)	2,900
Cash at bank and in hand (240 + (W2) 560)	800
	8,000
	12,366.7
Equity attributable to owners of the parent	
Share capital ($1)	118
Retained reserves (W5)	3,018.7
	3,136.7
Non-controlling interests (W6)	1,070.0
	4,206.7
Non-current liabilities	
Loans	1,920
Current liabilities	
Trade payables (5,030 + (W2) 1,210)	6,240
	12,366.7

(b)   CONSOLIDATED STATEMENT OF PROFIT OR LOSS AND OTHER COMPREHENSIVE INCOME
FOR YEAR ENDED 31 DECEMBER 20X5

	$'000
Revenue (40,425 + (W3) 25,900)	66,325
Cost of sales (35,500 + (W3) 20,680)	(56,180)
Gross profit	10,145
Distribution and administrative expenses (4,400 + (W3) 1,560)	(5,960)
Profit before tax	4,185
Income tax expense (300 + (W3) 1,260)	(1,560)
Profit for the year	2,625
Other comprehensive income:	
Exchange differences on translating foreign operations (W7)	316.7
Total comprehensive income for the year	2,941.7

	$'000
Profit attributable to:	
Owners of the parent (2,625 – 600)	2,025
Non-controlling interests ((W3) 2,400 × 25%)	600
	2,625
Total comprehensive income attributable to:	
Owners of the parent (2,941.7 – 675.5)	2,266.2
Non-controlling interests [((W3) 2,400 + (W7) 302) × 25%]	675.5
	2,941.7

Statement of changes in equity for the year ended 31 December 20X5 (extract)

	$'000 Owners of the parent
Balance at 1 January 20X5 (118 + 1,452.5(W5))	1,570.5
Dividends	(700)
Total comprehensive income for the year (per SPLOCI)	2,266.2
Balance at 31 December 20X5 (118 + 3,018.7(W5))	3,136.7

Workings

1   Group structure

Harvard

31.12.X2 | $\dfrac{1,011}{1,348}$ = 75%

Krakow   Pre-acq'n ret'd earnings = PLN 2,876,000

2   *Translation of Krakow – statement of financial position*

	PLN '000	Rate	$'000
Property, plant and equipment	4,860	3.6	1,350
Inventories	8,316	3.6	2,310
Trade receivables	4,572	3.6	1,270
Cash	2,016	3.6	560
	19,764		5,490
Share capital	1,348	4.4	306.4
Retained reserves			
– pre-acquisition	2,876	4.4	653.6
– post-acquisition (14,060 – 2,876)	11,184	β	3,320
	15,408		4,280
Trade payables	4,356	3.6	1,210
	19,764		5,490

3   *Translation of Krakow – statement of profit or loss and other comprehensive income*

	PLN '000	Rate	$'000
Revenue	97,125	3.75	25,900
Cost of sales	(77,550)	3.75	(20,680)
Gross profit	19,575		5,220
Distribution and administrative expenses	(5,850)	3.75	(1,560)
Profit before tax	13,725		3,660
Income tax expense	(4,725)	3.75	(1,260)
Profit for the year	9,000		2,400

4   Goodwill

	PLN '000	PLN '000	Rate	$'000
Consideration transferred (840 × 4.4)		3,696		840
Non-controlling interests (4,224 × 25%)		1,056		240
Less: Share of net assets at acquisition:			4.4	
Share capital	1,348			
Retained earnings	2,876			
		(4,224)		(960)
Goodwill at acquisition		528		120
Exchange gain 20X3 – 20X4		–	β	12
Goodwill at 31 December 20X4		528	4.0	132
Exchange gain 20X5		––	β	14.7
Goodwill at year end		528	3.6	146.7

5   Proof of retained reserves

(i)   At 31 December 20X5

	Harvard A$'000	Krakow A$'000
Per question/(W2)	502	3,974
Pre-acquisition (W2)		(654)
		3,320
Group share of Krakow post-acquisition (3,320 × 75%)	2,490	
Impairment losses to date	(0)	
Exchange differences on goodwill ((W4) 12 + 15)	27	
	3,019	

(ii)   At 31 December 20X4 *(find as a balancing figure in the exam)*

	Harvard A$'000	Krakow A$'000
Harvard reserves b/d ((502 – (945 – 700))	257	2,538
Krakow net assets b/d (B$15,408 – 9,000 + 3,744)/4)		
Pre-acquisition net assets (B$ (W2) (1,348 + 2,876)/4.4)		(960)
		1,578
Group share of Krakow post-acquisition (1,578 × 75%)	1,184	
Impairment losses to date	(0)	
Exchange differences on goodwill (W4)	12	
	1,453	

Note: Net assets rather than reserves are used for the foreign subsidiary to incorporate exchange differences.

6   Non-controlling interests

	$'000
NCI at acquisition (W4)	240
Add: NCI share of post-acquisition retained reserves of Krakow ((W2) 3,320 × 25%)	830
	1,070

7   *Exchange differences arising during the year*

	SOCI $'000
On translation of net assets of Krakow:	
Closing NA at CR (W2)	4,280
Opening NA @ OR [(15,408 – 9,000 + 3,744)/4.0]	(2,538)
	1,742
Less: retained profit as translated ((W3) 2,400 – 3,744/3.90)	(1,440)
	302
On goodwill (W4)	14.7
	316.7

30 Objective test questions: Consolidated statements of cash flow

30.1 **D**

	$m
B/f	410
Depreciation	(115)
Revaluation	80
Purchases (β)	305
C/f	680

30.2 **B**

	$'000
Balance b/f	1,860
Revaluation	100
Disposal	(240)
Depreciation	(280)
	1,440
Additions (β)	1,440
Balance c/f	2,880

30.3 **C**

	$'000
B/f (2,000 + 800)	2,800
Additions (6,500 – 2,500 + 1,800)	5,800
Payments made (β)	(2,100)
C/f (4,800 + 1,700)	6,500

30.4 **C**   The only cash inflow from TP is the dividend received by the shareholders. TP paid a dividend of $100,000 after NS had acquired its shares therefore NS received 30% of this dividend – $30,000.

31 AH Group

AH GROUP CONSOLIDATED STATEMENT OF CASH FLOWS FOR THE YEAR ENDED 30 JUNE 20X5

	$'000	$'000
Cash flows from operating activities		
Profit before taxation	19,450	
Adjustment for		
Depreciation	7,950	
Profit on disposal of property	(1,250)	
Interest expense	1,400	
	27,550	
Decrease in trade receivables (W2)	470	
Increase in inventories (W2)	(3,100)	
Decrease in trade payables (W2)	(1,420)	
Cash generated from operations	23,500	
Interest paid (W4)	(1,480)	
Income taxes paid (W5)	(5,850)	
Net cash from operating activities		16,170
Cash flows from investing activities		
Acquisition of subsidiary, net of cash acquired (2,000 – 50)	(1,950)	
Purchase of property, plant and equipment (W1)	(11,300)	
Proceeds from sale of property	2,250	
Net cash used in investing activities		(11,000)
Cash flows from financing activities		
Repayment of interest-bearing borrowings	(1,000)	
Dividends paid (6,000 + (W3) 200)	(6,200)	
Net cash used in financing activities		(7,200)
Net decrease in cash and cash equivalents		(2,030)
Cash and cash equivalents at beginning of period		3,900
Cash and cash equivalents at end of period		1,870

Note. Dividends paid could also be shown under financing activities and dividends paid to non-controlling interest could also be shown under either operating activities or under financing activities.

Workings

1   *Property, plant and equipment*

	$000
B/f	44,050
Depreciation	(7,950)
Disposal	(1,000)
Acquisition of subsidiary	4,200
	39,300
Additions (balancing figure)	11,300
C/f	50,600

PROPERTY, PLANT AND EQUIPMENT

	$'000		$'000
Opening balance	44,050	Depreciation	7,950
Acquisition of subsidiary	4,200	Disposal	1,000
Additions (bal fig)	11,300	Closing balance	50,600
	59,550		59,550

2   *Inventories, trade receivables and trade payables*

	Inventories $000	Trade receivables $000	Trade payables $000
B/f	28,750	26,300	32,810
Acquisition of subsidiary	1,650	1,300	1,950
	30,400	27,600	34,760
Increase/(decrease)(balancing figure)	3,100	(470)	(1,420)
C/f	33,500	27,130	33,340

3   *Non-controlling interest*

	$000
B/f	1,920
SPLOCI	655
Acquisition of subsidiary (5,000 x 25%)	1,250
	3,825
Dividends paid (balancing figure)	(200)
C/f	3,625

NON-CONTROLLING INTEREST

	$'000		$'000
Cash paid (bal fig)	200	Opening balance	1,920
		On acquisition (5,000 × 25%)	1,250
Closing balance	3,625	P/L	655
	3,825		3,825

4   *Interest payable*

	$000
B/f	1,440
SPLOCI	1,400
	2,840
Interest paid (balancing figure)	(1,480)
C/f	1,360

INTEREST PAYABLE

	$'000		$'000
Cash paid (bal fig)	1,480	Opening balance	1,440
Closing balance	1,360	SPLOCI	1,400
	2,840		2,840

5   *Income taxes paid*

	$000
B/f	5,450
SPLOCI	6,250
Acquisition of subsidiary	250
	11,950
Tax paid (balancing figure)	(5,850)
C/f	6,100

INCOME TAXES PAYABLE

	$'000		$'000
Cash paid (bal fig)	5,850	Opening balance	5,450
		Acquisition of subsidiary	250
Closing balance	6,100	P/L	6,250
	11,950		11,950

32 Objective test questions: Related parties

32.1 C   Providers of finance are not considered to be related parties simply by virtue of the normal dealings with the entity. Suppliers are also not related parties simply by virtue of the resulting economic dependence. Laura McRae, however, is a close family member of a person having control over the Linney – she is therefore a related party.

32.2 A   IAS 24 requires the financial statements to disclose the nature and information about the transactions and outstanding balances, including commitments and bad and doubtful debts. Junior employees are not key management personnel and therefore are not related parties. IAS 19 requires details of the pension scheme to be disclosed.

32.3 A   No disclosure is required of intragroup related party transactions in the consolidated financial statements, since they are eliminated.

32.4 B   Statement 1 is incorrect – all material related party transactions must be disclosed regardless of whether they are at market value.

Statement 3 is incorrect – two associates are not related as joint significant influence is not considered to be a close enough relationship. An associate and a joint venture are related because the power over a joint venture (joint control) is stronger than that over an associate (significant influence).

33 Objective test questions: Earnings per share

33.1 A

Earnings on dilution:	$'000
Basic	1,850
Add back interest (2,000 × 6% × 70%)	84
	1,934

Shares on dilution:	'000
Existing	10,000
Conversion (2m × 4/5)	1,600
	11,600

Basic EPS = 1,850 / 10,000 = 18.5c

Diluted EPS = 1,934 / 11,600 = 16.7c

33.2 A   TERP

5 × 1.8 =	9.0
1 × 1.5 =	1.5
	10.5 / 6 = $1.75

Shares:

	'000
5,000 × 5/12 × 1.8 / 1.75	2,143
6,000 × 7/12	3,500
	5,643

EPS = 7,600 / 5,643 = $1.35

33.3 **D**

	Shares '000
B/f (7,500 / 0.5)	15,000
Full market price issue (4,000 × 9/12)	3,000
Bonus issue (18,000 / 3)	6,000
	24,000

EPS = 12 / 24 = 50c

33.4 **D**

	Shares '000
B/f	4,000
Bonus issue	1,000
	5,000

EPS = 3.6/5 = 72c

EPS 20X7 = 70c × 4,000/5,000 = 56c

34 Pilum

(a)   Earnings per share

	$
Profit for the period	1,403,000
Less: Preference dividends	(276,000)
Earnings	1,127,000
Earnings per share =	1,127,000
	4,120,000
	27.4c

(b)   The first step is to calculate the theoretical ex-rights price. Consider the holder of five shares.

	$
Before rights issue (5 shares × $1.78)	8.90
Rights issue (1 share × $1.20)	1.20
After rights issue (6 shares)	10.10

The theoretical ex-rights price is therefore $10.10/6 = $1.68.

The number of shares in issue before the rights issue must be multiplied by the fraction:

$$\frac{\text{Fair value immediately before exercise of rights}}{\text{Theoretical ex - rights price}} = \frac{\$1.78}{\$1.68}$$

Number of shares in issue during the year

Date	Narrative	Shares	Time	Bonus fraction	Total
1.1.X4	B/f	4,120,000 ×	9/12 ×	1.78/1.68	3,273,929
1.10.X4	Rights issue (1 for 5)	824,000			
		4,944,000 ×	3/12 ×		1,236,000
					4,509,929

EPS = $\dfrac{\$1,127,000}{4,509,929}$

= 25.0c

(c)   The maximum number of shares into which the loan stock could be converted is on the 31 December 20X5 terms of 90 $1 ordinary shares for every $100 of loan stock (90/100 × 1,500,000 = 1,350,000 shares). The calculation of diluted EPS should be based on the assumption that such a conversion actually took place on 1 January 20X4. Shares in issue during the year would then have numbered:

	$
Basic number of shares	4,120,000
Maximum number of shares on conversion (90/100 x 1,500,000)	1,350,000
Diluted number of shares	5,470,000

And revised earnings would be as follows:

	$	$
Earnings from (a) above		1,127,000
Interest saved by conversion (1,320,975 × 8%)	105,678	
Less: attributable tax (105,678 × 30%)	(31,703)	
		73,975
		1,200,975

$$\therefore \text{ Diluted EPS} = \frac{\$1,200,975}{5,470,000}$$

$$= 22.0c$$

Tutorial note:

Proof of liability component given in question:

	$
Principal ($1,500,000 × 0.681 [5 year 8% DF])	1,021,500
Interest ($1,500,000 × 5% × 3.993 [5 year 8% AF])	299,475
	1,320,975

35 Objective test questions: Ethics in financial reporting

35.1 **B**   The directors' proposed course of action would not comply with the CIMA *Code of Ethics'* principle of professional competence. Providing for $75,000 does not comply with IAS 37 which requires the most likely outcome to be provided for when there is a single outcome. Here, this would be $150,000.

35.2 **A**   The directors have correctly complied with IAS 39. This is an available for sale financial asset and is initially recorded at fair value plus transaction costs at $240,000 [(100,0000 x $2.30) + $10,000]. At the year end, it must be recorded at its fair value of $180,000 with the loss of $60,000 ($180,000 - $240,000) recognised in other comprehensive income.

35.3 **D**   The CIMA fundamental principles state that a professional accountant should not disclose any information acquired as a result of professional or business relationships to third parties without proper and specific authority, unless there is a legal or professional right or duty to disclose. The CIMA Code of Ethics contains no requirement to disclose information when requested by the police or the tax authorities. In certain circumstances, a professional accountant may need to disclose information to third parties without obtaining consent (ie. whistleblowing).

35.4 **B**   John faces a self-review threat, as determining the appropriate accounting treatment of the business combination would require him to rely upon the work he had carried out himself previously.

35.5 **B**   IAS 7 does permit dividends paid to be either treated as an 'operating' or 'financing' cash flow which makes Statement 1 incorrect. However, IAS 8 only allows a change in accounting policy which results in information that is more relevant to the economic decision-making needs of users and more reliable rather than simply for the personal gain of the directors.

The bonus based on the predetermined operating cash flow target represents a self-interest threat because if the directors reclassify the dividends from 'operating' to 'financing', the operating cash flow will be higher and the directors more likely to earn their bonus.

Statement 4 is incorrect because whilst the directors have the option of contacting the CIMA Ethics Helpline, there is no obligation to do so and in this situation, given that the proposed treatment complies with IAS 7, appears a bit extreme.

36 Objective test questions: Analysis of financial performance and position

36.1 **D**   The low asset turnover suggests a capital-intensive industry. This rules out the estate agency or architectural practice. Supermarkets can also be capital-intensive but tend to operate on low profit margins.

36.2 **A**

	$'000
Profit before interest and tax	230
	%
Capital employed (3,500 + 1,000)	4,500
	= 5.1%

36.3 **C**   This will reduce working capital and means that it will take longer to build up working capital needed for production. The other options will all speed up the operating cycle.

36.4 **D**   (Dividends (3.4 + 11.1) / Share price) × 100 = 14.5/350 × 100 = 4.1%

36.5 **B**   EPS = 800/4,000 = 20c. P/E ratio = 150/20 = 7.5

37 DM

(a)   *Report to investor*

Date: October 20X5

This report has been prepared at your request based upon the financial statements of DM for the last two years to 31 December 20X4. A number of ratios have been calculated and these, together with some supermarket sector comparatives, are included in the appendix to this report.

Profitability – revenue

During 20X4 DM has opened 6 new stores which is an expansion rate of 17% although this has led to an increase in revenue of only 3%. It has also led to a fall in annual sales per store although the **annual store sales** for DM are still considerably higher than the sector average. However this may simply be due to the fact that DM has larger stores than the average. The reduction in annual sales per store may also be due to the fact that not all of the new stores were fully operational for the entire year.

Profitability – gross profit margin

Gross profit margin has remained the same for the last two years and is marginally **higher than the industry average**. In contrast the operating profit margin has increased 18% over the two year period although we have no sector comparative to compare this to. However we are told that the directors have reviewed the useful lives of the non-current assets and in most cases have increased them. This in turn will reduce the annual depreciation charge and therefore increase operating profit although there has been no real improvement in operating performance.

Profitability – net profit margin

Net profit margin for DM has increased from 2.9% to 3.7% and is now approaching the sector average. As the interest cost and tax expense have largely remained constant between the two

years then this increase in net profit margin is due to the increased operating margin which in turn may be due to the change in depreciation charges.

Asset utilisation – asset turnover

The overall non-current asset turnover has **increased slightly over last year** but is still lower than the sector average. This increase could be due to the new stores although the non-current asset figure has remained almost the same as last year which is surprising due to the opening of the new stores. However it is possible that most of the capital expenditure on the new stores was actually incurred last year before the stores were brought into operation.

Asset utilisation – current ratio

The **current ratio is low** in both years as would be expected in a supermarket but has improved. There is also a distinct increase in the amount of cash being held. The inventory turnover period has not changed although there has been a slight increase in the payables payment period which will have a positive effect on cash flow. Finally the level of gearing has remained fairly constant and would not appear to be a problem.

Conclusion

DM has been **expanding** in the last two year and has appeared to **maintain and indeed improve its profitability** during this period. Its gross profit margin compares well with the sector average as do sales per store although the net profit margin has not kept pace with the sector average. It is possible, however, that the increasing operating profit margin and therefore net profit margin have been **manipulated** by the directors by the **increase in useful lives of the non-current assets** and therefore reduction in depreciation charges, This may have been done in order to encourage a high offer in any takeover bid that might be made. The directors would of course benefit personally from the sale of their individual stakes in the company at a high price but from the evidence we have it is not possible to state conclusively that this is the case. Further information would be required.

APPENDIX – RATIOS

	20X4	20X3	Sector
Gross profit margin	78/1,255 × 100 = 6.2%	75/1,220 × 100 = 6.1%	5.9%
Operating profit margin	57/1,255 × 100 = 4.5%	46/1,220 × 100 = 3.8%	
Net profit margin	33/1,255 × 100 = 2.6%	23/1,220 × 100 = 1.9%	3.9%
Annual sales per store	1,255/42 = $29.9m	1,220/38 = $32.1m	$27.6m
Non-current asset turnover	1,255/680 = 1.85	1,220/675 = 1.81	1.93
Current ratio	105/317 = 0.33	71/309 = 0.23	
Inventory turnover	47/1,177 × 365 = 14.6 days	46/1,145 × 365 = 14.7 days	
Payables payment period	297/1,177 × 365 = 92 days	273/1,145 × 365 = 87 days	

(b)   Limitations

Sector comparatives can provide useful information in ratio analysis but as with all comparisons there are both general and specific drawbacks. These include the following.

(i)   The sector figures are an **average** figure for the sector and therefore can be easily **affected by** just a **few abnormal** results or figures.

(ii)   The companies included in the sector figures may be of **different sizes** which may affect their sector results.

(iii)   The companies included in the sector figures may have **different year ends** which may affect the statement of financial position figures used in a variety of ratios particularly in the retail business.

(iv) As with all comparisons the different companies in the sector may have **different accounting policies** which may mean that their results and resulting ratios are not strictly comparable.

(v) There are a number of **different ways of calculating various key ratios** and if different companies in the sector calculate them in these different ways they will not be comparable.

INDEX

Note: **Key Terms** and their page references are given in **bold**.

Review Form – Paper F2 Financial Management (7/14)

Please help us to ensure that the CIMA learning materials we produce remain as accurate and user-friendly as possible. We cannot promise to answer every submission we receive, but we do promise that it will be read and taken into account when we update this Study Text.

Name: _____   Address: _____

_____

_____

How have you used this Study Text?
(Tick one box only)

☐ Home study (book only)

☐ On a course: college _____

☐ With 'correspondence' package

☐ Other _____

Why did you decide to purchase this Study Text? *(Tick one box only)*

☐ Have used BPP Texts in the past

☐ Recommendation by friend/colleague

☐ Recommendation by a lecturer at college

☐ Saw information on BPP website

☐ Saw advertising

☐ Other _____

During the past six months do you recall seeing/receiving any of the following?
(Tick as many boxes as are relevant)

☐ Our advertisement in *Financial Management*

☐ Our advertisement in *Pass*

☐ Our advertisement in *PQ*

☐ Our brochure with a letter through the post

☐ Our website www.bpp.com

Which (if any) aspects of our advertising do you find useful?
(Tick as many boxes as are relevant)

☐ Prices and publication dates of new editions

☐ Information on Text content

☐ Facility to order books off-the-page

☐ None of the above

Which BPP products have you used?

Text	☑	Passcard	☐
Kit	☐	i-Pass	☐

Your ratings, comments and suggestions would be appreciated on the following areas.

	Very useful	Useful	Not useful
Introductory section	☐	☐	☐
Chapter introductions	☐	☐	☐
Key terms	☐	☐	☐
Quality of explanations	☐	☐	☐
Case studies and other examples	☐	☐	☐
Exam skills and alerts	☐	☐	☐
Questions and answers in each chapter	☐	☐	☐
Chapter overview and summary diagrams	☐	☐	☐
Quick quizzes	☐	☐	☐
Question Bank	☐	☐	☐
Answer Bank	☐	☐	☐
Index	☐	☐	☐

	Excellent	Good	Adequate	Poor
Overall opinion of this Study Text	☐	☐	☐	☐

Do you intend to continue using BPP products?   Yes ☐   No ☐

On the reverse of this page is space for you to write your comments about our Study Text We welcome your feedback.

The BPP Learning Media author team can be e-mailed at: yen-peichen@bpp.com

Please return this form to: CIMA Product Manager, BPP Learning Media Ltd, FREEPOST, London, W12 8BR

TELL US WHAT YOU THINK

Please note any further comments and suggestions/errors below. For example, was the text accurate, readable, concise, user-friendly and comprehensive?